TERRORISM

Documents of International and Local Control

VOLUME 30

U.S. PERSPECTIVES

Yonah Alexander
and
Donald J. Musch

OCEANA PUBLICATIONS, INC.   DOBBS FERRY, NEW YORK

Information contained in this work has been obtained by Oceana Publications from sources believed to be reliable. However, neither the Publisher nor its authors guarantee the accuracy or completeness of any information published herein, and neither Oceana nor its authors shall be responsible for any errors, omissions or damages arising from the use of this information. This work is published with the understanding that Oceana and its authors are supplying information, but are not attempting to render legal or other professional services. If such services are required, the assistance of an appropriate professional should be sought.

You may order this or any other Oceana publications by visiting Oceana's website at http://www.oceanalaw.com

ISSN 1062-4007

ISBN 0-379-00752-5 (v. 30)

Manufactured in the United States of America on acid-free paper.

TABLE OF CONTENTS

VOLUME 30

DOCUMENTS

EXECUTIVE BRANCH

The White House

Department of State

Director of Central Intelligence

LEGISLATIVE BRANCH

Reports

Testimony

INTERNATIONAL DOCUMENTS

United Nations

Canada

United Kingdom

PREFACE

Since the brutal and unprecedented attacks on September 11, 2001, killing some 3,000 people and wounding many others, the United States has continued to face terrorist threats at home and abroad. Usama bin Laden, the leader of al-Qaida, whose members perpetrated the operations of the "Day of Infamy," stated in a video broadcast on December 27, 2001 that "terrorism against America deserves to be praised because it was a response to injustice." He further declared that "the end of the United States is imminent, whether bin Laden or his followers are alive or dead, for the awakening of the Muslim *umma* (nation) has occurred."

In light of this reality, the United States developed a comprehensive strategy including political, legal, intelligence, law enforcement, diplomatic, economic, military, and public affairs responses. It is not surprising therefore that in the aftermath of September 11 a proliferation of official and unofficial documents dealing with both the nature of the threat and response options were generated. In fact, volumes 28 and 29 in *Terrorism: Documents of International and Local Control* recorded several American perspectives from this period. This volume focuses on the views of the United States as reflected in the documentation available from the executive and legislative branches. For example, the volume includes President George W. Bush's addresses to the Joint Session of Congress on September 20, 2001, to the Nation on October 7, 2001, and to the United Nations General Assembly on November 10, 2001.

The President's Executive Order 13224 (dated December 14 but originally issued on September 23 "Blocking Property and Prohibiting Transactions with Persons who Commit, threaten to Commit, or Support Terrorism" as well as the "Presidential Order on Military Trials in Terrorist Cases" (dated November 14, 2001) are also incorporated. In addition, a legal response presented by Secretary of State Colin Powell on "Designating Certain Organizations under the USA Patriot Act as part of the Terrorist Exclusion List" (dated December 6) and an unclassified report to Congress by Director of Central Intelligence, George Tenet, on "the Acquisition of Technology Relating to Weapons of Mass Destruction and Advanced Munitions" (that reflects an assessment prior to September 11) are included.

The legislative part of this volume contains both the reports and the testimony from several hearings. Two of the reports presented focus on "Terrorism: Automated Lookout Systems and Border Security Options and Issues" (Congressional Research study, prepared in June 2001) and the General Accounting Office (GAO) report on "Bioterrorism: Federal Research and Preparedness Activities" (issued in September 2001).

The testimony segment covers a wide range of topics such as "Homeland Defense"; "Defining Terrorism and Responding to the Terrorist Threat"; "Protecting the Homeland from Asymmetric/Conventional Threats"; "Al Qaida and the Global Reach of Terrorism"; "A Silent War: Are Federal, State and Local Government Prepared for Biological and Chemical Attacks?"

and "Federal Efforts to Coordinate and Prepare the United States for Bioterrorism: Are They Ready?"

The aforementioned topics were discussed at different hearings conducted by the U.S. Senate (Committee on the Judiciary and the Committee on Governmental Affairs) and House Committees (e.g. Permanent Select Committee on Intelligence) and Subcommittees (e.g. National Security, Veterans' Affairs and International Relations of the House Committee on Government Reform). Both government officials and private and academic experts participated in these discussions.

Because of the continuing war against terrorism that affects the United States as well the international community, the Editors decided to include relevant material in this volume, reflecting the nature of the terrorist challenge to civilizations and the responses available to reduce the risks both in the conventional and unconventional levels. Several documents are included: United Nations Security Council Resolutions 1368 (September 12, 2001) and 1373 (September 28, 2001), emphasizing the need for increased international cooperation in combating terrorism; the "Joint U.S.-Canada Declaration for the Creation of a Smart Border for the 21st Century"; the Canadian "Anti-Terrorism Act" (December 18, 2001); and the United Kingdom's "Anti-Terrorism, Crime and Security Bill" (introduced on November 13th in the House of Commons, UK Parliament).

Subsequent volumes in this series to be published in 2002 will provide additional documents highlighting American as well as international multi-faceted responses to terrorist threats domestically and globally.

We wish to thank Michael S. Swetnam, CEO and Chairman of the Board, (Potomac Institute for Policy Studies), for his continuing support. We also wish to acknowledge the assistance of Professor Herbert M. Levine, James T. Kirkhope, Kerrie J. Martin, the research team of Meredith Gilchrest, Alon Lanir, Vivek Narayanan, and Tyler Richardson and the support of the intern group, including: Jack L. Babcock, Jr., Winter Salembier, and Kristin L. Wilczynski at the International Center for Terrorism Studies (Potomac Institute for Policy Studies). Finally, thanks are due to Professor Edgar H. Brenner, Co-Director, Inter-University Center for Legal Studies (International Law Institute) who provided guidance to the research project.

Yonah Alexander
and
Donald Musch
Washington, D.C.

January 31, 2002

EXECUTIVE BRANCH

The White House

DOCUMENT NO. 1

PRESIDENT BUSH REMARKS AT
NATIONAL DAY OF PRAYER AND REMEMBRANCE

The National Cathedral
Washington, D.C.

September 14, 2001

COMMENTARY: *The comments in this Document, along with those in Documents Numbers 2, 3, and 5 which follow, provide a clear expression of the President's view subsequent to the terrorist attacks of September 11th.*

For Immediate Release
Office of the Press Secretary

THE PRESIDENT: We are here in the middle hour of our grief. So many have suffered so great a loss, and today we express our nation's sorrow. We come before God to pray for the missing and the dead, and for those who love them.

On Tuesday, our country was attacked with deliberate and massive cruelty. We have seen the images of fire and ashes, and bent steel.

Now come the names, the list of casualties we are only beginning to read. They are the names of men and women who began their day at a desk or in an airport, busy with life. They are the names of people who faced death, and in their last moments called home to say, be brave, and I love you.

They are the names of passengers who defied their murderers, and prevented the murder of others on the ground. They are the names of men and women who wore the uniform of the United States, and died at their posts.

They are the names of rescuers, the ones whom death found running up the stairs and into the fires to help others. We will read all these names. We will linger over them, and learn their stories, and many Americans will weep.

To the children and parents and spouses and families and friends of the lost, we offer the deepest sympathy of the nation. And I assure you, you are not alone.

Just three days removed from these events, Americans do not yet have the distance of history. But our responsibility to history is already clear: to answer these attacks and rid the world of evil.

War has been waged against us by stealth and deceit and murder. This nation is peaceful, but fierce when stirred to anger. This conflict was begun on the timing and terms of others. It will end in a way, and at an hour, of our choosing.

Our purpose as a nation is firm. Yet our wounds as a people are recent and unhealed, and lead us to pray. In many of our prayers this week, there is a searching, and an honesty. At St. Patrick's Cathedral in New York on Tuesday, a woman said, "I prayed to God to give us a sign that He is still here."Others have prayed for the same, searching hospital to hospital, carrying pictures of those still missing.

God's signs are not always the ones we look for. We learn in tragedy that his purposes are not always our own. Yet the prayers of private suffering, whether in our homes or in this great cathedral, are known and heard, and understood.

There are prayers that help us last through the day, or endure the night. There are prayers of friends and strangers, that give us strength for the journey. And there are prayers that yield our will to a will greater than our own.

This world He created is of moral design. Grief and tragedy and hatred are only for a time. Goodness, remembrance, and love have no end. And the Lord of life holds all who die, and all who mourn.

It is said that adversity introduces us to ourselves. This is true of a nation as well. In this trial, we have been reminded, and the world has seen, that our fellow Americans are generous and kind, resourceful and brave. We see our national character in rescuers working past exhaustion; in long lines of blood donors; in thousands of citizens who have asked to work and serve in any way possible.

And we have seen our national character in eloquent acts of sacrifice. Inside the World Trade Center, one man who could have saved himself stayed until the end at the side of his quadriplegic friend. A beloved priest died giving the last rites to a firefighter. Two office workers, finding a disabled stranger, carried her down sixty-eight floors to safety. A group of men drove through the night from Dallas to Washington to bring skin grafts for burn victims.

In these acts, and in many others, Americans showed a deep commitment to one another, and an abiding love for our country. Today, we feel what Franklin Roosevelt called the warm courage of national unity. This is a unity of every faith, and every background.

It has joined together political parties in both houses of Congress. It is evident in services of prayer and candlelight vigils, and American flags, which are displayed in pride, and wave in defiance.

Our unity is a kinship of grief, and a steadfast resolve to prevail against our enemies. And this unity against terror is now extending across the world.

America is a nation full of good fortune, with so much to be grateful for. But we are not spared from suffering. In every generation, the world has produced enemies of human freedom. They have attacked America, because we are freedom's home and defender. And the commitment of our fathers is now the calling of our time.

On this national day of prayer and remembrance, we ask almighty God to watch over our nation, and grant us patience and resolve in all that is to come. We pray that He will comfort and console those who now walk in sorrow. We thank Him for each life we now must mourn, and the promise of a life to come.

As we have been assured, neither death nor life, nor angels nor principalities nor powers, nor things present nor things to come, nor height nor depth, can separate us from God's love. May He bless the souls of the departed. May He comfort our own. And may He always guide our country.

God bless America.

DOCUMENT NO. 2

PRESIDENTIAL ADDRESS TO JOINT SESSION OF CONGRESS

United States Capitol
Washington, D.C.

September 20, 2001

For Immediate Release
Office of the Press Secretary

THE PRESIDENT: Mr. Speaker, Mr. President Pro Tempore, members of Congress, and fellow Americans:

In the normal course of events, Presidents come to this chamber to report on the state of the Union. Tonight, no such report is needed. It has already been delivered by the American people.

We have seen it in the courage of passengers, who rushed terrorists to save others on the ground—passengers like an exceptional man named Todd Beamer. And would you please help me to welcome his wife, Lisa Beamer, here tonight. (Applause.)

We have seen the state of our Union in the endurance of rescuers, working past exhaustion. We have seen the unfurling of flags, the lighting of candles, the giving of blood, the saying of prayers—in English, Hebrew, and Arabic. We have seen the decency of a loving and giving people who have made the grief of strangers their own.

My fellow citizens, for the last nine days, the entire world has seen for itself the state of our Union—and it is strong. (Applause.)

Tonight we are a country awakened to danger and called to defend freedom. Our grief has turned to anger, and anger to resolution. Whether we bring our enemies to justice, or bring justice to our enemies, justice will be done. (Applause.)

I thank the Congress for its leadership at such an important time. All of America was touched on the evening of the tragedy to see Republicans and Democrats joined together on the steps of this Capitol, singing "God Bless America."And you did more than sing; you acted, by delivering $40 billion to rebuild our communities and meet the needs of our military.

Speaker Hastert, Minority Leader Gephardt, Majority Leader Daschle and Senator Lott, I thank you for your friendship, for your leadership and for your service to our country. (Applause.)

And on behalf of the American people, I thank the world for its outpouring of support. America will never forget the sounds of our National Anthem playing at Buckingham Palace, on the streets of Paris, and at Berlin's Brandenburg Gate.

We will not forget South Korean children gathering to pray outside our embassy in Seoul, or the prayers of sympathy offered at a mosque in Cairo. We will not forget moments of silence and days of mourning in Australia and Africa and Latin America.

Nor will we forget the citizens of 80 other nations who died with our own:dozens of Pakistanis; more than 130 Israelis; more than 250 citizens of India; men and women from El Salvador, Iran, Mexico and Japan; and hundreds of British citizens. America has no truer friend than Great Britain. (Applause.) Once again, we are joined together in a great cause—so honored the British Prime Minister has crossed an ocean to show his unity of purpose with America. Thank you for coming, friend. (Applause.)

On September the 11th, enemies of freedom committed an act of war against our country. Americans have known wars—but for the past 136 years, they have been wars on foreign soil, except for one Sunday in 1941. Americans have known the casualties of war—but not at the center of a great city on a peaceful morning. Americans have known surprise attacks—but never before on thousands of civilians. All of this was brought upon us in a single day—and night fell on a different world, a world where freedom itself is under attack.

Americans have many questions tonight. Americans are asking:Who attacked our country? The evidence we have gathered all points to a collection of loosely affiliated terrorist organizations known as al Qaeda. They are the same murderers indicted for bombing American embassies in Tanzania and Kenya, and responsible for bombing the USS Cole.

Al Qaeda is to terror what the mafia is to crime. But its goal is not making money; its goal is remaking the world—and imposing its radical beliefs on people everywhere.

The terrorists practice a fringe form of Islamic extremism that has been rejected by Muslim scholars and the vast majority of Muslim clerics—a fringe movement that perverts the peaceful teachings of Islam. The terrorists' directive commands them to kill Christians and Jews, to kill all Americans, and make no distinction among military and civilians, including women and children.

This group and its leader—a person named Osama bin Laden—are linked to many other organizations in different countries, including the Egyptian Islamic Jihad and the Islamic Movement of Uzbekistan. There are thousands of these terrorists in more than 60 countries. They are recruited from their own nations and neighborhoods and brought to camps in places like Afghanistan, where they are trained in the tactics of terror. They are sent back to their homes or sent to hide in countries around the world to plot evil and destruction.

The leadership of al Qaeda has great influence in Afghanistan and supports the Taliban regime in controlling most of that country. In Afghanistan, we see al Qaeda's vision for the world.

Afghanistan's people have been brutalized—many are starving and many have fled. Women are not allowed to attend school. You can be jailed for owning a television. Religion can be practiced only as their leaders dictate. A man can be jailed in Afghanistan if his beard is not long enough.

The United States respects the people of Afghanistan—after all, we are currently its largest source of humanitarian aid—but we condemn the Taliban regime. (Applause.)It is not only repressing its own people, it is threatening people everywhere by sponsoring and sheltering and supplying terrorists. By aiding and abetting murder, the Taliban regime is committing murder.

And tonight, the United States of America makes the following demands on the Taliban:Deliver to United States authorities all the leaders of al Qaeda who hide in your land. (Applause.) Release all foreign nationals, including American citizens, you have unjustly imprisoned. Protect foreign journalists, diplomats and aid workers in your country. Close immediately and permanently every terrorist training camp in Afghanistan, and hand over every terrorist, and every person in their support structure, to appropriate authorities. (Applause.) Give the United States full access to terrorist training camps, so we can make sure they are no longer operating.

These demands are not open to negotiation or discussion. (Applause.) The Taliban must act, and act immediately. They will hand over the terrorists, or they will share in their fate.

I also want to speak tonight directly to Muslims throughout the world. We respect your faith. It's practiced freely by many millions of Americans, and by millions more in countries that America counts as friends. Its teachings are good and peaceful, and those who commit evil in the name of Allah blaspheme the name of Allah. (Applause.) The terrorists are traitors to their own faith, trying, in effect, to hijack Islam itself. The enemy of America is not our many Muslim friends; it is not our many Arab friends. Our enemy is a radical network of terrorists, and every government that supports them. (Applause.)

Our war on terror begins with al Qaeda, but it does not end there. It will not end until every terrorist group of global reach has been found, stopped and defeated. (Applause.)

Americans are asking, why do they hate us? They hate what we see right here in this chamber—a democratically elected government. Their leaders are self-appointed. They hate our freedoms—our freedom of religion, our freedom of speech, our freedom to vote and assemble and disagree with each other.

They want to overthrow existing governments in many Muslim countries, such as Egypt, Saudi Arabia, and Jordan. They want to drive Israel out of the Middle East. They want to drive Christians and Jews out of vast regions of Asia and Africa.

These terrorists kill not merely to end lives, but to disrupt and end a way of life. With every atrocity, they hope that America grows fearful, retreating from the world and forsaking our friends. They stand against us, because we stand in their way.

We are not deceived by their pretenses to piety. We have seen their kind before. They are the heirs of all the murderous ideologies of the 20th century. By sacrificing human life to serve their radical visions—by abandoning every value except the will to power—they follow in the path of fascism, and Nazism, and totalitarianism. And they will follow that path all the way, to where it ends:in history's unmarked grave of discarded lies. (Applause.)

Americans are asking:How will we fight and win this war? We will direct every resource at our command—every means of diplomacy, every tool of intelligence, every instrument of law enforcement, every financial influence, and every necessary weapon of war—to the disruption and to the defeat of the global terror network.

This war will not be like the war against Iraq a decade ago, with a decisive liberation of territory and a swift conclusion. It will not look like the air war above Kosovo two years ago, where no ground troops were used and not a single American was lost in combat.

Our response involves far more than instant retaliation and isolated strikes. Americans should not expect one battle, but a lengthy campaign, unlike any other we have ever seen. It may include dramatic strikes, visible on TV, and covert operations, secret even in success. We will starve terrorists of funding, turn them one against another, drive them from place to place, until there is no refuge or no rest. And we will pursue nations that provide aid or safe haven to terrorism. Every nation, in every region, now has a decision to make. Either you are with us, or you are with the terrorists. (Applause.) From this day forward, any nation that continues to harbor or support terrorism will be regarded by the United States as a hostile regime.

Our nation has been put on notice:We are not immune from attack. We will take defensive measures against terrorism to protect Americans. Today, dozens of federal departments and agencies, as well as state and local governments, have responsibilities affecting homeland security. These efforts must be coordinated at the highest level. So tonight I announce the creation of a Cabinet-level position reporting directly to me—the Office of Homeland Security.

And tonight I also announce a distinguished American to lead this effort, to strengthen American security: a military veteran, an effective governor, a true patriot, a trusted friend—Pennsylvania's Tom Ridge. (Applause.) He will lead, oversee and coordinate a comprehensive national strategy to safeguard our country against terrorism, and respond to any attacks that may come.

These measures are essential. But the only way to defeat terrorism as a threat to our way of life is to stop it, eliminate it, and destroy it where it grows. (Applause.)

Many will be involved in this effort, from FBI agents to intelligence operatives to the reservists we have called to active duty. All deserve our thanks, and all have our prayers. And tonight, a few miles from the damaged Pentagon, I have a message for our military:Be ready. I've called the Armed Forces to alert, and there is a reason. The hour is coming when America will act, and you will make us proud. (Applause.)

This is not, however, just America's fight. And what is at stake is not just America's freedom. This is the world's fight. This is civilization's fight. This is the fight of all who believe in progress and pluralism, tolerance and freedom.

We ask every nation to join us. We will ask, and we will need, the help of police forces, intelligence services, and banking systems around the world. The United States is grateful that many nations and many international organizations have already responded—with sympathy and with support. Nations from Latin America, to Asia, to Africa, to Europe, to the Islamic world. Perhaps the NATO Charter reflects best the attitude of the world:An attack on one is an attack on all.

The civilized world is rallying to America's side. They understand that if this terror goes unpunished, their own cities, their own citizens may be next. Terror, unanswered, can not only bring down buildings, it can threaten the stability of legitimate governments. And you know what—we're not going to allow it. (Applause.)

Americans are asking:What is expected of us?I ask you to live your lives, and hug your children. I know many citizens have fears tonight, and I ask you to be calm and resolute, even in the face of a continuing threat.

I ask you to uphold the values of America, and remember why so many have come here. We are in a fight for our principles, and our first responsibility is to live by them. No one should be singled out for unfair treatment or unkind words because of their ethnic background or religious faith. (Applause.)

I ask you to continue to support the victims of this tragedy with your contributions. Those who want to give can go to a central source of information, libertyunites. org, to find the names of groups providing direct help in New York, Pennsylvania, and Virginia.

The thousands of FBI agents who are now at work in this investigation may need your cooperation, and I ask you to give it.

I ask for your patience, with the delays and inconveniences that may accompany tighter security; and for your patience in what will be a long struggle.

I ask your continued participation and confidence in the American economy. Terrorists attacked a symbol of American prosperity. They did not touch its source. America is successful because of the hard work, and creativity, and enterprise of our people. These were the true strengths of our economy before September 11th, and they are our strengths today. (Applause.)

And, finally, please continue praying for the victims of terror and their families, for those in uniform, and for our great country. Prayer has comforted us in sorrow, and will help strengthen us for the journey ahead.

Tonight I thank my fellow Americans for what you have already done and for what you will do. And ladies and gentlemen of the Congress, I thank you, their representatives, for what you have already done and for what we will do together.

Tonight, we face new and sudden national challenges. We will come together to improve air safety, to dramatically expand the number of air marshals on domestic flights, and take new measures to prevent hijacking. We will come together to promote stability and keep our airlines flying, with direct assistance during this emergency. (Applause.)

We will come together to give law enforcement the additional tools it needs to track down terror here at home. (Applause.) We will come together to strengthen our intelligence capabilities to know the plans of terrorists before they act, and find them before they strike. (Applause.)

We will come together to take active steps that strengthen America's economy, and put our people back to work.

Tonight we welcome two leaders who embody the extraordinary spirit of all New Yorkers: Governor George Pataki, and Mayor Rudolph Giuliani. (Applause.)As a symbol of America's resolve, my administration will work with Congress, and these two leaders, to show the world that we will rebuild New York City. (Applause.)

After all that has just passed—all the lives taken, and all the possibilities and hopes that died with them—it is natural to wonder if America's future is one of fear. Some speak of an age of terror. I know there are struggles ahead, and dangers to face. But this country will define our times, not be defined by them. As long as the United States of America is determined and strong, this will not be an age of terror; this will be an age of liberty, here and across the world. (Applause.)

Great harm has been done to us. We have suffered great loss. And in our grief and anger we have found our mission and our moment. Freedom and fear are at war. The advance of human freedom—the great achievement of our time, and the great hope of every time—now depends on us. Our nation—this generation—will lift a dark threat of violence from our people and our future. We will rally the world to this cause by our efforts, by our courage. We will not tire, we will not falter, and we will not fail. (Applause.)

It is my hope that in the months and years ahead, life will return almost to normal. We'll go back to our lives and routines, and that is good. Even grief recedes with time and grace. But our resolve must not pass. Each of us will remember what happened that day, and to whom it happened. We'll remember the moment the news came—where we were and what we were doing. Some will remember an image of a fire, or a story of rescue. Some will carry memories of a face and a voice gone forever.

And I will carry this:It is the police shield of a man named George Howard, who died at the World Trade Center trying to save others. It was given to me by his mom, Arlene, as a proud memorial to her son. This is my reminder of lives that ended, and a task that does not end. (Applause.)

I will not forget this wound to our country or those who inflicted it. I will not yield; I will not rest; I will not relent in waging this struggle for freedom and security for the American people.

The course of this conflict is not known, yet its outcome is certain. Freedom and fear, justice and cruelty, have always been at war, and we know that God is not neutral between them. (Applause.)

Fellow citizens, we'll meet violence with patient justice—assured of the rightness of our cause, and confident of the victories to come. In all that lies before us, may God grant us wisdom, and may He watch over the United States of America.

Thank you. (Applause.)

DOCUMENT NO. 3

PRESIDENTIAL ADDRESS TO THE NATION

The Treaty Room
Washington, D. C.

October 7, 2001

For Immediate Release
Office of the Press Secretary

THE PRESIDENT: Good afternoon. On my orders, the United States military has begun strikes against al Qaeda terrorist training camps and military installations of the Taliban regime in Afghanistan. These carefully targeted actions are designed to disrupt the use of Afghanistan as a terrorist base of operations, and to attack the military capability of the Taliban regime.

We are joined in this operation by our staunch friend, Great Britain. Other close friends, including Canada, Australia, Germany and France, have pledged forces as the operation unfolds. More than 40 countries in the Middle East, Africa, Europe and across Asia have granted air transit or landing rights. Many more have shared intelligence. We are supported by the collective will of the world.

More than two weeks ago, I gave Taliban leaders a series of clear and specific demands:Close terrorist training camps; hand over leaders of the al Qaeda network; and return all foreign nationals, including American citizens, unjustly detained in your country. None of these demands were met. And now the Taliban will pay a price. By destroying camps and disrupting communications, we will make it more difficult for the terror network to train new recruits and coordinate their evil plans.

Initially, the terrorists may burrow deeper into caves and other entrenched hiding places. Our military action is also designed to clear the way for sustained, comprehensive and relentless operations to drive them out and bring them to justice.

At the same time, the oppressed people of Afghanistan will know the generosity of America and our allies. As we strike military targets, we'll also drop food, medicine and supplies to the starving and suffering men and women and children of Afghanistan.

The United States of America is a friend to the Afghan people, and we are the friends of almost a billion worldwide who practice the Islamic faith. The United States of America is an enemy of those who aid terrorists and of the barbaric criminals who profane a great religion by committing murder in its name.

This military action is a part of our campaign against terrorism, another front in a war that has already been joined through diplomacy, intelligence, the freezing of financial assets and the arrests of known terrorists by law enforcement agents in 38 countries. Given the nature and reach of our enemies, we will win this conflict by the patient accumulation of successes, by meeting a series of challenges with determination and will and purpose.

Today we focus on Afghanistan, but the battle is broader. Every nation has a choice to make. In this conflict, there is no neutral ground. If any government sponsors the outlaws and killers of innocents, they have become outlaws and murderers, themselves. And they will take that lonely path at their own peril.

I'm speaking to you today from the Treaty Room of the White House, a place where American Presidents have worked for peace. We're a peaceful nation. Yet, as we have learned, so suddenly and so tragically, there can be no peace in a world of sudden terror. In the face of today's new threat, the only way to pursue peace is to pursue those who threaten it.

We did not ask for this mission, but we will fulfill it. The name of today's military operation is Enduring Freedom. We defend not only our precious freedoms, but also the freedom of people everywhere to live and raise their children free from fear.

I know many Americans feel fear today. And our government is taking strong precautions. All law enforcement and intelligence agencies are working aggressively around America, around the world and around the clock. At my request, many governors have activated the National Guard to strengthen airport security. We have called up Reserves to reinforce our military capability and strengthen the protection of our homeland.

In the months ahead, our patience will be one of our strengths—patience with the long waits that will result from tighter security; patience and understanding that it will take time to achieve our goals; patience in all the sacrifices that may come.

Today, those sacrifices are being made by members of our Armed Forces who now defend us so far from home, and by their proud and worried families. A Commander-in-Chief sends America's sons and daughters into a battle in a foreign land only after the greatest care and a lot of prayer. We ask a lot of those who wear our uniform. We ask them to leave their loved ones, to travel great distances, to risk injury, even to be prepared to make the ultimate sacrifice of their lives. They are dedicated, they are honorable; they represent the best of our country. And we are grateful.

To all the men and women in our military—every sailor, every soldier, every airman, every coastguardsman, every Marine— I say this: Your mission is defined; your objectives are clear; your goal is just. You have my full confidence, and you will have every tool you need to carry out your duty.

I recently received a touching letter that says a lot about the state of America in these difficult times—a letter from a 4th-grade girl, with a father in the military: "As much as I don't want my Dad to fight," she wrote, "I'm willing to give him to you."

This is a precious gift, the greatest she could give. This young girl knows what America is all about. Since September 11, an entire generation of young Americans has gained new understanding of the value of freedom, and its cost in duty and in sacrifice.

The battle is now joined on many fronts. We will not waver; we will not tire; we will not falter; and we will not fail. Peace and freedom will prevail.

Thank you. May God continue to bless America.

DOCUMENT NO. 4

EXECUTIVE ORDER 13224
BLOCKING PROPERTY AND PROHIBITING TRANSACTIONS WITH PERSONS WHO COMMIT, THREATEN TO COMMIT, OR SUPPORT TERRORISM

**As Updated Through the Special Bulletin Dated
December 14, 2001**

COMMENTARY: The original Executive Order of September 23, 2001 is carried as Document No. 1 in Volume 29. This later version incorporates numerous additions to the listing of proscribed entities.

Executive Order 13224 blocking Terrorist Property and a summary of the Terrorism Sanctions Regulations (Title 31 Part 595 of the U.S. Code of Federal Regulations), Terrorism List Governments Sanctions Regulations (Title 31 Part 596 of the U.S. Code of Federal Regulations), and Foreign Terrorist Organizations Sanctions Regulations (Title 31 Part 597 of the U.S. Code of Federal Regulations)

By the authority vested in me as President by the Constitution and the laws of the United States of America, including the International Emergency Economic Powers Act (50 U.S.C. 1701 et seq.)(IEEPA), the National Emergencies Act (50 U.S.C. 1601 et seq.), section 5 of the United Nations Participation Act of 1945, as amended (22 U.S.C. 287c) (UNPA), and section 301 of title 3, United States Code, and in view of United Nations Security Council Resolution (UNSCR) 1214 of December 8, 1998, UNSCR 1267 of October 15, 1999, UNSCR 1333 of December 19, 2000, and the multilateral sanctions contained therein, and UNSCR 1363 of July 30, 2001, establishing a mechanism to monitor the implementation of UNSCR 1333,

I, GEORGE W. BUSH, President of the United States of America, find that grave acts of terrorism and threats of terrorism committed by foreign terrorists, including the terrorist attacks in New York, Pennsylvania, and the Pentagon committed on September 11, 2001, acts recognized and condemned in UNSCR 1368 of September 12, 2001, and UNSCR 1269 of October 19, 1999, and the continuing and immediate threat of further attacks on United States nationals or the United States constitute an unusual and extraordinary threat to the national security, foreign policy, and economy of the United States, and in furtherance of my proclamation of September 14, 2001, Declaration of National Emergency by Reason of Certain Terrorist Attacks, hereby declare a national emergency to deal with that threat. I also find that because of the pervasiveness and expansiveness of the financial foundation of foreign terrorists, financial sanctions may be appropriate for those foreign persons that support or otherwise associate with these foreign terrorists. I also find that a need exists for further consultation and cooperation with, and sharing of information by, United States and foreign financial institutions as an additional tool to enable the United States to combat the financing of terrorism.

I hereby order:

Section 1. Except to the extent required by section 203(b) of IEEPA (50 U.S.C. 1702(b)), or provided in regulations, orders, directives, or licenses that may be issued pursuant to this order, and notwithstanding any contract entered into or any license or permit granted prior to the effective date of this order, all property and interests in property of the following persons that are in the United States or that hereafter come within the United States, or that hereafter come within the possession or control of United States persons are blocked:

(a) foreign persons listed in the Annex to this order;

(b) foreign persons determined by the Secretary of State, in consultation with the Secretary of the Treasury and the Attorney General, to have committed, or to pose a significant risk of committing, acts of terrorism that threaten the security of U.S. nationals or the national security, foreign policy, or economy of the United States;

(c) persons determined by the Secretary of the Treasury, in consultation with the Secretary of State and the Attorney General, to be owned or controlled by, or to act for or on behalf of those persons listed in the Annex to this order or those persons determined to be subject to subsection 1(b), 1(c), or 1(d)(i) of this order;

(d) except as provided in section 5 of this order and after such consultation, if any, with foreign authorities as the Secretary of State, in consultation with the Secretary of the Treasury and the Attorney General, deems appropriate in the exercise of his discretion, persons determined by the Secretary of the Treasury, in consultation with the Secretary of State and the Attorney General;

(i) to assist in, sponsor, or provide financial, material, or technological support for, or financial or other services to or in support of, such acts of terrorism or those persons listed in the Annex to this order or determined to be subject to this order; or

(ii) to be otherwise associated with those persons listed in the Annex to this order or those persons determined to be subject to subsection 1(b), 1(c), or 1(d)(i) of this order.

Sec. 2. Except to the extent required by section 203(b) of IEEPA (50 U.S.C. 1702(b)), or provided in regulations, orders, directives, or licenses that may be issued pursuant to this order, and notwithstanding any contract entered into or any license or permit granted prior to the effective date:

(a) any transaction or dealing by United States persons or within the United States in property or interests in property blocked pursuant to this order is prohibited, including but not limited to the making or receiving of any contribution of funds, goods, or services to or for the benefit of those persons listed in the Annex to this order or determined to be subject to this order;

(b) any transaction by any United States person or within the United States that evades or avoids, or has the purpose of evading or avoiding, or attempts to violate, any of the prohibitions set forth in this order is prohibited; and

(c) any conspiracy formed to violate any of the prohibitions set forth in this order is prohibited.

Sec. 3. For purposes of this order:

(a) the term "person" means an individual or entity;

(b) the term "entity" means a partnership, association, corporation, or other organization, group, or subgroup;

(c) the term "United States person" means any United States citizen, permanent resident alien, entity organized under the laws of the United States (including foreign branches), or any person in the United States; and

(d) the term "terrorism" means an activity that—

(i) involves a violent act or an act dangerous to human life, property, or infrastructure; and

(ii) appears to be intended—

(A) to intimidate or coerce a civilian population;

(B) to influence the policy of a government by intimidation or coercion; or

(C) to affect the conduct of a government by mass destruction, assassination, kidnapping, or hostage-taking.

Sec. 4. I hereby determine that the making of donations of the type specified in section 203(b)(2) of IEEPA (50 U.S.C. 1702(b)(2)) by United States persons to persons determined to be subject to this order would seriously impair my ability to deal with the national emergency declared in this order, and would endanger Armed Forces of the United States that are in a situation where imminent involvement in hostilities is clearly indicated by the circumstances, and hereby prohibit such donations as provided by section 1 of this order. Furthermore, I hereby determine that the Trade Sanctions Reform and Export Enhancement Act of 2000 (title IX, Public Law 106387) shall not affect the imposition or the continuation of the imposition of any unilateral agricultural sanction or unilateral medical sanction on any person determined to be subject to this order because imminent involvement of the Armed Forces of the United States in hostilities is clearly indicated by the circumstances.

Sec. 5. With respect to those persons designated pursuant to subsection 1(d) of this order, the Secretary of the Treasury, in the exercise of his discretion and in consultation with the Secretary of State and the Attorney General, may take such other actions than the complete blocking of property or interests in property as the President is authorized to take under IEEPA and UNPA if the Secretary of the Treasury, in consultation with the Secretary of State and the Attorney General, deems such other actions to be consistent with the national interests of the United States, considering such factors as he deems appropriate.

Sec. 6. The Secretary of State, the Secretary of the Treasury, and other appropriate agencies shall make all relevant efforts to cooperate and coordinate with other countries, including through technical assistance, as well as bilateral and multilateral agreements and arrangements, to achieve the objectives of this order, including the prevention and suppression of acts of terrorism, the denial of financing and financial services to terrorists and terrorist organizations, and the sharing of intelligence about funding activities in support of terrorism.

Sec. 7. The Secretary of the Treasury, in consultation with the Secretary of State and the Attorney General, is hereby authorized to take such actions, including the promulgation of rules and regulations, and to employ all powers granted to the President by IEEPA and UNPA as may be necessary to carry out the purposes of this order. The Secretary of the Treasury may redelegate any of these functions to other officers and agencies of the United States Government. All agencies of the United States Government are hereby directed to take all appropriate measures within their authority to carry out the provisions of this order.

Sec. 8. Nothing in this order is intended to affect the continued effectiveness of any rules, regulations, orders, licenses, or other forms of administrative action issued, taken, or continued in effect heretofore or hereafter under 31 C.F.R. chapter V, except as expressly terminated, modified, or suspended by or pursuant to this order.

Sec. 9. Nothing contained in this order is intended to create, nor does it create, any right, benefit, or privilege, substantive or procedural, enforceable at law by a party against the United States, its agencies, officers, employees or any other person.

Sec. 10. For those persons listed in the Annex to this order or determined to be subject to this order who might have a constitutional presence in the United States, I find that because of the ability to transfer funds or assets instantaneously, prior notice to such persons of measures to be taken pursuant to this order would render these measures ineffectual. I therefore determine that for these measures to be effective in addressing the national emergency declared in this order, there need be no prior notice of a listing or determination made pursuant to this order.

Sec. 11. (a) This order is effective at 12:01 a.m. eastern daylight time on September 24, 2001.

(b) This order shall be transmitted to the Congress and published in the *Federal Register.*

THE WHITE HOUSE,

September 23, 2001.

ANNEX

Al Qaida/Islamic Army

Abu Sayyaf Group

Armed Islamic Group (GIA)

Harakat ul-Mujahidin (HUM)

Al-Jihad (Egyptian Islamic Jihad)

Islamic Movement of Uzbekistan (IMU)

Asbat al-Ansar

Salafist Group for Call and Combat (GSPC)

Libyan Islamic Fighting Group

Al-Itihaad al-Islamiya (AIAI)

Islamic Army of Aden

Usama bin Laden

Muhammad Atif (aka, Subhi Abu Sitta, Abu Hafs Al Masri)

Sayf al-Adl

Shaykh Sai'id (aka, Mustafa Muhammad Ahmad)

Abu Hafs the Mauritanian (aka, Mahfouz Ould al-Walid, Khalid Al-Shanqiti)

Ibn Al-Shaykh al-Libi

Abu Zubaydah (aka, Zayn al-Abidin Muhammad Husayn, Tariq)

Abd al-Hadi al-Iraqi (aka, Abu Abdallah)

Ayman al-Zawahiri

Thirwat Salah Shihata

Tariq Anwar al-Sayyid Ahmad (aka, Fathi, Amr al-Fatih)

Muhammad Salah (aka, Nasr Fahmi Nasr Hasanayn)

Makhtab Al-Khidamat/Al Kifah

Wafa Humanitarian Organization

Al Rashid Trust

Mamoun Darkazanli Import-Export Company

NAMES OF THOSE DESIGNATED ON 10-12-01

Abdullah Ahmed Abdullah

Haji Abdul Manan Agha

Al-Hamati Sweets Bakeries

Muhammad Al-Hamati

Amin Al-Haq

Saqar Al-Jadawi

Ahmad Sa'id Al-Kadr

Anas Al-Liby

Ahmad Ibrahim Al-Mughassil

Abdelkarim Hussein Mohamed Al-Nasser

Al-Nur Honey Press Shops

Yasin Al-Qadi

Sa'd Al-Sharif

Al-Shifa' Honey Press for Industry and Commerce

Ibrahim Salih Mohammed Al-Yacoub

Ahmed Mohammed Hamed Ali

Ali Atwa

Muhsin Musa Matwalli Atwah

Bilal Bin Marwan

Ayadi Chafiq Bin Muhammad

Mamoun Darkazanli

Ali Saed Bin Ali El-Hoorie

Mustafa Mohamed Fadhil

Ahmed Khalfan Ghailani

Riad Hijazi

Hasan Izz-Al-Din

Jaish-I-Mohammed

Jam'Yah Ta'Awun Al-Islamia

Mufti Rashid Ahmad Ladehyanoy

Fazul Abdullah Mohammed

Khalid Shaikh Mohammed

Fahid Mohammed Ally Msalam

Imad Fa'iz Mughniyah

Rabita Trust

Sheikh Ahmed Salim Swedan

Omar Mahmoud Uthman

Abdul Rahman Yasin

Tohir Yuldashev

Mohammad Zia

NAMES OF THOSE DESIGNATED ON 11-07-01

Aaran Money Wire Service Inc.

Abbas Abdi Ali

Abdi Abdulaziz Ali

Abdirisak Aden

Abdullahi Hussein Kahie

Ahmed Nur Ali Jim'ale (a.k.a. Ahmad Nur Ali Jim'ale; a.k.a. Ahmad Ali Jimale; a.k.a. Ahmed Nur Jumale; a.k.a. Ahmed Ali Jumali)

Al Baraka Exchange LLC

Al Taqwa Trade, Property and Industry Company Limited (f.k.a. Al Taqwa Trade, Property and Industry; f.k.a. Al Taqwa Trade, Property and Industry Establishment; f.k.a. Himmat Establishment)

Al-Barakaat (Mogadishu)

Al-Barakaat Bank (Mogadishu)

Al-Barakaat Bank of Somalia (a.k.a. Barakaat Bank of Somalia; a.k.a. BBS)

Al-Barakaat Group of Companies Somalia Limited (a.k.a. Al-Barakat Financial Company)

Al-Barakat Finance Group

Al-Barakat Financial Holding Company

Al-Barakat Global Telecommunications (a.k.a. Barakaat Globetelcompany)

Al-Barakaat Wiring Service (U.S.A.)

Al-Barakat International (a.k.a. Baraco Co.)

Al-Barakat Investments

Albert Friedrich Armand Huber (a.k.a. Ahmed Huber)

Ali Ghaleb Himmat

Asat Trust Reg.

Bank Al Taqwa Limited (a.k.a. Al Taqwa Bank; a.k.a. Bank Al Taqwa

Baraka Trading Company

Barakaat Boston (U.S.A.)

Barakaat Construction Company

Barakaat Enterprise (U.S.A.)

Barakaat Group of Companies

Barakaat International (Sweden)

Barakaat International Companies (BICO)

Barakaat International Foundation

Barakaat International, Inc. (U.S.A.)

Barakaat North America, Inc. (Canada & U.S.A.)

Barakaat Red Sea Telecommunications

Barakaat Telecommunications Co. Somalia, Ltd.

Barakat Telecommunications Company Limited (BTELCO)

Barakat Bank and Remittances

Barakat Computer Consulting (BCC)

Barakat Consulting Group (BCG)

Barakat Global Telephone Company

Barakat Post Express (BPE)

Barakat Refreshment Company

Barakat Wire Transfer Company (U.S.A.)

Barako Trading Company LLC

Dahir Ubeidullahi Aweys

Garad Jama (a.k.a. Garad K. Nor; a.k.a. Fartune Ahmed Wasrsame)

Global Service International (U.S.A.)

Hassan Dahir Aweys (a.k.a. Sheikh Hassan Dahir Aweys; a.k.a. Shaykh Hassan Dahir Awes)

Heyatul Ulya

Hussein Mahamud Abdullkadir

Liban Hussein

Mohamed Mansour (a.k.a. Dr. Mohamed Al-Mansour)

Nada Management Organization SA (f.k.a. Al Taqwa Management Organization SA)

Parka Trading Company

Red Sea Barakat Company Limited

Somali International Relief Organization (U.S.A.)

Somali Internet Company

Somali Network AB (a.k.a. SOM NET AB)

Youssef M. Nada

Youssef M. Nada & Co. Gesellschaft M.B.H.

Youssef Nada (a.k.a. Youssef M. Nada; a.k.a. Youssef Mustafa Nada)

Yusaf Ahmed Ali

Zeinab Mansour-Fattouh

NAMES OF THOSE DESIGNATED ON 12-04-01

Al-Aqsa Islamic Bank (A.K.A. Al-Aqsa Al-Islami Bank)

Beit El-Mal Holdings (A.K.A. Arab Palestinian Beit El-Mal Company; A.K.A. Beit Al Mal Holdings; A.K.A. Beit El Mal Al-Phalastini Al-Arabi Al-Mushima Al-Aama Al-Mahaduda Ltd.; A.K.A. Palestinian Arab Beit El Mal Corporation, Ltd.)

Holy Land Foundation For Relief And Development (F.K.A. Occupied Land Fund) (U.S.A.)

NAMES OF THOSE DESIGNATED ON 12-20-01

Lashkar E-Tayyiba (a.k.a. Army of the Righteous; a.k.a. Lashkar E-Toiba; a.k.a. Lashkar-I-Taiba)

Sultan Bashir-Ud-Din Mahmood (a.k.a. Sultan Bashiruddin Mahmood; a.k.a. Dr. Bashir Uddin Mehmood; a.k.a. Sultan Baishiruddin Mekmud)

Abdul Majeed (a.k.a. Chaudhry Abdul Majeed; a.k.a. Abdul Majid)

Mohammed Tufail (a.k.a. S.M. Tufail; a.k.a. Sheik Mohammed Tufail)

Ummah Tameer E-Nau (UTN) (a.k.a. Foundation for Construction; a.k.a. Nation Building; a.k.a. Reconstruction Foundation; a.k.a. Reconstruction of the Islamic Community; a.k.a. Reconstruction of the Muslim Ummah; a.k.a. Ummah Tameer I-Nau; a.k.a. Ummah Tameer E-Nau; a.k.a. Ummah Tamir I-Nau; a.k.a. Ummat Tamir E-Nau; a.k.a. Ummat Tamir I-Pau)

NAMES OF THOSE LISTED ON 12-31-01

Continuity IRA (CIRA)

Loyalist Volunteer Force (LVF)

Orange Volunteers

Red Hand Defenders (RHD)

Ulster Defence Association (a.k.a. Ulster Freedom Fighters)

First of October Antifascist Resistance Group (GRAPO)

Details of Specially Designated Global Terrorist [SDGT] Entities

17 NOVEMBER (a.k.a. REVOLUTIONARY ORGANIZATION 17 NOVEMBER; a.k.a. EPANASTATIKI ORGANOSI 17 NOEMVRI) [FTO] **also listed as [SDGT] on 10-31-01**

32 COUNTY SOVEREIGNTY COMMITTEE (a.k.a. 32 COUNTY SOVEREIGNTY MOVEMENT; a.k.a. IRISH REPUBLICAN PRISONERS WELFARE ASSOCIATION; a.k.a. REAL IRA; a.k.a. REAL IRISH REPUBLICAN ARMY; a.k.a. REAL OGLAIGH NA HEIREANN; a.k.a. RIRA) [FTO] **also listed as [SDGT] on 10-31-01**

32 COUNTY SOVEREIGNTY MOVEMENT (a.k.a. 32 COUNTY SOVEREIGNTY COMMITTEE; a.k.a. IRISH REPUBLICAN PRISONERS WELFARE ASSOCIATION; REAL IRA; a.k.a. REAL IRISH REPUBLICAN ARMY; a.k.a. REAL OGLAIGH NA HEIREANN; a.k.a. RIRA) [FTO] **also listed as [SDGT] on 10-31-01**

A.I.C. COMPREHENSIVE RESEARCH INSTITUTE (a.k.a. AUM SHINRIKYO; a.k.a. A.I.C. SOGO KENKYUSHO; a.k.a. ALEPH; a.k.a. AUM SUPREME TRUTH) [FTO] **also listed as [SDGT] on 10-31-01**

A.I.C. SOGO KENKYUSHO (a.k.a. AUM SHINRIKYO; a.k.a. A.I.C. COMPREHENSIVE RESEARCH INSTITUTE; a.k.a. ALEPH; a.k.a. AUM SUPREME TRUTH) [FTO] **also listed as [SDGT] on 10-31-01**

AARAN MONEY WIRE SERVICE INC., 1806 Riverside Ave., 2nd Floor, Minneapolis, Minnesota, U.S.A. [SDGT] **11-07-01**

ABU GHUNAYM SQUAD OF THE HIZBALLAH BAYT AL-MAQDIS (a.k.a. PALESTINE ISLAMIC JIHAD - SHAQAQI FACTION; a.k.a. AL-AWDAH BRIGADES; a.k.a. AL-QUDS BRIGADES; a.k.a. AL-QUDS SQUADS; a.k.a. ISLAMIC JIHAD IN PALESTINE; a.k.a. ISLAMIC JIHAD OF PALESTINE; a.k.a. PALESTINIAN ISLAMIC JIHAD; a.k.a. PIJ; a.k.a. PIJ-SHALLAH FACTION; a.k.a. PIJ-SHAQAQI FACTION; a.k.a. SAYARA AL-QUDS) [SDT] [FTO] also listed as [SDGT] on 10-31-01

ABU NIDAL ORGANIZATION (a.k.a. ANO; a.k.a. BLACK SEPTEMBER; a.k.a. FATAH REVOLUTIONARY COUNCIL; a.k.a. ARAB REVOLUTIONARY COUNCIL; a.k.a. ARAB REVOLUTIONARY BRIGADES; a.k.a. REVOLUTIONARY ORGANIZATION OF SOCIALIST MUSLIMS) [SDT] [FTO] also listed as [SDGT] on 10-31-01

ABU SAYYAF GROUP (a.k.a. AL HARAKAT AL ISLAMIYYA) [FTO] [SDGT] 09-24-01

AIAI (a.k.a. AL-ITIHAAD AL-ISLAMIYA) [SDGT] 09-24-01

AL-AWDAH BRIGADES (a.k.a. PALESTINE ISLAMIC JIHAD - SHAQAQI FACTION; a.k.a. ABU GHUNAYM SQUAD OF THE HIZBALLAH BAYT AL-MAQDIS; a.k.a AL-QUDS BRIGADES; a.k.a. AL-QUDS SQUADS; a.k.a. ISLAMIC JIHAD IN PALESTINE; a.k.a. ISLAMIC JIHAD OF PALESTINE; a.k.a. PALESTINIAN ISLAMIC JIHAD; a.k.a. PIJ; a.k.a. PIJ-SHALLAH FACTION; a.k.a. PIJ-SHAQAQI FACTION; a.k.a. SAYARA AL-QUDS) [SDT] [FTO] also listed as [SDGT] on 10-31-01

AL BARAKA EXCHANGE LLC, P.O. Box 20066, Dubai, U.A.E.; P.O. Box 3313, Deira, Dubai, U.A.E. [SDGT] 11-07-01

AL-FARAN (a.k.a. HARAKAT UL-MUJAHIDEEN; a.k.a. AL-HADID; a.k.a. AL-HADITH; a.k.a. HARAKAT UL-ANSAR; a.k.a. HARAKAT UL-MUJAHIDIN; a.k.a. HUA; a.k.a. HUM) [FTO] [SDGT] 09-24-01

AL-GAMA'AT (a.k.a. GI; a.k.a. ISLAMIC GROUP; a.k.a. IG; a.k.a. EGYPTIAN AL-GAMA'AT AL-ISLAMIYYA; a.k.a. ISLAMIC GAMA'AT; a.k.a. GAMA'A AL-ISLAMIYYA) [SDT][FTO] also listed as [SDGT] on 10-31-01

AL-HADID (a.k.a. HARAKAT UL-MUJAHIDEEN; a.k.a. AL-FARAN; a.k.a. AL-HADITH; a.k.a. HARAKAT UL-ANSAR; a.k.a. HARAKAT UL-MUJAHIDIN; a.k.a. HUA; a.k.a. HUM) [FTO] [SDGT] 09-24-01

AL-HADITH (a.k.a. HARAKAT UL-MUJAHIDEEN; a.k.a. AL-FARAN; a.k.a. AL-HADID; a.k.a. HARAKAT UL-ANSAR; a.k.a. HARAKAT UL-MUJAHIDIN; a.k.a. HUA; a.k.a. HUM) [FTO] [SDGT] 09-24-01

AL-HAMATI SWEETS BAKERIES, Al-Mukallah, Hadhramawt Governorate, Yemen [SDGT] 10-12-01

AL HARAKAT AL ISLAMIYYA (a.k.a. ABU SAYYAF GROUP) [FTO] [SDGT] 09-24-01

AL-ITIHAAD AL-ISLAMIYA (a.k.a. AIAI) [SDGT] 09-24-01

AL-JAMA'AH AL-ISLAMIYAH AL-MUSALLAH (a.k.a. ARMED ISLAMIC GROUP; a.k.a. GIA; a.k.a. GROUPEMENT ISLAMIQUE ARME) [FTO] [SDGT] 09-24-01

AL-JIHAD (a.k.a. EGYPTIAN AL-JIHAD; a.k.a. EGYPTIAN ISLAMIC JIHAD; a.k.a. JIHAD GROUP; a.k.a. NEW JIHAD) [SDT] [FTO] [SDGT] 09-24-01

AL-NUR HONEY CENTER (a.k.a. AL-NUR HONEY PRESS SHOPS), Sanaa, Yemen [SDGT] 10-12-01

AL-NUR HONEY PRESS SHOPS (a.k.a. AL-NUR HONEY CENTER), Sanaa, Yemen [SDGT] 10-12-01

AL QAEDA (a.k.a. ISLAMIC ARMY; a.k.a. "THE BASE;" a.k.a. AL QA'IDA; a.k.a. AL QAIDA; a.k.a. INTERNATIONAL FRONT FOR FIGHTING JEWS AND CRUSADES; a.k.a. ISLAMIC ARMY FOR THE LIBERATION OF HOLY SITES; a.k.a. ISLAMIC SALVATION FOUNDATION; a.k.a. THE GROUP FOR THE PRESERVATION OF THE HOLY SITES; a.k.a. THE ISLAMIC ARMY FOR THE LIBERATION OF THE HOLY PLACES; a.k.a. THE WORLD ISLAMIC FRONT FOR JIHAD AGAINST JEWS AND CRUSADERS; a.k.a. USAMA BIN LADEN NETWORK; a.k.a. USAMA BIN LADEN ORGANIZATION) [SDT] [FTO] [SDG] 09-24-01

AL QAIDA (a.k.a. ISLAMIC ARMY; a.k.a. "THE BASE;" a.k.a. AL QA'IDA; a.k.a. AL QAEDA; a.k.a. INTERNATIONAL FRONT FOR FIGHTING JEWS AND CRUSADES; a.k.a. ISLAMIC ARMY FOR THE LIBERATION OF HOLY SITES; a.k.a. ISLAMIC SALVATION FOUNDATION; a.k.a. THE GROUP FOR THE PRESERVATION OF THE HOLY SITES; a.k.a. THE ISLAMIC ARMY FOR THE LIBERATION OF THE HOLY PLACES; a.k.a. THE WORLD ISLAMIC FRONT FOR JIHAD AGAINST JEWS AND CRUSADERS; a.k.a. USAMA BIN LADEN NETWORK; a.k.a. USAMA BIN LADEN ORGANIZATION) [SDT] [FTO] [SDGT] 09-24-01

AL QA'IDA (a.k.a. ISLAMIC ARMY; a.k.a. "THE BASE;" a.k.a. AL QAEDA; a.k.a. AL QAIDA; a.k.a. INTERNATIONAL FRONT FOR FIGHTING JEWS AND CRUSADES; a.k.a. ISLAMIC ARMY FOR THE LIBERATION OF HOLY SITES; a.k.a. ISLAMIC SALVATION FOUNDATION; a.k.a. THE GROUP FOR THE PRESERVATION OF THE HOLY SITES; a.k.a. THE ISLAMIC ARMY FOR THE LIBERATION OF THE HOLY PLACES; a.k.a. THE WORLD ISLAMIC FRONT FOR JIHAD AGAINST JEWS AND CRUSADERS; a.k.a. USAMA BIN LADEN NETWORK; a.k.a. USAMA BIN LADEN ORGANIZATION) [SDT] [FTO] [SDGT] 09-24-01

AL-QUDS BRIGADES (a.k.a. PALESTINE ISLAMIC JIHAD - SHAQAQI FACTION; a.k.a. ABU GHUNAYM SQUAD OF THE HIZBALLAH BAYT AL-MAQDIS; a.k.a. AL-AWDAH BRIGADES; a.k.a. AL-QUDS SQUADS; a.k.a. ISLAMIC JIHAD IN PALESTINE; a.k.a. ISLAMIC JIHAD OF PALESTINE; a.k.a. PALESTINIAN ISLAMIC JIHAD; a.k.a. PIJ; a.k.a. PIJ-SHALLAH FACTION; a.k.a. PIJ-SHAQAQI FACTION; a.k.a. SAYARA AL-QUDS) [SDT] [FTO] **also listed as [SDGT] on 10-31-01**

AL-QUDS SQUADS (a.k.a. PALESTINE ISLAMIC JIHAD - SHAQAQI FACTION; a.k.a. ABU GHUNAYM SQUAD OF THE HIZBALLAH BAYT AL-MAQDIS; a.k.a. AL-AWDAH BRIGADES; a.k.a. AL-QUDS BRIGADES; a.k.a. ISLAMIC JIHAD IN PALESTINE; a.k.a. ISLAMIC JIHAD OF PALESTINE; a.k.a. PALESTINIAN ISLAMIC JIHAD; a.k.a. PIJ; a.k.a. PIJ-SHALLAH FACTION; a.k.a. PIJ-SHAQAQI FACTION; a.k.a. SAYARA AL-QUDS) [SDT] [FTO] **also listed as [SDGT] on 10-31-01**

AL-RASEED TRUST (a.k.a. AL RASHID TRUST; a.k.a. AL RASHEED TRUST; a.k.a. AL-RASHID TRUST), Kitab Ghar, 4 Dar-el-Iftah, Nazimabad, Karachi, Pakistan; Jamia Masjid, Sulaiman Park, Begum Pura, Lahore, Pakistan; Office Dha'rb-i-M'unin, opposite Khyber Bank, Abbottabad Road, Mansehra, Pakistan; Office Dha'rb-i-M'unin, Z.R. Brothers, Katchehry Road, Chowk Yadgaar, Peshawar, Pakistan; Office Dha'rb-i-M'unin, Room no. 3, Third Floor, Moti Plaza, near Liaquat Bagh, Murree Road, Rawalpindi, Pakistan; Office Dha'rb-i-M'unin, Top Floor, Dr. Dawa Khan Dental Clinic Surgeon, Main Baxar, Mingora, Swat, Pakistan <Operations in Afghanistan: Herat, Jalalabad, Kabul, Kandahar, Mazar Sharif. Also operations in: Kosovo, Chechnya> [SDGT] **09-24-01**

AL RASHEED TRUST (a.k.a. AL RASHID TRUST; a.k.a. AL-RASHEED TRUST; a.k.a. AL-RASHID TRUST), Kitab Ghar, 4 Dar-el-Iftah, Nazimabad, Karachi, Pakistan; Jamia Masjid, Sulaiman Park, Begum Pura, Lahore, Pakistan; Office Dha'rb-i-M'unin, opposite Khyber Bank, Abbottabad Road, Mansehra, Pakistan; Office Dha'rb-i-M'unin, Z.R. Brothers, Katchehry Road, Chowk Yadgaar, Peshawar, Pakistan; Office Dha'rb-i-M'unin, Room no. 3, Third Floor, Moti Plaza, near Liaquat Bagh, Murree Road, Rawalpindi, Pakistan; Office Dha'rb-i-M'unin, Top Floor, Dr. Dawa Khan Dental Clinic Surgeon, Main Baxar, Mingora, Swat, Pakistan <Operations in Afghanistan: Herat, Jalalabad, Kabul, Kandahar, Mazar Sharif. Also operations in: Kosovo, Chechnya> [SDGT] **09-24-01**

AL RASHID TRUST (a.k.a. AL RASHEED TRUST; a.k.a. AL-RASHEED TRUST; a.k.a. AL-RASHID TRUST), Kitab Ghar, 4 Dar-el-Iftah, Nazimabad, Karachi, Pakistan; Jamia Masjid, Sulaiman Park, Begum Pura, Lahore, Pakistan; Office Dha'rb-i-M'unin, opposite Khyber Bank, Abbottabad Road, Mansehra, Pakistan; Office Dha'rb-i-M'unin, Z.R. Brothers, Katchehry Road, Chowk Yadgaar, Peshawar, Pakistan; Office Dha'rb-i-M'unin, Room no. 3, Third Floor, Moti Plaza, near Liaquat Bagh, Murree Road,

Rawalpindi, Pakistan; Office Dha'rb-i-M'unin, Top Floor, Dr. Dawa Khan Dental Clinic Surgeon, Main Baxar, Mingora, Swat, Pakistan <Operations in Afghanistan: Herat, Jalalabad, Kabul, Kandahar, Mazar Sharif. Also operations in: Kosovo, Chechnya> [SDGT] **09-24-01**

AL-RASHID TRUST (a.k.a. AL RASHID TRUST; a.k.a. AL RASHEED TRUST; a.k.a. AL-RASHEED TRUST), Kitab Ghar, 4 Dar-el-Iftah, Nazimabad, Karachi, Pakistan; Jamia Masjid, Sulaiman Park, Begum Pura, Lahore, Pakistan; Office Dha'rb-i-M'unin, opposite Khyber Bank, Abbottabad Road, Mansehra, Pakistan; Office Dha'rb-i-M'unin, Z.R. Brothers, Katchehry Road, Chowk Yadgaar, Peshawar, Pakistan; Office Dha'rb-i-M'unin, Room no. 3, Third Floor, Moti Plaza, near Liaquat Bagh, Murree Road, Rawalpindi, Pakistan; Office Dha'rb-i-M'unin, Top Floor, Dr. Dawa Khan Dental Clinic Surgeon, Main Baxar, Mingora, Swat, Pakistan <Operations in Afghanistan: Herat, Jalalabad, Kabul, Kandahar, Mazar Sharif. Also operations in: Kosovo, Chechnya> [SDGT] **09-24-01**

AL-SHIFA' HONEY PRESS FOR INDUSTRY AND COMMERCE, P.O. Box 8089, Al-Hasabah, Sanaa, Yemen; by the Shrine Next to the Gas Station, Jamal Street, Ta'iz, Yemen; Al-'Arudh Square, Khur Maksar, Aden, Yemen; Al-Nasr Street, Doha, Qatar [SDGT] **10-12-01**

AL TAQWA BANK (a.k.a. BANK AL TAQWA; BANK AL TAQWA LIMITED), c/o Arthur D. Hanna & Company, 10 Deveaux Street, Nassau, Bahamas; P.O. Box N-4877, Nassau, Bahamas [SDGT] **11-07-01**

AL TAQWA MANAGEMENT ORGANIZATION SA (n.k.a. NADA MANAGEMENT ORGANIZATION SA), Viale Stefano Franscini 22, Lugano CH-6900 TI, Switzerland [SDGT] **11-07-01**

AL TAQWA TRADE, PROPERTY AND INDUSTRY (n.k.a. AL TAQWA TRADE, PROPERTY AND INDUSTRY COMPANY LIMITED; a.k.a. AL TAQWA TRADE, PROPERTY AND INDUSTRY ESTABLISHMENT; a.k.a. HIMMAT ESTABLISHMENT), c/o Asat Trust Reg., Altenbach 8, Vaduz 9490, Liechtenstein [SDGT] **11-07-01**

AL TAQWA TRADE, PROPERTY AND INDUSTRY COMPANY LIMITED (f.k.a. AL TAQWA TRADE, PROPERTY AND INDUSTRY; f.k.a. AL TAQWA TRADE, PROPERTY AND INDUSTRY ESTABLISHMENT; f.k.a. HIMMAT ESTABLISHMENT), c/o Asat Trust Reg., Altenbach 8, Vaduz 9490, Liechtenstein [SDGT] **11-07-01**

AL TAQWA TRADE, PROPERTY AND INDUSTRY ESTABLISHMENT (a.k.a. AL TAQWA TRADE, PROPERTY AND INDUSTRY; n.k.a. AL TAQWA TRADE, PROPERTY AND INDUSTRY COMPANY LIMITED; a.k.a. HIMMAT ESTABLISHMENT), c/o Asat Trust Reg., Altenbach 8, Vaduz 9490, Liechtenstein [SDGT] **11-07-01**

AL WAFA (a.k.a. WAFA HUMANITARIAN ORGANIZATION; a.k.a. AL WAFA ORGANIZATION; a.k.a. WAFA AL-IGATHA AL-ISLAMIA) [SDGT] **09-24-01**

AL WAFA ORGANIZATION (a.k.a. WAFA HUMANITARIAN ORGANIZATION; a.k.a. AL WAFA; a.k.a. WAFA AL-IGATHA AL-ISLAMIA) [SDGT] **09-24-01**

AL-AQSA AL-ISLAMI BANK (a.k.a. AL-AQSA ISLAMIC BANK), P.O. Box 3753 al-Beireh, West Bank; Ramallah II 970, West Bank [SDGT] **12-04-01**

AL-AQSA ISLAMIC BANK (a.k.a. AL-AQSA AL-ISLAMI BANK), P.O. Box 3753 al-Beireh, West Bank; Ramallah II 970, West Bank [SDGT] **12-04-01**

AL-BARAKAAT BANK, Mogadishu, Somalia [SDGT] **11-07-01**

AL-BARAKAAT BANK OF SOMALIA (a.k.a. BARAKAAT BANK OF SOMALIA; a.k.a. BBS), Bossaso, Somalia; Mogadishu, Somalia [SDGT] **11-07-01**

AL-BARAKAAT GROUP OF COMPANIES SOMALIA LIMITED (a.k.a. AL-BARAKAT FINANCIAL COMPANY), Mogadishu, Somalia; P.O. Box 3313, Dubai, U.A.E. [SDGT] **11-07-01**

AL-BARAKAAT, Mogadishu, Somalia; Dubai, U.A.E. [SDGT] **11-07-01**

AL-BARAKAAT WIRING SERVICE, 2940 Pillsbury Avenue, Suite 4, Minneapolis, Minnesota 55408, U.S.A. [SDGT] **11-07-01**

AL-BARAKAT FINANCE GROUP, Dubai, U.A.E.; Mogadishu, Somalia [SDGT] **11-07-01**

AL-BARAKAT FINANCIAL COMPANY (a.k.a. AL-BARAKAAT GROUP OF COMPANIES SOMALIA LIMITED), Mogadishu, Somalia; P.O. Box 3313, Dubai, U.A.E. [SDGT] **11-07-01**

AL-BARAKAT FINANCIAL HOLDING COMPANY, Dubai, U.A.E.; Mogadishu, Somalia [SDGT] **11-07-01**

AL-BARAKAT GLOBAL TELECOMMUNICATIONS (a.k.a. BARAKAAT GLOBETELCOMPANY), Hargeysa, Somalia; Mogadishu, Somalia; P.O. Box 3313, Dubai, U.A.E. [SDGT] **11-07-01**

AL-BARAKAT INTERNATIONAL (a.k.a. BARACO CO.), Box 2923, Dubai, U.A.E. [SDGT] **11-07-01**

AL-BARAKAT INVESTMENTS, P.O. Box 3313, Deira, Dubai, U.A.E. [SDGT] **11-07-01**

ALEPH (a.k.a. AUM SHINRIKYO; a.k.a. A.I.C. COMPREHENSIVE RESEARCH INSTITUTE; a.k.a. A.I.C. SOGO KENKYUSHO; a.k.a. AUM SUPREME TRUTH) [FTO] **also listed as [SDGT] on 10-31-01**

ANO (a.k.a. ABU NIDAL ORGANIZATION; a.k.a. BLACK SEPTEMBER; a.k.a. FATAH REVOLUTIONARY COUNCIL; a.k.a. ARAB REVOLUTIONARY COUNCIL; a.k.a. ARAB REVOLUTIONARY

BRIGADES; a.k.a. REVOLUTIONARY ORGANIZATION OF SOCIALIST MUSLIMS) [SDT] [FTO] **also listed as [SDGT] on 10-31-01**

ANSAR ALLAH (a.k.a. HIZBALLAH; a.k.a. ISLAMIC JIHAD; a.k.a. ISLAMIC JIHAD ORGANIZATION; a.k.a. REVOLUTIONARY JUSTICE ORGANIZATION; a.k.a. ORGANIZATION OF THE OPPRESSED ON EARTH; a.k.a. ISLAMIC JIHAD FOR THE LIBERATION OF PALESTINE; a.k.a. ORGANIZATION OF RIGHT AGAINST WRONG; a.k.a. PARTY OF GOD; a.k.a. FOLLOWERS OF THE PROPHET MUHAMMED) [SDT] [FTO] **also listed as [SDGT] on 10-31-01**

ARAB PALESTINIAN BEIT EL-MAL COMPANY (a.k.a. BEIT AL MAL HOLDINGS; a.k.a. BEIT EL MAL AL-PHALASTINI AL-ARABI AL-MUSHIMA AL-AAMA AL-MAHADUDA LTD.; a.k.a. BEIT EL-MAL HOLDINGS; a.k.a. PALESTINIAN ARAB BEIT EL MAL CORPORATION, LTD.), P.O. Box 662, Ramallah, West Bank [SDGT] **12-04-01**

ARAB REVOLUTIONARY BRIGADES (a.k.a. ANO; a.k.a. BLACK SEPTEMBER; a.k.a. FATAH REVOLUTIONARY COUNCIL; a.k.a. ARAB REVOLUTIONARY COUNCIL; a.k.a. ABU NIDAL ORGANIZATION; a.k.a. REVOLUTIONARY ORGANIZATION OF SOCIALIST MUSLIMS) [SDT] [FTO] **also listed as [SDGT] on 10-31-01**

ARAB REVOLUTIONARY COUNCIL (a.k.a. ANO; a.k.a. BLACK SEPTEMBER; a.k.a. FATAH REVOLUTIONARY COUNCIL; a.k.a. ABU NIDAL ORGANIZATION; a.k.a. ARAB REVOLUTIONARY BRIGADES; a.k.a. REVOLUTIONARY ORGANIZATION OF SOCIALIST MUSLIMS) [SDT] [FTO] **also listed as [SDGT] on 10-31-01**

ARMED ISLAMIC GROUP (a.k.a. AL-JAMA'AH AL-ISLAMIYAH AL-MUSALLAH; a.k.a. GIA; a.k.a. GROUPEMENT ISLAMIQUE ARME) [FTO] [SDGT] **09-24-01**

ARMY OF MOHAMMED (a.k.a. JAISH-I-MOHAMMED; a.k.a. MOHAMMED'S ARMY; a.k.a. TEHRIK UL-FURQAAN), Pakistan [FTO] [SDGT] **10-12-01**

ARMY OF THE RIGHTEOUS (a.k.a. LASHKAR E-TAYYIBA; a.k.a. LASHKAR E-TOIBA; a.k.a. LASHKAR-I-TAIBA), Pakistan [FTO] [SDGT] **[12-20-01]**

ASAT TRUST REG., Altenbach 8, Vaduz 9490, Liechtenstein [SDGT] **11-07-01**

ASBAT AL-ANSAR [SDGT] **09-24-01**

AUC (a.k.a. AUTODEFENSAS UNIDAS DE COLOMBIA; a.k.a. UNITED SELF-DEFENSE FORCES OF COLOMBIA) [FTO] **also listed as [SDGT] on 10-31-01**

AUM SHINRIKYO (a.k.a. A.I.C. COMPREHENSIVE RESEARCH INSTITUTE; a.k.a. A.I.C. SOGO KENKYUSHO; a.k.a. ALEPH; a.k.a. AUM SUPREME TRUTH) [FTO] also listed as [SDGT] on 10-31-01

AUM SUPREME TRUTH (a.k.a. AUM SHINRIKYO; a.k.a. A.I.C. COMPREHENSIVE RESEARCH INSTITUTE; a.k.a. A.I.C. SOGO KENKYUSHO; a.k.a. ALEPH) [FTO] also listed as [SDGT] on 10-31-01

AUTODEFENSAS UNIDAS DE COLOMBIA (a.k.a. AUC; a.k.a. UNITED SELF-DEFENSE FORCES OF COLOMBIA) [FTO] also listed as [SDGT] on 10-31-01

BANK AL TAQWA (a.k.a. AL TAQWA BANK; a.k.a. BANK AL TAQWA LIMITED), c/o Arthur D. Hanna & Company, 10 Deveaux Street, Nassau, Bahamas; P.O. Box N-4877, Nassau, Bahamas [SDGT] 11-07-01

BANK AL TAQWA LIMITED (a.k.a. AL TAQWA BANK; a.k.a. BANK AL TAQWA), c/o Arthur D. Hanna & Company, 10 Deveaux Street, Nassau, Bahamas; P.O. Box N-4877, Nassau, Bahamas [SDGT] 11-07-01

BARACO CO. (a.k.a. AL-BARAKAT INTERNATIONAL), Box 2923, Dubai, U.A.E. [SDGT] 11-07-01

BARAKA TRADING COMPANY, P.O. Box 3313, Dubai, U.A.E. [SDGT] 11-07-01

BARAKAAT BANK OF SOMALIA (a.a.k.a. AL-BARAKAAT BANK OF SOMALIA; a.k.a. BBS), Bossaso, Somalia; Mogadishu, Somalia [SDGT] 11-07-01

BARAKAAT BOSTON, 266 Neponset Ave., Apt 43, Dorchester, Massachusetts 02122-3224, U.S.A. [SDGT] 11-07-01

BARAKAAT CONSTRUCTION COMPANY, P.O. Box 3313, Dubai, U.A.E. [SDGT] 11-07-01

BARAKAAT ENTERPRISE, 1762 Huy Rd., Columbus, Ohio 43224-3550, U.S.A. [SDGT] 11-07-01

BARAKAAT GLOBETELCOMPANY (a.k.a. AL-BARAKAT GLOBAL TELECOMMUNICATIONS), Hargeysa, Somalia; Mogadishu, Somalia; P.O. Box 3313, Dubai, U.A.E. [SDGT] 11-07-01

BARAKAAT GROUP OF COMPANIES, Mogadishu, Somalia; P.O. Box 3313, Dubai, U.A.E. [SDGT] 11-07-01

BARAKAAT INTERNATIONAL COMPANIES (BICO), Mogadishu, Somalia; Dubai, U.A.E. [SDGT] 11-07-01

BARAKAAT INTERNATIONAL FOUNDATION, P.O. Box 4036, Spanga, Sweden; Rinkebytorget 1, Spanga 04, Sweden [SDGT] 11-07-01

BARAKAAT INTERNATIONAL, Hallbybacken 15, Spanga 70, Sweden [SDGT] 11-07-01

BARAKAAT INTERNATIONAL, INC., 1929 South 5th Street, Suite 205, Minneapolis, Minnesota, U.S.A. [SDGT] **11-07-01**

BARAKAAT NORTH AMERICA, INC., 2019 Bank St., Ottawa, Ontario, Canada; 925 Washington St., Dorchester, Massachusetts, U.S.A. [SDGT] **11-07-01**

BARAKAAT RED SEA TELECOMMUNICATIONS, Ala Aamin, Somalia; Bossaso, Somalia; Bubaarag, Somalia; Carafaat, Somalia; Gufure, Somalia; Guureeye, Somalia; Huruuse, Somalia; Kowthar, Somalia; Najax, Somalia; Nakhiil, Somalia; Noobir, Somalia; Raxmo, Somalia; Ticis, Somalia; Xuuxuule, Somalia [SDGT] **11-07-01**

BARAKAAT TELECOMMUNICATIONS COMPANY LIMITED (a.k.a. BTELCO), Bakara Market, Dar Salaam Buildings, Mogadishu, Somalia; Kievitlaan 16, T'veld, Noord-Holland, The Netherlands [SDGT] **11-07-01**

BARAKAAT TELECOMMUNICATIONS COMPANY SOMALIA, LIMITED, P.O. Box 3313, Dubai, U.A.E. [SDGT] **11-07-01**

BARAKAT BANK AND REMITTANCES, Mogadishu, Somalia; Dubai, U.A.E. [SDGT] **11-07-01**

BARAKAT COMPUTER CONSULTING (BCC), Mogadishu, Somalia [SDGT] **11-07-01**

BARAKAT CONSULTING GROUP (BCG), Mogadishu, Somalia [SDGT] **11-07-01**

BARAKAT GLOBAL TELEPHONE COMPANY, Mogadishu, Somalia; Dubai, U.A.E. [SDGT] **11-07-01**

BARAKAT POST EXPRESS (BPE), Mogadishu, Somalia [SDGT] **11-07-01**

BARAKAT REFRESHMENT COMPANY, Mogadishu, Somalia; Dubai, U.A.E. [SDGT] **11-07-01**

BARAKAT WIRE TRANSFER COMPANY, 4419 S. Brandon St., Seattle, Washington, U.S.A. [SDGT] **11-07-01**

BARAKO TRADING COMPANY LLC, P.O. Box 3313, Dubai, U.A.E. [SDGT] **11-07-01**

BASQUE FATHERLAND AND LIBERTY (a.k.a. ETA; a.k.a. EUZKADI TA ASKATASUNA)[FTO] **also listed as [SDGT] on 10-31-01**

BBS (a.k.a. AL-BARAKAAT BANK OF SOMALIA; BARAKAAT BANK OF SOMALIA), Bossaso, Somalia; Mogadishu, Somalia [SDGT] **11-07-01**

BEIT AL MAL HOLDINGS (a.k.a. ARAB PALESTINIAN BEIT EL-MAL COMPANY; a.k.a. BEIT EL MAL AL-PHALASTINI AL-ARABI AL-MUSHIMA AL-AAMA AL-MAHADUDA LTD.; a.k.a. BEIT EL-MAL

HOLDINGS; a.k.a. PALESTINIAN ARAB BEIT EL MAL CORPORATION, LTD.), P.O. Box 662, Ramallah, West Bank [SDGT] **12-04-01**

BEIT EL MAL AL-PHALASTINI AL-ARABI AL-MUSHIMA AL-AAMA AL-MAHADUDA LTD. (a.k.a. ARAB PALESTINIAN BEIT EL-MAL COMPANY; a.k.a. BEIT AL MAL HOLDINGS; a.k.a. BEIT EL-MAL HOLDINGS; a.k.a. PALESTINIAN ARAB BEIT EL MAL CORPORATION, LTD.), P.O. Box 662, Ramallah, West Bank [SDGT] **12-04-01**

BEIT EL-MAL HOLDINGS (a.k.a. ARAB PALESTINIAN BEIT EL-MAL COMPANY; a.k.a. BEIT AL MAL HOLDINGS; a.k.a. BEIT EL MAL AL-PHALASTINI AL-ARABI AL-MUSHIMA AL-AAMA AL-MAHADUDA LTD.; a.k.a. PALESTINIAN ARAB BEIT EL MAL CORPORATION, LTD.), P.O. Box 662, Ramallah, West Bank [SDGT] **12-04-01**

BLACK SEPTEMBER (a.k.a. ANO; a.k.a. ABU NIDAL ORGANIZATION; a.k.a. FATAH REVOLUTIONARY COUNCIL; a.k.a. ARAB REVOLUTIONARY COUNCIL; a.k.a. ARAB REVOLUTIONARY BRIGADES; a.k.a. REVOLUTIONARY ORGANIZATION OF SOCIALIST MUSLIMS) [SDT] [FTO] **also listed as [SDGT] on 10-31-01**

BTELCO (a.k.a. BARAKAAT TELECOMMUNICATIONS COMPANY LIMITED), Bakara Market, Dar Salaam Buildings, Mogadishu, Somalia; Kievitlaan 16, T'veld, Noord-Holland, The Netherlands [SDGT] **11-07-01**

COMMITTEE FOR THE SAFETY OF THE ROADS (a.k.a. KAHANE CHAI; a.k.a. DIKUY BOGDIM; a.k.a. DOV; a.k.a. FOREFRONT OF THE IDEA; a.k.a. JUDEA POLICE; a.k.a. KACH; a.k.a. KAHANE LIVES; a.k.a. KFAR TAPUAH FUND; a.k.a. KOACH; a.k.a. REPRESSION OF TRAITORS; a.k.a. STATE OF JUDEA; a.k.a. SWORD OF DAVID; a.k.a. THE JUDEAN LEGION; a.k.a. THE JUDEAN VOICE; a.k.a. THE QOMEMIYUT MOVEMENT; a.k.a. THE WAY OF THE TORAH; a.k.a. THE YESHIVA OF THE JEWISH IDEA) [SDT] [FTO] **also listed as [SDGT] on 10-31-01**

CONTINUITY IRA (CIRA); United Kingdom [SDGT] **12-31-01**

DARKAZANLI COMPANY (a.k.a. MAMOUN DARKAZANLI IMPORT-EXPORT COMPANY; a.k.a. DARKAZANLI EXPORT-IMPORT SONDERPOSTEN), Uhlenhorsterweg 34 11, Hamburg, Germany [SDGT] **09-24-01**

DARKAZANLI EXPORT-IMPORT SONDERPOSTEN (a.k.a. MAMOUN DARKAZANLI IMPORT-EXPORT COMPANY; a.k.a. DARKAZANLI COMPANY), Uhlenhorsterweg 34 11, Hamburg, Germany [SDGT] **09-24-01**

DEV SO ARMED REVOLUTIONARY UNITS (a.k.a. DEVRIMCI HALK KURTULUS PARTISI-CEPHESI; a.k.a. DHKP/C; a.k.a. DEVRIMCI SOL; a.k.a. REVOLUTIONARY LEFT; a.k.a. DEV SOL; a.k.a. DEV SOL SILAHLI DEVRIMCI BIRLIKLERI; a.k.a. DEV SOL SDB; a.k.a. REVOLUTIONARY

PEOPLE'S LIBERATION PARTY/FRONT) [FTO] **also listed as [SDGT]** **on 10-31-01**

DEV SOL (a.k.a. DEVRIMCI HALK KURTULUS PARTISI-CEPHESI; a.k.a. DHKP/C; a.k.a. DEVRIMCI SOL; a.k.a. REVOLUTIONARY LEFT; a.k.a. REVOLUTIONARY PEOPLE'S LIBERATION PARTY/FRONT; a.k.a. DEV SOL SILAHLI DEVRIMCI BIRLIKLERI; a.k.a. DEV SOL SDB; a.k.a. DEV SOL ARMED REVOLUTIONARY UNITS) [FTO] **also listed as [SDGT] on 10-31-01**

DEV SOL SDB (a.k.a. DEVRIMCI HALK KURTULUS PARTISI-CEPHESI; a.k.a. DHKP/C; a.k.a. DEVRIMCI SOL; a.k.a. REVOLUTIONARY LEFT; a.k.a. DEV SOL; a.k.a. DEV SOL SILAHLI DEVRIMCI BIRLIKLERI; a.k.a. REVOLUTIONARY PEOPLE'S LIBERATION PARTY/FRONT; a.k.a. DEV SOL ARMED REVOLUTIONARY UNITS) [FTO] **also listed as [SDGT] on 10-31-01**

DEV SOL SILAHLI DEVRIMCI BIRLIKLERI (a.k.a. DEVRIMCI HALK KURTULUS PARTISI-CEPHESI; a.k.a. DHKP/C; a.k.a. DEVRIMCI SOL; a.k.a. REVOLUTIONARY LEFT; a.k.a. DEV SOL; a.k.a. REVOLUTIONARY PEOPLE'S LIBERATION PARTY/FRONT; a.k.a. DEV SOL SDB; a.k.a. DEV SOL ARMED REVOLUTIONARY UNITS) [FTO] **also listed as [SDGT] on 10-31-01**

DEVRIMCI HALK KURTULUS PARTISI-CEPHESI (a.k.a. REVOLUTIONARY PEOPLE'S LIERATION PARTY/FRONT; a.k.a. DHKP/C; a.k.a. DEVRIMCI SOL; a.k.a. REVOLUTIONARY LEFT; a.k.a. DEV SOL; a.k.a. DEV SOL SILAHLI DEVRIMCI BIRLIKLERI; a.k.a. DEV SOL SDB; a.k.a. DEV SOL ARMED REVOLUTIONARY UNITS) [FTO] **also listed as [SDGT] on 10-31-01**

DEVRIMCI SOL (a.k.a. DEVRIMCI HALK KURTULUS PARTISI-CEPHESI; a.k.a. DHKP/C; a.k.a. REVOLUTIONARY PEOPLE'S LIBERATION PARTY/FRONT; a.k.a. REVOLUTIONARY LEFT; a.k.a. DEV SOL; a.k.a. DEV SOL SILAHLI DEVRIMCI BIRLIKLERI; a.k.a. DEV SOL SDB; a.k.a. DEV SOL ARMED REVOLUTIONARY UNITS) [FTO] **also listed as [SDGT] on 10-31-01**

DHKP/C (a.k.a. DEVRIMCI HALK KURTULUS PARTISI-CEPHESI; a.k.a. REVOLUTIONARY PEOPLE'S LIBERATION PARTY/FRONT; a.k.a. DEVRIMCI SOL; a.k.a. REVOLUTIONARY LEFT; a.k.a. DEV SOL; a.k.a. DEV SOL SILAHLI DEVRIMCI BIRLIKLERI; a.k.a. DEV SOL SDB; a.k.a. DEV SOL ARMED REVOLUTIONARY UNITS) [FTO] **also listed as [SDGT] on 10-31-01**

DIKUY BOGDIM (a.k.a. KAHANE CHAI; a.k.a. COMMITTEE FOR THE SAFETY OF THE ROADS; a.k.a. DOV; a.k.a. FOREFRONT OF THE IDEA; a.k.a. JUDEA POLICE; a.k.a. KACH; a.k.a. KAHANE LIVES; a.k.a. KFAR TAPUAH FUND; a.k.a. KOACH; a.k.a. REPRESSION OF TRAITORS; a.k.a. STATE OF JUDEA; a.k.a. SWORD OF DAVID; a.k.a. THE JUDEAN

LEGION; a.k.a. THE JUDEAN VOICE; a.k.a. THE QOMEMIYUT MOVEMENT; a.k.a. THE WAY OF THE TORAH; a.k.a. THE YESHIVA OF THE JEWISH IDEA) [SDT] [FTO] **also listed as [SDGT] on 10-31-01**

DOV (a.k.a. KAHANE CHAI; a.k.a. COMMITTEE FOR THE SAFETY OF THE ROADS; a.k.a. DIKUY BOGDIM; a.k.a. FOREFRONT OF THE IDEA; a.k.a. JUDEA POLICE; a.k.a. KACH; a.k.a. KAHANE LIVES; a.k.a. KFAR TAPUAH FUND; a.k.a. KOACH; a.k.a. REPRESSION OF TRAITORS; a.k.a. STATE OF JUDEA; a.k.a. SWORD OF DAVID; a.k.a. THE JUDEAN LEGION; a.k.a. THE JUDEAN VOICE; a.k.a. THE QOMEMIYUT MOVEMENT; a.k.a. THE WAY OF THE TORAH; a.k.a. THE YESHIVA OF THE JEWISH IDEA) [SDT] [FTO] **also listed as [SDGT] on 10-31-01**

EGP (a.k.a. SENDERO LUMINOSO; a.k.a. SL; a.k.a. PARTIDO COMUNISTA DEL PERU EN EL SENDERO LUMINOSO DE JOSE CARLOS MARIATGUI (COMMUNIST PARTY OF PERU ON THE SHINING PATH OF JOSE CARLOS MARIATEGUI); a.k.a. PARTIDO COMUNISTA DEL PERU (COMMUNIST PARTY OF PERU); a.k.a. PCP; a.k.a. SOCORRO POPULAR DEL PERU (PEOPLE'S AID OF PERU); a.k.a. SPP; a.k.a EJERCITO GUERRILLERO POPULAR (PEOPLE'S GUERRILLA ARMY); a.k.a. SHINING PATH; a.k.a. EJERCITO POPULAR DE LIBERACION (PEOPLE'S LIBERATION ARMY); a.k.a. EPL) [FTO] **also listed as [SDGT] on 10-31-01**

EGYPTIAN AL-GAMA'AT AL-ISLAMIYYA (a.k.a. GI; a.k.a. ISLAMIC GROUP; a.k.a. IG; a.k.a. AL-GAMA'AT; a.k.a. ISLAMIC GAMA'AT; a.k.a. GAMA'A AL-ISLAMIYYA) [SDT][FTO] **also listed as [SDGT] on 10-31-01**

EGYPTIAN AL-JIHAD (a.k.a. AL-JIHAD; a.k.a. EGYPTIAN ISLAMIC JIHAD; a.k.a. JIHAD GROUP; a.k.a. NEW JIHAD) [SDT] [FTO] [SDGT] **09-24-01**

EGYPTIAN ISLAMIC JIHAD (a.k.a. AL-JIHAD; a.k.a. EGYPTIAN AL-JIHAD; a.k.a. JIHAD GROUP; a.k.a. NEW JIHAD) [SDT] [FTO] [SDGT] **09-24-01**

EJERCITO DE LIBERACION NACIONAL (a.k.a. NATIONAL LIBERATION ARMY; a.k.a. ELN) [FTO] **also listed as [SDGT] on 10-31-01**

EJERCITO GUERRILLERO POPULAR (PEOPLE'S GUERRILLA ARMY) (a.k.a. SENDERO LUMINOSO; a.k.a. SL; a.k.a. PARTIDO COMUNISTA DEL PERU EN EL SENDERO LUMINOSO DE JOSE CARLOS MARIATEGUI (COMMUNIST PARTY OF PERU ON THE SHINING PATH OF JOSE CARLOS MARIATEGUI); a.k.a. PARTIDO COMUNISTA DEL PERU (COMMUNIST PARTY OF PERU); a.k.a. PCP; a.k.a. SOCORRO POPULAR DEL PERU (PEOPLE'S AID OF PERU); a.k.a. SPP; a.k.a SHINING PATH; a.k.a. EGP; a.k.a. EJERCITO POPULAR DE LIBERACION (PEOPLE'S LIBERATION ARMY); a.k.a. EPL) [FTO] **also listed as [SDGT] on 10-31-01**

EJERCITO POPULAR DE LIBERACION (PEOPLE'S LIBERATION ARMY) (a.k.a. SENDERO LUMINOSO; a.k.a. SL; a.k.a. PARTIDO COMUNISTA DEL PERU EN EL SENDERO LUMINOSO DE JOSE CARLOS MARIATEGUI (COMMUNIST PARTY OF ERU ON THE SHINING PATH OF JOSE CARLOS MARIATEGUI); a.k.a. PARTIDO COMUNISTA DEL PERU (COMMUNIST PARTY OF PERU); a.k.a. PCP; a.k.a. SOCORRO POPULAR DEL PERU (PEOPLE'S AID OF PERU); a.k.a. SPP; a.k.a EJERCITO GUERRILLERO POPULAR (PEOPLE'S GUERRILLA ARMY); a.k.a. EGP; a.k.a. SHINING PATH ; a.k.a. EPL) [FTO] **also listed as [SDGT] on 10-31-01**

ELA (a.k.a. POPULAR REVOLUTIONARY STRUGGLE; a.k.a. EPANASTATIKOS LAIKOS AGONAS; a.k.a. REVOLUTIONARY POPULAR STRUGGLE; a.k.a. REVOLUTIONARY PEOPLE'S STRUGGLE; a.k.a. JUNE 78; a.k.a. ORGANIZATION OF REVOLUTIONARY INTERNATIONALIST SOLIDARITY; a.k.a. REVOLUTIONARY NUCLEI; a.k.a. REVOLUTIONARY CELLS; a.k.a. LIBERATION STRUGGLE) [FTO] **also listed as [SDGT] on 10-31-01**

ELLALAN FORCE (a.k.a. LIBERATION TIGERS OF TAMIL EELAM; a.k.a. LTTE; a.k.a. TAMIL TIGERS) [FTO] **also listed as [SDGT] on 10-31-01**

ELN (a.k.a. NATIONAL LIBERATION ARMY; a.k.a. EJERCITO DE LIBERACION NACIONAL) [FTO] **also listed as [SDGT] on 10-31-01**

EPANASTATIKI ORGANOSI 17 NOEMVRI (a.k.a. REVOLUTIONARY ORGANIZATION 17 NOVEMBER; a.k.a. 17 NOVEMBER) [FTO] **also listed as [SDGT] on 10-31-01**

EPANASTATIKOS LAIKOS AGONAS (a.k.a. POPULAR REVOLUTIONARY STRUGGLE; a.k.a. ELA; a.k.a. REVOLUTIONARY POPLAR STRUGGLE; a.k.a. REVOLUTIONARY PEOPLE'S STRUGGLE; a.k.a. JUNE 78; a.k.a. ORGANIZATION OF REVOLUTIONARY INTERNATIONALIST SOLIDARITY; a.k.a. REVOLUTIONARY NUCLEI; a.k.a. REVOLUTIONARY CELLS; a.k.a. LIBERATION STRUGGLE) [FTO] **also listed as [SDGT] on 10-31-01**

EPL (a.k.a. SENDERO LUMINOSO; a.k.a. SL; a.k.a. PARTIDO COMUNISTA DEL PERU EN EL SENDERO LUMINOSO DE JOSE CARLOS MARIATEGUI (COMMUNIST PARTY OF PERU ON THE SHINING PATH OF JOSE CARLOS MARIATEGUI); a.k.a. PARTIDO COMUNISTA DEL PERU (COMMUNIST PARTY OF PERU); a.k.a. PCP; a.k.a. SOCORRO POPULAR DEL PERU (PEOPLE'S AID OF PERU); a.k.a. SPP; a.k.a EJERCITO GUERRILLERO POPULAR (PEOPLE'S GUERRILLA ARMY); a.k.a. EGP; a.k.a. EJERCITO POPULAR DE LIBERACION (PEOPLE'S LIBERATION ARMY); a.k.a. SHINING PATH) [FTO] **also listed as [SDGT] on 10-31-01**

ETA (a.k.a. EUZKADI TA ASKATASUNA; a.k.a. BASQUE FATHERLAND AND LIBERTY) [FTO] **also listed as [SDGT] on 10-31-01**

EUZKADI TA ASKATASUNA (a.k.a. BASQUE FATHERLAND AND LIBERTY; a.k.a. ETA) [FTO] **also listed as [SDGT] on 10-31-01**

FARC (a.k.a. REVOLUTIONARY ARMED FORCES OF COLOMBIA; a.k.a. FUERZAS ARMADAS REVOLUCIONARIAS DE COLOMBIA) [FTO] **also listed as [SDGT] on 10-31-01**

FATAH REVOLUTIONARY COUNCIL (a.k.a. ANO; a.k.a. BLACK SEPTEMBER; a.k.a. ABU NIDAL ORGANIZATION a.k.a. ARAB REVOLUTIONARY COUNCIL; a.k.a. ARAB REVOLUTIONARY BRIGADES; a.k.a. REVOLUTIONARY ORGANIZATION OF SOCIALIST MUSLIMS) [SDT] [FTO] **also listed as [SDGT] on 10-31-01**

FIRST OF OCTOBER ANTIFASCIST RESISTANCE GROUP (GRAPO); Spain [SDGT] **12-31-01**

FOLLOWERS OF THE PROPHET MUHAMMED (a.k.a. HIZBALLAH; a.k.a. ISLAMIC JIHAD; a.k.a. ISLAMIC JIHAD ORGANIZATION; a.k.a. REVOLUTIONARY JUSTICE ORGANIZATION; a.k.a. ORGANIZATION OF THE OPPRESSED ON EARTH; a.k.a. ISLAMIC JIHAD FOR THE LIBERATION OF PALESTINE; a.k.a. ORGANIZATION OF RIGHT AGAINST WRONG; a.k.a. PARTY OF GOD; a.k.a. ANAR ALLAH) [SDT] [FTO] **also listed as [SDGT] on 10-31-01**

FOREFRONT OF THE IDEA (a.k.a. KAHANE CHAI; a.k.a. COMMITTEE FOR THE SAFETY OF THE ROADS; a.k.a. DIKUY BOGDIM; a.k.a. DOV; a.k.a. JUDEA POLICE; a.k.a. KACH; a.k.a. KAHANE LIVES; a.k.a. KFAR TAPUAH FUND; a.k.a. KOACH; a.k.a. REPRESSION OF TRAITORS; a.k.a. STATE OF JUDEA; a.k.a. SWORD OF DAVID; a.k.a. THE JUDEAN LEGION; a.k.a. THE JUDEAN VOICE; a.k.a. THE QOMEMIYUT MOVEMENT; a.k.a. THE WAY OF THE TORAH; a.k.a. THE YESHIVA OF THE JEWISH IDEA) [SDT] [FTO] **also listed as [SDGT] on 10-31-01**

FOUNDATION FOR CONSTRUCTION (a.k.a. UMMAH TAMEER E-NAU (UTN); a.k.a. NATION BUILDING; a.k.a. RECONSTRUCTION FOUNDATION; a.k.a. RECONSTRUCTION OF THE ISLAMIC COMMUNITY; a.k.a. RECONSTRUCTION OF THE MUSLIM UMMAH; a.k.a. UMMAH TAMEER I-NAU; a.k.a. UMMAH TAMIR E-NAU; a.k.a. UMMAH TAMIR I-NAU; a.k.a. UMMAT TAMIR E-NAU; a.k.a. UMMAT TAMIR-I-PAU), Street 13, Wazir Akbar Khan, Kabul, Afghanistan; 60-C, Nazim Ud Din Road, Islamabad F 8/4, Pakistan [SDGT] [FTO] **12-20-01**

FUERZAS ARMADAS REVOLUCIONARIAS DE COLOMBIA (a.k.a. REVOLUTIONARY ARMED FORCES OF COLOMBIA; a.k.a. FARC) [FTO] **also listed as [SDGT] on 10-31-01**

GAMA'A AL-ISLAMIYYA (a.k.a. GI; a.k.a. ISLAMIC GROUP; a.k.a. IG; a.k.a. AL-GAMA'AT; a.k.a. ISLAMIC GAMA'AT; a.k.a. EGYPTIAN AL-GAMA'AT AL-ISLAMIYYA) [SDT][FTO] **also listed as [SDGT] on 10-31-01**

GI (a.k.a. AL-GAMA'AT; a.k.a. ISLAMIC GROUP; a.k.a. IG; a.k.a. EGYPTIAN AL-GAMA'AT AL-ISLAMIYYA; a.k.a. ISLAMIC GAMA'AT; a.k.a. GAMA'A AL-ISLAMIYYA) [SDT][FTO] **also listed as [SDGT] on 10-31-01**

GIA (a.k.a. ARMED ISLAMIC GROUP; a.k.a. AL-JAMA'AH AL-ISLAMIYAH AL-MUSALLAH; a.k.a. GROUPEMENT ISLAMIQUE ARME) [FTO] [SDGT] **09-24-01**

GLOBAL SERVICE INTERNATIONAL, 1929 5th St., Suite 204, Minneapolis, Minnesota, U.S.A. [SDGT] **11-07-01**

GROUPEMENT ISLAMIQUE ARME (a.k.a. ARMED ISLAMIC GROUP; a.k.a. AL-JAMA'AH AL-ISLAMIYAH AL-MUSALLAH; a.k.a. GIA) [FTO] [SDGT] **09-24-01**

GSPC (a.k.a. SALAFIST GROUP FOR CALL AND COMBAT; a.k.a. LE GROUPE SALAFISTE POUR LA PREDICATION ET LE COMBAT) [SDGT] **09-24-01**

HALHUL GANG (a.k.a. POPULAR FRONT FOR THE LIBERATION OF PALESTINE; a.k.a. HALHUL SQUAD; a.k.a. PALESTINIAN POPULAR RESISTANCE FORCES; a.k.a. PFLP; a.k.a. PPRF; a.k.a. RED EAGLE GANG; a.k.a. RED EAGLE GROUP; a.k.a. RED EAGLES) [SDT] [FTO] **also listed as [SDGT] on 10-31-01**

HALHUL SQUAD (a.k.a. POPULAR FRONT FOR THE LIBERATION OF PALESTINE; a.k.a. HALHUL GANG; a.k.a. PALESTINIAN POPULAR RESISTANCE FORCES; a.k.a. PFLP; a.k.a. PPRF; a.k.a. RED EAGLE GANG; a.k.a. RED EAGLE GROUP; a.k.a. RED EAGLES) [SDT] [FTO] **also listed as [SDGT] on 10-31-01**

HALU MESRU SAVUNMA KUVVETI (HSK) (a.k.a. KURDISTAN WORKERS' PARTY; a.k.a. PARTIYA KARKERAN KURDISTAN; a.k.a. PKK; a.k.a. THE PEOPLE'S DEFENSE FORCE) [FTO] **also listed as [SDGT] on 10-31-01**

HAMAS (a.k.a. ISLAMIC RESISTANCE MOVEMENT; a.k.a. HARAKAT AL-MUQAWAMA AL-ISLAMIYA; a.k.a. STUDENTS OF AYYASH; a.k.a. STUDENT OF THE ENGINEER; a.k.a. YAHYA AYYASH UNITS; a.k.a. IZZ AL-DIN AL-QASSIM BRIGADES; a.k.a. IZZ AL-DIN AL-QASSIM FORCES; a.k.a. IZZ AL-DIN AL-QASSIM BATTALIONS; a.k.a. IZZ AL-DIN AL QASSAM BRIGADES; a.k.a. IZZ AL-DIN AL QASSAM FORCES; a.k.a. IZZ AL-DIN AL QASSAM BATTALIONS) [SDT] [FTO] **also listed as [SDGT] on 10-31-01**

HARAKAT AL-MUQAWAMA AL-ISLAMIYA (a.k.a. ISLAMIC RESISTANCE MOVEMENT; a.k.a. HAMAS; a.k.a. STUDENTS OF AYYASH; a.k.a. STUDENTS OF THE ENGINEER; a.k.a. YAHYA AYYASH UNITS; a.k.a. IZZ AL-DIN AL-QASSIM BRIGADES; a.k.a. IZZ AL-DIN AL-QASSIM FORCES; a.k.a. IZZ AL-DIN AL-QASSIM BATTALIONS; a.k.a. IZZ AL-DIN AL QASSAM BRIGADES; a.k.a. IZZ AL-DIN AL

QASSAM FORCES; a.k.a. IZZ AL-DIN AL QASSAM BATTALIONS) [SDT] [FTO] **also listed as [SDGT] on 10-31-01**

HARAKAT UL-ANSAR (a.k.a. HARAKAT UL-MUJAHIDEEN; a.k.a. HARAKAT UL-MUJAHIDIN; a.k.a. HUA; a.k.a. HUM) [FTO] [SDGT] **09-24-01**

HARAKAT UL-MUJAHIDEEN (a.k.a. HARAKAT UL-ANSAR; a.k.a. HARAKAT UL-MUJAHIDIN; a.k.a. HUA; a.k.a. HUM) [FTO] [SDGT] **09-24-01**

HARAKAT UL-MUJAHIDIN (a.k.a. HARAKAT UL-MUJAHIDEEN; a.k.a. HARAKAT UL-ANSAR; a.k.a. HUA; a.k.a. HUM) [FTO] [SDGT] **09-24-01**

HEYATUL ULYA, Mogadishu, Somalia [SDGT] **11-07-01**

HIMMAT ESTABLISHMENT (a.k.a. AL TAQWA TRADE, PROPERTY AND INDUSTRY; n.k.a. AL TAQWA TRADE, PROPERTY AND INDUSTRY COMPANY LIMITED; a.k.a. AL TAQWA TRADE, PROPERTY AND INDUSTRY ESTABLISHMENT), c/o Asat Trust Reg., Altenbach 8, Vaduz 9490, Liechtenstein [SDGT] **11-07-01**

HIZBALLAH (a.k.a. PARTY OF GOD; a.k.a. ISLAMIC JIHAD; a.k.a. ISLAMIC JIHAD ORGANIZATION; a.k.a. REVOLUTIONARY JUSTICE ORGANIZATION; a.k.a. ORGANIZATION OF THE OPPRESSED ON EARTH; a.k.a. ISLAMIC JIHAD FOR THE LIBERATION OF PALESTINE; a.k.a. ORGANIZATION OF RIGHT AGAINST WRONG; a.k.a. ANSAR ALLAH; a.k.a. FOLLOWERS OF THE PROPHET MUHAMMED) [SDT] [FTO] **also listed as [SDGT] on 10-31-01**

HOLY LAND FOUNDATION FOR RELIEF AND DEVELOPMENT (f.k.a. OCCUPIED LAND FUND), 525 International Parkway, Suite 509, Richardson, Texas 75081, U.S.A.; P.O. Box 832390, Richardson, Texas 75083, U.S.A.; 9250 S. Harlem Avenue, Bridgeview, Illinois, U.S.A.; 345 E. Railway Avenue, Paterson, New Jersey 07503, U.S.A.; 12798 Ranco Penasquitos Blvd., Suite F, San Diego, California 92128, U.S.A.; Hebron, West Bank; Gaza; and other locations within the United States; U.S. FEIN: 95-4227517 [SDGT] **12-04-01**

HUA (a.k.a. HARAKAT UL-MUJAHIDEEN; a.k.a. HARAKAT UL-ANSAR; a.k.a. HARAKAT UL-MUJAHIDIN; a.k.a. HUM) [FTO] [SDGT] **09-24-01**

HUM (a.k.a. HARAKAT UL-MUJAHIDEEN; a.k.a. HARAKAT UL-ANSAR; a.k.a. HARAKAT UL-MUJAHIDIN; a.k.a. HUA) [FTO] [SDGT] **09-24-01**

IG (a.k.a. GI; a.k.a. ISLAMIC GROUP; a.k.a. GAMA'A AL-ISLAMIYYA; a.k.a. AL-GAMA'AT; a.k.a. ISLAMIC GAMA'AT; a.k.a. EGYPTIAN AL-GAMA'AT AL-ISLAMIYYA) [SDT][FTO] **also listed as [SDGT] on 10-31-01**

IMU (a.k.a. ISLAMIC MOVEMENT OF UZBEKISTAN) [FTO] [SDGT] **09-24-01**

INTERNATIONAL FRONT FOR FIGHTING JEWS AND CRUSADES (a.k.a. ISLAMIC ARMY; a.k.a. "THE BASE;" a.k.a. AL QA'IDA; a.k.a. AL QAEDA; a.k.a. AL QAIDA; a.k.a. ISLAMIC ARMY FOR THE LIBERATION

OF HOLY SITES; a.k.a. ISLAMIC SALVATION FOUNDATION; a.k.a. THE GROUP FOR THE PRESERVATION OF THE HOLY SITES; a.k.a. THE ISLAMIC ARMY FOR THE LIBERATION OF THE HOLY PLACES; a.k.a. THE WORLD ISLAMIC FRONT FOR JIHAD AGAINST JEWS AND CRUSADERS; a.k.a. USAMA BIN LADEN NETWORK; a.k.a. USAMA BIN LADEN ORGANIZATION) [SDT] [FTO] [SDGT] **09-24-01**

IRISH REPUBLICAN PRISONERS WELFARE ASSOCIATION (a.k.a. 32 COUNTY SOVEREIGNTY COMMITTEE; a.k.a. 32 COUNTY SOVEREIGNTY MOVEMENT; a.k.a. REAL IRA; a.k.a. REAL IRISH REPUBLICAN ARMY; a.k.a. REAL OGLAIGH NA HEIREANN; a.k.a. RIRA) [FTO] **also listed as [SDGT] on 10-31-01**

ISLAMIC ARMY (a.k.a. "THE BASE;" a.k.a. AL QA'IDA; a.k.a. AL QAEDA; a.k.a. AL QAIDA; a.k.a. INTERNATIONAL FRONT FOR FIGHTING JEWS AND CRUSADES; a.k.a. ISLAMIC ARMY FOR THE LIBERATION OF HOLY SITES; a.k.a. ISLAMIC SALVATION FOUNDATION; a.k.a. THE GROUP FOR THE PRESERVATION OF THE HOLY SITES; a.k.a. THE ISLAMIC ARMY FOR THE LIBERATION OF THE HOLY PLACES; a.k.a. THE WORLD ISLAMIC FRONT FOR JIHAD AGAINST JEWS AND CRUSADERS; a.k.a. USAMA BIN LADEN NETWORK; a.k.a. USAMA BIN LADEN ORGANIZATION) [SDT] [FTO] [SDGT] **09-24-01**

ISLAMIC ARMY FOR THE LIBERATION OF HOLY SITES (a.k.a. ISLAMIC ARMY; a.k.a. "THE BASE;" a.k.a. AL QA'IDA; a.k.a. AL QAEDA; a.k.a. AL QAIDA; a.k.a. INTERNATIONAL FRONT FOR FIGHTING JEWS AND CRUSADES; a.k.a. ISLAMIC SALVATION FOUNDATION; a.k.a. THE GROUP FOR THE PRESERVATION OF THE HOLY SITES; a.k.a. THE ISLAMIC ARMY FOR THE LIBERATION OF THE HOLY PLACES; a.k.a. THE WORLD ISLAMIC FRONT FOR JIHAD AGAINST JEWS AND CRUSADERS; a.k.a. USAMA BIN LADEN NETWORK; a.k.a. USAMA BIN LADEN ORGANIZATION) [SDT] [FTO] [SDGT] **09-24-01**

ISLAMIC ARMY OF ADEN [SDGT] **09-24-01**

ISLAMIC GAMA'AT (a.k.a. GI; a.k.a. ISLAMIC GROUP; a.k.a. IG; a.k.a. AL-GAMA'AT; a.k.a. GAMA'A AL-ISLAMIYYA; a.k.a. EGYPTIAN AL-GAMA'AT AL-ISLAMIYYA) [SDT][FTO] **also listed as [SDGT] on 10-31-01**

ISLAMIC GROUP (a.k.a. EGYPTIAN AL-GAMA'AT AL-ISLAMIYYA; a.k.a. GI; a.k.a. IG; a.k.a. AL-GAMA'AT; a.k.a. ISLAMIC GAMA'AT; a.k.a. GAMA'A AL-ISLAMIYYA) [SDT][FTO] **also listed as [SDGT] on 10-31-01**

ISLAMIC JIHAD (a.k.a. PARTY OF GOD; a.k.a. HIZBALLAH; a.k.a. ISLAMIC JIHAD ORGANIZATION; a.k.a. REVOLUTIONARY JUSTICE ORGANIZATION; a.k.a. ORGANIZATION OF THE OPPRESSED ON EARTH; a.k.a. ISLAMIC JIHAD FOR THE LIBERATION OF PALESTINE; a.k.a. ORGANIZATION OF RIGHT AGAINST WRONG; a.k.a. ANSAR

ALLAH; a.k.a. FOLLOWERS OF THE PROPHET MUHAMMED) [SDT] [FTO] **also listed as [SDGT] on 10-31-01**

ISLAMIC JIHAD FOR THE LIBERATION OF PALESTINE (a.k.a. PARTY OF GOD; a.k.a. ISLAMIC JIHAD; a.k.a. ISLAMIC JIHAD ORGANIZATION; a.k.a. REVOLUTIONARY JUSTICE ORGANIZATION; a.k.a. ORGANIZATION OF THE OPPRESSED ON EARTH; a.k.a. HIZBALLAH; a.k.a. ORGANIZATION OF RIGHT AGAINST WRONG; a.k.a. ANSAR ALLAH; a.k.a. FOLLOWERS OF THE PROPHET MUHAMMED) [SDT] [FTO] **also listed as [SDGT] on 10-31-01**

ISLAMIC JIHAD IN PALESTINE (a.k.a. PALESTINE ISLAMIC JIHAD - SHAQAQI FACTION; a.k.a. ABU GHUNAYM SQUAD OF THE HIZBALLAH BAYT AL-MAQDIS; a.k.a. AL-AWDAH BRIGADES; a.k.a. AL-QUDS BRIGADES; a.k.a. AL-QUDS SQUADS; a.k.a. ISLAMIC JIHAD OF PALESTINE; a.k.a. PALESTINIAN ISLAMIC JIHAD; a.k.a. PIJ; a.k.a. PIJ-SHALLAH FACTION; a.k.a. PIJ-SHAQAQI FACTION; a.k.a. SAYARA AL-QUDS) [SDT] [FTO] **also listed as [SDGT] on 10-31-01**

ISLAMIC JIHAD OF PALESTINE (a.k.a. PALESTINE ISLAMIC JIHAD - SHAQAQI FACTION; a.k.a. ABU GHUNAYM SQUAD OF THE HIZBALLAH BAYT AL-MAQDIS; a.k.a. AL-AWDAH BRIGADES; a.k.a. AL-QUDS BRIGADES; a.k.a. AL-QUDS SQUADS; a.k.a. ISLAMIC JIHAD IN PALESTINE; a.k.a. PALESTINIAN ISLAMIC JIHAD; a.k.a. PIJ; a.k.a. PIJ-SHALLAH FACTION; a.k.a. PIJ-SHAQAQI FACTION; a.k.a. SAYARA AL-QUDS) [SDT] [FTO] **also listed as [SDGT] on 10-31-01**

ISLAMIC JIHAD ORGANIZATION (a.k.a. PARTY OF GOD; a.k.a. HIZBALLAH; a.k.a. ISLAMIC JIHAD; a.k.a. REVOLUTIONARY JUSTICE ORGANIZATION; a.k.a. ORGANIZATION OF THE OPPRESSED ON EARTH; a.k.a. ISLAMIC JIHAD FOR THE LIBERATION OF PALESTINE; a.k.a. ORGANIZATION OF RIGHT AGAINST WRONG; a.k.a. ANSAR ALLAH; a.k.a. FOLLOWERS OF THE PROPHET MUHAMMED) [SDT] [FTO] **also listed as [SDGT] on 10-31-01**

ISLAMIC MOVEMENT OF UZBEKISTAN (a.k.a. IMU) [FTO] [SDGT] **9-24-01**

ISLAMIC RESISTANCE MOVEMENT (a.k.a. HAMAS; a.k.a. HARAKAT AL-MUQAWAMA AL-ISLAMIYA; a.k.a. STUDENTS OF AYYASH; a.k.a. STUDENTS OF THE ENGINEER; a.k.a. YAHYA AYYASH UNITS; a.k.a. IZZ AL-DIN AL-QASSIM BRIGADES; a.k.a. IZZ AL-DIN AL-QASSIM FORCES; a.k.a. IZZ AL-DIN AL-QASSIM BATTALIONS; a.k.a. IZZ AL-DIN AL QASSAM BRIGADES; a.k.a. IZZ AL-DIN AL QASSAM FORCES; a.k.a. IZZ AL-DIN AL QASSAM BATTALIONS) [SDT] [FTO] **also listed as [SDGT] on 10-31-01**

ISLAMIC SALVATION FOUNDATION (a.k.a. ISLAMIC ARMY; a.k.a. "THE BASE;" a.k.a. AL QA'IDA; a.k.a. AL QAEDA; a.k.a. AL QAIDA; a.k.a.

INTERNATIONAL FRONT FOR FIGHTING JEWS AND CRUSADES; a.k.a. ISLAMIC ARMY FOR THE LIBERATION OF HOLY SITES; a.k.a. THE GROUP FOR THE PRESERVATION OF THE HOLY SITES; a.k.a. THE ISLAMIC ARMY FOR THE LIBERATION OF THE HOLY PLACES; a.k.a. THE WORLD ISLAMIC FRONT FOR JIHAD AGAINST JEWS AND CRUSADERS; a.k.a. USAMA BIN LADEN NETWORK; a.k.a. USAMA BIN LADEN ORGANIZATION) [SDT] [FTO] [SDGT] **09-24-01**

IZZ AL-DIN AL QASSAM BATTALIONS (a.k.a. ISLAMIC RESISTANCE MOVEMENT; a.k.a. HARAKAT AL-MUQAWAMA AL-ISLAMIYA; a.k.a. STUDENTS OF AYYASH; a.k.a. STUDENTS OF THE ENGINEER; a.k.a. YAHYA AYYASH UNITS; a.k.a. IZZ AL-DIN AL-QASSIM BRIGADES; a.k.a. IZZ AL-DIN AL-QASSIM FORCES; a.k.a. IZZ AL-DIN AL-QASSM BATTALIONS; a.k.a. IZZ AL-DIN AL QASSAM BRIGADES; a.k.a. IZZ AL-DIN AL QASSAM FORCES; a.k.a. HAMAS) [SDT] [FTO] **also listed as [SDGT] on 10-31-01**

IZZ AL-DIN AL QASSAM BRIGADES (a.k.a. ISLAMIC RESISTANCE MOVEMENT; a.k.a. HARAKAT AL-MUQAWAMA AL-ISLAMIYA; a.k.a. STUDENTS OF AYYASH; a.k.a. STUDENTS OF THE ENGINEER; a.k.a. YAHYA AYYASH UNITS; a.k.a. IZZ AL-DIN AL-QASSIM BRIGADES; a.k.a. IZZ AL-DIN AL-QASSIM FORCES; a.k.a. IZZ AL-DIN AL-QASSIM BATTALIONS; a.k.a. HAMAS; a.k.a. IZZ AL-DIN AL QASSAM FORCES; a.k.a. IZZ AL-DIN AL QASSAM BATTALIONS) [SDT] [FTO] **also listed as [SDGT] on 10-31-01**

IZZ AL-DIN AL QASSAM FORCES (a.k.a. ISLAMIC RESISTANCE MOVEMENT; a.k.a. HARAKAT AL-MUQAWAMA AL-ISLAMIYA; a.k.a. STUDENTS OF AYYASH; a.k.a. STUDENTS OF THE ENGINEER; a.k.a. YAHYA AYYASH UNITS; a.k.a. IZZ AL-DIN AL-QASSIM BRIGADES; a.k.a. IZZ AL-DIN AL-QASSIM FORCES; a.k.a. IZZ AL-DIN AL-QASSIM BATTALIONS; a.k.a. IZZ AL-DIN AL QASSAM BRIGADES; a.k.a. HAMAS; a.k.a. IZZ AL-DIN AL QASSAM BATTALIONS) [SDT] [FTO] **also listed as [SDGT] on 10-31-01**

IZZ AL-DIN AL-QASSIM BATTALIONS (a.k.a. ISLAMIC RESISTANCE MOVEMENT; a.k.a. HARAKAT AL-MUQAWAMA AL-ISLAMIYA; a.k.a. STUDENTS OF AYYASH; a.k.a. STUDENTS OF THE ENGINEER; a.k.a. YAHYA AYYASH UNITS; a.k.a. IZZ AL-DIN AL-QASSIM BRIGADES; a.k.a. IZZ AL-DIN AL-QASSIM FORCES; a.k.a. HAMAS; a.k.a. IZZ AL-DIN AL QASSAM BRIGADES; a.k.a. IZZ AL-DIN AL QASSAM FORCES; a.k.a. IZZ AL-DIN AL QASSAM BATTALIONS) [SDT] [FTO] **also listed as [SDGT] on 10-31-01**

IZZ AL-DIN AL-QASSIM BRIGADES (a.k.a. ISLAMIC RESISTANCE MOVEMENT; a.k.a. HARAKAT AL-MUQAWAMA AL-ISLAMIYA; a.k.a. STUDENTS OF AYYASH; a.k.a. STUDENTS OF THE ENGINEER; a.k.a.

YAHYA AYYASH UNITS; a.k.a. HAMAS; a.k.a. IZZ AL-DIN AL-QASSIM FORCES; a.k.a. IZZ AL-DIN AL-QASSIM BATTALIONS; a.k.a. IZZ AL-DIN AL QASSAM BRIGADES; a.k.a. IZZ AL-DIN AL QASSAM FORCES; a.k.a. IZZ AL-DIN AL QASSAM BATTALIONS) [SDT] [FTO] **also listed as [SDGT] on 10-31-01**

IZZ AL-DIN AL-QASSIM FORCES (a.k.a. ISLAMIC RESISTANCE MOVEMENT; a.k.a. HARAKAT AL-MUQAWAMA AL-ISLAMIYA; a.k.a. STUDENTS OF AYYASH; a.k.a. STUDENTS OF THE ENGINEER; a.k.a. YAHYA AYYASH UNITS; a.k.a. IZZ AL-DIN AL-QASSIM BRIGADES; a.k.a. HAMAS; a.k.a. IZZ AL-DIN AL-QASSIM BATTALIONS; a.k.a. IZZ AL-DIN AL QASSAM BRIGADES; a.k.a. IZZ AL-DIN AL QASSAM FORCES; a.k.a. IZZ AL-DIN AL QASSAM BATTALIONS) [SDT] [FTO] **also listed as [SDGT] on 10-31-01**

JAISH-I-MOHAMMED (a.k.a. ARMY OF MOHAMMED; a.k.a. MOHAMMED'S ARMY; a.k.a. TEHRIK UL-FURQAAN), Pakistan [FTO] [SDGT] **10-12-01**

JAM'IYAT AL TA'AWUN AL ISLAMIYYA (a.k.a. JAM'YAH TA'AWUN AL-ISLAMIA; a.k.a. JIT; a.k.a. SOCIETY OF ISLAMIC COOPERATION), Qandahar City, Afghanistan [SDGT] **10-12-01**

JAM'YAH TA'AWUN AL-ISLAMIA (a.k.a. JAM'IYAT AL TA'AWUN AL ISLAMIYYA; a.k.a. JIT; a.k.a. SOCIETY OF ISLAMIC COOPERATION), Qandahar City, Afghanistan [SDGT] **10-12-01**

JIHAD GROUP (a.k.a. AL-JIHAD; a.k.a. EGYPTIAN AL-JIHAD; a.k.a. EGYPTIAN ISLAMIC JIHAD; a.k.a. NEW JIHAD) [SDT] [FTO] [SDGT] **09-24-01**

JIT (a.k.a. JAM'IYATAL TA'AWUN AL ISLAMIYYA; a.k.a. JAM'YAH TA'AWUN AL-ISLAMIA; a.k.a. SOCIETY OF ISLAMIC COOPERATION), Qandahar City, Afghanistan [SDGT] **10-12-01**

JUDEA POLICE (a.k.a. KAHANE CHAI; a.k.a. COMMITTEE FOR THE SAFETY OF THE ROADS; a.k.a. DIKUY BOGDIM; a.k.a. DOV; a.k.a. FOREFRONT OF THE IDEA; a.k.a. KACH; a.k.a. KAHANE LIVES; a.k.a. KFAR TAPUAH FUND; a.k.a. KOACH; a.k.a. REPRESSION OF TRAITORS; a.k.a. STATE OF JUDEA; a.k.a. SWORD OF DAVID; a.k.a. THE JUDEAN LEGION; a.k.a. THE JUDEAN VOICE; a.k.a. THE QOMEMIYUT MOVEMENT; a.k.a. THE WAY OF THE TORAH; a.k.a. THE YESHIVA OF THE JEWISH IDEA) [SDT] [FTO] **also listed as [SDGT] on 10-31-01**

JUNE 78 (a.k.a. POPULAR REVOLUTIONARY STRUGGLE; a.k.a. EPANASTATIKOS LAIKOS AGONAS; a.k.a. REVOLUTIONARY POPULAR STRUGGLE; a.k.a. REVOLUTIONARY PEOPLE'S STRUGGLE; a.k.a. ELA; a.k.a. ORGANIZATION OF REVOLUTIONARY INTERNATIONALIST SOLIDARITY; a.k.a. REVOLUTIONARY NUCLEI;

a.k.a. REVOLUTIONARY CELLS; a.k.a. LIBERATION STRUGGLE) [FTO] also listed as [SDGT] on 10-31-01

KACH (a.k.a. KAHANE CHAI; a.k.a. COMMITTEE FOR THE SAFETY OF THE ROADS; a.k.a. DIKUY BOGDIM; a.k.a. DOV; a.k.a. FOREFRONT OF THE IDEA; a.k.a. JUDEA POLICE; a.k.a. KAHANE LIVES; a.k.a. KFAR TAPUAH FUND; a.k.a. KOACH; a.k.a. REPRESSION OF TRAITORS; a.k.a. STATE OF JUDEA; a.k.a. SWORD OF DAVID; a.k.a. THE JUDEAN LEGION; a.k.a. THE JUDEAN VOICE; a.k.a. THE QOMEMIYUT MOVEMENT; a.k.a. THE WAY OF THE TORAH; a.k.a. THE YESHIVA OF THE JEWISH IDEA) [SDT] [FTO] also listed as [SDGT] on 10-31-01

KAHANE CHAI (a.k.a. COMMITTEE FOR THE SAFETY OF THE ROADS; a.k.a. DIKUY BOGDIM; a.k.a. DOV; a.k.a. FOREFRONT OF THE IDEA; a.k.a. JUDEA POLICE; a.k.a. KACH; a.k.a. KAHANE LIVES; a.k.a. KFAR TAPUAH FUND; a.k.a. KOACH; a.k.a. REPRESSION OF TRAITORS; a.k.a. STATE OF JUDEA; a.k.a. SWORD OF DAVID; a.k.a. THE JUDEAN LEGION; a.k.a. THE JUDEAN VOICE; a.k.a. THE QOMEMIYUT MOVEMENT; a.k.a. THE WAY OF THE TORAH; a.k.a. THE YESHIVA OF THE JEWISH IDEA) [SDT] [FTO] also listed as [SDGT] on 10-31-01

KAHANE LIVES (a.k.a. KAHANE CHAI; a.k.a. COMMITTEE FOR THE SAFETY OF THE ROADS; a.k.a. DIKUY BOGDIM; a.k.a. DOV; a.k.a. FOREFRONT OF THE IDEA; a.k.a. JUDEA POLICE; a.k.a. KACH; a.k.a. KFAR TAPUAH FUND; a.k.a. KOACH; a.k.a. REPRESSION OF TRAITORS; a.k.a. STATE OF JUDEA; a.k.a. SWORD OF DAVID; a.k.a. THE JUDEAN LEGION; a.k.a. THE JUDEAN VOICE; a.k.a. THE QOMEMIYUT MOVEMENT; a.k.a. THE WAY OF THE TORAH; a.k.a. THE YESHIVA OF THE JEWISH IDEA) [SDT] [FTO

KFAR TAPUAH FUND (a.k.a. KAHANE CHAI; a.k.a. COMMITTEE FOR THE SAFETY OF THE ROADS; a.k.a. DIKUY BOGDIM; a.k.a. DOV; a.k.a. FOREFRONT OF THE IDEA; a.k.a. JUDEA POLICE; a.k.a. KACH; a.k.a. KAHANE LIVES; a.k.a. KOACH; a.k.a. REPRESSION OF TRAITORS; a.k.a. STATE OF JUDEA; a.k.a. SWORD OF DAVID; a.k.a. THE JUDEAN LEGION; a.k.a. THE JUDEAN VOICE; a.k.a. THE QOMEMIYUT MOVEMENT; a.k.a. THE WAY OF THE TORAH; a.k.a. THE YESHIVA OF THE JEWISH IDEA) [SDT] [FTO] also listed as [SDGT] on 10-31-01

KOACH (a.k.a. KAHANE CHAI; a.k.a. COMMITTEE FOR THE SAFETY OF THE ROADS; a.k.a. DIKUY BOGDIM; a.k.a. DOV; a.k.a. FOREFRONT OF THE IDEA; a.k.a. JUDEA POLICE; a.k.a. KACH; a.k.a. KAHANE LIVES; a.k.a. KFAR TAPUAH FUND; a.k.a. REPRESSION OF TRAITORS; a.k.a. STATE OF JUDEA; a.k.a. SWORD OF DAVID; a.k.a. THE JUDEAN LEGION; a.k.a. THE JUDEAN VOICE; a.k.a. THE QOMEMIYUT MOVEMENT; a.k.a. THE WAY OF THE TORAH; a.k.a. THE YESHIVA OF THE JEWISH IDEA) [SDT] [FTO] also listed as [SDGT] on 10-31-01

KURDISTAN WORKERS' PARTY (a.k.a. HALU MESRU SAVUNMA KUVVETI (HSK); a.k.a. PARTIYA KARKERAN KURDISTAN; a.k.a. PKK; a.k.a. THE PEOPLE'S DEFENSE FORCE) [FTO] **also listed as [SDGT] on 10-31-01**

LASHKAR E-TAYYIBA (a.k.a. ARMY OF THE RIGHTEOUS; a.k.a. LASHKAR E-TOIBA; a.k.a. LASHKAR-I-TAIBA), Pakistan [FTO] [SDGT] **[12-20-01]**

LASHKAR E-TOIBA (a.k.a. LASHKAR E-TAYYIBA; a.k.a. ARMY OF THE RIGHTEOUS; a.k.a. LASHKAR-I-TAIBA), Pakistan [FTO] [SDGT] **[12-20-01]**

LASHKAR-I-TAIBA (a.k.a. LASHKAR E-TAYYIBA; a.k.a. ARMY OF THE RIGHTEOUS; a.k.a. LASHKAR E-TOIBA), Pakistan [FTO] [SDGT] **[12-20-01]**

LE GROUPE SALAFISTE POUR LA PREDICATION ET LE COMBAT (a.k.a. SALAFIST GROUP FOR CALL AND COMBAT; a.k.a. GSPC) [SDGT] **09-24-01**

LIBERATION STRUGGLE (a.k.a. POPULAR REVOLUTIONARY STRUGGLE; a.k.a. EPANASTATIKOS LAIKOS AGONAS; a.k.a. REVOLUTIONARY POPULAR STRUGGLE; a.k.a. REVOLUTIONARY PEOPLE'S STRUGGLE; a.k.a. JUNE 78; a.k.a. ORGANIZATION OF REVOLUTIONARY INTERNATIONALIST SOLIDARITY; a.k.a. REVOLUTIONARY NUCLEI; a.k.a. REVOLUTIONARY CELLS; a.k.a. ELA) [FTO] **also listed as [SDGT] on 10-31-01**

LIBERATION TIGERS OF TAMIL EELAM (a.k.a. LTTE; a.k.a. TAMIL TIGERS; a.k.a. ELLALAN FORCE) [FTO] **also listed as [SDGT] on 10-31-01**

LIBYAN ISLAMIC FIGHTING GROUP [SDGT] **09-24-01**

LOYALIST VOLUNTEER FORCE (LVF); United Kingdom [SDGT] **12-31-01**

LTTE (a.k.a. LIBERATION TIGERS OF TAMIL EELAM; a.k.a. TAMIL TIGERS; a.k.a. ELLALAN FORCE) [FTO] **also listed as [SDGT] on 10-31-01**

MAKHTAB AL-KHIDAMAT/AL KIFAH, House no. 125, Street 54, Phase II, Hayatabad, Peshawar, Pakistan [SDGT] **09-24-01**

MAMOUN DARKAZANLI IMPORT-EXPORT COMPANY (a.k.a. DARKAZANLI COMPANY; a.k.a. DARKAZANLI EXPORT-IMPORT SONDERPOSTEN), Uhlenhorsterweg 34 11, Hamburg, Germany [SDGT] **09-24-01**

MEK (a.k.a. MUJAHEDIN-E KHALQ ORGANIZATION; a.k.a. MKO; a.k.a. MUJAHEDIN-E KHALQ; a.k.a. NATIONAL COUNCIL OF RESISTANCE (NCR); a.k.a. NLA; a.k.a. ORGANIZATION OF THE PEOPLE'S HOLY WARRIORS OF IRAN; a.k.a. PEOPLE'S MUJAHEDIN ORGANIZATION OF IRAN; a.k.a. PMOI; a.k.a. SAZEMAN-E MUJAHEDIN-E KHALQ-E IRAN; a.k.a. THE NATIONAL LIBERATION ARMY OF IRAN) [FTO] **also listed as [SDGT] on 10-31-01**

MKO (a.k.a. MUJAHEDIN-E KHALQ ORGANIZATION; a.k.a. MEK; a.k.a. MUJAHEDIN-E KHALQ; a.k.a. NATIONAL COUNCIL OF RESISTANCE

(NCR); a.k.a. NLA; a.k.a. ORGANIZATION OF THE PEOPLE'S HOLY WARRIORS OF IRAN; a.k.a. PEOPLE'S MUJAHEDIN ORGANIZATION OF IRAN; a.k.a. PMOI; a.k.a. SAZEMAN-E MUJAHEDIN-E KHALQ-E IRAN; a.k.a. THE NATIONAL LIBERATION ARMY OF IRAN) [FTO] **also listed as [SDGT] on 10-31-01**

MOHAMMED'S ARMY (a.k.a. ARMY OF MOHAMMED; a.k.a. JAISH-I-MOHAMMED; a.k.a. TEHRIK UL-FURQAAN), Pakistan [FTO] [SDGT] **10-12-01**

MUJAHEDIN-E KHALQ (a.k.a. MUJAHEDIN-E KHALQ ORGANIZATION; a.k.a. MEK; a.k.a. MKO; a.k.a. NATIONAL COUNCIL OF RESISTANCE (NCR); a.k.a. NLA; a.k.a. ORGANIZATION OF THE PEOPLE'S HOLY WARRIORS OF IRAN; a.k.a. PEOPLE'S MUJAHEDIN ORGANIZATION OF IRAN; a.k.a. PMOI; a.k.a. SAZEMAN-E MUJAHEDIN-E KHALQ-E IRAN; a.k.a. THE NATIONAL LIBERATION ARMY OF IRAN) [FTO] **also listed as [SDGT] on 10-31-01**

MUJAHEDIN-E KHALQ ORGANIZATION (a.k.a. MEK; a.k.a. MKO; a.k.a. MUJAHEDIN-E KHALQ; a.k.a. NATIONAL COUNCIL OF RESISTANCE (NCR); a.k.a. NLA; a.k.a. ORGANIZATION OF THE PEOPLE'S HOLY WARRIORS OF IRAN; a.k.a. PEOPLE'S MUJAHEDIN ORGANIZATION OF IRAN; a.k.a. PMOI; a.k.a. SAZEMAN-E MUJAHEDIN-E KHALQ-E IRAN; a.k.a. THE NATIONAL LIBERATION ARMY OF IRAN) [FTO] **also listed as [SDGT] on 10-31-01**

NADA MANAGEMENT ORGANIZATION SA (f.k.a. AL TAQWA MANAGEMENT ORGANIZATION SA), Viale Stefano Franscini 22, Lugano CH-6900 TI, Switzerland [SDGT] **11-07-01**

NATION BUILDING (a.k.a. UMMAH TAMEER E-NAU (UTN); a.k.a. FOUNDATION FOR CONSTRUCTION; a.k.a. RECONSTRUCTION FOUNDATION; a.k.a. RECONSTRUCTION OF THE ISLAMIC COMMUNITY; a.k.a. RECONSTRUCTION OF THE MUSLIM UMMAH; a.k.a. UMMAH TAMEER I-NAU; a.k.a. UMMAH TAMIR E-NAU; a.k.a. UMMAH TAMIR I-NAU; a.k.a. UMMAT TAMIR E-NAU; a.k.a. UMMAT TAMIR-I-PAU), Street 13, Wazir Akbar Khan, Kabul, Afghanistan; 60-C, Nazim Ud Din Road, Islamabad F 8/4, Pakistan [SDGT] [FTO] **12-20-01**

NATIONAL COUNCIL OF RESISTANCE (NCR) (a.k.a. MUJAHEDIN-E KHALQ ORGANIZATION; a.k.a. MEK; a.k.a. MKO; a.k.a. MUJAHEDIN-E KHALQ; a.k.a. NLA; a.k.a. ORGANIZATION OF THE PEOPLE'S HOLY WARRIORS OF IRAN; a.k.a. PEOPLE'S MUJAHEDIN ORGANIZATION OF IRAN; a.k.a. PMOI; a.k.a. SAZEMAN-E MUJAHEDIN-E KHALQ-E IRAN; a.k.a. THE NATIONAL LIBERATION ARMY OF IRAN) [FTO] **also listed as [SDGT] on 10-31-01**

NATIONAL LIBERATION ARMY (a.k.a. ELN; a.k.a. EJERCITO DE LIBERACION NACIONAL) [FTO] also listed as [SDGT] on 10-31-01

NEW JIHAD (a.k.a. AL-JIHAD; a.k.a. EGYPTIAN AL-JIHAD; a.k.a. EGYPTIAN ISLAMIC JIHAD; a.k.a. JIHAD GROUP) [SDT] [FTO] [SDGT] 09-24-01

NLA (a.k.a. MUJAHEDIN-E KHALQ ORGANIZATION; a.k.a. MEK; a.k.a. MKO; a.k.a. MUJAHEDIN-E KHALQ; a.k.a. NATIONAL COUNCIL OF RESISTANCE (NCR); a.k.a. ORGANIZATION OF THE PEOPLE'S HOLY WARRIORS OF IRAN; a.k.a. PEOPLE'S MUJAHEDIN ORGANIZATION OF IRAN; a.k.a. PMOI; a.k.a. SAZEMAN-E MUJAHEDIN-E KHALQ-E IRAN; a.k.a. THE NATIONAL LIBERATION ARMY OF IRAN) [FTO] also listed as [SDGT] on 10-31-01

OCCUPIED LAND FUND (n.k.a. HOLY LAND FOUNDATION FOR RELIEF AND DEVELOPMENT), 525 International Parkway, Suite 509, Richardson, Texas 75081, U.S.A.; P.O. Box 832390, Richardson, Texas 75083, U.S.A.; 9250 S. Harlem Avenue, Bridgeview, Illinois, U.S.A.; 345 E. Railway Avenue, Paterson, New Jersey 07503, U.S.A.; 12798 Rancho Penasquitos Blvd., Suite F, San Diego, California, 92128 U.S.A.; Hebron, West Bank; Gaza; and other locations within the United States; U.S. FEIN: 95-4227517 [SDGT] 12-04-01

ORANGE VOLUNTEERS; United Kingdom [SDGT] 12-31-01

ORGANIZATION OF REVOLUTIONARY INTERNATIONALIST SOLIDARITY (a.k.a. POPULAR REVOLUTIONARY STRUGGLE; a.k.a. EPANASTATIKOS LAIKOS AGONAS; a.k.a. REVOLUTIONARY POPULAR STRUGGLE; a.k.a. REVOLUTIONARY PEOPLE'S STRUGGLE; a.k.a. JUNE 78; a.k.a. ELA; a.k.a. REVOLUTIONARY NUCLEI; a.k.a. REVOLUTIONARY CELLS; a.k.a. LIBERATION STRUGGLE) [FTO] also listed as [SDGT] on 10-31-01

ORGANIZATION OF RIGHT AGAINST WRONG (a.k.a. PARTY OF GOD; a.k.a. ISLAMIC JIHAD; a.k.a. ISLAMIC JIHAD ORGANIZATION; a.k.a. ISLAMIC JIHAD FOR THE LIBERATION OF PALESTINE; a.k.a. REVOLUTIONARY JUSTICE ORGANIZATION; a.k.a. HIZBALLAH; a.k.a. ORGANIZATION OF THE OPPRESSED ON EARTH ; a.k.a. ANSAR ALLAH; a.k.a. FOLLOWERS OF THE PROPHET MUHAMMED) [SDT] [FTO] also listed as [SDGT] on 10-31-01

ORGANIZATION OF THE OPPRESSED ON EARTH (a.k.a. PARTY OF GOD; a.k.a. ISLAMIC JIHAD; a.k.a. ISLAMIC JIHAD ORGANIZATION; a.k.a. ISLAMIC JIHAD FOR THE LIBERATION OF PALESTINE; a.k.a. REVOLUTIONARY JUSTICE ORGANIZATION; a.k.a. HIZBALLAH; a.k.a. ORGANIZATION OF RIGHT AGAINST WRONG; a.k.a. ANSAR ALLAH; a.k.a. FOLLOWERS OF THE PROPHET MUHAMMED) [SDT] [FTO] also listed as [SDGT] on 10-31-01

ORGANIZATION OF THE PEOPLE'S HOLY WARRIORS OF IRAN (a.k.a. MUJAHEDIN-E KHALQ ORGANIZATION; a.k.a. MEK; a.k.a. MKO; a.k.a. MUJAHEDIN-E KHALQ; a.k.a. NATIONAL COUNCIL OF RESISTANCE (NCR); a.k.a. NLA; a.k.a. PEOPLE'S MUJAHEDIN ORGANIZATION OF IRAN; a.k.a. PMOI; a.k.a. SAZEMAN-E MUJAHEDIN-E KHALQ-E IRAN; a.k.a. THE NATIONAL LIBERATION ARMY OF IRAN) [FTO] **also listed as [SDGT] on 10-31-01**

PALESTINE ISLAMIC JIHAD - SHAQAQI FACTION (a.k.a. ABU GHUNAYM SQUAD OF THE HIZBALLAH BAYT AL-MAQDIS; a.k.a. AL-AWDAH BRIGADES; a.k.a. AL-QUDS BRIGADES; a.k.a. AL-QUDS SQUADS; a.k.a. ISLAMIC JIHAD IN PALESTINE; a.k.a. ISLAMIC JIHAD OF PALESTINE; a.k.a. PALESTINIAN ISLAMIC JIHAD; a.k.a. PIJ; a.k.a. PIJ-SHALLAH FACTION; a.k.a. PIJ-SHAQAQI FACTION; a.k.a. SAYARA AL-QUDS) [SDT] [FTO] **also listed as [SDGT] on 10-31-01**

PALESTINE LIBERATION FRONT (a.k.a. PALESTINE LIBERATION FRONT - ABU ABBAS FACTION; a.k.a. PLF; a.k.a. PLF-ABU ABBAS) [SDT] [FTO] **also listed as [SDGT] on 10-31-01**

PALESTINE LIBERATION FRONT - ABU ABBAS FACTION (a.k.a. PALESTINE LIBERATION FRONT; a.k.a. PLF; a.k.a. PLF-ABU ABBAS) [SDT] [FTO] **also listed as [SDGT] on 10-31-01**

PALESTINIAN ARAB BEIT EL MAL CORPORATION, LTD. (a.k.a. ARAB PALESTINIAN BEIT EL-MAL COMPANY; a.k.a. BEIT AL MAL HOLDINGS; a.k.a. BEIT EL MAL AL-PHALASTINI AL-ARABI AL-MUSHIMA AL-AAMA AL-MAHADUDA LTD.; a.k.a. BEIT EL-MAL HOLDINGS), P.O. Box 662, Ramallah, West Bank [SDGT] **12-04-01**

PALESTINIAN ISLAMIC JIHAD (a.k.a. PALESTINE ISLAMIC JIHAD - SHAQAQI FACTION; a.k.a. ABU GHUNAYM SQUAD OF THE HIZBALLAH BAYT AL-MAQDIS; a.k.a. AL-AWDAH BRIGADES; a.k.a. AL-QUDS BRIGADES; a.k.a. AL-QUDS SQUADS; a.k.a. ISLAMIC JIHAD IN PALESTINE; a.k.a. ISLAMIC JIHAD OF PALESTINE; a.k.a. PIJ; a.k.a. PIJ-SHALLAH FACTION; a.k.a. PIJ-SHAQAQI FACTION; a.k.a. SAYARA AL-QUDS) [SDT] [FTO] **also listed as [SDGT] on 10-31-01**

PALESTINIAN POPULAR RESISTANCE FORCES (a.k.a. POPULAR FRONT FOR THE LIBERATION OF PALESTINE; a.k.a. HALHUL GANG; a.k.a. HALHUL SQUAD; a.k.a. PFLP; a.k.a. PPRF; a.k.a. RED EAGLE GANG; a.k.a. RED EAGLE GROUP; a.k.a. RED EAGLES) [SDT] [FTO] **also listed as [SDGT] on 10-31-01**

PARKA TRADING COMPANY, P.O. Box 3313, Deira, Dubai, U.A.E. [SDGT] **11-07-01**

PARTIDO COMUNISTA DEL PERU (COMMUNIST PARTY OF PERU) (a.k.a. SENDERO LUMINOSO; a..a. SL; a.k.a. PARTIDO COMUNISTA DEL PERU EN EL SENDERO LUMINOSO DE JOSE CARLOS

MARIATEGUI (COMMUNIST PARTY OF PERU ON THE SHINING PATH OF JOSE CARLOS MARIATEGUI); a.k.a. SHINING PATH; a.k.a. PCP; a.k.a. SOCORRO POPULAR DEL PERU (PEOPLE'S AID OF PERU); a.k.a. SPP; a.k.a EJERCITO GUERRILLERO POPULAR (PEOPLE'S GUERRILLA ARMY); a.k.a. EGP; a.k.a. EJERCITO POPULAR DE LIBERACION (PEOPLE'S LIBERATION ARMY); a.k.a. EPL) [FTO] **also listed as [SDGT] on 10-31-01**

PARTIDO COMUNISTA DEL PERU EN EL SENDERO LUMINOSO DE JOSE CARLOS MARIATEGUI (COMMUNIST PARTY OF PERU ON THE SHINING PATH OF JOSE CARLOS MARIATEGUI) (a.k.a. SENDERO LUMINOSO; a.k.a. SL; a.k.a. SHINING PATH; a.k.a. PARTIDO COMUNISTA DEL PERU (COMMUNIST PARTY OF PERU); a.k.a. PCP; a.k.a. SOCORRO POPULAR DEL PERU (PEOPLE'S AID OF PERU); a.k.a. SPP; a.k.a EJERITO GUERRILLERO POPULAR (PEOPLE'S GUERRILLA ARMY); a.k.a. EGP; a.k.a. EJERCITO POPULAR DE LIBERACION (PEOPLE'S LIBERATION ARMY); a.k.a. EPL) [FTO] **also listed as [SDGT] on 10-31-01**

PARTIYA KARKERAN KURDISTAN (a.k.a. KURDISTAN WORKERS' PARTY; a.k.a. HALU MESRU SAVUNMA KUVVETI (HSK); a.k.a. PKK; a.k.a. THE PEOPLE'S DEFENSE FORCE) [FTO] **also listed as [SDGT] on 10-31-01**

PARTY OF GOD (a.k.a. HIZBALLAH; a.k.a. ISLAMIC JIHAD; a.k.a. ISLAMIC JIHAD ORGANIZATION; a.k.a. REVOLUTIONARY JUSTICE ORGANIZATION; a.k.a. ORGANIZATION OF THE OPPRESSED ON EARTH; a.k.a. ISLAMIC JIHAD FOR THE LIBERATION OF PALESTINE; a.k.a. ORGANIZATION OF RIGHT AGAINST WRONG; a.k.a. ANSAR ALLAH; a.k.a. FOLLOWERS OF THE PROPHET MUHAMMED) [SDT] [FTO] **also listed as [SDGT] on 10-31-01**

PCP (a.k.a. SENDERO LUMINOSO; a.k.a. SL; a.k.a. PARTIDO COMUNISTA DEL PERU EN EL SENDERO LUMINOSO DE JOSE CARLOS MARIATEGUI (COMMUNIST PARTY OF PERU ON THE SHINING PATH OF JOSE CARLOS MARIATEGUI); a.k.a. PARTIDO COMUNISTA DEL PERU (COMMUNIST PARTY OF PERU); a.k.a. SHINING PATH; a.k.a. SOCORRO POPULAR DEL PERU (PEOPLE'S AID OF PERU); a.k.a. SPP; a.k.a EJERCITO GUERRILLERO POPULAR (PEOPLE'S GUERRILLA ARMY); a.k.a. EGP; a.k.a. EJERCITO POPULAR DE LIBERACION (PEOPLE'S LIBERATION ARMY); a.k.a. EPL) [FTO] **also listed as [SDGT] on 10-31-01**

PEOPLE'S MUJAHEDIN ORGANIZATION OF IRAN (a.k.a. MUJAHEDIN-E KHALQ ORGANIZATION; a.k.a. MEK; a.k.a. MKO; a.k.a. MUJAHEDIN-E KHALQ; a.k.a. NATIONAL COUNCIL OF RESISTANCE (NCR); a.k.a. NLA; a.k.a. ORGANIZATION OF THE PEOPLE'S HOLY WARRIORS OF IRAN; a.k.a. PMOI; a.k.a. SAZEMAN-E MUJAHEDIN-E

KHALQ-E IRAN; a.k.a. THE NATIONAL LIBERATION ARMY OF IRAN) [FTO] **also listed as [SDGT] on 10-31-01**

PFLP (a.k.a. POPULAR FRONT FOR THE LIBERATION OF PALESTINE; a.k.a. HALHUL GANG; a.k.a. HALHUL SQUAD; a.k.a. PALESTINIAN POPULAR RESISTANCE FORCES; a.k.a. PPRF; a.k.a. RED EAGLE GANG; a.k.a. RED EAGLE GROUP; a.k.a. RED EAGLES) [SDT] [FTO] **also listed as [SDGT] on 10-31-01**

PFLP-GC (a.k.a. POPULAR FRONT FOR THE LIBERATION OF PALESTINE - GENERAL COMMAND) [SDT] [FTO] **also listed as [SDGT] on 10-31-01**

PIJ (a.k.a. PALESTINE ISLAMIC JIHAD - SHAQAQI FACTION; a.k.a. ABU GHUNAYM SQUAD OF THE HIZBALLAH BAYT AL-MAQDIS; a.k.a. AL-AWDAH BRIGADES; a.k.a. AL-QUDS BRIGADES; a.k.a. AL-QUDS SQUADS; a.k.a. ISLAMIC JIHAD IN PALESTINE; a.k.a. ISLAMIC JIHAD OF PALESTINE; a.k.a. PALESTINIAN ISLAMIC JIHAD; a.k.a. PIJ-SHALLAH FACTION; a.k.a. PIJ-SHAQAQI FACTION; a.k.a. SAYARA AL-QUDS) [SDT] [FTO] **also listed as [SDGT] on 10-31-01**

PIJ-SHALLAH FACTION (a.k.a. PALESTINE ISLAMIC JIHAD - SHAQAQI FACTION; a.k.a. ABU GHUNAYM SQUAD OF THE HIZBALLAH BAYT AL-MAQDIS; a.k.a. AL-AWDAH BRIGADES; a.k.a. AL-QUDS BRIGADES; a.k.a. AL-QUDS SQUADS; a.k.a. ISLAMIC JIHAD IN PALESTINE; a.k.a. ISLAMIC JIHAD OF PALESTINE; a.k.a. PALESTINIAN ISLAMIC JIHAD; a.k.a. PIJ; a.k.a. PIJ-SHAQAQI FACTION; a.k.a. SAYARA AL-QUDS) [SDT] [FTO] **also listed as [SDGT] on 10-31-01**

PIJ-SHAQAQI FACTION (a.k.a. PALESTINE ISLAMIC JIHAD - SHAQAQI FACTION; a.k.a. ABU GHUNAYM SQUAD OF THE HIZBALLAH BAYT AL-MAQDIS; a.k.a. AL-AWDAH BRIGADES; a.k.a. AL-QUDS BRIGADES; a.k.a. AL-QUDS SQUADS; a.k.a. ISLAMIC JIHAD IN PALESTINE; a.k.a. ISLAMIC JIHAD OF PALESTINE; a.k.a. PALESTINIAN ISLAMIC JIHAD; a.k.a. PIJ; a.k.a. PIJ-SHALLAH FACTION; a.k.a. SAYARA AL-QUDS) [SDT] [FTO] **also listed as [SDGT] on 10-31-01**

PKK (a.k.a. KURDISTAN WORKERS' PARTY; a.k.a. HALU MESRU SAVUNMA KUVVETI (HSK); a.k.a. PARTIYA KARKERAN KURDISTAN; a.k.a. THE PEOPLE'S DEFENSE FORCE) [FTO] **also listed as [SDGT] on 10-31-01**

PLF (a.k.a. PALESTINE LIBERATION FRONT - ABU ABBAS FACTION; a.k.a. PALESTINE LIBERATION FRONT; a.k.a. PLF-ABU ABBAS) [SDT] [FTO] **also listed as [SDGT] on 10-31-01**

PLF-ABU ABBAS (a.k.a. PALESTINE LIBERATION FRONT - ABU ABBAS FACTION; a.k.a. PALESTINE LIBERATION FRONT; a.k.a. PLF) [SDT] [FTO] **also listed as [SDGT] on 10-31-01**

PMOI (a.k.a. MUJAHEDIN-E KHALQ ORGANIZATION; a.k.a. MEK; a.k.a. MKO; a.k.a. MUJAHEDIN-E KHALQ; a.k.a. NATIONAL COUNCIL OF RESISTANCE (NCR); a.k.a. NLA; a.k.a. ORGANIZATION OF THE PEOPLE'S HOLY WARRIORS OF IRAN; a.k.a. PEOPLE'S MUJAHEDIN ORGANIZATION OF IRAN; a.k.a. SAZEMAN-E MUJAHEDIN-E KHALQ-E IRAN; a.k.a. THE NATIONAL LIBERATION ARMY OF IRAN) [FTO] also listed as [SDGT] on 10-31-01

POPULAR FRONT FOR THE LIBERATION OF PALESTINE (a.k.a. HALHUL GANG; a.k.a. HALHUL SQUAD; a.k.a. PALESTINIAN POPULAR RESISTANCE FORCES; a.k.a. PFLP; a.k.a. PPRF; a.k.a. RED EAGLE GANG; a.k.a. RED EAGLE GROUP; a.k.a. RED EAGLES) [SDT] [FTO] also listed as [SDGT] on 10-31-01

POPULAR FRONT FOR THE LIBERATION OF PALESTINE - GENERAL COMMAND (a.k.a. PFLP-GC) [SDT] [FTO] also listed as [SDGT] on 10-31-01

POPULAR REVOLUTIONARY STRUGGLE (a.k.a. EPANASTATIKOS LAIKOS AGONA; a.k.a. ELA; a.k.a. REVOLUTIONARY POPULAR STRUGGLE; a.k.a. REVOLUTIONARY PEOPLE'S STRUGGLE; a.k.a. JUNE 78; a.k.a. ORGANIZATION OF REVOLUTIONARY INTERNATIONALIST SOLIDARITY; a.k.a. REVOLUTIONARY NUCLEI; a.k.a. REVOLUTIONARY CELLS; a.k.a. LIBERATION STRUGGLE) [FTO] also listed as [SDGT] on 10-31-01

PPRF (a.k.a. POPULAR FRONT FOR THE LIBERATION OF PALESTINE; a.k.a. HALHUL GANG; a.k.a. HALHUL SQUAD; a.k.a. PALESTINIAN POPULAR RESISTANCE FORCES; a.k.a. PFLP; a.k.a. RED EAGLE GANG; a.k.a. RED EAGLE GROUP; a.k.a. RED EAGLES) [SDT] [FTO] also listed as [SDGT] on 10-31-01

RABITA TRUST, Room 9A, 2nd Floor, Wahdat Road, Education Town, Lahore, Pakistan; Wares Colony, Lahore, Pakistan [SDGT] 10-12-01

REAL IRA (a.k.a. 32 COUNTY SOVEREIGNTY COMMITTEE; a.k.a. 32 COUNTY SOVEREIGNTY MOVEMENT; a.k.a. IRISH REPUBLICAN PRISONERS WELFARE ASSOCIATION; a.k.a. REAL IRISH REPUBLICAN ARMY; a.k.a. REAL OGLAIGH NA HEIREANN; a.k.a. RIRA) [FTO] also listed as [SDGT] on 10-31-01

REAL IRISH REPUBLICAN ARMY (a.k.a. 32 COUNTY SOVEREIGNTY COMMITTEE; a.k.a. 32 COUNTY SOVEREIGNTY MOVEMENT; a.k.a. IRISH REPUBLICAN PRISONERS WELFARE ASSOCIATION; a.k.a. REAL IRA; a.k.a. REAL OGLAIGH NA HEIREANN; a.k.a. RIRA) [FTO] also listed as [SDGT] on 10-31-01

REAL OGLAIGH NA HEIREANN (a.k.a. 32 COUNTY SOVEREIGNTY COMMITTEE; a.k.a. 32 COUNTY SOVEREIGNTY MOVEMENT; a.k.a.

IRISH REPUBLICAN PRISONERS WELFARE ASSOCIATION; a.k.a. REAL IRA; a.k.a. REAL IRISH REPUBLICAN ARMY; a.k.a. RIRA) [FTO] **also listed as [SDGT] on 10-31-01**

RECONSTRUCTION FOUNDATION (a.k.a. UMMAH TAMEER E-NAU (UTN); a.k.a. FOUNDATION FOR CONSTRUCTION; a.k.a. NATION BUILDING; a.k.a. RECONSTRUCTION OF THE ISLAMIC COMMUNITY; a.k.a. RECONSTRUCTION OF THE MUSLIM UMMAH; a.k.a. UMMAH TAMEER I-NAU; a.k.a. UMMAH TAMIR E-NAU; a.k.a. UMMAH TAMIR I-NAU; a.k.a. UMMAT TAMIR E-NAU; a.k.a. UMMAT TAMIR-I-PAU), Street 13, Wazir Akbar Khan, Kabul, Afghanistan; 60-C, Nazim Ud Din Road, Islamabad F 8/4, Pakistan [SDGT] [FTO] **12-20-01**

RECONSTRUCTION OF THE ISLAMIC COMMUNITY (a.k.a. UMMAH TAMEER E-NAU (UTN); a.k.a. FOUNDATION FOR CONSTRUCTION; a.k.a. NATION BUILDING; a.k.a. RECONSTRUCTION FOUNDATION; a.k.a. RECONSTRUCTION OF THE MUSLIM UMMAH; a.k.a. UMMAH TAMEER I-NAU; a.k.a. UMMAH TAMIR E-NAU; a.k.a. UMMAH TAMIR I-NAU; a.k.a. UMMAT TAMIR E-NAU; a.k.a. UMMAT TAMIR-I-PAU), Street 13, Wazir Akbar Khan, Kabul, Afghanistan; 60-C, Nazim Ud Din Road, Islamabad F 8/4, Pakistan [SDGT] [FTO] **12-20-01**

RECONSTRUCTION OF THE MUSLIM UMMAH (a.k.a. UMMAH TAMEER E-NAU (UTN); a.k.a. FOUNDATION FOR CONSTRUCTION; a.k.a. NATION BUILDING; a.k.a. RECONSTRUCTION FOUNDATION; a.k.a. RECONSTRUCTION OF THE ISLAMIC COMMUNITY; a.k.a. UMMAH TAMEER I-NAU; a.k.a. UMMAH TAMIR E-NAU; a.k.a. UMMAH TAMIR I-NAU; a.k.a. UMMAT TAMIR E-NAU; a.k.a. UMMAT TAMIR-I-PAU), Street 13, Wazir Akbar Khan, Kabul, Afghanistan; 60-C, Nazim Ud Din Road, Islamabad F 8/4, Pakistan [SDGT] [FTO] **12-20-01**

RED EAGLE GANG (a.k.a. POPULAR FRONT FOR THE LIBERATION OF PALESTINE; a.k.a. HALHUL GANG; a.k.a. HALHUL SQUAD; a.k.a. PALESTINIAN POPULAR RESISTANCE FORCES; a.k.a. PFLP; a.k.a. PPRF; a.k.a. RED EAGLE GROUP; a.k.a. RED EAGLES) [SDT] [FTO] **also listed as [SDGT] on 10-31-01**

RED EAGLE GROUP (a.k.a. POPULAR FRONT FOR THE LIBERATION OF PALESTINE; a.k.a. HALHUL GANG; a.k.a. HALHUL SQUAD; a.k.a. PALESTINIAN POPULAR RESISTANCE FORCES; a.k.a. PFLP; a.k.a. PPRF; a.k.a. RED EAGLE GANG; a.k.a. RED EAGLES) [SDT] [FTO] **also listed as [SDGT] on 10-31-01**

RED EAGLES (a.k.a. POPULAR FRONT FOR THE LIBERATION OF PALESTINE; a.k.a. HALHUL GANG; a.k.a. HALHUL SQUAD; a.k.a. PALESTINIAN POPULAR RESISTANCE FORCES; a.k.a. PFLP; a.k.a. PPRF; a.k.a. RED EAGLE GANG; a.k.a. RED EAGLE GROUP) [SDT] [FTO] **also listed as [SDGT] on 10-31-01**

RED HAND DEFENDERS (RHD); United Kingdom [SDGT] **12-31-01**

RED SEA BARAKAT COMPANY LIMITED, Mogadishu, Somalia; Dubai, U.A.E. [SDGT] **11-07-01**

REPRESSION OF TRAITORS (a.k.a. KAHANE CHAI; a.k.a. COMMITTEE FOR THE SAFETY OF THE ROADS; a.k.a. DIKUY BOGDIM; a.k.a. DOV; a.k.a. FOREFRONT OF THE IDEA; a.k.a. JUDEA POLICE; a.k.a. KACH; a.k.a. KAHANE LIVES; a.k.a. KFAR TAPUAH FUND; a.k.a. KOACH; a.k.a. STATE OF JUDEA; a.k.a. SWORD OF DAVID; a.k.a. THE JUDEAN LEGION; a.k.a. THE JUDEAN VOICE; a.k.a. THE QOMEMIYUT MOVEMENT; a.k.a. THE WAY OF THE TORAH; a.k.a. THE YESHIVA OF THE JEWISH IDEA) [SDT] [FTO] **also listed as [SDGT] on 10-31-01**

REVOLUTIONARY ARMED FORCES OF COLOMBIA (a.k.a. FARC; a.k.a. FUERZAS ARMADAS REVOLUCIONARIAS DE COLOMBIA) [FTO] **also listed as [SDGT] on 10-31-01**

REVOLUTIONARY CELLS (a.k.a. POPULAR REVOLUTIONARY STRUGGLE; a.k.a. EPANASTATIKOS LAIKOS AGONAS; a.k.a. REVOLUTIONARY POPULAR STRUGGLE; a.k.a. REVOLUTIONARY PEOPLE'S STRUGGLE; a.k.a. JUNE 78; a.k.a. ORGANIZATION OF REVOLUTIONARY INTERNATIONALIST SOLIDARITY; a.k.a. REVOLUTIONARY NUCLEI; a.k.a. ELA; a.k.a. LIBERATION STRUGGLE) [FTO] **also listed as [SDGT] on 10-31-01**

REVOLUTIONARY JUSTICE ORGANIZATION (a.k.a. PARTY OF GOD; a.k.a. ISLAMIC JIHAD; a.k.a. ISLAMIC JIHAD ORGANIZATION; a.k.a. ISLAMIC JIHAD FOR THE LIBERATION OF PALESTINE; a.k.a. ORGANIZATION OF THE OPPRESSED ON EARTH; a.k.a. HIZBALLAH; a.k.a. ORGANIZATION OF RIGHT AGAINST WRONG; a.k.a. ANSAR ALLAH; a.k.a. FOLLOWERS OF THE PROPHET MUHAMMED) [SDT] [FTO] **also listed as [SDGT] on 10-31-01**

REVOLUTIONARY LEFT (a.k.a. DEVRIMCI HALK KURTULUS PARTISI-CEPHESI; a.k.a. DHKP/C; a.k.a. DEVRIMCI SOL; a.k.a. REVOLUTIONARY PEOPLE'S LIBERATION PARTY/FRONT; a.k.a. DEV SOL; a.k.a. DEV SOL SILAHLI DEVRIMCI BIRLIKLERI; a.k.a. DEV SOL SDB; a.k.a. DEV SOL ARMED REVOLUTIONARY UNITS) [FTO] **also listed as [SDGT] on 10-31-01**

REVOLUTIONARY NUCLEI (a.k.a. POPULAR REVOLUTIONARY STRUGGLE; a.k.a. EPANASTATIKOS LAIKOS AGONAS; a.k.a. REVOLUTIONARY POPULAR STRUGGLE; a.k.a. REVOLUTIONARY PEOPLE'S STRUGGLE; a.k.a. JUNE 78; a.k.a. ORGANIZATION OF REVOLUTIONARY INTERNATIONALIST SOLIDARITY; a.k.a. ELA; a.k.a. REVOLUTIONARY CELLS; a.k.a. LIBERATION STRUGGLE) [FTO] **also listed as [SDGT] on 10-31-01**

REVOLUTIONARY ORGANIATION OF SOCIALIST MUSLIMS (a.k.a. ANO; a.k.a. BLACK SEPTEMBER; a.k.a. FATAH REVOLUTIONARY COUNCIL; a.k.a. ARAB REVOLUTIONARY COUNCIL; a.k.a. ABU NIDAL ORGANIZATION; a.k.a. ARAB REVOLUTIONARY BRIGADES) [SDT] [FTO] also listed as [SDGT] on 10-31-01

REVOLUTIONARY ORGANIZATION 17 NOVEMBER (a.k.a. 17 NOVEMBER; a.k.a. EPANASTATIKI ORGANOSI 17 NOEMVRI) [FTO] also listed as [SDGT] on 10-31-01

REVOLUTIONARY PEOPLE'S LIBERATION PARTY/FRONT (a.k.a. DEVRIMCI HALK KURTULUS PARTISI-CEPHESI; a.k.a. DHKP/C; a.k.a. DEVRIMCI SOL; a.k.a. REVOLUTIONARY LEFT; a.k.a. DEV SOL; a.k.a. DEV SOL SILAHLI DEVRIMCI BIRLIKLERI; a.k.a. DEV SOL SDB; a.k.a. DEV SOL ARMED REVOLUTIONARY UNITS) [FTO] also listed as [SDGT] on 10-31-01

REVOLUTIONARY PEOPLE'S STRUGGLE (a.k.a. EPANASTATIKOS LAIKOS AGONAS; a.k.a. ELA; a.k.a. REVOLUTIONARY POPULAR STRUGGLE; a.k.a. POPULAR REVOLUTIONARY STRUGGLE; a.k.a. JUNE 78; a.k.a. ORGANIZATION OF REVOLUTIONARY INTERNATIONALIST SOLIDARITY; a.k.a. REVOLUTIONARY NUCLEI; a.k.a. REVOLUTIONARY CELS; a.k.a. LIBERATION STRUGGLE) [FTO] also listed as [SDGT] on 10-31-01

REVOLUTIONARY POPULAR STRUGGLE (a.k.a. EPANASTATIKOS LAIKOS AGONAS; a.k.a. ELA; a.k.a. REVOLUTIONARY PEOPLE'S STRUGGLE; a.k.a. POPULAR REVOLUTIONARY STRUGGLE; a.k.a. JUNE 78; a.k.a. ORGANIZATION OF REVOLUTIONARY INTERNATIONALIST SOLIDARITY; a.k.a. REVOLUTIONARY NUCLEI; a.k.a. REVOLUTIONARY CELLS; a.k.a. LIBERATION STRUGGLE) [FTO] also listed as [SDGT] on 10-31-01

RIRA (a.k.a. 32 COUNTY SOVEREIGNTY COMMITTEE; a.k.a. 32 COUNTY SOVEREIGNTY MOVEMENT; a.k.a. IRISH REPUBLICAN PRISONERS WELFARE ASSOCIATION; a.k.a. REAL IRA; a.k.a. REAL IRISH REPUBLICAN ARMY; a.k.a. REAL OGLAIGH NA HEIREANN) [FTO] also listed as [SDGT] on 10-31-01

SALAFIST GROUP FOR CALL AND COMBAT (a.k.a. GSPC; a.k.a. LE GROUPE SALAFISTE POUR LA PREDICATION ET LE COMBAT) [SDGT] 09-24-01

SAYARA AL-QUDS (a.k.a. PALESTINE ISLAMIC JIHAD - SHAQAQI FACTION; a.k.a. ABU GHUNAYM SQUAD OF THE HIZBALLAH BAYT AL-MAQDIS; a.k.a. AL-AWDAH BRIGADES; a.k.a. AL-QUDS BRIGADES; a.k.a. AL-QUDS SQUADS; a.k.a. ISLAMIC JIHAD IN PALESTINE; a.k.a. ISLAMIC JIHAD OF PALESTINE; a.k.a. PALESTINIAN ISLAMIC JIHAD;

a.k.a. PIJ; a.k.a. PIJ-SHALLAH FACTION; a.k.a. PIJ-SHAQAQI FACTION) [SDT] [FTO] also listed as [SDGT] on 10-31-01

SAZEMAN-E MUJAHEDIN-E KHALQ-E IRAN (a.k.a. MUJAHEDIN-E KHALQ ORGANIZATION; a.k.a. MEK; a.k.a. MKO; a.k.a. MUJAHEDIN-E KHALQ; a.k.a. NATIONAL COUNCIL OF RESISTANCE (NCR); a.k.a. NLA; a.k.a. ORGANIZATION OF THE PEOPLE'S HOLY WARRIORS OF IRAN; a.k.a. PEOPLE'S MUJAHEDIN ORGANIZATION OF IRAN; a.k.a. PMOI; a.k.a. THE NATIONAL LIBERATION ARMY OF IRAN) [FTO] also listed as [SDGT] on 10-31-01

SENDERO LUMINOSO (a.k.a. SHINING PATH; a.k.a. SL; a.k.a. PARTIDO COMUNISTA DEL PERU EN EL SENDERO LUMINOSO DE JOSE CARLOS MARIATEGUI (COMMUNIST PARTY OF PERU ON THE SHINING PATH OF JOSE CARLOS MARIATEGUI); a.k.a. PARTIDO COMUNISTA DEL PERU (COMMUNIST PARTY OF PERU); a.k.a. PCP; a.k.a. SOCORRO POPULAR DEL PERU (PEOPLE'S AID OF PERU); a.k.a. SPP; a.k.a EJERCITO GUERRILLERO POPULAR (PEOPLE'S GUERRILLA ARMY); a.k.a. EGP; a.k.a. EJERCITO POPULAR DE LIBERACION (PEOPLE'S LIBERATION ARMY); a.k.a. EPL) [FTO] also listed as [SDGT] on 10-31-01

SHINING PATH (a.k.a. SENDERO LUMINOSO; a.k.a. SL; a.k.a. PARTIDO COMUNISTA DEL PERU EN EL SENDERO LUMINOSO DE JOSE CARLOS MARIATEGUI (COMMUNIST PARTY OF PERU ON THE SHINING PATH OF JOSE CARLOS MARIATEGUI); a.k.a. PARTIDO COMUNISTA DEL PERU (COMMUNIST PARTY OF PERU); a.k.a. PCP; a.k.a. SOCORRO POPULAR DEL PERU (PEOPLE'S AID OF PERU); a.k.a. SPP; a.k.a EJERCITO GUERRILLERO POPULAR (PEOPLE'S GUERRILLA ARMY); a.k.a. EGP; a.k.a. EJERCITO POPULAR DE LIBERACION (PEOPLE'S LIBERATION ARMY); a.k.a. EPL) [FTO] also listed as [SDGT] on 10-31-01

SL (a.k.a. SENDERO LUMINOSO; a.k.a. SHINING PATH; a.k.a. PARTIDO COMUNISTA DEL PERU EN EL SENDERO LUMINOSO DE JOSE CARLOS MARIATEGUI (COMMUNIST PARTY OF PERU ON THE SHINING PATH OF JOSE CARLOS MARIATEGUI); a.k.a. PARTIDO COMUNISTA DEL PERU (COMMUNIST PARTY OF PERU); a.k.a. PCP; a.k.a. SOCORRO POPULAR DEL PERU (PEOPLE'S AID OF PERU); a.k.a. SPP; a.k.a EJERCITO GUERRILLERO POPULAR (PEOPLE'S GUERRILLA ARMY); a.k.a. EGP; a.k.a. EJERCITO POPULAR DE LIBERACION (PEOPLE'S LIBERATION ARMY); a.k.a. EPL) [FTO] also listed as [SDGT] on 10-31-01

SOCIETY OF ISLAMIC COOPERATION (a.k.a. JAM'IYAT AL TA'AWUN AL ISLAMIYYA; a.k.a. JAM'YAH TA'AWUN AL-ISLAMIA; a.k.a. JIT), Qandahar City, Afghanistan [SDGT] 10-12-01

SOCORRO POPULAR DEL PERU (PEOPLE'S AID OF PERU) (a.k.a. SENDERO LUMINOSO; a.k.a. SL; a.k.a. PARTIDO COMUNISTA DEL PERU EN EL SENDERO LUMINOSO DE JOSE CARLOS MARIATEGUI (COMMUNIST PARTY OF PERU ON THE SHINING PATH OF JOSE CARLOS MARIATEGUI); a.k.a. PARTIDO COMUNISTA DEL PERU (COMMUNIST PARTY OF PERU); a.k.a. PCP; a.k.a. SHINING PATH; a.k.a. SPP; a.k.a EJERCITO GUERRILLERO POPULAR (PEOPLE'S GUERRILLA ARMY); a.k.a. EGP; a.k.a. EJERCITO POPULAR DE LIBERACION (PEOPLE'S LIBERATION ARMY); a.k.a. EPL) [FTO] **also listed as [SDGT] on 10-31-01**

SOM NET AB (a.k.a. SOMALI NETWORK AB), Hallbybacken 15, Spanga 70, Sweden [SDGT] **11-07-01**

SOMALI INTERNATIONAL RELIEF ORGANIZATION, 1806 Riverside Ave., 2nd Floor, Minneapolis, Minnesota, U.S.A. [SDGT] **11-07-01**

SOMALI INTERNET COMPANY, Mogadishu, Somalia [SDGT] **11-07-01**

SOMALI NETWORK AB (a.k.a. SOM NET AB), Hallbybacken 15, Spanga 70, Sweden [SDGT] **11-07-01**

SPP (a.k.a. SENDERO LUMINOSO; a.k.a. SL; a.k.a. PARTDO COMUNISTA DEL PERU EN EL SENDERO LUMINOSO DE JOSE CARLOS MARIATEGUI (COMMUNIST PARTY OF PERU ON THE SHINING PATH OF JOSE CARLOS MARIATEGUI); a.k.a. PARTIDO COMUNISTA DEL PERU (COMMUNIST PARTY OF PERU); a.k.a. PCP; a.k.a. SOCORRO POPULAR DEL PERU (PEOPLE'S AID OF PERU); a.k.a. SHINING PATH; a.k.a EJERCITO GUERRILLERO POPULAR (PEOPLE'S GUERRILLA ARMY); a.k.a. EGP; a.k.a. EJERCITO POPULAR DE LIBERACION (PEOPLE'S LIBERATION ARMY); a.k.a. EPL) [FTO] **also listed as [SDGT] on 10-31-01**

STATE OF JUDEA (a.k.a. KAHANE CHAI; a.k.a. COMMITTEE FOR THE SAFETY OF THE ROADS; a.k.a. DIKUY BOGDIM; a.k.a. DOV; a.k.a. FOREFRONT OF THE IDEA; a.k.a. JUDEA POLICE; a.k.a. KACH; a.k.a. KAHANE LIVES; a.k.a. KFAR TAPUAH FUND; a.k.a. KOACH; a.k.a. REPRESSION OF TRAITORS; a.k.a. SWORD OF DAVID; a.k.a. THE JUDEAN LEGION; a.k.a. THE JUDEAN VOICE; a.k.a. THE QOMEMIYUT MOVEMENT; a.k.a. THE WAY OF THE TORAH; a.k.a. THE YESHIVA OF THE JEWISH IDEA) [SDT] [FTO] **also listed as [SDGT] on 10-31-01**

STUDENTS OF AYYASH (a.k.a. ISLAMIC RESISTANCE MOVEMENT; a.k.a. HARAKAT AL-MUQAWAMA AL-ISLAMIYA; a.k.a. HAMAS; a.k.a. STUDENTS OF TH ENGINEER; a.k.a. YAHYA AYYASH UNITS; a.k.a. IZZ AL-DIN AL-QASSIM BRIGADES; a.k.a. IZZ AL-DIN AL-QASSIM FORCES; a.k.a. IZZ AL-DIN AL-QASSIM BATTALIONS; a.k.a. IZZ AL-DIN AL QASSAM BRIGADES; a.k.a. IZZ AL-DIN AL QASSAM

FORCES; a.k.a. IZZ AL-DIN AL QASSAM BATTALIONS) [SDT] [FTO] **also listed as [SDGT] on 10-31-01**

STUDENTS OF THE ENGINEER (a.k.a. ISLAMIC RESISTANCE MOVEMENT; a.k.a. HARAKAT AL-MUQAWAMA AL-ISLAMIYA; a.k.a. STUDENTS OF AYYASH; a.k.a. HAMAS; a.k.a. YAHYA AYYASH UNITS; a.k.a. IZZ AL-DIN AL-QASSIM BRIGADES; a.k.a. IZZ AL-DIN AL-QASSIM FORCES; a.k.a. IZZ AL-DIN AL-QASSIM BATTALIONS; a.k.a. IZZ AL-DIN AL QASSAM BRIGADES; a.k.a. IZZ AL-DIN AL QASSAM FORCES; a.k.a. IZZ AL-DIN AL QASSAM BATTALIONS) [SDT] [FTO] **also listed as [SDGT] on 10-31-01**

SWORD OF DAVID (a.k.a. KAHANE CHAI; a.k.a. COMMITTEE FOR THE SAFETY OF THE ROADS; a.k.a. DIKUY BOGDIM; a.k.a. DOV; a.k.a. FOREFRONT OF THE IDEA; a.k.a. JUDEA POLICE; a.k.a. KACH; a.k.a. KAHANE LIVES; a.k.a. KFAR TAPUAH FUND; a.k.a. KOACH; a.k.a. REPRESSION OF TRAITORS; a.k.a. STATE OF JUDEA; a.k.a. THE JUDEAN LEGION; a.k.a. THE JUDEAN VOICE; a.k.a. THE QOMEMIYUT MOVEMENT; a.k.a. THE WAY OF THE TORAH; a.k.a. THE YESHIVA OF THE JEWISH IDEA) [SDT] [FTO] **also listed as [SDGT] on 10-31-01**

TAMIL TIGERS (a.k.a. LIBERATION TIGERS OF TAMIL EELAM; a.k.a. LTTE; a.k.a. ELLALAN FORCE) [FTO] **also listed as [SDGT] on 10-31-01**

TEHRIK UL-FURQAAN (a.k.a. ARMY OF MOHAMMED; a.k.a. JAISH-I-MOHAMMED; a.k.a. MOHAMMED'S ARMY), Pakistan [FTO] [SDGT] **10-12-01**

"THE BASE" (a.k.a. ISLAMIC ARMY; a.k.a. AL QA'IDA; a.k.a. AL QAEDA; a.k.a. AL QAIDA; a.k.a. INTERNATIONAL FRONT FOR FIGHTING JEWS AND CRUSADES; a.k.a. ISLAMIC ARMY FOR THE LIBERATION OF HOLY SITES; a.k.a. ISLAMIC SALVATION FOUNDATION; a.k.a. THE GROUP FOR THE PRESERVATION OF THE HOLY SITES; a.k.a. THE ISLAMIC ARMY FOR THE LIBERATION OF THE HOLY PLACES; a.k.a. THE WORLD ISLAMIC FRONT FOR JIHAD AGAINST JEWS AND CRUSADERS; a.k.a. USAMA BIN LADEN NETWORK; a.k.a. USAMA BIN LADEN ORGANIZATION) [SDT] [FTO] [SDGT] **09-24-01**

THE GROUP FOR THE PRESERVATION OF THE HOLY SITES (a.k.a. ISLAMIC ARMY; a.k.a. "THE BASE;" a.k.a. AL QA'IDA; a.k.a. AL QAEDA; a.k.a. AL QAIDA; a.k.a. INTERNATIONAL FRONT FOR FIGHTING JEWS AND CRUSADES; a.k.a. ISLAMIC ARMY FOR THE LIBERATION OF HOLY SITES; a.k.a. ISLAMIC SALVATION FOUNDATION; a.k.a. THE ISLAMIC ARMY FOR THE LIBERATION OF THE HOLY PLACES; a.k.a. THE WORLD ISLAMIC FRONT FOR JIHAD AGAINST JEWS AND CRUSADERS; a.k.a. USAMA BIN LADEN NETWORK; a.k.a. USAMA BIN LADEN ORGANIZATION) [SDT] [FTO] [SD T] **09-24-01**

THE ISLAMIC ARMY FOR THE LIBERATION OF THE HOLY PLACES (a.k.a. ISLAMIC ARMY; a.k.a. "THE BASE;" a.k.a. AL QA'IDA; a.k.a. AL QAEDA; a.k.a. AL QAIDA; a.k.a. INTERNATIONAL FRONT FOR FIGHTING JEWS AND CRUSADES; a.k.a. ISLAMIC ARMY FOR THE LIBERATION OF HOLY SITES; a.k.a. ISLAMIC SALVATION FOUNDATION; a.k.a. THE GROUP FOR THE PRESERVATION OF THE HOLY SITES; a.k.a. THE WORLD ISLAMIC FRONT FOR JIHAD AGAINST JEWS AND CRUSADERS; a.k.a. USAMA BIN LADEN NETWORK; a.k.a. USAMA BIN LADEN ORGANIZATION) [SDT] [FTO] [SDGT] **09-24-01**

THE JUDEAN LEGION (a.k.a. KAHANE CHAI; a.k.a. COMMITTEE FOR THE SAFETY OF THE ROADS; a.k.a. DIKUY BOGDIM; a.k.a. DOV; a.k.a. FOREFRONT OF THE IDEA; a.k.a. JUDEA POLICE; a.k.a. KACH; a.k.a. KAHANE LIVES; a.k.a. KFAR TAPUAH FUND; a.k.a. KOACH; a.k.a. REPRESSION OF TRAITORS; a.k.a. STATE OF JUDEA; a.k.a. SWORD OF DAVID; a.k.a. THE JUDEAN VOICE; a.k.a. THE QOMEMIYUT MOVEMENT; a.k.a. THE WAY OF THE TORAH; a.k.a. THE YESHIVA OF THE JEWISH IDEA) [SDT] [FTO] **also listed as [SDGT] on 10-31-01**

THE JUDEAN VOICE (a.k.a. KAHANE CHAI; a.k.a. COMMITTEE FOR THE SAFETY OF THE ROADS; a.k.a. DIKUY BOGDIM; a.k.a. DOV; a.k.a. FOREFRONT OF THE IDEA; a.k.a. JUDEA POLICE; a.k.a. KACH; a.k.a. KAHANE LIVES; a.k.a. KFAR TAPUAH FUND; a.k.a. KOACH; a.k.a. REPRESSION OF TRAITORS; a.k.a. STATE OF JUDEA; a.k.a. SWORD OF DAVID; a.k.a. THE JUDEAN LEGION; a.k.a. THE QOMEMIYUT MOVEMENT; a.k.a. THE WAY OF THE TORAH; a.k.a. THE YESHIVA OF THE JEWISH IDEA) [SDT] [FTO] **also listed as [SDGT] on 10-31-01**

THE NATIONAL LIBERATION ARMY OF IRAN (a.k.a. MUJAHEDIN-E KHALQ ORGANIZATION; a.k.a. MEK; a.k.a. MKO; a.k.a. MUJAHEDIN-E KHALQ; a.k.a. NATIONAL COUNCIL OF RESISTANCE (NCR); a.k.a. NLA; a.k.a. ORGANIZATION OF THE PEOPLE'S HOLY WARRIORS OF IRAN; a.k.a. PEOPLE'S MUJAHEDIN ORGANIZATION OF IRAN; a.k.a. PMOI; a.k.a. SAZEMAN-E MUJAHEDIN-E KHALQ-E IRAN) [FTO] **also listed as [SDGT] on 10-31-01**

THE PEOPLE'S DEFENSE FORCE (a.k.a. KURDISTAN WORKERS' PARTY; a.k.a. HALU MESRU SAVUNMA KUVVETI (HSK); a.k.a. PARTIYA KARKERAN KURDISTAN; a.k.a. PKK) [FTO] **also listed as [SDGT] on 10-31-01**

THE QOMEMIYUT MOVEMENT (a.k.a. KAHANE CHAI; a.k.a. COMMITTEE FOR THE SAFETY OF THE ROADS; a.k.a. DIKUY BOGDIM; a.k.a. DOV; a.k.a. FOREFRONT OF THE IDEA; a.k.a. JUDEA POLICE; a.k.a. KACH; a.k.a. KAHANE LIVES; a.k.a. KFAR TAPUAH FUND; a.k.a. KOACH; a.k.a. REPRESSION OF TRAITORS; a.k.a. STATE OF JUDEA; a.k.a. SWORD OF DAVID; a.k.a. THE JUDEAN LEGION; a.k.a.

THE JUDEAN VOICE; a.k.a. THE WAY OF THE TORAH; a.k.a. THE YESHIVA OF THE JEWISH IDEA) [SDT] [FTO] **also listed as [SDGT] on 10-31-01**

THE WAY OF THE TORAH (a.k.a. KAHANE CHAI; a.k.a. COMMITTEE FOR THE SAFETY OF THEROADS; a.k.a. DIKUY BOGDIM; a.k.a. DOV; a.k.a. FOREFRONT OF THE IDEA; a.k.a. JUDEA POLICE; a.k.a. KACH; a.k.a. KAHANE LIVES; a.k.a. KFAR TAPUAH FUND; a.k.a. KOACH; a.k.a. REPRESSION OF TRAITORS; a.k.a. STATE OF JUDEA; a.k.a. SWORD OF DAVID; a.k.a. THE JUDEAN LEGION; a.k.a. THE JUDEAN VOICE; a.k.a. THE QOMEMIYUT MOVEMENT; a.k.a. THE YESHIVA OF THE JEWISH IDEA) [SDT] [FTO] **also listed as [SDGT] on 10-31-01**

THE WORLD ISLAMIC FRONT FOR JIHAD AGAINST JEWS AND CRUSADERS (a.k.a. ISLAMIC ARMY; a.k.a. "THE BASE;" a.k.a. AL QA'IDA; a.k.a. AL QAEDA; a.k.a. AL QAIDA; a.k.a. INTERNATIONAL FRONT FOR FIGHTING JEWS AND CRUSADES; a.k.a. ISLAMIC ARMY FOR THE LIBERATION OF HOLY SITES; a.k.a. ISLAMIC SALVATION FOUNDATION; a.k.a. THE GROUP FOR THE PRESERVATION OF THE HOLY SITES; a.k.a. THE ISLAMIC ARMY FOR THE LIBERATION OF THE HOLY PLACES; a.k.a. USAMA BIN LADEN NETWORK; a.k.a. USAMA BIN LADEN ORGANIZATION) [SDT] [FTO] [SDGT] **09-24-01**

THE YESHIVA OF THE JEWISH IDEA (a.k.a. KAHANE CHAI; a.k.a. COMMITTEE FOR THE SAFETY OF THE ROADS; a.k.a. DIKUY BOGDIM; a.k.a. DOV; a.k.a. FOREFRONT OF THE IDEA; a.k.a. JUDEA POLICE; a.k.a. KACH; a.k.a. KAHANE LIVES; a.k.a. KFAR TAPUAH FUND; a.k.a. KOACH; a.k.a. REPRESSION OF TRAITORS; a.k.a. STATE OF JUDEA; a.k.a. SWORD OF DAVID; a.k.a. THE JUDEAN LEGION; a.k.a. THE JUDEAN VOICE; a.k.a. THE QOMEMIYUT MOVEMENT; a.k.a. THE WAY OF THE TORAH) [SDT] [FTO] **also listed as [SDGT] on 10-31-01**

ULSTER DEFENCE ASSOCIATION (a.k.a. ULSTER FREEDOM FIGHTERS); United Kingdom [SDGT] **12-31-01**

ULSTER FREEDOM FIGHTERS (a.k.a. ULSTER DEFENCE ASSOCIATION); United Kingdom [SDGT] **12-31-01**

UMMAH TAMEER E-NAU (UTN) (a.k.a. FOUNDATION FOR CONSTRUCTION; a.k.a. NATION BUILDING; a.k.a. RECONSTRUCTION FOUNDATION; a.k.a. RECONSTRUCTION OF THE ISLAMIC COMMUNITY; a.k.a. RECONSTRUCTION OF THE MUSLIM UMMAH; a.k.a. UMMAH TAMEER I-NAU; a.k.a. UMMAH TAMIR E-NAU; a.k.a. UMMAH TAMIR I-NAU; a.k.a. UMMAT TAMIR E-NAU; a.k.a. UMMAT TAMIR-I-PAU), Street 13, Wazir Akbar Khan, Kabul, Afghanistan; 60-C, Nazim Ud Din Road, Islamabad F 8/4, Pakistan [SDGT] [FTO] **12-20-01**

UMMAH TAMEER I-NAU (a.k.a. UMMAH TAMEER E-NAU (UTN); a.k.a. FOUNDATION FOR CONSTRUCTION; a.k.a. NATION BUILDING; a.k.a. RECONSTRUCTION FOUNDATION; a.k.a. RECONSTRUCTION OF THE ISLAMIC COMMUNITY; a.k.a. RECONSTRUCTION OF THE MUSLIM UMMAH; a.k.a. UMMAH TAMIR E-NAU; a.k.a. UMMAH TAMIR I-NAU; a.k.a. UMMAT TAMIR E-NAU; a.k.a. UMMAT TAMIR-I-PAU), Street 13, Wazir Akbar Khan, Kabul, Afghanistan; 60-C, Nazim Ud Din Road, Islamabad F 8/4, Pakistan [SDGT] [FTO] 12-20-01

UMMAH TAMIR E-NAU (a.k.a. UMMAH TAMEER E-NAU (UTN); a.k.a. FOUNDATION FOR CONSTRUCTION; a.k.a. NATION BUILDING; a.k.a. RECONSTRUCTION FOUNDATION; a.k.a. RECONSTRUCTION OF THE ISLAMIC COMMUNITY; a.k.a. RECONSTRUCTION OF THE MUSLIM UMMAH; a.k.a. UMMAH TAMEER I-NAU; a.k.a. UMMAH TAMIR I-NAU; a.k.a. UMMAT TAMIR E-NAU; a.k.a. UMMAT TAMIR-I-PAU), Street 13, Wazir Akbar Khan, Kabul, Afghanistan; 60-C, Nazim Ud Din Road, Islamabad F 8/4, Pakistan [SDGT] [FTO] 12-20-01

UMMAH TAMIR I-NAU (a.k.a. UMMAH TAMEER E-NAU (UTN); a.k.a. FOUNDATION FOR CONSTRUCTION; a.k.a. NATION BUILDING; a.k.a. RECONSTRUCTION FOUNDATION; a.k.a. RECONSTRUCTION OF THE ISLAMIC COMMUNITY; a.k.a. RECONSTRUCTION OF THE MUSLIM UMMAH; a.k.a. UMMAH TAMEER I-NAU; a.k.a. UMMAH TAMIR E-NAU; a.k.a. UMMAT TAMIR E-NAU; a.k.a. UMMAT TAMIR-I-PAU), Street 13, Wazir Akbar Khan, Kabul, Afghanistan; 60-C, Nazim Ud Din Road, Islamabad F 8/4, Pakistan [SDGT] [FTO] 12-20-01

UMMAT TAMIR E-NAU (a.k.a. UMMAH TAMEER E-NAU (UTN); a.k.a. FOUNDATION FOR CONSTRUCTION; a.k.a. NATION BUILDING; a.k.a. RECONSTRUCTION FOUNDATION; a.k.a. RECONSTRUCTION OF THE ISLAMIC COMMUNITY; a.k.a. RECONSTRUCTION OF THE MUSLIM UMMAH; a.k.a. UMMAH TAMEER I-NAU; a.k.a. UMMAH TAMIR E-NAU; a.k.a. UMMAH TAMIR I-NAU; a.k.a. UMMAT TAMIR-I-PAU), Street 13, Wazir Akbar Khan, Kabul, Afghanistan; 60-C, Nazim Ud Din Road, Islamabad F 8/4, Pakistan [SDGT] [FTO] 12-20-01

UMMAT TAMIR-I-PAU (a.k.a. UMMAH TAMEER E-NAU (UTN); a.k.a. FOUNDATION FOR CONSTRUCTION; a.k.a. NATION BUILDING; a.k.a. RECONSTRUCTION FOUNDATION; a.k.a. RECONSTRUCTION OF THE ISLAMIC COMMUNITY; a.k.a. RECONSTRUCTION OF THE MUSLIM UMMAH; a.k.a. UMMAH TAMEER I-NAU; a.k.a. UMMAH TAMIR E-NAU; a.k.a. UMMAH TAMIR I-NAU; a.k.a. UMMAT TAMIR E-NAU), Street 13, Wazir Akbar Khan, Kabul, Afghanistan; 60-C, Nazim Ud Din Road, Islamabad F 8/4, Pakistan [SDGT] [FTO] 12-20-01

UNITED SELF-DEFENSE FORCES OF COLOMBIA (a.k.a. AUC; a.k.a. AUTODEFENSAS UNIDAS DE COLOMBIA) [FTO] **also listed as [SDGT] on 10-31-01**

USAMA BIN LADEN NETWORK (a.k.a. ISLAMIC ARMY; a.k.a. "THE BASE;" a.k.a. AL QA'IDA; a.k.a. AL QAEDA; a.k.a. AL QAIDA; a.k.a. INTERNATIONAL FRONT FOR FIGHTING JEWS AND CRUSADES; a.k.a. ISLAMIC ARMY FOR THE LIBERATION OF HOLY SITES; a.k.a. ISLAMIC SALVATION FOUNDATION; a.k.a. THE GROUP FOR THE PRESERVATION OF THE HOLY SITES; a.k.a. THE ISLAMIC ARMY FOR THE LIBERATION OF THE HOLY PLACES; a.k.a. THE WORLD ISLAMIC FRONT FOR JIHAD AGAINST JEWS AND CRUSADERS; a.k.a. USAMA BIN LADEN ORGANIZATION) [SDT] [FTO] [SDGT] **09-24-01**

USAMA BIN LADEN ORGANIZATION (a.k.a. ISLAMIC ARMY; a.k.a. "THE BASE;" a.k.a. AL QA'IDA; a.k.a. AL QAEDA; a.k.a. AL QAIDA; a.k.a. INTERNATIONAL FRONT FOR FIGHTING JEWS AND CRUSADES; a.k.a. ISLAMIC ARMY FOR THE LIBERATION OF HOLY SITES; a.k.a. ISLAMIC SALVATION FOUNDATION; a.k.a. THE GROUP FOR THE PRESERVATION OF THE HOLY SITES; a.k.a. THE ISLAMIC ARMY FOR THE LIBERATION OF THE HOLY PLACES; a.k.a. THE WORLD ISLAMIC FRONT FOR JIHAD AGAINST JEWS AND CRUSADERS; a.k.a. USAMA BIN LADEN NETWORK) [SDT] [FTO] [SDGT] **09-24-01**

WAFA AL-IGATHA AL-ISLAMIA (a.k.a. WAFA HUMANITARIAN ORGANIZATION; a.k.a. AL WAFA; a.k.a. AL WAFA ORGANIZATION) [SDGT] **09-24-01**

WAFA HUMANITARIAN ORGANIZATION (a.k.a. AL WAFA; a.k.a. AL WAFA ORGANIZATION; a.k.a. WAFA AL-IGATHA AL-ISLAMIA) [SDGT] 09-24-01

YAHYA AYYASH UNITS (a.k.a. ISLAMIC RESISTANCE MOVEMENT; a.k.a. HARAKAT AL-MUQAWAMA AL-ISLAMIYA; a.k.a. STUDENTS OF AYYASH; a.k.a. STUDENTS OF THE ENGINEER; a.k.a. HAMAS; a.k.a. IZZ AL-DIN AL-QASSIM BRIGADES; a.k.a. IZZ AL-DIN AL-QASSIM FORCES; a.k.a. IZZ AL-DIN AL-QASSIM BATTALIONS; a.k.a. IZZ AL-DIN AL QASSAM BRIGADES; a.k.a. IZZ AL-DIN AL QASSAM FORCES; a.k.a. IZZ AL-DIN AL QASSAM BATTALIONS) [SDT] [FTO] **also listed as [SDGT] on 10-31-01**

YOUSSEF M. NADA & CO. GESELLSCHAFT M.B.H., Kaernter Ring 2/2/5/22, Vienna 1010, Austria [SDGT] **11-07-01**

YOUSSEF M. NADA, Via Riasc 4, Campione d'Italia I, CH-6911, Switzerland [SDGT] **11-07-01**

Details of Specially Designated Global Terrorist [SDGT] Individuals:

"AHMED THE TANZANIAN" (a.k.a. GHAILANI, Ahmed Khalfan; a.k.a. "FOOPIE;" a.k.a. "FUPI;" a.k.a. AHMAD, Abu Bakr; a.k.a. AHMED, A.; a.k.a. AHMED, Abubakar; a.k.a. AHMED, Abubakar K.; a.k.a. AHMED, Abubakar Khalfan; a.k.a. AHMED, Abubakary K.; a.k.a. AHMED, Ahmed Khalfan; a.k.a. AL TANZANI, Ahmad; a.k.a. ALI, Ahmed Khalfan; a.k.a. BAKR, Abu; a.k.a. GHAILANI, Abubakary Khalfan Ahmed; a.k.a. GHAILANI, Ahmed; a.k.a. GHILANI, Ahmad Khalafan; a.k.a. HUSSEIN, Mahafudh Abubakar Ahmed Abdallah; a.k.a. KHABAR, Abu; a.k.a. KHALFAN, Ahmed; a.k.a. MOHAMMED, Shariff Omar); DOB 14 Mar 1974; alt. DOB 13 Apr 1974; alt. DOB 14 Apr 1974; alt. DOB 1 Aug 1970; POB Zanzibar, Tanzania; citizen Tanzania (individual) [SDGT] **10-12-01**

"FOOPIE" (a.k.a. GHAILANI, Ahmed Khalfan; a.k.a. "AHMED THE TANZANIAN;" a.k.a. "FUPI;" a.k.a. AHMAD, Abu Bakr; a.k.a. AHMED, A.; a.k.a. AHMED, Abubakar; a.k.a. AHMED, Abubakar K.; a.k.a. AHMED, Abubakar Khalfan; a.k.a. AHMED, Abubakary K.; a.k.a. AHMED, Ahmed Khalfan; a.k.a. AL TANZANI, Ahmad; a.k.a. ALI, Ahmed Khalfan; a.k.a. BAKR, Abu; a.k.a. GHAILANI, Abubakary Khalfan Ahmed; a.k.a. GHAILANI, Ahmed; a.k.a. GHILANI, Ahmad Khalafan; a.k.a. HUSSEIN, Mahafudh Abubakar Ahmed Abdallah; a.k.a. KHABAR, Abu; a.k.a. KHALFAN, Ahmed; a.k.a. MOHAMMED, Shariff Omar); DOB 14 Mar 1974; alt. DOB 13 Apr 1974; alt. DOB 14 Apr 1974; alt. DOB 1 Aug 1970; POB Zanzibar, Tanzania; citizen Tanzania (individual) [SDGT] **10-12-01**

"FUPI" (a.k.a. GHAILANI, Ahmed Khalfan; a.k.a. "AHMED THE TANZANIAN;" a.k.a. "FOOPIE;" a.k.a. AHMAD, Abu Bakr; a.k.a. AHMED, A.; a.k.a. AHMED, Abubakar; a.k.a. AHMED, Abubakar K.; a.k.a. AHMED, Abubakar Khalfan; a.k.a. AHMED, Abubakary K.; a.k.a. AHMED, Ahmed Khalfan; a.k.a. AL TANZANI, Ahmad; a.k.a. ALI, Ahmed Khalfan; a.k.a. BAKR, Abu; a.k.a. GHAILANI, Abubakary Khalfan Ahmed; a.k.a. GHAILANI, Ahmed; a.k.a. GHILANI, Ahmad Khalafan; a.k.a. HUSSEIN, Mahafudh Abubakar Ahmed Abdallah; a.k.a. KHABAR, Abu; a.k.a. KHALFAN, Ahmed; a.k.a. MOHAMMED, Shariff Omar); DOB 14 Mar 1974; alt. DOB 13 Apr 1974; alt. DOB 14 Apr 1974; alt. DOB 1 Aug 1970; POB Zanzibar, Tanzania; citizen Tanzania (individual) [SDGT] **10-12-01**

ABDALLA, Fazul (a.k.a. MOHAMMED, Fazul Abdullah; a.k.a. ADBALLAH, Fazul; a.k.a. AISHA, Abu; a.k.a. AL SUDANI, Abu Seif; a.k.a. ALI, Fadel Abdallah Mohammed; a.k.a. FAZUL, Abdalla; a.k.a. FAZUL, Abdallah; a.k.a. FAZUL, Abdallah Mohammed; a.k.a. FAZUL, Haroon; a.k.a. FAZUL, Harun; a.k.a. HAROON; a.k.a. HAROUN, Fadhil; a.k.a. HARUN; a.k.a. LUQMAN, Abu; a.k.a. MOHAMMED, Fazul; a.k.a. MOHAMMED, Fazul Abdilahi; a.k.a. MOHAMMED, Fouad; a.k.a. MUHAMAD, Fadil Abdallah); DOB 25 Aug 1972; alt. DOB 25 Dec 1974; alt.

DOB 25 Feb 1974; POB Moroni, Comoros Islands; citizen Comoros; alt. citizen Kenya (individual) [SDGT] **10-12-01**

ABDALLAH, Tarwat Salah (a.k.a. SHIHATA, Thirwat Salah; a.k.a. THIRWAT, Salah Shihata; a.k.a. THIRWAT, Shahata); DOB 29 Jun 60; POB Egypt (individual) [SDGT] **09-24-01**

ABDEL RAHMAN (a.k.a. ATWAH, Muhsin Musa Matwalli; a.k.a. ABDUL RAHMAN; a.k.a. AL-MUHAJIR, Abdul Rahman; a.k.a. AL-NAMER, Mohammed K.A.), Afghanistan; DOB 19 Jun 1964; POB Egypt; citizen Egypt (individual) [SDGT] **10-12-01**

ABDUL RAHMAN (a.k.a. ATWAH, Muhsin Musa Matwalli; a.k.a. ABDEL RAHMAN; a.k.a. AL-MUHAJIR, Abdul Rahman; a.k.a. AL-NAMER, Mohammed K.A.), Afghanistan; DOB 19 Jun 1964; POB Egypt; citizen Egypt (individual) [SDGT] **10-12-01**

ABDULLAH, Abdullah Ahmed (a.k.a. ABU MARIAM; a.k.a. AL-MASRI, Abu Mohamed; a.k.a. SALEH), Afghanistan; DOB 1963; POB Egypt; citizen Egypt (individual) [SDGT] **10-12-01**

ABDULLAH, Sheikh Taysir (a.k.a. AL-MASRI, Abu Hafs; a.k.a. ABU HAFS; a.k.a. ABU SITTA, Subhi; a.k.a. ATEF, Muhammad; a.k.a. ATIF, Mohamed; a.k.a. ATIF, Muhammad; a.k.a. EL KHABIR, Abu Hafs el Masry; a.k.a. TAYSIR); DOB 1951; Alt. DOB 1956; Alt. DOB 1944; POB Alexandria, Egypt (individual) [SDT] [SDGT] **09-24-01**

ABDULLKADIR, Hussein Mahamud, Florence, Italy (individual) [SDGT] **11-07-01**

ABDUREHMAN, Ahmed Mohammed (a.k.a. ALI, Ahmed Mohammed Hamed; a.k.a. ABU FATIMA; a.k.a. ABU ISLAM; a.k.a. ABU KHADIIJAH; a.k.a. AHMED HAMED; a.k.a. Ahmed The Egyptian; a.k.a. AHMED, Ahmed; a.k.a. AL-MASRI, Ahmad; a.k.a. AL-SURIR, Abu Islam; a.k.a. ALI, Ahmed Mohammed; a.k.a. ALI, Hamed; a.k.a. HEMED, Ahmed; a.k.a. SHIEB, Ahmed; a.k.a. SHUAIB), Afghanistan; DOB 1965; POB Egypt; citizen Egypt (individual) [SDGT] **10-12-01**

ABU ABDALLAH (a.k.a. AL-IRAQI, Abd al-Hadi; a.k.a. AL-IRAQI, Abdal al-Hadi) (individual) [SDGT] **09-24-01**

ABU FATIMA (a.k.a. ALI, Ahmed Mohammed Hamed; a.k.a. ABDUREHMAN, Ahmed Mohammed; a.k.a. ABU ISLAM; a.k.a. ABU KHADIIJAH; a.k.a. AHMED HAMED; a.k.a. Ahmed The Egyptian; a.k.a. AHMED, Ahmed; a.k.a. AL-MASRI, Ahmad; a.k.a. AL-SURIR, Abu Islam; a.k.a. ALI, Ahmed Mohammed; a.k.a. ALI, Hamed; a.k.a. HEMED, Ahmed; a.k.a. SHIEB, Ahmed; a.k.a. SHUAIB), Afghanistan; DOB 1965; POB Egypt; citizen Egypt (individual) [SDGT] **10-12-01**

ABU HAFS (a.k.a. AL-MASRI, Abu Hafs; a.k.a. ABDULLAH, Sheikh Taysir; a.k.a. ABU SITTA, Subhi; a.k.a. ATEF, Muhammd; a.k.a. ATIF, Mohamed; a.k.a. ATIF, Muhammad; a.k.a. EL KHABIR, Abu Hafs el Masry; a.k.a. TAYSIR); DOB 1951; Alt. DOB 1956; Alt. DOB 1944; POB Alexandria, Egypt (individual) [SDT] [SDGT] **9-24-01**

ABU HAFS THE MAURITANIAN (a.k.a. AL-SHANQITI, Khalid; a.k.a. AL-WALID, Mafouz Walad; a.k.a. AL-WALID, Mahfouz Ould; a.k.a. SLAHI, Mahamedou Ould); DOB 1 Jan 75 (individual) [SDGT] **09-24-01**

ABU ISLAM (a.k.a. ALI, Ahmed Mohammed Hamed; a.k.a. ABDUREHMAN, Ahmed Mohammed; a.k.a. ABU FATIMA; a.k.a. ABU KHADIIJAH; a.k.a. AHMED HAMED; a.k.a. Ahmed The Egyptian; a.k.a. AHMED, Ahmed; a.k.a. AL-MASRI, Ahmad; a.k.a. AL-SURIR, Abu Islam; a.k.a. ALI, Ahmed Mohammed; a.k.a. ALI, Hamed; a.k.a. HEMED, Ahmed; a.k.a. SHIEB, Ahmed; a.k.a. SHUAIB), Afghanistan; DOB 1965; POB Egypt; citizen Egypt (individual) [SDGT] **10-12-01**

ABU ISMAIL (a.k.a. ABU UMAR, Abu Omar; a.k.a. AL-FILISTINI, Abu Qatada; a.k.a. TAKFIRI, Abu #Umr; a.k.a. UMAR, Abu Umar; a.k.a. UTHMAN, Ali-Samman; a.k.a. UTHMAN, Omar Mahmoud; a.k.a. UTHMAN, Umar), London, England; DOB 30 Dec 1960; alt. DOB 13 Dec 1960 (individual) [SDGT] **10-12-01**

ABU KHADIIJAH (a.k.a. ALI, Ahmed Mohammed Hamed; a.k.a. ABDUREHMAN, Ahmed Mohammed; a.k.a. ABU FATIMA; a.k.a. ABU ISLAM; a.k.a. AHMED HAMED; a.k.a. Ahmed The Egyptian; a.k.a. AHMED, Ahmed; a.k.a. AL-MASRI, Ahmad; a.k.a. AL-SURIR, Abu Islam; a.k.a. ALI, Ahmed Mohammed; a.k.a. ALI, Hamed; a.k.a. HEMED, Ahmed; a.k.a. SHIEB, Ahmed; a.k.a. SHUAIB), Afghanistan; DOB 1965; POB Egypt; citizen Egypt (individual) [SDGT] **10-12-01**

ABU MARIAM (a.k.a. ABDULLAH, Abdullah Ahmed; a.k.a. AL-MASRI, Abu Mohamed; a.k.a. SALEH), Afghanistan; DOB 1963; POB Egypt; citizen Egypt (individual) [SDGT] **10-12-01**

ABU OMRAN (a.k.a. AL-MUGHASSIL, Ahmad Ibrahim; a.k.a. AL-MUGHASSIL, Ahmed Ibrahim); DOB 26 Jun 1967; POB Qatif-Bab al Shamal, Saudi Arabia; citizen Saudi Arabia (individual) [SDGT] **10-12-01**

ABU SITTA, Subhi (a.k.a. AL-MASRI, Abu Hafs; a.k.a. ABDULLAH, Sheikh Taysir; a.k.a. ABU HAFS; a.k.a. ATEF, Muhammad; a.k.a. ATIF, Mohamed; a.k.a. ATIF, Muhammad; a.k.a. EL KHABIR, Abu Hafs el Masry; a.k.a. TAYSIR); DOB 1951; Alt. DOB 1956; Alt. DOB 1944; POB Alexandria, Egypt (individual) [SDT] [SDGT] **09-24-01**

ABU UMAR, Abu Omar (a.k.a. ABU ISMAIL; a.k.a. AL-FILISTINI, Abu Qatada; a.k.a. TAKFIRI, Abu'Umr; a.k.a. UMAR, Abu Umar; a.k.a. UTHMAN, Omar Mahmoud; a.k.a. UTHMAN, Al-Samman; a.k.a.

UTHMAN, Umar), London, England; DOB 30 Dec 1960; DOB 13 Dec 1960 (individual) [SDGT] **10-12-01**

ABU ZUBAIDA (a.k.a. ABU ZUBAYDAH; a.k.a. AL-WAHAB, Abd Al-Hadi; a.k.a. HUSAIN, Zain Al-Abidin Muhahhad; a.k.a. HUSAYN, Zayn al-Abidin Muhammad; a.k.a. TARIQ); DOB 12 Mar 71; POB Riyadh, Saudi Arabia (individual) [SDGT] **09-24-01**

ABU ZUBAYDAH (a.k.a. ABU ZUBAIDA; a.k.a. AL-WAHAB, Abd Al-Hadi; a.k.a. HUSAIN, Zain Al-Abidin Muhahhad; a.k.a. HUSAYN, Zayn al-Abidin Muhammad; a.k.a. TARIQ); DOB 12 Mar 71; POB Riyadh, Saudi Arabia (individual) [SDGT] **09-24-01**

ADBALLAH, Fazul (a.k.a. MOHAMMED, Fazul Abdullah; a.k.a. ABDALLA, Fazul; a.k.a. AISHA, Abu; a.k.a. AL SUDANI, Abu Seif; a.k.a. ALI, Fadel Abdallah Mohammed; a.k.a. FAZUL, Abdalla; a.k.a. FAZUL, Abdallah; a.k.a. FAZUL, Abdallah Mohammed; a.k.a. FAZUL, Haroon; a.k.a. FAZUL, Harun; a.k.a. HAROON; a.k.a. HAROUN, Fadhil; a.k.a. HARUN; a.k.a. LUQMAN, Abu; a.k.a. MOHAMMED, Fazul; a.k.a. MOHAMMED, Fazul Abdilahi; a.k.a. MOHAMMED, Fouad; a.k.a. MUHAMAD, Fadil Abdallah); DOB 25 Aug 1972; alt. DOB 25 Dec 1974; alt. DOB 25 Feb 1974; POB Moroni, Comoros Islands; citizen Comoros; alt. citizen Kenya (individual) [SDGT] **10-12-01**

ADEN, Abdirisak, Skaftingebacken 8, Spanga 163 67, Sweden; DOB 01 Jun 1968 (individual) [SDGT] **11-07-01**

AGHA, Haji Abdul Manan (a.k.a. SAIYID, Abd Al-Man'am), Pakistan (individual) [SDGT] **10-12-01**

AH HAQ, Dr. Amin (a.k.a. AL-HAQ, Amin; a.k.a. AMIN, Muhammad; a.k.a. UL-HAQ, Dr. Amin); DOB 1960; POB Nangahar Province, Afghanistan (individual) [SDGT] **10-12-01**

AHMAD, Abu Bakr (a.k.a. GHAILANI, Ahmed Khalfan; a.k.a. "AHMED THE TANZANIAN;" a.k.a. "FOOPIE;" a.k.a. "FUPI;" a.k.a. AHMED, A.; a.k.a. AHMED, Abubakar; a.k.a. AHMED, Abubakar K.; a.k.a. AHMED, Abubakar Khalfan; a.k.a. AHMED, Abubakary K.; a.k.a. AHMED, Ahmed Khalfan; a.k.a. AL TANZANI, Ahmad; a.k.a. ALI, Ahmed Khalfan; a.k.a. BAKR, Abu; a.k.a. GHAILANI, Abubakary Khalfan Ahmed; a.k.a. GHAILANI, Ahmed; a.k.a. GHILANI, Ahmad Khalafan; a.k.a. HUSSEIN, Mahafudh Abubakar Ahmed Abdallah; a.k.a. KHABAR, Abu; a.k.a. KHALFAN, Ahmed; a.k.a. MOHAMMED, Shariff Omar); DOB 14 Mar 1974; alt. DOB 13 Apr 1974; alt. DOB 14 Apr 1974; alt. DOB 1 Aug 1970; POB Zanzibar, Tanzania; citizen Tanzania (individual) [SDGT] **10-12-01**

AHMAD, Mufti Rasheed (a.k.a. LADEHYANOY, Mufti Rashid Ahmad; a.k.a. LUDHIANVI, Mufti Rashid Ahmad; a.k.a. WADEHYANOY, Mufti Rashid Ahmad), Karachi, Pakistan (individual) [SDGT] **10-12-01**

AHMAD, Musafa Muhammad (a.k.a. SAI'ID, Shaykh); POB Egypt (individual) [SDGT] **09-24-01**

AHMAD, Tariq Anwar al-Sayyid (a.k.a. FARAG, Hamdi Ahmad; a.k.a. FATHI, Amr Al-Fatih); DOB 15 Mar 63; POB Alexandria, Egypt (individual) [SDGT] **09-24-01**

Ahmed the Tall (a.k.a. SWEDAN, Sheikh Ahmed Salim; a.k.a. ALLY, Ahmed; a.k.a. BAHAMAD; a.k.a. BAHAMAD, Sheik; a.k.a. BAHAMADI, Sheikh; a.k.a. SUWEIDAN, Sheikh Ahmad Salem; a.k.a. SWEDAN, Sheikh; a.k.a. SWEDAN, Sheikh Ahmed Salem); DOB 9 Apr 1969; alt. DOB 9 Apr 1960; POB Mombasa, Kenya; citizen Kenya (individual) [SDGT] **10-12-01**

Ahmed The Egyptian (a.k.a. ALI, Ahmed Mohammed Hamed; a.k.a. ABDUREHMAN, Ahmed Mohammed; a.k.a. ABU FATIMA; a.k.a. ABU ISLAM; a.k.a. ABU KHADIIJAH; a.k.a. AHMED HAMED; a.k.a. AHMED, Ahmed; a.k.a. AL-MASRI, Ahmad; a.k.a. AL-SURIR, Abu Islam; a.k.a. ALI, Ahmed Mohammed; a.k.a. ALI, Hamed; a.k.a. HEMED, Ahmed; a.k.a. SHIEB, Ahmed; a.k.a. SHUAIB), Afghanistan; DOB 1965; POB Egypt; citizen Egypt (individual) [SDGT] **10-12-01**

AHMED, A. (a.k.a. GHAILANI, Ahmed Khalfan; a.k.a. "AHMED THE TANZANIAN;" a.k.a. "FOOPIE;" a.k.a. "FUPI;" a.k.a. AHMAD, Abu Bakr; a.k.a. AHMED, Abubakar; a.k.a. AHMED, Abubakar K.; a.k.a. AHMED, Abubakar Khalfan; a.k.a. AHMED, Abubakary K.; a.k.a. AHMED, Ahmed Khalfan; a.k.a. AL TANZANI, Ahmad; a.k.a. ALI, Ahmed Khalfan; a.k.a. BAKR, Abu; a.k.a. GHAILANI, Abubakary Khalfan Ahmed; a.k.a. GHAILANI, Ahmed; a.k.a. GHILANI, Ahmad Khalafan; a.k.a. HUSSEIN, Mahafudh Abubakar Ahmed Abdallah; a.k.a. KHABAR, Abu; a.k.a. KHALFAN, Ahmed; a.k.a. MOHAMMED, Shariff Omar); DOB 14 Mar 1974; alt. DOB 13 Apr 1974; alt. DOB 14 Apr 1974; alt. DOB 1 Aug 1970; POB Zanzibar, Tanzania; citizen Tanzania (individual) [SDGT] **10-12-01**

AHMED, Abubakar (a.k.a. GHAILANI, Ahmed Khalfan; a.k.a. "AHMED THE TANZANIAN;" a.k.a. "FOOPIE;" a.k.a. "FUPI;" a.k.a. AHMAD, Abu Bakr; a.k.a. AHMED, A.; a.k.a. AHMED, Abubakar K.; a.k.a. AHMED, Abubakar Khalfan; a.k.a. AHMED, Abubakary K.; a.k.a. AHMED, Ahmed Khalfan; a.k.a. AL TANZANI, Ahmad; a.k.a. ALI, Ahmed Khalfan; a.k.a. BAKR, Abu; a.k.a. GHAILANI, Abubakary Khalfan Ahmed; a.k.a. GHAILANI, Ahmed; a.k.a. GHILANI, Ahmad Khalafan; a.k.a. HUSSEIN, Mahafudh Abubakar Ahmed Abdallah; a.k.a. KHABAR, Abu; a.k.a. KHALFAN, Ahmed; a.k.a. MOHAMMED, Shariff Omar); DOB 14 Mar 1974; alt. DOB 13 Apr 1974; alt. DOB 14 Apr 1974; alt. DOB 1 Aug 1970; POB Zanzibar, Tanzania; citizen Tanzania (individual) [SDGT] **10-12-01**

AHMED, Abubakar K. (a.k.a. GHAILANI, Ahmed Khalfan; a.k.a. "AHMED THE TANZANIAN;" a.k.a. "FOOPIE;" a.k.a. "FUPI;" a.k.a. AHMAD, Abu Bakr; a.k.a. AHMED, A.; a.k.a. AHMED, Abubakar; a.k.a. AHMED,

Abubakar Khalfan; a.k.a. AHMED, Abubakary K.; a.k.a. AHMED, Ahmed Khalfan; a.k.a. AL TANZANI, Ahmad; a.k.a. ALI, Ahmed Khalfan; a.k.a. BAKR, Abu; a.k.a. GHAILANI, Abubakary Khalfan Ahmed; a.k.a. GHAILANI, Ahmed; a.k.a. GHILANI, Ahmad Khalafan; a.k.a. HUSSEIN, Mahafudh Abubakar Ahmed Abdallah; a.k.a. KHABAR, Abu; a.k.a. KHALFAN, Ahmed; a.k.a. MOHAMMED, Shariff Omar); DOB 14 Mar 1974; alt. DOB 13 Apr 1974; alt. DOB 14 Apr 1974; alt. DOB 1 Aug 1970; POB Zanzibar, Tanzania; citizen Tanzania (individual) [SDGT] **10-12-01**

AHMED, Abubakar Khalfan (a.k.a. GHAILANI, Ahmed Khalfan; a.k.a. "AHMED THE TANZANIAN;" a.k.a. "FOOPIE;" a.k.a. "FUPI;" a.k.a. AHMAD, Abu Bakr; a.k.a. AHMED, A.; a.k.a. AHMED, Abubakar; a.k.a. AHMED, Abubakar K.; a.k.a. AHMED, Abubakary K.; a.k.a. AHMED, Ahmed Khalfan; a.k.a. AL TANZANI, Ahmad; a.k.a. ALI, Ahmed Khalfan; a.k.a. BAKR, Abu; a.k.a. GHAILANI, Abubakary Khalfan Ahmed; a.k.a. GHAILANI, Ahmed; a.k.a. GHILANI, Ahmad Khalafan; a.k.a. HUSSEIN, Mahafudh Abubakar Ahmed Abdallah; a.k.a. KHABAR, Abu; a.k.a. KHLFAN, Ahmed; a.k.a. MOHAMMED, Shariff Omar); DOB 14 Mar 1974; alt. DOB 13 Apr 1974; alt. DOB 14 Apr 1974; alt. DOB 1 Aug 1970; POB Zanzibar, Tanzania; citizen Tanzania (individual) [SDGT] **10-12-01**

AHMED, Abubakary K. (a.k.a. GHAILANI, Ahmed Khalfan; a.k.a. "AHMED THE TANZANIAN;" a.k.a. "FOOPIE;" a.k.a. "FUPI;" a.k.a. AHMAD, Abu Bakr; a.k.a. AHMED, A.; a.k.a. AHMED, Abubakar; a.k.a. AHMED, Abubakar K.; a.k.a. AHMED, Abubakar Khalfan; a.k.a. AHMED, Ahmed Khalfan; a.k.a. AL TANZANI, Ahmad; a.k.a. ALI, Ahmed Khalfan; a.k.a. BAKR, Abu; a.k.a. GHAILANI, Abubakary Khalfan Ahmed; a.k.a. GHAILANI, Ahmed; a.k.a. GHILANI, Ahmad Khalafan; a.k.a. HUSSEIN, Mahafudh Abubakar Ahmed Abdallah; a.k.a. KHABAR, Abu; a.k.a. KHALFAN, Ahmed; a.k.a. MOHAMMED, Shariff Omar); DOB 14 Mar 1974; alt. DOB 13 Apr 1974; alt. DOB 14 Apr 1974; alt. DOB 1 Aug 1970; POB Zanzibar, Tanzania; citizen Tanzania (individual) [SDGT] **10-12-01**

AHMED, Ahmed (a.k.a. ALI, Ahmed Mohammed Hamed; a.k.a. ABDUREHMAN, Ahmed Mohammed; a.k.a. ABU FATIMA; a.k.a. ABU ISLAM; a.k.a. ABU KHADIIJAH; a.k.a. AHMED HAMED; a.k.a. Ahmed The Egyptian; a.k.a. AL-MASRI, Ahmad; a.k.a. AL-SURIR, Abu Islam; a.k.a. ALI, Ahmed Mohammed; a.k.a. ALI, Hamed; a.k.a. HEMED, Ahmed; a.k.a. SHIEB, Ahmed; a.k.a. SHUAIB), Afghanistan; DOB 1965; POB Egypt; citizen Egypt (individual) [SDGT] **10-12-01**

AHMED, Ahmed Khalfan (a.k.a. GHAILANI, Ahmed Khalfan; a.k.a. "AHMED THE TANZANIAN;" a.k.a. "FOOPIE;" a.k.a. "FUPI;" a.k.a. AHMAD, Abu Bakr; a.k.a. AHMED, A.; a.k.a. AHMED, Abubakar; a.k.a. AHMED, Abubakar K.; a.k.a. AHMED, Abubakar Khalfan; a.k.a. AHMED, Abubakary K.; a.k.a. AL TANZANI, Ahmad; a.k.a. ALI, Ahmed Khalfan; a.k.a. BAKR, Abu; a.k.a. GHAILANI, Abubakary Khalfan Ahmed; a.k.a.

GHAILANI, Ahmed; a.k.a. GHILANI, Ahmad Khalafan; a.k.a. HUSSEIN, Mahafudh Abubakar Ahmed Abdallah; a.k.a. KHABAR, Abu; a.k.a. KHALFAN, Ahmed; a.k.a. MOHAMMED, Shariff Omar); DOB 14 Mar 1974; alt. DOB 13 Apr 1974; alt. DOB 14 Apr 1974; alt. DOB 1 Aug 1970; POB Zanzibar, Tanzania; citizen Tanzania (individual) [SDGT] **10-12-01**

AHMED HAMED (a.k.a. ALI, Ahmed Mohammed Hamed; a.k.a. ABDUREHMAN, Ahmed Mohammed; a.k.a. ABU FATIMA; a.k.a. ABU ISLAM; a.k.a. ABU KHADIIJAH; a.k.a. Ahmed The Egyptian; a.k.a. AHMED, Ahmed; a.k.a. AL-MASRI, Ahmad; a.k.a. AL-SURIR, Abu Islam; a.k.a. ALI, Ahmed Mohammed; a.k.a. ALI, Hamed; a.k.a. HEMED, Ahmed; a.k.a. SHIEB, Ahmed; a.k.a. SHUAIB), Afghanistan; DOB 1965; POB Egypt; citizen Egypt (individual) [SDGT] **10-12-01**

AIADI, Ben Muhammad (a.k.a. AIADY, Ben Muhammad; a.k.a. AYADI CHAFIK, Ben Muhammad; a.k.a. AYADI SHAFIQ, Ben Muhammad; a.k.a. BIN MUHAMMAD, Ayadi Chafiq), Helene Meyer Ring 10-1415-80809, Munich, Germany; 129 Park Road, NW8, London, England; 28 Chaussee de Lille, Mouscron, Belgium; Darvingasse 1/2/58-60, Vienna, Austria; Tunisia; DOB 21 Jan 1963; POB Safais (Sfax), Tunisia (individual) [SDGT] **10-12-01**

AIADY, Ben Muhammad (a.k.a. AIADI, Ben Muhammad; a.k.a. AYADI CHAFIK, Bn Muhammad; a.k.a. AYADI SHAFIQ, Ben Muhammad; a.k.a. BIN MUHAMMAD, Ayadi Chafiq), Helene Meyer Ring 10-1415-80809, Munich, Germany; 129 Park Road, NW8, London, England; 28 Chaussee de Lille, Mouscron, Belgium; Darvingasse 1/2/58-60, Vienna, Austria; Tunisia; DOB 21 Jan 1963; POB Safais (Sfax), Tunisia (individual) [SDGT] **10-12-01**

AISHA, Abu (a.k.a. MOHAMMED, Fazul Abdullah; a.k.a. ABDALLA, Fazul; a.k.a. ADBALLAH, Fazul; a.k.a. AL SUDANI, Abu Seif; a.k.a. ALI, Fadel Abdallah Mohammed; a.k.a. FAZUL, Abdalla; a.k.a. FAZUL, Abdallah; a.k.a. FAZUL, Abdallah Mohammed; a.k.a. FAZUL, Haroon; a.k.a. FAZUL, Harun; a.k.a. HAROON; a.k.a. HAROUN, Fadhil; a.k.a. HARUN; a.k.a. LUQMAN, Abu; a.k.a. MOHAMMED, Fazul; a.k.a. MOHAMMED, Fazul Abdilahi; a.k.a. MOHAMMED, Fouad; a.k.a. MUHAMAD, Fadil Abdallah); DOB 25 Aug 1972; alt. DOB 25 Dec 1974; alt. DOB 25 Feb 1974; POB Moroni, Comoros Islands; citizen Comoros; alt. citizen Kenya (individual) [SDGT] **10-12-01**

AL-ADL, Sayf (a.k.a. AL-'ADIL, Saif); DOB 1963; POB Egypt (individual) [SDGT] **09-24-01**

AL-AHDAL, Mohammad Hamdi Sadiq (a.k.a. AL-HAMATI, Muhammad; a.k.a. AL-MAKKI, Abu Asim), Yemen (individual) [SDGT] **10-12-01**

AL-AMRIKI, Abu-Ahmad (a.k.a. AL-HAWEN, Abu-Ahmad; a.k.a. AL-MAGHRIBI, Rashid; a.k.a. AL-SHAHID, Abu-Ahmad; a.k.a. HIJAZI,

Raed M.; a.k.a. HIJAZI, Riad), Jordan; DOB 1968; POB California, U.S.A.; SSN: 548-91-5411 (USA) (individual) [SDGT] **10-12-01**

AL-FILISTINI, Abu Qatada (a.k.a. ABU ISMAIL; a.k.a. ABU UMAR, Abu Omar; a.k.a. TAKFIRI, Abu #Umr; a.k.a. UMAR, Abu Umar; a.k.a. UTHMAN, Al-Samman; a.k.a. UTHMAN, Omar Mahmoud; a.k.a. UTHMAN, Umar), London, England; DOB 30 Dec 1960; alt. DOB 13 Dec 1960 (individual) [SDGT] **10-12-01**

AL-HAMATI, Muhammad (a.k.a. AL-AHDAL, Mohammad Hamdi Sadiq; a.k.a. AL-MAKKI, Abu Asim), Yemen (individual) [SDGT] **10-12-01**

AL-HAQ, Amin (a.k.a. AH HAQ, Dr. Amin; a.k.a. AMIN, Muhammad; a.k.a. UL-HAQ, Dr. Amin); DOB 1960; POB Nangahar Province, Afghanistan (individual) [SDGT] **10-12-01**

AL-HAWEN, Abu-Ahmad (a.k.a. AL-AMRIKI, Abu-Ahmad; a.k.a. AL-MAGHRIBI, Rashid; a.k.a. AL-SHAHID, Abu-Ahmad; a.k.a. HIJAZI, Raed M.; a.k.a. HIJAZI, Riad), Jordan; DOB 1968; POB California, U.S.A.; SSN: 548-91-5411 (USA) (individual) [SDGT] **10-12-01**

AL-HOURI, Ali Saed Bin Ali (a.k.a. EL-HOORIE, Ali Saed Bin Ali; a.k.a. EL-HOURI, Ali Saed Bin Ali); DOB 10 Jul 1965; alt. DOB 11 Jul 1965; POB El Dibabiya, Saudi Arabia; citizen Saudi Arabia (individual) [SDGT] **10-12-01**

AL-IRAQI, Abd al-Hadi (a.k.a. ABU ABDALLAH; a.k.a. AL-IRAQI, Abdal al-Hadi) (individual) [SDGT] **09-24-01**

AL-IRAQI, Abdal al-Hadi (a.k.a. AL-IRAQI, Abd al-Hadi; a.k.a. ABU ABDALLAH) (individual) [SDGT] **09-24-01**

AL-JADAWI, Saqar; DOB 1965 (individual) [SDGT] **10-12-01**

AL-KADR, Ahmad Sa'id (a.k.a. AL-KANADI, Abu Abd Al-Rahman); DOB 01 Mar 1948; POB Cairo, Egypt (individual) [SDGT] **10-12-01**

AL-KANADI, Abu Abd Al-Rahman (a.k.a. AL-KADR, Ahmad Sa'id); DOB 01 Mar 1948; POB Cairo, Egypt (individual) [SDGT] **10-12-01**

AL-KINI, Usama (a.k.a. MSALAM, Fahid Mohammed Ally; a.k.a. ALLY, Fahid Mohammed; a.k.a. MSALAM, Fahad Ally; a.k.a. MSALAM, Fahid Mohammed Ali; a.k.a. MSALAM, Mohammed Ally; a.k.a. MUSALAAM, Fahid Mohammed Ali; a.k.a. SALEM, Fahid Muhamad Ali); DOB 19 Feb 1976; POB Mombasa, Kenya; citizen Kenya (individual) [SDGT] **10-12-01**

AL-LIBI, Anas (a.k.a. AL-LIBY, Anas; a.k.a. AL-RAGHIE, Nazih; a.k.a. AL-RAGHIE, Nazih Abdul Hamed; a.k.a. AL-SABAI, Anas), Afghanistan; DOB 30 Mar 1964; alt. DOB 14 May 1964; POB Tripoli, Libya; citizen Libya (individual) [SDGT] **10-12-01**

AL-LIBI, Ibn Al-Shaykh (individual) [SDGT] **09-24-01**

AL-LIBY, Anas (a.k.a. AL-LIBI, Anas; a.k.a. A-RAGHIE, Nazih; a.k.a. AL-RAGHIE, Nazih Abdul Hamed; a.k.a. AL-SABAI, Anas), Afghanistan; DOB 30 Mar 1964; alt. DOB 14 May 1964; POB Tripoli, Libya; citizen Libya (individual) [SDGT] **10-12-01**

AL-MAGHRIBI, Rashid (a.k.a. AL-AMRIKI, Abu-Ahmad; a.k.a. AL-HAWEN, Abu-Ahmad; a.k.a. AL-SHAHID, Abu-Ahmad; a.k.a. HIJAZI, Raed M.; a.k.a. HIJAZI, Riad), Jordan; DOB 1968; POB California, U.S.A.; SSN: 548-91-5411 (USA) (individual) [SDGT] **10-12-01**

AL-MAKKI, Abu Asim (a.k.a. AL-AHDAL, Mohammad Hamdi Sadiq; a.k.a. AL-HAMATI, Muhammad), Yemen (individual) [SDGT] **10-12-01**

AL MASRI, Abd Al Wakil (a.k.a. FADHIL, Mustafa Mohamed; a.k.a. AL-NUBI, Abu; a.k.a. ALI, Hassan; a.k.a. ANIS, Abu; a.k.a. ELBISHY, Moustafa Ali; a.k.a. FADIL, Mustafa Muhamad; a.k.a. FAZUL, Mustafa; a.k.a. HUSSEIN; a.k.a. JIHAD, Abu; a.k.a. KHALID; a.k.a. MAN, Nu; a.k.a. MOHAMMED, Mustafa; a.k.a. YUSSRR, Abu); DOB 23 Jun 1976; POB Cairo, Egypt; citizen Egypt; alt. citizen Kenya; Kenyan ID No. 12773667; Serial No. 201735161 (individual) [SDGT] **10-12-01**

AL-MASRI, Abu Hafs (a.k.a. ABDULLAH, Sheikh Taysir; a.k.a. ABU HAFS; a.k.a. ABU SITTA, Subhi; a.k.a. ATEF, Muhammad; a.k.a. ATIF, Mohamed; a.k.a. ATIF, Muhammad; a.k.a. EL KHABIR, Abu Hafs el Masry; a.k.a. TAYSIR); DOB 1951; Alt. DOB 1956; Alt. DOB 1944; POB Alexandria, Egypt (individual) [SDT] [SDGT] **9-24-01**

AL-MASRI, Abu Mohamed (a.k.a. ABDULLAH, Abdullah Ahmed; a.k.a. ABU MARIAM; a.k.a. SALEH), Afghanistan; DOB 1963; POB Egypt; citizen Egypt (individual) [SDGT] **10-12-01**

AL-MASRI, Ahmad (a.k.a. ALI, Ahmed Mohammed Hamed; a.k.a. ABDUREHMAN, Ahmed Mohammed; a.k.a. ABU FATIMA; a.k.a. ABU ISLAM; a.k.a. ABU KHADIIJAH; a.k.a. AHMED HAMED; a.k.a. Ahmed The Egyptian; a.k.a. AHMED, Ahmed; a.k.a. AL-SURIR, Abu Islam; a.k.a. ALI, Ahmed Mohammed; a.k.a. ALI, Hamed; a.k.a. HEMED, Ahmed; a.k.a. SHIEB, Ahmed; a.k.a. SHUAIB), Afghanistan; DOB 1965; POB Egypt; citizen Egypt (individual) [SDGT] **10-12-01**

AL-MUGHASSIL, Ahmad Ibrahim (a.k.a. ABU OMRAN; a.k.a. AL-MUGHASSIL, Ahmed Ibrahim); DOB 26 Jun 1967; POB Qatif-Bab al Shamal, Saudi Arabia; citizen Saudi Arabia (individual) [SDGT] **10-12-01**

AL-MUGHASSIL, Ahmed Ibrahim (a.k.a. AL-MUGHASSIL, Ahmad Ibrahim; a.k.a. ABU OMRAN); DOB 26 Jun 1967; POB Qatif-Bab al Shamal, Saudi Arabia; citizen Saudi Arabia (individual) [SDGT] **10-12-01**

AL-MUHAJIR, Abdul Rahman (a.k.a. ATWAH, Muhsin Musa Matwalli; a.k.a. ABDEL RAHMAN; a.k.a. ABDUL RAHMAN; a.k.a. AL-NAMER,

Mohammed K.A.), Afghanistan; DOB 19 Jun 1964; POB Egypt; citizen Egypt (individual) [SDGT] **10-12-01**

AL-NAMER, Mohammed K.A. (a.k.a. ATWAH, Muhsin Musa Matwalli; a.k.a. ABDEL RAHMAN; a.k.a. ABDUL RAHMAN; a.k.a. AL-MUHAJIR, Abdul Rahman), Afghanistan; DOB 19 Jun 1964; POB Egypt; citizen Egypt (individual) [SDGT] **10-12-01**

AL-NASSER, Abdelkarim Hussein Mohamed; POB Al Ihsa, Saudi Arabia; citizen Saudi Arabia (individual) [SDGT] **10-12-01**

AL-NUBI, Abu (a.k.a. FADHIL, Mustafa Mohamed; a.k.a. AL MASRI, Abd Al Wakil; a.k.a. ALI, Hassan; a.k.a. ANIS, Abu; a.k.a. ELBISHY, Moustafa Ali; a.k.a. FADIL, Mustafa Muhamad; a.k.a. FAZUL, Mustafa; a.k.a. HUSSEIN; a.k.a. JIHAD, Abu; a.k.a. KHALID; a.k.a. MAN, Nu; a.k.a. MOHAMMED, Mustafa; a.k.a. YUSSRR, Abu); DOB 23 Jun 1976; POB Cairo, Egypt; citizen Egypt; alt. citizen Kenya; Kenyan ID No. 12773667; Serial No. 201735161 (individual) [SDGT] **10-12-01**

AL-QADI, Yasin (a.k.a. KADI, Shaykh Yassin Abdullah; a.k.a. KAHDI, Yasin), Jeddah, Saudi Arabia (individual) [SDGT] **10-12-01**

AL-RAGHIE, Nazih (a.k.a. AL-LIBY, Anas; a.k.a. AL-LIBI, Anas; a.k.a. AL-RAGHIE, Nazih Abdul Hamed; a.k.a. AL-SABAI, Anas), Afghanistan; DOB 30 Mar 1964; alt. DOB 14 May 1964; POB Tripoli, Libya; citizen Libya (individual) [SDGT **10-12-01**

AL-RAGHIE, Nazih Abdul Hamed (a.k.a. AL-LIBY, Anas; a.k.a. AL-LIBI, Anas; a.k.a. AL-RAGHIE, Nazih; a.k.a. AL-SABAI, Anas), Afghanistan; DOB 30 Mar 1964; alt. DOB 14 May 1964; POB Tripoli, Libya; citizen Libya (individual) [SDGT] **10-12-01**

AL-SABAI, Anas (a.k.a. AL-LIBY, Anas; a.k.a. AL-LIBI, Anas; a.k.a. AL-RAGHIE, Nazih; a.k.a. AL-RAGHIE, Nazih Abdul Hamed), Afghanistan; DOB 30 Mar 1964; alt. DOB 14 May 1964; POB Tripoli, Libya; citizen Libya (individual) [SDGT] **10-12-01**

AL-SHAHID, Abu-Ahmad (a.k.a. AL-AMRIKI, Abu-Ahmad; a.k.a. AL-HAWEN, Abu-Ahmad; a.k.a. AL-MAGHRIBI, Rashid; a.k.a. HIJAZI, Raed M.; a.k.a. HIJAZI, Riad), Jordan; DOB 1968; POB California, U.S.A.; SSN: 548-91-5411 (USA) (individual) [SDGT] **10-12-01**

AL-SHANQITI, Khalid (a.k.a. ABU HAFS THE MAURITANIAN; a.k.a. AL-WALID, Mafouz Walad; a.k.a. AL-WALID, Mahfouz Ould; a.k.a. SLAHI, Mahamedou Ould); DOB 1 Jan 75 (individual) [SDGT] **09-24-01**

AL-SHARIF, Sa'd; DOB 1969; POB Saudi Arabia (individual) [SDGT] **10-12-01**

AL SUDANI, Abu Seif (a.k.a. MOHAMMED, Fazul Abdullah; a.k.a. ABDALLA, Fazul; a.k.a. ADBALLAH, Fazul; a.k.a. AISHA, Abu; a.k.a. ALI, Fadel Abdallah Mohammed; a.k.a. FAZUL, Abdalla; a.k.a. FAZUL, Abdallah; a.k.a. FAZUL, Abdallah Mohammed; a.k.a. FAZUL, Haroon; a.k.a. FAZUL, Harun; a.k.a. HAROON; a.k.a. HAROUN, Fadhil; a.k.a. HARUN; a.k.a. LUQMAN, Abu; a.k.a. MOHAMMED, Fazul; a.k.a. MOHAMMED, Fazul Abdilahi; a.k.a. MOHAMMED, Fouad; a.k.a. MUHAMAD, Fadil Abdallah); DOB 25 Aug 1972; alt. DOB 25 Dec 1974; alt. DOB 25 Feb 1974; POB Moroni, Comoros Islands; citizen Comoros; alt. citizen Kenya (individual) [SDGT] **10-12-01**

AL-SURIR, Abu Islam (a.k.a. ALI, Ahmed Mohammed Hamed; a.k.a. ABDUREHMAN, Ahmed Mohammed; a.k.a. ABU FATIMA; a.k.a. ABU ISLAM; a.k.a. ABU KHADIIJAH; a.k.a. AHMED HAMED; a.k.a. Ahmed The Egyptian; a.k.a. AHMED, Ahmed; a.k.a. AL-MASRI, Ahmad; a.k.a. ALI, Ahmed Mohammed; a.k.a. ALI, Hamed; a.k.a. HEMED, Ahmed; a.k.a. SHIEB, Ahmed; a.k.a. SHUAIB), Afghanistan; DOB 1965; POB Egypt; citizen Egypt (individual) [SDGT] **10-12-01**

AL TANZANI, Ahmad (a.ka. GHAILANI, Ahmed Khalfan; a.k.a. "AHMED THE TANZANIAN;" a.k.a. "FOOPIE;" a.k.a. "FUPI;" a.k.a. AHMAD, Abu Bakr; a.k.a. AHMED, A.; a.k.a. AHMED, Abubakar; a.k.a. AHMED, Abubakar K.; a.k.a. AHMED, Abubakar Khalfan; a.k.a. AHMED, Abubakary K.; a.k.a. AHMED, Ahmed Khalfan; a.k.a. ALI, Ahmed Khalfan; a.k.a. BAKR, Abu; a.k.a. GHAILANI, Abubakary Khalfan Ahmed; a.k.a. GHAILANI, Ahmed; a.k.a. GHILANI, Ahmad Khalafan; a.k.a. HUSSEIN, Mahafudh Abubakar Ahmed Abdallah; a.k.a. KHABAR, Abu; a.k.a. KHALFAN, Ahmed; a.k.a. MOHAMMED, Shariff Omar); DOB 14 Mar 1974; alt. DOB 13 Apr 1974; alt. DOB 14 Apr 1974; alt. DOB 1 Aug 1970; POB Zanzibar, Tanzania; citizen Tanzania (individual) [SDGT] **10-12-01**

AL-WAHAB, Abd Al-Hadi (a.k.a. ABU ZUBAYDAH; a.k.a. ABU ZUBAIDA; a.k.a. HUSAIN, Zain Al-Abidin Muhahhad; a.k.a. HUSAYN, Zayn al-Abidin Muhammad; a.k.a. TARIQ); DOB 12 Mar 71; POB Riyadh, Saudi Arabia (individual) [SDGT] **09-24-01**

AL-WALID, Mafouz Walad (a.k.a. ABU HAFS THE MAURITANIAN; a.k.a. AL-SHANQITI, Khalid; a.k.a. AL-WALID, Mahfouz Ould; a.k.a. SLAHI, Mahamedou Ould); DOB 1 Jan 75 (individual) [SDGT] **09-24-01**

AL-WALID, Mahfouz Ould (a.k.a. ABU HAFS THE MAURITANIAN; a.k.a. AL-SHANQITI, Khalid; a.k.a. AL-WALID, Mafouz Walad; a.k.a. SLAHI, Mahamedou Ould); DOB 1 Jan 75 (individual) [SDGT] **09-24-01**

AL-YACOUB, Ibrahim Salih Mohammed; DOB 16 Oct 1966; POB Tarut, Saudi Arabia; citizen Saudi Arabia (individual) [SDGT] **10-12-01**

AL-ZAWAHIRI, Aiman Muhammad Rabi (a.k.a. AL ZAWAHIRI, Dr. Ayman; a.k.a. AL-ZAWAHIRI, Ayman; a.k.a. SALIM, Ahmad Fuad), Operational and Military Leader of JIHAD GROUP; DOB 19 Jun 1951; POB Giza, Egypt; Passport No. 1084010 (Egypt), Alt. No. 19820215 (individual) [SDT] [SDGT] **09-24-01**

AL-ZAWAHIRI, Ayman (a.k.a. AL ZAWAHIRI, Dr. Ayman; a.k.a. AL-ZAWAHIRI, Aiman Muhammad Rabi; a.k.a. SALIM, Ahmad Fuad), Operational and Military Leader of JIHAD GROUP; DOB 19 Jun 1951; POB Giza, Egypt; Passport No. 1084010 (Egypt); Alt. No. 19820215 (individual) [SDT] [SDGT] **09-24-01**

AL ZAWAHIRI, Dr. Ayman (a.k.a. AL-ZAWAHIRI, Aiman Muhammad Rabi; a.k.a. AL-ZAWAHIRI, Ayman; a.k.a. SALIM, Ahmad Fuad), Operational and Military Leader of JIHAD GROUP; DOB 19 Jun 1951; POB Giza, Egypt; Passport No. 1084010 (Egypt), Alt. No. 19820215 (individual) [SDT] [SDGT] **09-24-01**

AL-'ADIL, Saif (a.k.a. AL-ADL, Sayf); DOB 1963; POB Egypt (individual) [SDGT] **09-24-01**

AL-MANSOUR, Dr. Mohamed (a.k.a. MANSOUR, Mohamed), Ob. Heslibachstr. 20, Kusnacht, Switzerland; Zurich, Switzerland; DOB 1928; POB U.A.E.; alt. POB Egypt (individual) [SDGT] **11-07-01**

ALI, Abbas Abdi, Mogadishu, Somalia (individual) [SDGT] **11-07-01**

ALI, Abdi Abdulaziz, Drabantvagen 21, Spanga 177, 50, Sweden; DOB 01 Jan 1955 (individual) [SDGT] **11-07-01**

ALI, Ahmed Khalfan (a.k.a. GHAILANI, Ahmed Khalfan; a.k.a. "AHMED THE TANZANIAN;" a.k.a. "FOOPIE;" a.k.a. "FUPI;" a.k.a. AHMAD, Abu Bakr; a.k.a. AHMED, A.; a.k.a. AHMED, Abubakar; a.k.a. AHMED, Abubakar K.; a.k.a. AHMED, Abubakar Khalfan; a.k.a. AHMED, Abubakary K.; a.k.a. AHMED, Ahmed Khalfan; a.k.a. AL TANZANI, Ahmad; a.k.a. BAKR, Abu; a.k.a. GHAILANI, Abubakary Khalfan Ahmed; a.k.a. GHAILANI, Ahmed; a.k.a. GHILANI, Ahmad Khalafan; a.k.a. HUSSEIN, Mahafudh Abubakar Ahmed Abdallah; a.k.a. KHABAR, Abu; a.k.a. KHALFAN, Ahmed; a.k.a. MOHAMMED, Shariff Omar); DOB 14 Mar 1974; alt. DOB 13 Apr 1974; alt. DOB 14 Apr 1974; alt. DOB 1 Aug 1970; POB Zanzibar, Tanzania; citizen Tanzania (individual) [SDGT] **10-12-01**

ALI, Ahmed Mohammed (a.k.a. ALI, Ahmed Mohammed Hamed; a.k.a. ABDUREHMAN, Ahmed Mohammed; a.k.a. ABU FATIMA; a.k.a. ABU ISLAM; a.k.a. ABU KHADIIJAH; a.k.a. AHMED HAMED; a.k.a. Ahmed The Egyptian; a.k.a. AHMED, Ahmed; a.k.a. AL-MASRI, Ahmad; a.k.a. AL-SURIR, Abu Islam; a.k.a. ALI, Hamed; a.k.a. HEMED, Ahmed; a.k.a. SHIEB, Ahmed; a.k.a. SHUAIB), Afghanistan; DOB 1965; POB Egypt; citizen Egypt (individual) [SDGT] **10-12-01**

ALI, Ahmed Mohammed Hamed (a.k.a. ABDUREHMAN, Ahmed Mohammed; a.k.a. ABU FATIMA; a.k.a. ABU ISLAM; a.k.a. ABU KHADIIJAH; a.k.a. AHMED HAMED; a.k.a. Ahmed The Egyptian; a.k.a. AHMED, Ahmed; a.k.a. AL-MASRI, Ahmad; a.k.a. AL-SURIR, Abu Islam; a.k.a. ALI, Ahmed Mohammed; a.k.a. ALI, Hamed; a.k.a. HEMED, Ahmed; a.k.a. SHIEB, Ahmed; a.k.a. SHUAIB), Afghanistan; DOB 1965; POB Egypt; citizen Egypt (individual) [SDGT] **10-12-01**

ALI, Fadel Abdallah Mohammed (a.k.a. MOHAMMED, Fazul Abdullah; a.k.a. ABDALLA, Fazul; a.k.a. ADBALLAH, Fazul; a.k.a. AISHA, Abu; a.k.a. AL SUDANI, Abu Seif; a.k.a. FAZUL, Abdalla; a.k.a. FAZUL, Abdallah; a.k.a. FAZUL, Abdallah Mohammed; a.k.a. FAZUL, Haroon; a.k.a. FAZUL, Harun; a.k.a. HAROON; a.k.a. HAROUN, Fadhil; a.k.a. HARUN; a.k.a. LUQMAN, Abu; a.k.a. MOHAMMED, Fazul; a.k.a. MOHAMMED, Fazul Abdilahi; a.k.a. MOHAMMED, Fouad; a.k.a. MUHAMAD, Fadil Abdallah); DOB 25 Aug 1972; alt. DOB 25 Dec 1974; alt. DOB 25 Feb 1974; POB Moroni, Comoros Islands; citizen Comoros; alt. citizen Kenya (individual) [SDGT] **10-12-01**

ALI, Hamed (a.k.a. ALI, Ahmed Mohammed Hamed; a.k.a. ABDUREHMAN, Ahmed Mohammed; a.k.a. ABU FATIMA; a.k.a. ABU ISLAM; a.k.a. ABU KHADIIJAH; a.k.a. AHMED HAMED; a.k.a. Ahmed The Egyptian; a.k.a. AHMED, Ahmed; a.k.a. AL-MASRI, Ahmad; a.k.a. AL-SURIR, Abu Islam; a.k.a. ALI, Ahmed Mohammed; a.k.a. HEMED, Ahmed; a.k.a. SHIEB, Ahmed; a.k.a. SHUAIB), Afghanistan; DOB 1965; POB Egypt; citizen Egypt (individual) [DGT] **10-12-01**

ALI, Hassan (a.k.a. FADHIL, Mustafa Mohamed; a.k.a. AL MASRI, Abd Al Wakil; a.k.a. AL-NUBI, Abu; a.k.a. ANIS, Abu; a.k.a. ELBISHY, Moustafa Ali; a.k.a. FADIL, Mustafa Muhamad; a.k.a. FAZUL, Mustafa; a.k.a. HUSSEIN; a.k.a. JIHAD, Abu; a.k.a. KHALID; a.k.a. MAN, Nu; a.k.a. MOHAMMED, Mustafa; a.k.a. YUSSRR, Abu); DOB 23 Jun 1976; POB Cairo, Egypt; citizen Egypt; alt. citizen Kenya; Kenyan ID No. 12773667; Serial No. 201735161 (individual) [SDGT] **10-12-01**

ALI, Salem (a.k.a. MOHAMMED, Khalid Shaikh; a.k.a. BIN KHALID, Fahd Bin Adballah; a.k.a. HENIN, Ashraf Refaat Nabith; a.k.a. WADOOD, Khalid Adbul); DOB 14 Apr 1965; alt. DOB 1 Mar 1964; POB Kuwait; citizen Kuwait (individual) [SDGT] **10-12-01**

ALI, Sheikh Hassan Dahir Aweys (a.k.a. AWES, Shaykh Hassan Dahir; AWEYS, Hassan Dahir), DOB 1935; citizen Somalia (individual) [SDGT] **11-07-01**

ALI, Yusaf Ahmed, Hallbybacken 15, Spanga 70, Sweden; DOB 20 Nov 1974 (individual) [SDGT] **11-07-01**

ALLY, Ahmed (a.k.a. SWEDAN, Sheikh Ahmed Salim; a.k.a. Ahmed the Tall; a.k.a. BAHAMAD; a.k.a. BAHAMAD, Sheik; a.k.a. BAHAMADI, Sheikh; a.k.a. SUWEIDAN, Sheikh Ahmad Salem; a.k.a. SWEDAN, Sheikh; a.k.a. SWEDAN, Sheikh Ahmed Salem); DOB 9 Apr 1969; alt. DOB 9 Apr 1960; POB Mombasa, Kenya; citizen Kenya (individual) [SDGT] **10-12-01**

ALLY, Fahid Mohammed (a.k.a. MSALAM, Fahid Mohammed Ally; a.k.a. AL-KINI, Usama; a.k.a. MSALAM, Fahad Ally; a.k.a. MSALAM, Fahid Mohammed Ali; a.k.a. MSALAM, Mohammed Ally; a.k.a. MUSALAAM, Fahid Mohammed Ali; a.k.a. SALEM, Fahid Muhamad Ali); DOB 19 Feb 1976; POB Mombasa, Kenya; citizen Kenya (individual) [SDGT] **10-12-01**

AMIN, Muhammad (a.k.a. AH HAQ, Dr. Amin; a.k.a. AL-HAQ, Amin; a.k.a. UL-HAQ, Dr. Amin); DOB 1960; POB Nangahar Province, Afghanistan (individual) [SDGT] **10-12-01**

ANIS, Abu (a.k.a. FADHIL, Mustafa Mohamed; a.k.a. AL MASRI, Abd Al Wakil; a.k.a. AL-NUBI, Abu; a.k.a. ALI, Hassan; a.k.a. ELBISHY, Moustafa Ali; a.k.a. FADIL, Mustafa Muhamad; a.k.a. FAZUL, Mustafa; a.k.a. HUSSEIN; a.k.a. JIHAD, Abu; a.k.a. KHALID; a.k.a. MAN, Nu; a.k.a. MOHAMMED, Mustafa; a.k.a. YUSSRR, Abu); DOB 23 Jun 1976; POB Cairo, Egypt; citizen Egypt; alt. citizen Kenya; Kenyan ID No. 12773667; Serial No. 201735161 (individual) [SDGT] **10-12-01**

ATEF, Muhammad (a.k.a. AL-MASRI, Abu Hafs; a.k.a. ABDULLAH, Sheikh Taysir; a.k.a. ABU HAFS; a.k.a ABU SITTA, Subhi; a.k.a. ATIF, Mohamed; a.k.a. ATIF, Muhammad; a.k.a. EL KHABIR, Abu Hafs el Masry; a.k.a. TAYSIR); DOB 1951; Alt. DOB 1956; Alt. DOB 1944; POB Alexandria, Egypt (individual) [SDT] [SDGT] **9-24-01**

ATIF, Mohamed (a.k.a. AL-MASRI, Abu Hafs; a.k.a. ABDULLAH, Sheikh Taysir; a.k.a. ABU HAFS; a.k.a. ABU SITTA, Subhi; a.k.a. ATEF, Muhammad; a.k.a. ATIF, Muhammad; a.k.a. EL KHABIR, Abu Hafs el Masry; a.k.a. TAYSIR); DOB 1951; Alt. DOB 1956; Alt. DOB 1944; POB Alexandria, Egypt (individual) [SDT] [SDGT] **09-24-01**

ATIF, Muhammad (a.k.a. AL-MASRI, Abu Hafs; a.k.a. ABDULLAH, Sheikh Taysir; a.k.a. ABU HAFS; a.k.a. ABU SITTA, Subhi; a.k.a. ATEF, Muhammad; a.k.a. ATIF, Mohamed; a.k.a. EL KHABIR, Abu Hafs el Masry; a.k.a. TAYSIR); DOB 1951; Alt. DOB 1956; Alt. DOB 1944; POB Alexandria, Egypt (individual) [SDT] [SDGT] **09-24-01**

ATWA, Ali (a.k.a. BOUSLIM, Ammar Mansour; a.k.a. SALIM, Hassan Rostom), Lebanon; DOB 1960; POB Lebanon; citizen Lebanon (individual) [SDGT] **10-12-01**

ATWAH, Muhsin Musa Matwalli (a.k.a. ABDEL RAHMAN; a.k.a. ABDUL RAHMAN; a.k.a. AL-MUHAJIR, Abdul Rahman; a.k.a. AL-NAMER,

Mohammed K.A.), Afghanistan; DOB 19 Jun 1964; POB Egypt; citizen Egypt (individual) [SDGT] **10-12-01**

AWES, Shaykh Hassan Dahir (a.k.a. ALI, Sheikh Hassan Dahir Aweys; a.k.a. AWEYS, Hassan Dahir), DOB 1935; citizen Somalia (individual) [SDGT] **11-07-01**

AWEYS, Dahir Ubeidullahi, Via Cipriano Facchinetti 84, Rome, Italy (individual) [SDGT] **11-07-01**

AWEYS, Hassan Dahir (a.k.a. ALI, Sheikh Hassan Dahir Aweys; a.k.a. AWES, Shaykh Hassan Dahir), DOB 1935; citizen Somalia (individual) [SDGT] **11-07-01**

AYADI CHAFIK, Ben Muhammad (a.k.a. AIADI, Ben Muhammad; a.k.a. AIADY, Ben Muhammad; a.k.a. AYADI SHAFIQ, Ben Muhammad; a.k.a. BIN MUHAMMAD, Ayadi Chafiq), Helene Meyer Ring 10-1415-80809, Munich, Germany; 129 Park Road, NW8, London, England; 28 Chaussee de Lille, Mouscron, Belgium; Darvingasse 1/2/58-60, Vienna, Austria; Tunisia; DOB 21 Jan 1963; POB Safais (Sfax), Tunisia (individual) [SDGT] **10-12-01**

AYADI SHAFIQ, Ben Muhammad (a.k.a. AIADI, Ben Muhammad; a.k.a. AIADY, Ben Muhammad; a.k.a. AYADI CHAFIK, Ben Muhammad; a.k.a. BIN MUHAMMAD, Ayadi Chafiq), Helene Meyer Ring 10-1415-80809, Munich, Germany; 129 Park Road, NW8, London, England; 28 Chaussee de Lille, Mouscron, Belgium; Darvingasse 1/2/58-60, Vienna, Austria; Tunisia; DOB 21 Jan 1963; POB Safais (Sfax), Tunisia (individual) [SDGT] **10-12-01**

BAHAMAD (a.k.a. SWEDAN, Sheikh Ahmed Salim; a.k.a. Ahmed the Tall; a.k.a. ALLY, Ahmed; a.k.a. BAHAMAD, Sheik; a.k.a. BAHAMADI, Sheikh; a.k.a. SUWEIDAN, Sheikh Ahmad Salem; a.k.a. SWEDAN, Sheikh; a.k.a. SWEDAN, Sheikh Ahmed Salem); DOB 9 Apr 1969; alt. DOB 9 Apr 1960; POB Mombasa, Kenya; citizen Kenya (individual) [SDGT] **10-12-01**

BAHAMAD, Sheik (a.k.a. SWEDAN, Sheikh Ahmed Salim; a.k.a. Ahmed the Tall; a.k.a. ALLY, Ahmed; a.k.a. BAHAMAD; a.k.a. BAHAMADI, Sheikh; a.k.a. SUWEIDAN, Sheikh Ahmad Salem; a.k.a. SWEDAN, Sheikh; a.k.a. SWEDAN, Sheikh Ahmed Salem); DOB 9 Apr 1969; alt. DOB 9 Apr 1960; POB Mombasa, Kenya; citizen Kenya (individual) [SDGT] **10-12-01**

BAHAMADI, Sheikh (a.k.a. SWEDAN, Sheikh Ahmed Salim; a.k.a. Ahmed the Tall; a.k.a. ALLY, Ahmed; a.k.a. BAHAMAD; a.k.a. BAHAMAD, Sheik; a.k.a. SUWEIDAN, Sheikh Ahmad Salem; a.k.a. SWEDAN, Sheikh; a.k.a. SWEDAN, Sheikh Ahmed Salem); DOB 9 Apr 1969; alt. DOB 9 Apr 1960; POB Mombasa, Kenya; citizen Kenya (individual) [SDGT] **10-12-01**

BAKR, Abu (a.k.a. GHAILANI, Ahmed Khalfan; a.k.a. "AHMED THE TANZANIAN;" a.k.a. "FOOPIE;" a.k.a. "FUPI;" a.k.a. AHMAD, Abu Bakr; a.k.a. AHMED, A.; a.k.a. AHMED, Abubakar; a.k.a. AHMED, Abubakar K.;

a.k.a. AHMED, Abubakar Khalfan; a.k.a. AHMED, Abubakary K.; a.k.a. AHMED, Ahmed Khalfan; a.k.a. AL TANZANI, Ahmad; a.k.a. ALI, Ahmed Khalfan; a.k.a. GHAILANI, Abubakary Khalfan Ahmed; a.k.a. GHAILANI, Ahmed; a.k.a. GHILANI, Ahmad Khalafan; a.k.a. HUSSEIN, Mahafudh Abubakar Ahmed Abdallah; a.k.a. KHABAR, Abu; a.k.a. KHALFAN, Ahmed a.k.a. MOHAMMED, Shariff Omar); DOB 14 Mar 1974; alt. DOB 13 Apr 1974; alt. DOB 14 Apr 1974; alt. DOB 1 Aug 1970; POB Zanzibar, Tanzania; citizen Tanzania (individual) [SDGT] 10-12-01

BIN KHALID, Fahd Bin Adballah (a.k.a. MOHAMMED, Khalid Shaikh; a.k.a. ALI, Salem; a.k.a. HENIN, Ashraf Refaat Nabith; a.k.a. WADOOD, Khalid Adbul); DOB 14 Apr 1965; alt. DOB 1 Mar 1964; POB Kuwait; citizen Kuwait (individual) [SDGT] 10-12-01

BIN LADEN, Osama (a.k.a. BIN LADIN, Usama bin Muhammad bin Awad; a.k.a. BIN LADEN, Usama; a.k.a. BIN LADIN, Osama; a.k.a. BIN LADIN, Osama bin Muhammad bin Awad; a.k.a. BIN LADEN, Usama), Afghanistan; DOB 30 Jul 57; Alt. DOB 1958; POB Jeddah, Saudi Arabia; Alt. POB Yemen (individual) [SDT] [SDGT] 09-24-01

BIN LADEN, Usama (a.k.a. BIN LADIN, Usama bin Muhammad bin Awad; a.k.a. BIN LADEN, Osama; a.k.a. BIN LADIN, Osama; a.k.a. BIN LADIN, Osama bin Muhammad bin Awad; a.k.a. BIN LADIN, Usama), Afghanistan; DOB 30 Jul 57; Alt. DOB 1958; POB Jeddah, Saudi Arabia; Alt. POB Yemen (individual) [SDT] [SDGT] 09-24-01

BIN LADIN, Osama (a.k.a. BIN LADIN, Usama bin Muhammad bin Awad; a.k.a. BIN LADEN, Osama; a.k.a. BIN LADEN, Usama; a.k.a. BIN LADIN, Osama bin Muhammad bin wad; a.k.a. BIN LADIN, Usama), Afghanistan; DOB 30 Jul 57; Alt. DOB 1958; POB Jeddah, Saudi Arabia; Alt. POB Yemen (individual) [SDT] [SDGT] 09-24-01

BIN LADIN, Osama bin Muhammad bin Awad (a.k.a. BIN LADIN, Usama bin Muhammad bin Awad; a.k.a. BIN LADEN, Osama; a.k.a. BIN LADEN, Usama; a.k.a. BIN LADIN, Osama; a.k.a. BIN LADIN, Usama), Afghanistan; DOB 30 Jul 57; Alt. DOB 1958; POB Jeddah, Saudi Arabia; Alt. POB Yemen (individual) [SDT] [SDGT] 09-24-01

BIN LADIN, Usama (a.k.a. BIN LADIN, Usama bin Muhammad bin Awad; a.k.a. BIN LADEN, Osama; a.k.a. BIN LADEN, Usama; a.k.a. BIN LADIN, Osama; a.k.a. BIN LADIN, Osama bin Muhammad bin Awad); DOB 30 Jul 57; Alt. DOB 1958; POB Jeddah, Saudi Arabia; Alt. POB Yemen (individual) [SDT] [SDGT] 09-24-01

BIN LADIN, Usama bin Muhammad bin Awad (a.k.a. BIN LADEN, Osama; a.k.a. BIN LADEN, Usama; a.k.a. BIN LADIN, Osama; a.k.a. BIN LADIN, Osama bin Muhammad bin Awad; a.k.a. BIN LADIN, Usama);

DOB 30 Jul 57; Alt. DOB 1958; POB Jeddah, Saudi Arabia; Alt. POB Yemen (individual) [SDT] [SDGT] **09-24-01**

BIN MARWAN, Bilal; DOB 1947 (individual) [SDGT] **10-12-01**

BIN MUHAMMAD, Ayadi Chafiq (a.k.a. AIADI, Ben Muhammad; a.k.a. AIADY, Ben Muhammad; a.k.a. AYADI CHAFIK, Ben Muhammad; a.k.a. AYADI SHAFIQ, Ben Muhammad), Helene Meyer Ring 10-1415-80809, Munich, Germany; 129 Park Road, NW8, London, England; 28 Chaussee de Lille, Mouscron, Belgium; Darvingasse 1/2/58-60, Vienna, Austria; Tunisia; DOB 21 Jan 1963; POB Safais (Sfax), Tunisia (individual) [SDGT] **10-12-01**

BOUSLIM, Ammar Mansour (a.k.a. ATWA, Ali; a.k.a. SALIM, Hassan Rostom), Lebanon; DOB 1960; POB Lebanon; citizen Lebanon (individual) [SDGT] **10-12-01**

DARKAZANLI, Mamoun, Uhlenhorsterweg 34 11, Hamburg, 22085 Germany; DOB 4 Aug 1958; POB Aleppo, Syria; Passport No. 1310636262 (Germany) (individual) [SDGT] **10-12-01**

EL-HOORIE, Ali Saed Bin Ali (a.k.a. AL-HOURI, Ali Saed Bin Ali; a.k.a. EL-HOURI, Ali Saed Bin Ali); DOB 10 Jul 1965; alt. DOB 11 Jul 1965; POB El Dibabiya, Saudi Arabia; citizen Saudi Arabia (individual) [SDGT] **10-12-01**

EL-HOURI, Ali Saed Bin Ali (a.k.a. EL-HOORIE, Ali Saed Bin Ali; a.k.a. AL-HOURI, Ali Saed Bin Ali); DOB 10 Jul 1965; alt. DOB 11 Jul 1965; POB El Dibabiya, Saudi Arabia; citizen Saudi Arabia (individual) [SDGT] **10-12-01**

EL KHABIR, Abu Hafs el Masry (a.k.a. AL-MASRI, Abu Hafs; a.k.a. ABDULLAH, Sheikh Taysir; a.k.a. ABU HAFS; a.k.a. ABU SITTA, Subhi; a.k.a. ATEF, Muhammad; a.k.a. ATIF, Mohamed; a.k.a. ATIF, Muhammad; a.k.a. TAYSIR); DOB 1951; Alt. DOB 1956; Alt. DOB 1944; POB Alexandria, Egypt (individual) [SDT] [SDGT] **09-24-01**

ELBISHY, Moustafa Ali (a.k.a. FADHIL, Mustafa Mohamed; a.k.a. AL MASRI, Abd Al Wakil; a.k.a. AL-NUBI, Abu; a.k.a. ALI, Hassan; a.k.a. ANIS, Abu; a.k.a. FADIL, Mustafa Muhamad; a.k.a. FAZUL, Mustafa; a.k.a. HUSSEIN; a.k.a. JIHAD, Abu; a.k.a. KHALID; a.k.a. MAN, Nu; a.k.a. MOHAMMED, Mustafa; a.k.a. YUSSRR, Abu); DOB 23 Jun 1976; POB Cairo, Egypt; citizen Egypt; alt. citizen Kenya; Kenyan ID No. 12773667; Serial No. 201735161 (individual) [SDGT] **10-12-01**

FADHIL, Mustafa Mohamed (a.k.a. AL MASRI, Abd Al Wakil; a.k.a. AL-NUBI, Abu; a.k.a. ALI, Hassan; a.k.a. ANIS, Abu; a.k.a. ELBISHY, Moustafa Ali; a.k.a. FADIL, Mustafa Muhamad; a.k.a. FAZUL, Mustafa; a.k.a. HUSSEIN; a.k.a. JIHAD, Abu; a.k.a. KHALID; a.k.a. MAN, Nu; a.k.a. MOHAMMED, Mustafa; a.k.a. YUSSRR, Abu); DOB 23 Jun 1976; POB

Cairo, Egypt; citizen Egypt; alt. citizen Kenya; Kenyan ID No. 12773667; Serial No. 201735161 (individual) [SDGT] **10-12-01**

FADIL, Mustafa Muhamad (a.k.a. FADHIL, Mustafa Mohamed; a.k.a. AL MASRI, Abd Al Wakil; a.k.a. AL-NUBI, Abu; a.k.a. ALI, Hassan; a.k.a. ANIS, Abu; a.k.a. ELBISHY, Moustafa Ali; a.k.a. FAZUL, Mustafa; a.k.a. HUSSEIN; a.k.a. JIHAD, Abu; a.k.a. KHALID; a.k.a. MAN, Nu; a.k.a. MOHAMMED, Mustafa; a.k.a. YUSSRR, Abu); DOB 23 Jun 1976; POB Cairo, Egypt; citizen Egypt; alt. citizen Kenya; Kenyan ID No. 12773667; Serial No. 201735161 (individual) [SDGT] **10-12-01**

FARAG, Hamdi Ahmad (a.k.a. AHMAD, Tariq Anwar al-Sayyid; a.k.a. FATHI, Amr Al-Fatih); DOB 15 Mar 63; POB Alexandria, Egypt (individual) [SDGT] **09-24-01**

FATHI, Amr Al-Fatih (a.k.a. AHMAD, Tariq Anwar al-Sayyid; a.k.a. FARAG, Hamdi Ahmad); DOB 15 Mar 63; POB Alexandria, Egypt (individual) [SDGT] **09-24-01**

FAZUL, Abdalla (a.k.a. MOHAMMED, Fazul Abdullah; a.k.a. ABDALLA, Fazul; a.k.a. ADBALLAH, Fazul; a.k.a. AISHA, Abu; a.k.a. AL SUDANI, Abu Seif; a.k.a. ALI, Fadel Abdallah Mohammed; a.k.a. FAZUL, Abdallah; a.k.a. FAZUL, Abdallah Mohammed; a.k.a. FAZUL, Haroon; a.k.a. FAZUL, Harun; a.k.a. HAROON; a.k.a. HAROUN, Fadhil; a.k.a. HARUN; a.k.a. LUQMAN, Abu; a.k.a. MOHAMMED, Fazul; a.k.a. MOHAMMED, Fazul Abdilahi; a.k.a. MOHAMMED, Fouad; a.k.a. MUHAMAD, Fadil Abdallah); DOB 25 Aug 1972; alt. DOB 25 Dec 1974; alt. DOB 25 Feb 1974; POB Moroni, Comoros Islands; citizen Comoros; alt. citizen Kenya (individual) [SDGT] **10-12-01**

FAZUL, Abdallah (a.k.a. MOHAMMED, Fazul Abdullah; a.k.a. ABDALLA, Fazul; a.k.a. ADBALLAH, Fazul; a.k.a. AISHA, Abu; a.k.a. AL SUDANI, bu Seif; a.k.a. ALI, Fadel Abdallah Mohammed; a.k.a. FAZUL, Abdalla; a.k.a. FAZUL, Abdallah Mohammed; a.k.a. FAZUL, Haroon; a.k.a. FAZUL, Harun; a.k.a. HAROON; a.k.a. HAROUN, Fadhil; a.k.a. HARUN; a.k.a. LUQMAN, Abu; a.k.a. MOHAMMED, Fazul; a.k.a. MOHAMMED, Fazul Abdilahi; a.k.a. MOHAMMED, Fouad; a.k.a. MUHAMAD, Fadil Abdallah); DOB 25 Aug 1972; alt. DOB 25 Dec 1974; alt. DOB 25 Feb 1974; POB Moroni, Comoros Islands; citizen Comoros; alt. citizen Kenya (individual) [SDGT] **10-12-01**

FAZUL, Abdallah Mohammed (a.k.a. MOHAMMED, Fazul Abdullah; a.k.a. ABDALLA, Fazul; a.k.a. ADBALLAH, Fazul; a.k.a. AISHA, Abu; a.k.a. AL SUDANI, Abu Seif; a.k.a. ALI, Fadel Abdallah Mohammed; a.k.a. FAZUL, Abdalla; a.k.a. FAZUL, Abdallah; a.k.a. FAZUL, Haroon; a.k.a. FAZUL, Harun; a.k.a. HAROON; a.k.a. HAROUN, Fadhil; a.k.a. HARUN; a.k.a. LUQMAN, Abu; a.k.a. MOHAMMED, Fazul; a.k.a. MOHAMMED, Fazul Abdilahi; a.k.a. MOHAMMED, Fouad; a.k.a. MUHAMAD, Fadil

Abdallah); DOB 25 Aug 1972; alt. DOB 25 Dec 1974; alt. DOB 25 Feb 1974; POB Moroni, Comoros Islands; citizen Comoros; alt. citizen Kenya (individual) [SDGT] **10-12-01**

FAZUL, Haroon (a.k.a. MOHAMMED, Fazul Abdullah; a.k.a. ABDALLA, Fazul; a.k.a. ADBALLAH, Fazul; a.k.a. AISHA, Abu; a.k.a. AL SUDANI, Abu Seif; a.k.a. ALI, Fadel Abdallah Mohammed; a.k.a. FAZUL, Abdalla; a.k.a. FAZUL, Abdallah; a.k.a. FAZUL, Abdallah Mohammed; a.k.a. FAZUL, Harun; a.k.a. HAROON; a.k.a. HAROUN, Fadhil; a.k.a. HARUN; a.k.a. LUQMAN, Abu; a.k.a. MOHAMMED, Fazul; a.k.a. MOHAMMED, Fazul Abdilahi; a.k.a. MOHAMMED, Fouad; a.k.a. MUHAMAD, Fadil Abdallah); DOB 25 Aug 1972; alt. DOB 25 Dec 1974; alt. DOB 25 Feb 1974; POB Moroni, Comoros Islands; citizen Comoros; alt. citizen Kenya (individual) [SDGT] **10-12-01**

FAZUL, Harun (a.k.a. MOHAMMED, Fazul Abdullah; a.k.a. ABDALLA, Fazul; a.k.a. ADBALLAH, Fazul; a.k.a. AISHA, Abu; a.k.a. AL SUDANI, Abu Seif; a.k.a. ALI, Fadel Abdallah Mohammed; a.k.a. FAZUL, Abdalla; a.k.a. FAZUL, Abdallah; a.k.a. FAZUL, Abdallah Mohammed; a.k.a. FAZUL, Haroon; a.k.a. HAROON; a.k.a. HAROUN, Fadhil; a.k.a. HARUN; a.k.a. LUQMAN, Abu; a.k.a. MOHAMMED, Fazul; a.k.a. MOHAMMED, Fazul Abdilahi; a.k.a. MOHAMMED, Fouad; a.k.a. MUHAMAD, Fadil Abdallah); DOB 25 Aug 1972; alt. DOB 25 Dec 1974; alt. DOB 25 Feb 1974; POB Moroni, Comoros Islands; citizen Comoros; alt. citizen Kenya (individual) [SDGT] **10-12-01**

FAZUL, Mustafa (a.k.a. FADHIL, Mustafa Mohamed; a.k.a. AL MASRI, Abd Al Wakil; a.k.a. AL-NUBI, Abu; a.k.a. ALI, Hassan; a.k.a. ANIS, Abu; a.k.a. ELBISHY, Moustafa Ali; a.k.a. FADIL, Mustafa Muhamad; a.k.a. HUSSEIN; a.k.a. JIHAD, Abu; a.k.a. KHALID; a.k.a. MAN, Nu; a.k.a. MOHAMMED, Mustafa; a.k.a. YUSSRR, Abu); DOB 23 Jun 1976; POB Cairo, Egypt; citizen Egypt; alt. citizen Kenya; Kenyan ID No. 12773667; Serial No. 201735161 (individual) [SDGT] **10-12-01**

GARBAYA, AHMED (a.k.a. IZZ-AL-DIN, Hasan; a.k.a. SA-ID; a.k.a. SALWWAN, Samir), Lebanon; DOB 1963; POB Lebanon; citizen Lebanon (individual) [SDGT] **10-12-01**

GHAILANI, Ahmed (a.k.a. GHAILANI, Ahmed Khalfan; a.k.a. "AHMED THE TANZANIAN;" a.k.a. "FOOPIE;" a.k.a. "FUPI;" a.k.a. AHMAD, Abu Bakr; a.k.a. AHMED, A.; a.k.a. AHMED, Abubakar; a.k.a. AHMED, Abubakar K.; a.k.a. AHMED, Abubakar Khalfan; a.k.a. AHMED, Abubakary K.; a.k.a. AHMED, Ahmed Khalfan; a.k.a. AL TANZANI, Ahmad; a.k.a. ALI, Ahmed Khalfan; a.k.a. BAKR, Abu; a.k.a. GHAILANI, Abubakary Khalfan Ahmed; a.k.a. GHILANI, Ahmad Khalafan; a.k.a. HUSSEIN, Mahafudh Abubakar Ahmed Abdallah; a.k.a. KHABAR, Abu; a.k.a. KHALFAN, Ahmed; a.k.a. MOHAMMED, Shariff Omar); DOB 14

Mar 1974; alt. DOB 13 Apr 1974; alt. DOB 14 Apr 1974; alt. DOB 1 Aug 1970; POB Zanzibar, Tanzania; citizen Tanzania (individual) [SDGT] **10-12-01**

GHAILANI, Ahmed Khalfan (a.k.a. "AHMED THE TANZANIAN;" a.k.a. "FOOPIE;" a.k.a. "FUPI;" a.k.a. AHMAD, Abu Bakr; a.k.a. AHMED, A.; a.k.a. AHMED, Abubakar; a.k.a. AHMED, Abubakar K.; a.k.a. AHMED, Abubakar Khalfan; a.k.a. AHMED, Abubakary K.; a.k.a. AHMED, Ahmed Khalfan; a.k.a. AL TANZANI, Ahmad; a.k.a. ALI, Ahmed Khalfan; a.k.a. BAKR, Abu; a.k.a. GHAILANI, Abubakary Khalfan Ahmed; a.k.a. GHAILANI, Ahmed; a.k.a. GHILANI, Ahmad Khalafan; a.k.a. HUSSEIN, Mahafudh Abubakar Ahmed Abdallah; a.k.a. KHABAR, Abu; a.k.a. KHALFAN, Ahmed; a.k.a. MOHAMMED, Shariff Omar); DOB 14 Mar 1974; alt. DOB 13 Apr 1974; alt. DOB 14 Apr 1974; alt. DOB 1 Aug 1970; POB Zanzibar, Tanzania; citizen Tanzania (individual) [SDGT] **10-12-01**

GHAILNI, Abubakary Khalfan Ahmed (a.k.a. GHAILANI, Ahmed Khalfan; a.k.a. "AHMED THE TANZANIAN;" a.k.a. "FOOPIE;" a.k.a. "FUPI;" a.k.a. AHMAD, Abu Bakr; a.k.a. AHMED, A.; a.k.a. AHMED, Abubakar; a.k.a. AHMED, Abubakar K.; a.k.a. AHMED, Abubakar Khalfan; a.k.a. AHMED, Abubakary K.; a.k.a. AHMED, Ahmed Khalfan; a.k.a. AL TANZANI, Ahmad; a.k.a. ALI, Ahmed Khalfan; a.k.a. BAKR, Abu; a.k.a. GHAILANI, Ahmed; a.k.a. GHILANI, Ahmad Khalafan; a.k.a. HUSSEIN, Mahafudh Abubakar Ahmed Abdallah; a.k.a. KHABAR, Abu; a.k.a. KHALFAN, Ahmed; a.k.a. MOHAMMED, Shariff Omar); DOB 14 Mar 1974; alt. DOB 13 Apr 1974; alt. DOB 14 Apr 1974; alt. DOB 1 Aug 1970; POB Zanzibar, Tanzania; citizen Tanzania (individual) [SDGT] **10-12-01**

GHILANI, Ahmad Khalafan (a.k.a. GHAILANI, Ahmed Khalfan; a.k.a. "AHMED THE TANZANIAN;" a.k.a. "FOOPIE;" a.k.a. "FUPI;" a.k.a. AHMAD, Abu Bakr; a.k.a. AHMED, A.; a.k.a. AHMED, Abubakar; a.k.a. AHMED, Abubakar K.; a.k.a. AHMED, Abubakar Khalfan; a.k.a. AHMED, Abubakary K.; a.k.a. AHMED, Ahmed Khalfan; a.k.a. AL TANZANI, Ahmad; a.k.a. ALI, Ahmed Khalfan; a.k.a. BAKR, Abu; a.k.a. GHAILANI, Abubakary Khalfan Ahmed; a.k.a. GHAILANI, Ahmed; a.k.a. HUSSEIN, Mahafudh Abubakar Ahmed Abdallah; a.k.a. KHABAR, Abu; a.k.a. KHALFAN, Ahmed; a.k.a. MOHAMMED, Shariff Omar); DOB 14 Mar 1974; alt. DOB 13 Apr 1974; alt. DOB 14 Apr 1974; alt. DOB 1 Aug 1970; POB Zanzibar, Tanzania; citizen Tanzania (individual) [SDGT] **10-12-01**

HAROON (a.k.a. MOHAMMED, Fazul Abdullah; a.k.a. ABDALLA, Fazul; a.k.a. ADBALLAH, Fazul; a.k.a. AISHA, Abu; a.k.a. AL SUDANI, Abu Seif; a.k.a. ALI, Fadel Abdallah Mohammed; a.k.a. FAZUL, Abdalla; a.k.a. FAZUL, Abdallah; a.k.a. FAZUL, Abdallah Mohammed; a.k.a. FAZUL, Haroon; a.k.a. FAZUL, Harun; a.k.a. HAROUN, Fadhil; a.k.a. HARUN; a.k.a. LUQMAN, Abu; a.k.a. MOHAMMED, Fazul; a.k.a. MOHAMMED, Fazul Abdilahi; a.k.a. MOHAMMED, Fouad; a.k.a. MUHAMAD, Fadil Abdallah); DOB 25 Aug 1972; alt. DOB 25 Dec 1974; alt. DOB 25 Feb 1974;

POB Moroni, Comoros Islands; citizen Comoros; alt. citizen Kenya (individual) [SDGT] **10-12-01**

HAROUN, Fadhil (a.k.a. MOHAMMED, Fazul Abdullah; a.k.a. ABDALLA, Fazul; a.k.a. ADBALLAH, Fazul; a.k.a. AISHA, Abu; a.k.a. AL SUDANI, Abu Seif; a.k.a. ALI, Fadel Abdallah Mohammed; a.k.a. FAZUL, Abdalla; a.k.a. FAZUL, Abdallah; a.k.a. FAZUL, Abdallah Mohammed; a.k.a. FAZUL, Haroon; a.k.a. FAZUL, Harun; a.k.a. HAROON; a.k.a. HARUN; a.k.a. LUQMAN, Abu; a.k.a. MOHAMMED, Fazul; a.k.a. MOHAMMED, Fazul Abdilahi; a.k.a. MOHAMMED, Fouad; a.k.a. MUHAMAD, Fadil Abdallah); DOB 25 Aug 1972; alt. DOB 25 Dec 1974; alt. DOB 25 Feb 1974; POB Moroni, Comoros Islands; citizen Comoros; alt. citizen Kenya (individual) [SDGT] **10-12-01**

HARUN (a.k.a. MOHAMMED, Fazul Abdullah; a.k.a. ABDALLA, Fazul; a.k.a. ADBALLAH, Fazul; a.k.a. AISHA, Abu; a.k.a. AL SUDANI, Abu Seif; a.k.a. ALI, Fadel Abdallah Mohammed; a.k.a. FAZUL, Abdalla; a.k.a. FAZUL, Abdallah; a.k.a. FAZUL, Abdallah Mohammed; a.k.a. FAZUL, Haroon; a.k.a. FAZUL, Harun; a.k.a. HAROON; a.k.a. HAROUN, Fadhil; a.k.a. LUQMAN, Abu; a.k.a. MOHAMMED, Fazul; a.k.a. MOHAMMED, Fazul Abdilahi; a.k.a. MOHAMMED, Fouad; a.k.a. MUHAMAD, Fadil Abdallah); DOB 25 Aug 1972; alt. DOB 25 Dec 1974; alt. DOB 25 Feb 1974; POB Moroni, Comoros Islands; citizen Comoros; alt. citizen Kenya (individual) [SDGT] **10-12-01**

HASANAYN, Nasr Fahmi Nasr (a.k.a. SALAH, Muhammad) (individual) [SDGT] **09-24-01**

HEMED, Ahmed (a.k.a. ALI, Ahmed Mohammed Hamed; a.k.a. ABDUREHMAN, Ahmed Mohammed; a.k.a. ABU FATIMA; a.k.a. ABU ISLAM; a.k.a. ABU KHADIIJAH; a.k.a. AHMED HAMED; a.k.a. Ahmed The Egyptian; ak.a. AHMED, Ahmed; a.k.a. AL-MASRI, Ahmad; a.k.a. AL-SURIR, Abu Islam; a.k.a. ALI, Ahmed Mohammed; a.k.a. ALI, Hamed; a.k.a. SHIEB, Ahmed; a.k.a. SHUAIB), Afghanistan; DOB 1965; POB Egypt; citizen Egypt (individual) [SDGT] **10-12-01**

HENIN, Ashraf Refaat Nabith (a.k.a. MOHAMMED, Khalid Shaikh; a.k.a. ALI, Salem; a.k.a. BIN KHALID, Fahd Bin Adballah; a.k.a. WADOOD, Khalid Adbul); DOB 14 Apr 1965; alt. DOB 1 Mar 1964; POB Kuwait; citizen Kuwait (individual) [SDGT] **10-12-01**

HIJAZI, Raed M. (a.k.a. AL-AMRIKI, Abu-Ahmad; a.k.a. AL-HAWEN, Abu-Ahmad; a.k.a. AL-MAGHRIBI, Rashid; a.k.a. AL-SHAHID, Abu-Ahmad; a.k.a. HIJAZI, Riad), Jordan; DOB 1968; POB California, U.S.A.; SSN: 548-91-5411 (USA) (individual) [SDGT] **10-12-01**

HIJAZI, Riad (a.k.a. AL-AMRIKI, Abu-Ahmad; a.k.a. AL-HAWEN, Abu-Ahmad; a.k.a. AL-MAGHRIBI, Rashid; a.k.a. AL-SHAHID,

Abu-Ahmad; a.k.a. HIJAZI, Raed M.), Jordan; DOB 1968; POB California, U.S.A.; SSN: 548-91-5411 (USA) (individual) [SDGT] **10-12-01**

HIMMAT, Ali Ghaleb, Via Posero 2, Campione d'Italia CH-6911, Switzerland; DOB 16 Jun 1938; POB Damascus, Syria; citizen Switzerland; alt. citizen Tunisia (individual) [SDGT] **11-07-01**

HUBER, Ahmed (a.k.a. HUBER, Albert Friedrich Armand), Mettmenstetten, Switzerland; DOB 1927 (individual) [SDGT] **11-07-01**

HUBER, Albert Friedrich Armand (a.k.a. HUBER, Ahmed), Mettmenstetten, Switzerland; DOB 1927 (individual) [SDGT] **11-07-01**

HUSAIN, Zain Al-Abidin Muhahhad (a.k.a. ABU ZUBAYDAH; a.k.a. ABU ZUBAIDA; a.k.a. AL-WAHAB, Abd Al-Hadi; a.k.a. HUSAYN, Zayn al-Abidin Muhammad; a.k.a. TARIQ); DOB 12 Mar 71; POB Riyadh, Saudi Arabia (individual) [SDGT] **09-24-01**

HUSAYN, Zayn al-Abidin Muhammad (a.k.a. ABU ZUBAYDAH; a.k.a. ABU ZUBAIDA; a.k.a. AL-WAHAB, Abd Al-Hadi; a.k.a. HUSAIN, Zain Al-Abidin Muhahhad; a.k.a. TARIQ); DOB 12 Mar 71; POB Riyadh, Saudi Arabia (individual) [SDGT] **09-24-01**

HUSSEIN (a.k.a. FADHIL, Mustafa Mohamed; a.k.a. AL MASRI, Abd Al Wakil; a.k.a. AL-NUBI, Abu; a.k.a. ALI, Hassan; a.k.a. ANIS, Abu; a.k.a. ELBISHY, Moustafa Ali; a.k.a. FADIL, Mustafa Muhamad; a.k.a. FAZUL, Mustafa; a.k.a. JIHAD, Abu; a.k.a. KHALID; a.k.a. MAN, Nu; a.k.a. MOHAMMED, Mustafa; a.k.a. YUSSRR, Abu); DOB 23 Jun 1976; POB Cairo, Egypt; citizen Egypt; alt. citizen Kenya; Kenyan ID No. 12773667; Serial No. 201735161 (individual) [SDGT] **10-12-01**

HUSSEIN, Liban, 2019 Bank St., Ottawa, Ontario, Canada; 925 Washington St., Dorchester, Massachusetts, U.S.A. (individual) [SDGT] **11-07-01**

HUSSEIN, Mahafudh Abubakar Ahmed Abdallah (a.k.a. GHAILANI, Ahmed Khalfan; a.k.a. "AHMED THE TANZANIAN;" a.k.a. "FOOPIE;" a.k.a. "FUPI;" a.k.a. AHMAD, Abu Bakr; a.k.a. AHMED, A.; a.k.a. AHMED, Abubakar; a.k.a. AHMED, Abubakar K.; a.k.a. AHMED, Abubakar Khalfan; a.k.a. AHMED, Abubakary K.; a.k.a. AHMED, Ahmed Khalfan; a.k.a. AL TANZANI, Ahmad; a.k.a. ALI, Ahmed Khalfan; a.k.a. BAKR, Abu; a.k.a. GHAILANI, Abubakary Khalfan Ahmed; a.k.a. GHAILANI, Ahmed; a.k.a. GHILANI, Ahmad Khalafan; a.k.a. KHABAR, Abu; a.k.a. KHALFAN, Ahmed; a.k.a. MOHAMMED, Shariff Omar); DOB 14 Mar 1974; alt. DOB 13 Apr 1974; alt. DOB 14 Apr 1974; alt. DOB 1 Aug 1970; POB Zanzibar, Tanzania; citizen Tanzania (individual) [SDGT] **10-12-01**

IZZ-AL-DIN, Hasan (a.k.a. GARBAYA, AHMED; a.k.a. SA-ID; a.k.a. SALWWAN, Samir), Lebanon; DOB 1963; POB Lebanon; citizen Lebanon (individual) [SDGT] **10-12-01**

JAMA, Garad (a.k.a. NOR, Garad K.; a.k.a. WASRSAME, Fartune Ahmed), 2100 Bloomington Ave., Minneapolis, Minnesota, U.S.A.; 1806 Riverside Ave., 2nd Floor, Minneapolis, Minnesota, U.S.A.; DOB 26 Jun 1974 (individual) [SDGT] 11-07-01

JIHAD, Abu (a.k.a. FADHIL, Mustafa Mohamed; a.k.a. AL MASRI, Abd Al Wakil; a.k.a. AL-NUBI, Abu; a.k.a. ALI, Hassan; a.k.a. ANIS, Abu; a.k.a. ELBISHY, Moustafa Ali; a.k.a. FADIL, Mustafa Muhamad; a.k.a. FAZUL, Mustafa; a.k.a. HUSSEIN; a.k.a. KHALID; a.k.a. MAN, Nu; a.k.a. MOHAMMED, Mustafa; a.k.a. YUSSRR, Abu); DOB 23 Jun 1976; POB Cairo, Egypt; citizen Egypt; alt. citizen Kenya; Kenyan ID No. 12773667; Serial No. 201735161 (individual) [SDGT] 10-12-01

JIM'ALE, Ahmad Nur Ali (a.k.a. JIM'ALE, Ahmed Nur Ali; a.k.a. JIMALE, Ahmad Ali; a.k.a. JUMALE, Ahmed Nur; a.k.a. JUMALI, Ahmed Ali), Mogadishu, Somalia; P.O. Box 3312, Dubai, U.A.E. (individual) [SDGT] 11-07-01

JIM'ALE, Ahmed Nur Ali (a.k.a. JIM'ALE, Ahmad Nur Ali; a.k.a. JIMALE, Ahmad Ali; a.k.a. JUMALE, Ahmed Nur; a.k.a. JUMALI, Ahmed Ali), Mogadishu, Somalia; P.O. Box 3312, Dubai, U.A.E. (individual) [SDGT] 11-07-01

JIMALE, Ahmad Ali (a.k.a. JIM'ALE, Ahmad Nur Ali; a.k.a. JIM'ALE, Ahmed Nur Ali; a.k.a. JUMALE, Ahmed Nur; a.k.a. JUMALI, Ahmed Ali), Mogadishu, Somalia; P.O. Box 3312, Dubai, U.A.E. (individual) [SDGT] 11-07-01

JUMALE, Ahmed Nur (a.k.a. JIM'ALE, Ahmad Nur Ali; a.k.a. JIM'ALE, Ahmed Nur Ali; a.k.a. JIMALE, Ahmad Ali; a.k.a. JUMALI, Ahmed Ali), Mogadishu, Somalia; P.O. Box 3312, Dubai, U.A.E. (individual) [SDGT] 11-07-01

JUMALI, Ahmed Ali (a.k.a. JIM'ALE, Ahmad Nur Ali; a.k.a. JIM'ALE, Ahmed Nur Ali; a.k.a. JIMALE, Ahmad Ali; a.k.a. JUMALE, Ahmed Nur), Mogadishu, Somalia; P.O. Box 3312, Dubai, U.A.E. (individual) [SDGT] 11-07-01

KADI, Shaykh Yassin Abdullah (a.k.a. AL-QADI, Yasin; a.k.a. KAHDI, Yasin), Jeddah, Saudi Arabia (individual) [SDGT] 10-12-01

KAHDI, Yasin (a.k.a. AL-QADI, Yasin; a.k.a. KADI, Shaykh Yassin Abdullah), Jeddah, Saudi Arabia (individual) [SDGT] 10-12-01

KAHIE, Abdullahi Hussein, Bakara Market, Dar Salaam Buildings, Mogadishu, Somalia (individual) [SDGT] 11-07-01

KHABAR, Abu (a.k.a. GHAILANI, Ahmed Khalfan; a.k.a. "AHMED THE TANZANIAN;" a.k.a. "FOOPIE;" a.k.a. "FUPI;" a.k.a. AHMAD, Abu Bakr; a.k.a. AHMED, A.; a.k.a. AHMED, Abubakar; a.k.a. AHMED, Abubakar K.; a.k.a. AHMED, Abubakar Khalfan; a.k.a. AHMED, Abubakary K.; a.k.a. AHMED, Ahmed Khalfan; a.k.a. AL TANZANI, Ahmad; a.k.a. ALI, Ahmed Khalfan; a.k.a. BAKR, Abu; a.k.a. GHAILANI, Abubakary Khalfan Ahmed; a.k.a. GHAILANI, Ahmed; a.k.a. GHILANI, Ahmad Khalafan; a.k.a. HUSSEIN, Mahafudh Abubakar Ahmed Abdallah; a.k.a. KHALFAN, Ahmed; a.k.a. MOHAMMED, Shariff Omar); DOB 14 Mar 1974; alt. DOB

13 Apr 1974; alt. DOB 14 Apr 1974; alt. DOB 1 Aug 1970; POB Zanzibar, Tanzania; citizen Tanzania (individual) [SDGT] **10-12-01**

KHALFAN, Ahmed (a.k.a. GHAILANI, Ahmed Khalfan; a.k.a. "AHMED THE TANZANIAN;" a.k.a. "FOOPIE;" a.k.a. "FUPI;" a.k.a. AHMAD, Abu Bakr; a.k.a. AHMED, A.; a.k.a. AHMED, Abubakar; a.k.a. AHMED, Abubakar K.; a.k.a. AHMED, Abubakar Khalfan; a.k.a. AHMED, Abubakary K.; a.k.a. AHMED, Ahmed Khalfan; a.k.a. AL TANZANI, Ahmad; a.k.a. ALI, Ahmed Khalfan; a.k.a. BAKR, Abu; a.k.a. GHAILANI, Abubakary Khalfan Ahmed; a.k.a. GHAILANI, Ahmed; a.k.a. GHILANI, Ahmad Khalafan; a.k.a. HUSSEIN, Mahafudh Abubakar Ahmed Abdallah; a.k.a. KHABAR, Abu; a.k.a. MOHAMMED, Shariff Omar); DOB 14 Mar 1974; alt. DOB 13 Apr 1974; alt. DOB 14 Apr 1974; alt. DOB 1 Aug 1970; POB Zanzibar, Tanzania; citizen Tanzania (individual) [SDGT] **10-12-01**

KHALID (a.k.a. FADHIL, Mustafa Mohamed; a.k.a. AL MASRI, Abd Al Wakil; a.k.a. AL-NUBI, Abu; a.k.a. ALI, Hassan; a.k.a. ANIS, Abu; a.k.a. ELBISHY, Moustafa Ali; a.k.a. FADIL, Mustafa Muhamad; a.k.a. FAZUL, Mustafa; a.k.a. HUSSEIN; a.k.a. JIHAD, Abu; a.k.a. MAN, Nu; a.k.a. MOHAMMED, Mustafa; a.k.a. YUSSRR, Abu); DOB 23 Jun 1976; POB Cairo, Egypt; citizen Egypt; alt. citizen Kenya; Kenyan ID No. 12773667; Serial No. 201735161 (individual) [SDGT] **10-12-01**

LADEHYANOY, Mufti Rashid Ahmad (a.k.a. AHMAD, Mufti Rasheed; a.k.a. LUDHIANVI, Mufti Rashid Ahmad; a.k.a. WADEHYANOY, Mufti Rashid Ahmad), Karachi, Pakistan (individual) [SDGT] **10-12-01**

LUDHIANVI, Mufti Rashid Ahmad (a.k.a. AHMAD, Mufti Rasheed; a.k.a. LADEHYANOY, Mufti Rashid Ahmad; a.k.a. WADEHYANOY, Mufti Rashid Ahmad), Karachi, Pakistan (individual) [SDGT] **10-12-01**

LUQMAN, Abu (a.k.a. MOHAMMED, Fazul Abdullah; a.k.a. ABDALLA, Fazul; a.k.a. ADBALLAH, Fazul; a.k.a. AISHA, Abu; a.k.a. AL SUDANI, Abu Seif; a.k.a. ALI, Fadel Abdallah Mohammed; a.k.a. FAZUL, Abdalla; a.k.a. FAZUL, Abdallah; a.k.a. FAZUL, Abdallah Mohammed; a.k.a. FAZUL, Haroon; a.k.a. FAZUL, Harun; a.k.a. HAROON; a.k.a. HAROUN, Fadhil; a.k.a. HARUN; a.k.a. MOHAMMED, Fazul; a.k.a. MOHAMMED, Fazul Abdilahi; a.k.a. MOHAMMED, Fouad; a.k.a. MUHAMAD, Fadil Abdallah); DOB 25 Aug 1972; alt. DOB 25 Dec 1974; alt. DOB 25 Feb 1974; POB Moroni, Comoros Islands; citizen Comoros; alt. citizen Kenya (individual) [SDGT] **10-12-01**

MAHMOOD, Sultan Bashir-Ud-Din (a.k.a. MAHMOOD, Sultan Bashiruddin; a.k.a. MEHMOOD, Dr. Bashir Uddin; a.k.a. MEKMUD, Sultan Baishiruddin), Street 13, Wazir Akbar Khan, Kabul, Afghanistan; alt. DOB 1937; alt. DOB 1938; alt. DOB 1939; alt. DOB 1940; alt. DOB 1941; alt. DOB 1942; alt. DOB 1943; alt. DOB 1944; alt. DOB 1945; nationality Pakistani (individual) [SDGT] **[12-20-01]**

MAHMOOD, Sultan Bashiruddin (a.k.a. MAHMOOD, Sultan Bashir-Ud-Din; a.k.a. MEHMOOD, Dr. Bashir Uddin; a.k.a. MEKMUD, Sultan Baishiruddin), Street 13, Wazir Akbar Khan, Kabul, Afghanistan; alt. DOB 1937; alt. DOB 1938; alt. DOB 1939; alt. DOB 1940; alt. DOB 1941; alt. DOB 1942; alt. DOB 1943; alt. DOB 1944; alt. DOB 1945; nationality Pakistani (individual) [SDGT] **[12-20-01]**

MAJEED, Abdul (a.k.a. MAJEED, Chaudhry Abdul; a.k.a. MAJID, Abdul); DOB 13 Apr 1939; alt.DOB 1938; nationality Pakistani (individual) [SDGT] **[12-20-01]**

MAJEED, Chaudhry Abdul (a.k.a. MAJEED, Abdul; a.k.a. MAJID, Abdul); DOB 15 Apr 1939; alt. DOB 1938; nationality Pakistani (individual) [SDGT] **[12-20-01]**

MAJID, Abdul (a.k.a. MAJEED, Abdul; a.k.a. MAJEED Chaudhry Abdul); DOB 15 Apr 1939; alt. DOB 1938; nationality Pakistani (individual) [SDGT] **[12-20-01]**

MAN, Nu (a.k.a. FADHIL, Mustafa Mohamed; a.k.a. AL MASRI, Abd Al Wakil; a.k.a. AL-NUBI, Abu; a.k.a. ALI, Hassan; a.k.a. ANIS, Abu; a.k.a. ELBISHY, Moustafa Ali; a.k.a. FADIL, Mustafa Muhamad; a.k.a. FAZUL, Mustafa; a.k.a. HUSSEIN; a.k.a. JIHAD, Abu; a.k.a. KHALID; a.k.a. MOHAMMED, Mustafa; a.k.a. YUSSRR, Abu); DOB 23 Jun 1976; POB Cairo, Egypt; citizen Egypt; alt. citizen Kenya; Kenyan ID No. 12773667; Serial No. 201735161 (individual) [SDGT] **10-12-01**

MANSOUR, Mohamed (a.k.a. AL-MANSOUR, Dr. Mohamed), Ob. Heslibachstr. 20, Kusnacht, Switzerland; Zurich, Switzerland; DOB 1928; POB U.A.E.; alt. POB Egypt (individual) [SDGT] **11-07-01**

MANSOUR-FATTOUH, Zeinab, Zurich, Switzerland (individual) [SDGT] **11-07-01**

MEHMOOD, Dr. Bashir Uddin (a.k.a. MAHMOOD, Sultan Bashir-Ud-Din; a.k.a. MAHMOOD, Sultan Bashiruddin; a.k.a. MEKMUD, Sultan Baishiruddin), Street 13, Wazir Akbar Khan, Kabul, Afghanistan; alt. DOB 1937; alt. DOB 1938; alt. DOB 1939; alt. DOB 1940; alt. DOB 1941; alt. DOB 1942; alt. DOB 1943; alt. DOB 1944; alt. DOB 1945; nationality Pakistani (individual) [SDGT] **[12-20-01]**

MEKMUD, Sultan Baishiruddin (a.k.a. MAHMOOD, Sultan Bashir-Ud-Din; a.k.a. MAHMOOD, Sultan Bashiruddin; a.k.a. MEHMOOD, Dr. Bashir Uddin), Street 13, Wazir Akbar Khan, Kabul, Afghanistan; alt. DOB 1937; alt. DOB 1938; alt. DOB 1939; alt. DOB 1940; alt. DOB 1941; alt. DOB 1942; alt. DOB 1943; alt. DOB 1944; alt. DOB 1945; nationality Pakistani (individual) [SDGT] **[12-20-01]**

MOHAMMED, Fazul (a.k.a. MOHAMMED, Fazul Abdullah; a.k.a. ABDALLA, Fazul; a.k.a. ADBALLAH, Fazul; a.k.a. AISHA, Abu; a.k.a. AL SUDANI, Abu Seif; a.k.a. ALI, Fadel Abdallah Mohammed; a.k.a. FAZUL, Abdalla; a.k.a. FAZUL, Abdallah; a.k.a. FAZUL, Abdallah Mohammed; ak.a. FAZUL, Haroon; a.k.a. FAZUL, Harun; a.k.a. HAROON; a.k.a. HAROUN, Fadhil; a.k.a. HARUN; a.k.a. LUQMAN, Abu; a.k.a. MOHAMMED, Fazul Abdilahi; a.k.a. MOHAMMED, Fouad; a.k.a.

MUHAMAD, Fadil Abdallah); DOB 25 Aug 1972; alt. DOB 25 Dec 1974; alt. DOB 25 Feb 1974; POB Moroni, Comoros Islands; citizen Comoros; alt. citizen Kenya (individual) [SDGT] **10-12-01**

MOHAMMED, Fazul Abdilahi (a.k.a. MOHAMMED, Fazul Abdullah; a.k.a. ABDALLA, Fazul; a.k.a. ADBALLAH, Fazul; a.k.a. AISHA, Abu; a.k.a. AL SUDANI, Abu Seif; a.k.a. ALI, Fadel Abdallah Mohammed; a.k.a. FAZUL, Abdalla; a.k.a. FAZUL, Abdallah; a.k.a. FAZUL, Abdallah Mohammed; a.k.a. FAZUL, Haroon; a.k.a. FAZUL, Harun; a.k.a. HAROON; a.k.a. HAROUN, Fadhil; a.k.a. HARUN; a.k.a. LUQMAN, Abu; a.k.a. MOHAMMED, Fazul; a.k.a. MOHAMMED, Fouad; a.k.a. MUHAMAD, Fadil Abdallah); DOB 25 Aug 1972; alt. DOB 25 Dec 1974; alt. DOB 25 Feb 1974; POB Moroni, Comoros Islands; citizen Comoros; alt. citizen Kenya (individual) [SDGT] **10-12-01**

MOHAMMED, Fazul Abdullah (a.k.a. ABDALLA, Fazul; a.k.a. ADBALLAH, Fazul; a.k.a. AISHA, Abu; a.k.a. AL SUDANI, Abu Seif; a.k.a. ALI, Fadel Abdallah Mohammed; a.k.a. FAZUL, Abdalla; a.k.a. FAZUL, Abdallah; a.k.a. FAZUL, Abdallah Mohammed; a.k.a. FAZUL, Haroon; a.k.a. FAZUL, Harun; a.k.a. HAROON; a.k.a. HAROUN, Fadhil; a.k.a. HARUN; a.k.a. LUQMAN, Abu; a.k.a. MOHAMMED, Fazul; a.k.a. MOHAMMED, Fazul Abdilahi; a.k.a. MOHAMMED, Fouad; a.k.a. MUHAMAD, Fadil Abdallah); DOB 25 Aug 1972; alt. DOB 25 Dec 1974; alt. DOB 25 Feb 1974; POB Moroni, Comoros Islands; citizen Comoros; alt. citizen Kenya (individual) [SDGT] **10-12-01**

MOHAMMED, Fouad (a.k.a. MOHAMMED, Fazul Abdullah; a.k.a. ABDALLA, Fazul; a.k.a. ADBALLAH, Fazul; a.k.a. AISHA, Abu; a.k.a. AL SUDANI, Abu Seif; a.k.a. ALI, Fadel Abdallah Mohammed; a.k.a. FAZUL, Abdalla; a.k.a. FAZUL, Abdallah; a.k.a. FAZUL, Abdallah Mohammed; a.k.a. FAZUL, Haroon; a.k.a. FAZUL, Harun; a.k.a. HAROON; a.k.a. HAROUN, Fadhil; a.k.a. HARUN; a.k.a. LUQMAN, Abu; a.k.a. MOHAMMED, Fazul; a.k.a. MOHAMMED, Fazul Abdilahi; a.k.a. MUHAMAD, Fadil Abdallah); DOB 25 Aug 1972; alt. DOB 25 Dec 1974; alt. DOB 25 Feb 1974; POB Moroni, Comoros Islands; citizen Comoros; alt. citizen Kenya (individual) [SDGT] **10-12-01**

MOHAMMED, Khalid Shaikh (a.k.a. ALI, Salem; a.k.a. BIN KHALID, Fahd Bin Adballah; a.k.a. HENIN, Ashraf Refaat Nabith; a.k.a. WADOOD, Khalid Adbul); DOB 14 Apr 1965; alt. DOB 1 Mar 1964; POB Kuwait; citizen Kuwait (individual) [SDGT] **10-12-01**

MOHAMMED, Mustafa (a.k.a. FADHIL, Mustafa Mohamed; a.k.a. AL MASRI, Abd Al Wakil; a.k.a. AL-NUBI, Abu; a.k.a. ALI, Hassan; a.k.a. ANIS, Abu; a.k.a. ELBISHY, Moustafa Ali; a.k.a. FADIL, Mustafa Muhamad; a.k.a. FAZUL, Mustafa; a.k.a. HUSSEIN; a.k.a. JIHAD, Abu; a.k.a. KHALID; a.k.a. MAN, Nu; a.k.a. YUSSRR, Abu); DOB 23 Jun 1976; POB Cairo, Egypt;

citizen Egypt; alt. citizen Kenya; Kenyan ID No. 12773667; Serial No. 201735161 (individual) [SDGT] **10-12-01**

MOHAMMED, Shariff Omar (a.k.a. GHAILANI, Ahmed Khalfan; a.k.a. "AHMED THE TANZANIAN;" a.k.a. "FOOPIE;" a.k.a. "FUPI;" a.k.a. AHMAD, Abu Bakr; a.k.a. AHMED, A.; a.k.a. AHMED, Abubakar; a.k.a. AHMED, Abubakar K.; a.k.a. AHMED, Abubakar Khalfan; a.k.a. AHMED, Abubakary K.; a.k.a. AHMED, Ahmed Khalfan; a.k.a. AL TANZANI, Ahmad; a.k.a. ALI, Ahmed Khalfan; a.k.a. BAKR, Abu; a.k.a. GHAILANI, Abubakary Khalfan Ahmed; a.k.a. GHAILANI, Ahmed; a.k.a. GHILANI, Ahmad Khalafan; a.k.a. HUSSEIN, Mahafudh Abubakar Ahmed Abdallah; a.k.a. KHABAR, Abu; a.k.a. KHALFAN, Ahmed); DOB 14 Mar 1974; alt. DOB 13 Apr 1974; alt. DOB 14 Apr 1974; alt. DOB 1 Aug 1970; POB Zanzibar, Tanzania; citizen Tanzania (individual) [SDGT] **10-12-01**

MSALAM, Fahad Ally (a.k.a. MSALAM, Fahid Mohammed Ally; a.k.a. AL-KINI, Usama; a.k.a. ALLY, Fahid Mohammed; a.k.a. MSALAM, Fahid Mohammed Ali; a.k.a. MSALAM, Mohammed Ally; a.k.a. MUSALAAM, Fahid Mohammed Ali; a.k.a. SALEM, Fahid Muhamad Ali); DOB 19 Feb 1976; POB Mombasa, Kenya; citizen Kenya (individual) [SDGT] **10-12-01**

MSALAM, Fahid Mohammed Ali (a.k.a. MSALAM, Fahid Mohammed Ally; a.k.. AL-KINI, Usama; a.k.a. ALLY, Fahid Mohammed; a.k.a. MSALAM, Fahad Ally; a.k.a. MSALAM, Mohammed Ally; a.k.a. MUSALAAM, Fahid Mohammed Ali; a.k.a. SALEM, Fahid Muhamad Ali); DOB 19 Feb 1976; POB Mombasa, Kenya; citizen Kenya (individual) [SDGT] **10-12-01**

MSALAM, Fahid Mohammed Ally (a.k.a. AL-KINI, Usama; a.k.a. ALLY, Fahid Mohammed; a.k.a. MSALAM, Fahad Ally; a.k.a. MSALAM, Fahid Mohammed Ali; a.k.a. MSALAM, Mohammed Ally; a.k.a. MUSALAAM, Fahid Mohammed Ali; a.k.a. SALEM, Fahid Muhamad Ali); DOB 19 Feb 1976; POB Mombasa, Kenya; citizen Kenya (individual) [SDGT] **10-12-01**

MSALAM, Mohammed Ally (a.k.a. MSALAM, Fahid Mohammed Ally; a.k.a. AL-KINI, Usama; a.k.a. ALLY, Fahid Mohammed; a.k.a. MSALAM, Fahad Ally; a.k.a. MSALAM, Fahid Mohammed Ali; a.k.a. MUSALAAM, Fahid Mohammed Ali; a.k.a. SALEM, Fahid Muhamad Ali); DOB 19 Feb 1976; POB Mombasa, Kenya; citizen Kenya (individual) [SDGT] **10-12-01**

MUGHNIYAH, Imad Fayiz (a.k.a. MUGHNIYAH, Imad Fa'iz); Senior Intelligence Officer of HIZBALLAH; DOB 07 Dec 1962; POB Tayr Dibba, Lebanon; Passport No. 432298 (Lebanon) (individual) [SDT] [SDGT] **10-12-01**

MUGHNIYAH, Imad Fa'iz (a.k.a. MUGHNIYAH, Imad Fayiz); Senior Intelligence Officer of HIZBALLAH; DOB 07 Dec 1962; POB Tayr Dibba, Lebanon; Passport No. 432298 (Lebanon) (inividual) [SDT] [SDGT] **10-12-01**

MUHAMAD, Fadil Abdallah (a.k.a. MOHAMMED, Fazul Abdullah; a.k.a. ABDALLA, Fazul; a.k.a. ADBALLAH, Fazul; a.k.a. AISHA, Abu; a.k.a. AL

SUDANI, Abu Seif; a.k.a. ALI, Fadel Abdallah Mohammed; a.k.a. FAZUL, Abdalla; a.k.a. FAZUL, Abdallah; a.k.a. FAZUL, Abdallah Mohammed; a.k.a. FAZUL, Haroon; a.k.a. FAZUL, Harun; a.k.a. HAROON; a.k.a. HAROUN, Fadhil; a.k.a. HARUN; a.k.a. LUQMAN, Abu; a.k.a. MOHAMMED, Fazul; a.k.a. MOHAMMED, Fazul Abdilahi; a.k.a. MOHAMMED, Fouad); DOB 25 Aug 1972; alt. DOB 25 Dec 1974; alt. DOB 25 Feb 1974; POB Moroni, Comoros Islands; citizen Comoros; alt. citizen Kenya (individual) [SDGT] **10-12-01**

MUSALAAM, Fahid Mohammed Ali (a.k.a. MSALAM, Fahid Mohammed Ally; a.k.a. AL-KINI, Usama; a.k.a. ALLY, Fahid Mohammed; a.k.a. MSALAM, Fahad Ally; a.k.a. MSALAM, Fahid Mohammed Ali; a.k.a. MSALAM, Mohammed Ally; a.k.a. SALEM, Fahid Muhamad Ali); DOB 19 Feb 1976; POB Mombasa, Kenya; citizen Kenya (individual) [SDGT] **10-12-01**

NADA, Youssef (a.k.a. NADA, Youssef M.; a.k.a. NADA, Youssef Mustafa), Via Arogno 32, Campione d'Italia 6911, Italy; Via Riasc 4, Campione d'Italia 6911, Switzerland; Via Per Arogno 32, Campione d'Italia CH-6911, Switzerland; DOB 17 May 1931; alt. DOB 17 May 1937; POB Alexandria, Egypt; citizen Tunisia (individual) [SDGT] **11-07-01**

NADA, Youssef M. (a.k.a. NADA, Youssef; a.k.a. NADA, Youssef Mustafa), Via Arogno 32, Campione d'Italia 6911, Italy; Via Riasc 4, Campione d'Italia 6911, Switzerland; Via Per Arogno 32, Campione d'Italia CH-6911, Switzerland; DOB 17 May 1931; alt. DOB 17 May 1937; POB Alexandria, Egypt; citizen Tunisia (individual) [SDGT] **11-07-01**

NADA, Youssef Mustafa (a.k.a. NADA, Youssef; a.k.a. NADA, Youssef M.), Via Arogno 32, Campione d'Italia 6911, Italy; Via Riasc 4, Campione d'Italia 6911, Switzerland; Via Per Arogno 32, Campione d'Italia CH-6911, Switzerland; DOB 17 May 1931; alt. DOB 17 May 1937; POB Alexandria, Egypt; citizen Tunisia (individual) [SDGT] **11-07-01**

NOR, Garad K. (a.k.a. JAMA, Garad; a.k.a. WASRSAME, Fartune Ahmed), 2100 Bloomington Ave., Minneapolis, Minnesota, U.S.A.; 1806 Riverside Ave., 2nd Floor, Minneapolis, Minnesota, U.S.A.; 26 Jun 1974 (individual) [SDGT] **11-07-01**

SA-ID (a.k.a. IZZ-AL-DIN, Hasan; a.k.a. GARBAYA, AHMED; a.k.a. SALWWAN, Samir), Lebanon; DOB 1963; POB Lebanon; citizen Lebanon (individual) [SDGT] **10-12-01**

SAIYID, Abd Al-Man'am (a.k.a. AGHA, Haji Abdul Manan), Pakistan (individual) [SDGT] **10-12-01**

SAI'ID, Shaykh (a.k.a. AHMAD, Mustafa Muhammad) (POB Egypt) (individual) [SDGT] **09-24-01**

SALAH, Muhammad (a.k.a. HASANAYN, Nasr Fahmi Nasr) (individual) [SDGT] **09-24-01**

SALEH (a.k.a. ABDULLAH, Abdullah Ahmed; a.k.a. ABU MARIAM; a.k.a. AL-MASRI, Abu Mohamed), Afghanistan; DOB 1963; POB Egypt; citizen Egypt (individual) [SDGT] 10-12-01

SALEM, Fahid Muhamad Ali (a.k.a. MSALAM, Fahid Mohammed Ally; a.k.a. AL-KINI, Usama; a.k.a. ALLY, Fahid Mohammed; a.k.a. MSALAM Fahad Ally; a.k.a. MSALAM, Fahid Mohammed Ali; a.k.a. MSALAM, Mohammed Ally; a.k.a. MUSALAAM, Fahid Mohammed Ali); DOB 19 Feb 1976; POB Mombasa, Kenya; citizen Kenya (individual) [SDGT] 10-12-01

SALIM, Ahmad Fuad (a.k.a. AL ZAWAHIRI, Dr. Ayman; a.k.a. AL-ZAWAHIRI, Aiman Muhammad Rabi; a.k.a. AL-ZAWAHIRI, Ayman), Operational and Military Leader of JIHAD GROUP; DOB 19 Jun 1951; POB Giza, Egypt; Passport No. 1084010 (Egypt); Alt No. 19820215 (individual) [SDT] [SDGT] 09-24-01

SALIM, Hassan Rostom (a.k.a. ATWA, Ali; a.k.a. BOUSLIM, Ammar Mansour), Lebanon; DOB 1960; POB Lebanon; citizen Lebanon (individual) [SDGT] 10-12-01

SALWWAN, Samir (a.k.a. IZZ-AL-DIN, Hasan; a.k.a. GARBAYA, AHMED; a.k.a. SA-ID), Lebanon; DOB 1963; POB Lebanon; citizen Lebanon (individual) [SDGT] 10-12-01

SHIEB, Ahmed (a.k.a. ALI, Ahmed Mohammed Hamed; a.k.a. ABDUREHMAN, Ahmed Mohammed; a.k.a. ABU FATIMA; a.k.a. ABU ISLAM; a.k.a. ABU KHADIIJAH; a.k.a. AHMED HAMED; a.k.a. Ahmed The Egyptian; a.k.a. AHMED, Ahmed; a.k.a. AL-MASRI, Ahmad; a.k.a. AL-SURIR, Abu Islam; a.k.a. ALI, Ahmed Mohammed; a.k.a. ALI, Hamed; a.k.a. HEMED, Ahmed; a.k.a. SHUAIB), Afghanistan; DOB 1965; POB Egypt; citizen Egypt (individual) [SDGT] 10-12-01

SHIHATA, Thirwat Salah (a.k.a. ABDALLAH, Tarwat Salah; a.k.a. THIRWAT, Salah Shihata; a.k.a. THIRWAT, Shahata); DOB 29 Jun 60; POB Egypt (individual) [SDGT] 09-24-01

SHUAIB (a.k.a. ALI, Ahmed Mohammed Hamed; a.k.a. ABDUREHMAN, Ahmed Mohammed; a.k.a. ABU FATIMA; a.k.a. ABU ISLAM; a.k.a. ABU KHADIIJAH; a.k.a. AHMED HAMED; a.k.a. Ahmed The Egyptian; a.k.a. AHMED, Ahmed; a.k.a. AL-MASRI, Ahmad; a.k.a. AL-SURIR, Abu Islam; a.k.a. ALI, Ahmed Mohammed; a.k.a. ALI, Hamed; a.k.a. HEMED, Ahmed; a.k.a. SHIEB, Ahmed), Afghanistan; DOB 1965; POB Egypt; citizen Egypt (individual) [SDGT] 10-12-01

SLAHI, Mahamedou Ould (a.k.a. ABU HAFS THE MAURITANIAN; a.k.a. AL-SHANQITI, Khalid; a.k.a. AL-WALID, Mafouz Walad; a.k.a. AL-WALID, Mahfouz Ould); DOB 1 Jan 75 (individual) [SDGT] 09-24-01

SUWEIDAN, Sheikh Ahmad Salem (a.k.a. SWEDAN, Sheikh Ahmed Salim; a.k.a. Ahmed the Tall; a.k.a. ALLY, Ahmed; a.k.a. BAHAMAD; a.k.a. BAHAMAD, Sheik; a.k.a. BAHAMADI, Sheikh; a.k.a. SWEDAN, Sheikh;

a.k.a. SWEDAN, Sheikh Ahmed Salem); DOB 9 Apr 1969; alt. DOB 9 Apr 1960; POB Mombasa, Kenya; citizen Kenya (individual) [SDGT] **10-12-01**

SWEDAN, Sheikh (a.k.a. SWEDAN, Sheikh Ahmed Salim; a.k.a. Ahmed the Tall; a.k.a. ALLY, Ahmed; a.k.a. BAHAMAD; a.k.a. BAHAMAD, Sheik; a.k.a. BAHAMADI, Sheikh; a.k.a. SUWEIDAN, Sheikh Ahmad Salem; a.k.a. SWEDAN, Sheikh Ahmed Salem); DOB 9 Apr 1969; alt. DOB 9 Apr 1960; POB Mombasa, Kenya; citizen Kenya (individual) [SDGT] **10-12-01**

SWEDAN, Sheikh Ahmed Salem (a.k.a. SWEDAN, Sheikh Ahmed Salim; a.k.a. Ahmed the Tall; a.k.a. ALLY, Ahmed; a.k.a. BAHAMAD; a.k.a. BAHAMAD, Sheik; a.k.a. BAHAMADI, Sheikh; a.k.a. SUWEIDAN, Sheikh Ahmad Salem; a.k.a. SWEDAN, Sheikh); DOB 9 Apr 1969; alt. DOB 9 Apr 1960; POB Mombasa, Kenya; citizen Kenya (individual) [SDGT] **10-12-01**

SWEDAN, Sheikh Ahmed Salim (a.k.a. Ahmed the Tall; a.k.a. ALLY, Ahmed; a.k.a. BAHAMAD; a.k.a. BAHAMAD, Sheik; a.k.a. BAHAMADI, Sheikh; a.k.a. SUWEIDAN, Sheikh Ahmad Salem; a.k.a. SWEDAN, Sheikh; a.k.a. SWEDAN, Sheikh Ahmed Salem); DOB 9 Apr 1969; alt. DOB 9 Apr 1960; POB Mombasa, Kenya; citizen Kenya (individual) [SDGT] **10-12-01**

TAHA, Abdul Rahman S. (a.k.a. YASIN, Abdul Rahman; a.k.a. TAHER, Abdul Rahman S.; a.k.a. YASIN, Abdul Rahman Said; a.k.a. YASIN, Aboud); DOB 10 Apr 1960; POB Bloomingon, Indiana U.S.A.; SSN 156-92-9858 (U.S.A.); Passport No. 27082171 (U.S.A. [issued 21 Jun 1992 in Amman, Jordan]); alt. Passport No. M0887925 (Iraq); citizen U.S.A. (individual) [SDGT] **10-12-01**

TAHER, Abdul Rahman S. (a.k.a. YASIN, Abdul Rahman; a.k.a. TAHA, Abdul Rahman S.; a.k.a. YASIN, Abdul Rahman Said; a.k.a. YASIN, Aboud); DOB 10 Apr 1960; POB Bloomington, Indiana U.S.A.; SSN 156-92-9858 (U.S.A.); Passport No. 27082171 (U.S.A. [issued 21 Jun 1992 in Amman, Jordan]); alt. Passport No. M0887925 (Iraq); citizen U.S.A. (individual) [SDGT] **10-12-01**

TAKFIRI, Abu #Umr (a.k.a. ABU ISMAIL; a.k.a. ABU UMAR, Abu Omar; a.k.a. AL-FILISTINI, Abu Qatada; a.k.a. UMAR, Abu Umar; a.k.a. UTHMAN, Al-Samman; a.k.a. UTHMAN, Omar Mahmoud; a.k.a. UTHMAN, Umar), London, England; DOB 30 Dec 1960; alt. DOB 13 Dec 1960 (individual) [SDGT] **10-12-01**

TARIQ (a.k.a. ABU ZUBAYDAH; a.k.a. ABU ZUBAIDA; a.k.a. AL-WAHAB, Abd Al-Hadi; a.k.a. HUSAIN, Zain Al-Abidin Muhahhad; a.k.a. HUSAYN, Zayn al-Abidin Muhammad); DOB 12 Mar 71; POB Riyadh, Saudi Arabia (individual) [SDGT] **09-24-01**

TAYSIR (a.k.a. AL-MASRI, Abu Hafs; a.k.a. ABDULLAH, Sheikh Taysir; a.k.a. ABU HAFS; a.k.a. ABU SITTA, Subhi; a.k.a. ATEF, Muhammad; a.k.a. ATIF, Mohamed; a.k.a. ATIF, Muhammad; a.k.a. EL KHABIR, Abu Hafs el Masry); DOB 1951; Alt. DOB 1956; Alt. DOB 1944; POB Alexandria, Egypt (individual) [SDT] [SDGT] **09-24-01**

THIRWAT, Salah Shihata (a.k.a. SHIHATA, Thirwat Salah; a.k.a. ABDALLAH, Tarwat Salah; a.k.a. THIRWAT, Shahata); DOB 29 Jun 60; POB Egypt (individual) [SDGT] 09-24-01

THIRWAT, Shahata (a.k.a. SHIHATA, Thirwat Salah; a.k.a. ABDALLAH, Tarwat Salah; a.k.a. THIRWAT, Salah Shihata); DOB 29 Jun 60; POB Egypt (individual) [SDGT] 09-24-01

TUFAIL, Mohammed (a.k.a. TUFAIL, S.M.; a.k.a. TUFAIL, Sheik Mohammed); nationality Pakistani (individual) [SDGT] [12-20-01]

TUFAIL, S.M. (a.k.a. TUFAIL, Mohammed; a.k.a. TUFAIL, Sheik Mohammed); nationality Pakistani (individual) [SDGT] [12-20-01]

TUFAIL, Sheik Mohammed (a.k.a. TUFAIL, Mohammed; a.k.a. TUFAIL, S.M.); nationality Pakistani (individual) [SDGT] [12-20-01]

UL-HAQ, Dr. Amin (a.k.a. AH HAQ, Dr. Amin; a.k.a. AL-HAQ, Amin; a.k.a. AMIN, Muhammad); DOB 1960; POB Nangahar Province, Afghanistan (individual) [SDGT] 10-12-01

UMAR, Abu Umar (a.k.a. ABU ISMAIL; a.k.a. ABU UMAR, Abu Omar; a.k.a. AL-FILISTINI, Abu Qatada; a.k.a. TAKFIRI, Abu #Umr; a.k.a. UTHMAN, Al-Samman; a.k.a. UTHMAN, Omar Mahmoud; a.k.a. UTHMAN, Umar), London, England; DOB 30 Dec 1960; DOB 13 Dec 1960 (individual) [SDGT] 10-12-01

UTHMAN, Al-Samman (a.k.a. ABU ISMAIL; a.k.a. ABU UMAR, Abu Omar; a.k.a. AL-FILISTINI, Abu Qatada; a.k.a. TAKFIRI, Abu #Umr; a.k.a. UMAR, Abu Umar; a.k.a. UTHMAN, Omar Mahmoud; a.k.a. UTHMAN, Umar), London, England; DOB 30 Dec 1960; DOB 13 Dec 1960 (individual) [SDGT] 10-12-01

UTHMAN, Omar Mahmoud (a.k.a. ABU ISMAIL; a.k.a. ABU UMAR, Abu Omar; a.k.a. AL-FILISTINI, Abu Qatada; a.k.a. TAKFIRI, Abu #Umr; a.k.a. UMAR, Abu Umar; a.k.a. UTHMAN, Al-Samman; a.k.a. UTHMAN, Umar), London, England; DOB 30 Dec 1960; DOB 13 Dec 1960 (individual) [SDGT] 10-12-01

UTHMAN, Umar (a.k.a. ABU ISMAIL; a.k.a. ABU UMAR, Abu Omar; a.k.a. AL-FILISTINI, Abu Qatada; a.k.a. TAKFIRI, Abu #Umr; a.k.a. UMAR, Abu Umar; a.k.a. UTHMAN, Al-Samman; a.k.a. UTHMAN, Omar Mahmoud), London, England; DOB 30 Dec 1960; DOB 13 Dec 1960 (individual) [SDGT] 10-12-01

WADEHYANOY, Mufti Rashid Ahmad (a.k.a. AHMAD, Mufti Rasheed; a.k.a. LADEHYANOY, Mufti Rashid Ahmad; a.k.a. LUDHIANVI, Mufti Rashid Ahmad), Karachi, Pakistan (individual) [SDGT] 10-12-01

WADOOD, Khalid Adbul (a.k.a. OHAMMED, Khalid Shaikh; a.k.a. ALI, Salem; a.k.a. BIN KHALID, Fahd Bin Adballah; a.k.a. HENIN, Ashraf Refaat Nabith); DOB 14 Apr 1965; alt. DOB 1 Mar 1964; POB Kuwait; citizen Kuwait (individual) [SDGT] 10-12-01

WASRSAME, Fartune Ahmed (a.k.a. JAMA, Garad; a.k.a. NOR, Garad K.), 2100 Bloomington Ave., Minneapolis, Minnesota, U.S.A.; 1806 Riverside Ave., 2nd Floor, Minneapolis, Minnesota, U.S.A.; 26 Jun 1974 (individual) [SDGT] **11-07-01**

YASIN, Abdul Rahman (a.k.a. TAHA, Abdul Rahman S.; a.k.a. TAHER, Abdul Rahman S.; a.k.a. YASIN, Abdul Rahman Said; a.k.a. YASIN, Aboud); DOB 10 Apr 1960; POB Bloomington, Indiana U.S.A.; SSN 156-92-9858 (U.S.A.); Passport No. 27082171 (U.S.A. [issued 21 Jun 1992 in Amman, Jordan]); alt. Passport No. M0887925 (Iraq); citizen U.S.A. (individual) [SDGT] **10-12-01**

YASIN, Abdul Rahman Said (a.k.a. YASIN, Abdul Rahman; a.k.a. TAHA, Abdul Rahman S.; a.k.a. TAHER, Abdul Rahman S.; a.k.a. YASIN, Aboud); DOB 10 Apr 1960; POB Bloomington, Indiana U.S.A.; SSN 156-92-9858 (U.S.A.); Passport No. 27082171 (U.S.A. [issued 21 Jun 1992 in Amman, Jordan]); alt. Passport No. M0887925 (Iraq); citizen U.S.A. (individual) [SDGT] **10-12-01**

YASIN, Aboud (a.k.a. YASIN, Abdul Rahman; a.k.a. TAHA, Abdul Rahman S.; a.k.a. TAHER, Abdul Rahman S.; a.k.a. YASIN, Abdul Rahman Said); DOB 10 Apr 1960; POB Bloomington, Indiana U.S.A.; SSN 156-92-9858 (U.S.A.); Passport No. 27082171 (U.S.A. [issued 21 Jun 1992 in Amman, Jordan]); alt. Passport No. M0887925 (Iraq); citizen U.S.A. (individual) [SDGT] **10-12-01**

YULDASHEV, Takhir (a.k.a. YULDASHEV, Tohir), Uzbekistan (individual) [SDGT] **10-12-01**

YULDASHEV, Tohir (a.k.a. YULDASHEV, Takhir), Uzbekistan (individual) [SDGT] **10-12-01**

YUSSRR, Abu (a.k.a. FADHIL, Mustafa Mohamed; a.k.a. AL MASRI, Abd Al Wakil; a.k.a. AL-NUBI, Abu; a.k.a. ALI, Hassan; a.k.a. ANIS, Abu; a.k.a. ELBISHY, Moustafa Ali; a.k.a. FADIL, Mustafa Muhamad; a.k.a. FAZUL, Mustafa; a.k.a. HUSSEIN; a.k.a. JIHAD, Abu; a.k.a. KHALID; a.k.a. MAN, Nu; a.k.a. MOHAMMED, Mustafa); DOB 23 Jun 1976; POB Cairo, Egypt; citizen Egypt; alt. citizen Kenya; Kenyan ID No. 12773667; Serial No. 201735161 (individual) [SDGT] **10-12-01**

ZIA, Ahmad (a.k.a. ZIA, Mohammad), c/o Ahmed Shah s/o Painda Mohammad al-Karim Set, Peshawar, Pakistan; c/o Alam General Store Shop 17, Awami Market, Peshawar, Pakistan; c/o Zahir Shah s/o Murad Khan Ander Sher, Peshawar, Pakistan (individual) [SDGT] **10-12-01**

ZIA, Mohammad (a.k.a. ZIA, Ahmad), c/o Ahmed Shah s/o Painda Mohammad al-Karim Set, Peshawar, Pakistan; c/o Alam General Store Shop 17, Awami Market, Peshawar, Pakistan; c/o Zahir Shah s/o Murad Khan Ander Sher, Peshawar, Pakistan (individual) [SDGT] **10-12-01**

TERRORISM SANCTIONS REGULATIONS

On January 23, 1995, pursuant to the International Emergency Economic Powers Act, 50 U.S.C. 1701-06 ("IEEPA"), President Clinton signed Executive Order 12947, "Prohibiting Transactions with Terrorists Who Threaten to Disrupt the Middle East Peace Process." The Order blocked all property subject to U.S. jurisdiction in which there is any interest of 12 Middle East terrorist organizations included in an Annex to the Order. On August 20, 1998, the President signed Executive Order 13099 to amend Executive Order 12947, adding additional names. Executive Order 12947 blocks the property and interests in property of persons designated by the Secretary of State, in coordination with the Secretary of the Treasury and the Attorney General, who are found (1) to have committed or to pose a significant risk of disrupting the Middle East peace process, or (2) to assist in, sponsor or provide financial, material, or technological support for, or services in support of, such acts of violence. The Order further blocks all property and interests in property subject to U.S. jurisdiction in which there is any interest of persons determined by the Secretary of the Treasury, in coordination with the Secretary of State and the Attorney General, to be owned or controlled by, or to act for or on behalf of any other person designated pursuant to the Order (collectively "Specially Designated Terrorists" or "SDTs"), designated by an "[SDT]" on OFAC's SDN list. The Order prohibits any transaction or dealing by a United States person or within the United States in property or interests in property of SDTs, including the making or receiving of any contribution of funds, goods, or services to or for the benefit of such persons.

Blockings must be reported within 10 days by fax to OFAC's Compliance Programs Division at 202/622-1657. Blocked accounts must be interest-bearing, at rates similar to those currently offered other depositors on deposits of comparable size and maturity. Maturities on blocked accounts may not exceed 90 days. Debits to blocked customer accounts are prohibited, although credits are authorized.

Corporate criminal penalties for violations of IEEPA range up to $500,000; individual penalties range up to $250,000 and/or 10 years in jail. Civil penalties of up to $11,000 may also be imposed administratively.

TERRORISM LIST GOVERNMENTS SANCTIONS REGULATIONS

On April 24, 1996, President Clinton signed into law the Antiterrorism and Effective Death Penalty Act of 1996, Public Law 104-132, 110 Stat. 1214-1319. Section 321 of the Act makes it a criminal offense for U.S. persons, except as provided in regulations issued by the Secretary of the Treasury in consultation with the Secretary of State, to engage in financial transactions with the governments of countries designated under section 6(j) of the Export Administration Act of 1979, 50 U.S.C. App. 2405, as supporting international terrorism. U.S. persons who engage in such transactions are subject to criminal penalties under title 18, United States Code. In implementation of section 321, the Treasury Department has issued the Terrorism List Governments Sanctions Regulations.

The countries currently designated under section 6(j) of the Export Administration Act are Cuba, Iran, Iraq, Libya, North Korea, Sudan, and Syria. The provisions of existing OFAC regulations governing Cuba, Iran, Iraq, Libya, North Korea, and Sudan continue in effect with the added authority of section 321. Financial transactions of U.S. persons with the governments of those six countries are governed by the separate parts of Title 31 Chapter V of the U.S. Code of Federal Regulations imposing economic sanctions on those countries and information about those programs is available in separate OFAC brochures.

Regarding the governments of countries designated under section 6(j) that are not otherwise subject to economic sanctions administered by OFAC, at present the government of Syria, the Terrorism List Governments Sanctions Regulations prohibit U.S. persons from receiving unlicensed donations and from engaging in financial transactions with respect to which the U.S. person knows or has reasonable cause to believe that the financial transaction poses a risk of furthering terrorist acts in the United States. Banks located in the United States and U.S. banks located offshore must reject transfers in the form of gifts or charitable contributions from the government of Syria, or from entities owned or controlled by the government of Syria, unless the bank knows or has reasonable cause to believe that the transaction poses a risk of furthering terrorism in the United States, in which case the funds must be retained by the bank. Banks should immediately notify OFAC Compliance about any retained items. Reject items must be reported within 10 business days of rejection. For the purposes of this program only, a financial transaction not originated by the government of Syria (including its central bank and government owned-or-controlled banks acting for their own accounts), but transferred to the United States *through* one of those banks, is not considered to be a prohibited financial transaction with the government of Syria.

FOREIGN TERRORIST ORGANIZATIONS SANCTIONS REGULATIONS

Section 302 of the Antiterrorism and Effective Death Penalty Act of 1996 also authorizes the Secretary of State to designate organizations as "Foreign Terrorist Organizations" ("FTOs"). The Act makes it a criminal offense for U.S. persons to provide material support or resources to FTOs and requires financial institutions to block all funds in which FTOs or their agents have an interest. The term "financial institutions" comes from 31 U.S.C. 5312(a)(2) and is defined very broadly. Among the types of businesses covered by Treasury's Foreign Terrorist Organizations Sanctions Regulations, which implement Sections 302 and 303 of the Act, are banks, securities and commodities broker/dealers, investment companies, currency exchanges, issuers, redeemers, and cashiers of traveler's checks, checks, money orders, or similar instruments, credit card system operators, insurance companies, dealers in precious metals, stones or jewels, pawnbrokers, loan and finance companies, travel agencies, licensed money transmitters, telegraph companies, businesses engaged in vehicle sales, including automobile, airplane or boat sales, persons involved in real estate closings or settlements, and casinos. Such "financial institutions" must notify OFAC Compliance about any blocked funds within ten days of blocking. The Act provides for civil penalties to be assessed against financial institutions for failing to block or report the blocking of FTO funds in an amount equal to $50,000 per violation or twice the amount which ought to have been blocked or reported, whichever is greater. Foreign Terrorist Organizations and their agents are identified by an "[FTO]" on OFAC's SDN list.

Other Named Terrorist Entities

DEMOCRATIC FRONT FOR THE LIBERATION OF PALESTINE (a.k.a. DEMOCRATIC FRONT FOR THE LIBERATION OF PALESTINE—HAWATMEH FACTION; a.k.a. DFLP; a.k.a. RED STAR FORCES; a.k.a. RED STAR BATTALIONS) [SDT]

DEMOCRATIC FRONT FOR THE LIBERATION OF PALESTINE—HAWATMEH FACTION (a.k.a. DEMOCRATIC FRONT FOR THE LIBERATION OF PALESTINE; a.k.a. DFLP; a.k.a. RED STAR FORCES; a.k.a. RED STAR BATTALIONS) [SDT]

DFLP (a.k.a. DEMOCRATIC FRONT FOR THE LIBERATION OF PALESTINE; a.k.a. DEMOCRATIC FRONT FOR THE LIBERATION OF PALESTINE - HAWATMEH FACTION; a.k.a. RED STAR FORCES; a.k.a. RED STAR BATTALIONS) [SDT]

NATIONAL COUNCIL OF RESISTANCE OF IRAN (a.k.a. MUJAHEDIN-E KHALQ ORGANIZATION; a.k.a. MEK; a.k.a. MKO; a.k.a. MUJAHEDIN-E KHALQ; a.k.a. NATIONAL COUNCIL OF RESISTANCE (NCR); a.k.a. NCRI; a.k.a. NLA; a.k.a. ORGANIZATION OF THE PEOPLE'S HOLY WARRIORS OF IRAN; a.k.a. PEOPLE'S MUJAHEDIN ORGANIZATION OF IRAN; a.k.a. PMOI; a.k.a. SAZEMAN-E MUJAHEDIN-E KHALQ-E IRAN; a.k.a. THE NATIONAL LIBERATION ARMY OF IRAN) [FTO]

NCRI (a.k.a. MUJAHEDIN-E KHALQ ORGANIZATION; a.k.a. MEK; a.k.a. MKO; a.k.a. MUJAHEDIN-E KHALQ; a.k.a. NATIONAL CONCIL OF RESISTANCE (NCR); a.k.a. NATIONAL COUNCIL OF RESISTANCE OF IRAN; a.k.a. NLA; a.k.a. ORGANIZATION OF THE PEOPLE'S HOLY WARRIORS OF IRAN; a.k.a. PEOPLE'S MUJAHEDIN ORGANIZATION

OF IRAN; a.k.a. PMOI; a.k.a. SAZEMAN-E MUJAHEDIN-E KHALQ-E IRAN; a.k.a. THE NATIONAL LIBERATION ARMY OF IRAN) [FTO]

RED STAR BATTALIONS (a.k.a. DEMOCRATIC FRONT FOR THE LIBERATION OF PALESTINE; a.k.a. DFLP; a.k.a. RED STAR FORCES; a.k.a. DEMOCRATIC FRONT FOR THE LIBERATION OF PALESTINE—HAWATMEH FACTION) [SDT]

RED STAR FORCES (a.k.a. DEMOCRATIC FRONT FOR THE LIBERATION OF PALESTINE; a.k.a. DFLP; a.k.a. DEMOCRATIC FRONT FOR THE LIBERATION OF PALESTINE—HAWATMEH FACTION; a.k.a. RED STAR BATTALIONS) [SDT]

Other Named Individuals

'ABD-AL-'IZ (a.k.a. ABD-AL-WAHAB, Abd-al-Hai Ahmad; a.k.a. ABU YASIR; a.k.a. 'ABD ALLAH, 'Issam 'Ali Muhammad; a.k.a. AL-KAMEL, Salah 'Ali; a.k.a. MUSA, Rifa'i Ahmad Taha; a.k.a. TAHA, Rifa'i Ahmad; a.k.a. TAHA MUSA, Rifa'i Ahmad; a.k.a. THABIT 'IZ); DOB 24 Jun 1954; POB Egypt; Passport No. 83860 (Sudan), 30455 (Egypt), 1046403 (Egypt) (individual) [SDT]

'ABD ALLAH, 'Issam 'Ali Muhammad (a.k.a. 'ABD-AL-'IZ; a.k.a. ABD-AL-WAHAB, Abd-al-Hai Ahmad; a.k.a. ABU YASIR; a.k.a. AL-KAMEL, Salah 'Ali; a.k.a. MUSA, Rifa'i Ahmad Taha; a.k.a. TAHA, Rifa'i Ahmad; a.k.a. TAHA MUSA, Rifa'i Ahmad; a.k.a. THABIT 'IZ); DOB 24 Jun 1954; POB Egypt; Passport No. 83860 (Sudan), 30455 (Egypt), 1046403 (Egypt) (individual) [SDT]

ABBAS, Abu (a.k.a. ZAYDAN, Muhammad); Director of PALESTINE LIBERATION FRONT—ABU ABBAS FACTION; DOB 10 Dec 1948 (individual) [SDT]

ABD-AL-WAHAB, Abd-al-Hai Ahmad (a.k.a. 'ABD-AL-'IZ; a.k.a. ABU YASIR; a.k.a. 'ABD ALLAH, 'Issam 'Ali Muhammad; a.k.a. AL-KAMEL, Salah 'Ali; a.k.a. MUSA, Rifa' Ahmad Taha; a.k.a. TAHA, Rifa'i Ahmad; a.k.a. TAHA MUSA, Rifa'i Ahmad; a.k.a. THABIT 'IZ); DOB 24 Jun 1954; POB Egypt; Passport No. 83860 (Sudan), 30455 (Egypt), 1046403 (Egypt) (individual) [SDT]

ABDALLAH, Ramadan (a.k.a. ABDULLAH, Dr. Ramadan; a.k.a. SHALLAH, Dr. Ramadan Abdullah; a.k.a. SHALLAH, Ramadan Abdalla Mohamed), Damascus, Syria; Secretary General of the PALESTINIAN ISLAMIC JIHAD; DOB 01 Jan 1958; POB Gaza City, Gaza Strip; SSN 589-17-6824 (U.S.A.); Passport No. 265 216 (Egypt) (individual) [SDT]

ABDULLAH, Dr. Ramadan (a.k.a. ABDALLAH, Ramadan; a.k.a. SHALLAH, Dr. Ramadan Abdullah; a.k.a. SHALLAH, Ramadan Abdalla Mohamed), Damascus, Syria; Secretary General of the PALESTINIAN

ISLAMIC JIHAD; DOB 01 Jan 1958; POB Gaza City, Gaza Strip; SSN 589-17-6824 (U.S.A.); Passport No. 265 216 (Egypt) (individual) [SDT]

ABU YASIR (a.k.a. 'ABD-AL-'IZ; a.k.a. ABD-AL-WAHAB, Abd-al-Hai Ahmad; a.k.a. 'ABD ALLAH, 'Issam 'Ali Muhammad; a.k.a. AL-KAMEL, Salah 'Ali; a.k.a. MUSA, Rifa'i Ahmad Taha; a.k.a. TAHA, Rifa'i Ahmad; a.k.a. TAHA MUSA, Rifa'i Ahmad; a.k.a. THABIT 'IZ); DOB 24 Jun 1954; POB Egypt; Passport No. 83860 (Sudan), 30455 (Egypt), 1046403 (Egypt) (individual) [SDT]

ABU MARZOOK, Mousa Mohammed (a.k.a. ABU-MARZUQ, Dr. Musa; a.k.a. ABU-MARZUQ, Sa'id; a.k.a. ABU-'UMAR; a.k.a. MARZOOK, Mousa Mohamed Abou; a.k.a. MARZUK, Musa Abu), Political Leader in Amman, Jordan and Damascus, Syria for HAMAS; DOB 09 Feb 1951; POB Gaza, Egypt; SSN 523-33-8386 (U.S.A.); Passport No. 92/664 (Egypt) (individual) [SDT]

ABU-MARZUQ, Dr. Musa (a.k.a. ABU MARZOOK, Mousa Mohammed; a.k.a. ABU-MARZUQ, Sa'id; a.k.a. ABU-'UMAR; a.k.a. MARZOOK, Mousa Mohamed Abou; a.k.a. MARZUK, Musa Abu), Political Leader in Amman, Jordan and Damascus, Syria for HAMAS; DOB 09 Feb 1951; POB Gaza, Egypt; SSN 523-33-8386 (U.S.A.); Passport No. 92/664 (Egypt) (individual) [SDT]

ABU-MARZUQ, Sa'id (a.k.a. ABU MARZOOK, Mousa Mohammed; a.k.a. ABU-MARZUQ, Dr. Musa; a.k.a. ABU-'UMAR; a.k.a. MARZOOK, Mousa Mohamed Abou; a.k.a. MARZUK, Musa Abu), Political Leader in Amman, Jordan and Damascus, Syria for HAMAS; DOB 09 Feb 1951; POB Gaza, Egypt; SSN 523-33-8386 (U.S.A.); Passport No. 92/664 (Egypt) (individual) [SDT]

ABU-'UMAR (a.k.a. ABU MARZOOK, Mousa Mohammed; a.k.a. ABU-MARZUQ, Dr. Musa; a.k.a. ABU-MARZUQ, Sa'id; a.k.a. MARZOOK, Mousa Mohamed Abou; a.k.a. MARZUK, Musa Abu), Political Leader in Amman, Jordan and Damascus, Syria for HAMAS; DOB 09 Feb 1951; POB Gaza, Egypt; SSN 523-33-8386 (U.S.A.); Passport No. 92/664 (Egypt) (individual) [SDT]

AHMAD, Abu (a.k.a. AHMED, Abu; a.k.a. SALAH, Mohammad Abd El-Hamid Khalil; a.k.a. SALAH, Mohammad Abdel Hamid Halil; a.k.a. SALAH, Muhammad A.), 9229 South Thomas, Bridgeview, Illinois 60455, U.S.A.; P.O. Box 2578, Bridgeview, Illinois 60455, U.S.A.; P.O. Box 2616, Bridgeview, Illinois 60455-6616, U.S.A.; Israel; DOB 30 May 1953; SSN 342-52-7612; Passport No. 024296248 (U.S.A.) (individual) [SDT]

AHMED, Abu (a.k.a. AHMAD, Abu; a.k.a. SALAH, Mohammad Abd El-Hamid Khalil; a.k.a. SALAH, Mohammad Abdel Hamid Halil; a.k.a. SALAH, Muhammad A.), 9229 South Thomas, Bridgeview, Illinois 60455,U.S.A.; P.O. Box 2578, Bridgeview, Illinois 60455, U.S.A.; P.O. Box 2616, Bridgeview, Illinois 60455-6616, U.S.A.; Israel; DOB 30 May 1953; SSN 342-52-7612; Passport No. 024296248 (U.S.A.) (individual) [SDT]

AL RAHMAN, Shaykh Umar Abd; Chief Ideological Figure of ISLAMIC GAMA'AT; DOB 03 May 1938; POB Egypt (individual) [SDT]

AL-ZUMAR, Abbud (a.k.a. ZUMAR, Colonel Abbud); Factional Leader of JIHAD GROUP; Egypt; POB Egypt (individual) [SDT]

AL-KAMEL, Salah 'Ali (a.k.a. 'ABD-AL-'IZ; a.k.a. ABD-AL-WAHAB, Abd-al-Hai Ahmad; a.k.a. ABU YASIR; a.k.a. 'ABD ALLAH, 'Issam 'Ali Muhammad; a.k.a. MUSA, Rifa'i Ahmad Taha; a.k.a. TAHA, Rifa'i Ahmad; a.k.a. TAHA MUSA, Rifa'i Ahmad; a.k.a. THABIT 'IZ); DOB 24 Jun 1954; POB Egypt; Passport No. 83860 (Sudan), 30455 (Egypt), 1046403 (Egypt) (individual) [SDT]

AL BANNA, Sabri Khalil Abd Al Qadir (a.k.a. NIDAL, Abu); Founder and Secretary General of ABU NIDAL ORGANIZATION; DOB May 1937 or 1940; POB Jaffa, Israel (individual) [SDT]

AWDA, Abd Al Aziz; Chief Ideological Figure of PALESTINIAN ISLAMIC JIHAD - SHIQAQI; DOB 1946 (individual) [SDT]

FADLALLAH, Shaykh Muhammad Husayn; Leading Ideological Figure of HIZBALLAH; DOB 1938 or 1936; POB Najf Al Ashraf (Najaf), Iraq (individual) [SDT]

HABASH, George (a.k.a. HABBASH, George); Secretary General of POPULAR FRONT FOR THE LIBERATION OF PALESTINE (individual) [SDT]

HABBASH, George (a.k.a. HABASH, George); Secretary General of POPULAR FRONT FOR THE LIBERATION OF PALESTINE (individual) [SDT]

HAWATMA, Nayif (a.k.a. HAWATMEH, Nayif; a.k.a. HAWATMAH, Nayif; a.k.a. KHALID, Abu); Secretary General of DEMOCRATIC FRONT FOR THE LIBERATION OF PALESTINE—HAWATMEH FACTION; DOB 1933 (individual) [SDT]

HAWATMAH, Nayif (a.k.a. HAWATMA, Nayif; a.k.a. HAWATMEH, Nayif; a.k.a. KHALID, Abu); Secretary General of DEMOCRATIC FRONT FOR THE LIBERATION OF PALESTINE—HAWATMEH FACTION; DOB 1933 (individual) [SDT]

HAWATMEH, Nayif (a.k.a. HAWATMA, Nayif; a.k.a. HAWATMAH, Nayif; a.k.a. KHALID, Abu); Secretary General of DEMOCRATIC FRONT FOR THE LIBERATION OF PALESTINE—HAWATMEH FACTION; DOB 1933 (individual) [SDT]

ISLAMBOULI, Mohammad Shawqi; Military Leader of ISLAMIC GAMA'AT; DOB 15 Jan 1955; POB Egypt; Passport No. 304555 (Egypt) (individual) [SDT]

JABRIL, Ahmad (a.k.a. JIBRIL, Ahmad); Secretary General of POPULAR FRONT FOR THE LIBERATION OF PALESTINE—GENERAL COMMAND; DOB 1938; POB Ramleh, Israel (individual) [SDT]

JIBRIL, Ahmad (a.k.a. JABRIL, Ahmad); Secretary General of POPULAR FRONT FOR THE LIBERATION OF PALESTINE—GENERAL COMMAND; DOB 1938; POB Ramleh, Israel (individual) [SDT]

KHALID, Abu (a.k.a. HAWATMEH, Nayif; a.k.a. HAWATMA, Nayif; a.k.a. HAWATMAH, Nayif); Secretary General of DEMOCRATIC FRONT FOR THE LIBERATION OF PALESTINE—HAWATMEH FACTION; DOB 1933 (individual) [SDT]

MARZOOK, Mousa Mohamed Abou (a.k.a. ABU MARZOOK, Mousa Mohammed; a.k.a. ABU-MARZUQ, Dr. Musa; a.k.a. ABU-MARZUQ, Sa'id; a.k.a. ABU-'UMAR; a.k.a. MARZUK, Musa Abu), Political Leader in Amman, Jordan and Damascus, Syria for HAMAS; DOB 09 Feb 1951; POB Gaza, Egypt; SSN 523-33-8386 (U.S.A.); Passport No. 92/664 (Egypt) (individual) [SDT]

MARZUK, Musa Abu (a.k.a. ABU MARZOOK, Mousa Mohammed; a.k.a. ABU-MARZUQ, Dr. Musa; a.k.a. ABU-MARZUQ, Sa'id; a.k.a. ABU-'UMAR; a.k.a. MARZOOK, Mousa Mohamed Abou), Political Leader in Amman, Jordan and Damascus, Syria for HAMAS; DOB 09 Feb 1951; POB Gaza, Egypt; SSN 523-33-8386 (U.S.A.); Passport No. 92/664 (Egypt) (individual) [SDT]

MUSA, Rifa'i Ahmad Taha (a.k.a. 'ABD-AL-'IZ; a.k.a. ABD-AL-WAHAB, Abd-al-Hai Ahmad; a.k.a. ABU YASIR; a.k.a. 'ABD ALLAH, 'Issam 'Ali Muhammad; a.k.a. AL-KAMEL, Salah 'Ali; a.k.a. TAHA, Rifa'i Ahmad; a.k.a. TAHA MUSA, Rifa'i Ahmad; a.k.a. THABIT 'IZ); DOB 24 Jun 1954; POB Egypt; Passport No. 83860 (Sudan), 30455 (Egypt), 1046403 (Egypt) (individual) [SDT]

NAJI, Talal Muhammad Rashid; Principal Deputy of POPULAR FRONT FOR THE LIBERATION OF PALESTINE - GENERAL COMMAND; DOB 1930; POB Al Nasiria, Palestine (individual) [SDT]

NASRALLAH, Hasan; Secretary General of HIZBALLAH; DOB 31 Aug 1960 or 1953 or 1955 or 1958; POB Al Basuriyah, Lebanon; Passport No. 042833 (Lebanon) (individual) [SDT]

NIDAL, Abu (a.k.a. AL BANNA, Sabri Khalil Abd Al Qadir); Founder and Secretary General of ABU NIDAL ORGANIZATION; DOB May 1937 or 1940; POB Jaffa, Israel (individual) [SDT]

QASEM, Talat Fouad; Propaganda Leader of ISLAMIC GAMA'AT; DOB 02 Jun 1957 or 03 Jun 1957; POB Al Mina, Egypt (individual) [SDT]

SALAH, Mohammad Abdel Hamid Halil (a.k.a. AHMAD, Abu; a.k.a. AHMED, Abu; a.k.a. SALAH, Mohammad Abd El-Hamid Khalil; a.k.a. SALAH, Muhammad A.), 9229 South Thomas, Bridgeview, Illinois 60455, U.S.A.; P.O. Box 2578, Bridgeview, Illinois 60455, U.S.A.; P.O. Box 2616, Bridgeview, Illinois 60455-6616, U.S.A.; Israel; DOB 30 May 1953; SSN 342-52-7612; Passport No. 024296248 (U.S.A.) (individual) [SDT]

SALAH, Mohammad Abd El-Hamid Khalil (a.k.a. AHMAD, Abu; a.k.a. AHMED, Abu; a.k.a. SALAH, Mohammad Abdel Hamid Halil; a.k.a. SALAH, Muhammad A.), 9229 South Thomas, Bridgeview, Illinois 60455, U.S.A.; P.O. Box 2578, Bridgeview, Illinois 60455, U.S.A.; P.O. Box 2616, Bridgeview, Illinois 60455-6616, U.S.A.; Israel; DOB 30 May 1953; SSN 342-52-7612; Passport No. 024296248 (U.S.A.) (individual) [SDT]

SALAH, Muhammad A. (a.k.a. AHMAD, Abu; a.k.a. AHMED, Abu; a.k.a. SALAH, Mohammad Abd El-Hamid Khalil; a.k.a. SALAH, Mohammad Abdel Hamid Halil), 9229 South Thomas, Bridgeview, Illinois 60455, U.S.A.; P.O. Box 2578, Bridgeview, Illinois 60455, U.S.A.; P.O. Box 2616, Bridgeview, Illinois 60455-6616, U.S.A.; Israel; DOB 30 May 1953; SSN 342-52-7612; Passport No. 024296248 (U.S.A.) (individual) [SDT]

SHALLAH, Dr. Ramadan Abdullah (a.k.a. ABDALLAH, Ramadan; a.k.a. ABDULLAH, Dr. Ramadan; a.k.a. SHALLAH, Ramadan Abdalla Mohamed), Damascus, Syria; Secretary General of the PALESTINIAN ISLAMIC JIHAD; DOB 01 Jan 1958; POB Gaza City, Gaza Strip; SSN 589-17-6824 (U.S.A.); Passport No. 265 216 (Egypt) (individual) [SDT]

SHALLAH, Ramadan Abdalla Mohamed (a.k.a. ABDALLAH, Ramadan; a.k.a. ABDULLAH, Dr. Ramadan; a.k.a. SHALLAH, Dr. Ramadan Abdullah), Damascus, Syria; Secretary General of the PALESTINIAN ISLAMIC JIHAD; DOB 01 Jan 1958; POB Gaza City, Gaza Strip; SSN 589-17-6824 (U.S.A.); Passport No. 265 216 (Egypt) (individual) [SDT]

SHAQAQI, Fathi; Secretary General of PALESTINIAN ISLAMIC JIHAD -SHIQAQI (individual) [SDT]

TAHA, Rifa'i Ahmad (a.k.a. 'ABD-AL-'IZ; .k.a. ABD-AL-WAHAB, Abd-al-Hai Ahmad; a.k.a. ABU YASIR; a.k.a. 'ABD ALLAH, 'Issam 'Ali Muhammad; a.k.a. AL-KAMEL, Salah 'Ali; a.k.a. MUSA, Rifa'i Ahmad Taha; a.k.a. TAHA MUSA, Rifa'i Ahmad; a.k.a. THABIT 'IZ); DOB 24 Jun 1954; POB Egypt; Passport No. 83860 (Sudan), 30455 (Egypt), 1046403 (Egypt) (individual) [SDT]

TAHA MUSA, Rifa'i Ahmad (a.k.a. 'ABD-AL-'IZ; a.k.a. ABD-AL-WAHAB, Abd-al-Hai Ahmad; a.k.a. ABU YASIR; a.k.a. 'ABD ALLAH, 'Issam 'Ali Muhammad; a.k.a. AL-KAMEL, Salah 'Ali; a.k.a. MUSA, Rifa'i Ahmad Taha; a.k.a. TAHA, Rifa'i Ahmad; a.k.a. THABIT 'IZ); DOB 24 Jun 1954; POB

Egypt; Passport No. 83860 (Sudan), 30455 (Egypt), 1046403 (Egypt) (individual) [SDT]

THABIT 'IZ (a.k.a. 'ABD-AL-'IZ; a.k.a. ABD-AL-WAHAB, Abd-al-Hai Ahmad; a.k.a. ABU YASIR; a.k.a. 'ABD ALLAH, 'Issam 'Ali Muhammad; a.k.a. AL-KAMEL, Salah 'Ali; a.k.a. MUSA, Rifa'i Ahmad Taha; a.k.a. TAHA, Rifa'i Ahmad; a.k.a. TAHA MUSA, Rifa'i Ahmad); DOB 24 Jun 1954; POB Egypt; Passport No. 83860 (Sudan), 30455 (Egypt), 1046403 (Egypt) (individual) [SDT]

TUFAYLI, Subhi; Former Secretary General and Current Senior Figure of HIZBALLAH; DOB 1947; POB Biqa Valley, Lebanon (individual) [SDT]

YASIN, Shaykh Ahmad; Founder and Chief Ideological Figure of HAMAS; DOB 1931 (individual) [SDT]

ZAYDAN, Muhammad (a.k.a. ABBAS, Abu); Director of PALESTINE LIBERATION FRONT - ABU ABBAS FACTION; DOB 10 Dec 1948 (individual) [SDT]

ZUMAR, Colonel Abbud (a.k.a. AL-ZUMAR, Abbud); Factional Leader of JIHAD GROUP; Egypt; POB Egypt (individual) [SDT]

A Bulletin from the Office of Foreign Assets Control
December 14, 2001: 4:30pm

All financial assets and all records of BENEVOLENCE INTERNATIONAL FOUNDATION, INC. and GLOBAL RELIEF FOUNDATION, INC. wherever located are blocked pending investigation pursuant to Section 106 of the U.S.A. Patriot Act of 2001, 107 Public Law 56 (October 26, 2001). BENEVOLENCE is known to have offices in Illinois and New Jersey. Global is known to have offices in Illinois. Although these entities are not now SDNs, their names have been integrated into OFAC's SDN list with the descriptor "[BPI-PA]" to indicate that their financial assets and all records are currently blocked.

BENEVOLENCE INTERNATIONAL FOUNDATION, INC., 20-24 Branford Place, Suite 705, Newark, NJ 07102, U.S.A.; 9838 S. Roberts Road, Suite 1-W, Palos Hills, IL 60465, U.S.A.; P.O. Box 548, Worth, IL 60482, U.S.A.; U.S. FEIN: 36-3823186 (all financial assets and all records are blocked) [BPI-PA]

GLOBAL RELIEF FOUNDATION, INC., 9935 S. 76th Avenue, #1, Bridgeview, IL 60455, U.S.A.; P.O. Box 1406, Bridgeview, IL 60455, U.S.A.; U.S. FEIN: 36-3804626 (all financial assets and all records are blocked) [BPI-PA]

This document is explanatory only and does not have the force of law. Executive Order 13224 is reprinted here. Executive Order 12947, as amended, and the implementing Terrorism Sanctions Regulations (31 C.F.R Part 595) contain the legally binding provisions governing the sanctions against terrorists who threaten to disrupt the Middle East peace process. Section 321 (18 U.S.C. 2332d) of the Antiterrorism and Effective Death Penalty Act of 1996, Pub.L. 104-132, 110 Stat. 1214-1319 (the "Antiterrorism Act") and the implementing Terrorism List Governments Sanctions Regulations (31 C.F.R. Part 596) contain the legally binding provisions governing sanctions against the governments of countries designated under section 6(j) of the Export Administration Act of 1979, 50 U.S.C. App. 2405, as supporting international terrorism. Sections 302 and 303 of the Antiterrorism Act (new 8 U.S.C. 1189 and 18 U.S.C. 2339B, respectively) and the implementing Foreign Terrorist Organizations Sanctions Regulations (31 C.F.R. Part 597) contain the legally binding provisions governing the sanctions against foreign terrorist organizations. This document does not supplement or modify Executive Order 13224, Executive Order 12947, as amended, the Antiterrorism Act, or 31 C.F.R. Parts 595, 596, or 597.

The Treasury Department's Office of Foreign Assets Control also administers sanctions programs involving Libya, Iraq, the Balkans, the Federal Republic of Yugoslavia (Serbia and Montenegro), Cuba, the National Union for the Total Independence of Angola (UNITA), North Korea, Iran, Burma (Myanmar), Sudan, the Taliban in Afghanistan, Sierra Leone, Liberia, highly enriched uranium transactions, international narcotics traffickers, and designated foreign persons who have engaged in activities related to the proliferation of weapons of mass destruction. For additional information about these programs or about sanctions involving transactions with terrorists, terrorist organizations, or their agents, please contact the:

OFFICE OF FOREIGN ASSETS CONTROL

U.S. Department of the Treasury
Washington, D.C. 20220
202/622-2520

(12-31-2001)

DOCUMENT NO. 5

PRESIDENTIAL ADDRESS TO
THE UNITED NATIONS GENERAL ASSEMBLY

U.N. Headquarters
New York, N.Y.

November 10, 2001

For Immediate Release
Office of the Press Secretary

THE PRESIDENT: Thank you. Mr. Secretary General, Mr. President, distinguished delegates, and ladies and gentlemen. We meet in a hall devoted to peace, in a city scarred by violence, in a nation awakened to danger, in a world uniting for a long struggle. Every civilized nation here today is resolved to keep the most basic commitment of civilization: We will defend ourselves and our future against terror and lawless violence.

The United Nations was founded in this cause. In a second world war, we learned there is no isolation from evil. We affirmed that some crimes are so terrible they offend humanity, itself. And we resolved that the aggressions and ambitions of the wicked must be opposed early, decisively, and collectively, before they threaten us all. That evil has returned, and that cause is renewed.

A few miles from here, many thousands still lie in a tomb of rubble. Tomorrow, the Secretary General, the President of the General Assembly, and I will visit that site, where the names of every nation and region that lost citizens will be read aloud. If we were to read the names of every person who died, it would take more than three hours.

Those names include a citizen of Gambia, whose wife spent their fourth wedding anniversary, September the 12th, searching in vain for her husband. Those names include a man who supported his wife in Mexico, sending home money every week. Those names include a young Pakistani who prayed toward Mecca five times a day, and died that day trying to save others.

The suffering of September the 11th was inflicted on people of many faiths and many nations. All of the victims, including Muslims, were killed with equal indifference and equal satisfaction by the terrorist leaders. The terrorists are violating the tenets of every religion, including the one they invoke.

Last week, the Sheikh of Al-Azhar University, the world's oldest Islamic institution of higher learning, declared that terrorism is a disease, and that

Islam prohibits killing innocent civilians. The terrorists call their cause holy, yet, they fund it with drug dealing; they encourage murder and suicide in the name of a great faith that forbids both. They dare to ask God's blessing as they set out to kill innocent men, women and children. But the God of Isaac and Ishmael would never answer such a prayer. And a murderer is not a martyr; he is just a murderer.

Time is passing. Yet, for the United States of America, there will be no forgetting September the 11th. We will remember every rescuer who died in honor. We will remember every family that lives in grief. We will remember the fire and ash, the last phone calls, the funerals of the children.

And the people of my country will remember those who have plotted against us. We are learning their names. We are coming to know their faces. There is no corner of the Earth distant or dark enough to protect them. However long it takes, their hour of justice will come.

Every nation has a stake in this cause. As we meet, the terrorists are planning more murder—perhaps in my country, or perhaps in yours. They kill because they aspire to dominate. They seek to overthrow governments and destabilize entire regions.

Last week, anticipating this meeting of the General Assembly, they denounced the United Nations. They called our Secretary General a criminal and condemned all Arab nations here as traitors to Islam.

Few countries meet their exacting standards of brutality and oppression. Every other country is a potential target. And all the world faces the most horrifying prospect of all:These same terrorists are searching for weapons of mass destruction, the tools to turn their hatred into holocaust. They can be expected to use chemical, biological and nuclear weapons the moment they are capable of doing so. No hint of conscience would prevent it.

This threat cannot be ignored. This threat cannot be appeased. Civilization, itself, the civilization we share, is threatened. History will record our response, and judge or justify every nation in this hall.

The civilized world is now responding. We act to defend ourselves and deliver our children from a future of fear. We choose the dignity of life over a culture of death. We choose lawful change and civil disagreement over coercion, subversion, and chaos. These commitments—hope and order, law and life—unite people across cultures and continents. Upon these commitments depend all peace and progress. For these commitments, we are determined to fight.

The United Nations has risen to this responsibility. On the 12th of September, these buildings opened for emergency meetings of the General Assembly and the Security Council. Before the sun had set, these attacks on the world stood condemned by the world. And I want to thank you for this strong and principled stand.

I also thank the Arab Islamic countries that have condemned terrorist murder. Many of you have seen the destruction of terror in your own lands. The terrorists are increasingly isolated by their own hatred and extremism. They cannot hide behind Islam. The authors of mass murder and their allies have no place in any culture, and no home in any faith.

The conspiracies of terror are being answered by an expanding global coalition. Not every nation will be a part of every action against the enemy. But every nation in our coalition has duties. These duties can be demanding, as we in America are learning. We have already made adjustments in our laws and in our daily lives. We're taking new measures to investigate terror and to protect against threats.

The leaders of all nations must now carefully consider their responsibilities and their future. Terrorist groups like al Qaeda depend upon the aid or indifference of governments. They need the support of a financial infrastructure, and safe havens to train and plan and hide.

Some nations want to play their part in the fight against terror, but tell us they lack the means to enforce their laws and control their borders. We stand ready to help. Some governments still turn a blind eye to the terrorists, hoping the threat will pass them by. They are mistaken. And some governments, while pledging to uphold the principles of the U.N. , have cast their lot with the terrorists. They support them and harbor them, and they will find that their welcome guests are parasites that will weaken them, and eventually consume them.

For every regime that sponsors terror, there is a price to be paid. And it will be paid. The allies of terror are equally guilty of murder and equally accountable to justice.

The Taliban are now learning this lesson—that regime and the terrorists who support it are now virtually indistinguishable. Together they promote terror abroad and impose a reign of terror on the Afghan people. Women are executed in Kabal's soccer stadium. They can be beaten for wearing socks that are too thin. Men are jailed for missing prayer meetings.

The United States, supported by many nations, is bringing justice to the terrorists in Afghanistan. We're making progress against military targets, and that is our objective. Unlike the enemy, we seek to minimize, not maximize, the loss of innocent life.

I'm proud of the honorable conduct of the American military. And my country grieves for all the suffering the Taliban have brought upon Afghanistan, including the terrible burden of war. The Afghan people do not deserve their present rulers. Years of Taliban misrule have brought nothing but misery and starvation. Even before this current crisis, 4 million Afghans depended on food from the United States and other nations, and millions of Afghans were refugees from Taliban oppression.

I make this promise to all the victims of that regime:The Taliban's days of harboring terrorists and dealing in heroin and brutalizing women are drawing to a close. And when that regime is gone, the people of Afghanistan will say with the rest of the world:good riddance.

I can promise, too, that America will join the world in helping the people of Afghanistan rebuild their country. Many nations, including mine, are sending food and medicine to help Afghans through the winter. America has air-dropped over 1. 3 million packages of rations into Afghanistan. Just this week, we air-lifted 20,000 blankets and over 200 tons of provisions into the region. We continue to provide humanitarian aid, even while the Taliban tried to steal the food we send.

More help eventually will be needed. The United States will work closely with the United Nations and development banks to reconstruct Afghanistan after hostilities there have ceased and the Taliban are no longer in control. And the United States will work with the U.N. to support a post-Taliban government that represents all of the Afghan people.

In this war of terror, each of us must answer for what we have done or what we have left undone. After tragedy, there is a time for sympathy and condolence. And my country has been very grateful for both. The memorials and vigils around the world will not be forgotten. But the time for sympathy has now passed; the time for action has now arrived.

The most basic obligations in this new conflict have already been defined by the United Nations. On September the 28th, the Security Council adopted Resolution 1373. Its requirements are clear:Every United Nations member has a responsibility to crack down on terrorist financing. We must pass all necessary laws in our own countries to allow the confiscation of terrorist assets. We must apply those laws to every financial institution in every nation.

We have a responsibility to share intelligence and coordinate the efforts of law enforcement. If you know something, tell us. If we know something, we'll tell you. And when we find the terrorists, we must work together to bring them to justice. We have a responsibility to deny any sanctuary, safe haven or transit to terrorists. Every known terrorist camp must be shut down, its operators apprehended, and evidence of their arrest presented to the United Nations. We have a responsibility to deny weapons to terrorists and to actively prevent private citizens from providing them.

These obligations are urgent and they are binding on every nation with a place in this chamber. Many governments are taking these obligations seriously, and my country appreciates it. Yet, even beyond Resolution 1373, more is required, and more is expected of our coalition against terror.

We're asking for a comprehensive commitment to this fight. We must unite in opposing all terrorists, not just some of them. In this world there are good causes and bad causes, and we may disagree on where the line is drawn. Yet, there is no such thing as a good terrorist. No national aspiration, no remembered wrong can ever justify the deliberate murder of the innocent. Any government that rejects this principle, trying to pick and choose its terrorist friends, will know the consequences.

We must speak the truth about terror. Let us never tolerate outrageous conspiracy theories concerning the attacks of September the 11th; malicious lies that attempt to shift the blame away from the terrorists, themselves, away from the guilty. To inflame ethnic hatred is to advance the cause of terror.

The war against terror must not serve as an excuse to persecute ethnic and religious minorities in any country. Innocent people must be allowed to live their own lives, by their own customs, under their own religion. And every nation must have avenues for the peaceful expression of opinion and dissent. When these avenues are closed, the temptation to speak through violence grows.

We must press on with our agenda for peace and prosperity in every land. My country is pledged to encouraging development and expanding trade. My country is pledged to investing in education and combatting AIDS and other infectious diseases around the world. Following September 11th, these pledges are even more important. In our struggle against hateful groups that exploit poverty and despair, we must offer an alternative of opportunity and hope.

The American government also stands by its commitment to a just peace in the Middle East. We are working toward a day when two states, Israel and Palestine, live peacefully together within secure and recognize borders as called for by the Security Council resolutions. We will do all in our power to bring both parties back into negotiations. But peace will only come when all have sworn off, forever, incitement, violence and terror.

And, finally, this struggle is a defining moment for the United Nations, itself. And the world needs its principled leadership. It undermines the credibility of this great institution, for example, when the Commission on Human Rights offers seats to the world's most persistent violators of human rights. The United Nations depends, above all, on its moral authority—and that authority must be preserved.

The steps I described will not be easy. For all nations, they will require effort. For some nations, they will require great courage. Yet, the cost of inaction is far greater. The only alternative to victory is a nightmare world where every city is a potential killing field.

As I've told the American people, freedom and fear are at war. We face enemies that hate not our policies, but our existence; the tolerance of openness and creative culture that defines us. But the outcome of this conflict is certain:There is a current in history and it runs toward freedom. Our enemies resent it and dismiss it, but the dreams of mankind are defined by liberty—the natural right to create and build and worship and live in dignity. When men and women are released from oppression and isolation, they find fulfillment and hope, and they leave poverty by the millions.

These aspirations are lifting up the peoples of Europe, Asia, Africa and the Americas, and they can lift up all of the Islamic world.

We stand for the permanent hopes of humanity, and those hopes will not be denied. We're confident, too, that history has an author who fills time and eternity with his purpose. We know that evil is real, but good will prevail against it. This is theteaching of many faiths, and in that assurance we gain strength for a long journey.

It is our task—the task of this generation—to provide the response to aggression and terror. We have no other choice, because there is no other peace.

We did not ask for this mission, yet there is honor in history's call. We have a chance to write the story of our times, a story of courage defeating cruelty and light overcoming darkness. This calling is worthy of any life, and worthy of every nation. So let us go forward, confident, determined, and unafraid.

Thank you very much. (Applause.)

DOCUMENT NO. 6

PRESIDENTIAL ORDER ON MILITARY TRIALS IN TERRORIST CASES

November 14, 2001

COMMENTARY: This order prompted more adverse comments than virtually any other action taken by President Bush. Though the President and the Executive Branch have stressed their intention to preserve personal freedoms and follow the rule of law, individuals and groups in the legislative branch and outside government have expressed distinct reservations concerning this practice.

President Bush on November 13 signed an order allowing special military tribunals to try foreigners accused of terrorist attacks.

Under the order, the president himself will determine who is an accused terrorist and therefore subject to trial by the tribunal. The order states that the president may "determine from time to time in writing that there is reason to believe" that an individual is or was a member of al Qaida, "has engaged in, aided or abetted, or conspired to commit" acts of international terrorism, or has "knowingly harbored" a terrorist.

The order gives Secretary of Defense Donald Rumsfeld the authority to establish the courts, similar to those established by President Franklin D. Roosevelt during World War II.

Bush said in the order that, "Having fully considered the magnitude of the potential deaths, injuries, and property destruction that would result from potential acts of terrorism against the United States, and the probability that such acts will occur, I have determined that an extraordinary emergency exists for national defense purposes, that this emergency constitutes an urgent and compelling government interest, and that issuance of this order is necessary to meet the emergency."

Following is the text of the military order, which was issued by the White House:

THE WHITE HOUSE
Office of the Press Secretary
November 13, 2001

MILITARY ORDER

DETENTION, TREATMENT, AND TRIAL OF CERTAIN NON-CITIZENS IN THE WAR AGAINST TERRORISM

By the authority vested in me as President and as Commander in Chief of the Armed Forces of the United States by the Constitution and the laws of the United States of America, including the Authorization for Use of Military Force Joint Resolution (Public Law 107-40, 115 Stat. 224) and sections 821 and 836 of title 10, United States Code, it is hereby ordered as follows:

Section 1. Findings.

(a) International terrorists, including members of al Qaida, have carried out attacks on United States diplomatic and military personnel and facilities abroad and on citizens and property within the United States on a scale that has created a state of armed conflict that requires the use of the United States Armed Forces.

(b) In light of grave acts of terrorism and threats of terrorism, including the terrorist attacks on September 11, 2001, on the headquarters of the United States Department of Defense in the national capital region, on the World Trade Center in New York, and on civilian aircraft such as in Pennsylvania, I proclaimed a national emergency on September 14, 2001 (Proc. 7463, Declaration of National Emergency by Reason of Certain Terrorist Attacks).

(c) Individuals acting alone and in concert involved in international terrorism possess both the capability and the intention to undertake further terrorist attacks against the United States that, if not detected and prevented, will cause mass deaths, mass injuries, and massive destruction of property, and may place at risk the continuity of the operations of the United States Government.

(d) The ability of the United States to protect the United States and its citizens, and to help its allies and other cooperating nations protect their nations and their citizens, from such further terrorist attacks depends in significant part upon using the United States Armed Forces to identify terrorists and those who support them, to disrupt their activities, and to eliminate their ability to conduct or support such attacks.

(e) To protect the United States and its citizens, and for the effective conduct of military operations and prevention of terrorist attacks, it is necessary for individuals subject to this order pursuant to section 2 hereof to be detained, and, when tried, to be tried for violations of the laws of war and other applicable laws by military tribunals.

(f) Given the danger to the safety of the United States and the nature of international terrorism, and to the extent provided by and under this order, I find consistent with section 836 of title 10, United States Code, that it is not practicable to apply in military commissions under this order the principles of law and the rules of evidence generally recognized in the trial of criminal cases in the United States district courts.

(g) Having fully considered the magnitude of the potential deaths, injuries, and property destruction that would result from potential acts of terrorism against the United States, and the probability that such acts will occur, I have determined that an extraordinary emergency exists for national defense purposes, that this emergency constitutes an urgent and compelling government interest, and that issuance of this order is necessary to meet the emergency.

Section 2. Definition and Policy.

(a) The term "individual subject to this order" shall mean any individual who is not a United States citizen with respect to whom I determine from time to time in writing that:

(1) there is reason to believe that such individual, at the relevant times,

(i) is or was a member of the organization known as al Qaida;

(ii) has engaged in, aided or abetted, or conspired to commit, acts of international terrorism, or acts in preparation therefor, that have caused, threaten to cause, or have as their aim to cause, injury to or adverse effects on the United States, its citizens, national security, foreign policy, or economy; or

(iii) has knowingly harbored one or more individuals described in subparagraphs (i) or (ii) of subsection 2(a)(1) of this order; and

(2) it is in the interest of the United States that such individual be subject to this order.

(b) It is the policy of the United States that the Secretary of Defense shall take all necessary measures to ensure that any individual subject to this order is detained in accordance with section 3, and, if the individual is to be tried, that such individual is tried only in accordance with section 4.

(c) It is further the policy of the United States that any individual subject to this order who is not already under the control of the Secretary of Defense but who is under the control of any other officer or agent of the United States or any State shall, upon delivery of a copy of such written determination to such officer or agent, forthwith be placed under the control of the Secretary of Defense.

Section 3. Detention Authority of the Secretary of Defense. Any individual subject to this order shall be—

(a) detained at an appropriate location designated by the Secretary of Defense outside or within the United States;

(b) treated humanely, without any adverse distinction based on race, color, religion, gender, birth, wealth, or any similar criteria;

(c) afforded adequate food, drinking water, shelter, clothing, and medical treatment;

(d) allowed the free exercise of religion consistent with the requirements of such detention; and

(e) detained in accordance with such other conditions as the Secretary of Defense may prescribe.

Section 4. Authority of the Secretary of Defense Regarding Trials of Individuals Subject to this Order.

(a) Any individual subject to this order shall, when tried, be tried by military commission for any and all offenses triable by military commission that such individual is alleged to have committed, and may be punished in accordance with the penalties provided under applicable law, including life imprisonment or death.

(b) As a military function and in light of the findings in section 1, including subsection (f) thereof, the Secretary of Defense shall issue such orders and regulations, including orders for the appointment of one or more military commissions, as may be necessary to carry out subsection (a) of this section.

(c) Orders and regulations issued under subsection (b) of this section shall include, but not be limited to, rules for the conduct of the proceedings of military commissions, including pretrial, trial, and post-trial procedures, modes of proof, issuance of process, and qualifications of attorneys, which shall at a minimum provide for—

(1) military commissions to sit at any time and any place, consistent with such guidance regarding time and place as the Secretary of Defense may provide;

(2) a full and fair trial, with the military commission sitting as the triers of both fact and law;

(3) admission of such evidence as would, in the opinion of the presiding officer of the military commission (or instead, if any other member of the commission so requests at the time the presiding officer renders that opinion, the opinion of the commission rendered at that time by a majority of the commission), have probative value to a reasonable person;

(4) in a manner consistent with the protection of information classified or classifiable under Executive Order 12958 of April 17, 1995, as amended, or any successor Executive Order, protected by statute or rule from unauthorized disclosure, or otherwise protected by law, (A) the handling of, admission into evidence of, and access to materials and information, and (B) the conduct, closure of, and access to proceedings;

(5) conduct of the prosecution by one or more attorneys designated by the Secretary of Defense and conduct of the defense by attorneys for the individual subject to this order;

(6) conviction only upon the concurrence of two-thirds of the members of the commission present at the time of the vote, a majority being present;

(7) sentencing only upon the concurrence of two-thirds of the members of the commission present at the time of the vote, a majority being present; and

(8) submission of the record of the trial, including any conviction or sentence, for review and final decision by me or by the Secretary of Defense if so designated by me for that purpose.

Section 5. Obligation of Other Agencies to Assist the Secretary of Defense.

Departments, agencies, entities, and officers of the United States shall, to the maximum extent permitted by law, provide to the Secretary of Defense such assistance as he may request to implement this order.

Section 6. Additional Authorities of the Secretary of Defense.

(a) As a military function and in light of the findings in section 1, the Secretary of Defense shall issue such orders and regulations as may be necessary to carry out any of the provisions of this order.

(b) The Secretary of Defense may perform any of his functions or duties, and may exercise any of the powers provided to him under this order (other than under section 4(c)(8) hereof) in accordance with section 113(d) of title 10, United States Code.

Section 7. Relationship to Other Law and Forums.

(a) Nothing in this order shall be construed to—

(1) authorize the disclosure of state secrets to any person not otherwise authorized to have access to them;

(2) limit the authority of the President as Commander in Chief of the Armed Forces or the power of the President to grant reprieves and pardons; or

(3) limit the lawful authority of the Secretary of Defense, any military commander, or any other officer or agent of the United States or of any State to detain or try any person who is not an individual subject to this order.

(b) With respect to any individual subject to this order—

(1) military tribunals shall have exclusive jurisdiction with respect to offenses by the individual; and

(2) the individual shall not be privileged to seek any remedy or maintain any proceeding, directly or indirectly, or to have any such remedy or proceeding sought on the individual's behalf, in (i) any court of the United States, or any State thereof, (ii) any court of any foreign nation, or (iii) any international tribunal.

(c) This order is not intended to and does not create any right, benefit, or privilege, substantive or procedural, enforceable at law or equity by any party, against the United States, its departments, agencies, or other entities, its officers or employees, or any other person.

(d) For purposes of this order, the term "State" includes any State, district, territory, or possession of the United States.

(e) I reserve the authority to direct the Secretary of Defense, at any time hereafter, to transfer to a governmental authority control of any individual subject to this order. Nothing in this order shall be construed to limit the authority of any such governmental authority to prosecute any individual for whom control is transferred.

Section 8. Publication.

This order shall be published in the Federal Register.

GEORGE W. BUSH

THE WHITE HOUSE,
November 13, 2001.

EXECUTIVE BRANCH

Department of State

DOCUMENT NO. 7

STATEMENT BY SECRETARY OF STATE POWELL DESIGNATING 39 ORGANIZATIONS ON THE USA PATRIOT ACT'S 'TERRORIST EXCLUSION LIST'.

COMMENTARY: Inclusion in this listing triggers additional controls over the actions by the designated individuals and organizations and it represents a further tightening by the U.S. Government over the actions of suspected terrorist entities.

Philip T. Reeker, Deputy Spokesman
Washington, DC
December 6, 2001

To further protect the safety of the United States and its citizens, Secretary of State Colin L. Powell, in consultation with the Attorney General, on December 5 designated 39 groups as Terrorist Exclusion List (TEL) organizations under section 212 of the Immigration and Nationality Act, as amended by the new USA PATRIOT Act. By designating these groups, the Secretary has strengthened the United States' ability to exclude supporters of terrorism from the country or to deport them if they are found within our borders.

The campaign against terrorism will be a long one, using all the tools of statecraft. We are taking a methodical approach to all aspects of the campaign to eliminate terrorism as a threat to our way of life. This round of Terrorist Exclusion List designations is by no means the last. We will continue to expand the list as we identify and confirm additional entities that provide support to terrorists.

Terrorist Exclusion List Designees: December 5, 2001
- AlIttihad al-Islami (AIAI)
- Al-Wafa al-Igatha al-Islamia
- Asbat al-Ansar
- Darkazanli Company
- Salafist Group for Call and Combat (GSPC)
- Islamic Army of Aden
- Libyan Islamic Fighting Group

- Makhtab al-Khidmat
- Al-Hamati Sweets Bakeries
- Al-Nur Honey Center
- Al-Rashid Trust
- Al-Shifa Honey Press for Industry and Commerce
- Jaysh-e-Mohammed
- Jamiat al-Ta'awun al-Islamiyya
- Alex Boncayao Brigade (ABB)
- Army for the Liberation of Rwanda (ALIR)—AKA: Interahamwe, Former Armed Forces (EX-FAR)
- First of October Antifascist Resistance Group (GRAPO)—AKA: Grupo de Resistencia Anti-Fascista Premero De Octubre
- Lashkar-e-Tayyiba (LT)—AKA: Army of the Righteous
- Continuity Irish Republican Army (CIRA)—AKA: Continuity Army Council
- Orange Volunteers (OV)
- Red Hand Defenders (RHD)
- New People's Army (NPA)
- People Against Gangsterism and Drugs (PAGAD)
- Revolutionary United Front (RUF)
- Al-Ma'unah
- Jayshullah
- Black Star
- Anarchist Faction for Overthrow
- Red Brigades-Combatant Communist Party (BR-PCC)
- Revolutionary Proletarian Nucleus
- Turkish Hizballah
- Jerusalem Warriors
- Islamic Renewal and Reform Organization
- The Pentagon Gang
- Japanese Red Army (JRA)
- Jamiat ul-Mujahideen (JUM)
- Harakat ul Jihad i Islami (HUJI)
- The Allied Democratic Forces (ADF)
- The Lord's Resistance Army (LRA)

EXECUTIVE BRANCH

Director of Central Intelligence

DOCUMENT NO. 8

UNCLASSIFIED REPORT TO CONGRESS ON THE ACQUISITION OF TECHNOLOGY RELATING TO WEAPONS OF MASS DESTRUCTION AND ADVANCED CONVENTIONAL MUNITIONS 1 JULY THROUGH 31 DECEMBER 2000

Director of Central Intelligence

Issued September 7, 2001

COMMENTARY: This is the latest submission by the DCI of an unclassified Report for Congress. Though issued in September of 2001, it covers the last six months of 2000 and follows the Report carried in Volume 24, Document No. 8.

SCOPE NOTE

The Director of Central Intelligence (DCI) hereby submits this report in response to a Congressionally directed action in Section 721 of the FY 97 Intelligence Authorization Act, which requires:

"(a) Not later than 6 months after the date of the enactment of this Act, and every 6 months thereafter, the Director of Central Intelligence shall submit to Congress a report on

(1) the acquisition by foreign countries during the preceding 6 months of dual-use and other technology useful for the development or production of weapons of mass destruction (including nuclear weapons, chemical weapons, and biological weapons) and advanced conventional munitions; and

(2) trends in the acquisition of such technology by such countries."

At the DCI's request, the DCI Weapons Intelligence, Nonproliferation, and Arms Control Center (WINPAC) drafted this report and coordinated it throughout the Intelligence Community. As directed by Section 721, subsection (b) of the Act, it is unclassified. As such, the report does not present the details of the Intelligence Community's assessments of weapons of mass destruction and advanced conventional munitions programs that are available in other classified reports and briefings for the Congress.

ACQUISITION BY COUNTRY:

As required by Section 721 of the FY 97 Intelligence Authorization Act, the following are summaries by country of acquisition activities (solicitations, negotiations, contracts, and deliveries) related to weapons of mass destruction (WMD) and advanced conventional weapons (ACW) that occurred from 1 July through 31 December 2000. We excluded countries that already have substantial WMD programs, such as China and Russia, as well as countries that demonstrated little WMD acquisition activity of concern.

Iran

Iran remains one of the most active countries seeking to acquire WMD and ACW technology from abroad. In doing so, Tehran is attempting to develop a domestic capability to produce various types of weapons—chemical, biological, and nuclear—and their delivery systems. During the reporting period, the evidence indicates determined Iranian efforts to acquire WMD- and ACW-related equipment, materials, and technology focused primarily on entities in Russia, China, North Korea, and Western Europe.

Iran, a Chemical Weapons Convention (CWC) States party, already has manufactured and stockpiled chemical weapons—including blister, blood, choking, and probably nerve agents, and the bombs and artillery shells for delivering them. During the second half of 2000, Tehran continued to seek production technology, training, expertise, equipment, and chemicals that could be used as precursor agents in its chemical warfare (CW) program from entities in Russia and China.

Tehran continued its efforts to seek considerable dual-use biotechnical materials, equipment, and expertise from abroad—primarily from entities in Russia and Western Europe—ostensibly for civilian uses. We judge that this equipment and know-how could be applied to Iran's biological warfare (BW) program. Iran probably began its offensive BW program during the Iran-Iraq war, and it may have some limited capability for BW deployment.

Iran sought nuclear-related equipment, material, and technical expertise from a variety of sources, especially in Russia. Work continues on the construction of a 1,000-megawatt nuclear power reactor at Bushehr that will be subject to International Atomic Energy Agency (IAEA) safeguards. In addition, Russian entities continued to interact with Iranian research centers on various activities. These projects will help Iran augment its nuclear technology infrastructure, which in turn would be useful in supporting nuclear weapons research and development. The expertise and technology gained, along with the commercial channels and contacts established—particularly through the Bushehr nuclear power plant project—could be used to advance Iran's nuclear weapons research and development program.

Beginning in January 1998, the Russian Government took a number of steps to increase its oversight of entities involved in dealings with Iran and other states of proliferation concern. In 1999, it pushed a new export control law through the Duma. Russian firms, however, faced economic pressures to circumvent these controls and did so in some cases. The Russian Government, moreover, failed to enforce its export controls in some cases regarding Iran. A component of the Russian Ministry of Atomic Energy (MINATOM) contracted with Iran to provide equipment clearly intended for Atomic Vapor Laser Isotope Separation (AVLIS). The laser equipment was to have been delivered in late 2000 but continues to be held up as a result of US protests. AVLIS technology could provide Iran the means to produce weapons quantities of highly enriched uranium.

China pledged in October 1997 to halt cooperation on a uranium conversion facility (UCF) and not to engage in any new nuclear cooperation with Iran but said it would complete cooperation on two nuclear projects: a small research reactor and a zirconium production facility at Esfahan that Iran will use to produce cladding for reactor fuel. As a party to the Nuclear Nonproliferation Treaty (NPT), Iran is required to apply IAEA safeguards to nuclear fuel, but safeguards are not required for the zirconium plant or its products.

Iran has attempted to use its civilian energy program, which is quite modest in scope, to justify its efforts to establish domestically or otherwise acquire assorted nuclear fuel-cycle capabilities. But such capabilities can also support fissile material production for a weapons program, and we believe it is this objective that drives Iran's efforts to acquire relevant facilities. For example, Iran has sought to obtain turnkey facilities, such as the UCF, that ostensibly would be used to support fuel production for the Bushehr power plant. But the UCF could be used in any number of ways to support fissile material production needed for a nuclear weapon—specifically, production of uranium hexafluoride for use as a feedstock for uranium enrichment operations and production of uranium compounds suitable for use as fuel in a plutonium production reactor. In addition, we suspect that Tehran most likely is interested in acquiring foreign fissile material and technology for weapons development as part of its overall nuclear weapons program.

During the second half of 2000, entities in Russia, North Korea, and China continued to supply crucial ballistic missile–related equipment, technology, and expertise to Iran. Tehran is using assistance from foreign suppliers and entities to support current development and production programs and to achieve its goal of becoming self-sufficient in the production of ballistic missiles. Iran already is producing Scud short-range ballistic missiles (SRBMs) and is in the late stages of developing the Shahab-3 medium-range ballistic missile (MRBM). Iran has built and publicly displayed prototypes for the Shahab-3 and has tested the Shahab-3 three times—July

1998, July 2000, and September 2000. In addition, Iran has publicly acknowledged the development of a Shahab-4, originally calling it a more capable ballistic missile than the Shahab-3 but later categorizing it as solely a
space launch vehicle with no military applications. Iran's Defense Minister
also has publicly mentioned plans for a "Shahab-5". Such statements, made
against the backdrop of sustained cooperation with Russian, North Korean, and Chinese entities, strongly suggest that Tehran intends to develop
a longer-range ballistic missile capability.

Iran continues to seek and acquire conventional weapons and production
technologies primarily from Russia and China. Following Russia's public
abrogation of the 1995 Gore-Chernomyrdin Agreement in November 2000,
Iran has expressed interest in acquiring a variety of Russian air, naval and
ground weapons. Russia has continued to deliver on contracts signed prior
to the 1995 agreement. During the second half of 2000, Iran continued to
negotiate for and receive Mi-171 helicopters form Russia. Naval acquisitions from a variety of countries continue. Tehran also has been able to
keep operational at least part of its existing fleet of Western-origin aircraft
and helicopters supplied before the 1979 Iranian Revolution and continues
to develop limited capabilities to produce armor, artillery, tactical missiles,
munitions, and aircraft with foreign assistance.

Iraq

Since Operation Desert Fox in December 1998, Baghdad has refused to allow United Nations inspectors into Iraq as required by Security Council
Resolution 687. In spite of ongoing UN efforts to establish a follow-on inspection regime comprising the UN Monitoring, Verification, and Inspection Commission (UNMOVIC) and the IAEA's Iraq Action Team, no UN
inspections occurred during this reporting period. Moreover, the automated video monitoring system installed by the UN at known and suspect
WMD facilities in Iraq is no longer operating. Having lost this
on-the-ground access, it is more difficult for the UN or the US to accurately
assess the current state of Iraq's WMD programs.

Given Iraq's past behavior, it is likely that Iraq has used the period since
Desert Fox to reconstitute prohibited programs. We assess that since the
suspension of UN inspections in December of 1998, Baghdad has had the
capability to reinitiate both its CW and BW programs within a few weeks to
months. Without an inspection-monitoring program, however, it is more
difficult to determine if Iraq has done so.

Since the Gulf war, Iraq has rebuilt key portions of its chemical production
infrastructure for industrial and commercial use, as well as its missile production facilities. It has attempted to purchase numerous dual-use items
for, or under the guise of, legitimate civilian use. This equipment—in principle subject to UN scrutiny—also could be diverted for WMD purposes.

Since the suspension of UN inspections in December 1998, the risk of diversion has increased. After Desert Fox, Baghdad again instituted a reconstruction effort on those facilities destroyed by the US bombing, including several critical missile production complexes and former dual-use CW production facilities. In addition, Iraq appears to be installing or repairing dual-use equipment at CW-related facilities. Some of these facilities could be converted fairly quickly for production of CW agents.

UNSCOM reported to the Security Council in December 1998 that Iraq also continued to withhold information related to its CW program. For example, Baghdad seized from UNSCOM inspectors an Air Force document discovered by UNSCOM that indicated that Iraq had not consumed as many CW munitions during the Iran-Iraq war in the 1980s as had been declared by Baghdad. This discrepancy indicates that Iraq may have hidden an additional 6,000 CW munitions.

In 1995, Iraq admitted to having an offensive BW program and submitted the first in a series of Full, Final, and Complete Disclosures (FFCDs) that were supposed to reveal the full scope of its BW program. According to UNSCOM, these disclosures are incomplete and filled with inaccuracies. Since the full scope and nature of Iraq's BW program was not verified, UNSCOM had assessed that Iraq continued to maintain a knowledge base and industrial infrastructure that could be used to produce quickly a large amount of BW agents at any time, if the decision is made to do so. In the absence of UNSCOM or other inspections and monitoring since late 1998, we remain concerned that Iraq may again be producing biological warfare agents.

Iraq has continued working on its L-29 unmanned aerial vehicle (UAV) program, which involves converting L-29 jet trainer aircraft originally acquired from Eastern Europe. It is believed that Iraq has conducted flights of the L-29, possibly to test system improvements or to train new pilots. These refurbished trainer aircraft are believed to have been modified for delivery of chemical or, more likely, biological warfare agents.

We believe that Iraq has probably continued low-level theoretical R&D associated with its nuclear program. A sufficient source of fissile material remains Iraq's most significant obstacle to being able to produce a nuclear weapon. Although we were already concerned about a reconstituted nuclear weapons program, our concerns were increased last September when Saddam publicly exhorted his "Nuclear Mujahidin" to "defeat the enemy."

Iraq continues to pursue development of SRBM systems that are not prohibited by the United Nations and may be expanding to longer-range systems. Pursuit of UN-permitted missiles continues to allow Baghdad to develop technological improvements and infrastructure that could be applied to a longer-range missile program. We believe that development of the liquid-propellant Al-Samoud SRBM probably is maturing and that a low-level operational capability could be achieved in the near term — which is further suggested by the appearance of four Al Samoud transporter-erector-launchers (TELs) with airframes at the 31 December Al Aqsa Cal parade. The solid-propellant missile development program may now be receiving a higher priority, and development of the Ababil-100 SRBM – two of such airframes and TELs were paraded on 31 December—and possibly longer range systems may be moving ahead rapidly. If economic sanctions against Iraq were lifted, Baghdad probably would increase its attempts to acquire missile-related items from foreign sources, regardless of any future UN monitoring and continuing restrictions on long-range ballistic missile programs. Iraq probably retains a small, covert force of Scud-type missiles.

Iraq's ACW acquisitions remain low due to the generally successful enforcement of the UN arms embargo. The weapons and ACW-related goods which have been delivered to Iraq tend to be smaller arms transported over porous land borders. Iraq continues, however, to aggressively seek ACW equipment and technology.

North Korea

During this time frame, North Korea continued procurement of raw materials and components for its ballistic missile programs from various foreign sources, especially through North Korean firms based in China. We assess that North Korea is capable of producing and delivering via munitions a wide variety of chemical and biological agents.

During the remainder of 2000, P'yongyang continued its attempts to procure technology worldwide that could have applications in its nuclear program, but we do not know of any procurement directly linked to the nuclear weapons program. We assess that North Korea has produced enough plutonium for at least one, and possibly two, nuclear weapons. The United States and North Korea completed the canning of all accessible spent fuel rods and rod fragments in April 2000 in accordance with the 1994 Agreed Framework. That reactor fuel contains enough plutonium for several more weapons.

Libya

Libya is continuing its efforts to obtain ballistic missile–related equipment, materials, technology, and expertise from foreign sources. Outside assistance—particularly Serbian, Indian, North Korean and Chinese—is critical to it ballistic missile development programs, and the suspension of UN sanctions in 1999 has allowed Tripoli to expand its procurement effort. Libya's current capability probably remains limited to its Scud B missiles, but with continued foreign assistance it may achieve an MRBM capability—a long-desired goal—or extended-range Scud capability.

Libya remains heavily dependent on foreign suppliers for precursor chemicals and other key CW-related equipment. Following the suspension of UN sanctions in April 1999, Tripoli reestablished contacts with sources of expertise, parts, and precursor chemicals abroad, primarily in Western Europe. Libya still appears to have a goal of establishing an offensive CW capability and an indigenous production capability for weapons. Evidence suggests Libya also is seeking to acquire the capability to develop and produce BW agents.

Libya—an NPT party with full scope IAEA safeguards—continues to develop its nuclear research and development program but would still require significant foreign assistance to advance a nuclear weapons option. The suspension of UN sanctions has accelerated the pace of procurement efforts in Libya's drive to rejuvenate its ostensibly civilian nuclear program. In January and November 2000, for example, Tripoli and Moscow renewed talks on cooperation at the Tajura Nuclear Research Center and discussed a potential power reactor deal. Should such civil-sector work come to fruition, Libya could gain opportunities to pursue technologies that could be diverted for military purposes.

Following the suspension of UN sanctions, Libya has negotiated—and perhaps completed—contracts with Russian firms for conventional weapons, munitions, and upgrades and refurbishment for its existing inventory of Soviet-era weapons.

Syria

Syria sought CW-related precursors and expertise from foreign sources during the reporting period. Damascus already has a stockpile of the nerve agent sarin, and it would appear that Syria is trying to develop more toxic and persistent nerve agents. Syria remains dependent on foreign sources for key elements of its CW program, including precursor chemicals and key production equipment. It is highly probable that Syria also is developing an offensive BW capability.

We will continue to monitor the potential for Syria's nuclear R&D program to expand.

During the second half of 2000, Damascus continued work on establishing a solid-propellant rocket motor development and production capability with help from outside countries. Foreign equipment and assistance to its liquid-propellant missile program—primarily from North Korean entities, but also from firms in Russia—have been and will continue to be essential for Syria's effort. Damascus also continued its efforts to assemble—probably with considerable North Korean assistance—liquid-fueled Scud C missiles.

Syria continues to acquire ACW—mainly from Russia and other FSU suppliers—although at a reduced level from the early 1990s. During the past few years, Syria has received Kornet-E (AT-14), Metis-M (AT-13), Konkurs (AT-5), and Bastion-M (AT-10B) antitank guided missiles, RPG-29 rocket launchers, and small arms. Damascus has expressed interest in acquiring Russian Su-27 and MiG-29 fighters and air defense systems, but its outstanding debt to Moscow and inability to fund large purchases have hampered negotiations.

Sudan

In the WMD arena, Sudan, a CWC States Party, has been developing the capability to produce chemical weapons for many years. In this pursuit, it historically has obtained help from entities in other countries, principally Iraq. Sudan may be interested in a BW program as well.

During the reporting period, Sudan sought to acquire a variety of military equipment from various sources. Khartoum is seeking older, less expensive ACW and conventional weapons that nonetheless are advanced compared with the capabilities of the weapons possessed by its opponents and their supporters in neighboring countries in the long-running civil war.

India

India continues its nuclear weapons development program, for which its underground nuclear tests in May 1998 were a significant milestone. The acquisition of foreign equipment will benefit New Delhi in its efforts to develop and produce more sophisticated nuclear weapons. During this reporting period, India continued to obtain foreign assistance for its civilian nuclear power program, primarily from Russia.

India continues to rely on foreign assistance for key missile technologies, where it still lacks engineering or production expertise. Entities in Russia and Western Europe remained the primary conduits of missile-related and dual-use technology transfers during the latter half of 2000.

India continues an across-the-board modernization of its armed forces through ACW acquisitions, mostly from Russia, although many of its key programs have been plagued by delays. During the reporting period, New Delhi concluded a $3 billion contract with Russia to produce under license 140 Su-30 multirole fighters and continued negotiations with Moscow for 310 T-90S main battle tanks, A-50 Airborne Early Warning and Control (AWACS) aircraft, Tu-22M Backfire maritime strike bombers, and an aircraft carrier. India also continues to explore options for leasing or purchasing several AWACS systems from other entities. India also signed a contract with France for 10 additional Mirage 2000H multirole fighters and is considering offers for jet trainer aircraft from France and the United Kingdom. In addition to helping India with the development of its indigenous nuclear-powered submarine, Russia is negotiating with India the possible lease of a Russian nuclear-powered attack submarine.

Pakistan

Chinese entities continued to provide significant assistance to Pakistan's ballistic missile program during the reporting period. With Chinese assistance, Pakistan is moving toward serial production of solid-propellant SRBMs, such as the Shaheen-I and Haider-I. Pakistan flight-tested the Shaheen-I in 1999 and plans to flight-test the Haider-I in 2001. Successful development of the two-stage Shaheen-II MRBM will require continued Chinese assistance or assistance from other potential sources.

Pakistan continued to acquire nuclear-related and dual-use equipment and materials from various sources—principally in Western Europe. Islamabad has a well-developed nuclear weapons program, as evidenced by its first nuclear weapons tests in late May 1998. Acquisition of nuclear-related goods from foreign sources will remain important if Pakistan chooses to develop more advanced nuclear weapons. China, which has provided extensive support in the past to Islamabad's nuclear weapons and ballistic missile programs, in May 1996 pledged that it would not provide assistance to unsafeguarded nuclear facilities in any state, including Pakistan. We cannot rule out, however, some unspecified contacts between Chinese entities and entities involved in Pakistan's nuclear weapons development.

Pakistan continues to rely on China and France for its ACW requirements and negotiated to purchase an additional 40 F-7 fighters from China.

Egypt

During the last half of 2000, Egypt maintained a relationship with North Korea on ballistic missiles and maintained a Scud inventory. Egypt's ACW acquisition trends aim toward modernizing its Soviet-era equipment and acquiring newer, mostly US weapons.

KEY SUPPLIERS:

Russia

Despite improvements in Russia's economy, the state-run defense and nuclear industries remain strapped for funds, even as Moscow looks to them for badly needed foreign exchange through exports. We remain very concerned about the proliferation implications of such sales in several areas. Monitoring Russian proliferation behavior, therefore, will remain a very high priority.

Russian entities during the reporting period continued to supply a variety of ballistic missile-related goods and technical know-how to countries such as Iran, India, China, and Libya. Iran's earlier success in gaining technology and materials from Russian entities has helped to accelerate Iranian development of the Shahab-3 MRBM, and continuing Russian assistance likely supports Iranian efforts to develop new missiles and increase Tehran's self-sufficiency in missile production.

Russia also remained a key supplier for civilian nuclear programs in Iran, primarily focused on the Bushehr Nuclear Power Plant project. With respect to Iran's nuclear infrastructure, Russian assistance enhances Iran's ability to support a nuclear weapons development effort, even though the ostensible purpose of most of this assistance is for civilian applications. Despite Iran's NPT status, the United States is convinced Tehran is pursuing a nuclear weapons program. The Intelligence Community will be closely monitoring Tehran's nuclear cooperation with Moscow for any direct assistance in support of a nuclear weapons program.

In January 2000, Moscow approved a draft cooperative program with Syria that included civil use of nuclear power. Broader access to Russian scientists and Russia's large nuclear infrastructure could provide opportunities to solicit fissile material production expertise and other nuclear-related assistance if Syria decided to pursue nuclear weapons. In addition, Russia supplied India with material for its civilian nuclear program during this reporting period.

President Putin in May 2000 amended the presidential decree on nuclear exports to allow the export in exceptional cases of nuclear materials, technology, and equipment to countries that do not have full-scope IAEA safeguards. The move could clear the way for expanding nuclear exports to certain countries that do not have full-scope safeguards, such as India.

During the second half of 2000, Russian entities remained a significant source of dual-use biotechnology, chemicals, production technology, and equipment for Iran. Russia's biological and chemical expertise makes it an attractive target for Iranians seeking technical information and training on BW and CW agent production processes.

Russia continues to be a major supplier of conventional arms. It is the primary source of ACW for China and India, it continues to supply ACW to Iran and Syria, and it has negotiated new contracts with Libya and North Korea.

Russia continues to be the main supplier of technology and equipment to India and China's naval nuclear propulsion programs. In addition, Russia has discussed leasing nuclear-powered attack submarines to India.

The Russian Government's commitment, willingness, and ability to curb proliferation-related transfers remain uncertain. The export control bureaucracy was reorganized again as part of President Putin's broader government reorganization in May 2000. The Federal Service for Currency and

Export Controls (VEK) was abolished and its functions assumed by a new department in the Ministry of Economic Development and Trade. VEK had been tasked with drafting the implementing decrees for Russia's July 1999 export control law; the status of these decrees is not known. Export enforcement continues to need improvement. In February 2000, Sergey Ivanov, then Secretary of Russia's Security Council, said that during 1998-99 the government had obtained convictions for unauthorized technology transfers in three cases. The Russian press has reported on cases where advanced equipment is simply described as something else in the export documentation and is exported. Enterprises sometimes falsely declare goods to avoid government taxes.

North Korea

Throughout the second half of 2000, North Korea continued to export significant ballistic missile–related equipment, components, materials, and technical expertise to countries in the Middle East, South Asia, and North Africa. P'yongyang attaches a high priority to the development and sale of ballistic missiles, equipment, and related technology. Exports of ballistic missiles and related technology are one of the North's major sources of hard currency, which fuel continued missile development and production.

China

During this reporting period, Beijing continued to take a very narrow interpretation of its bilateral nonproliferation commitments with the United States. In the case of missile-related transfers, Beijing has on several occasions pledged not to sell Missile Technology Control Regime (MTCR) Category I systems but has not recognized the regime's key technology annex. China is not a member of the MTCR.

In November 2000, China committed not to assist, in any way, any country in the development of ballistic missiles that can be used to deliver nuclear weapons, and to enact at an early date a comprehensive missile-related export control system.

During the reporting period, Chinese entities provided Pakistan with missile-related technical assistance. Pakistan has been moving toward domestic serial production of solid-propellant SRBMs with Chinese help. Pakistan also needs continued Chinese assistance to support development of the two-stage Shaheen-II MRBM. In addition, firms in China have provided dual-use missile-related items, raw materials, and/or assistance to several other countries of proliferation concern—such as Iran, North Korea, and Libya.

In the nuclear area, China has made bilateral pledges to the United States that go beyond its 1992 NPT commitment not to assist any country in the acquisition or development of nuclear weapons. For example, in May 1996 Beijing pledged that it would not provide assistance to unsafeguarded nuclear facilities.

With respect to Pakistan, Chinese entities in the past provided extensive support to unsafeguarded as well as safeguarded nuclear facilities, which enhanced substantially Pakistan's nuclear weapons capability. We cannot rule out some continued contacts between Chinese entities and entities associated with Pakistan's nuclear weapons program subsequent to Beijing's 1996 pledge and during this reporting period.

In October 1997, China gave the United States assurances regarding its nuclear cooperation with Iran. China agreed to end cooperation with Iran on supply of a uranium conversion facility and undertake no new cooperation with Iran after completion of two existing projects—a zero-power reactor and a zirconium production plant. Although the Chinese appear to have lived up to these commitments, we are aware of some interactions between Chinese and Iranian entities that have raised questions about its "no new nuclear cooperation" pledge. According to the State Department, the Administration is seeking to address these questions with appropriate Chinese authorities.

Prior to the reporting period, Chinese firms had supplied dual-use CW-related production equipment and technology to Iran. The US sanctions imposed in May 1997 on seven Chinese entities for knowingly and materially contributing to Iran's CW program remain in effect. Evidence during the current reporting period shows Iran continues to seek such assistance from Chinese entities, but it is unclear to what extent these efforts have succeeded.

China is a primary supplier of advanced conventional weapons to Pakistan, Iran, and Sudan, among others. Sudan received military vehicles, naval equipment, guns, ammunition, and tanks from Chinese suppliers in the latter half of 2000.

Western Countries

As was the case in 1998 and 1999, entities in Western countries in 2000 were not as important as sources for WMD- and missile- related goods and materials as in past years. However, Iran and Libya continued to approach entities in Western Europe to provide needed acquisitions for their WMD and missile programs. Increasingly rigorous and effective export controls and cooperation among supplier countries have led the other foreign WMD and missile programs to look elsewhere for many controlled dual-use goods. Machine tools, spare parts for dual-use equipment, and widely available materials, scientific equipment, and specialty metals were the most common items sought. In addition, several Western countries announced their willingness to negotiate ACW sales to Libya.

TRENDS

As in previous reports, countries determined to maintain WMD and missile programs over the long term have been placing significant emphasis on increased self-sufficiency and attempts to insulate their programs against interdiction and disruption, as well as trying to reduce their dependence on imports by developing domestic production capabilities. Although these capabilities may not always be a good substitute for foreign imports—particularly for more advanced technologies—in many cases they may prove to be adequate. In addition, as their domestic capabilities grow, traditional recipients of WMD and missile technology could emerge as new suppliers of technology and expertise. Many of these countries—such as India, Iran and Pakistan—are not members of supplier groups such as the Nuclear Suppliers Group, Australia Group and the Missile Technology Control Regime and do not adhere to their export constraints. In addition, private companies, scientists, and engineers in Russia, China, and India may be increasing their involvement in WMD- and missile-related assistance, taking advantage of weak or unenforceable national export controls and the growing availability of technology.

Some countries of proliferation concern are continuing efforts to develop indigenous designs for advanced conventional weapons and expand production capabilities, although most of these programs usually rely heavily on foreign technical assistance. Many of these countries—unable to obtain newer or more advanced arms—are pursuing upgrade programs for existing inventories.

LEGISLATIVE BRANCH

Reports

DOCUMENT NO. 9

TERRORISM: AUTOMATED LOOKOUT SYSTEMS AND BORDER SECURITY OPTIONS AND ISSUES

CRS REPORT FOR CONGRESS

WILLIAM J. KROUSE
ANALYST IN SOCIAL LEGISLATION
DOMESTIC SOCIAL POLICY DIVISION

RAPHAEL F. PERL
SPECIALIST IN INTERNATIONAL AFFAIRS FOREIGN AFFAIRS, DEFENSE, AND TRADE DIVISION

June 18, 2001

COMMENTARY: *Though produced a good time before the September 11th attacks, this Report proposes a number of actions which are, to some extent, being introduced by the Administration to cope with terrorist movements into and out of the United States. The Report can be read in tandem with the Canadian-U.S. Border Declaration carried as Document number 20 in this Volume.*

SUMMARY

Border security and the threat of international terrorism are issues of intense congressional concern, as is evidenced by recent congressional hearings held to examine these issues in the 107th Congress. The challenge for policy makers is to provide for a level of border security that is commensurate with threats from abroad, while facilitating legitimate cross-border travel and commerce, and protecting civil liberties. To provide border security, a number of federal agencies work in tandem. The State Department and the federal inspection services, principally the Immigration and Naturalization Service and the U.S. Customs Service, have long maintained lookout books for the purpose of excluding "undesirable" persons, including suspected terrorists, from entry into the United States. While automated lookout books are an integral part of the border security equation, other measures can be taken to increase border security.

This report presents five options that have been discussed by international security specialists for strengthening the processes by which persons who are known to be members or supporters of foreign terrorist organizations are excluded from entry into the United States. Those options include (1) making it more difficult to counterfeit and alter international travel documents, (2) increasing entry/exit control mechanisms at international ports of entry, (3) increasing staff and technology for consular and federal inspection services, (4) enhancing recordkeeping on the visa status and whereabouts of foreign students in the United States, and (5) expanding the current visa lookout system to include data on members of international organized crime groups. While some, or perhaps all, of these options could theoretically be implemented by the Administration, adoption would most likely require congressional support through legislative mandates, directed appropriations, or report language.

Clearly, border control is vital to the security of the nation and its citizens. Notwithstanding, increasing border security has significant financial and social costs. Indeed, the exclusion of persons from entry into the United States for ideological or political beliefs has long been a source of controversy. Moreover, the options listed above could prove controversial, if adopted and implemented without careful consideration for facilitating legitimate cross-border travel and commerce. Furthermore, many view the inclusion of personal biometric identifiers in travel documents, monitoring foreign students, and increased entry/exit control as examples of greater government intrusion. Finally, hiring additional staff and developing force- multiplying technologies are expensive propositions as well.

This report examines options and issues related to improving border security by strengthening the automated "lookout" systems and processes employed to exclude persons who are known to be members or supporters of foreign terrorist organizations from entry into the United States.[1]

INTRODUCTION

Border security and the threat of international terrorism are issues of intense congressional concern, as is evidenced by recent congressional hearings held to examine these issues in the 107th Congress. The challenge for policy makers is to provide for a level of border security that is commensurate with threats from abroad, while facilitating legitimate cross-border travel and commerce, as well as, protecting civil liberties.

A number of federal agencies work in tandem to provide border security. The State Department and the federal inspection services,[2] principally the Immigration and Naturalization Service (INS) and the U.S. Customs Service, have long maintained lookout books for the purpose of excluding "undesirable" persons, including suspected terrorists, from entry into the United States. The exclusion of persons from entry into the United States for ideological or political beliefs, however, has long been a source of controversy. While it is clearly within the public interest and the federal government's mandate to exclude persons who are intent on inciting or engaging in terrorist activities, the determination of who may be a member or supporter of a foreign terrorist organization and, therefore, inadmissible is ultimately a subjective consideration made by intelligence analysts and consular officers and based on the best information available. As such, these considerations are likely to be controversial and change over time.

The administration and enforcement of immigration law has been viewed by some as a series of concentric circles. The first circle, or line of defense, is made up of the State Department's consular posts overseas, where consular officers adjudicate visa applications for foreign nationals wishing to come to the United States. Under current law, any alien (non-citizen) who is known to have engaged in terrorist activity, is likely to engage in terrorist activity, or who is a member/supporter of a foreign terrorist organization is inadmissible into the United States.[3]

Over the last decade, Congress has enacted legislation directing the State Department to computerize and expand its visa lookout books.[4] The computerized lookout system maintained by the State Department is the Consular Lookout and Support System (CLASS). With input from the intelligence community, the State Department enters the names and other biographical data of known and suspected members and supporters of foreign terrorist organizations into CLASS. As required by law, before issuing a visa to any foreign national, consular officers must certify, in writing, that a lookout check has been made and that there is no reason to exclude the applicant from admission to the United States.[5]

The second circle is composed of designated international ports of entry where travelers are screened for admission into the United States by INS immigration and Customs inspectors. It is unlawful for any person to enter the United States at any place other than a designated port of entry. The primary objective of inspections is twofold: to facilitate legal entries of admissible persons on the one hand, and to intercept *mala fide* applicants for admission on the other. INS and Customs inspectors use the Interagency Border Inspection System (IBIS) to quickly verify that applicants for admission are not known to be inadmissible and to check that they are not wanted by federal law enforcement officials. IBIS not only interfaces with CLASS, it also interfaces with databases maintained by other federal law enforcement agencies like the Federal Bureau of Investigation (FBI) and the Drug Enforcement Administration (DEA).

For the most part, once foreign nationals are admitted to the United States, they are not monitored unless they come under the scrutiny of the FBI's foreign counterintelligence operations, or the scrutiny of some other federal law enforcement agency because of some other suspected illegal activity

STATUTORY AUTHORITIES

The following discussion sets out the relevant federal authorities, the grounds of inadmissibility, the statutory definition of "terrorist activity," and the process by which the State Department designates foreign terrorist organizations.

The Roles of the Attorney General and Secretary of State

The Immigration and Nationality Act of 1952 (INA; 8 U.S.C. Section 1101 *et seq.*) is the main body of law governing immigration to the United States. Section 103 of the INA gives primary responsibility for the administration and enforcement of immigration law at the border and within the United States to the Attorney General. All persons seeking entry into the United States must apply for admission at a designated port of entry. With limited exceptions, any non-citizen seeking to enter the United States is required to present valid documentation as required by the Attorney General in regulation. Most of that authority is delegated to the INS Commissioner. The issuance of passports and visas, however, is the responsibility of the Secretary of State.

Section 104 of the INA gives responsibility for the administration and enforcement of immigration law to the Secretary of State as it relates to the duties and functions of diplomatic and consular officers. The Secretary of State oversees 250 diplomatic and consular posts around the world from which visas are issued to immigrants seeking permanent residence and nonimmigrants seeking authorization for a temporary stay in the United States. The Bureau of Consular Affairs is the branch of State that manages the issuance of passports to citizens and visas to non-citizens. U.S. consular officers abroad issue about 6 million visas annually to foreign nationals who wish to visit the United States and almost 500,000 immigrant visas to those who wish to reside here permanently.

Consular officers are given wide discretion whether to grant or refuse a visa, this decision is subject to very limited review, and there is no avenue for administrative appeal. Moreover, a visa (immigrant or nonimmigrant) is not a guarantee of entry into the United States; INS inspectors at ports of entry may find cause to exclude a visaed alien from entry, although this seldom occurs.

Grounds for Inadmissibility

During both the visa and admissions process, aliens must satisfy consular and immigration officers that they are not inadmissible under any of the grounds outlined in Section 212(a) of the INA. Grounds for inadmissibility are currently divided into 10 categories: (1) health-related grounds; (2) criminal grounds; (3) security grounds; (4) public charge proscription; (5) unauthorized employment; (6) illegal entrants and immigration violators proscription; (7) documentation requirements; (8) ineligibility for citizenship; (9) unlawful presence; and (10) miscellaneous.

Section 212(a)(3) of the INA makes any alien inadmissible if the Secretary of State or the Attorney General has reasonable grounds to believe that the alien seeks to enter the United States to engage in espionage or sabotage, to attempt to unlawfully overthrow the U.S. government, or to engage in any other unlawful activity.

Section 212(a)(3)(B)(i) of the INA makes any alien inadmissible if there is reasonable ground to believe the alien (1) has engaged in terrorist activity; (2) is or is likely to be engaged in terrorist activity; (3) has, under certain circumstances, indicated an intention to cause death or serious bodily harm, or incited terrorist activity; (4) is a representative of a foreign terrorist organization as designated by the Secretary of State, which the alien knows or should have known is a terrorist organization; or (5) is a member of a foreign terrorist organization as designated by the Secretary of State.

Visa Denial Waivers. The inadmissibility of members and supporters of foreign terrorist organizations under Section 212(a)(3)(B) can be waived under Section 212(d), which provides the Attorney General with that authority, if he deems that it is in the national interest to do so. Such waivers are usually granted at the request of the Secretary of State, with the concurrence of the Attorney General.

Terrorist Activity Defined. Section 212(a)(3)(B)(ii) defines "terrorist activity" as being comprised of the following six examples: (1) the highjacking or sabotage of any conveyance (including an aircraft, vessel, or vehicle); (2) the seizing or detaining, and threatening to kill, injure, or continue to detain, another individual in order to compel a third person (including a governmental organization) to do or abstain from doing any act as an explicit or implicit condition for the release of the individual seized or detained; (3) a violent attack upon an internationally protected person (as defined in Section 1116(b)(4) of Title 18) or upon the liberty of such a person; (4) an assassination; (5) the use of any—(a) biological agent, chemical agent, or nuclear weapon or device, or (b) explosive or firearm (other than for mere personal monetary gain), with intent to endanger, directly or indirectly, the safety of one or more individuals or to cause substantial damage to property; (6) a threat, attempt, or conspiracy to do any of the foregoing. In addition, such activity must be unlawful in the place where it is committed or, if committed in the United States, would be unlawful under the laws of the United States.

Designation of Foreign Terrorist Organizations. Section 219(a) of the INA governs the process by which the Secretary of State designates a foreign terrorist organization. Such an organization must (1) be foreign, (2) be engaged in an activity as defined under Section 212(a)(B)(ii) (described above), and (3) threaten the security of U.S. nationals or the security of the United States. In addition, State is required by law to inform Congress of its intent to designate a particular organization as terrorist in the *Federal Register*. An organization may appeal such designation within 30 days before the U.S. Court of Appeals for the District of Columbia Circuit.

VISA ISSUANCE, ADMISSIONS, AND LOOKOUT CHECKS

The State Department and the federal inspectional services have taken a number of steps to improve and computerize their lookout systems. Although efforts were already underway in the early 1990s to improve these systems, the bombing of the World Trade Center in February 1993 prompted federal officials to accelerate these efforts, since many of those involved in the conspiracy were visaed foreign nationals. The following discussion provides a brief description of these systems.

State Department

Consular officers are required by law to certify in writing that they have checked State's lookout system, CLASS, and that there is no basis to exclude an alien before issuing a visa.[6] The CLASS database contains approximately 4 million records, including limited biographical information on terrorists, narco-traffickers, and international criminals. Following the World Trade Center bombing, State directed consular offices to form "Visa

Viper" committees to ensure that the names of possible terrorist are forwarded by consular officers to the State Department.

In addition, State's Bureau of Intelligence and Research maintains a database known as TIPOFF. By screening highly classified holdings on international terrorists, State Department analysts compile files on persons who may be considered terrorists and may be subject to exclusion under Section 212(a)(3). Such information may prove useful to consular and immigration officers when making decisions regarding visa issuance and admissions. The bottom line criterion for inclusion in TIPOFF is whether a reasonable suspicion exists that a person, if admitted, is or would be engaged in terrorist activities.

The holdings of TIPOFF are classified. Essential components of TIPOFF data needed to identify and exclude persons on terrorist grounds have been added into CLASS. State Department employees, who maintain the TIPOFF system, check TIPOFF database hits and related intelligence reports. Names are periodically removed from TIPOFF. Reasons for removal include: (1) death; (2) attaining 99 years of age; (3) weakness of original information as confirmed by lack of activity over a sustained period of time; (4) subsequent ascertainment that the original information was incorrect; and (5) an individual has become an immigrant or U.S. citizen. Since 1987, when TIPOFF was established, several hundred names have been removed from TIPOFF, according to the State Department.

It is important to note that not all persons who are in CLASS are denied visas. A suspected or confirmed terrorist may be granted a visa denial waiver when requested by the Secretary of State and approved by the Attorney General. Such waivers may be granted for political purposes, as is now often the case with members of the Palestinian Liberation Organization (PLO) visiting the United States on diplomatic business. Waivers are also granted for intelligence gathering and law enforcement purposes. For example, a suspected terrorist may be admitted to the country so as to determine where and to whom his trail leads. Indeed, according to the Foreign Affairs Manual, all visa applications involving possible inadmissibility as a terrorist must be submitted to the State Department for a security advisory opinion, which State's Visa Office attempts to turn around with 15 days. Furthermore, the Secretary of State is required by law to report to Congress the denial of all visas on these grounds.

INS and Customs Service

With certain exceptions, INS immigration inspectors are instructed to check the name of every person 14 years of age or older in the Interagency Border Inspection System (IBIS). IBIS is maintained by the INS and the U.S. Customs Service and provides lookout information to the federal inspection services. While INS provides the largest number of lookout records through its National Automated Immigration Lookout System II (NAILS II), many different agencies feed information into IBIS. Some of these agencies include the Department of State, the Federal Bureau of Investigation (FBI), the Office of Special Investigations (OSI), the International Crime Police Organization (INTERPOL), and the Department of Agriculture. About 30 different agencies and approximately 3,000 government employees have access to IBIS.

NAILS II, the INS lookout system, contains biographical and case data on persons who may be inadmissible or are being sought by INS for other reasons related to immigration law and enforcement. It may be searched by name, variations of the name (soundex), alien registration number, or date of birth. Names are downloaded from TIPOFF into NAILS II. Conversely, NAILS lookout data is fed into CLASS on a daily basis.

The Treasury Enforcement and Communications System (TECS) II serves as the centralized database for IBIS. Through TECS II, IBIS interfaces with many other databases maintained by many other state, federal, and international law enforcement agencies, e.g., the FBI's National Crime Information Center (NCIC), the National Law Enforcement Telecommunications System (NLETS), and the California Law Enforcement Telecommunications System (CLETS). Through these interfaces, IBIS contains approximately 5 million names and birth dates of individuals who may be inadmissible into the United States. Most of these persons, however, are potentially inadmissible for reasons other than suspected terrorist activity. Persons may be included in IBIS for reasons ranging from suspected organized crime activity to nonpayment of child support.

OPTIONS AND ISSUES FOR CONGRESS

As international travel to the United States increases, Congress is likely to continue to focus on issues related to border security and the facilitation of legitimate cross-border travel. While automated lookout books are an integral part of the border security equation, other measures can be taken to increase border security. Enumerated below are five technology-based options for increasing border security along with related issues, such as economic and social costs. Options include (1) making it more difficult to counterfeit and alter international travel documents, (2) increasing entry/exit control mechanisms at international ports of entry, (3) increasing staff and technology for consular and federal inspection services, (4) enhancing record keeping on the visa status and whereabouts of foreign students in the United States, and (5) expanding the current visa lookout system to include data on members of international organized crime groups.

Certainly, these border security options are not without consequence. Related issues include the degree to which these measures: 1) encroach upon civil liberties, 2) impede legitimate cross-border travel and commerce, 3) increase fiscal costs, and 4) are responsive to emerging threats.

Travel Document Integrity

Increasing travel document integrity by making it more difficult to counterfeit and alter those documents could lead to two desirable outcomes. First, border security could be enhanced. Second, legitimate international travel could be expedited. Indeed, Congress has recently enacted legislation (P.L. 106-396) that makes permanent the Visa Waiver program. This program allows nationals from certain countries to enter the United States as temporary visitors for business or pleasure without first obtaining a visa from a U.S. consulate abroad. By eliminating the visa requirement, this program facilitates international travel and commerce and eases consular workloads, but it bypasses the first step by which international visitors are screened for admissibility when seeking to enter the United States.

This legislation also requires all countries participating in the Visa Waiver Program to issue machine readable passports to its citizens by October 2007. Machine readable passports not only facilitate international travel, but they also expedite lookout system queries. They also facilitate entry of international travelers by allowing carriers and the federal inspection services to pre-clear passengers through the use of electronic passenger manifests.[7]

Machine readable passports, however, do not address the issue of identity fraud. Another option by which border security could be enhanced is by upgrading lookout systems and travel documents to include biometric data. Indeed, INS and State have incorporated digitized fingerprints into the Green Card (I-551) carried by immigrants and the new Border Crossing Card (Laser Visa). In the case of the Green Card, INS administratively determined that a digitized fingerprint should be incorporated into that document. Congress has also enacted legislation requiring that a new Border Crossing Card be developed that would include a personal biometric identifier. The cost of producing and issuing these travel documents are covered by user fees. One option that has been mentioned is to legislatively require that passports include biometric identifiers. Such a course would likely require additional appropriations or higher passport fees.

With new technologies, a traveler's identity could be quickly and definitively verified by matching their identity with biometric identifiers like facial geometry, iris scans, and fingerprints that could be incorporated into passports, visas, and other travel documents. While biometric data is being collected for many purposes in the private sector, its use in the public sector has been controversial, for it is viewed by many as a government intrusion on individual privacy.[8]

Entry/Exit Control

Increasing entry/exit control mechanisms at international ports of entry is another measure that could be used to enhance border security. Provisions to require increased entry/exit control included in the Illegal Immigrations and Immigrant Responsibility Act of 1996 (IIRIRA; P.L. 104-208) have proved controversial and were amended by the 106th Congress. Section 110 of IIRIRA required the Attorney General to develop an automated entry/exit control system that would create a record for every alien arriving in the United States and match it with the record for the alien departing the United States. The Department of Justice (DOJ) encountered significant difficulty in implementing Section 110, because INS had not previously tracked arrivals and departures of immigrants and only had limited success in tracking arrivals and departures for nonimmigrants.

In addition, Canada and many congressional delegations from northern border states strongly opposed the implementation of Section 110 at the northern land border, since it would have represented a significant departure from the status quo. Canadians who enter the United States through land border ports were and are usually not required to obtain a visa, nor present a passport. Some were concerned that, if Section 110 were implemented at northern land border ports of entry, additional documents would have been required.

The principal focus of Section 110 was the enumeration and identification of nonimmigrant overstays (i.e., those persons who are legally admitted to the United States on a temporary basis and subsequently overstay the terms of their admission). Such a system, however, if linked to visa lookout systems and law enforcement databases, would serve as an extremely enhanced means of more closely screening aliens who may be subject to exclusion from the United States. Because of difficulties in developing such a system and concerns that it would impede legitimate international travel and commerce, Congress enacted the Immigration and Naturalization Service Data Management and Improvement Act of 2000(P.L. 106-215), amending Section 110 to require the development of an integrated entry and exit data system, which will use available data to record alien arrivals and departures, without establishing additional documentary requirements. Consequently, the scope of Section 110 is much narrower than originally enacted under P.L. 104-208.[9]

For reasons of immigration control and border security, entry/exit control could reemerge as an issue. Measures taken to increase border security, however, would be less controversial if they could be implemented in such a way as to facilitate legitimate cross border traffic and not greatly inconvenience the traveling public.

Increasing Staff and Technology for Consular and Federal Inspection Services

Increasing staff and technology for consular and federal inspection services is one option, albeit costly, that may warrant congressional attention. At the present time, the most effective mix of staff and technology necessary to achieve an optimal level of border security is under study by federal inspection services and is not yet known. Moreover, automated lookout systems and other technologies, which serve as force multipliers will, if not upgraded, be quickly outpaced by growth in cross- border traffic. It is undisputed that well trained and experienced staff are an essential component of the border security equation. Congress, however, may well want a clear assessment that agency personnel are being allocated efficiently and automated lookout systems are being properly and economically developed, before considering requests for increased funding.

According to State, demand for consular services is increasing. In FY2001, State anticipates that approximately 3,702 consular officers will provide services at overseas posts and domestically, processing over 7.5 million non-immigrant visa applications, about 500,000 immigrant visa applications, and over 7.8 million passports.[10] Under State's border security program, equipment and systems, including CLASS and TIPOFF, that support consular activities are being maintained and upgraded. Furthermore, increasing cooperation between consular officials with representatives of law enforcement agencies and the intelligence community is an ongoing part of the border security program. These efforts are funded through the machine readable visa (MRV) fee.[11]

At international airports of entry, INS is mandated by law to clear all international flights through primary inspections within 45 minutes. INS inspections at air and sea ports of entry are funded through user fees. While the 45 minute mandate expedites inspections, if a port is understaffed it probably leads to less thorough inspections, diminishing border security. The Administration's FY2002 request includes an increase in $70 million in user fees to hire an additional 539 positions to increase INS inspections staff at air and sea ports of entry, and $5 million to upgrade automated lookout systems.[12] The FY2002 request includes no additional funding for Customs inspectors at air ports of entry.

Regarding staffing and land border port infrastructure, the Customs Service has recently delivered to Congress two statutorily mandated reports. Regarding resource allocation Customs contracted with PricewaterhouseCoopers (PwC) in 1998 to develop a resource allocation model (RAM) to determine the most effective deployment of its inspectors and canine enforcement officers at its more than 300 international ports of entry. Such an analysis was necessary in order to identify opportunities to reduce passenger inspection wait time and cargo examination times, while maintaining some level of border security.

The RAM report includes a finding that, to meet its multifaceted mission, Customs staffing would need to be increased by 14,776 positions over its FY1998 base. The largest increases would be in inspector (6,481), special agent (2,041), and canine enforcement officer (650) positions. GAO testified in April 2000 that they found some weaknesses (data reliability issues) in the resource allocation model.[13] Nevertheless, the resource allocation model is the most comprehensive staffing analysis available to date, and it is very likely that Customs staffing will be an issue for the 107th Congress, as congestion and wait times at land border ports increase.

Regarding land border port infrastructure, the Customs Service, in consultation with the General Service Administration (GSA) and the federal inspection service (FIS) agencies, was directed in report language to assess the current infrastructure needs at ports of entry on the Northern and Southwest borders of the United States.[14] Customs identified 822 projects and projected that their costs would be around $784 million.[15] The agency also expects that imports and exports will nearly double in the next 5 years.[16] Customs anticipates that if the infrastructure at these ports is not improved in the next few years, the result is likely to be traffic backups and longer lines. In addition, the mission capabilities of federal inspection service agencies will be dangerously impaired, adversely affecting the level of border management.

Land border ports of entry pose greater border security challenges. Many people who cross the land border frequently reside in the region. Therefore, inspections process at land border ports is not conducted with the same level of intensity as at airports. At land border ports, inspectors visually screen applicants for admission in primary inspections lanes. As the vehicle approaches the inspections booth, the inspector usually enters the automobile license plate number into IBIS to check whether there is a lookout record on it. If there is a record, the vehicle is detoured into secondary inspection for further examination. In addition, the inspector queries the vehicle's occupants for documentation, intended destination, and length of stay.

If in the inspector's judgement no further examination is warranted, the vehicle and its occupants are waved through.

Unlike inspections at airports, wait times for inspections at land border ports have increased as cross border commerce has grown on both our northern and southern borders, largely as a consequence of the Canadian Free Trade Agreement and North American Free Trade Agreement. On the southern land border, inspection staff has increased dramatically, but on the northern land border, staffing has not increased significantly in the past 10 years.[17] The Administration's FY2002 request includes no funding for additional Immigration and Customs inspectors at land border ports. While statistical data are not readily available, it is generally acknowledged that both licit and illicit cross border commerce has increased on both the

northern and southern land borders in the past decade. Without corresponding increases in staffing and new technologies, however, the frequency and
rigor of inspections at land border ports of entry is likely to diminish.

Monitoring the Status of International Students

One of the recommendations of the National Commission on Terrorism,[18]
a congressionally-mandated bipartisan body, was to expand an existing
computerized program known as the Coordinated InterAgency Partnership Regulating International Students (CIPRIS).[19] This program is designed to facilitate data retrieval capability by establishing an automated
database to more efficiently monitor the immigration/visa status and
whereabouts of students from abroad. The Commission's report noted that
one of the convicted terrorists involved in the World Trade Center bombing entered the United States on a student visa, dropped out, and remained illegally thereafter.

In June 1997, INS implemented the program on a pilot basis at 21 educational institutions inGeorgia, Alabama, North Carolina, and South
Carolina, and at Atlanta's Hartsfield Airport. The program's automated
system was designed to not only monitor foreign students, but to support
screening foreign students at Consular Posts and processing their inspection at U.S. Ports-of-Entry. The pilot phase of the program officially ended
in October 1999, but INS reports that the program's automated system is
still a prototype.

Although enjoying strong support in the national security and counter-terrorism community, this program has drawn strong criticism from civil liberty groups and higher education administrators as a costly administrative
requirement that represents an overreach of governmental authority.[20]

An International Organized Crime Tipoff System

Many in the international law enforcement community perceive a growing
opportunistic and often symbiotic relationship between terrorist and international organized crime groups.[21] In light of such developments, expanding the Tipoff system to include identified members of international
criminal organizations may warrant congressional attention, they contend.
Such a database would undoubtedly expand the number of files included in
Tipoff and would increase the costs for the Department of State of maintaining such a system. While it would arguably provide national security benefits,
it could potentially result in challenges from the civil liberties community.

Endnotes

[1]It is important to note that lookout systems are only one of a number of tools available to federal officials carrying out border control functions. Alert and experienced consular staff and inspectors, such as the Customs inspectors who interdicted suspected terrorist Ahmed Ressam at the U.S.-Canada border in December 1999, are essential.

[2]"Federal inspection services" is a term of art. These services include: the Department of the Treasury's U.S. Customs Service, the Department of Justice's Immigration and Naturalization Service, the Department of Agriculture's Animal and Plant Health Inspection Service, and the Department of Health and Human Services' Public Health Service. Inspectors from all of these agencies are stationed at international ports of entry, but under certain circumstances, inspectors of one agency perform the functions of one or more of the other agencies.

[3]*See* Immigration and Nationality Act (INA) Section 212(a)(3)(B).

[4]See Section 140 of P.L. 103-236 (Foreign Relations Authorization Act, FY1994 and FY1995, as amended). Subsection (a) of this provision authorized the State Department to collect a fee to recover the costs of providing consular services. Subsection (b) directed the State Department to include a surcharge in the fee to upgrade and computerize visa lookout systems.

[5] *See* Section 140(c) of P.L. 103-236.

[6]Section 140(c) of P.L. 103-236, the Foreign Relations Authorization Act, FY1994 and FY1995.

[7]For further information, see CRS Report RS20546, *Immigration: Visa Waiver Permanent Program Act (P.L. 106-396)*, by William J. Krouse.

[8]For related information, see CRS Report RL30084, *Biometric Science and Technology for Personal Identification: Devices, Uses, Organizations and Congressional Intent*, by William C. Boesman.

[9]For further information, see CRS Report RS20627, *Immigration: Integrated Entry and Exit Data System*, by William J. Krouse.

[10]U.S. Department of State, *The Budget in Brief, Fiscal Year 2002*, (Washington, Winter 2001), p. 18.

[11]Machine readable visa (MRV) fees were authorized by the Foreign Relations Authorization Act, Fiscal Years 1994 and 1995 (P.L. 102-236). For FY2002, State has reported that it will obligate $414 million in offsetting receipts generated by the MRV fee for border security—a $23 million increase over FY2001 funding. The FY2002 request also includes a legislative proposal to make the MRV fee authorization permanent. It is currently authorized in 3-year cycles.

[12]For further information, see CRS Report RS20908, *Immigration and Naturalization Service's FY2002 Budget*, by William J. Krouse.

[13]U.S. General Accounting Office, Testimony before the House Committee on Government Reform Subcommittee on Government Management, Information and Technology, *U.S. Customs Service: Observations on Selected Operations and Program Issues*, TGGD/AIMD-00-150 (Washington, April 20, 2000), p. 6.

[14]Report language accompanying the FY2000 Treasury-Postal Appropriations Act (P.L. 106-58); S.Rept. 106-87 (S. 1282), p. 23.

[15]*Ports of Entry Infrastructure Assessment*, p. 1 of overview.

[16]U.S. General Accounting Office, *Major Management Challenges and Program Risks: Department of the Treasury*, (Washington, January 2001), p. 32.

[17]From FY1992 to FY1999, the number of immigration inspectors deployed on the southern land border increased from 666 to 1,893, an increase of 184%, while those deployed on the northern land border increased from 451 to 490, an increase of 9%. Meanwhile, immigration inspectors deployed at air and sea ports of entry nationwide went from 1,748 to 2,925, an increase of 67%. A breakout of Customs personnel deployed to the southern and northern land borders, and air and sea ports of entry, is not available; however, there are staffing sta-

tistics available nationwide. From FY1992 to FY1999, Customs inspectors deployed nationwide increased from 6,159 to 7,812, an increase of 27%, while canine enforcement officers increased from 405 to 644, an increase of 59%.

[18]For further information, see CRS Report RS20598, *National Commission on Terrorism Report: Background and Issues for Congress*, by Raphael Perl.

[19]Note that this pilot program was authorized by the Illegal Immigration and Immigrant Responsibility Act of 1996 (P.L. 104-208; IRRIRA). It was amended by the 106th Congress (P.L. 106-396; Title IV-Miscellaneous Provisions, Section 404) to eliminate the fee collection role for schools and exchange visitor programs by having the student/exchange visitor pay the fee directly to the federal government or a designated third party contractor.

[20]NAFSA: Association of International Educators, *Issue Brief: Repeal Section 641(CIPRIS): Illegal Immigration Reform and Immigrant Responsibility Act of 1996 (IIRIRA)*. (See: [http://www.nafsa.org/]. Click on "Public Policy," "Advocacy Topics," "For the Media," "NAFSA on the Issues," "CIPRIS") (This site was last visited on June 18, 2001.)

[21]For further information, see U.S. Congress. House Committee on the Judiciary. *Threat Posed by the Convergence of Organized Crime, Drug Trafficking, and Terrorism*. Hearing before the Subcommittee on Crime, December 13, 2000 (Serial No. 148).

DOCUMENT NO. 10

BIOTERRORISM:
FEDERAL RESEARCH AND PREPAREDNESS ACTIVITIES

GAO REPORT TO CONGRESSIONAL COMMITTEES

September 2001

COMMENTARY: *Here is a lengthy and informative Report which describes what Actions the U.S. Government has been taking to cope with Bioterrorism. It has Particular relevance in light of the Anthrax mailings of recent past and of the U.S. Government initiatives to counter such possibilities.*

Abbreviations

AHRQ	Agency for Healthcare Research and Quality
CDC	Centers for Disease Control and Prevention
CONPLAN	U.S. Government Interagency Domestic Terrorism Concept of Operations Plan
DOD	Department of Defense
DOE	Department of Energy
DOJ	Department of Justice
DOT	Department of Transportation
EPA	Environmental Protection Agency
FBI	Federal Bureau of Investigation
FDA	Food and Drug Administration
FEMA	Federal Emergency Management Agency
HHS	Department of Health and Human Services
NIAID	National Institute of Allergy and Infectious Diseases
NIH	National Institutes of Health
OEP	Office of Emergency Preparedness
OJP	Office of Justice Programs
TOPOFF 2000	Top Officials 2000 exercise
USDA	U.S. Department of Agriculture
VA	Department of Veterans Affairs
WMD	weapon of mass destruction

September 28, 2001

Congressional Committees

A number of incidents involving biological agents, including at least one completed bioterrorist act and numerous threats and hoaxes,[1] have occurred domestically. In 1984, a group intentionally contaminated salad bars in local restaurants in Oregon with salmonella bacteria[2] to prevent people from voting in a local election.[3] Although no one died, 751 people were diagnosed with foodborne illness. As was the case with this incident, determining whether an outbreak occurred naturally or was the product of an intentional release may be difficult unless someone announces the release beforehand or claims responsibility for it. Given the terrorist attacks of September 11, 2001, in addition to the terrorist bombings in New York City in 1993 and in Oklahoma City in 1995, some experts predict that domestic bioterrorist attacks are likely to occur. Others consider the likelihood of bioterrorist attacks to be low because of various difficulties, including those involved in processing the biological agents into lethal forms and successfully delivering them to achieve large-scale casualties. However, the ease with which these agents can be concealed and their potential to affect large segments of the population beyond those initially exposed may increase their appeal to terrorists.

Bioterrorism is the threat or intentional release of biological agents (viruses, bacteria, or their toxins) for the purpose of influencing the conduct of government, or intimidating or coercing a civilian population. These agents can be released by way of the air (as aerosols), food, water, or insects. The intentional release of a biological agent may not be recognized for several days, if ever, during which time a communicable biological agent (such as smallpox) can spread to others who were not initially exposed. Some biological agents (such as anthrax and plague) produce symptoms that can be easily confused with influenza or other, less virulent illnesses, leading to a delay in diagnosis or identification. In addition to widespread medical consequences, a bioterrorist attack also could bring about behavioral, social, economic, and psychological consequences, such as mass panic. Health care providers could be the first authorities to see victims as they seek treatment of their symptoms. If large numbers of people are affected, local and state officials may turn to the federal government for assistance with disease surveillance,[4] epidemiologic investigation,[5] health care delivery, quarantine management, remediation, and mass fatality management.

Many federal departments and agencies, including the Departments of Health and Human Services (HHS) and Justice (DOJ), would have roles in responding to a domestic bioterrorist attack against the U.S. population. These departments and agencies are involved in a range of activities related to the public health and medical consequences of a bioterrorist attack on the civilian population.[6] These activities are part of the federal government's overall effort to combat terrorism.

Because of the concerns about bioterrorism, the Public Health Improvement Act of 2000 (P.L. 106-505, sec. 102) mandates that we describe federal activities related to the public health and medical consequences of a bioterrorist attack against the civilian population. We are therefore providing information on (1) federal activities and funding related to the public health and medical consequences of a bioterrorist attack against the civilian population, (2) how these activities are coordinated among federal agencies and whether there are any shortcomings in the current coordination structure, and (3) existing evaluations of the effectiveness of these activities in preparing state and local authorities.

In carrying out our work, we relied on federal departments and agencies to identify relevant programs and provide budget information.[7] We have not audited or otherwise verified the information provided. We interviewed agency officials, obtained documents, and reviewed reports prepared by others (such as *Ataxia: The Chemical and Biological Terrorism Threat and the U.S. Response*[8] and *Toward a National Strategy for Combating Terrorism*[9]), as well as our previous reports (see Related GAO Products at the end of this report). Although there are generally no specific appropriations for activities on bioterrorism, some departments and agencies did provide estimates of the funds they were devoting to activities on bioterrorism. Other departments and agencies provided estimates for overall terrorism activities but were unable to provide funding amounts for activities on bioterrorism specifically. Still others stated that their activities were relevant for bioterrorism, but they were unable to specify the funding amounts. As a result, departments and agencies provided funding information in various forms—appropriations, obligations, expenditures. For a given fiscal year, this information is not necessarily additive across agencies.[10] For this reason, we have summarized funding by agency, but not across the federal government.[11] (See app. II for details regarding our scope and methodology.) We conducted our work from January through September 2001 in accordance with generally accepted government auditing standards.

Results in Brief

A variety of federal research and preparedness activities related to the public health and medical consequences of a bioterrorist attack are under way. Research activities focus on various biological agents that could be used as weapons of terrorism; detection of such agents; development of new or improved vaccines, antibiotics, and antivirals; and performance standards for emergency response equipment. Preparedness activities include increasing state and local response capabilities, improving federal response capacity, developing response teams, increasing the availability of medical treatments, participating in and sponsoring exercises, aiding victims, and providing support at special events, such as presidential inaugurations and Olympic games. Activities in many departments and agencies have a dual use, being not only relevant for bioterrorism but also for other types of terrorism, emergencies, and infectious disease surveillance. For example, the Federal Emergency Management Agency (FEMA) has a broad emergency and terrorist response system, which includes a bioterrorist response system. HHS has programs on emerging infectious diseases that benefit its activities on bioterrorism as well as research endeavors such as research on diagnoses, vaccines, and new therapies.

Federal departments and agencies use a variety of methods to coordinate their activities to combat terrorism. Departments and agencies are developing interagency response plans, participating in a variety of interagency work groups, and entering into formal agreements with other agencies to share resources and capabilities in order to improve coordination. However, coordination of federal terrorism research, preparedness, and response programs is fragmented, as we have discussed in a previous report.[12] As we noted, several different agencies are responsible for various coordination functions, which limits accountability and hinders unity of effort. For bioterrorism, different agencies have developed separate threat lists of biological agents, several agencies have not been included in bioterrorism-related policy and response planning, and agencies have developed programs to provide assistance to state and local governments that are similar and potentially duplicative. However, the Office of Management and Budget and the National Security Council have created a process to reduce overlap and improve coordination as part of the annual budget cycle. In addition, the Vice President was asked by the President in May 2001 to lead an interagency effort to improve coordination. Also, on September 20, 2001, the President announced the creation of the Office of Homeland Security to lead, oversee, and coordinate a comprehensive national strategy to safeguard the country against terrorism.

The reports that we reviewed identified concerns about the preparedness of states and local areas to respond to a bioterrorist attack. These concerns include insufficient state and local planning for response to terrorist events and a lack of hospital participation in training on terrorism and emergency response planning. Some federal programs have begun to provide funding to state and local governments to improve preparedness.

We provided a draft of this report to the eleven departments and agencies for their review in August 2001. HHS stated that many of the services needed in response to a bioterrorist attack would be needed to respond to other emergencies, including natural disasters and other types of terrorist attacks, and we added this information to the report. We also modified the report in response to a DOJ comment that it is appropriate for different agencies to maintain separate lists of biological threats, noting that such lists may have different purposes. Most agencies provided technical comments.

Background

Although the probability of a domestic bioterrorist attack has been considered to be low, some characteristics of biological agents may make them appealing to terrorists. The information for the production of agents is readily available on the Internet, and the agents are relatively easy to grow and conceal. According to intelligence agencies, the possibility that terrorists may use chemical or biological materials may increase over the next decade.[13]

However, other characteristics of biological agents may limit their appeal to terrorists. For example, they are difficult to obtain, process into a lethal form, and deliver to achieve large-scale casualties. Processing biological agents into the right particle size and delivering them effectively require expertise in a wide range of scientific disciplines. Additional hurdles to deployment include disruptions caused by environmental and meteorological conditions. For example, if wind conditions are too strong or erratic, agents released as aerosols might dissipate rapidly or fail to reach the desired area.

With any emergency, including natural disasters and terrorist attacks, states can call upon services related to emergency management, public safety, emergency medical services, health care delivery, and fatality management. Most states rely on local public health agencies to identify and respond to naturally occurring disease outbreaks, and these are the same agencies that are responsible for bioterrorism preparedness and response. Just as in naturally occurring outbreaks, a bioterrorist attack could involve public health officials in disease surveillance, epidemiologic investigation, health care delivery, quarantine management, remediation, and mass fatality management.

Unless a terrorist announces the release of a biological agent, the cause of an outbreak might be detected only after an epidemiologic investigation and laboratory identification. Officials from the Centers for Disease Control and Prevention (CDC) and the National Association of County and City Health Officials have stated that the capacities needed by local public health agencies to prepare for a bioterrorist incident should be built on the systems used to respond to naturally occurring disease outbreaks. Such a "dual-use" response infrastructure improves the capacity of local public health agencies to respond to all hazards.

In response to past domestic terrorist events and bioterrorism cases, including hoaxes, the federal government has become more involved in bioterrorism preparedness. From 1989 through 1996, Congress passed several laws aimed at preventing the acquisition and use of chemical or biological weapons by groups or individuals. In addition, the National

Defense Authorization Act for Fiscal Year 1997 (P.L. 104-201) authorized $97 million for domestic emergency assistance programs, including the implementation of programs providing advice, training, and the loan of equipment to state and local emergency response agencies and assistance to major cities in establishing medical strike teams. The act also authorized the Department of Defense (DOD) to establish military domestic terrorism rapid response teams. In the event of a bioterrorist attack against the civilian population, DOD will use these teams to provide support to the primary federal agency as defined under the Federal Response Plan.

The Federal Response Plan, originally drafted in 1992 and updated in 1999, is authorized under the Robert T. Stafford Disaster Relief and Emergency Assistance Act (Stafford Act; P.L. 93-288, as amended). The plan lays out the manner in which the federal government responds to domestic situations in which the President has declared an emergency requiring federal disaster assistance. Presidential Decision Directive 39, which was issued after the Oklahoma City bombing in 1995, provides a framework for how the federal government will respond to weapons of mass destruction (WMD)[14] terrorism within the United States, reaffirming the Federal Response Plan. The plan is an "all-hazards" (that is, for any emergency or disaster) approach document, with an annex specific to terrorism, which was added by FEMA in 1997. In 1998, Presidential Decision Directive 62 was issued, which describes federal agency roles in preparing for and responding to WMD terrorism. In 2001, the U.S. Government Interagency Domestic Terrorism Concept of Operations Plan was issued, which explains agencies' responsibilities under Presidential Decision Directives 39 and 62 in more detail. HHS is currently developing a bioterrorism annex to this plan. (See app. III for more information on these federal policy and planning documents.)

Departments and Agencies Reported a Variety of Actions and Funding for Research and Preparedness Activities

The federal government is conducting a variety of activities related to research on and preparedness for the public health and medical consequences of a bioterrorist attack against the civilian population. Research activities focus on detection, treatment, vaccination, and emergency response equipment. Preparedness efforts include increasing state and local response capabilities, improving federal response capacity, developing response teams, increasing availability of medical treatments, participating in and sponsoring exercises, planning for victim aid, and providing support during special events such as presidential inaugurations and Olympic games.

Research Activities Focus on Detection, Treatment, Vaccination, and Equipment

The federal government is involved in a range of research activities related to the public health and medical consequences of a bioterrorist attack on the civilian population. Studies are currently being done to enable the rapid identification of biological agents in a variety of settings; develop new or improved vaccines, antibiotics, and antivirals to improve treatment and vaccination for infectious diseases caused by biological agents; and develop and test emergency response equipment. Table 1 provides information on the total reported funding for all the departments and agencies carrying out research and examples of this research for these departments and agencies. In addition, DOD and the Department of Transportation (DOT) have some relevant research activities, but were not able to specify the associated funding. More detail on each department's and agency's activities is provided in appendixes IV through XIV.

Table 1: Total Reported Funding for Research on Bioterrorism and Terrorism by Federal Departments and Agencies, Fiscal Year 2000 and Fiscal Year 2001 (Dollars in millions)

Department or agency	Fiscal year 2000 funding	Fiscal year 2001 funding	Sample activities
U.S. Department of Agriculture—Agricultural Research Service	0	$0.5	Improving detection of biological agents
Department of Energy	$35.5	$39.6	Developing technologies for detecting and responding to a bioterrorist attack Developing models of the spread of and exposure to a biological agent after release
HHS—Agency for Healthcare Research and Quality	$5.0	0	Examining clinical training and ability of front-line medical staff to detect and respond to a bioterrorist threat Studying use of information systems and decision support systems to enhance preparedness for medical care in the event of a bioterrorist event
HHS—CDC	$48.2	$46.6	Developing equipment performance standards Conducting research on smallpox and anthrax viruses and therapeutics

Department or agency	Fiscal year 2000 funding	Fiscal year 2001 funding	Sample activities
HHS—Food and Drug Administration	$8.8	$9.1	Licensing of vaccines for anthrax and smallpox Determining procedures for allowing use of not yet approved drugs and specifying data needed for approval and labeling
HHS—National Institutes of Health	$43.0	$49.7	Developing new therapies for smallpox virus Developing smallpox and bacterial antigen detection system
HHS—Office of Emergency Preparedness	0	$4.6	Overseeing a study on response systems
DOJ—Office of Justice Programs	$0.7	$4.6	Developing a biological agent detector
DOJ—Federal Bureau of Investigation	0	$1.1	Conducting work on detection and characterization of biological materials
Department of the Treasury—Secret Service	0	$0.5	Developing a biological agent detector
Environmental Protection Agency	0	$0.5	Improving detection of biological agents

Note: Total reported funding refers to budget data we received from agencies. Agencies reported appropriations, actual or estimated obligations, or actual or estimated expenditures. An agency providing appropriations is not necessarily indicating the level of its commitments (that is, obligations) or expenditures for that year—only the amount of budget authority made available to it by the Congress. Similarly, an agency which provided expenditure information for fiscal year 2000 may have obligated the funds in fiscal year 1999 based on an appropriation for fiscal year 1998.

Source: Information obtained from departments and agencies.

The U.S. Department of Agriculture (USDA), DOD, Department of Energy (DOE), HHS, DOJ, Department of the Treasury, and the Environmental Protection Agency (EPA) have all sponsored or conducted projects to improve the detection and characterization of biological agents. These detection devices and tests are designed to identify biological agents in food, the environment, and clinical samples (such as blood). For example, EPA is sponsoring research to improve its ability to detect biological agents in the water supply.

Departments and agencies are also conducting or sponsoring studies to improve treatment and vaccination for diseases caused by biological agents. These projects include basic research to develop drugs and diagnostics and applied research to improve health care delivery systems. Several agencies also reported working to develop vaccines to prevent infection caused by biological agents. For example, HHS funded research to determine if the currently available stock of smallpox vaccine could be extended by dilution and yet remain effective. HHS is also developing a new vaccine for smallpox and collaborating with DOD on the development of a new anthrax vaccine.

In addition, several agencies are conducting research that focuses on developing performance standards and methods for testing the performance of emergency response equipment, such as respirators, personal protective equipment, and chemical and biological agent detectors and decontamination equipment.

Preparedness Efforts Include Multiple Actions

Departments and agencies are undertaking activities to increase preparedness for the public health and medical consequences of a bioterrorist attack. Preparing for a bioterrorist attack includes activities such as planning, purchasing equipment, training, and participating in exercises simulating a bioterrorist attack. Federal departments and agencies have undertaken the following preparedness activities: increasing state and local response capabilities, improving federal response capacity, developing response teams, increasing availability of medical treatments, participating in and sponsoring exercises, planning for victim aid, and providing support during special events. Table 2 contains information on total reported funding for all the departments and agencies with bioterrorism preparedness activities in fiscal year 2000 and fiscal year 2001 and examples of preparedness activities for these departments and agencies. In addition, the Department of the Treasury has some relevent preparedness activities, but was not able to specify the associated funding. More information on these activities is given in appendix IV through appendix XIV.

Table 2: Total Reported Funding for Preparedness Activities on Bioterrorism and Terrorism by Federal Departments and Agencies, Fiscal Year 2000 and Fiscal Year 2001 (Dollars in millions)

Department or agency	Fiscal year 2000 funding	Fiscal year 2001 funding	Sample activities
USDA—Animal and Plant Health Inspection Service	0	$0.2	Developing educational materials and training programs specifically dealing with bioterrorism
DOD—Joint Task Force for Civil Support	$3.4	$8.7	Planning, and when directed, commanding and controlling DOD's WMD and high-yield explosive consequence management capabilities in support of FEMA
DOD—National Guard	$70.0	$93.3	Managing response teams that would enter a contaminated area to gather samples for on-site evaluation
DOD—U.S. Army	$29.5	$11.7	Maintaining a repository of information about chemical and biological weapons and agents, detectors, and protection and decontamination equipment
HHS—CDC	$124.9	$147.3	Awarding planning grants to state and local health departments to prepare bioterrorism response plans Improving surveillance methods for detecting disease outbreaks Increasing communication capabilities in order to improve the gathering and exchanging of information related to bioterrorist incidents
HHS—Food and Drug Administration	$0.1	$2.1	Improving capabilities to identify and characterize foodborne pathogens Identifying biological agents using animal studies and microbiological surveillance

Department or agency	Fiscal year 2000 funding	Fiscal year 2001 funding	Sample activities
HHS—Office of Emergency Preparedness	$35.3	$46.1	Providing contracts to increase local emergency response capabilities Developing and managing response teams that can provide support at the site of a disaster
DOJ—Office of Justice Programs	$7.6	$5.3	Helping prepare state and local emergency responders through training, exercises, technical assistance, and equipment programs Developing a data collection tool to assist states in conducting their threat, risk, and needs assessments, and develop their preparedness strategy for terrorism, including bioterrorism
EPA	$0.1	$2.0	Providing technical assistance in identifying and decontaminating biological agents
FEMA	$25.1	$30.3	Providing grant assistance and guidance to states for planning and training Maintaining databases of safety precautions for biological, chemical, and nuclear agents

Note: Total reported funding refers to budget data we received from agencies. Agencies reported appropriations, actual or estimated obligations, or actual or estimated expenditures. An agency providing appropriations is not necessarily indicating the level of its commitments (that is, obligations) or expenditures for that year—only the amount of budget authority made available to it by the Congress. Similarly, an agency which provided expenditure information for fiscal year 2000 may have obligated the funds in fiscal year 1999 based on an appropriation for fiscal year 1998.

Source: Information obtained from departments and agencies.

Several federal departments and agencies have programs to increase the ability of state and local authorities to successfully respond to a bioterrorist attack. Some of these programs have focused on developing plans for dealing with a terrorist attack or emergency in general. Departments and agencies also contribute to state and local jurisdictions by helping them pay for equipment, providing technical assistance, increasing communications capabilities, and conducting training courses.

In addition to increasing the preparedness of state and local entities, federal departments and agencies have been increasing their own capacity to identify and deal with a bioterrorist incident. They are improving surveillance methods for detecting disease outbreaks in humans and animals. They have also established laboratory response networks to maintain state-of-the-art capabilities for biological agent identification and characterization of human clinical samples, as well as attempted to increase their communications capabilities in order to improve the gathering and exchanging of information related to a bioterrorist incident as well as other events.

Some federal departments and agencies have developed teams to directly respond to terrorist events. HHS' Office of Emergency Preparedness (OEP) and DOD have created response teams that would provide medical treatment and assistance in the event of a bioterrorist attack against the civilian population in the United States. Four teams led by OEP, known as National Medical Response Teams, are specially trained and equipped to respond to incidents involving WMDs—chemical, biological, radiological, or nuclear agents or weapons. The DOD teams would assist a local incident commander in case of a domestic bioterrorist incident. DOD coordinates with OEP in planning medical support for a civilian bioterrorist incident.

Several agencies are involved in increasing the availability of medical supplies that could be used in the event of a bioterrorist attack. CDC and OEP maintain repositories of pharmaceutical and other supplies that can be delivered to the site of a terrorist incident. CDC's National Pharmaceutical Stockpile Program consists of two components. The first component is the 12-Hour Push Packages, which contain pharmaceuticals, antidotes, and medical supplies and can be delivered to any site in the United States within 12 hours of a federal decision to deploy assets. These supplies are prepackaged and cannot be tailored to an individual incident.[15] The second component is the Vendor Managed Inventory. Through the Department of Veterans Affairs (VA), CDC has contracted with vendors to store pharmaceutical and medical supplies that could be used in a terrorist incident. These products can be tailored to an individual incident (that is, only pharmaceuticals and supplies needed for a particular incident would be sent) and would be available 24 to 36 hours after the National Pharmaceutical Stockpile staff notifies the appropriate vendors.[16] OEP's National Medical Response Teams have stockpiles that can be deployed with the teams. Each team has the capability of carrying enough pharmaceutical and medical supplies to treat up to 5,000 people, with the focus on the medical response to chemical incidents. The Food and Drug Administration (FDA) also has initiatives to increase the availability of medical countermeasures. For example, FDA is developing an approach that would allow drugs still in the FDA approval system to be used in the field during a bioterrorist attack. FDA is also working with CDC to implement a shelf-life extension program for the maintenance of stockpiled pharmaceuticals and medical supplies.

Bioterrorism response exercises are conducted across the country, both as on-site and as "tabletop" exercises. For example, in May 2000, many departments and agencies took part in the Top Officials 2000 exercise (TOPOFF 2000) in Denver, Colorado, which featured the simulated release of a biological agent.[17] Participants included local fire departments, police, area hospitals, the Colorado Department of Public Health and the Environment, the Colorado Office of Emergency Management, the Colorado National Guard, the American Red Cross, the Salvation Army, HHS, DOD, FEMA, the Federal Bureau of Investigation (FBI), and EPA. DOJ reported funding that facilitated 52 tabletop exercises on bioterrorism in fiscal year 2001. These 1-day exercises involve public health, fire, law enforcement, and emergency management agencies. Participants work through a simulation of a bioterrorism incident, starting with the incubation period (the time between initial exposure to a biological agent and onset of symptoms), followed by the recognition and initial response, and finally the challenges of integrating federal assets with local response and recovery efforts. Medical surveillance, epidemiologic investigation, quarantine management, remediation, and mass fatality management are addressed.

Under the Victims of Crime Act of 1984, DOJ's Office of Justice Programs (OJP) manages a program that provides assistance to victims of terrorism, including a bioterrorist attack. Under this program, funds can be used to provide mental health services. In addition, FEMA can provide supplemental funds to state and local mental health agencies to provide crisis counseling to eligible survivors of presidentially declared major disasters.[18]

Federal departments and agencies also provide support at special events to improve response in case of an emergency.[19] For example, OEP deployed teams from the National Disaster Medical System to provide medical services if required during the presidential inauguration of 2001. In addition, CDC is developing a surveillance system to provide increased surveillance and epidemiological capacity before, during, and after a special event. Besides improving emergency response at the events, department and agency participation provides them with valuable experience working together to develop and practice plans to combat terrorism. OEP reported funding of $2 million in fiscal year 2001 for special events. It was the only agency that reported funding for these activities.

Despite Efforts to Coordinate Federal Programs, Fragmentation Remains

Federal departments and agencies are using a variety of methods to coordinate their activities to combat terrorism. Departments and agencies are developing interagency response plans, participating in a variety of interagency work groups, and entering into formal agreements with other agencies to share resources and capabilities in order to improve coordination. However, during this and our previous work we found evidence that coordination of federal terrorism research, preparedness, and response programs is fragmented. Several different agencies are responsible for various coordination functions, which limits accountability and hinders unity of effort. Different agencies have developed separate threat lists of biological agents, several agencies have not been included in bioterrorism-related policy and response planning, and agencies have developed programs to provide assistance to state and local governments that are similar and potentially duplicative. For example, FEMA, DOJ, CDC, and OEP all offer separate assistance to state and local governments in planning for emergencies, including potential bioterrorist incidents. Congress and the President have recently taken steps to improve oversight and coordination. For example, in May 2001, the President asked the Vice President to lead an interagency effort to improve coordination of federal programs to deal with the consequences of a potential use of a WMD.

Departments and Agencies Use a Variety of Methods to Coordinate Activities

Departments and agencies use several approaches to coordinate their activities on terrorism. Interagency plans for responding to a terrorist incident help outline agency responsibilities and identify resources that could be used during a response. For example, the Federal Response Plan, which has been in effect for almost a decade, provides a broad framework for coordinating the delivery of federal disaster assistance to state and local governments when a major disaster or emergency, including a bioterrorist attack, overwhelms their ability to respond effectively.[20] The Federal Response Plan designates primary and supporting federal agencies for a variety of emergency support operations. For example, HHS is the primary agency for coordinating federal assistance to supplement state and local resources in response to public health and medical care needs in an emergency, including a bioterrorist attack. HHS could receive support from USDA, DOD, DOE, DOJ, DOT, VA, EPA, FEMA, and other agencies and organizations to assist state and local jurisdictions.

Interagency work groups are being used by federal departments and agencies to attempt to minimize duplication of funding and effort in federal activities on terrorism. For example, the Technical Support Working Group,[21] which receives funds from DOD and other agencies, is chartered to coordinate interagency and international research and development requirements for combating terrorism—including efforts to reduce vulnerability, collect and disseminate terrorism-related information, and prevent, deter, and respond to terrorist acts of any kind—in order to prevent duplication of effort between agencies.[22] The Technical Support Working

Group, among other projects, helped to identify research needs and fund a project to develop a means to detect biological agents in the food supply that can be used by both DOD and USDA. Another example of an inter-agency work group was provided by OEP officials, who told us that DOD, DOJ, DOE, OEP, FEMA, and VA meet as necessary to review equipment requests of state and local jurisdictions to ensure that duplicative funding is not being given for the same activities.

Formal agreements between departments and agencies are being used to share resources and knowledge. For example, CDC contracts with VA to purchase drugs and medical supplies for the National Pharmaceutical Stockpile because of VA's purchasing power and ability to negotiate large discounts from manufacturers that sell pharmaceuticals, equipment, and supplies to the VA hospital system. USDA's Animal and Plant Health Inspection Service is negotiating an agreement with DOD's Armed Forces Medical Intelligence Center to share information and expertise on tracking diseases that can be transmitted from animals to people and could be used in a bioterrorist attack.

Coordination Remains Fragmented Within the Federal Government

Overall coordination of federal programs to combat terrorism, including bioterrorism, is fragmented within the federal government.[23] For example, several agencies have coordination functions, including DOJ, FBI, FEMA, and the Office of Management and Budget. Officials from a number of the agencies that combat terrorism told us that the coordination roles of these various agencies are not always clear and sometimes overlap, leading to a fragmented approach. The Advisory Panel to Assess Domestic Response Capabilities for Terrorism Involving Weapons of Mass Destruction (also known as the Gilmore Panel) also concluded that the current coordination structure does not provide for the requisite authority or accountability to make policy changes and to impose the discipline necessary among the numerous federal agencies involved.[24]

The multiplicity of federal assistance programs requires focus and attention to minimize redundancy of effort.[25] Table 3 describes some of the federal programs providing assistance to state and local governments for emergency planning that would be relevant to responding to a bioterrorist attack. While the programs vary somewhat in their target audiences, the potential redundancy of these federal efforts highlights the need for scrutiny. In a recent report, we recommended that the President, working closely with Congress, consolidate some of the activities of the DOJ's OJP under FEMA.[26]

Table 3: Selected Federal Activities Providing Assistance to State and Local Governments for Emergency Planning Relevant to a Bioterrorist Attack

Department or agency	Activities	Target audience
HHS—CDC	Provides grants, technical support, and performance standards to support bioterrorism preparedness and response planning.	State and local health agencies
HHS—OEP	Enters into contracts to enhance medical response capability. The program includes a focus on response to bioterrorism, including early recognition, mass postexposure treatment, mass casualty care, and mass fatality management.	Local jurisdictions, including fire, police, emergency medical services, hospitals, and public health agencies
DOJ—OJP	Assists states in developing strategic plans. Includes funding for training, equipment acquisition, technical assistance, and exercise planning and execution to enhance state and local capabilities to respond to terrorist incidents.	States, including fire, law enforcement, emergency medical services, hazardous materials response services, hospitals, and public health departments
FEMA	Provides grant assistance to support state and local consequence management planning, training, and exercises for all types of terrorism, including bioterrorism.	State emergency management agencies

Source: Information obtained from departments and agencies.

Fragmentation is also evident in the different threat lists of biological agents developed by federal departments and agencies. Several different agencies have or are in the process of developing biological agent threat lists, which differ based on the agencies' focus. For example, CDC collaborated with law enforcement, intelligence, and defense agencies to develop a critical agent list that focuses on the biological agents that would have the greatest impact on public health. The FBI, the National Institute of Justice, and the Technical Support Working Group are completing a report that lists biological agents that may be more likely to be used by a terrorist group working in the United States that is not foreign sponsored. In addition, an official at USDA's Animal and Plant Health Inspection Service told us that it uses two lists of agents of concern for a potential bioterrorist attack developed through an international process (although only some of these agents are capable of making both animals and humans sick). According to agency officials, separate threat lists are appropriate because of the different focuses of these agencies. In prior reports, we have recommended that the federal government conduct multidisciplinary and analytically sound threat and risk assessments to define and prioritize requirements and properly focus programs and investments in combating terrorism.[27]

Fragmentation has also hindered unity of effort. Officials at USDA, FDA, and DOT told us that their departments and agencies have often been overlooked in bioterrorism-related planning and policy. USDA officials told us that as federal policy and coordination were developed in Presidential Decision Directive 62, the department was not included even though it would have key responsibilities if terrorists targeted the food supply. FDA officials told us that FDA was involved in some issues with the National Pharmaceutical Stockpile, but was not involved in the selection of all items procured for the stockpile. DOT officials noted that even though its programs cross many areas and the nation's transportation centers for a significant percentage of potential terrorist targets, the department was not part of the founding group of agencies that worked on bioterrorism issues and has not been included in bioterrorism response plans. DOT officials also told us that the department is supposed to deliver supplies for FEMA under the Federal Response Plan, but it was not brought in early enough to understand the extent of its responsibilities in the transportation process. It did not learn these details until its participation in TOPOFF 2000.

Recent Actions Seek to Improve Coordination Across Federal Departments and Agencies

In 1997, we reported that the amount of funds being spent to combat terrorism was unknown and difficult to determine and no priorities had been set for funding terrorism-related programs.[28] As a result, there was no assurance that agencies' requests were funded through a coordinated and focused approach. Subsequently, Congress required the Office of Management and Budget to establish a reporting system on the budgeting and expenditure of funds to combat terrorism.[29] The Office of Management and Budget and the National Security Council created a process to reduce overlap and improve coordination as part of the annual budget cycle in 1999. As part of this process, the Office of Management and Budget started issuing an *Annual Report to Congress on Combating Terrorism*, which details agency activities and funding. These reports potentially represent a significant step toward improved coordination by providing strategic oversight of the magnitude and direction of spending for activities on terrorism. However, as we have testified, we have not yet seen evidence that these reports have established priorities or identified duplication of effort.[30]

In May 2001, the President asked the Vice President to oversee the development of a coordinated national effort dealing with WMDs.[31] At the same time, the President asked the Director of FEMA to establish an Office of

National Preparedness to implement the results of this effort that deal with programs within DOD, HHS, DOJ, DOE, EPA, and other federal agencies that address consequence management resulting from the use of WMDs. The purpose of this effort is to better focus policies and ensure that programs and activities are fully coordinated and integrated in support of building the needed preparedness and response capabilities.[32] We have previously recommended that the President appoint a single focal point for all critical leadership and coordination functions to combat terrorism.[33]

On September 20, 2001, the President announced the creation of the Office of Homeland Security. The head of the office will lead, oversee, and coordinate a comprehensive national strategy to safeguard the country against terrorism and respond to any attacks that may occur.

Despite Federal Efforts, Concerns Exist Regarding Preparedness at State and Local Levels

The reports that we reviewed identified concerns about the preparedness of states and local areas to respond to a bioterrorist attack. These concerns include insufficient state and local planning for response to terrorist events, inadequacies in the public health infrastructure, a lack of hospital participation in training on terrorism and emergency response planning, insufficient capacity for treating mass casualties from a terrorist act, and the timely availability of medical teams and resources in an emergency. Some federal programs have begun to provide funding to state and local governments to try to improve preparedness.

Questions exist regarding how much progress has been made in improving terrorism preparedness at the state and local levels. Most of the states surveyed by the National Governors' Association in 1996 reported that they had neither the equipment and trained personnel to detect a biological hazard nor the protective equipment that would be necessary during an attack. In 1997, FEMA identified planning and equipment for response to nuclear, biological, and chemical incidents as an area in need of significant improvement at the state level. The federal government has several programs to train and equip state and local authorities to respond to terrorist WMD incidents.[34] All 50 states and approximately 255 local jurisdictions will receive at least some federal assistance, including training and equipment grants, to help them prepare for a terrorist WMD incident. However, survey results presented in an October 2000 report indicated that even those cities receiving federal aid are still not adequately prepared to respond to a bioterrorist attack.[35]

According to the October 2000 report, components of the nation's infectious disease surveillance system are still not well prepared to detect a covert bioterrorist attack.[36] This report concluded that reductions in public health laboratory staffing and training have affected the ability of state and local authorities to identify biological agents. CDC began taking steps to improve the nation's public health infrastructure for responding to bioterrorism in fiscal year 1999. In fiscal year 2000, CDC awarded grants totaling approximately $11 million to 48 states and four major urban health departments to improve and upgrade their surveillance and epidemiological capabilities.

As we previously reported, even the initial West Nile virus outbreak in 1999, which was relatively small and occurred in an area with one of the nation's largest local public health agencies, taxed the federal, state, and local laboratory resources.[37] Both the New York state and CDC laboratories were quickly inundated with requests for tests during the West Nile outbreak, and because of the limited capacity at the New York laboratories, the CDC laboratory handled the bulk of the testing. Officials indicated that the CDC laboratory would have been unable to respond to another outbreak, had one occurred at the same time. In order to improve laboratory capacity for biological agents, CDC awarded grants during fiscal year 2000 totaling approximately $6 million to 42 states and two major urban health departments. At the same time, it began to upgrade its own laboratory capacity. CDC officials told us that the grants are beginning to improve state and local public health agencies' abilities to detect and identify biological agents. We plan to examine the efforts in preparing state and local authorities to address the public health and medical consequences of a bioterrorist attack in a future report.

Inadequate training and planning for bioterrorism response by hospitals is a major problem, according to recent reports and to federal officials. The Gilmore Panel concluded that the level of expertise in recognizing and dealing with a terrorist attack involving a chemical or biological agent is problematic in many hospitals.[38] Other recent reports have concluded that hospitals need to improve their preparedness for mass casualty incidents, such as a bioterrorist attack.[39] In addition, a recent study found that hospitals often lack the basic tools, such as Internet access, to communicate effectively with field units, health departments, and laboratories.[40] Local officials told us that it has been difficult to get hospitals and medical personnel to participate in local training, planning, and exercises to improve their preparedness.

Several federal and local officials reported that there is little or no excess capacity in the health care system in most communities for accepting and treating mass casualty patients. A recent study concluded that the patient load of a regular influenza season in the late 1990s overtaxed primary care facilities,[41] and other studies have reported that emergency rooms in major metropolitan areas such as Boston are routinely filled and unable to accept patients in need of urgent care.[42] According to a local official, the health care system might not be able to handle the aftermath of a disaster, attack, or epidemic because of the problems caused by overcrowding and the lack of additional capacity. OEP officials told us that its Metropolitan Medical Response System (a program to improve local medical response capabilities) can assist communities in planning, including identifying alternative care facilities for treating victims, identifying reserve medical personnel that could be brought in during an emergency, and planning to treat mass casualties within and outside of hospitals.[43] CDC, working with the Association for Professionals in Infection Control and Epidemiology, has developed guidance for individual hospitals on how to plan for a sudden and significant increase in infectious disease patients, relevant for the handling of anthrax, botulism, plague, and smallpox cases.

According to one report, local officials are also concerned about whether the federal government could quickly deliver enough medical teams and resources to help after a biological attack.[44] Federal officials said that assets, such as the Disaster Medical Assistance Teams, could be on site within 12 to 24 hours. Local officials who have deployed with such teams said that cities would probably be on their own for the first 24 to 72 hours, and that the number of medical workers that could arrive even in that time frame might fall far short of what would be needed.[45] Local officials also told us that they were concerned about the time and resources required to prepare and distribute drugs from the National Pharmaceutical Stockpile during an emergency. Partially in response to these concerns, CDC has developed training for state and local officials on using the stockpile and will deploy a small staff with the supplies to assist the local jurisdiction with distribution.

Agency Comments

We provided a draft of this report to the eleven departments and agencies for their review in August 2001. The Department of Commerce, DOD, HHS, and DOJ submitted written comments that are provided in appendixes XV through XVIII. They also provided technical comments. The Department of the Treasury, VA, and FEMA provided technical comments only. The audit liaison from DOT provided oral technical comments on a draft of this report; the audit liaison from EPA responded that the agency had no comments on the report. The technical liaison from DOE provided oral comments noting the department's concurrence with the draft report. USDA did not provide comments on the report. Written and oral comments from all of these agencies have been incorporated in the report, as appropriate.

The Department of Commerce stated that the report did not sufficiently discuss its integrated efforts with DOD, DOJ, and FEMA to develop chemical and biological protective equipment standards. We have provided additional detail on this activity in appendix V. In its technical comments DOD expressed a concern that the report did not reflect some of DOD's bioterrorism research and preparedness activities which are focused on battlefield scenarios and crisis management. We have not included these activities because they are outside the scope of our work, which focuses on the public health and medical consequences of a bioterrorist attack on the civilian population. HHS noted the importance of the systems and programs described in the report that could provide assistance to state and local governments in the event of a bioterrorist attack. HHS also stated that many of the services needed in response to a bioterrorist attack would be needed to respond to other emergencies, including natural disasters and other types of terrorist attacks, and we added this information to the report. In response to a DOJ technical comment, we also modified the report to indicate that the department stated it is appropriate for different agencies to maintain separate lists of biological threats, noting that such lists may have different purposes.

We are sending copies of this report to the Secretaries of Agriculture, Commerce, Defense, Energy, Health and Human Services, Transportation, the Treasury, and Veterans Affairs; the Attorney General; the Administrator of the Environmental Protection Agency; the Director of the Federal Emergency Management Agency; and other interested officials.

If you or your staffs have any questions about this report, please call me at (202) 512-7118. Another contact and key contributors are listed in appendix XIX.

Janet Heinrich
Director, Health Care—Public Health Issues

List of Committees

The Honorable Edward M. Kennedy
Chairman
The Honorable Judd Gregg
Ranking Minority Member
Committee on Health, Education,
Labor, and Pensions
United States Senate

The Honorable Robert C. Byrd
Chairman
The Honorable Ted Stevens
Ranking Minority Member
Committee on Appropriations
United States Senate

The Honorable W. J. "Billy" Tauzin
Chairman
The Honorable John D. Dingell
Ranking Minority Member
Committee on Energy and Commerce
House of Representatives

The Honorable C.W. Bill Young
Chairman
The Honorable David Obey
Ranking Minority Member
Committee on Appropriations
House of Representatives

Appendix I
Biological Agents and Pathogens Mentioned in This Report

Agent/pathogen	Description
Anthrax (*Bacillus anthracis*)	Transmission is possible through three different routes: direct skin contact with contaminated animals, ingestion of contaminated meat, or inhalation of airborne particles. Cutaneous anthrax causes itching, followed by papular lesions (red elevation on skin) and then vesicular lesions (blisterlike elevation on skin containing fluid). Untreated infections may spread to lymph nodes and to the bloodstream, leading to septicemia (presence of pathogenic microorganisms in the blood). Untreated cutaneous anthrax has a case fatality rate between 5 and 20 percent. Gastrointestinal anthrax has a mortality rate of 25 to 60 percent. Patients present with nausea, vomiting, severe diarrhea, fever, abdominal pain, and gastrointestinal bleeding. Inhalatory anthrax causes necrotizing hemorrhagic mediastinitis (destruction of the structures of the middle chest caused by the toxin). Initial presentation resembles viral syndrome—fever, malaise, fatigue, nonproductive cough. Treatment after onset of symptoms of inhalatory anthrax is not effective, with mortality of 90 percent.
Plague (*Yersinia pestis*)	Transmission is through the bite of infected fleas or handling of tissues of infected animals, such as rodents and rabbits. After bite of infected flea, patient usually develops bubonic plague, in which patients present with malaise, high fever, and tender lymph nodes. This may progress spontaneously to septicemic plague, with fever, chills, absolute exhaustion, abdominal pain, shock, and bleeding into skin and other organs. Neither bubonic nor septicemic plague spreads person-to-person. A small percentage of patients go on to develop pneumonic plague, which can be spread by respiratory droplet. For untreated pneumonic plague, mortality approaches 100 percent.
Salmonellosis (*Salmonella*)	Transmission is by ingestion of infected food, including food contaminated by feces of an infected animal or person. Symptoms include headache, nausea, vomiting, chills, diarrhea, fever, and abdominal cramping. Deaths are uncommon.

Agent/pathogen	Description
Smallpox (*variola major*)	Transmission is person-to-person, and the disease is highly contagious. The disease was eradicated, and routine immunizations have ceased. Any immunity conferred by the vaccine has waned. Patients present with high fever, malaise, absolute exhaustion, headache, and backache. A maculopapular rash (discolored spots on skin; some raised, some not raised) appears on mucosa of the mouth and pharynx, face, and forearms and spreads to trunk and legs. Within 1 to 2 days, the rash becomes vesicular, and later, pustular (small elevation on skin containing pus), which leaves pitting scars after recovery. Mortality rate is 30 percent or more.
Tularemia (*Francisella tularensis*)	Transmission is through the bite of infected ticks, by drinking contaminated water, or rarely through the bite of coyote, squirrel, skunk, hog, cat, or dog whose mouth presumably was contaminated by eating an infected animal. Most times, patients present with painless ulcers at the site of introduction and swelling regional lymph node. Ingestion of organisms in contaminated water or food may produce painful pharyngitis (inflammation of the throat area), abdominal pain, diarrhea, and vomiting. Inhalation of infectious material may be followed with pneumonic involvement or a primary septicemic syndrome with a 30 to 60 percent mortality rate if untreated.
West Nile virus (*flavivirus*)	Transmission is through the bite of an infected mosquito. Most infections are mild, and symptoms include fever, headache, and body aches, often with skin rash and swollen lymph glands. More severe infections may be marked with headache, high fever, neck stiffness, stupor, disorientation, coma, tremors, convulsions, muscle weakness, and paralysis. The virus is rarely fatal.

Appendix II
Scope and Methodology

We began our work by identifying the federal departments and agencies that have a role in the public health and medical consequences of a bioterrorist attack on the civilian population. We reviewed the Office of Management and Budget's *Annual Report to Congress on Combating Terrorism* to determine which federal agencies receive funding for activities on terrorism.[1] We then reviewed the Federal Response Plan to understand the roles of each agency in the consequence management of a possible bioterrorist attack. See appendix III for more information regarding the Federal Response Plan. We also reviewed each agency's performance plan to determine its specific activities on bioterrorism.

We identified the following federal departments and agencies as having a role in the public health and medical consequences of a bioterrorist attack on the civilian population: the Departments of Agriculture (USDA), Commerce, Defense (DOD), Energy (DOE), Health and Human Services (HHS), Justice (DOJ), Transportation (DOT), the Treasury, and Veterans Affairs (VA); the Environmental Protection Agency (EPA); and the Federal Emergency Management Agency (FEMA). We interviewed program directors at each department and agency about their activities related to the research on and preparedness for the public health and medical consequences of a bioterrorist attack against the civilian population in fiscal year 1998 through fiscal year 2001. We asked them to identify activities with dual-use purposes, such as preparedness activities for biological and chemical attacks, and surveillance activities for emerging infectious diseases. We also asked program directors about the coordination of interagency activities and requested copies of memorandums of understanding and memorandums of agreement to identify working relationships between departments and agencies.

We asked the program directors to provide the amount of authorized, appropriated, and obligated federal funds for activities on bioterrorism in fiscal year 1998 through fiscal year 2001. Some departments and agencies could not provide the categories of funding we requested. For example, some agencies could only provide appropriations estimates, while others could only provide expenditure data. Because these different characterizations of budget data are not necessarily additive across agencies for specific fiscal years, we have provided budgetary information summarized only by agency and refer to this generally as "funding information." We relied on the departments and agencies to identify relevant programs and to provide funding information. We have not audited or otherwise verified the information provided.

Information concerning the effectiveness of federal efforts to prepare state and local authorities for a bioterrorist event was obtained by reviewing our previous work, as well as reports from training exercises, including the multiagency Top Officials 2000 exercise (TOPOFF 2000). We interviewed officials who participated in TOPOFF 2000. We also reviewed reports by the Advisory Panel to Assess Domestic Response Capabilities for Terrorism Involving Weapons of Mass Destruction (also known as the Gilmore Panel), and the Henry L. Stimson Center and articles from peer-reviewed journals.

We conducted our work from January through September 2001 in accordance with generally accepted government auditing standards.

Appendix III
Summaries of Selected Federal Policy and Planning Documents

The Federal Response Plan, originally drafted in 1992 and updated in 1999, is authorized under the Robert T. Stafford Disaster Relief and Emergency Assistance Act (P.L. 93-288, as amended). The Stafford Act authorizes the President to provide financial and other forms of assistance to state and local governments, certain private nonprofit organizations, and individuals to support response, recovery, and mitigation efforts following presidentially declared major disasters and emergencies. The Federal Response Plan lays out the manner in which the federal government responds to domestic situations in which the President has declared an emergency requiring federal disaster assistance. Presidential Decision Directive 39 was issued after the Oklahoma City bombing in 1995, and it provides a framework for how the federal government will respond to weapons of mass destruction (WMD) terrorism within the United States, reaffirming the Federal Response Plan. The Federal Response Plan is an all-hazards approach document, with an annex specific to terrorism added by FEMA in 1997. In 1998, Presidential Decision Directive 62 was issued, which further describes the federal agency roles in preparing for and responding to WMD terrorism. In 2001, the U.S. Government Interagency Domestic Terrorism Concept of Operations Plan (CONPLAN) was issued, which explains agencies' responsibilities under Presidential Decision Directives 39 and 62 in more detail.[1]

Federal Response Plan with Terrorism Incident Annex

The Federal Response Plan lays out the manner in which the federal government responds to domestic situations in which the President has declared an emergency requiring federal disaster assistance. The plan outlines the planning assumptions, policies, concept of operations, organizational structures, and specific assignment of responsibilities to lead departments and agencies in providing federal assistance. The plan is intended to be the single source for an all-hazards response to terrorism, categorizing the types of federal assistance into specific emergency support functions. Primary and supporting agencies are listed for each emergency support function. Emergency support function number 8 is the Health and Medical Services Annex. HHS is the primary agency for this annex and could receive support from USDA, DOD, DOE, DOJ, DOT, VA, EPA, FEMA, and other agencies and organizations to assist state and local jurisdictions. Through the Health and Medical Services Annex, coordinated federal assistance is provided to supplement state and local resources in response to public health and medical care needs following a major disaster or emergency. The Terrorism Incident Annex establishes a general concept of operations for the federal response to a terrorist incident, including the concurrent operation under other federal plans.

Presidential Decision Directive 39, U.S. Policy on Counterterrorism

Under Presidential Decision Directive 39, which was issued in 1995, DOJ, acting through the Federal Bureau of Investigation (FBI), is the overall lead federal agency for domestic terrorist incidents. The FBI is the lead agency for crisis management and FEMA is the lead agency for consequence management in cases of terrorism.[2] This directive states that the director of FEMA shall ensure that the Federal Response Plan is adequate to respond to the consequences of terrorism, including terrorism involving WMDs directed against the U.S. population.

Presidential Decision Directive 62, Combating Terrorism

Presidential Decision Directive 62, which was issued in 1998, organizes and clarifies the roles and activities of many agencies responsible for combating a wide range of terrorism preparedness and response activities. This directive calls for the provision of necessary equipment and training to state and local responders and the development of stockpiles of vaccines and specialized medicines. It also created a category of special events called National Security Special Events, which are events of such significance that they warrant greater federal planning and protection than other special events. Such events have included presidential inaugurations, major political party conventions, and Olympic games. The U.S. Secret Service is responsible for the design, planning, and implementation of security at designated National Security Special Events.

U.S. Government Interagency Domestic Terrorism Concept of Operations Plan

The U.S. Government Interagency Domestic Terrorism Concept of Operations Plan (CONPLAN) was primarily developed through the efforts of DOD, DOE, HHS, DOJ, EPA, and FEMA. It was ratified in January 2001 and is designed to provide overall guidance to federal, state, and local agencies concerning how the federal government would respond to a potential or actual terrorist threat or incident that occurs in the United States, particularly one involving a WMD. As a follow-up to the Federal Response Plan Terrorism Incident Annex, it facilitates interdepartmental coordination of crisis and consequence management activities and states in more detail the responsibilities of primary and supporting agencies during a terrorist attack. HHS is currently developing a bioterrorism annex to this plan, which will address issues concerning the appropriate response to acts of bioterrorism.

Appendix IV
Department of Agriculture

USDA has become involved in activities on bioterrorism because of the increasing realization that the food supply may become a vehicle for a biological attack against the civilian population.[1] Biological attacks on the health of animals and plants are also important to recognize because there are a number of diseases and toxins that can cause illness or death in humans, such as West Nile virus, that can be carried or spread by animals and plants. However, USDA receives little funding specifically for activities on bioterrorism. Most of the agency's activities on terrorism are conducted using general program funds (see table 4).

Table 4: Reported Funding for Activities on Bioterrorism at USDA (Dollars in millions)

Program/initiative	Fiscal year 1998	Fiscal year 1999	Fiscal year 2000	Fiscal year 2001
Agricultural Research Service				
Research activities				
Detection of biological agents	0	0	0	$0.5
Animal and Plant Health Inspection Service			0	0
Preparedness activities				
Education and training programs	0	0	0	$0.2
Total	**0**	**0**	**0**	**$0.7**

Note: We have not audited or otherwise verified the information provided.

Source: USDA.

Office of Crisis Planning and Management

The Office of Crisis Planning and Management is a department-level office under the Assistant Secretary for Administration. The office is responsible for coordinating activities on terrorism across USDA. The Director of the Office of Crisis Planning and Management serves as the department's Emergency Coordinator and coordinates USDA's response to all disasters, crises, and emergencies. The office coordinates emergency management activities with other federal agencies, including FEMA, and coordinates USDA's role under the Federal Response Plan. The office also operates the department's Emergency Operations Centers, where representatives of organizational elements of USDA gather to manage and coordinate emergency response functions.

Agricultural Research Service

The Agricultural Research Service conducts research for several federal agencies, including agencies within USDA, such as the Animal and Plant Health Inspection Service and the Food Safety and Inspection Service.

Research Activities

The Agricultural Research Service is working on a system to improve on-site rapid detection of biological agents in animals, plants, and food in cooperation with DOD and HHS. The agency received $500,000 in fiscal year 2001 to sponsor this research (see table 4).

Preparedness Activities

The Agricultural Research Service is also repairing and modernizing the Plum Island Animal Disease Center in New York state to improve detection capacity for diseases and toxins that could affect animals and humans. The center provides definitive diagnoses of foreign animal diseases in North America.

Animal and Plant Health Inspection Service

The Animal and Plant Health Inspection Service is responsible for the health of animals and plants and has a role in responding to biological agents that are zoonotic, that is, capable of infecting both animals and humans.

Preparedness Activities

If a disease outbreak occurred in humans, this agency would work with other federal, state, and local departments and agencies to determine the source of the exposure to the disease. If the exposure was determined to be related to an animal, the agency's veterinary epidemiologists would be responsible for tracing back the source of the animal exposure. They would then be responsible for controlling and eradicating the outbreak to minimize further exposure to both animals and humans. The Animal and Plant Health Inspection Service reported funding of $150,000 in fiscal year 2001 to develop educational materials and training programs specifically dealing with activities on bioterrorism (see table 4).

Food Safety Inspection Service

The Food Safety Inspection Service provides emergency preparedness for foodborne incidents, including a bioterrorist attack.

Preparedness Activities

The Food Safety Inspection Service routinely responds to actual and potential food-borne disease outbreaks. Its response to a bioterrorist incident
would be the same as its response to any food-borne disease outbreak. The
Food Safety Inspection Service has not received any funding for activities
on bioterrorism.

Appendix V
Department of Commerce

Activities on bioterrorism within the Department of Commerce center on developing performance standards for emergency response equipment and are carried out in conjunction with DOD, DOJ, and HHS.

Office of Law Enforcement Standards

The Office of Law Enforcement Standards at the Department of Commerce's National Institute of Standards and Technology is the principal agent for equipment standards development for the criminal justice and public safety communities, including biological response equipment. The office develops standards, test procedures, and user guides that helps ensure that the equipment the communities purchase and the technologies they use are safe, dependable, and effective. The department reported receiving $0.5 million in fiscal year 2000 and $4.6 million in fiscal year 2001 from DOJ for research. It reported funding, also from DOJ, of $0.3 million annually in fiscal year 1999 and fiscal year 2000 for preparedness activities.

Research Activities

The Office of Law Enforcement Standards develops performance standards and evaluates test methods and procedures for WMD and explosive emergency response equipment. The office manages research projects with the National Institute for Occupational Safety and Health and the U.S. Army Soldier Biological and Chemical Command to develop standards for respiratory and other personal protective equipment, and detectors and decontamination equipment designed to protect against biological and chemical agents

Preparedness Activities

The Office of Law Enforcement Standards also issues technical reports and publishes user guides for WMD and explosive response equipment. The office is the executive agent of the Standards Coordination Committee of the Interagency Board for Equipment Standardization and Interoperability. The Interagency Board, which is co-chaired by DOD and DOJ, develops and maintains a Standardized Equipment List, which lists essential items for responding to terrorist WMD attacks. Other agencies participating in this effort include HHS, DOE, DOT, EPA, and FEMA. The Standardized Equipment List can be used by local public safety organizations when developing response plans and acquiring response equipment.

Appendix VI
Department of Defense

Although DOD is primarily responsible for service members in the battle-field, it would provide support to the primary federal agency under the Federal Response Plan in the event of an emergency, including a bioterrorist attack on the civilian population. Research at DOD is targeted for the battlefield, but is often shared with other agencies to benefit the civilian population. DOD has civil support responsibilities through the Defense Advanced Research Projects Agency, the Joint Task Force for Civil Support, the National Guard, and the U.S. Army. The Assistant Secretary of Defense for Special Operations and Low-Intensity Conflict provides oversight by supervising policy, requirements, priorities, resources, and programs to ensure adherence to approved policy and planning guidelines. See table 5 for DOD's reported funding for activities on domestic terrorism. In addition, we provide information on other activities for which DOD could not provide funding data

Table 5: Reported Funding for Activities on Domestic Terrorism at DOD (Dollars in millions)

Program/initiative	Fiscal year 1998	Fiscal year 1999	Fiscal year 2000	Fiscal year 2001
Joint Task Force for Civil Support				
Preparedness activities				
Training, exercises, travel, contingency operations, garrison support, communications, support contracts	0	0	$3.4	$6.5
Communication link system	0	0	0	$2.2
National Guard				
Preparedness activities				
Weapons of Mass Destruction—Civil Support Teams	0	$73.0	$70.0	$93.3
U.S. Army				
Preparedness activities[a]				
Program management	$3.0	$2.5	$3.3	$0.9
Expert assistance	$6.3	$4.8	$4.7	$1.9
Training	$21.6	$30.8	$10.9	0

Program/initiative	Fiscal year 1998	Fiscal year 1999	Fiscal year 2000	Fiscal year 2001
Director of military support travel	0	0	$0.3	$0.1
Exercises and testing	$10.2	$7.9	$8.4	$6.2
Chemical Biological—Rapid Response Teams	$1.9	$1.9	$1.9	$2.6
Total	$43.0	$120.9	$102.9	$113.7

Note: We have not audited or otherwise verified the information provided.

[a]Funding for preparedness activities has decreased over time due to a transfer of responsibility for these activities under the Domestic Preparedness Program from DOD to DOJ beginning October 1, 2000.

Source: DOD.

Defense Advanced Research Projects Agency

The Defense Advanced Research Projects Agency is the central research and development organization for DOD. It manages and directs basic and applied research and development projects for the department. Success of the projects may provide military advances as well as civilian applications.

Research Activities

The Defense Advance Research Projects Agency's current work includes genetic sequencing to enable the identification of molecular targets for the design of detection, diagnostic, and therapeutic strategies that will aid service members and may be used for the civilian population. The agency's objectives include developing the capacity to detect the presence of infection by a biological agent, differentiate the agent from other pathogens, and identify the pathogen in the absence of recognizable clinical signs. The agency often shares research results with other agencies to benefit the civilian population. DOD has initiated discussions on how best to evaluate and transition select technology for bioterrorism defense. The agency does not receive funding to conduct research on the public health and medical consequences of a bioterrorist attack against civilian populations.

Joint Task Force for Civil Support

The mandate of the Joint Task Force for Civil Support at the Joint Forces Command is to plan for and integrate DOD's support to FEMA for WMD events in the continental United States.

Preparedness Activities

The Joint Task Force for Civil Support plans and, when directed, commands and controls DOD's WMD and high-yield explosive consequence management capabilities in providing support during a domestic bioterrorist incident. The Joint Task Force for Civil Support provides support through FEMA and the Federal Response Plan during an incident and works with other federal agencies on planning and exercises. The Joint Task Force for Civil Support and the Joint Forces Command are working in support of FEMA and HHS' Office of Emergency Preparedness (OEP) to plan Force Packages, which are groupings of units that the military would designate to respond to an incident. It also coordinates with OEP on the planning for medical support for any WMD incident. Reported funding for Joint Task Force activities on terrorism was $3.4 million for fiscal year 2000 (see table 5). It rose to $8.7 million for fiscal year 2001, including $6.5 million for individual unit training, exercises, travel, contingency operations, garrison support, purchased communications, and general support contracts, and $2.2 million for the establishment of a communication link system.

National Guard

The National Guard Weapons of Mass Destruction—Civil Support Teams are meant to deploy to assist local responders in determining the precise nature of an attack and provide medical and technical advice. The teams also help pave the way for the identification and arrival of follow-on state and federal military response assets.

Preparedness Activities

The National Guard Weapons of Mass Destruction—Civil Support Team program is intended to help prepare the United States against terrorist use of WMDs. Originally, 10 civil support teams (formerly called Rapid Assessment and Initial Detection teams) were located in alignment with the 10 FEMA regional offices.[1] Congress authorized an additional 17 civil support teams in fiscal year 2000, and another 5 in fiscal year 2001.[2] DOD reported funding of $70 million and $93.3 million for these teams in fiscal year 2000 and fiscal year 2001, respectively (see table 5).

Although the teams are federally funded and trained, they are primarily under the command and control of the governors of the states in which they are located, to facilitate their rapid deployment. Their roles can include entering a contaminated area to gather air, soil, and other samples for on-site evaluation. They also are to assist a local incident commander in determining the nature and extent of an attack or incident, provide expert technical advice on WMD response operations, and help identify and support the arrival of follow-on state and federal military response assets. Teams are designed to be ready to deploy within 4 hours to anywhere within their area of responsibility, with their own detection and decontamination equipment, medical supplies, and protective gear. As of August 15, 2001, six civil support teams have been certified as fully mission capable.

U.S. Army

The U.S. Army engages in research and preparedness activities on bioterrorism that have benefits for both military and civilian populations.

Research Activities

The U.S. Army Medical Research Institute of Infectious Diseases is a biological research facility that deals with militarily relevant infectious diseases and biological agents. The institute conducts research to develop vaccines, drugs, and diagnostics for laboratory and field use, as well as formulates strategies, information, procedures, and training programs for medical defense against biological agents. The institute has a Biosafety Level 4 laboratory, which is used for dangerous, exotic agents that pose a high risk of life-threatening diseases and have no vaccines or drugs available for treatment. The institute also provides definitive identification of biological agents and diagnosis of the diseases they produce. It provides professional expertise on issues related to technologies, therapeutics, prophylactics, and education that could be used to support readiness for a bioterrorist incident.

The institute helps supply diagnostic reagent[3] sets to the Centers for Disease Control and Prevention (CDC) and serves CDC's Laboratory Response Network as a confirmatory diagnostic laboratory and subject matter expert.[4] It provides support for the development of an anthrax vaccine by the National Institutes of Health (NIH). Other ongoing work with CDC and NIH includes the development of a database for genetically engineered threats. It works with CDC and the FBI to assist with potential bioterrorism incidents on a consultation or confirmatory basis. The institute, along with the U.S. Army Soldier Biological and Chemical Command, the Director of Military Support, and the Joint Task Force for Civil Support, is currently working on plans to provide support in the event of a domestic bioterrorist incident. The institute does not receive funding to conduct research on the public health and medical consequences of a bioterrorist attack against civilian populations.

Preparedness Activities

The Domestic Preparedness Program5 was formed in response to the National Defense Authorization Act of Fiscal Year 1997 (P.L. 104-201) and required DOD to enhance the capability of federal, state, and local emergency responders regarding terrorist incidents involving WMDs and high-yield explosives.

The program was developed through work groups with expertise with WMD response skills. Work groups were composed of experts from municipalities, counties, and states and federal first responders having responsibility for responding to WMD terrorism incidents. The work groups developed courses and training in accordance with the Occupational Safety and Health Administration, the National Fire Protection Agency, and standards set by the Joint Commission for the Accreditation of Healthcare Organizations.

DOD created the Domestic Preparedness Program with four major elements: the City Training Program, the Exercises Program, the Expert Assistance Program, and the Chemical Biological—Rapid Response Team. The City Training Program provides training for senior local officials and emergency first responders and trainers in 120 cities. It includes equipment loans to the local areas by DOD.

The Exercises Program includes the federal, state, and local exercise and the Biological Warfare—Improved Response Program. The Improved Response Program is a multiagency, intergovernmental, and interdisciplinary effort designed to improve our nation's ability to respond to domestic acts of terrorism involving biological agents. Program activities include testing and evaluating biological agent response concepts, developing technical and operational requirements for first responder equipment, and conducting exercises to test the major components and integrated response plan. Lessons learned from biological weapons tabletop exercises[6] on the medical consequence management of a biological attack have been applied to the Improved Response Program.

Expert Assistance Program activities include the emergency responders' WMD help line (which provides nonemergency planning and technical information), a hot line (a component of the National Response Center, which is located at the Coast Guard's Headquarter Command Center and allows the caller to alert federal agencies and speak with technical experts who can provide critical incident management information), a Web page (which provides information about the Domestic Preparedness Program), equipment testing and reports, a chemical-biological database (a repository of information about chemical and biological weapons and agents, detectors, and protection and decontamination equipment), and subject matter experts (who provide support for technical inquiries).

The Chemical Biological—Rapid Response Team coordinates and manages all DOD technical capabilities tasked to support a crisis response or consequence management operation. The Rapid Response Team delivers skills, training, and equipment to the scene of a chemical or biological incident.

As of October 1, 2000, the City Training Program, portions of the Improved Response Program, and the help line, hot line, and Web page elements of the Expert Assistance Program were transferred from DOD to DOJ. DOD will retain responsibility for the chemical-biological database and equipment testing and the Chemical Biological—Rapid Response Team. DOD also will retain responsibility for the annual federal, state, and local exercise through fiscal year 2001. DOD will share responsibility for the Improved Response Program with DOJ.

Appendix VII
Department of Energy

DOE is developing new capabilities to counter chemical and biological threats. DOE expects the results of its research to be public and possibly lead to the development of commercial products in the domestic market. Table 6 lists funding for DOE's research activities on terrorism.

Table 6: Reported Funding for Activities on Terrorism at DOE
(Dollars in millions)

Program/initiative	Fiscal year 1998	Fiscal year 1999	Fiscal year 2000	Fiscal year 2001
Chemical and Biological National Security Program				
Research activities				
Chemical and biological detection	$7.3	$7.5	$9.5	$10.9
Modeling and prediction	$2.3	$3.0	$4.7	$5.5
Decontamination and restoration	$1.8	$1.7	$2.2	$1.5
Biological foundations	$4.5	$5.0	$10.0	$10.9
System analysis (includes Domestic Demonstration and Application Programs)	$1.7	$1.8	$5.5	$9.1
Other	$0.4	0	$3.6	$1.7
Total	**$18.0**	**$19.0**	**$35.5**	**$39.6**

Note: We have not audited or otherwise verified the information provided.
Source: DOE.

The Office of Defense Nuclear Nonproliferation

Among other duties, the Office of Defense Nuclear Nonproliferation is responsible for reducing global danger from WMDs. Within this office is the Chemical and Biological National Security Program, which participates in research related to bioterrorism.

Research Activities

The mission of the Chemical and Biological National Security Program is to develop, demonstrate, and deliver technologies and systems that will lead to major improvements in the United States' capability to prepare for and respond to chemical or biological attacks. The program was begun in 1997 to involve DOE and its laboratories in research and demonstrations of terrorism preparedness, including, but not limited to, bioterrorism.

The Chemical and Biological National Security Program is divided into three components: analytical studies, technology development, and Domestic Demonstration and Application Programs. Analytical studies help guide the overall program direction as well as individual technical areas. In general, these studies use analytical and simulation models to assess the value of technology in system applications. Technology development is the core research and development program element, with the purpose of enhancing response capabilities across the full spectrum of chemical and biological terrorism. In general, development is focused on technologies for which the basic science is already understood. Technology development is categorized into four areas: (1) chemical and biological detection, (2) modeling and prediction, (3) decontamination and restoration, and (4) biological foundations (that is, molecular biology- based capabilities to support efforts in advanced detection, attribution, and medical countermeasures). Finally, Domestic Demonstration and Application Programs seek to integrate current technology into capable, prototype operational systems directed at specific applications in 2 to 3 years.

One current demonstration project is the Biological Aerosol Sentry and Information System. This portable system is intended to provide early warning of airborne biological incidents for special events such as large assemblies and dignitary visits. This system is planned for use in civilian settings to detect a biological incident within a few hours of an attack, early enough to mount an effective medical response. This system is intended to estimate where an attack occurred, exposure levels, and duration, all of which would assist the public health system in identifying the population requiring treatment.

Appendix VIII
Department of Health and Human Services

Within HHS, five agencies or offices work on bioterrorism issues. The Agency for Healthcare Research and Quality (AHRQ), the Food and Drug Administration (FDA), and NIH are primarily involved in research activities, and CDC and OEP are primarily concerned with preparedness activities. HHS is the primary federal agency for the medical and public health response to emergencies, including major disasters and terrorist events, under the Federal Response Plan. In addition, the Secretary of HHS has recently appointed a Special Assistant for Bioterrorism to coordinate antibioterrorism efforts across the department.

The Secretary of HHS was authorized $221 million in fiscal year 2001 through the Public Health Improvement Act of 2000 for the medical and public health consequences of a bioterrorist attack. However, despite this authorization, there were no specific appropriations for such activities.

Agency for Healthcare Research and Quality

AHRQ's mission is to support research designed to improve the outcomes and quality of health care, reduce its costs, address safety and medical errors, and broaden access to effective services. Working through an informal interagency workgroup, AHRQ included officials across HHS (such as those in CDC, OEP, and the Office of the Assistant Secretary for Planning and Evaluation) in its anti-bioterrorism research planning efforts.

Research Activities

AHRQ received $5 million in fiscal year 2000 to develop research initiatives to identify effective and specific strategies for improving the clinical preparedness of health care providers and health care systems for a bioterrorist attack. For example, the agency funded research on the use of information systems and decision support systems to enhance preparedness for the delivery of medical care in the event of such an attack. AHRQ, along with other HHS agency partners, also provided funding to support a bioterrorism symposium sponsored by the Center for Civilian Biodefense Studies at Johns Hopkins University.

Centers for Disease Control and Prevention

HHS was designated to lead an effort to work with governmental and nongovernmental partners to upgrade the nation's capacity to respond to bioterrorism. Several centers, institutes, and offices within CDC work together on bioterrorism preparedness and response efforts. The principal priority of the Bioterrorism Preparedness and Response Program is to upgrade infrastructure and capacity to respond to a large-scale epidemic, regardless of whether it is the result of a bioterrorist attack or a naturally occurring infectious disease outbreak. The program was started in fiscal year 1999 and was tasked with building and enhancing national, state, and local capacity; developing a national pharmaceutical stockpile; and con-ducting several independent studies on bioterrorism. It has focused on helping states with planning for a bioterrorist event; enhancing surveil-lance and laboratory capacity at the national, state, and local levels; and improving communications and training for bioterrorism preparedness. Examples of CDC's internal research activities include work on anthrax and smallpox. The agency also oversees a number of studies being con-ducted by universities and hospitals. Table 7 lists CDC's reported bioterrorism funding for fiscal years 1998 through 2001.

Table 7: Reported Funding for Activities on Bioterrorism at CDC
(Dollars in millions)

Program/initiative[a]	Fiscal year 1998	Fiscal year 1999	Fiscal year 2000	Fiscal year 2001
Research activities				
Research and development	0	0	$40.5	$42.9
Independent studies[b]	0	$1.8	$7.7	$2.6
Worker safety	0	0	0	$1.1
Preparedness activities				
Upgrading state and local capacity	0	**$55.0**	**$56.9**	**$66.7**
Preparedness planning	0	$2.0	$1.9	$5.8
Surveillance and epidemiology	0	$12.0	$15.8	$16.1
Laboratory capacity	0	$13.0	$9.5	$12.8
Communications	0	$28.0	$29.7	$32.0
Upgrading CDC capacity	0	**$12.0**	**$13.9**	**$20.4**
Epidemiologic capacity	0	$2.0	$1.8	$4.0
Laboratory capacity	0	$5.0	$7.6	$11.4
Rapid toxic screen	0	$5.0	$4.5	$5.0
Preparedness and response planning	0	**$1.0**	**$2.3**	**$9.2**
Building the National Pharmaceutical Stockpile	0	**$51.0**	**$51.8**	**$51.0**
Total	0	$120.8	$173.1	$193.9

Note: We have not audited or otherwise verified the information provided.

ªCDC received funding in fiscal year 1999, fiscal year 2000, and fiscal year 2001 for bioterrorism deterrence activities, such as implementing regulations restricting the importation of certain biological agents. However, since deterrence is outside the scope of our study, that funding is not included here.

ᵇFor instance, $1 million was specified in the fiscal year 2000 appropriations conference report for the Carnegie Mellon Research Institute to study health and bioterrorism threats.

Source: CDC.

The Bioterrorism Preparedness and Response Program was placed within the National Center for Infectious Diseases because of the likely similarity between a bioterrorist attack and a naturally occurring infectious disease outbreak. The National Center for Infectious Diseases oversees research, surveillance, laboratory, and epidemiological response efforts. The National Center for Environmental Health manages the National Pharmaceutical Stockpile Program and associated emergency preparedness and planning activities. Several other offices and institutes also contribute to the Bioterrorism Preparedness and Response Program, including the Epidemiology Program Office; the Public Health Practice Program Office, which focuses on communications and training; and the National Institute of Occupational Safety and Health. Program staff are responsible for coordination within CDC and with other federal agencies and for policy development.

Research Activities

In fiscal year 2001, CDC was allocated $18 million to continue research on an anthrax vaccine and associated issues, such as scheduling and dosage. The agency also received $22.4 million in fiscal year 2001 to conduct smallpox research. In addition, CDC oversees a number of independent studies, which are specific lines in the budget that fund specific universities and hospitals to do research and other work on bioterrorism. For example, the Carnegie Mellon Research Institute received $1 million in fiscal year 2000 to study health and bioterrorism threats. Finally, CDC's National Institute for Occupational Safety and Health is developing standards for respiratory protection equipment used against biological agents by firefighters, laboratory technicians, and other potentially affected workers.

Preparedness Activities

Most of CDC's activities to counter bioterrorism are focused on building and expanding multipurpose public health infrastructure at the national, state, and local levels. For example, CDC reported receiving funding of $66.7 million in fiscal year 2001 to upgrade state and local capacity to detect and respond to a bioterrorist attack. CDC received an additional $20.4 million to upgrade its own capacity in these areas, $9.2 million for planning and response, and another $51 million for developing the National Pharmaceutical Stockpile. These activities may have a dual use, such as identifying and containing a naturally occurring emerging infectious disease in addition to responding to a bioterrorism attack.

Upgrading State and Local Capacity

In fiscal year 2000, CDC received $56.9 million to award to 50 states and 4 major metropolitan health departments for preparedness and response activities. CDC also provides technical assistance to these agencies to assist preparedness efforts. CDC is developing planning guidance for state public health officials to upgrade state and local public health departments' preparedness and response capabilities. In addition, CDC has worked with DOJ to complete a public health assessment tool, which is being used to determine the ability of state and local public health agencies to respond to biological and chemical agents, as well as other public health emergencies.

States have received funding from CDC to increase staff, provide better access to data sources, enhance capacity to detect the release of a biological agent or an emerging infectious disease, and improve communications infrastructure. In fiscal year 1999, for example, a total of $7.8 million was awarded to 41 state and local health agencies to improve the state and local public health agencies' ability to link different sources of data, such as sales of certain pharmaceuticals, which could be helpful in detecting a covert bioterrorist event.

Rapid identification and confirmatory diagnosis of biological agents are critical to ensuring that prevention and treatment measures can be implemented quickly. CDC was allocated $13 million in fiscal year 1999 to enhance state and local laboratory capacity. CDC has established a Laboratory Response Network that maintains state-of-the-art capabilities for biological agent identification and characterization. CDC has provided technical assistance and training in identification techniques to state and local public health laboratories. In addition, five state health departments received awards totaling $3 million in fiscal year 2000 to enhance chemical laboratory capabilities. These funds were used to purchase equipment and provide training.

CDC is working with state and local health agencies to build a modern electronic infrastructure for public health communications that will improve the collection and transmission of information related to a bioterrorism incident as well as other events. For example, $21 million was awarded to states in fiscal year 1999 to begin implementation of the Health Alert Network, which will support the exchange of key information over the Internet and provide a foundation for distance training that could potentially reach a large segment of the public health community.

Upgrading CDC Capacity

CDC is upgrading its own epidemiologic and disease surveillance capacity. It has deployed, and is continuing to develop, a surveillance system to increase surveillance and epidemiological capacities before, during, and after special events (such as the 1999 World Trade Organization meeting in Seattle, Washington). The agency is also increasing its veterinary surveillance. In addition, CDC monitors unusual clusters of illnesses, such as influenza in June. While these clusters may not be a cause for concern, they can indicate a potential problem.

CDC has strengthened its own laboratory capacity. For example, it is developing and validating diagnostic tests as well as creating agent-specific protocols. In collaboration with the Association of Public Health Laboratories and DOD, CDC has operationalized a secure Internet-based network that allows state, local, and other public health laboratories access to guidelines for analyzing biological agents. The site also allows authenticated users to order critical reagents needed in performing laboratory analysis of samples.

The agency has also operationalized a Rapid Response and Advance Technology Laboratory, which screens samples for the presence of suspicious biological agents and evaluates new technology and protocols for the detection of biological agents. These technology assessments and protocols, as well as reagents and reference samples, are being shared with state and local public health laboratories.

Preparedness and Response Planning

In fiscal year 1999, at the start of CDC's bioterrorism program, the agency received funding to develop an overall preparedness plan. CDC received $2.3 million in fiscal year 2000 for preparedness and response training and $9.2 million in fiscal year 2001. Among the activities to be undertaken is the initial implementation of a national bioterrorism response training plan. This plan will focus on preparing CDC officials to respond to bioterrorism and will include the development of exercises to assess progress in achieving bioterrorism preparedness at the federal, state, and local levels. The agency will also develop a crisis communications/media response curriculum for bioterrorism as well as core capabilities guidelines to assist states and localities in their efforts to build comprehensive anti- bioterrorism programs.

CDC has developed a bioterrorism Web site. This site provides emergency contact information for possible bioterrorism events, a list of critical agents, summaries of state and local bioterrorism projects, general information about CDC's bioterrorism initiative, and links to documents on bioterrorism preparedness and response.

Building the National Pharmaceutical Stockpile Program

The National Pharmaceutical Stockpile Program maintains a repository of life-saving pharmaceuticals, antidotes, and medical supplies, known as 12-Hour Push Packages, that can be delivered to the site of a biological (or other) attack within 12 hours of deployment for the treatment of civilians. These Push Packages are prepackaged and contain products that could be used in a variety of scenarios.[1] Additional antibiotics, antidotes, other drugs, medical equipment, and supplies known as Vendor Managed Inventory, can be delivered within 24 to 36 hours after the appropriate vendors are notified. The Vendor Managed Inventory can be tailored to an individual incident (that is, only products needed for a particular incident would be sent). The program received $51.0 million in fiscal year 1999, $51.8 million in fiscal year 2000, and $51.0 million in fiscal year 2001. CDC and OEP have encouraged state and local representatives to consider stockpile assets in their emergency planning for a biological attack and have trained representatives from state and local authorities in using the stockpile. The program also provides technical advisers in response to an event to ensure the appropriate and timely transfer of stockpile contents to authorized state representatives.[2]

Food and Drug Administration

FDA's responsibilities and activities on bioterrorism are spread throughout the agency. These activities include safeguarding the food supply, ensuring that new vaccines and drugs are safe and effective, and conducting research for diagnostic tools and treatment of disease outbreaks.

Under the Health and Medical Services Annex of the Federal Response Plan, FDA is the lead HHS agency for ensuring the safety of regulated foods, drugs, medical devices, and biological products. In an emergency, FDA would arrange for the seizure, removal, and/or destruction of any contaminated and unsafe products. FDA is revising its Emergency Operations Response Plan to include bioterrorism preparedness and response elements.

Congress has earmarked $5 million for FDA for activities on bioterrorism in fiscal year 2001. These funds were for FDA to continue previously initiated work on bioterrorism that had been supported by departmental and general purpose funds. HHS has allocated other funds to FDA's activities on bioterrorism. For example, the Center for Biologics Evaluation and Research received $7.5 million in fiscal year 2000 from departmental funds specifically for vaccine projects (see table 8).

Table 8: Reported Funding for Activities on Bioterrorism at FDA
(Dollars in millions)

Program/initiative	Fiscal year 1998[a]	Fiscal year 1999	Fiscal year 2000	Fiscal year 2001
Center for Biologics Evaluation and Research				
Research activities				
Premarket evaluation of vaccines, Develop vaccines	a	$1.2	$7.5	$7.0
Center for Devices and Radiological Health				
Research activities				
Develop data requirements for approving devices intended to detect exposure to or infection with biological agents	a	$0.1	$0.8	$0.9
Center for Drug Evaluation and Research				
Research activities				
Determine procedures for allowing use of not-yet-approved drugs, specify data needed for approval and labeling, gather and supply information	a	$0.2	$0.4	$0.7
Center for Food Safety and Applied Nutrition				
Preparedness activities				
Monitor food supply, communicate with state and local officials	a	0	0	$0.3
Center for Veterinary Medicine				
Preparedness activities				
Communicate with state officials, held meeting on bioterrorism risk	a	$0.1	$0.1	$0.3
National Center for Toxicological Research				
Research activities				

Define biological mechanisms [a] of action underlying toxicity of products, identify indications of toxicity associated with biological agents	$0.2	$0.1	$0.5
Preparedness activities			
Participate in training meetings [a]	[b]	[b]	[b]
Office of Regulatory Affairs			
Preparedness activities			
Communicate with other agencies and the public, conduct investigations [c]	[c]	[c]	$1.5
Total[d] [a]	$1.9	$9.0	$11.2

Note: We have not audited or otherwise verified the information provided.

[a]Agency officials told us that in fiscal year 1998 funds were expended on bioterrorism-related activities, but they did not report these levels to us.

[b]We were unable to allocate funding within this program for research and preparedness based on the information provided by FDA. Instead, we list all the funding under research because the preponderance of activities within that program are best categorized there.

[c]FDA reported that activities on bioterrorism were conducted by the Office of Regulatory Affairs, but it did not specify how much was spent on them.

[d]Individual entries may not sum to totals because of rounding.

Source: FDA.

Center for Biologics Evaluation and Research

The mission of the Center for Biologics Evaluation and Research is to ensure the safety, efficacy, potency, and purity of biological and related products, including vaccines, that could be used in case of a bioterrorist attack.

Research Activities

Among its responsibilities, the Center for Biologics Evaluation and Research regulates the development and licensure of new vaccines for anthrax, smallpox, and the associated vaccinia immune globulin used to treat serious vaccinia infections or other adverse events caused by the smallpox vaccine. In addition to premarketing evaluation, vaccine products require review of lot release data, inspection of manufacturing facilities, assessment of product availability, and surveillance and compliance activities. The center works closely with other government agencies such as CDC and DOD to assist in ensuring that sufficient quantities of medical products are available for military and civilian use during a bioterrorism attack, and that the use is controlled under an acceptable clinical protocol when the biological product is not licensed by FDA or is being used "off label."[3] It also coordinates with industry and government agencies to prepare surveillance methods for adverse event monitoring associated with the use of biological products in a bioterrorism attack. The center engages in vaccine research activities related to the regulation of the development of vaccines for plague, tularemia, and encephalitis-causing viruses.[4] (See app. I for a discussion of specific biological agents mentioned in this report.)

Since high-risk bioterrorism pathogens either do not exist naturally or do not cause significant disease in large populations, the traditional human testing and ultimate approval of products for mitigating a disease in humans caused by a bioterrorist pathogen is neither ethical nor feasible. The center is working with CDC, NIH, and DOD, as well as academia and industry to develop regulations that will define the type of nonhuman research data required to demonstrate the potential efficacy of new products on humans affected by biological WMDs.

Officials have noted that while there is a clear need to develop vaccines for biological agents, there are limited commercial interests or market incentives for addressing the problem. Consequently, it falls upon the federal government to develop such vaccines. The Center for Biologics Evaluation and Research has research projects under way dealing with vaccines for anthrax, plague, and smallpox.

Center for Devices and Radiological Health

The mission of the Center for Devices and Radiological Health is to ensure the safety and effectiveness of medical devices, including those that could be used in the event of a bioterrorist attack.

Research Activities

The center provided comments on a research protocol to evaluate a device intended to identify anthrax in human specimens. It has also conducted an advisory panel meeting to discuss data requirements for approval of devices intended to detect exposure to or infection with biological agents. In addition, the center is working with CDC on a process that would allow the use of investigational diagnostic devices in the event of a bioterrorist attack.

Center for Drug Evaluation and Research

The Center for Drug Evaluation and Research helps ensure the availability of safe and effective human drugs. The center reviews research to take appropriate action on the marketing of drugs, including those that would be used in the event of a bioterrorist attack.

Research Activities

The center is working with CDC on a process that would satisfy the re-quirements for allowing the use of investigational drugs (not approved by FDA) in the event of a bioterrorist attack. Testing drugs that might be used in case of a bioterrorist attack is difficult because the diseases caused by the biological agents rarely occur naturally and it would be unethical to infect healthy volunteers with the disease when there is no known cure. The center is working with other government agencies and the manufacturers of these drugs to determine what studies are needed to generate sufficient safety and efficacy data to permit labeling of these drugs. For products that might still be in the investigational stage, but potentially the only therapies available for a specific disease caused by a bioterrorist event, the center is working with CDC to determine additional methods of data col-lection and analysis to evaluate the products' safety and efficacy if it were necessary for them to be used.

Although some drugs that would be used in the case of a bioterrorist attack have been approved to treat diseases caused by a biological agent, use of a number of these drugs would be "off-label." The center is determining what data are needed to enable approval of a label indicating that a drug would treat a disease that might be caused by a bioterrorist attack. It has a program in this area, but there has been limited funding for these activities. The center has worked to facilitate the labeling of ciproflaxacin for the treatment of inhalational anthrax and is now working to assess what is needed in the way of studies to produce sufficient data for labeling gentamicin to treat pneumonic plague. It is also determining what types of nonclinical (nonhuman) data are acceptable for product marketing ap-proval if traditional clinical studies are not feasible or ethical.

At the request of the National Security Council, the center has compiled a list of and information on drugs that might be effective in case of a bioterrorist attack. The information includes manufacturers, inventories, lead time for producing the drugs, and bulk suppliers. Center officials noted that they do not regularly collect this information. It is also working with CDC to implement a shelf-life extension program for the maintenance of stockpiled supplies.

Center for Food Safety and Applied Nutrition

The Center for Food Safety and Applied Nutrition is responsible for pro-moting and protecting the public's health by ensuring that the nation's food supply is safe, sanitary, wholesome, and appropriately labeled. The center has been involved in preparing for a bioterrorist attack on the food supply.

Preparedness Activities

The Center for Food Safety and Applied Nutrition has undertaken activities regarding contaminated food that are important for bioterrorism response readiness. For example, the agency has developed a procedures manual for dealing with foodborne attacks. The center works with other federal and state agencies to monitor the safety of the U.S. food supply. The agency has been involved in the development and support of two surveillance systems for identifying and characterizing contaminated food, FoodNet and PulseNet. FoodNet is a collaborative project of FDA, CDC, USDA, and nine state health departments. It is an effort to capture a more accurate and complete picture of trends in the occurrence of foodborne illness and provides information about the number of persons who were diagnosed with specific infections that are likely to be foodborne. PulseNet is a collaborative project of FDA, CDC, USDA, and state health department food safety laboratories to facilitate subtyping bacterial foodborne pathogens for epidemiological purposes.

The center (along with the Office of Regulatory Affairs) is leading an effort to improve coordination and communication among federal, state, and local public health and food regulatory officials. The efforts are targeted at outbreaks of illness caused by foodborne pathogens and are meant to contribute to more effective implementation of existing food safety programs.

Center for Veterinary Medicine

The Center for Veterinary Medicine regulates the manufacture and distribution of food additives and drugs that will be given to animals. These include animals from which human foods are derived as well as food additives and drugs for pet (or companion) animals. Since animals raised for food are a potential target for a bioterrorist attack, the center has initiated activities to increase its preparedness.

Preparedness Activities

The Center for Veterinary Medicine has established and maintains lines of communication with state regulatory officials and personnel in state veterinary diagnostic laboratories. The center co-sponsored a meeting to review the risks to U.S. and world food and agriculture from plant and animal disease and bioterrorism.

National Center for Toxicological Research

The National Center for Toxicological Research conducts scientific research that supports and anticipates FDA's current and future regulatory needs. This involves fundamental and applied research on biological mechanisms of action underlying the toxicity of products regulated by FDA.

Research Activities

The National Center for Toxicological Research has examined proteins in food to determine the existence of bacteria. It has also worked on approaches to identify indications of toxicity associated with biological agents.

Preparedness Activities

In the event of an attack, the center has the ability to respond with animal studies and microbiological surveillance to identify the agent.

Representatives from the National Center for Toxicological Research participate in meetings with FEMA and Arkansas public health officials to plan training activities for responding to bioterrorism threats.

Office of Regulatory Affairs

Among its responsibilities, the Office of Regulatory Affairs responds to emergencies involving products regulated by FDA. If a bioterrorist event were to take place, the office would be involved in the investigation.

Preparedness Activities

FDA would be involved in the management of a response to any attack that targets a FDA-regulated product. The Office of Regulatory Affairs' Office of Criminal Investigations would conduct the criminal investigation and serve as the liaison to the FBI and other law enforcement agencies.

The Office of Regulatory Affairs maintains a 24-hour emergency hotline, in part for receiving information about a bioterrorist attack. It has also established a notification system with the FBI for bioterrorist events.

National Institutes of Health

NIH conducts medical research in its own laboratories and supports the research of nonfederal scientists in universities, medical schools, hospitals, and research institutions throughout the United States and abroad. NIH is composed of 27 separate institutes and centers. One of these is the National Institute of Allergy and Infectious Diseases (NIAID), which has a program to support research related to organisms likely to be used as biological weapons. This program includes research devoted to the development of (1) rapid, accurate diagnostics, (2) effective therapy for those infected, and (3) vaccines for those at risk of exposure.

All of NIH's research on bioterrorism has been funded out of general appropriations. Table 9 gives the amounts of reported funding for NIH's activities on bioterrorism for fiscal year 1998 through fiscal year 2001.

Table 9: Reported Funding for Activities on Bioterrorism at NIH
(Dollars in millions)

Program/initiative	Fiscal year 1998	Fiscal year 1999	Fiscal year 2000	Fiscal year 2001 (estimate)
Research activities				
Diagnostics	$0.3	$1.3	$0.9	$1.1
Vaccines	$3.0	$6.6	$6.8	$7.0
Antibiotics/antivirals	$0.4	$3.3	$5.6	$6.1
Basic research (genomics and pathogenesis)	$13.2	$21.4	$29.7	$35.4
Total[a]	$17.0	$32.6	$43.0	$49.7

Note: We have not audited or otherwise verified the information provided.

[a]Individual entries may not sum to totals because of rounding.

Source: NIH.

Research Activities

The initial focus of NIAID's research efforts on bioterrorism was on small-pox and anthrax. The agency collaboratively funded (along with DOD, DOE, and CDC) activities on smallpox, including research to develop and test antiviral drugs against smallpox viruses, extend the usefulness of the currently available, older vaccine, and to develop a vaccine that can be used in all segments of the civilian population (for instance, pregnant women and the immune-suppressed). For anthrax, NIAID has formed the Working Group on Anthrax Vaccines to develop and test a new vaccine that could be used to replace the currently licensed vaccine.

In addition to these ongoing activities, NIAID provided support to se-quence the genomes of all bacterial pathogens considered by CDC to have the potential to be used as bioterrorism agents. The results of such re-search, along with other information, are expected to facilitate pursuit of a variety of critical goals, including the development of rapid diagnostic methods, antimicrobial therapies, and new vaccines for the most likely bioterrorist agents.

NIAID also conducts and sponsors research in the areas of diagnostics, therapeutics, and vaccines, as well as basic research on the origination and development of diseases from biological agents. In diagnostics research, the development of detection systems for smallpox antigens has been em-phasized. Therapeutics research has covered a number of areas including the development of a replacement therapy for treating the serious complications that would result from immunizing the civilian population against smallpox. NIAID continues to work on vaccines for smallpox and anthrax to prevent illness resulting from a terrorist attack. The agency has collaborated with the U.S. Army Medical Research Institute of Infectious Diseases on the development of a new anthrax vaccine to protect the American public. NIAID is also conducting basic research in a number of areas, including the genetic basis for the virulence of potential bioterrorist agents.

Office of Emergency Preparedness

OEP coordinates the medical and public health response to emergencies, including all kinds of terrorist attacks and natural disasters. OEP has taken an "all-hazards" approach to emergency preparedness and response because it is involved in the health response to many different types of situations, including bioterrorism. See table 10 for OEP's reported funding for activities on terrorism.

Table 10: Reported Funding for Activities on Terrorism at OEP
(Dollars in millions)

Program/initiative	Fiscal year 1998	Fiscal year 1999	Fiscal year 2000	Fiscal year 2001
Research activities				
Infrastructure—research and development	$0.1	$0.1	0	0
Smallpox study	$0.1	0	0	0
Special activities	0	0	0	$4.6
Preparedness activities				
Combating terrorism	$0.3	$19.0	$20.0	$27.2
National Medical Response Teams	0	$1.5	$1.5	$1.5
U.S. Public Health Service Noble Training Center	0	$3.0	$1.0	$2.9
VA WMD training	0	0	0	$0.8
Pharmaceutical Cache	0	0	$1.0	$1.2
Metropolitan Medical Response System	0	$14.5	$16.5	$17.4
Special events	0	0	0	$2.0
Surveillance and laboratory support	$0.3ª	0	0	0
Special activities	0	0	0	$1.4

Program/initiative	Fiscal year 1998	Fiscal year 1999	Fiscal year 2000	Fiscal year 2001
Infrastructure	$9.7	$12.6	$15.3	$18.9
Office/regions	$5.0	$7.5	$8.8	$12.3
Planning and evaluation	$1.2	$1.0	$1.0	$1.0
Training and exercises	0	$0.8	$2.5	$2.5
Disaster Medical Assistance Team development	$2.5	$2.5	$2.5	$2.6
Communications	$1.0	$0.8	$0.5	$0.5
Total[b]	$10.2	$31.7	$35.3	$50.7

Note: We have not audited or otherwise verified the information provided.

[a]This money was transferred to CDC, FDA, and HHS' Agency for Toxic Substances and Disease Registry. This funding stopped once these agencies began receiving bioterrorism funding.

[b]Individual entries may not sum to totals because of rounding.

Source: OEP.

Research Activities

OEP has participated in research and evaluation activities. It has worked with the Institute of Medicine to develop an assessment methodology and performance measures for the Metropolitan Medical Response System. OEP also oversees $4.6 million in fiscal year 2001 for research special activities, which are earmarks in the budget for specific universities, hospitals, or response systems to conduct studies (see table 10).

Preparedness Activities

HHS coordinates many of its medical response activities with other agencies through the National Disaster Medical System. OEP leads this system, a partnership among HHS, DOD, VA, FEMA, state and local governments, and the private sector, which is intended to ensure that resources are available to provide medical services following a disaster that overwhelms the local health care resources. The overall purpose of the system is to establish a single, integrated national medical response capability to (1) assist state and local authorities in dealing with the medical and health effects of major peacetime disasters and (2) provide support to the military and VA medical systems in caring for casualties evacuated to the United States from overseas armed conflicts. About 2,000 civilian hospitals have pledged resources that could be marshaled in any domestic emergency under the system.

In addition to providing additional capacity in the event of an emergency, the National Disaster Medical System also has response teams that can provide support at the site of a disaster. Disaster Medical Assistance Teams can deploy to disaster sites with sufficient supplies and equipment to sustain themselves for 72 hours while providing medical care at a fixed or temporary site.[5] In mass casualty events, the teams would perform triage, provide medical care, and prepare patients for evacuation. In other types of situations, the teams may also provide primary health care and/or serve to augment overloaded local health care staffs.

There are also specialized Disaster Medical Assistance Teams. Some of the specialized teams deal with specific medical conditions, such as burns or mental health. Disaster Mortuary Operational Response Teams provide mortuary services and victim identification. There are four National Medical Response Teams located around the country that are specially equipped and trained to provide medical care for victims of WMDs. Three of these are deployable anywhere in the country, and all four teams have a stockpile of pharmaceuticals and medical supplies to treat up to 5,000 people. However, these stockpiles are primarily for treating victims of a chemical weapon.

OEP received $2 million in fiscal year 2001 that was transferred to VA to provide funding for VA to manage caches of pharmaceuticals for the National Medical Response Teams and for training of National Disaster Medical System hospitals in response to WMD events. OEP also received approximately $2.9 million in fiscal year 2001 to provide management staff and operating funds for the U.S. Public Health Service Noble Training Center in Alabama. This center is developing curricula and providing training activities for physicians, nurses, and emergency medical technicians. This facility will primarily provide training in response to a chemical incident, but will also have some bioterrorism response duties.

The office received $2.6 million in fiscal year 2001 for Disaster Medical Assistance Team development, which funds training programs for the teams and other specialty teams (see table 10 for detailed budget information). OEP received an additional $1.5 million to expand the National Medical Response Teams, primarily by providing additional team members and purchasing equipment. Some funding from both of these sources was also used to provide management and oversight of the annual National Disaster Medical System conference.

OEP was allocated received $2.5 million in fiscal year 2001 to provide additional training and exercise activities for Disaster Medical Assistance Teams and local responders to ensure that teams are operational in a field setting, and that the community and response teams can work together to achieve an integrated approach to medical care during a terrorist event. These funds also provide for coordinated training and exercises with other departments, such as DOD and DOE, during response to special events.

The office also deploys teams from the National Disaster Medical System to high-security events, such as visits by heads of state. In fiscal year 2001, OEP received $2 million to support the costs of deploying teams to a number of special events, including $1 million for the Olympic games and $1 million for other special events, such as the presidential inauguration.

OEP's Metropolitan Medical Response System emphasizes enhancement of local planning and response capability, tailored to each jurisdiction, to care for victims of a terrorist incident involving WMDs. The program includes a focus on response to bioterrorism, including disease surveillance, mass casualty care, and mass fatality management. OEP, under the Metropolitan Medical Response System, has entered into contracts with 97 local areas to develop and coordinate local medical response capabilities. This program works at the local level because of the rapid response time that would be required to manage the consequences of a terrorist attack. OEP received approximately $17 million in fiscal year 2001 to expand the program to 25 additional communities and continue development in 25 existing areas begun in fiscal year 2000. In addition, 47 of the areas received additional funding to plan for an appropriate health system response to a bioterrorist attack. Planning and evaluation funds were used, in part, to provide oversight and technical assistance for response system activities. In fiscal year 2001, OEP is overseeing $1.4 million that was earmarked in the budget for the Charlotte, North Carolina, Metropolitan Medical Response System. The funds will be used to coordinate and enhance preparedness of community health care facilities, for provider training, and to integrate the public health system into a mass casualty response system.

OEP received approximately $12 million in fiscal year 2001 for general emergency preparedness infrastructure development and maintenance. This includes headquarters and regional staff salaries, rent, and other operating costs. It also received $500,000 to maintain and enhance systems to communicate during disasters and special events.

Appendix IX
Department of Justice

DOJ has a variety of responsibilities for combating terrorism. The Office of Justice Programs (OJP) administers programs to provide equipment, training, exercises, and technical assistance to first responders, including some components of the Domestic Preparedness Program that were transferred from DOD,[1] and to provide assistance to victims of terrorism. Under Presidential Decision Directive 39, DOJ, acting through the FBI, is the overall lead federal agency for domestic terrorism incidents. The FBI is the lead agency for crisis management of any terrorist incident within the domestic United States and houses the National Domestic Preparedness Office, which was established to coordinate all federal efforts to assist state and local first responders in preparing for a terrorist incident. See table 11 for DOJ's reported funding for activities on bioterrorism.

Table 11: Reported Funding for Activities on Bioterrorism at DOJ
(Dollars in millions)

Program/initiative	Fiscal year 1998	Fiscal year 1999	Fiscal year 2000	Fiscal year 2001
OJP				
Research activities				
Biological agent detection	$0.2	$1.1	$0.2	0
Development of equipment performance standards and test protocols for emergency response equipment	0	0	$0.5	$4.6
Preparedness activities				
Development of chemical/biological agent list	$0.3	0	0	0
Exercises	0	0	$6.1[a]	$3.2
Development of an emergency response to domestic biological incidents	0	0	$0.5	$1.0
Metropolitan Medical Response System outreach plan	0	0	$0.3	0

Program/initiative	Fiscal year 1998	Fiscal year 1999	Fiscal year 2000	Fiscal year 2001
Veterinary Laboratory Network for rapid analysis of biological agents	0	0	$0.4	0
Hospital Provider Course Development And Delivery	0	0	0	$0.9
Biological Planning Guide	0	0	0	$0.2
Development of equipment guides	0	$0.3	$0.3	0
FBI				
Research activities				
Detecting and characterizing biological agents	0	0	0	$1.1
Total	**$0.5**	**$1.4**	**$8.3**	**$11.0**

Note: We have not audited or otherwise verified the information provided.

aOJP could not report how much of $6.1 million for exercises was only for activities on bioterrorism.

Source: DOJ.

Office of Justice Programs

OJP sponsors research on emergency response equipment, provides grants and technical assistance, and can provide assistance to victims of terrorism.

Research Activities

The National Institute of Justice within OJP conducts research activities on terrorism. Among its programs, the institute conducts operational testing and assessment of new technologies and supports efforts to develop lower cost, more effective emergency response equipment. It is also working with the Office of State and Local Domestic Preparedness Support, the FBI, and the Technical Support Working Group on a study to determine the chemical and biological agents that terrorists are most likely to use.

Preparedness Activities

The Anti-Terrorism and Effective Death Penalty Act of 1996 (P.L. 104-132, sec. 822) authorized OJP and FEMA to fund and develop a terrorism emergency response training program for fire, emergency medical service, and public safety personnel. The 1998 Commerce, Justice, and State

Appropriations Act (P.L. 105-119) provided funding used to create an equipment acquisition grant program as well as two training centers for emergency responders. The grant and training programs target the nation's 120 largest metropolitan jurisdictions. The Office for State and Local Domestic Preparedness Support administers the Domestic Preparedness Program and the grant and training programs. This office assists state and local jurisdictions in enhancing their domestic preparedness capabilities by providing assistance to jurisdictions to acquire equipment, technical assistance, exercises, and training. For example, this office has developed an on-line data collection tool to assist states in conducting their threat, risk, and needs assessments2 and to develop their WMD preparedness strategy, which is designed to be used by the states to target grant funds in order to improve preparedness.

OJP reported $5.3 million in fiscal year 2001 as being related to the public health and medical consequences of a bioterrorist attack against the civilian population, as shown in table 11. However, the funding in table 11 represents only part of DOJ's more general-purpose spending on activities on terrorism, which could also benefit preparedness for a bioterrorism event. DOJ reported $3.2 million was used to facilitate biological tabletop exercises in 52 cities in fiscal year 2001. These 1-day exercises involve public health, fire, law enforcement, and emergency management agencies. Participants work through a simulation of a bioterrorism incident, starting with the incubation period (the time between initial exposure to a biological agent and the first onset of symptoms), followed by the recognition and initial response, and finally the challenges of integrating federal assets in the response and recovery efforts. Medical surveillance, epidemiology, quarantine, patient tracking, remediation, and mass fatality management are addressed.

OJP also reported funding of $1.0 million in fiscal year 2001 to develop and deliver a course on planning a response to a bioterrorist attack (see table 11). The office reported about $0.3 million to develop a plan to enhance awareness of the Metropolitan Medical Response System and approximately $0.4 million to establish a Veterinary Laboratory Network for the rapid analysis of biological and infectious disease agents in fiscal year 2000.[3]

OJP may also provide assistance to victims of terrorism under the Victims of Crime Act of 1984 (P.L. 98-473, ch. 14, as amended). These funds could be used, for example, to provide mental health treatment to victims of terrorism.

Federal Bureau of Investigation

The FBI conducts some bioterrorism-related research, is the lead agency for crisis management, and houses the National Domestic Preparedness Office.

Research Activities

The Hazardous Materials Response Unit conducts research on detecting and characterizing biological materials for law enforcement reasons, such as associating some person, group, or geographical region with the biological material. This research could also have benefits in identifying biological agents for public health and medical systems. In fiscal year 2001, the Hazardous Materials Response Unit awarded $500,000 for research activities related to detection and characterization of biological materials ($250,000 each to the Massachusetts Institute of Technology and the U.S. Soldier Biological and Chemical Command). It has an additional $585,000 in awards pending. This amount includes $150,000 for CDC's Laboratory Response Network for bioterrorism.[4] The FBI participated in the creation of protocols used by the Laboratory Response Network to ensure uniformity in testing and the establishment of the proper chain of custody for biological, evidentiary samples.

Preparedness Activities

In the FBI's role as lead agency for crisis management, it conducts interagency threat assessments of WMDs (a process established to determine the credibility of WMD threats), and provides a situational assessment during a WMD incident. The FBI has designated a WMD coordinator in each of its 56 field offices. If necessary, the FBI coordinates deployment of the Domestic Emergency Support Team in response to an emergency under the U.S. Government Interagency Domestic Terrorism Concept of Operations Plan (CONPLAN).

The FBI also houses the National Domestic Preparedness Office, which was established to coordinate all federal efforts to assist state and local emergency responders with planning, training, equipment, medical and health, and exercise needs necessary to respond to a WMD incident. The office serves as a single point of contact and clearinghouse for WMD- related information for state and local responders, including fire, hazardous materials, law enforcement, public health, and medical personnel. It also provides emergency responders with access to subject matter experts and links to federal resources.

The FBI and CDC are engaged in a series of four regional meetings to identify the core capacities required to prepare for and respond to an act of bioterrorism. These sessions will assist in prioritizing the capabilities of the public health community and identify how law enforcement can promote and benefit from these programs. The FBI and CDC are also developing guidelines that will assist CDC in disseminating information to the public health departments through the communications system, Epi-X. Epi-X is a secure, moderated, Web-based communications network for public health officials that is intended to simplify and expedite the exchange of routine and emergency public health information between CDC and state health departments. Following the guidelines should allow the public health community to obtain necessary information without releasing case specific or law enforcement sensitive information not relevant to the health related concerns.

Appendix X
Department of Transportation

DOT is responsible for reducing vulnerabilities to terrorism affecting the security of all airports in the United States, all aircraft and passengers, and all maritime shipping under the U.S. flag or registration, or operating within the territory of the United States. DOT also coordinates security measures for rail, highway, mass transit, and pipeline facilities. Through the National Response Center, which is staffed by the Coast Guard and located in the Coast Guard's Headquarters Command Center, DOT also serves as the sole national point of contact for reporting all biological, oil, chemical, radiological, and disease-causing discharges into the environment anywhere in the United States and its territories. DOT received $800,000 in fiscal year 1999 and $800,000 in fiscal year 2000 for preparedness activities on bioterrorism from DOD.

Research Activities

DOT is conducting research on the ability of metropolitan areas to respond to attacks on local transit systems. Most of the WMD research at DOT is focused on chemical, not biological, agents.

Preparedness Activities

The National Response Center serves as the first-alert center for all releases of biological agents, maintains incident databases, and provides private and secure conferencing for the law enforcement, emergency response, and public health sectors on an incident-specific basis. It is also the communications and operations center for the National Response Team. Both the National Response Center and the National Response Team are components of the National Response System. The system is the government's mechanism for emergency response to discharges of oil and the release of chemicals into the navigable waters or environment of the United States and its territories. It provides a framework for coordination among federal, state, and local responders and responsible parties. The National Response Team provides a national planning, policy, and coordinating body to provide guidance before and assistance during an incident. Its membership consists of 16 federal agencies[1] with expertise in various aspects of emergency response to pollution incidents. The National Response Center participates in terrorism exercises as requested by other agencies. Some emergency response and management training courses at DOT have a bioterrorism component, but there are no training courses dedicated to bioterrorism.

Appendix XI
Department of the Treasury

Within the Department of the Treasury, the U.S. Secret Service receives funding for activities on bioterrorism.

U.S. Secret Service

The U.S. Secret Service is responsible for the protection of the President, the Vice President, and their families; heads of state and other designated individuals; the investigation of threats against these protectees; and protection of the White House, the Vice President's Residence, foreign missions, and other buildings within Washington, D.C. The U.S. Secret Service is also responsible for design, planning, and implementation of security at designated National Security Special Events.

Research Activities

The U.S. Secret Service reported funding of $450,000 for fiscal year 2001 to support the development of a biological agent detector. It reported funding of an additional $60,000 for laboratory identification of biological and chemical agents.

Preparedness Activities

The Hazardous Agent Mitigation and Medical Emergency Response teams, which are part of the Secret Service's Chemical, Biological, Radiological, and Nuclear Countermeasures program, travel with the presidential motorcade and respond to chemical and biological events. The Secret Service has a role to protect the civilian population in special events such as the Olympic games.

Appendix XII
Department of Veterans Affairs

VA manages one of the nation's largest health care systems and is the nation's largest drug purchaser. The department purchases pharmaceuticals and medical supplies for the National Pharmaceutical Stockpile Program and the National Medical Response Team stockpiles and it participates in other bioterrorism preparedness activities.

Preparedness Activities

VA purchases pharmaceuticals and medical supplies for federal stockpiles because of its purchasing power and ability to negotiate large discounts from manufacturers that sell pharmaceuticals, equipment, and supplies to the VA hospital system.[1] VA is under contract with CDC to purchase drugs for the National Pharmaceutical Stockpile Program and manages a spectrum of contracts for the storage, rotation, security, and transportation of the stockpile. The CDC contracts included an estimated $14 million for fiscal year 2000 and another $60 million for fiscal year 2001.

VA also works with OEP by agreement to purchase, store, and maintain drugs for the four National Medical Response Teams, and to train the National Disaster Medical System civilian hospital staff. VA received $0.9 million in fiscal year 2000 and $1.2 million in fiscal year 2001 from OEP for the purchase, storage, and maintenance of drugs. Also in fiscal year 2001, VA received $0.8 million from OEP to begin developing training for staff in the National Disaster Medical System hospitals.

In addition, VA hospitals throughout the United States participate in local community emergency planning. VA personnel have been deployed to many presidentially declared emergencies (for example, the Oklahoma City bombing).

Appendix XIII
Environmental Protection Agency

EPA has responsibilities to prepare for and respond to emergencies involving oil, hazardous substances, pollutants, or contaminants (which include chemical, biological, and radiological materials) that also could be components of a WMD attack. If necessary, EPA can assist the FBI in determining what sort of hazardous substance may be, or has been, released in a terrorist incident. Following an incident, EPA can help with environmental monitoring, sampling, decontamination efforts, and long- term site cleanup activities. In addition, Presidential Decision Directive 63 gives EPA responsibility for the protection of the U.S. water supply from terrorist attack, including the protection of water supplies from biological contamination.

EPA's participation in a potential bioterrorist event would vary on a case-by-case basis. EPA might advise the national, state, or local government on what the agent might be and could have a role in the potential cleanup and decontamination if asked to assist by other agencies. For example, this might include testing the water system for contaminants, including biological agents, if an outbreak of a disease occurred. EPA works with CDC on a case-by-case basis to tailor its response to address the specific agent.

EPA received little funding specifically for activities on bioterrorism during fiscal year 1998 through fiscal year 2001 (see table 12).

Table 12: Reported Funding for Activities on Bioterrorism at EPA (Dollars in millions)

Program/initiative	Fiscal year 1998	Fiscal year 1999	Fiscal year 2000	Fiscal year 2001
Research activities				
Detection of biological agents	0	0	0	$0.5
Preparedness activities				
Vulnerability assessments	$0.01	0	$0.1	$2.0
Total	**$0.01**	**0**	**$0.1**	**$2.5**

Note: We have not audited or otherwise verified the information provided.

Source: EPA.

Research Activities

EPA reported funding of $500,000 in fiscal year 2001 to sponsor research to investigate methods to detect and identify biological agents in water.

Preparedness Activities

EPA is training its staff to respond to a WMD incident. EPA has approximately 220 On-Scene Coordinators across the country, who are the on-location staff responsible for coordinating EPA's response to a hazardous material spill or release into the environment. The coordinators are responsible for bringing in the necessary resources, including EPA contractors, or tasking other agencies for support. The coordinators and EPA contractors are receiving training on WMD agents, especially biological agents, in order to get more specific, in-depth knowledge to enhance their overall ability to handle a bioterrorist incident. EPA is coordinating with CDC to add a bioterrorism module to EPA's training on terrorism. EPA is considering additional training for its coordinators to provide them with the in-depth knowledge they need to lead an appropriate response. However, because situations with biological agents are unique, it is hard to make generalizations about how to respond. For example, weather conditions can alter the need to decontaminate a site because temperature, among other factors, can render biological agents harmless.

EPA has also been working with DOE and the American Water Works Association—Research Foundation to develop a vulnerability assessment methodology for the water supply sector. In fiscal year 1998, EPA received $10,000 to partially fund the development of the National Infrastructure Assurance Plan—Water Supply (see table 12). EPA received $66,000 in fiscal year 2000 to fund the development of the vulnerability assessment methodology and to co-sponsor a workshop on water infrastructure protection with DOE. EPA reported funding of $2.0 million to continue the development of this methodology and related water issues in fiscal year 2001.

Appendix XIV
Federal Emergency Management Agency

FEMA is the lead federal agency for consequence management preparedness and response to terrorist incidents involving WMDs, and it is helping
to build a bioterrorist response system that is part of a broader terrorist response system. FEMA reported funding for activities on terrorism of $25.1
million for fiscal year 2000 and $30.3 million for fiscal year 2001 (see table 13).

Table 13: Reported Funding for Activities on Terrorism at FEMA
(Dollars in millions)

Program/initiative	Fiscal year 1998	Fiscal year 1999	Fiscal year 2000	Fiscal year 2001
Preparedness activities				
Response and recovery	a	$2.0	$2.0	$6.3
Preparedness, training, and exercises	a	$0.5	$1.8	$2.3
Fire prevention and training	a	$4.0	$4.9	$5.1
Emergency management planning grants	a	$8.3	$16.4	$16.6
Total		**$14.8**	**$25.1**	**$30.3**

Note: We have not audited or otherwise verified the information provided.

aFEMA did not supply us with funding amounts for fiscal year 1998. Source: FEMA.

Preparedness Activities

At the federal level, FEMA is involved with preparedness activities in coordination with other departments and agencies, using the structures of the Federal
Response Plan. At the state and local levels, preparedness activities include the
provision of grants to the states and the delivery of first-responder and emergency management training programs to support their terrorism-related planning, training, exercise, equipment, and assessment requirements.

Planning

FEMA works with other departments and agencies to support consequence management planning at the national and regional levels. FEMA
coordinates the federal response planning through the Emergency Support Functions Leaders Group, which is the principal body that addresses
Federal Response Plan planning and implementation at the working level,
and the Catastrophic Disaster Response Group, which provides guidance
and policy direction on response coordination and operational issues. Also,

FEMA plans and participates in activities to address consequence management for special events such as the Olympic games. FEMA has been actively engaged in the development and review of major organizational
and operational support documents, such as the CONPLAN (see app. III
for details regarding the CONPLAN). FEMA and DOJ's OJP are working to incorporate a bioterrorist response element into their terrorist response system.

At the state and local levels, FEMA provides assistance to support terrorism-related emergency response planning. FEMA gives Emergency Management Planning grants to support the development of terrorism- specific
annexes to existing state and local emergency operations plans. The grant
money can be used for activities such as planning, training, and conducting exercises. FEMA negotiates a work plan for funding with each state,
and states have been given wide latitude in targeting this assistance.
FEMA can also provide supplemental funds to state and local mental
health agencies to provide crisis counseling to eligible survivors of
presidentially declared major disasters.

FEMA also updates and maintains the Rapid Response Information System, which is authorized under the National Defense Authorization Act of
Fiscal Year 1997 (P.L. 104-201, sec. 1417). This information system contains
databases of characteristics and safety precautions for nuclear, biological,
and chemical agents and materials and can be used as a resource guide for
response to such an incident.

Training

FEMA has developed and delivered terrorism-related courses for state and
local emergency management personnel and first responders. It has provided grant assistance to the states to support this training. Training is provided through the Emergency Management Institute and the National
Fire Academy. The Institute also conducts a Senior Officials Course for local government officials as part of the Domestic Preparedness Program.[1]

Exercises

FEMA participates in federal interagency terrorism response exercises
sponsored by the FBI, DOD, and others. FEMA also provides funding to
states to support terrorism response exercises. FEMA participates in special
events such as the Olympic games, where it has the opportunity to detect
and correct weaknesses in its system.

Equipment

FEMA, in conjunction with DOD and DOJ, assisted in the development
and is currently helping to refine the Standardized Equipment List to support acquisition of equipment for fire, police, and emergency medical responders. This equipment will conform to appropriate and applicable

laws, regulations, and to-be-developed national standards including those issued by the National Institute of Justice, the National Institute for Occupational Safety and Health, and the National Fire Protection Association.

Assessment

FEMA and the National Emergency Management Association have created a partnership to develop an emergency management readiness and capability assessment system for state and local emergency managers. This self-assessment is intended to help governments determine strengths and weaknesses of their emergency management program. The baseline report was released on March 2, 1998. In summary, it found that although states have the basic capabilities in place to effectively respond to disasters that normally confront them, there are areas that require attention and improvement, such as planning and equipment for response to a terrorist incident.

Appendix XV
Comments From the Department of Commerce

THE SECRETARY OF COMMERCE
Washington, D.C. 20230

SEP 1 4 2001

Ms. Janet Heinrich
Director, Health Care-Public Health Issues
U.S. General Accounting Office
441 G Street, N.W., Room 5A14
Washington, D.C. 20548

Dear Ms. Heinrich:

Thank you for your letter requesting our review and comments on the General Accounting Office (GAO) draft report entitled "Bioterrorism: Federal Research and Preparedness Activities" (GAO-01-915).

The Office of Law Enforcement Standards of the National Institute of Standards and Technology (NIST) has reviewed the GAO draft report. Our comments on this report are enclosed. We hope these suggestions strengthen your final report and assist you in addressing this important issue.

If you have any questions or require additional information regarding our comments, please contact Albert Conerly of the NIST Management and Organization Division at (301) 975-4050.

Warm regards,

Donald L. Evans

Enclosure

Department of Commerce Comments on Draft GAO Report - Bioterrorism: Federal Research and Preparedness Activities (GAO-01-915)

The National Institute of Standards and Technology (NIST) Electronics and Electrical Engineering Laboratory, Office of Law Enforcement Standards (OLES) has reviewed the draft GAO Report entitled: Bioterrorism: Federal Research and Preparedness Activities (GAO-01-915), and is providing the following comments.

General Comment: The integrated nature of the ongoing program to develop a suite of chemical and biological protective national standards is not reflected in this report. The major player within NIST, the Office of Law Enforcement Standards, is managing programs through interagency agreements with the National Institute for Occupational Safety and Health (NIOSH), and the U.S. Army Soldier Biological and Chemical Command (SBCCOM) and is participating in the Interagency Board for Equipment Standardization and Interoperability (IAB). The IAB is co-chaired by representatives from DOD and DOJ (FBI). OLES's efforts are conducted with funding from DOJ's National Institute of Justice. However, discussion of the NIOSH involvement is absent from the CDC portion of Appendix VIII; and there is no mention of either DOD's or DOJ's roles as co-chairs of the IAB in Appendix VI or Appendix IX. The document does not show the funding provided by DOD to support the IAB, nor does it show the funding provided by NIJ to OLES. In many cases, current funding levels and programs do not reflect purely bioterrorism research and preparedness activities, but many of the chemical agent protective measures will be directly applied to bioterrorism prevention standards development, or can be built upon in subsequent programs. The current document makes it difficult to cross-reference multi-agency programs or to gain appreciation for the integrated efforts currently under way to develop chemical and biological agent protective standards.

Appendix XVI
Comments From the Department of Defense

OFFICE OF THE ASSISTANT SECRETARY OF DEFENSE

WASHINGTON, D.C. 20301-2500

SPECIAL OPERATIONS/
LOW-INTENSITY CONFLICT

SEP   4 2001

Ms. Janet Heinrich
Director
Health Care – Public Health Issues
United States General Accounting Office
441 G. Street, NW, Rm 5A14
Washington, DC 20548

Dear Ms. Heinrich:

    This is the Department of Defense (DoD) response to the General Accounting Office (GAO) draft report, "BIOTERRORISM: Federal Research and Preparedness Activities," undated (GAO Code 290018/OSD Case 01-915). There are no specific recommendations expressed in this report for our concurrence or comment. However, we would like to emphasize that DoD is working to improve biological terrorism response capabilities, and many are already in place, trained, and available to bolster federal, state and local bioterrorism preparedness efforts. This support and cooperative effort is key – our servicemembers and their families are as vulnerable to attack as the general populace and may be called upon to support worldwide operations at a moment's notice. Keeping them safe at our installations and in the surrounding communities is vital to national security. By facilitating federal agency cooperation and resource sharing, to include DOD, the safety of all U.S. citizens is enhanced.

    Technical comments for accuracy and clarification of the report have been provided separately. The Department appreciates the opportunity to comment on the draft report.

Sincerely,

Daniel J. Gallington
Special Assistant to the Secretary for Policy
   Matters (Performing the Duties of
   ASD/SOLIC)

Appendix XVII
Comments From the Department of Health and Human Services

 DEPARTMENT OF HEALTH & HUMAN SERVICES   Office of Inspector General

Washington, D.C. 20201

SEP 13 2001

Ms. Janet Heinrich
Director, Health Care--Public
  Health Issues
United States General
  Accounting Office
Washington, D.C. 20548

Dear Ms. Heinrich:

Enclosed are the Department's comments on your draft report,
"Bioterrorism: Federal Research and Preparedness Activities."
The comments present the tentative position of the Department and
are subject to reevaluation when the final version of this report
is received. ·

The Department also provided extensive technical comments
directly to your staff.

The Department appreciates the opportunity to comment on this
draft report before its publication.

Sincerely,

Michael Mangano

Michael F. Mangano
Principal Deputy Inspector General

The Office of Inspector General (OIG) is transmitting the   .
Department's response to this draft report in our capacity as
the Department's designated focal point and coordinator for
General Accounting Office reports. The OIG has not conducted
an independent assessment of these comments and therefore
expresses no opinion on them.

Comments of the Department of Health and Human Services
on the Draft GAO Report Entitled,
"Bioterrorism: Federal Research and Preparedness Activities"

The Department of Health and Human Services appreciates the opportunity to comment on the General Accounting Office's (GAO) draft report on bioterrorism. We believe that GAO has provided substantial factual information about Federal preparations should a significant bioterrorism attack against the civilian population occur in the United States. However, we would like to make several general observations about the draft report.

First, the Department is the principal public health agency in the Federal Government and therefore has an important role in providing technical advice to law enforcement agencies dealing with a bioterrorism crisis and in assisting State and local authorities respond to the human health consequences of an attack. Unlike other agencies that participate in the United States' Federal Response Plan, the Department brings to bioterrorism preparedness our unique capabilities and expertise in infectious disease surveillance and control that are unequaled elsewhere in the Federal Government. The Secretary of Health and Human Services has also recently appointed a Special Assistant for Bioterrorism to coordinate anti-bioterrorism efforts across the Department.

Quite possibly a bioterrorist attack may initially be observed as a naturally-occurring epidemic of unknown origin. In this case, the Department, and particularly our Centers for Disease Control and Prevention (CDC), would likely assist State and local governments in their disease surveillance, identification, and control efforts before a determination of terrorist origins was made. Should local health care resources be overwhelmed, the Department, through our Office of Emergency Preparedness (OEP), would already be assisting State and local authorities in providing care for massive numbers of casualties. The Department appreciates GAO's recognition of these systems and possible event characteristics.

Second, the capacity to respond to a bioterrorism event is dependent, at all levels, and in large part, on the ability of governments and health agencies to perform effective outbreak detection, control an epidemic, and respond to mass casualty-producing emergencies, whatever the cause. There are unique requirements for an effective response to a bioterrorist attack, including those related to disease surveillance, detection, laboratory identification, population prophylaxis, public health information, and possibly victim isolation and quarantine. However, there are additional aspects of an effective bioterrorism response that are dependent on effective preparations to respond to other types of emergencies, as well, including those related to emergency management, public safety, emergency medical services, health care delivery and fatality management. The report might benefit from clearly describing these commonalities and distinctions.

Third, because there are many common features of responses to biological, chemical, and other emergencies that can overwhelm local resources, the Federal Government takes an all-hazards approach to emergency response planning and management. Frequently it is difficult to partition budgets among preparations to respond to one or another type of emergency. Therefore, we have suggested changes to the report's resource table presentations to clarify, as much as possible, these allocations and expenditures.

Fourth, one of the most important aspects of State and local capacity-building is response planning for biological, chemical and other causes of mass casualty-producing events. In general, effective responses must include the community's public safety, public health and health care delivery resources. Because of the complex nature of coordinating these responses, the Department's OEP and CDC have emphasized preparedness and response planning in their systems development support.

Fifth, the Department has met with Federal law enforcement and intelligence agencies in our analyses of the most consequential chemical and biological agent threats. From these meetings, lists of agents were developed which were used as the basis for pharmaceutical stockpile acquisitions. Part of the consideration for stockpile planning is the potential size of the population that might be affected and the likely inadequacy of local resources to be able to meet the demand for pharmaceuticals.

The Department has emphasized public health and medical response planning and capacity-building at Federal, State, and local levels. Unfortunately, health concerns have frequently been under-emphasized in emergency management planning, resource development and exercise execution. Therefore, the Department appreciates the efforts of GAO to focus attention once again on the all-important need to assure that the Nation's health infrastructure will be able to respond to whatever challenge may confront it.

Appendix XVIII
Comments From the Department of Justice

 U. S. Department of Justice

Washington, DC 20530

August 31, 2001

Janet Heinrich
Director
Health Care - Public Health Issues
U.S. General Accounting Office
441 G Street, NW
Washington, DC   20548

Dear Ms. Heinrich:

On August 10, 2001, the General Accounting Office (GAO) provided the Department of Justice copies of its draft report entitled "BIOTERRORISM: Federal Research and Preparedness Activities." The draft was reviewed by representatives of the Office of Justice Programs, the Criminal Division, and the Federal Bureau of Investigation. While the Department generally agreed with the substance of the document, it believed some areas could be clarified or strengthened. We are providing several comments for these purposes. We understand that they will be incorporated as appropriate.

I hope the comments will be beneficial in completing the final document. If you have any questions concerning the Department's comments, you may contact me on (202) 514-0469.

Sincerely,

Vickie L. Sloan
Director, Audit Liaison Office
Justice Management Division

Enclosure

Appendix XIX
GAO Contacts and Staff Acknowledgments

GAO Contacts

Janet Heinrich, (202) 512-7118
Marcia Crosse, (202) 512-3407

Acknowledgments

In addition to those named above, Barbara Chapman, Robert Copeland, Greg Ferrante, LaKesha Jimmerson, Deborah Miller, and Roseanne Price made key contributions to this report.

Related GAO Products

Combating Terrorism: Selected Challenges and Related Recommendations (GAO-01-822, Sept. 20, 2001).

Combating Terrorism: Comments on H.R. 525 to Create a President's Council on Domestic Terrorism Preparedness (GAO-01-555T, May 9, 2001).

Combating Terrorism: Accountability Over Medical Supplies Needs Further Improvement (GAO-01-666T, May 1, 2001).

Combating Terrorism: Observations on Options to Improve the Federal Response (GAO-01-660T, Apr. 24, 2001).

Combating Terrorism: Accountability Over Medical Supplies Needs Further Improvement (GAO-01-463, Mar. 30, 2001).

Combating Terrorism: Comments on Counterterrorism Leadership and National Strategy (GAO-01-556T, Mar. 27, 2001).

Combating Terrorism: FEMA Continues to Make Progress in Coordinating Preparedness and Response (GAO-01-15, Mar. 20, 2001).

Combating Terrorism: Federal Response Teams Provide Varied Capabilities; Opportunities Remain to Improve Coordination (GAO-01- 14, Nov. 30, 2000).

West Nile Virus Outbreak: Lessons for Public Health Preparedness (GAO/HEHS-00-180, Sept. 11, 2000).

Combating Terrorism: Linking Threats to Strategies and Resources (GAO/T-NSIAD-00-218, July 26, 2000).

Chemical and Biological Defense: Observations on Nonmedical Chemical and Biological R&D Programs (GAO/T-NSIAD-00-130, Mar. 22, 2000).

Combating Terrorism: Need to Eliminate Duplicate Federal Weapons of Mass Destruction Training (GAO/NSIAD-00-64, Mar. 21, 2000).

Combating Terrorism: Chemical and Biological Medical Supplies are Poorly Managed (GAO/T-HEHS/AIMD-00-59, Mar. 8, 2000).

Combating Terrorism: Chemical and Biological Medical Supplies Are Poorly Managed (GAO/HEHS/AIMD-00-36, Oct. 29, 1999).

Food Safety: Agencies Should Further Test Plans for Responding to Deliberate Contamination (GAO/RCED-00-3, Oct. 27, 1999).

Endnotes

[1]For example, in January 2000, threatening letters were sent to a variety of recipients, including the Planned Parenthood office in Naples, Florida, warning of the release of anthrax. Federal authorities found no signs of anthrax or any other traces of harmful substances and determined these incidences to be hoaxes.

[2]See app. I for a description of salmonella and other biological agents and pathogens mentioned in this report.

[3]See *Food Safety: Agencies Should Further Test Plans for Responding to Deliberate Contamination* (GAO/RCED-00-3, Oct. 27, 1999), p. 4.

[4]Disease surveillance systems provide for the ongoing collection, analysis, and dissemination of data to prevent and control disease.

[5]Epidemiological investigation is the study of patterns of health or disease and the factors that influence these patterns.

[6]Public health and medical consequences refers to the effects of a biological agent on the population as well as on the individual. See app. I for the medical effects of the biological agents and pathogens mentioned in this report.

[7]We conducted interviews with and obtained information from the Departments of Agriculture, Commerce, Defense, Energy, Health and Human Services, Justice, Transportation, the Treasury, and Veterans Affairs; the Environmental Protection Agency; and the Federal Emergency Management Agency.

[8]Amy Smithson and Leslie-Ann Levy, *Ataxia: The Chemical and Biological Terrorism Threat and the U.S. Response* (Washington, DC: The Henry L. Stimson Center, Oct. 2000).

[9]Advisory Panel to Assess Domestic Response Capabilities for Terrorism Involving Weapons of Mass Destruction, *Toward a National Strategy for Combating Terrorism*, Second Annual Report (Arlington, VA: RAND, Dec. 15, 2000).

[10]For example, an agency providing appropriations is not necessarily indicating the level of its commitments (that is, obligations) or expenditures for that year—only the amount of budget authority made available to it by the Congress. Similarly, an agency which provided expenditure information for fiscal year 2000 may have obligated the funds in fiscal year 1999 based on an appropriation for fiscal year 1998. To simplify presentation, we generally refer to the budget data we received from agencies as "reported funding" and report this information for the agencies separately.

[11]Funding levels for activities on terrorism, including bioterrorism, were reported for activities prior to September 11, 2001 and do not include any funds approved by the Congress after that date.

[12]See *Combating Terrorism: Selected Challenges and Related Recommendations* (GAO-01-822, Sept. 20, 2001), p. 40.

[13]See *Combating Terrorism: Need for Comprehensive Threat and Risk Assessments of Chemical and Biological Attacks* (GAO/NSIAD-99-163, Sept. 14, 1999), p. 17.

[14]Throughout this report, we use the term WMDs to refer to chemical, biological, radiological, or nuclear agents or weapons. Some agencies define it to include large conventional explosives as well.

[15]The first emergency use of the National Pharmaceutical Stockpile occurred on September 11, 2001. In response to the terrorist attack on the World Trade Center, CDC released one of the eight Push Packages.

[16]For more information on management of the National Pharmaceutical Stockpile Program, see *Combating Terrorism: Accountability Over Medical Supplies Needs Further Improvement* (GAO-01-463, Mar. 30, 2001).

[17]In addition to simulating a bioterrorism attack in Denver, the exercise also portrayed a chemical weapons incident in Portsmouth, New Hampshire. A concurrent exercise, referred to as National Capital Region 2000, simulated a radiological event in the greater Washington, D.C., area.

[18]HHS can also address emotional and mental health consequences of terrorist attacks. On September 13, 2001, in response to the attack on the World Trade Center, HHS released $1 million in funding for New York to support mental health services and strategic planning for comprehensive and long-term support.

[19]Presidential Decision Directive 62 created a category of special events called National Security Special Events, which are events of such significance that they warrant greater federal planning and protection than other special events. Such events include presidential inaugurations and major political party conventions.

[20]See app. III for more details on selected federal policy and planning documents.

[21]A description of the funding for the Technical Support Working Group is not included in this report because it does not primarily focus on the public health and medical consequences of a bioterrorist attack.

[22]See GAO-01-822, Sept. 20, 2001, p. 79. Coordination of federal research and development efforts to combat terrorism is still limited by a number of factors, raising the potential for duplicative efforts among federal agencies.

[23]See also *Combating Terrorism: Comments on Counterterrorism Leadership and National Strategy* (GAO-01-556T, Mar. 27, 2001), p. 1.

[24]See Advisory Panel to Assess Domestic Response Capabilities for Terrorism Involving Weapons of Mass Destruction, p. 7.

[25]See also *Combating Terrorism: Issues in Managing Counterterrorist Programs* (GAO/TNSIAD-00-145, Apr. 6, 2000), p. 8.

[26]See GAO-01-822, Sept. 20, 2001, p. 104.

[27]See *Combating Terrorism: Threat and Risk Assessments Can Help Prioritize and Target Program Investments* (GAO/NSIAD-98-74, Apr. 9, 1998), *Combating Terrorism: Need for Comprehensive Threat and Risk Assessments of Chemical and Biological Attacks* (GAO/NSIAD-99-163, Sept. 14, 1999), and *Combating Terrorism: Selected Challenges and Related Recommendations* (GAO-01-822, Sept. 20, 2001).

[28]See *Combating Terrorism: Spending on Governmentwide Programs Requires Better Management and Coordination* (GAO/NSIAD-98-39, Dec. 1, 1997), pp. 3-5.

[29]Section 1051 of the National Defense Authorization Act for Fiscal Year 1998 (P.L. 105-85).

[30]See *Combating Terrorism: Observations on Options to Improve the Federal Response* (GAO-01-660T, Apr. 24, 2001), p. 8.

[31]According to the Office of the Vice President, as of June 2001, details on the Vice President's efforts had not yet been determined.

[32]See GAO-01-822, Sept. 20, 2001, p. 36.

[33]See GAO-01-822, Sept. 20, 2001, p. 41.

[34]See GAO-01-822, Sept. 20, 2001, p. 90

[35]Smithson and Levy, p. 245.

[36]Smithson and Levy, p. 245.

[37]See *West Nile Virus Outbreak: Lessons for Public Health Preparedness* (GAO/HEHS-00-180, Sept. 11, 2000), p. 21.

[38]Advisory Panel to Assess Domestic Response Capabilities for Terrorism Involving Weapons of Mass Destruction, p. 32.

[39]American Hospital Association, *Hospital Preparedness for Mass Casualties*, Summary of an Invitational Forum, Aug. 2000. D.C. Wetter, W.E. Daniell, and C.D. Treser, "Hospital Preparedness for Victims of Chemical or Biological Terrorism," *American Journal of Public Health*, Vol. 91 (2001), pp. 710-16.

[40]Smithson and Levy, p. 273.

[41]Smithson and Levy, p. 262.

[42]J. Richards, M. Navarro, and R. Derlet, "Survey of Directors of Emergency Departments in California on Overcrowding," *Western Journal of Medicine*, Vol. 172 (2000), pp. 385-388. R. Derlet, J. Richards, and R. Kravitz, "Frequent Overcrowding in U.S. Emergency Departments," *Academic Emergency Medicine*, Vol. 8, No. 2 (2001), pp. 151-55.

[43]See app. VIII for a description of the Metropolitan Medical Response System.

[44]Smithson and Levy, p. 227.

[45]Disaster Medical Assistance Teams were dispatched to the New York City and Washington, D.C., areas on September 11, 2001. The initial units included more than 300 medical and mortuary personnel.

Appendix II

[1]The report does not differentiate between biological, chemical, nuclear, and radiological terrorism.

Appendix III

[1]For a more complete discussion on these and other documents, see *Combating Terrorism: Selected Challenges and Related Recommendations* (GAO-01-822, Sept. 20, 2001), pp. 131-136.

[2]Crisis management is predominantly a law enforcement function and includes measures to identify, acquire, and plan the use of resources needed to anticipate, prevent, and/or resolve a threat or act of terrorism. Crisis management also includes assurance of public health and safety. Consequence management includes measures to protect public health, safety, and the environment; to restore essential government services; and to provide emergency relief to governments, businesses, and individuals affected by the consequences of terrorism.

Appendix IV

[1]For example, USDA and DOD jointly planned and conducted a multiagency simulation of a terrorist deliberately contaminating food with a biological agent. See *Food Safety: Agencies Should Further Test Plans for Responding to Deliberate Contamination* (GAO/RCED-00-3, Oct. 27, 1999).

Appendix VI

[1]The civil support teams are located in California, Colorado, Georgia, Illinois, Massachusetts, Missouri, New York, Pennsylvania, Texas, and Washington.

[2]The 17 additional teams for fiscal year 2000 are located in Alaska, Arizona, Arkansas, California (creating a second team), Florida, Hawaii, Idaho, Iowa, Kentucky, Louisiana, Maine, Minnesota, New Mexico, Ohio, Oklahoma, South Carolina, and Virginia. As of January 2001, team locations had not been determined for the additional five teams for fiscal year 2001.

[3]A reagent is a substance used to detect the presence of another substance.

[4]For more information on the Laboratory Response Network, see app. VIII.

[5]For more information concerning the Domestic Preparedness Program, see *Combating Terrorism: Opportunities to Improve Domestic Preparedness Program Focus and Efficiency* (GAO/NSIAD-99-3, Nov. 12, 1998).

[6]With tabletop exercises, participants work through a simulation of a bioterrorism incident, starting with the incubation period (the time between initial exposure to a biological agent and the onset of symptoms), followed by the recognition and initial response, and finally the challenges of integrating federal assets in the response and recovery efforts.

Appendix VIII

[1]The first emergency use of the National Pharmaceutical Stockpile occurred on September 11, 2001. In response to the terrorist attack on the World Trade Center, CDC released one of the eight Push Packages.

[2]For more information on the National Pharmaceutical Stockpile Program, see *Combating Terrorism: Accountability Over Medical Supplies Needs Further Improvement* (GAO-01- 463, Mar. 30, 2001).

[3]"Off label" refers to the treatment of conditions other than those listed on FDA's approved drug label.

[4]Encephalitis is inflammation of the brain.

[5]Disaster Medical Assistance Teams were dispatched to the New York City and Washington, D.C., areas on September 11, 2001. The initial units included more than 300 medical and mortuary personnel.

Appendix IX

[1]See app. VI for more information on the Domestic Preparedness Program.

[2]During the threat and risk assessment process, states identify the threat and risk posed to a community by the terrorist use of a WMD device and integrate vulnerability, threat, and public health performance information to yield a risk profile. The needs assessment outlines a state's needs for training, equipment, and other resources.

[3]See app. VII for more information on the Metropolitan Medical Response System.

[4]See app. VII for more information on the Laboratory Response Network.

Appendix X

[1]The 16 federal agencies are the Departments of Agriculture, Commerce, Defense, Energy, Health and Human Services, the Interior, Justice, Labor, State, Transportation, and the Treasury; the Environmental Protection Agency; the Federal Emergency Management Agency; the General Services Administration; the Nuclear Regulatory Commission, and the U.S. Coast Guard.

Appendix XII

[1]See app. VIII for more information on the stockpiles.

Appendix XIV

[1]See app. VI for more information on the Domestic Preparedness Program.

LEGISLATIVE BRANCH

Testimony

DOCUMENT NO. 11

STATEMENTS AT A HEARING BEFORE THE
U.S. SENATE COMMITTEE ON THE JUDICIARY
ON
"HOMELAND DEFENSE"

THE HONORABLE JOHN ASHCROFT
SENATOR PATRICK LEAHY
SENATOR ORRIN G. HATCH
SENATOR JON KYL

September 25, 2001

COMMENTARY: *These comments are setting the stage for legislative and executive initiatives which can counter the threat of terrorism. They followed closely the September 11th attacks and they illustrate the bipartisan support for new weapons to fight terrorism.*

TESTIMONY OF THE HONORABLE JOHN ASHCROFT
ATTORNEY GENERAL
UNITED STATES DEPARTMENT OF JUSTICE

September 25, 2001

Chairman Leahy, Senator Hatch, Senators: thank you for the opportunity to discuss the Administration's proposed changes in the law to give law enforcement the tools we need to fight terrorism.

In his address to Congress and the nation last Thursday, President Bush declared war on terrorism. As Attorney General, it is my duty to respond to this call to action by ensuring the capacity of United States law enforcement to perform two related critical tasks: First, prevent more terrorism, and second, to bring terrorists to justice.

The American people do not have the luxury of unlimited time in erecting the necessary defenses to future terrorist acts. The danger that darkened the United States of America and the civilized world on September 11 did not pass with the atrocities committed that day. Terrorism is a clear and present danger to Americans today.

Intelligence information available to the FBI indicates a potential for additional terrorist incidents. I testified before the House Judiciary Committee yesterday regarding the possibility of attacks using crop dusting aircraft.

Today I can report to you that our investigation has uncovered several individuals, including individuals who may have links to the hijackers, who fraudulently have obtained, or attempted to obtain, hazardous material transportation licenses.

Given the current threat environment, the FBI has advised all law enforcement agencies to remain alert to this threat.

And, I urge Americans to notify immediately the FBI of any suspicious circumstances that may come to your attention regarding hazardous materials, crop dusting aircraft or any other possible terrorist threat. The FBI website is www.ifccfbi.~tov. That's www.ifccfbi.uov. Our toll-free telephone number is 866-483-5137. Again, the toll-free number is 866-483-5137.

This new terrorist threat to Americans on our soil is a turning point in America's history. It is a new challenge for law enforcement. Our fight against terrorism is not merely or primarily a criminal justice endeavor—it is defense of our nation and its citizens. We cannot wait for terrorists to strike to begin investigations and make arrests. The death tolls are too high, the consequences too great. We must prevent first, prosecute second.

I can assure the Committee and the American people we are conducting this effort with a total commitment to protect the rights and privacy of all Americans and the Constitutional protections we hold dear.

In the past, when American law enforcement confronted challenges to our safety and security from espionage, drug trafficking and organized crime, we met those challenges in ways that preserved our fundamental freedoms and civil liberties.

Today we seek to meet the challenge of terrorism with the same careful regard for the Constitutional rights of Americans and respect for all human beings. Just as American rights and freedoms have been preserved throughout previous law enforcement campaigns, they must be preserved throughout this war on terrorism.

This Justice Department will never waiver in our defense of the Constitution nor relent our defense of civil rights.

As the members of this Committee understand, the deficiencies of our current laws on terrorism reflect two facts:

First, our laws fail to make defeating terrorism a national priority. Indeed, we have tougher laws against organized crime and drug trafficking than terrorism.

Second, technology has dramatically outpaced our statutes. Law enforcement tools created decades ago were crafted for rotary telephones - not email, the internet, mobile communications and voice mail.

Every day that passes with outdated statutes and the old rules of engagement is a day that terrorists have a competitive advantage. Until Congress makes these changes, we are fighting an unnecessarily uphill battle. Members of the Committee, I regret to inform you that we are today sending our troops into the modern field of battle with antique weapons.

The anti-terrorism proposals that have been submitted by the Administration represent careful, balanced, and long overdue improvements to our capacity to combat terrorism, it is not a wish list: It is a modest set of essentials, focusing on five broad objectives, which I will briefly summarize.

First, law enforcement needs a strengthened and streamlined ability for our intelligence gathering agencies to gather the information necessary to disrupt, weaken and eliminate the infrastructure of terrorist organizations. Critically, we also need the authority for law enforcement to share vital information with our national security agencies in order to prevent future terrorist attacks.

Terrorist organizations have increasingly used technology to facilitate their criminal acts and hide their communications from law enforcement. Intelligence gathering laws that were written for the era of land-line telephone communications are ill-adapted for use in communications over multiple cell phones and computer networks.

Our proposal creates a more efficient, technology-neutral standard for intelligence gathering, ensuring law enforcement's ability to trace the communications of terrorists over cell-phones, computer networks and new technologies that may be developed in the coming years.

These changes would streamline intelligence gathering procedures only. We do not seek changes in the underlying protections in the law for the privacy of law-abiding citizens. The information captured by the proposed technology-neutral standard would be limited to the kind of information you might find in a phone bill. The content of these communications would remain off-limits to monitoring by intelligence authorities, except for under current legal standards.

Our proposal would allow a federal court to issue a single order that would apply to all providers in a communications chain, including those outside the region where the court is located. We need speed in identifying and tracking down terrorists. Time is of the essence. The ability of law enforcement to trace communications into different jurisdictions without obtaining an additional court order can be the difference between life and death for American citizens.

Second, we must make fighting terrorism a national priority in our criminal justice system.

Our current laws make it easier to prosecute members of organized crime than to crack down on terrorists who can kill thousands of Americans in a single day. The same is true of drug traffickers and individuals involved in espionage—our laws treat these criminals and those who aid and abet them more severely than terrorists.

We would make harboring a terrorist a crime. Currently, for instance, harboring persons engaged in espionage is a criminal offense, but harboring terrorists is not.

Third, we seek to enhance the authority of the Immigration and Naturalization Service to detain or remove suspected alien terrorists from within our borders.

The ability of terrorists to move freely across borders and operate within the United States is critical to their capacity to inflict damage on the citizens and facilities in the United States. Under current law, the existing grounds for removal of aliens for terrorism are limited to direct material support of an individual terrorist. We propose to expand these grounds for removal to include material support to terrorist organizations.

Fourth, law enforcement must be able to "follow the money" in order to identify and neutralize terrorist networks.

We need the capacity for more than a freeze. We must be able to seize. Consistent with the President's action yesterday, our proposal gives law enforcement the ability to seize their terrorist assets.

Finally, we seek the ability for the President and the Department of Justice to provide swift emergency relief to the victims of terrorism and their families.

Mr. Chairman, I also want to report to you on the status of the DOJ's activities regarding protecting the civil rights of all Americans. Since September 11, the Civil Rights Division, working closely with the United States Attorneys and the FBI, has opened over 60 investigations into acts involving force or threats of force committed in retaliation for the events of September 11. All of these acts include killings, assaults, the destruction or attempted destruction of businesses, attacks on mosques and worshipers and death threats.

The Department of Justice is firmly committed to pursuing these misguided wrongdoers vigorously. The Civil Rights Division and FBI officials have met with leaders of the Arab American, Muslim and Sikh communities and we have established in the Civil Rights Division an initiative to combat post-terrorism discrimination to ensure that all allegations of violence or discrimination are addressed promptly and effectively.

Let there be no mistakes the Department of Justice will not tolerate acts of violence or discrimination against people in this country based on their race, national origin or religion.

Among the high honors of my life has been the opportunity I have had over the past days and weeks to be in the company of these heroes, these friends of freedom; to meet with and work side-by-side with men and women who have exerted themselves beyond fatigue, who have set aside their own personal agendas and their personal safety to answer our nation's call. The nation has found new leaders—and new role models—in these brave Americans.

Now it falls to us, in the name of freedom and those who cherish it, to ensure our nation's capacity to defend ourselves from terrorists. Today I call upon Congress to act to strengthen our ability to fight this evil wherever it exists, and to ensure that the line between the civil and the savage, so brightly drawn on September 11, is never crossed again.

SENATOR PATRICK LEAHY
HEARING STATEMENT ON HOMELAND DEFENSE

September 25, 2001

We meet today to do the people's business, at a time of great national loss and singleness of purpose. This morning, this Committee and the American people will have the opportunity to hear directly from the Attorney General of the United States regarding the status of the investigations underway regarding the terrorist attacks of September 11. Those hijackings resulting in senseless loss of life and destruction were crimes against humanity.

With the cooperation of the Attorney General over the past two weeks we have been able to arrange briefings from time to time. We have also begun a constructive effort to work together on legislative proposals to improve law enforcement tools in the fight against terrorism. Less than a week ago, on Wednesday, along with Senator Hatch and Senator Specter, I met with the Attorney General and other leaders in the House and Senate to put legislative proposals on the table for us all to consider.

We arranged meetings about these proposals in order to construct a consensus package of legislative proposals last Thursday, which meetings continued on Friday and into the weekend. We have made some progress, and I have confidence that working together we can make many improvements in the law and maintain a proper balance between the desires of law enforcement and the need to maintain fidelity to our constitutional rights and way of life. We cannot allow terrorism to prevail by curtailing our constitutional democracy or constricting our freedoms.

We are making progress with respect to a number of areas of law:

Authorizing use of "roving" or "multi-point" wiretaps in intelligence investigations [under FISA], as we already do for criminal investigations;

Updating the money laundering, RICO and wiretap laws, to make terrorism offenses predicates for exercising the authorities under those laws;

Making certain that we are doing all we can for the families of the police, firefighters and other law enforcement and public safety personnel on whom we depend and who have sacrificed so much;

Ensuring that our definition of "terrorism" fits the crime;

Reviewing the penalty structure for terrorism crimes;

Reviewing immigration authorities and seeing how they can be improved;

Increasing federal agents and capabilities along our Northern Border;

Authorizing expedited hiring of needed translators at the FBI;

Condemning hate crimes and ethnic and religious discrimination in the strongest terms.

There are scores of items in agreement that we hope to consider very soon that can help. I have sought to avoid setting unrealistic or artificial deadlines for our efforts. After the meeting last Wednesday, the Attorney General emerged and endorsed the time frame of "as soon as possible" and we have all been working together and coming together to do that. We have shown the ability to act quickly and together in the last several days, most recently with the transportation and victims assistance package enacted on Friday. Working together Democrats and Republicans from the Senate and the House have acted responsibly, expeditiously and together.

After the killing of 168 in the destruction of the federal building in Oklahoma City in 1995, this Committee held a series of hearings beginning with that chaired by Senator Specter two weeks after the incident and proceeding with additional full Committee and subcommittee hearings over the ensuing weeks. The Senate considered a bill quickly, within two months of the incident, but the House-Senate conference on that measure extended over the next year. In the wake of the violence at Columbine High School and the rash of school violence a few years ago, the House-Senate conference never reconciled the conflicting measures and Congress never completed its work on that legislation. To avoid extended proceedings or the risk that reconciliation never occurs, I intend to reach out to Chairman Sensenbrenner and Representative Conyers to see whether we might not combine our efforts in a coordinated and consolidated way from the outset to resolve to enact the best consensus measure we can design before Congress adjourns this year.

The Attorney General and every Member of this Committee and of the Senate have taken the same oath: to "support and defend the Constitution of the United States." In these difficult days, I caution that we should not lose touch with those constitutional values that make this the strongest, most vibrant democracy the world has even known. That will be a fundamental part of our mandate as we continue to shape the nation's legislative reaction. This challenge to our freedom is going to be answered by the strength of our democracy.

Trial by fire can refine us or it can coarsen us. If we hold to our ideals and values, then it will strengthen us. Americans are united and all the free world, all civilized nations, all caring people join together with us. I trust that we will seek and serve justice and demonstrate to the world not only by our resolve but by our commitment to our constitutional principles that the United States remains strong even in the face of these terrorist atrocities.

Like Pearl Harbor, these horrible events have galvanized our country and united our people with other nations throughout the world. I am confident we will work together to devise new and more effective means to defeat terrorists. This time we need to be smarter. We have to be vigilant to constitutional principles, not vigilantes. We need to focus our response on those responsible for the wrongdoing and to shun stereotyping and guilt by association.

The scope and sophistication of the recent terrorist attacks on American soil call for all the ingenuity, energy, and determination we possess. The actions that we will have to consider may include a combination of military, law enforcement, intelligence, diplomatic and security measures. Developing a comprehensive response may take a little time, but needs to be done right. The President sounded the chord in his address to the Joint Session of Congress and the American people last week. I trust that as we go forward all United States Senators will work together in this effort.

Building on the suggestions of many Members of this Committee and working with Senator Hatch and representatives of the Administration, we have been able over the course of the last week to assemble an impressive list of items on which we have agreement. I thank all Members from both sides of the aisle who have worked with us through the days and evenings and weekends to make significant progress. We are working to be in position without the passage of much time to pass significant legislation containing those consensus items. To the extent other complex proposals are in disagreement, we can continue working on them in the weeks and months ahead. Even if Congress were to adjourn next month, we can hold hearings and continue our work together during the recess.

I have tried to be mindful of the demands on the time of the Attorney General and FBI Director. I have tried not to distract them from their important responsibilities in the investigation and in the immediate aftermath of September 11. We all appreciate the Attorney General making time to be with the Committee this morning.

STATEMENT OF SENATOR ORRIN G. HATCH
BEFORE THE SENATE COMMITTEE ON THE JUDICIARY

September 25, 2001

Mr. Chairman, last Thursday, our President, with the undivided support of this Congress and the American People, announced a war on terrorism.

As the President made clear in his address, we did not seek this war. This war was thrust upon us—thrust upon us by an unprovoked attack upon our civilian population in the very midst of our greatest cities.

Each of us has, in different ways, had our lives touched by the awful events of September 11th. Each of us has, in the days since the attack, been shocked and appalled by the terrible images of destruction that have reached us, by television, by newspaper—and in many cases by our own eyes—from the sites of the attacks at the World Trade Center and the Pentagon. Paradoxically, each of us has also been uplifted by the stories of heroism and self-sacrifice that have emerged from around the country in the wake of these terrible events.

A scant three weeks ago, we could not have contemplated that today, September 25th, 2001, we would be at war. It is true that, for years, some of us in this Congress, and around the country, have warned that there were powerful, well-financed individuals located throughout the world who were dedicated to the destruction of our way of life. But there were few of us who comprehended the true depths of the hatred directed at us by these evil men. Few of us could predict the horrific methods that these men would employ in an effort to destroy us, destroy our liberties and destroy our democratic institutions.

On September 11th, all that changed.

In the last few days, we have all come to acknowledge that we live in a different and more dangerous world than the world we perceived when we woke up on the morning of September 11th. A different world—not only because thousands of our county-men are dead as a result of the September 11th attacks.

A different world—not only because many of our neighbors now hesitate to get on an airplane, or ride in an elevator, or engage in any one of a number of activities that we used to take for granted before the attacks.

But a different world, also, because we must acknowledge that there remains an ongoing and serious threat to our way of life and, in fact, to our health and well-being as a society.

As has been reported in the national media, the investigation into the September 11th attacks has revealed that there are terrorist cells that continue to operate actively among us. It is a chilling thought, but it is true.

The war to which we have collectively committed is a war unlike any war in the history of this country. It is different because a substantial part of this war must be fought on our own soil. This is not a circumstance of our choosing. The enemy has brought the war to us. But we must not flinch from acknowledging the fact that, because this is a different kind of war, it is a war that will require different kinds of tools, and different kinds of tactics.

The United States Attorney General will be the individual principally responsible for leading us in that part of the fight that will be conducted on American soil. The Department of Justice, and its investigatory components including the FBI, the INS, and the Border Patrol, will continue to have the principal responsibility for identifying and eradicating terrorist activity within our national borders.

The Attorney General has communicated to us, and in no uncertain terms, has told us that he does not currently have the adequate weapons to fight this war. He appears before us today—and General Ashcroft I want to personally thank you for appearing here today, and for your tireless efforts in managing this investigation over the last couple of weeks. The Attorney General will again request today that he be given the basic weapons, that many of us have supported over the years, that he requires to wage effectively this vital war against terrorism. I urge my colleagues to heed his words.

Mr. Chairman, I want to thank and commend you for this prompt hearing and for proceeding in a bipartisan manner. You and your staff have worked diligently and in good faith throughout the past week, and indeed over the years on these matters. This is not a partisan issue and it will not be. Some of us may disagree at the end of the day and I will respect each of my colleague's views. That is each of our principled beliefs and it is based on our views on the proper balance between the role of law enforcement and our civil liberties. And I should also note that the bulk of these proposals have been requested by the Department of Justice for years – under both Republican and Democratic Administrations. Unfortunately, they have languished in Congress, for one reason or another.

Back to the proposal before us—I have reviewed the Attorney General's proposal, and I can say without reservation, that the Administration's requested authorities reflects a measured and cautious response to the events of the last couple of weeks. We have been carefully examining this and other proposed reforms. I applaud the Attorney General for moving responsibly in this area, and taking care to ensure that the requested reforms—as promised a week ago—fit well within the bounds of the Constitution and do not compromise the basic liberties that all of us as citizens of this great nation cherish.

As the Attorney General has recognized, we must not change our way of life, because to do so would be to signal our defeat. That is exactly what our enemy seeks to bring about.

We must not repeal or impinge upon our cherished constitutional liberties, because to do would only bring us closer to the joyless totalitarian society espoused by our enemy.

The Attorney General's proposal properly takes these concerns into account and, at the same time, does what people around America have been calling upon Congress to do—that is, to give our law enforcement community the tools they need to keep us safe in our homes and in our places of business.

If we do not prevent terrorists from taking away our liberties, we will have no freedom.

I would like to briefly comment on the general thrust of the more familiar proposals in the Administrations legislation—namely, electronic surveillance.

Electronic surveillance, conducted under the supervision of a federal judge, is one of the most powerful tools at the disposal of our law enforcement community. It is simply unfortunate that the laws currently on the books which govern such surveillance were enacted before the fax machine came into common usage, and well before the advent of cellular telephones, e-mail, and instant messaging. All of these modern modes of communication we now know were principal tools used by the terrorists to coordinate their deadly attacks.

The Department of Justice has asked us for years to update these laws to reflect the new technologies, but there has always been a reason to go slow, to seek more information, to order further studies. We simply cannot afford to wait anymore!

I would like to dispel a myth that the reforms somehow require an abridgment of the Constitutional freedoms enjoyed by law-abiding American citizens. Many in the media have portrayed this issue as a choice between individual liberties on the one hand, and on the other hand, enhanced powers for our law enforcement institutions. This is a false dichotomy. The reforms requested by the Attorney General are primarily directed at allowing law enforcement agents to work smarter and more efficiently—in no case do they, as I have reviewed them, curtail the precious civil liberties protected by our Constitution.

Mr. Chairman, there have been few, if any, times in our nation's great history where an event has brought home to so many of our citizens, so quickly, and in such a graphic fashion, a sense of our own mortality, and a sense of our vulnerability to unexpected attack. I believe we all took some comfort last week, when the President promised us that our law enforcement institutions would have the tools necessary to protect us from the danger that we are just beginning to perceive.

I look forward to working with our colleagues to ensure that happens.

SENATOR JON KYL
STATEMENT FOR THE RECORD:
JUDICIARY COMMITTEE HEARING

September 25, 2001

I commend the Chairman for wasting no time in calling this hearing on the counter-terrorism recommendations presented to Congress by the Attorney General last week. As we are all aware, we are in a race to ensure the safety and security of our citizens, and there is literally no time to lose.

Sadly, the events of September 11 demonstrated, as no other recent occurrence has been able to do, that we must put aside the typical, painfully-slow process that often seems to rule here in times of peace. We cannot continue to yield the advantage of time to those who will continue to murder Americans and our allies until we stop them.

Fortunately, we are not rushing forward with ill-conceived legislation. We are finally putting in place important tools that will enable our nation's law- enforcement personnel to more effectively investigate and prevent further attacks on the people of the United States. Since September of 1998, the Senate Judiciary Committee or its Subcommittee on Technology, Terrorism and Government Information has held thirteen hearings on terrorism. The witnesses who appeared before the Committee in those hearings included Louis Freeh, former Director of the FBI, and representatives of all three of the congressionally-mandated commissions on terrorism that have issued reports over the last two years.

Most of the provisions contained in the Attorney General's proposed legislation have already been examined by the committee of jurisdiction. These provisions mirror the recommendations of one or more of the major terrorism commissions. In fact, some of these provisions have already been voted on and passed by the Senate.

The language sent forward by the Attorney General to establish nation-wide trap and trace authority is included, verbatim, in the Hatch-Feinstein-Kyl Amendment to the recently passed Commerce, Justice, State Appropriations Bill. Much of the remaining language in that amendment was included in a bill we passed in the Senate last fall, entitled the "Counterterrorism Act of 2000." We passed that bill, S. 3205, after significant debate and numerous hearings.

Nearly a year after we passed it the first time, and two full weeks after the unspeakable acts of terror that occurred on September 11, we still have members of this body dragging their feet and saying we are moving too quickly to pass counter-terrorism legislation. Thursday's New York Times included an article that quoted one of my colleagues saying he, "would not be rushed, noting that Congress took almost two months to pass antiterrorism legislation in response to the Oklahoma City bombing in 1995."

I appreciate the fact that some of my colleagues do not like to be rushed, but we are talking about legislation that has been requested by both Democratic and Republican administrations (and debated ad nauseum) since 1995. Some of it, the Senate has already voted to enact. My friends, taking two months to pass antiterrorism legislation in response to the Oklahoma City bombing is not something of which we should be proud. And if we take another two months to act after an even more heinous act of terrorism, we will be giving terrorists who are already around the first turn, a full lap advantage in this race. That is not what the American people are expecting from their leaders at this time.

Let me address briefly the concerns voiced by some of my colleagues. Namely, that we are in danger of "trampling civil liberties" in our rush to pass counter-terrorism legislation. I reiterate that we are not rushing. The legislation we have already passed, and the legislation now offered by the administration, was under consideration long before the events of September 11. We have already held numerous hearings on these issues. Most importantly, there is nothing being requested that broadly impinges on the rights and liberties of U.S. citizens or raises any constitutional questions.

Most of what is being requested would give federal agencies fighting terrorism the same tools we have given those fighting illicit drugs, or even postal fraud. In most instances, the Attorney General is not asking for new authority, he is simply asking to apply existing authority to the crime of terrorism. The powers requested, in almost every case, would be subject to the ruling of a federal judge before action could be taken by law-enforcement personnel. That is entirely consistent with the system of checks and balances provided by the Constitution.

I support the request of the Attorney General, and I urge my colleagues to give this body due credit for the work that has already been done over the last six years, in several committees, to bring credible counter-terrorism legislation to the floor. I urge the Senate conferrees to the upcoming Commerce, Justice, State appropriations conference to support the carefully-crafted language included in the Hatch-Feinstein-Kyl Amendment. We have a responsibility to the people of this nation to act, and to act with all prudent haste, to ensure that those who are charged with protecting us from future terrorist attacks are empowered to do so.

My friends, we cannot afford to lose this race against terror, and we cannot afford to give the enemy in this war a full lap head-start.

DOCUMENT NO. 12

STATEMENTS AT A HEARING BEFORE THE SUBCOMMITTEE ON TERRORISM AND HOMELAND SECURITY OF THE HOUSE PERMANENT SELECT COMMITTEE ON INTELLIGENCE

"DEFINING TERRORISM AND RESPONDING TO THE TERRORIST THREAT"

CHAIRMAN SAXBY CHAMBLISS
THE HONORABLE JANE HARMAN
GOVERNOR JAMES GILMORE
DR. JOHN J. HAMRE, CSIS
DR. BRUCE HOFFMAN, RAND

September 26, 2001

COMMENTARY: *One of the results of the September 11th attacks was the formation of this Subcommittee which had formerly been a Working Group. It has moved ahead aggressively to publicize problems and potential solutions in the terrorism arena. In these contributions one will find thoughtful and useful comments on this topic from men and women who are particularly gifted in addressing the subject of terrorism.*

STATEMENT OF CHAIRMAN SAXBY CHAMBLISS

September 26, 2001

This hearing of the Subcommittee on Terrorism and Homeland Security of the House Intelligence Committee will come to order.

At the start of the 107th Congress, the Speaker of the House established a Working Group on Terrorism and Homeland Security within the Permanent Select Committee on Intelligence. The Speaker understood prophetically that changes needed to be made not only in the way in which government agencies combat terrorism, but also in the way the House conducts its counterterrorism oversight.

Our Group was placed within the confines of the Intelligence Committee to ensure that we had unfettered access to the full range of classified intelligence information to better inform ourselves in preparation for making our decisions and recommendations. Our status within the Intelligence Committee also gave us the formal oversight portfolio for intelligence-related counterterrorism programs that we subsequently funded in the Fiscal Year 2002 Intelligence Authorization Act reported out of Committee on Monday night.

I was honored to be selected as Chairman of the Group, and my distinguished Ranking Democrat, Jane Harman, and I have worked closely together ever since in a wholly bipartisan fashion. We were charged with examining the many complex facets of international and domestic terrorism, including the means by which Federal, State, and Local entities cooperate in the event of a major terrorist incident. In addition, we were asked to recommend major changes in the way in which oversight of counterterrorism programs in the House of Representatives is conducted, with the objective of streamlining the process, better rationalizing resources for counterterrorism across government, eliminating duplication, and qualitatively improving our overall capabilities. Most of our initial work was done in closed session and consisted of regular briefings by a range of terrorism experts from the intelligence and law enforcement communities, meetings with outside experts, and travel overseas to consult with counterterrorism officials from select foreign governments.

The horrific terrorist attacks on the World Trade Center, the Pentagon, and on U.S. civilian airliners on September 11, 2001 significantly enhanced the urgency of our task. Speaker Hastert and Minority Leader Gephardt moved swiftly to convert the Working Group into a full subcommittee of the Intelligence Committee, with subpoena power and authority to hold open and closed hearings. The Speaker and Mr. Gephardt then directed the subcommittee to spearhead all House efforts to respond to the September 11 attacks, and to coordinate the work and witnesses of   the othercommittees of oversight jurisdiction on terrorism to ensure that we are all working in unison towards the same goal. We look forward to working closely with all of the various committees and subcommittees of jurisdiction, and with Governor Ridge in his new role as Director of Homeland Security for the President.

In the immediate aftermath of the September 11 attacks, the subcommittee organized a series of seminars on terrorism and the threat from Usama Bin Ladan and his Al-Qaeda network for all Members of Congress and key staff. We then visited the Pentagon and World Trade Center sites to assess the damage and to meet with those heroic firefighters, police officers, FBI agents, volunteer rescue workers, City officials, military personnel, and those who make up the Joint Terrorism Task Force. I was both humbled and awestruck not only by the magnitude of the tragedy, but by the extraordinary dedication and feats of heroism of those charged with rescuing possible survivors, finding those responsible, and preventing future attacks. These special individuals are working around the clock for all of us and they deserve our full support.

As a former firefighter, I am acutely aware of the bravery, sense of duty, and sense of self-sacrifice demonstrated on September 11 by those first responders who decided to enter the shattered World Trade Center, even when it was unsafe, in a desperate attempt to save lives. Sadly ironic is the fact that one of those brave people who died trying to save others at the World Trade Center was Mr. John O'Neill, one of the FBI's leading counterterrorism experts. John was to testify before our subcommittee at the World Trade Center and City Hall in New York on October 29. Whatever we achieve as a result of our deliberations will be dedicated in my mind to helping to repay the debt we as Americans owe those fallen heroes and their grieving families for showing the world what is best about the American spirit.

Throughout the crisis, we, as part of the Intelligence Committee, expedited passage through the full committee of the Intelligence Authorization for Fiscal Year 2002. As part of the package of measures we approved on Monday night, we substantially increased funding for FBI counterterrorism efforts, investing in both long and short-term activities. In addition, we increased funding for language training across the Intelligence Community, which directly enhances our counterterrorism capabilities. We have found ways in this year's Bill to creatively promote a more focused analytic effort against the terrorist target, particularly as regards threat reporting, and we have significantly enhanced the capabilities and focus of CIA's Counterterrorism Center. Moreover, we have asked the Director of Central Intelligence to take a more aggressive approach to recruiting terrorist agents by rescinding restrictive internal CIA guidelines, and by providingnew guidelines that more appropriately weigh and incentivize risks to achieve successful operations.

Now, I would like to turn to today's hearing on defining terrorism and responding to the terrorist threat. The Intelligence Committee and its subcommittees rarely hold public hearings. Most of our work is done behind closed doors due to the sensitive and classified nature of the discussions. But due to the extraordinary nature of the problem we are now facing, we felt it was important that part of our debate be conducted in the open before the American public. Open debate is particularly important because part of our mandate is to better inform the American public about the dangers of terrorism, the groups involved, and the role state governments and local communities can play in the war against terrorism. Today's hearing will be the first of a series of open hearings that we plan to hold over the next few months, culminating in a field hearing in New York with Mayor Giuliani and several key governors tentatively scheduled for October 29.

We thought we would begin our open work by inviting the leaders of the four expert groups that have been focused on the terrorism problem and have issued reports over the last year recommending structural and other changes in the way we address the terrorist threat, both domestically and overseas. Our first witness is Virginia's Governor Jim Gilmore, who is the Chairman of the Advisory Panel to Assess Domestic Response Capabilities for Terrorism Involving Weapons of Mass Destruction. Thank you for agreeing to share your thoughts with us today, Jim. We look forward to your comments.

Our second witness is former Chairman of the House Committee on Foreign Affairs, Lee Hamilton, who was a key commissioner on the U.S. Commission on National Security in the 21st Century that was co-chaired by Warren Rudman and Gary Hart. It's good to see you again, Lee, and we very much appreciate your hard work on the commission.

Our third witness is former Ambassador-at-Large for Counterterrorism, Paul Bremer, who was the Chairman of the National Commission on Terrorism. Welcome, Paul. You are certainly no stranger to our subcommittee, and your commission produced a fine report.

Our fourth witness is former Deputy Secretary of Defense, John Hamre, who as President of the Center for Strategic and International Studies, led his organization's task force on terrorism, produced a very useful study, and conducted the recent "Dark Winter" bioterrorism exercise. Thank you for coming, John, and for all the work you have done on terrorism.

Our final witness is Dr. Bruce Hoffman, Vice President of the RAND Corporation and a leading expert on terrorism. Dr. Hoffman is the author of Inside Terrorism, and we have asked him to help us to define what terrorism and counterterrorism are, and what they are not. Thank you for agreeing to testify today.

Before turning over the floor to my distinguished Ranking Democrat, Jane Harman, I would like to point out that due to time considerations and the number of witnesses, Jane and I have decided to limit opening remarks by Members to the Chairman and Ranking Member only. That said, all Members are invited to submit written remarks for the record.

We have also invited the Chairmen and Ranking Members of the five key committees with oversight jurisdiction over terrorism and related issues to participate with us today. We welcome your participation, and will continue to reach out to you to participate in our other open hearings and in regular meetings to ensure that we coordinate our activities. This is particularly important given that Executive Branch witnesses will be in short supply, especially as we begin to strike back against the terrorists, and we need to make sure that we can do our job in such a way that leaves the Executive Branch free to do its job. Thank you in advance for your cooperation in this endeavor.

With that, I will now turn to Jane Harman for whatever opening remarks she would care to make. And I would remind the witnesses that their opening testimony should be limited to no more than ten minutes, so that we will have plenty of time for questions.

STATEMENT OF THE HONORABLE JANE HARMAN

September 26, 2001

Last year, during my "sabbatical" from Congress, I was sitting where our witnesses are—joining Ambassador Bremer as a member of the National Commission on Terrorism to warn Congress of the real threat of international terrorism on the U.S. homeland.

On September 10 of this year, Jerry and I had lunch at the Red River Grill on Capitol Hill—a place I later learned was Barbara Olson's favorite—to review pending legislation and lament that Congress was still moving too slowly.

One day later, the world changed.

Today, this Subcommittee begins its critical public exploration to review and modernize our intelligence capacity and our laws and regulations for collecting and acting upon intelligence, and prosecuting terrorist suspects.

The horrors visited upon the World Trade Center and the Pentagon, both of which this Subcommittee has visited, are indelibly inked in our collective mind.

The images sear and hurt and we cannot calculate, nor can we fathom, the enormous loss of life, innocence, and self-assurance as a nation. Our prayers are with those who perished. To their families and friends—you do not grieve or suffer alone. We all lost so much on September 11.

The terrorist assaults instilled fear in our citizenry—but we will respond wisely and with fearless determination. The same determination will be reflected in the work of this Subcommittee.

We will be bold and bipartisan in fulfilling the charge given us by Speaker Hastert and Leader Gephardt.

We will undertake a complete investigation. Identifying the vulnerabilities exploited by the terrorists will be a complicated and lengthy process.

Identifying intelligence failures will require introspection, a critical eye, and the ability to appreciate that talented women and men who work in our intelligence agencies are devastated too.

We must and will be thorough—not only because the world expects us to be fair—but because such thoroughness is necessary to restore our nation's own sense of security and confidence.

We must get it right. We will get it right.

We will respond as a united people—focused on a task like no other. We will protect and defend our liberties against those who despise them.

We will root out terrorism—punishing not only those terrorists responsible but also their sponsors, and also addressing terrorism's underlying causes. We will "drain the swamp" where terrorism breeds and lay the groundwork for freedom, hope and opportunity.

We have an enormous task—and we are humble, yet ready.

Today's witnesses have been describing for years the face of terrorism and the steps necessary to protect ourselves. They have been proposing important legislative and regulatory reform, and will aid the Subcommittee in fashioning a strong and effective legislative response. I welcome them back at this critical time in our history.

TESTIMONY OF GOVERNOR JAMES S. GILMORE, III GOVERNOR OF THE COMMONWEALTH OF VIRGINIA AND CHAIRMAN, ADVISORY PANEL TO ASSESS THE CAPABILITIES FOR DOMESTIC RESPONSE TO TERRORISM INVOLVING WEAPONS OF MASS DESTRUCTION

September 26, 2001

Introduction

Chairman Chambliss, Ranking Member Harman, and distinguished Committee Members, thank you for inviting me to discuss recommendations of the Advisory Panel to Assess Domestic Response Capabilities for Terrorism Involving Weapons of Mass Destruction, a national commission established by Congress in 1999 (P.L. 105-261). The Advisory Panel has assessed our Nation's combined federal, state and local capabilities to detect, deter, prevent—and respond to and recover from—a terrorist attack inside America's borders, and to offer recommendations for preparing the Nation to address terrorist threats.

For almost three years, I have served as Chairman of the bi-partisan Advisory Panel, and it has been my privilege to work with experts in a broad range of fields, including current and former federal, state and local officials and specialists in terrorism, intelligence, the military, law enforcement, emergency management, fire services, medicine and public health.

I am saddened to report that, as of today, one member of our Panel is reported as missing at ground zero in New York. Ray Downey, Chief of Special Operations for the New York City Fire Department, was one of the first emergency responders to arrive at the World Trade Center on September 11. Firemen from California to Virginia to New York know Ray Downey as a man of great courage and skill and commitment. Our prayers go out to Ray and his family.

Attack on American Freedom

Ladies and gentlemen, for many generations to come, September 11, 2001, is a day that will stand out in the history of the United States and, indeed, the entire world, as the day tyranny attacked freedom. The criminals who committed these attacks on the people of the United States, in New York and Virginia, sought a decisive strike, one that was designed to remake the world and the post-Cold War era.

The picture of two commercial airplanes careening into two off ce towers and a wounded Pentagon—recorded for posterity—forever will remind our children and grandchildren of how precious freedom is and that freedom can never be taken for granted.

The goal of these terrorists was to prove that the great democracies are not the way of the future. The goal was, in fact, to establish the dominance of tyranny, force, and fear—and to blot out a love of freedom and individual liberty, which has been growing consistently since the Enlightenment centuries ago. In the 21st century, the United States stands as the ultimate statement and symbol of that human freedom and liberty across the world; and, therefore, the United States was the country attacked.

Ladies and gentlemen, the evil people who committed these crimes, with those goals in mind, have failed. They have failed in their attacks. They have not blotted out the United States as the ultimate formation and symbol of liberty. They have not diminished the resolve of the United States. They have not created fear and terror in the United States.

Yes, we grieve as a civilized people for the people who have died. Freedom-loving people in New York at the World Trade Center—a stunning loss of life in the nation's largest city. At the Pentagon, across the river in Virginia. The people who died on the airplanes, totally innocent victims. As I recall, having read the manifest on the airplanes, there were fathers with their young daughters on those planes. Barbara Olson, who we all knew and loved. She was a personal friend mine. We lost our firemen and emergency rescue responders, who gave their lives attempting to save the lives of their fellow Americans. Ray Downey, another personal friend, may be one who gave the last measure of commitment. Yes, I grieve. The American people grieve. Any civilized people would grieve.

But, in the eternal conflict between freedom and tyranny, the people of the United States shall never retreat. President Bush has spoken most eloquently and cogently to the American people on the state of the current crisis. "Freedom and fear are at war," the President said. Freedom shall prevail.

Work of the Advisory Panel

Sooner or later, those who inflicted these injuries will feel the full weight of justice and the free world's combined efforts to hold them responsible.

We cannot undo their evil actions now. If only we could. Be we can, and must, move forward to do everything we can to prevent a tragedy of this magnitude from striking again in our homeland.

That brings me to the work of the Advisory Panel. The Advisory Panel was established by Section 1405 of the National Defense Authorization Act for Fiscal Year 1999, Public Law 105-261 (H.R. 3616, 105`}' Congress, 2"d Session) (October 17, 1998).

For the last three years I have worked with a distinguished panel of experts, with staff support from the RAND Corporation, to draw up a blueprin for American preparedness. Our commission has been a three-year commission. The Panel has issued two reports to the President and Congress. The first report was issued in December of 1999, and the second report in December of 2000. Both of these reports can be downloaded from RAND's website: *www.rand.org/organization/nsrd/terrpanel.*

Mare recently, on Monday of this week, the Panel issued a third set of recommendations for consideration by Congress and the President.

The work of our Advisory Panel is significantly and qualitatively different from any previous terrorism commission. Our panel includes a unique combination of experts from all three levels of government representing the intelligence community, front-line local emergency responders, military experts, and state and Iocal law enforcement. We also have leaders from the health care community. Reflective of the broad array of experts and a strong "outside-thebeltway" perspective, our panel has addressed the full realm of issues from assessment of the risk to prescriptions for detection, prevention, response and recovery. We have focused a tremendous amount of attention upon state and local first-responders, as well as intelligence issues and national coordination topics. Other commissions have not covered as wride a realm of topics.

Conclusions & Recommendations Issued in First and Second Reports

In our first report (December 1999), we provided a comprehensive assessment of the actual threat of a terrorist attack on U.S. soil. Among our findings were the following:

- First and foremost, the threat of a terrorist attack on some level inside our borders was inevitable, and the United States must prepare.

- In assessing the kind of attack the United States could expect; we concluded that a conventional attacks (such as the one that occurred on September 11) had a high probability of occurrence and should receive more attention than they were receiving at that time. We concluded that an attack using weapons of mass destruction, while threatening a high impact, had a lower probability of occurrence in the near term, but could not be ignored. While we should prepare, first and foremost, for the most likely conventional terrorist attack scenario (such as the conventional attack we recently witnessed), we must also heed the threat of a more exotic attack by weapons of mass destruction. Regardless of the kind of attack, we called for a national strategy to address the full spectrum of possible attacks.

- We also said that the terrorist threat would be more lethal than ever before because the trend among terrorists is toward greater and greater lethality.

- We concluded that the real weapon is not the device or the material involved, but the terrorist delivery capacity and capability. Unfortunately, I am afraid that this point has been borne out by the events of September 11.

- Our review revealed that counter-terrorism efforts to date had been largely reactionary, to a threat not clearly understood. We concluded that a clear comprehensive national vision and strategy for large or small events must be developed and put into place, but that such a vision and strategy did not presently exist as of the time of that report. We recognized that a coordinated national strategy could be built upon the well-tested system that already exists for responding to natural and man-made disasters, such as hurricanes, earthquakes, toxic chemical spills and nuclear accidents. That is, firefighters, emergency medical providers, public health offices and private hospitals, police and the National Guard.

- And we stressed the paramount importance of preserving our citizens' constitutional rights and civil Liberties. We said, "[T]he Panel urges officials at all levels of government to ensure that the civil liberties of our citizens are protected." We can meet this terrorist threat without trampling the Constitution. In fact, the goal of the enemy would be to have us trample our constitutional rights. We don't have to do that and we should never ask the people of the United States to give up their freedoms because of an attack like this.

Our second report, issued a year Later (December 2000), contained about 50 recommendations for improving our nation's preparedness against the threat of terrorism identified in our first report. Most importantly, the second report underscored the need for something more than a *federal* strategy. The federal government's role represents only one component of a *national* strategy. The distinction here is an important one. The federal government cannot address this threat alone. We need new public and private partnerships. Every state and local community has capabilities, resources, assets, experience and training that must be brought to bear in addressing this threat.

Among our most important recommendations in our second repo~2 are the following recommendations:

- First, we concluded that the current federal bureaucratic structure, with numerous agencies and offices bearing responsibilities touching upon the domestic and international terrorist threat, lacks the requisite coordination, accountability and authority to address the terrorist threat. Therefore, we recommended creation of a National Office for Combating Terrorism to serve as a senior level coordinating entity in the Executive Office of the President. We further recommended that the office would be vested with responsibility for developing both *domestic* and *international* policy as well as coordinating the Nation's vast counter-terrorism programs and budgets. The Director of this office should be a high ranking "Cabinet-Level" appointee of the President. Foremost, the office should assume responsibility for developing a comprehensive national strategy approved by the President.

I am heartened that President Bush has acted on this recommendation and has appointed Governor Ridge to head this office. It is now incumbent upon the Congress to give Governor Ridge its utmost support. But there is more the Congress can do.

- We proposed that Congress create a "Special Committee for Combating Terrorism." This could be a joint committee of senators and congressmen to create a unified legislative view or it could encompass two distinct committees, one for the House and one for the Senate. Of course, we do not presume to instruct the Congress on how it should conduct its affairs, but we offer that recommendation in the best interests of the people of the United States. The Special Committee should have a direct link to the Executive Branch`s National Office for Combating Terrorism, and it should be the first referral for legislation preparing our nation for terrorist attacks.

On this point, I would like to commend Speaker Hasten for taking decisive action in establishing this special Subcommittee of the Intelligence Committee. This Subcommittee can provide precisely the kind of streamlined parliamentary process that is needed to address the nature of the current crisis and the unique threat posed by terrorism.

- Next, we addressed the issue of intelligence-sharing and focused on the fact that it is very typical in the intelligence community to hold information so close it can often not be communicated to those responsible parties who need to know. This is particularly true of sharing intelligence information with state and local authorities. Thus, we need to develop a comprehensive national intelligence system based on sound need-to-know principles.

- We found our federal intelligence apparatus was lacking critical tools it needs to detect terrorist plots, so we recommended improvements to human intelligence capabilities such as, for example, rescinding the CIA guidelines on paying foreign informants engaged in terrorist or criminal activity.

- We recognized the importance of state and local agencies in responding to and recovering from terrorist attacks and insisted they be included in the plotting of a national strategy. Thus, the panel recommended a number of ways to strengthen the nation's first responders: firemen, law enforcement, emergency medical services and emergency management.

- We also called for improvement of health and medical response capabilities and I think everybody is very proud of the hospitals and medical services that have been called into action over the past weeks. Our report, however, recognized that our public and private hospitals are prepared for the routine, but in the case of a high concentration of traumas resulting from a weapon of mass destruction—especially biological in nature—or a catastrophic conventional attack such as we have seen, our medical system might become overloaded. Therefore, we intend to address this issue further in our final report.

- And, finally, we have focused a great deal of attention on the use of the Armed Forces, their appropriate role and how they should be used. We expressly recommended that the U.S. military *not* serve as the lead federal agency in responding to a domestic terrorist action. Although it is generally accepted that events could occur where the military needs to be engaged, particularly the National Guard, nonetheless, we have expressed an abiding caution about deploying a military response to a domestic situation and only then in support of a civilian federal agency like FEMA.

More recently, on Monday, September 24, the Advisory Panel issued our third set of recommendations for your consideration. Among the topics we addressed in our third round of recommendations are the critical issues of U.S. border security, cyber terrorism, the proper role of the military in domestic response scenarios, and necessary medical strategies to plan for a biological or chemical weapons.

Our Panel accelerated issuance of these recommendations in order to afford the Congress the benefit of our three-year study as you consider and respond to the current crisis, and I would like to highlight the key recommendations issued earlier this week.

These recommendations address four major topical areas:

- First, how our Nation can improve *health and medical capabilities* to respond to terrorist attacks.

- Second, how the United States can improve its *immigration and border controls* to prevent terrorists or their weapons from entering the United States.

- Third, how we should clarify the *role of the U.S. military* in responding to domestic terrorist attacks.

- Fourth, measures the public and private sectors should take to guard against *cyber-terrorism*.

Improve Health & Medical Capabilities

Terrorists attack innocent civilians. In the unfortunate event that terrorists evade our detection and prevention mechanisms, the United States' health system must be prepared to care for thousands of injured civilians. The health threats are complex and could arise from either or bath conventional weapons or more exotic weapons of mass destruction, including biological or chemical agents. Therefore, the Advisory Panel recommends the following actions:

- Implement the American Medical Association (AMA) "Report and Recommendations on Medical Preparedness for Terrorism and Other Disasters."

- Establish a national advisory board on health and medicine to work with Governor Ridge's new national office.

- Fully implement the "Biological and Chemical Terrorism: Strategic Plan for Preparedness and Response" issued by the Centers for Disease Control and Prevention in order to:

    a. Enhance epidemiologic capacity to detect and respond

    b. Establish surveillance for critical biologic and chemical agents

    c. Improve training of public health professionals

    d. Foster communication and public education programs e. Promote research efforts

- Fully implement the "Laboratory Response Network for Bioterrorism" of the Centers for Disease Control and Prevention, including the following measures:

    a. Develop critical laboratory capacity in public health entities

    b. Faster appropriate linkage with clinical laboratories

    c. Integrate these capacities into overall emergency preparedness d.Implement rapid detection, analysis, and communication of the findings to appropriate health and medical entities nationwide

- Fully implement CDC's Health Alert Network, designed to improve communications within the public health community and with other emergency response entities, especially law enforcement.

- U.S. Department of Health and Human Services (HHS), in coordination with Governor Ridge's new national office, should develop additional all-hazards model response standards and other planning templates, as well as training and exercise programs, for use at Federal, State, and local levels.

- HHS should re-establish a pre-hospital Emergency Medical Services program office.

- Congress should increase Federal resources available for exercises that are informed by and targeted at State and local health and medical entities, both public and private.

- Congress should establish a government-owned, contractor-operated national facility for the research, development, and production of vaccines for specified infections diseases—especially contagious diseases.

- Governor Ridge's new national office, in coordination with HHS and the Department of Veteran's Affairs, should review and recommend appropriate changes to plans for the manufacture and stockpiles of:

    a. Vaccines

    b. Antidotes

    c. Other prophylaxes

    d. Other critical supplies

    e. Triage

    f. Distribution process

- Governor Ridge's new national office, with the advice of national advisory panels, and in coordination with the responsible Federal agencies, should develop a comprehensive plan for the full spectrum of medical and health research, development, testing, and evaluation as it relates to terrorism, including detection, diagnosis, prophylaxis, and therapeutics.

- Governor Ridge's new national office, in conjunction HHS, other appropriate Federal agencies, and a national advisory board formed to advise that office on these issues, should conduct a thorough review of the authorities, structures, and capabilities available under the Metropolitan Medical Response System and the National Disaster Medical System.

- Governor Ridge's new national office should develop an information and education program on the legal and procedural problems involved in a health and medical response to terrorism. Additionally, in coordination with the Department of Justice, the American Bar Association and the Federalist Society, should consider the efficacy of model laws or other programs to enhance future responses to such events.

- Governor Ridge's new national office should develop, as part of the implementation of plans under the national strategy, a framework for public education, including the media, on terrorism causes and effects prior to terrorist events and coordination of initial and continuing public pronouncements during and following an attack. Special attention should be given to educating the public on issues related to health-related quarantines.

U.S. Immigration & Border Control

As many of you know, several of the September 11 hijackers may have entered the United States on forged visas or by car from Canada. A truck carrying explosive materials bound for Seattle's New Year's Eve 2000 celebration was stopped at the Canadian border.

If America is to be secure, we must have a coordinated policy of immigration enforcement and border security, and it must address the totality of all avenues of entry into the United States—land, air, and sea. This effort will require unprecedented coordination between the U.S. Border Patrol, the Immigration & Naturalization Service, U.S. Customs Service, the Coast Guard, and the Federal Aviation Administration—as well as state and local law enforcement.

In its previous two reports, this panel acknowledged that the laws and traditions of the United States creating and maintaining a very open society make us vulnerable to terrorist attacks. Some statistics emphasize this stark reality:

- Over 100,000 miles of national coastline
- Almost 2000 miles of land border with Mexico, another 4000 miles with Canada, most of it essentially open to transit
- Almost 500 million people cross our borders annually
- Over 127 million automobile crossings annually
- Over 11.5 million truck crossings annually
- Over 2. I million rail cars annually
- Almost 1 million commercial and private aircraft enter annually
- Over 200,000 ships annually dock in maritime
- Over 5.8 million containers enter annually from maritime sources

The movement of goods, people, and vehicles through our border facilities is characterized by vast transportation, logistics, and services systems that are extremely complex, essentially decentralized, and almost exclusively owned by the private sector. Despite valiant efforts by personnel of the U.S. Customs Service, the U.S. Coast Guard, the U.S. Immigration and Naturalization Service (including the U.S. Border Patrol), the Federal Aviation Administration, and other Federal entities, as well as State and local enforcement authorities, the challenge is seemingly insurmountable. Those efforts are further hampezed by a lack of full interagency connectivity and information sharing.

With adequate coordination of effort and resources—and primarily through information sharing—these agencies could significantly improve a seamless enforcement and detection system without unduly hindering the flow of goods and people. However, still, simply increasing enforcement of current laws and regulations through existing mechanisms may not provide the ultimate solution. That activity could result in further delays at very busy ports of entry. The likely "domino" effect of further delays will generate opposition from many U.S. commercial interests whose businesses depend on carefully timed delivery of goods, political pressure from states and localities whose job markets would likely be affected, potential retaliation from foreign countries who export goods to the United States, and increased complaints from the millions of business and tourist passengers transiting our border—many of whom are already unhappy about the queues at airports of entry.

Given the nature and complexity of the problem, the panel recognizes that we as a nation will not likely find the "100% solution" for our borders. We should, nevertheless, search for ways to make it harder to exploit our borders for the purpose of doing harm—physical or economic—to our citizens. The confluence of these issues calls for new, innovative approaches that will strike an appropriate *and* more effective balance between valid enforcement activities, the interests of commerce, and civil liberties.

Among the Advisory Panel's recommendations to accomplish these objectives are the following proposals:

- First, we must improve intelligence collection and dissemination between and among agencies responsible for some aspect of border protection. This panel is strongly committed to the proposition that relevant, timely intelligence is crucial in the campaign to combat terrorism. That is especially so in the arena of enhancing the security of our borders. New and better ways must be developed to track terrorist groups and their activities through transportation and logistics systems. All agencies with border responsibilities must be included as full partners in the intelligence collection, analysis, and dissemination process, as related to border security. This process is a "two-way street;" all entities involved must be willing to share information, horizontally and vertically. This will represent a departure from the current "culture" of many agencies to cloister information. The structure and procedures that the panel recommended in its second report, for the establishment of intelligence oversight through an advisory board under the National Office for Combating terrorism could facilitate a new paradigm in this area.

The fact is that no single framework exists to look at terrorist and security threats across all the various agency functions. And what is critically needed is connectivity across agencies to create a virtual national data repository of data that will serve as the focal point for the fusion and distribution of information on all border security matters.

Although some interagency agreements for border security do exist, notably the Memorandum of Agreement on Maritime Domain Awareness among the Department of Defense, the U.S. Coast Guard, the U.S. Immigration and Naturalization Service; and the Department of State, all affected agencies are not involved in a fully coordinated and integrated process. Therefore, we recommend that the Maritime Domain Awareness model be expanded to create an interactive and fully-integrated database system for "Border Security Awareness." It should include participation from all relevant U.S. government agencies, and State and local partners. Congress should mandate participation of all related

Federal agencies in this activity, and provide sufficient resources to fund its implementation. The development and implementation of such a system, including appropriate resources for systems integration to be provided by the Congress, can be accomplished by the National Office for Combating Terrorism.

- Second, a necessary corollary to inter-agency intelligence sharing is the need to expand intelligence sharing with state and Local agencies responsible for critical aspects of law enforcement and customs checks. This concept may break with "inside-the-beltway" culture, but state and local agencies must be trusted with important intelligence and information if our border security effort is to be successful. The point is plain and simple: The full, timely dissemination and sharing of information among effected Federal, State, and local agencies will be critical in preventing the movement of foreign terrorists and their weapons across our borders.

- Third, we must foster intensive coordination between and among the relevant agencies. Information and intelligence sharing is just a start. The next level of interagency cooperation will mean coordinated *operations* between federal and state agencies with border responsibilities. Again, this coordination could be led by the National Office for Combating Terrorism, which would bring to bear the power and authority of the White House to establish a special inter-agency advisory panel on border security, ensure cooperation and eliminate turf struggles. That entity could be an expansion of the Border Interdiction Committee, formed in the late 1980s to address the problem of drug trafficking across U.S. borders. This advisory board can assist the director of the NOCT in developing program and resource priorities as part of the national strategy for combating terrorism and the related budget processes.

- Fourth, we should enhance sensor and other detection and warning systems of the various agencies—but in a coordinated fashion to ensure each agency's system compliments the others' systems. Individual agencies have one or more activities underway that are intended to enhance enforcement and interdiction capabilities, through the use of static or mobile sensors and other detection devices. Valuable research and development is also underway in multiple agencaes to extend such capabilities, especially in the area of non-intrusive inspection systems. There is, nevertheless, no comprehensive and fully-vetted plan among related agencies for critical aspects of such activities. Therefore, the National Office for Combating Terrorism should coordinate a plan for research and development among the agencies, and for fielding and integration of sensor and other detection and warning systems, as well as elevation of priority for the application of resources for the execution of such a plan.

- Finally, no border security plan will be successful unless we improve our cooperation with Mexico and Canada. It will be imperative for the U.S. to implement more comprehensive agreements on combating terrorism with the governments of Mexico and Canada. Some agreements and protocols with both countries already exist, but more needs to be done. We know from open-source material and from other sources that Canada has been a country of choice for certain elements who have engaged or who may seek to engage in terrorist activities against the United States. Unfortunately, the laws of Canada do not explicitly make terrorist activities a crime *per se*. As a result, Canada has been unable to take action against certain individuals who may, for example, be conspiring to perpetrate a terrorist attack against the United States. Country-to-country negotiations should be designed to strengthen laws that will enhance our collective ability to deter, prevent, and respond to terrorist activities, to exchange information on terrorist activities, and to assist in the apprehension of known terrorists before they can strike.

Clarify Military Roles and Missions on Use of the Military

In our second report, we emphatically concluded that the U.S. military should **not** serve as the lead federal agency in responding to a domestic terrorist action. The reason for this conclusion was the paramount importance the Panel places upon the protection of civil liberties and Constitutional rights of American citizens. Even during trying times, civilian agencies, be they law enforcement or FEMA, should take the lead role in addressing a crisis. While each member of the Advisory Panel could imagine a domestic terrorism scenario which would require use of the U.S. military, even then the Panel concluded the military's involvement should be in support of a civilian federal agency such as the FBI or FEMA. Building upon that conclusion, we have offered several recommendations to clarify more precisely the role the U.S. military should assume in times of terrorist crises.

- The National Command Authority should implement a single, unified command and control structure for all functions for providing military support or assistance to civil authorities.

- The Secretary of Defense should direct the development of more detailed plans for the use of the military domestically across the spectrum of potential activities, and coordinate with State and other Federal agencies in the creation of more State-or regional-specific plans.

- The Secretary of Defense should direct the Military Departments to institute specif c training in military units most likely to be involved in military support to civil authorities, and to expand military involvement in related exercises with Federal, State, and local agencies.

- The Secretary of Defense should direct specific new mission areas for the use of the National Guard for providing support to civil authorities for combating domestic terrorism.

- The Secretary of Defense should clarify and provide specific guidance on Active Duty and Title 10 Reserve Component roles and missions, especially inside the United States.

- The President should always designate a Federal civilian agency other than the Department of Defense (DoD) as the Lead Federal Agency in response to a terrorist threat within the United States.

- Governor Ridge's new national office should coordinate publication of a compendium, in layman's terms, of the statutory authorities for use of the military domestically to combat terrorism, with detailed explanations about the procedures for implementing those authorities.

- The Department of Defense should expand and elevate full time military liaisons with the ten FEMA regional offices. Military liaisons must be trained on all aspects of legislative and operational responsibilities and must have clearly defined responsibilities for coordination of plans, training, and preparedness exercises.

Improve America's Security Against Cyber Attacks

The Advisory Panel noted in both its first report and second report the evolving threat posed by the potential use of computer technologies. We concluded that a cyber-attack could potentially impact our national economy, infrastructures, businesses and our citizens in very harmful ways. Whether perpetrated as the single method for destruction or disruption, or in conjunction with some other weapon, the effects could be substantial and devastating.

The Panel recognized the topic of cyber-terrorism is exceptionally complex. It spans issues of national security, law enforcement, civil rights, and it implicates the vast technological operations of the entire private sector. Over 80 percent of our Nation's information systems are owned and operated by the private sector. Furthermore, rapid technological advancements complicate the development of policy solutions. Compounding the technical complexities is the important value we placed upon protection of civil rights and Liberties. Qur Panel quickly recognized the lack of precedents in this area (with the possible exception of Y2K) or easy solutions, as well as the need for new and carefully crafted government-private partnerships.

With these caveats in mind, we have recommended the following steps be taken:

- Any entity formed to advise the President on cyber security issues must include broad representation from those constituencies that have direct interests in the issue, especially State and local government representatives, and those sectors of private industry who are dependent upon information assurance.

- The Congress should create an independent advisory body, which should be tasked with evaluating programs designed to promote cyber security, with developing recommended strategies for addressing the issues, and with the requirement to report its findings to the President and the Congress.

- The Congress should establish a government-funded, not-for-profit entity that can represent the interests of all affected stakeholders, including public and private interests, national security agencies, law enforcement agencies, other government functions, and business and industry interests to provide cyber detection, alert, and warning functions.

- The Congress and President should convene an urgent Congressional-Executive Branch "summit" to address necessary changes to a wide range of federal statutes, in order to provide necessary protection and incentives for enhancing cyber assurance.

- Congress should establish a special federal "Cyber Court" patterned after the court established in the Foreign Intelligence Surveillance Act (FISA), with jurisdiction dedicated to criminal cyber conduct to recognize and act more quickly and appropriately in approving or disapproving special authority for investigative activities. Furthermore, the "Cyber Court" should facilitate an electronic, real-time, on-line, secure method for U.S. Attorneys anywhere in the country to contact a cyber judge on short notice. Use of the court should be subject to a prior expedited review (using a similar process to FISA applications) by the Department of Justice.

- Congress should establish a government-funded consortium of not-for-profit entities with expertise in the field to develop and implement a comprehensive plan for research, development, test, and evaluation to enhance cyber security.

- All federal, state and local government agencies, as well as private sector businesses and entities, should re-establish operational capabilities that were eliminated after Y2K, and rename these operations "cyber security."

Conclusion

Mr. Chairman, Ranking Member Merman, we must start preparing our Nation to defend freedom within our borders today. The President and the Congress face solemn decisions about how we proceed and there is little time for deliberation.

As our great democratic institutions move forward toward a solution, allow me to offer a couple of observations. This is not a partisan political issue. It transcends partisanship. It is about the preservation of freedom and the American way of life.

After a generation of moral relativity an equivocation, let there be no debate or doubt that the hijacking of four commercial airplanes and the tragedies that followed on September 11 clearly demonstrated that evil exists in our world.

Regardless of how we as a democracy decide to approach this evil force, we must always remember that terrorism is tyranny. Its aim is to strip away our rights and liberties and replace them with fear. As Americans, it is our duty and our destiny to strike down tyranny wherever it may arise. We did so in World War I, again in World War II, in Korea, and Later in Kuwait. The battlefields and warriors change, but the enemy is always the same.

In the face of this evil, we will not be afraid, but strong. We will not divide, but unite. We will not doubt, but affirm our faith in freedom, each other, and the grace of God. And freedom shall prevail.

DR. JOHN J. HAMRE
PRESIDENT AND CEO
CENTER FOR STRATEGIC AND INTERNATIONAL STUDIES
WASHINGTON, D.C.

September 26, 2001

Introduction to the Problem

The United States faces a series of serious threats to its homeland. These emerging challenges come from missile proliferation in rogue states; the potential use by terrorists of chemical, biological, radiological, and nuclear (CBRN) devices; and various threats to the nation's critical information and economic infrastructure. These threats, although low in probability, have potentially high consequences. Some of them, particularly those involving nuclear or biological weapons, have the potential to cause mass destruction.

Although they are not new, these threats are to a large degree novel. It will take unprecedented efforts by the military and civilian federal, state, and local officials, as well as elements of the private sector, to meet them. Adding to the complexity, neither the federal government nor the U.S. military will usually be the lead actor in meeting these threats. Today, the "first to fight" may well be a police officer, a firefighter, or an information security technician. New actors must become part of the national security equation.

To date, U.S. homeland defense efforts have been like the proverbial glass that is both half full and half empty. Over the past five years, U.S. efforts to address these new challenges have been prodigious yet inadequate. We have fallen well short of putting into place the resources and organizational structure necessary to meet the new threats. The most pressing needs today are for a revised plan for national missile defense (NMD) as well as major organizational changes that will allow comprehensive planning and better training to meet the terrorist and cyber threats. The United States cannot wait for these threats to emerge full grown before taking effective steps to deal with them. The report that follows assesses the nation's progress in meeting these threats to the U.S. homeland and makes recommendations to solve this complex set of problems.

Several recent major strategic assessments—including the Quadrennial Defense Review, the report of the National Defense Panel, and the reports of the U.S. Commission on National Security in the 21st Century—contain strong warnings about new threats to the American homeland. The U.S. Commission issued this stark prediction:

> America will become increasingly vulnerable to hostile attack on our homeland, and our military superiority will not protect us. . . . States, terrorists, and other disaffected groups will acquire weapons of mass

destruction, and some will use them. Americans will likely die on American soil, possibly in large numbers.[1]

Other senior officials have arrived at the same conclusion. In fact, a highly placed official on the National Security Council (NSC) staff reported that President Bill Clinton believes that "within the next ten years, there was a 100 percent chance of a chemical or biological attack in our country."[2]

To many, homeland defense appears to be a new requirement. But the perception of homeland defense as a new mission strips it of an important part of its context. Homeland defense—the defense of the United States' territory, critical infrastructure, and population from direct attack by terrorists or foreign enemies operating on our soil—was, is, and will always be the most essential function of our government.

What is changing, however, is not only the level and type of threat, but also how the United States accomplishes homeland defense. Today, the shape of homeland defense has been influenced by three factors:

- the uniquely dominant power position of the United States,

- the technological development of certain states hostile to the United States, and

- the onset of the information age, which has empowered individuals and non-state actors.

First, after the end of the Cold War, the United States became the world's sole superpower. Its technological prowess—especially in precision attack and information systems—is unmatched and unprecedented. For most competitors, the overriding lesson of recent operations is that successful challenges to the United States must be indirect or asymmetrical. For rogue states and some non-state actors, attacking the United States at home may even be easier than trying to attack a small element of U.S. forces at sea or in the field.

The second factor is the technological development of many nations that pose a potential threat to the United States. Many rogue states—a shorthand expression for about a half dozen states hostile to U.S. interests, including Iran, Iraq, and North Korea—are entering the latter stages of the industrial age and gaining the ability to develop chemical, biological, nuclear, and missile technology. At the same time, for both strategic and economic reasons, Russia, China, and North Korea have compounded the

---

1   United States Commission on National Security/21st Century, *New World Coming: American Security in the 21st Century* (Arlington, Va.: The Commission, 1999), p. 141.

2   Richard Clarke in an interview with Lesley Stahl on *60 Minutes*, CBS Television, October 22, 2000.

proliferation problem. Today, for most analysts, the focal point for national missile defense is protection from accidental attacks from great powers or small attacks from Iran, Iraq, or North Korea.

Information technology and globalization constitute a third factor. The onset of the information age—marked by the development of the personal computer and the expansion of the Internet—has decreased the power of states and other mass hierarchical organizations and increased the capabilities of markets, individuals, small groups, and networks. Individuals and nongovernmental organizations (NGOs)—the logical, issue-oriented extension of empowered individuals—have become important subsidiary actors in international relations. Economic and even social relations have become subject to globalization, a force outside the control of even the most powerful states.[3]

These factors present a set of threats that are steadily becoming more serious. In an era of global communications and expanding trade and travel, states or small groups of terrorists—of foreign or domestic vintage—can directly attack the United States' homeland. The knowledge that empowers them to do this is often free to all on the Internet. The resulting attacks can be by conventional means (gun, knife, or bomb), or they can exploit the growing body of knowledge about CBRN (chemical, biological, radiological, or nuclear) weapons or information and the vulnerability of telecommunication systems.[4] As noted above, a small number of states also represent a potential ballistic or cruise missile threat to the U.S. homeland.

The potential use of biological agents—anthrax, plague, mycotoxins, for example—is particularly troubling. Such agents may well become a more attractive option for a hostile state or terrorist bent on mass destruction. Ounce for ounce, the lethality of these agents is many times that of chemical agents or nuclear weapons. Pounds or possibly ounces of biological agent can do a job that would require tons of a chemical agent.

- In one study, 30 kilograms of anthrax spores applied in a densely populated area at maximum effectiveness created 500 times the number of deaths that could have been produced by 300 kilograms of deadly sarin nerve gas.

---

3   Thomas L. Friedman, *The Lexus and the Olive Tree* (New York: Anchor Books, 2000), pp. 29–72 ; and Thomas L. Friedman, "Parsing the Protests," *New York Times*, April 14, 2000, p. A31.

4   This report will use CBRN for accuracy. It clearly denotes the classes of weapons under discussion. CBRN weapons do not always achieve mass destruction. The less precise term "weapons of mass destruction" (WMD) couples an ambiguous set of weapons with the effects that these weapons may or may not achieve. Moreover, conventional ordnance may well achieve mass destruction under certain circumstances.

- A 12.5 kiloton (thousand tons of TNT equivalent) nuclear device—close to the potency of the bomb dropped on Hiroshima—employed in the same area would likely have produced 20 percent fewer deaths than well-dispersed anthrax under relatively ideal climactic conditions.[5]

- Another study suggested that the lethality of 250 pounds of anthrax, spread efficiently over the Washington, D.C., metropolitan area, could cause up to 3 million deaths, significantly more than would likely result from a 1 megaton (a million tons of TNT equivalent) hydrogen bomb.[6]

While the effects of biological agents are subject to varying estimates, there is little doubt that biological weapons in the hands of state or non-state actors have the potential to create much greater destruction than any society can tolerate.

Many recent studies have pointed out the difficulties that terrorists would incur if they wanted to use biological agents. Several factors, however, make the use of biological agents by terrorists a substantial danger in the future. First, in the near term, non-state actors may be helped by rogue states, removing technological obstacles to the efficient use of any kind of CBRN weapons. Second, proliferation in the developing world or the insecurity of the Russian or Iraqi CBRN arsenal may provide a ready source of agent to terrorists. Third, future advances in genetics may make it easier to create more potent and more easily useable agents. Fourth, technological barriers to the effective dispersal of biological agents are disappearing, and knowledge of these advances will inevitably spread.[7] Finally, our medical and public health systems do not have the capacity to handle a large-scale, CBRN terrorist attack. In the future, terrorists using biological weapons are likely to have a much greater capacity for mass destruction.

Enemies of the United States, opponents of its armed forces, or those in opposition to U.S.-based multinational corporations can also choose cyber crime, cyber vandalism or cyber attacks against U.S. public or private interests, turning our reliance on information systems into a strategic vulnerability.[8] Cyber vulnerability is magnified by the fact that 95 percent of all U.S. military traffic moves over civilian telecommunications and computer

---

5   Anthony Cordesman, *The Risks and Effects of Indirect, Covert, Terrorist, and Extremist Attacks with Weapons of Mass Destruction: Challenges for Defense and Response*, September 1, 2000, webu6102.ntx.net/homeland/reports/EffectsTerrWMD.pdf (accessed November 2000).

6   Tara O'Toole, "Biological Weapons: National Security Threat and Public Health Emergency," a presentation at CSIS, August 22, 2000.

7   Randall J. Larson and Ruth A. David, "Homeland Defense: Assumptions First, Strategy Second," *Strategic Review* (Fall 2000): 6–8.

8   Frank Cilluffo and Bruce Berkowitz, eds., *Cybercrime, Cyberterrorism, and Cyberwarfare: Averting an Electronic Waterloo* (Washington, D.C.: CSIS, 1998), pp. 1-72.

systems. A terrorist can combat U.S. military forces, disrupt a military operation, or hurt the U.S. economy by hindering our vulnerable civilian telecommunications systems.

Some terrorists are already practicing: In 1999, there were more than 22,000 attacks against unclassified military computer systems, a threefold increase over the number reported in the previous year. A few experts believe that number to have reached a few hundred thousand per year.[9] Some estimates suggest that only 10 percent of penetrations are detected.

The cyber threat in particular will present new organizational issues. As Richard Clarke, National Coordinator for Security, Counterterrorism, and Infrastructure Protection, told a CSIS audience:

There is a unique challenge here. For the first time in our history, the Armed Forces cannot defend us from the foreign threat. They cannot surround the power grid. . . . Therefore, we are asking the private sector to defend not only itself, but the country as well.[10]

In all, a challenging scenario might be a large-scale CBRN terrorist attack or series of attacks, backed up by an intensive cyber attack on the U.S. government and civil telecommunications infrastructure. Such an attack might be timed to coincide with a deployment of military forces to an overseas contingency. To meet such a multidimensional threat, federal, state, and local governments as well as the private sector must pay more attention to unconventional and transnational threats to the U.S. homeland. In the process, this nation will have to change the way it does much of the business of national defense.

The set of instruments that the United States must use to combat threats to our security will have to become much broader. In the past, the first line of defense might be a ship at sea, a fighter aircraft on patrol, or an infantryman walking point. Today, the "first to fight" may well be a police officer, a volunteer firefighter, a hazardous material technician, a nurse, or even an information security technician. Compounding the problem, there may be a significant period of time between the attack and its discovery. Cyber and CBRN terrorists may not leave a clear "return address," making deterrence, attribution, and even retaliation after attacks on the U.S. homeland increasingly difficult. A delay in identifying such attacks could be very costly.

---

9   Jim Wolf, "Hacking of Pentagon Computers Persists; Pace Undiminished This Year, Complicating Security Efforts," Washington Post, August 23, 2000, p. A23; and comments by Richard Clarke at a lecture for MIT Alumni Association, October 10, 2000.

10   Richard Clarke, "Homeland Defense: Proceedings of the April 5 Senior Advisory Group Meeting and Participants List," 2000, webu6102.ntx.net/homeland/reports/sag040500.html (accessed November 2000).

The United States must view homeland defense as a partnership among federal, state, local, and private-sector organizations. It must reorganize vertically—federal, state, and local—as well as horizontally within the executive branch. While these threats are legitimate national security problems, they are not—except for national missile defense—primarily the domain of the Pentagon or even the federal government. State and local officials will primarily be in charge. Federal officials will usually find themselves in support of state and local officials. New Jersey governor Christine Todd Whitman, reminded a Capitol Hill audience that state governors were the commander in chief in their states:

> As is true so often . . . it comes back to the governors to manage the . . . fallout, literally or figuratively, of any kind of terrorist attack. . . . We are the ones along with our mayors and our local government officials, who actually must deal with people. It is fine to deal with the theory, and we want to be part of that process, but ultimately, we are the ones who are responsible for dealing with the people.[11]

Legal authority to act in nontraditional areas of homeland defense presents another dilemma. In routine operations, the president and the secretary of defense (the "National Command Authority") have sufficient legal authority to use the armed forces at home. For example, *posse comitatus*, the law that prohibits most military personnel from engaging in law enforcement, is sufficiently flexible to permit exceptions for riots, civil disturbances, and even support for counternarcotics programs.

There are, however, more complex, unresolved legal issues concerning homeland defense. Because meeting contemporary threats may involve extensive information gathering at home, homeland defense tasks will be especially sensitive to a nation that jealously guards its civil rights. The specter of massive federal involvement in terrorist incidents has been the subject of a few major motion pictures but no significant political debate.[12] In one of his valedictory speeches, Secretary of Defense William Cohen highlighted the sensitivity of homeland defense issues:

I believe that we as a democratic society have yet to come to grips with the tension that exists between our constitutional protection of the right to privacy [and] the demand that we made . . . to protect us.[13]

---

11 Governor Christine Whitman, as recorded in "Homeland Defense: Proceedings of the April 5th Senior Advisory Group Meeting," 2000, webu6102.ntx.net/homeland/reports/sag040500.html (accessed November 2000).

12 A recent movie, *Siege*, for example, highlighted the difficulties of seeking military solutions to urban terrorism and highlighted concerns for civil rights in domestic terrorist incidents.

13 Secretary of Defense William S. Cohen in a speech delivered at CSIS, October 2, 2000.

The issue of legal authority during mass destruction incidents in urban areas is especially problematic. In the case of such an unlikely but not impossible scenario, it is not even clear what the legal questions are, never mind the answers. Expanding homeland defense roles for the Department of Defense (DOD) may make sense; it will also set off alarms. Policy architects will have to balance individual rights with the need to protect society under difficult and potentially unique circumstances.

In summary, homeland defense can be viewed as the defense of the most vital of all of the nation's traditional interests. It also comprises a new set of priority defense activities to meet novel threats that have in common the potential for direct impact on the United States. These threats have appeared in the form of missile proliferation in hostile states, the emergence of CBRN terrorism, and a variety of threats to the nation's critical information and economic infrastructure. Each of these threats is in many ways unique. New national strategies will have to deal with a wide range of both new and old challenges.

These new threats in their worst forms are low-probability but high-impact threats. All of them carry a high element of unpredictability about them. Indeed, the threat of mass destruction inherent in a missile attack or CBRN terrorism—especially in the mid- to long-term future—is such that either one, if it occurred, could literally change the course of U.S. history. The effects of either of these attacks on contemporary foreign and domestic policy would be profound.

Clearly, the United States must do whatever is possible to prevent or deter these threats. The nation must also continue to refine its ability to deal with them if they do occur. The more unprepared we are, the more we encourage attacks on the homeland. The more prepared we are, the higher the likelihood that we can prevent, deter, or effectively cope with the effects of an attack.

The following material—digested from four CSIS working group reports posted on *www.csis.org*—suggests that in the latter half of the 1990s the nation made significant progress on many issues of homeland defense, but still must dramatically improve policy, programs, and organization for homeland defense against diverse threats. Memories of the repeated failures, for example, to develop and test successfully the United States' controversial national missile defense system remain fresh. Equally salient are the unresolved missile defense issues that concern U.S. allies, as well as China and Russia. At the same time, vigorous efforts to improve the United States' ability to deal with CBRN terrorist threats or threats to its critical infrastructure remain incoherent and inadequate. As one group of experts noted after a simulation of a relatively unsophisticated, single-point, bioterrorist attack: ". . . the systems and resources now in place would be hard-pressed to successfully manage a bio-weapons attack such as that portrayed in [one scenario of the federal government's] 'TOPOFF' exercise."[14]

While the Office of Management and Budget (OMB) has improved the transparency of the budget process, there is only limited coordination, little long-term planning, inadequate programmatic development, and a near total lack of net assessments. Annual budgets are in search of long-term programs, which, in turn, are in search of the national plans that would give them objectives and priorities. We have only begun to understand all that we are doing and not doing for homeland defense. We do not have adequate threat estimates, technical assessments, or net assessments to guide our policymakers.

The four working group reports of this project tell us that, compared to the U.S. posture five years ago, there has been measurable progress in missile defense, the protection of critical infrastructure, and defense against CBRN terrorism. To get to where we need to be, however, much work needs to be done. Not only are programmatic and policy fixes in order, but many aspects of U.S. homeland defense policy need to be reconsidered, and others need a plan to tie them together. This kind of defense planning is hard enough to do when it entails coordinating the responsibilities of five disciplined, uniformed military services. It is far more complex when it involves wide interagency cooperation on the federal level and also includes state, local, and private actors. We must do more for homeland defense, but, more importantly, we must do it better.

Conclusions

Among the most important findings of the four working group reports on homeland defense are the following:

- There is a priority need to reevaluate our national missile defense goals, programs, and testing program.

- The most obvious need in the area of homeland defense is a national plan and a comprehensive, multiyear program. To develop and enforce such a plan, however, will require major organizational changes in the federal government and new organizations to spur state-federal and state-state dialog.

- The homeland defense effort must fit into the U.S. system of laws and concept of federalism. At the same time, given the possibility of mass

---

14   Thomas Inglesby, Rita Grossman, and Tara O'Toole, "A Plague on Your City: Observations from TOPOFF," *Biodefense Quarterly* 2, no. 2 (September 2000): 9. TOPOFF is the code name for a Defense Department nationwide counterterrorism exercise.

destruction and mass disruption, we need to explore areas where new legal authorities may be necessary.

- It will be increasingly important to assess where policies and programs for homeland defense fit in terms of national priorities. Conceptually, homeland defense tasks are related to but do not replace current tasks for deterrence, engagement, presence, and power projection. A failure in any of those tasks may well increase risks to the homeland. Likewise, a failure to build appropriate homeland defense capabilities might encourage an attack that could jeopardize a deployment for an overseas operation.

- U.S. homeland defense efforts have been reactive, disjointed, and focused on post facto consequence management. In addition to the critically important issues of crisis and consequence management, we must see homeland defense in terms of preventing, deterring, disrupting, and attributing attacks on the homeland.

- The U.S. intelligence apparatus is geared primarily to assess major foreign threats in the form of overt attacks on the United States and its allies. While there have been significant improvements in intelligence work on terrorist issues, the United States must continue to redirect efforts at gaining, processing, and analyzing intelligence across the full spectrum of terrorist and cyber threat actions from early planning through execution to attribution of the event.

- In a similar vein, we need to sharpen our knowledge of the effects of the evolving cyber threat and CBRN weapons. The United States urgently requires a net technical assessment that looks not only at threats but also at U.S. capabilities to meet them.

- There is a critical need to train more people to prepare for and deal with cyber security and homeland defense issues.

- There is a critical need in the field of cyber security for the government to improve cooperation with the private sector, create incentives for the private sector to better protect its own systems, and improve its own credibility by improving its internal operations.

Recommendations

The recommendations that follow are those of the four separately constituted reports prepared by the working groups. The recommendations have been modified slightly for this comprehensive executive summary. For detailed discussion and explanation of each recommendation, the reader is referred to the report in question.

Missile Defense

The next administration must develop a new plan for missile defense. The threat assessment needs recalibration, and current missile defense plans may not make sense in terms of the technological possibilities. Future air and cruise missile defenses must also be taken into account. Moreover, the next administration will also have to improve coordination with U.S. allies, come to some final agreement (or disagreement) with Russia over the Anti-Ballistic Missile (ABM) Treaty, and link national missile defense to an overall approach to arms control and efforts to reshape strategic offensive forces. Much useful research and development has taken place during the past decade. Now we must develop an architecture that reflects new strategic requirements and encompasses the threat, the infrastructure, and the technology.

President Clinton's decision to postpone NMD deployment provides the opportunity to reevaluate the path to national missile defense and the criteria for future systems. The next administration will undoubtedly conduct a review of programs and options. In light of program delays, there will be time, probably several years, before a decision on NMD will be required if a deployment is to take place as soon as a defense is judged feasible.

The decision on program direction should be based on a return to first principle: a clearly stated administration goal that the United States should deploy as soon as possible an effective NMD. An initial deployment, however, need not, indeed it probably cannot, provide the same level of effectiveness as a robust system. Any system must have sufficient growth potential to address new missions. The planned NMD architecture should allow for capabilities beyond those associated with an initial deployment, capabilities that will enable it to be effective against not only a near-term North Korean threat but also advanced threats posed by North Korea and simple or complex threats from other nations.

To develop and demonstrate an effective NMD capability at the earliest possible date, the next administration should:

- Consider an initial NMD deployment, as soon as practical, at Grand Forks, North Dakota. Such a deployment would serve as a test-bed for the planned system, allow for testing of the integrated command, control, and communications (C3), and permit crew training.

- Restructure the NMD test and evaluation program. More tests and more realistic testing of the system are required.

- Address the countermeasures (CM) issue through a program to develop and test representative CMs.

- Ensure the successful development and deployment of the Space-Based Infrared System (SBIRS). Space-based surveillance will be required both as an alternative to land-based radar and as a means of defeating some countermeasures.

A program that can meet the requirement of effective defense against initial threats with growth potential will require, at a minimum, the following elements:

- Multiple sites for ground-based interceptors (three to five)
- An interceptor inventory in the several hundreds
- Freedom to deploy sensors
- Freedom to test and develop advanced defenses (e.g., directed energy)
- Freedom to deploy theater defenses (abandonment of demarcation)

The next administration should consider additional measures to refine the set of potential options for responding to an emerging ballistic missile threat. These include the following:

- Evaluate options for enhancing an initial NMD system by the deployment of additional defensive layers (e.g., boost-phase, naval NMD, point defenses). Such an evaluation should not be permitted to delay efforts to deploy a land-based national missile defense.

- Improve intelligence collection and analysis of states possessing or acquiring ballistic missiles. Traditional assessments of proliferants' capabilities, intentions, and behaviors are inadequate. In addition, there is little understanding of potential adversaries' military plans regarding ballistic missiles and weapons of mass destruction (WMD).

- Develop a new strategy for addressing the ABM Treaty that recognizes the limits the treaty imposes on development of missile defenses. Effective nationwide defense against anticipated threats is not possible within the ABM Treaty. Modest amendments to the treaty will not permit the development or deployment of the robust system needed if a sophisticated threat emerges. The choices are to modify "early and often," pursue a "Big Bang" revision, or, if Moscow refuses to negotiate changes to the ABM Treaty, withdrawal.

- Provide significant additional funding, on the order of several billion dollars annually, to ensure that the proposed program can be achieved.

Organization to Meet CBRN and Cyber Threats

A national plan for these aspects of homeland defense must encompass federal-, state-, and local-level responsibilities. This plan must include threat assessments, objectives, key concepts, and means. It would cover all details of the nation's defense against terrorists, as well as plans for critical infrastructure protection. Missile defense is more of a classical defense responsibility, but the U.S. homeland defense plan would also include provisions for consequence management against a foreign missile strike on the territory of the United States.

Today, such an overarching plan is not possible because no one has the authority to write one and make it stick. Today, the nation has up to $12 billion of federal budget authority, in search of long-term programs, which, in turn, are in search of coordinated and prioritized objectives. Recent suggestions about super coordinators or new deputy attorneys general ignore the complexity of this problem. The United States cannot rely on super coordinators or subcabinet officers to build new federal-state bridges or to ride herd on cabinet departments.

We recommend that the president make the vice president responsible for most aspects of homeland defense. In performing this function, the vice president would be assisted by an "Emergency Planning Staff," or EPS, drawn from a reinforced national coordinator's staff and selected Department of Justice organizations. The National Coordinator for Security, Critical Infrastructure and Counterterrorism would retain the current title and would become the principal deputy to the vice president for homeland defense issues. He or she would also continue to be a member of the NSC staff. The national coordinator would also become the chief of the Emergency Planning staff. The head of the Federal Emergency Management Agency (FEMA) would report through the national coordinator to the vice president. Both of these positions would be confirmable by the United States Senate.

Among his or her principal responsibilities, the vice president would chair a new National Emergency Planning Council that would include representatives from all departments, agencies, states, and territories. This council would be the senior body for federal and state coordination on matters relating to critical infrastructure protection or response to terrorist incidents. Private-sector organizations would be invited to participate on issues related to critical infrastructure protection. The council would meet twice yearly, once at the principal level (vice president, governors, CEOs), once at the subordinate level. The national coordinator would be the vice chair of the council.

Under this reorganization, there would be no changes to the principal State Department, Justice Department, and FEMA responsibilities for crisis management and consequence management. Federal Bureau of Investigation and CIA counterterrorist coordination efforts would remain unchanged. Neither the national coordinator nor the vice president would supervise ongoing counterterrorism or counterintelligence operations. The National Infrastructure Protection Center (NIPC) would remain under the auspices of the FBI, and the Critical Infrastructure Assurance Office (CIAO) would remain at the Department of Commerce.

Some consolidation of offices and/or functions would take place to support new EPS in the Office of the Vice President. The National Defense Preparedness Office (NDPO), a Department of Justice clearinghouse for domestic preparedness, would be transferred to FEMA. Selected divisions of the Office of State and Local Domestic Preparedness Support, currently in the Office of Justice Programs, would also become a part of FEMA or the Emergency Planning Staff. The EPS and FEMA would also absorb responsibility for running training programs under the Nunn-Lugar-Domenici Act that were recently been transferred from the Defense Department to the Justice Department.

At the same time, the president and Congress should augment FEMA with personnel as well as administrative and logistical support to play a lead role in domestic CBRN preparedness. FEMA is already well integrated into state- and local-level activity, and it makes little sense to take away training for consequence management from the very organization that has been assigned that function.

The Pentagon must also realign offices so that it has one coherent system for civil support to natural disasters and to terrorism, as opposed to the two distinct systems that it has today. The Directorate of Military Support (DOMS) should no longer work for the Secretary of the Army, but instead be aligned with the Joint Staff and Joint Task Force Civil Support. In the next administration, the Assistant to the Secretary of Defense for Civil Support should become a confirmable Assistant or Deputy Under Secretary of Defense. When confirmed, this official needs to ensure that lines of responsibility within the Office of the Secretary of Defense are clarified and that any overlap in the functions of the Assistant Secretary of Defense for Reserve Affairs and the Assistant Secretary of Defense for Special Operations and Low Intensity Conflict is corrected.

To foster more effective oversight, a bipartisan congressional task force should study ways to improve and simplify the oversight of selected homeland defense tasks. The objective would be for each legislative body to have only one authorization and one appropriations committee for cyber threats, CBRN terrorism, and critical infrastructure protection. The leadership of the House and the Senate should also appoint a minority and majority staff specialist in each of the appropriations and authorization committees to follow all counterterrorism programs. These staffers can educate members who are voting on a specific agency's counterterrorism program about how that program or policy fits into the overall U.S. counterterrorism effort.

Planning for CBRN and Cyber Threats

Among the key, recurring tasks for the vice president, the national coordinator, and the Emergency Planning Staff would be the following:

- Develop an Annual Preparedness Report, to include evaluations of the nation's ability to prevent, deter, and respond to attacks on the homeland.

- Coordinate or otherwise participate in the development of threat assessments, technical assessments, and net assessments relating to homeland defense.

- Coordinate the development of future programs in each related federal department or agency and institute coherent and effective annual budgetary reviews.

- Coordinate national plans for critical infrastructure protection and domestic terrorism response.

- Supervise all aspects of emergency planning and policy development for the federal government.

The vice president, the national coordinator, and the EPS should also accomplish the following projects on a priority basis.

As soon as practical, the vice president and the national coordinator, in conjunction with OMB, should assess the budgetary programs of federal agencies for homeland defense. The objective here, as noted above, would be to create annual budgets that clearly support long-term programs that, in turn, support the major objectives outlined in the national plans.

Early on, the vice president and the national coordinator need to assess the United States' present and future needs against its ongoing research efforts and make detailed recommendations to the president and the Congress. While the CSIS working groups on homeland defense have not made a detailed assessment of R&D needs, many experts believe that the federal government should foster an acceleration of research in immunology and genetics with the objective of putting improvements in immune responses ahead of the ability to create new and more deadly biological agents.[15] A net technical assessment is needed on this set of options, as well as on others that include an analysis of potential deployment costs and requirements, countermeasures, and relative costs and benefits.

The vice president and his new staff should develop a new and comprehensive series of exercises, simulations, and evaluations. The purpose of these activities will be to identify and improve the readiness of the government to carry out potential tasks and coordinate an effective response to all incidents, especially those that involve CBRN weapons or that might otherwise create mass destruction. At the same time, these exercises should be specifically designed to identify and help to resolve conflicts of legal authority and potential civil rights issues.

---

15 Conversation between Joseph Collins of CSIS and Dr. Tara O'Toole of the John Hopkins Center for Civilian Biodefense Studies, Washington, D.C., August 22, 2000.

In conjunction with this series of exercises, the federal government must develop ways (see below) to improve the lessons-learned process so as to ensure that learning from exercises takes place and that the resulting knowledge receives the widest possible dissemination.

As soon as practical, the president should also direct the vice president and the director of Central Intelligence (DCI) to assess the country's ability to gain, process, analyze, and disseminate intelligence on cyber and terrorism issues. CBRN counterterrorism poses unique challenges to the U.S. intelligence community. Terrorist groups are difficult to penetrate and less susceptible to technological collection techniques. Continuing to widen the circle of intelligence consumers to included Health and Human Services (HHS) and selected state and local officials will be an important task. It is clear also that FBI and CIA guidelines about recruiting terrorists as informants must be simplified to make it easier to recruit terrorists to provide information.[16] Several specific steps to strengthen the intelligence community need urgent examination and may require important changes to intelligence programs and budgets:

- Invest in all source intelligence capabilities. Multidisciplinary intelligence collection is crucial to provide indications and warning of a possible attack as well as insights into the cultures and mindsets of terrorist organizations, and to identify key vulnerabilities that can be exploited and leveraged to disrupt terrorist activities before they occur. To date, signal intelligence (SIGINT) has provided decisionmakers with the lion's share of operational counterterrorism intelligence. National technical means cannot be allowed to atrophy further. While a robust technical intelligence capability is crucial, our human intelligence capability must also be enhanced. This is especially needed against terrorists, who operate in small groups with less technical paraphernalia to monitor and who are less vulnerable to satellite reconnaissance.

- Invest in intelligence analytical capabilities. The intelligence community, including the FBI, must invest in expertise—linguists, CBRN experts, and regional experts—to buttress its analytical ability to track terrorists considering using CBRN weapons. Moreover, the intelligence community must think creatively in structuring its analytic capabilities to track the CBRN terrorist threat.

- Tighten coordination among the nonproliferation, counterproliferation and counterterrorism communities. Rotational assignments at the analyst level would in part serve this end.

---

16   This issue was first publicized in L.Paul Bremer III, et al., *Countering the Changing Threat of International Terrorism*: *Report of the National Commission on Terrorism* (Washington, D.C., July 13, 2000), pp. 7-10

- Tap the scientific and biomedical research communities. Develop networking relationships with the scientific and biomedical research communities, whose knowledge of emerging capabilities and of other information gleaned from the open scientific literature, international scientific collaborations, and conferences could prove invaluable to the intelligence community—particularly with respect to the bioterrorism threat. Indeed, some of the most critical intelligence related to bioterrorism may be derived through the ongoing and open-source practice of international public health and surveillance activities, such as those run by the World Health Organization.

- Invest in detection and attribution capabilities. A credible retaliatory capability, essential for effective deterrence, depends on a strong attribution capability to identify the perpetrators and their supporters. These capabilities include laboratory facilities, other equipment, and the personnel necessary for CBRN attribution.

- Strengthen the U.S. warning capability. Facilitate rapid communications for conveying information concerning warning and preemptive attack. Conduct a lessons-learned study of U.S. government warning across the entire intelligence cycle (collection, processing, analysis, and dissemination).

- Carry out a "Net Assessment of Intelligence Capabilities to Deal with Asymmetric and Terrorist Attacks." Develop a comprehensive net assessment of current and projected U.S. intelligence capabilities to deal with the problems of warning, detection, defense, targeting, and damage assessment, with a supporting net technical assessment of the capabilities to use national technical means and the current and future capabilities of key organizations like the National Security Agency and the National Reconnaissance Office, and the role of human intelligence.

- Develop "Annual Net Threat Assessments of the Foreign and Domestic Threat of CBRN Attacks and Terrorism." Provide federal planners with the basis for assessing the emerging risk of such attacks and develop an integrated analysis structure for planning U.S. programs and response.

The vice president and the EPS should join with the Defense and State Departments to review the United States' arms control posture to see if a more effective enforcement regime could put teeth into the prohibitions on the development of biological weapons. Even though its verification procedures will have serious limits, the Biological Weapons Convention is useful because it strengthens the international norm against development of biological weapons and creates an impediment to nations bent on acquiring biological warfare capabilities.

Finally, the vice president and the EPS should study other ways to build up the nation's prevention and deterrent capabilities against terrorists and cyber attack. For example, a well-conceived, effective, and well-publicized exercise program that demonstrates U.S. capability to deal with attacks could help to deter hostile states or terrorists from choosing biological or chemical weapons or attacking our critical infrastructure.

Similarly, the vice president and the national coordinator should support the continuation of the Nunn-Lugar Threat Reduction Act. In the future, to help prevent threats to the West, Nunn-Lugar needs to redouble its efforts to assist the Russian government to destroy chemical stocks and related equipment.

CBRN Terrorism and Other Homeland Defense Training

An inadequate number of people in the United States are trained for cyber security and to combat CBRN terrorism.

In the cyber area, in 1999 only 10 U.S. citizens received the highest academic degrees in computer security. Majoring in other aspects of computer science or related disciplines carries much greater financial rewards. Clearly, the federal government will have to establish incentives for people to move into this field and stay in government service. In this regard, CSIS applauds the appropriation in FY2001 of $11 million of scholarship money, administered by the National Science Foundation, for students who will serve in government cyber security positions.

In the area of CBRN terrorism, the focus should be on training emergency responders, emergency room personnel, and public health officials. Only about 3 percent of the total number of emergency responders have been trained in the past five years. To assist in training at their level, emergency responders need a single doctrinal focal point for manuals and training programs for civilian CBRN terrorism responders.

To move toward these goals in the near term, the federal government should examine such options as the following:

- Fund the Justice Department's Center for Domestic Preparedness (CDP) at Anniston, Alabama, to allow it to achieve full capacity of 10,000 trainees per year. Also, continue to fund the U.S. Public Health Service's Noble Training Facility at the same location. Both of these new institutions are special national assets and should be carefully nurtured and protected.

- Encourage departments who use the CDP to assign all of their graduates to training roles within the local departments.

- Continue to coordinate with the U.S. Army Chemical School at Fort Leonard Wood, Missouri, to share training techniques and lessons learned on dealing with chemical and biological devices and defense operations.[17]

- Continue at a minimum the same level of interagency effort at mobile training after the Domestic Preparedness Program goes under Justice Department control in FY2001.

- State Department-sponsored training of host nation personnel is chronically underfunded and should be drastically increased. In other areas, the president and secretary of state should do whatever is necessary to assure full funding for protection of United States embassies and installations overseas.

- As a separate entity, fully fund the National Defense Preparedness Office clearinghouse for information on WMD preparedness planning and policy.

In the long term, the federal government should:

- Continue to reassess equipment and training needs across the country.

- Determine the steady state number of people that will have to be trained to deal with terrorism and weapons of mass destruction.

- As initial needs are met, gradually abolish mobile training teams and replace them to the greatest extent possible with multilevel institutional training at full capacity CDPs or other fixed training institutions. The focus of this institutional training should be to train local trainers and officials.

- Develop a WMD "training and doctrine center" in Anniston, Alabama, or some other suitable facility. This center could also become the hub of the cyber attack and CBRN terrorism lessons-learned process. Also, organize a series of conferences, as well as a private Internet site, to facilitate the sharing of ideas and lessons-learned among emergency responders throughout the United States.

- Study the need and feasibility of establishing a second CDP-type of live agent training facility, probably in the western United States, to allow a greater number of responders to be trained expeditiously in a toxic agent environment.

- Foster greater organizational collaboration between the health sector and emergency management officials. Such collaboration is critical for survival at the local level during an epidemic. FEMA and HHS should

---

17   CSIS questioned whether there was excess capacity at the USA Chemical School at Fort Leonard Wood that could be used to train first responders. An extensive estimate was conducted on-site and Army experts determined that there was very little excess capacity there. See correspondence from the USA Chemical School to CSIS, dated October 4, 2000.

develop an equivalent national preparedness program together to foster such collaboration. Linkage at the county and city level is critical and will not happen until FEMA and HHS are well-connected by a common doctrine guiding bioterrorism preparedness and response at the top level.

Medical Training and Preparedness

In a similar vein, we need to continue to improve the ability of U.S. hospitals, public health services, and health care providers to deal with mass casualties and the effects of chemical and biological weapons. This will entail the examination of the most cost-effective approach to equipment and drug stockpiling. All of this will be especially difficult in an environment where a third of all civilian hospitals are already losing money. The federal government will have to continue to leverage the public health and Veterans Administration (VA) medical systems to help local hospitals adapt to the threat. The core capacity for public health and medical care needs to be greatly enhanced with respect to detection and treatment of infectious disease. The biomedical and public health communities should be working in greater partnership with each other and should be integrated more effectively into the larger national security community. Once again, the federal government needs to determine the most cost-effective program to achieve the following:

- Capitalize the public health structure. Core functions of public health (e.g., disease surveillance and laboratory capability) will form the foundation of detection, investigation, and response for bioterrorist threats. Development of these core functions requires investing in communications facilities, administrative support, and surge personnel capabilities so that public health offices are capable of leading the effort to contain and eradicate epidemics. Run exercises to test capabilities and determine what is cost-effective.

- Direct FEMA and CDC to develop the national response capacity for the rapid assessment of a bioterrorist emergency occurring anywhere in the United States. These agencies will need to develop a Biological Emergency Support Team (BEST) that can rapidly assess and set priorities following the consequences of a bioterrorist event. This will ensure that FEMA can rapidly galvanize other federal departments around a common assessment and set of response priorities during a national emergency. Furthermore, this arrangement links state and local infectious disease control agencies through CDC to the disaster management skills of FEMA.

- Expand the provisions on biological terrorism in the Terrorism Annex of the Federal Response Plan. The current U.S. plan for an organized response must be updated to include preparedness for a biological attack, which presents a host of unique and complicated challenges and requires reexamining lead agency roles and missions. The National Disaster Medical System (NDMS), which is composed of FEMA, the Defense Department, HHS, and the VA, has no strategy to rapidly augment medical resources at the state and local levels in the event of a biological attack. The NDMS has never been resourced properly, nor has it been properly focused on the issue of bioterrorism response. The NDMS needs to be funded adequately, and FEMA should be designated the lead federal agency to coordinate the NDMS's activities.

- Increase physicians' awareness of the symptoms of biological weapons. Physicians are the tripwire for recognizing a biological attack and must be trained to spot symptoms of exotic diseases and rapidly report unusual manifestations or clusters of disease to the appropriate public health authorities. HHS should work with pertinent infectious disease professional societies and medical specialists to further this goal.

- Develop a national bioterrorism surveillance capacity. Surveillance is the touchstone of public health and organizes the other capacities within the public health sector. A national bioterrorism surveillance system should allow public health and emergency managers to monitor the general health status of their populations, track outbreaks, monitor health service utilization, and serve as an alerting vehicle for a bioterrorist attack. There should be linkage between public health and clinical medicine, hospitals and health departments, local health officers, and local, state, and federal health authorities. This capacity does not exist at this time; an emergency mobilization toward this end is urgently needed.

- Develop suitable diagnostic capabilities and systems. Develop rapid and more reliable diagnostic capabilities, build regional diagnostic centers, and upgrade hospital diagnostic laboratories. Create a "library" of strains of diseases that is linked—in real time and via a safe intranet—to public health and medical systems worldwide. Rapid and "gold standard" diagnostic capabilities are critical to catching a biological attack in time to prevent massive casualties. Expand CDC's national bioterrorism laboratory response network and laboratory standardization efforts under way with the states. Full implementation of this multidepartment effort (the Defense, Energy, and Agriculture Departments as well as the FBI) will come close to full coverage of the entire nation. CDC's rapid response and technology transfer laboratory activities in support of this network should be dramatically expanded. The development of standardized assays and public health laboratory detection should be a priority.

- Stockpile antibiotics, vaccines, and other related pharmaceuticals and materiel. Currently, CDC is developing a fledgling stockpile of pharmaceuticals for civilian use. DOD also has major stockpile activities in progress. These efforts must be more fully supported and extended to match evolving needs and emerging technologies. At the same time, because of the administrative complexities and financial costs (in the billions of dollars) associated with developing a national pharmaceutical stockpile of vaccines, drugs, and equipment, a standing board (which reports to the president) composed of scientists, stockpile managers, federal government representatives, and private-sector pharmaceutical administrators should ensure that the bioterrorism threat to civilian populations lines up with the national R&D efforts and the requirements of the pharmaceutical stockpile.

- Develop a comprehensive plan for assuring surge capacity for health care. Through both regional and national planning efforts, identify all existing assets and how they would be mobilized to address mass casualty care. In addition, develop working strategies for rapid expansion of care as needed, including potential mobilization of field hospitals or establishment of auxiliary care facilities (e.g., in school gymnasiums, armories, or hotels). This would also need to include strategies for rapid mobilization of critical equipment needs (e.g., ventilators or respiratory isolation capacity) on a regional basis.

- Increase R&D for new vaccines, antidotes, and medicines. Harness the power of the U.S. academic and business communities to research and develop better understanding of basic pathogens and immunology; new antidotes/vaccines, especially for unknown/"designer" toxins; ways to lengthen the shelf life of existing antidotes/vaccines; and improved biological detection capability (for both human and environmental samples). Provide incentives, utilize contracts, and adopt an "In-Q-Tel" style format with universities and companies. Strengthen applied R&D programs and ensure that R&D is not concentrated solely on military needs.

- Develop an integrated plan for biomedical research capabilities of the Departments of Defense and Health and Human Services. Ensure that applied research receives adequate focus as compared to long-term bench research projects.

- Legislate emergency supplemental funding authority (akin to FEMA natural disaster supplementals) for CBRN response activities reimbursement.

- Engage the pharmaceutical industry and the private sector as a whole. Explore new funding strategies to "incentivize" broader participation of the private sector, including ways to encourage greater engagement of hospitals/medical care providers in preparedness planning and capability building, and ways to more fully engage the pharmaceutical industry in developing and supplying new diagnostics, antibiotics, antivirals, and vaccines.

- Prepare a communications and information strategy. Information concerning medicine and diseases should be developed, in various languages, before the event so as to be readily available. Public health and other governmental personnel who will engage in media relations during a biological attack should train for the role and should build trust with the media.

- Identify and remedy legal ambiguities or inadequate authority. An interagency task force, with state and local representation, should immediately begin efforts to identify legal issues raised by a CBRN threat or attack and work to resolve those issues, whether through proposing new laws or simply clarifying the application of existing laws and authorities.

Special Recommendations on Cyber Issues

As has been noted, to create improved cyber security, the government must improve cooperation with the private sector, create incentives for the private sector to better protect its own systems, and improve its own credibility by improving its internal operations.

Government can improve cooperation with the private sector in many ways. Options that deserve high priority consideration include the following:

- Conduct information-sharing on vulnerabilities and warnings of ongoing attacks or threats; share information on hacker modus operandi and on solutions and defenses to established threats and attacks.

- Continue to facilitate discussions within industry sectors, interaction with information sharing and analysis centers (ISACs), and assistance in collecting, "sanitizing," and disseminating pertinent warnings of threats and attacks.

- Build on the successful elements of the National Information Protection Center (NIPC) model while learning from its mistakes (most notably, its failure to reciprocate information sharing, and its tendency to demand private-sector action using national security language rather than business concerns).

- Establish a single point of national coordination for cyber concerns and alerts, specifically, the creation of both an office for a cyber "commander" (or "national CIO") and a "cyber-911" virtual center that would issue warnings, provide security-related information, and coordinate multiple-agency responses in emergencies. Unlike NIPC, this new virtual center would not be housed within the Department of Justice, but rather within an organization less restricted by its own information-protection and law-enforcement mission.

Government also can provide specific incentives to the private sector to better protect its own systems. Suggested approaches include the following:

- Collaborate in collecting and sharing risk-data information, and acting as the catalyst for the establishment of industrywide standards for information security in different business sectors.

- Grant relief from specific provisions of antitrust laws to companies that share information specifically related to vulnerabilities or threats.

- Establish liability limits against disruption of service for companies using security "best practices."

- Establish clear corporate liability for disruptions to consumers (i.e., limit consumer liability in ways similar to the Electronic Fund Transfer Act).

- Provide extraordinary liability relief to the private sector in the case of cyber warfare, similar to the indemnification authorities set up in case of destruction of commercial assets through conventional warfare.

- Provide specific awards or credits for information leading to hacker arrests.

- Enact intermediate regulatory steps (both domestic and international) governing shared systems.

Government can also increase its credibility with the private sector by taking certain internal measures:

- Generate an agreement across agencies on a clear definition of the problem and a clear breakdown of responsibilities (e.g., warning vs. defense vs. prosecution).

- Improve internal security practices, including strengthening the requirements for system upgrades and timely anti-virus software upgrades, tightening personal security requirements, and instituting personal accountability for the handling of sensitive government data.

- Improve information-sharing processes and incentives within and between agencies.

- At the agency level, establish policies that focus not only on remediation but also on reconstitution and continuity of operations.

- Work toward altering the incentive structure in the law enforcement and intelligence communities so that prevention becomes as important as prosecution.

- Vastly improve education and training not only of security professionals, but of all government employees handling sensitive data on government information systems.

- Provide direct financial incentives to universities to develop information security curricula, and to integrate information security not only into their current information science programs, but into their humanities and public policy courses as well.

- Finally, work toward more comprehensive legislation for international collaboration on both the prevention and prosecution of cyber crimes and cyber aggressions.

TESTIMONY OF DR. BRUCE HOFFMAN*
VICE PRESIDENT, EXTERNAL AFFAIRS, AND
DIRECTOR, RAND WASHINGTON OFFICE

RE-THINKING TERRORISM IN LIGHT OF A WAR ON TERRORISM

September 26, 2001

The opinions and conclusions expressed in this written testimony are the author's alone and should not be interpreted as representing those of RAND or any of the sponsors of its research.

Thank you, Mr. Chairman, for the privilege and opportunity to testify before the Subcommittee as it begins its important deliberations on this critical issue.

The 9/11 Attacks In Context

Until last Tuesday, terrorists either in this country or abroad had killed no more than approximately 1,000 Americans total, since 1968. The enormity and sheer scale of the simultaneous suicide attacks of September 11th dwarf anything we have previously seen—either individually or in aggregate. Indeed, by the time the rubble and debris is cleared from New York City's World Trade Center, the collapsed walls of the Pentagon are stabilized and the last of the bodies are retrieved from the field in rural Pennsylvania where a fourth suicide aircraft crashed, the death toll is likely to be exponentially higher. Accordingly, for that reason alone, the events of September 11th argue for nothing less than a re-configuration of both our thinking about terrorism and of our national security architecture as well. Such a change is amply justified by the unique constellation of operational capabilities evident in that day's tragic attacks: showing a level of planning, professionalism and tradecraft rarely seen among the vast majority of terrorists and terrorist movements we have known.[1] Among the most significant characteristics of the operation were its:

- ambitious scope and dimensions;
- consummate coordination and synchronization;
- professionalism and tradecraft that kept so large an operation so secret; and

---

*The preparation of this testimony was supported entirely by RAND funds, and was neither funded nor supported by federal government grants or monies. It should also be emphasized that the opninions and conclusions expressed both in this testimony and the published work from which it is derived are entirely my own and therefore should not be interpreted as representing those of RAND or any of the sponsors of its reserach.

- the unswerving dedication and determination of the 19 aircraft hijackers who willingly and wantonly killed themselves, the passengers and crews of the four aircraft they commandeered and the thousands of the persons working or visiting both the World Trade Center and the Pentagon.

To give you some idea of the significance of the September 11th incidents from a terrorist operational perspective, simultaneous attacks—using far more prosaic and arguably conventional means of attack (such as car bombs, for example)—are relatively uncommon. For reasons not well understood, terrorists typically have not undertaken such coordinated operations. This was doubtless less of a choice than a reflection of the logistical and other organizational hurdles that most terrorist groups are not able to overcome. Indeed, this was one reason why we were so galvanized by the synchronized attacks on the American embassies in Nairobi and Dar-es-Salaam three years ago. The orchestration of that operation, coupled with its unusually high death and casualty tolls, stood out in a way that, until September 11th, few other terrorists had: bringing bin Laden as much renown as infamy in many quarters. During the 1990s, perhaps only one other (presumably unrelated) terrorist incident evidenced those same characteristics of coordination and high lethality: the series of attacks that occurred in Bombay in March 1993, where a dozen or so simultaneous car bombings rocked the city, killing nearly 300 persons and wounding more than 700 others.[2] Indeed, apart from the IRA's near simultaneous assassination of Lord Mounbatten and remote-control mine attack on British troops in Warrenpoint, Northern Ireland in 1979, it is hard to recall any other significant incidents reflecting such operational expertise.

Accordingly, we were perhaps lulled into believing that mass, simultaneous attacks in general and those of such devastating potential as we saw in New York and Washington on September 11th were likely beyond most capabilities of most terrorists—including those directly connected to or associated with Usama bin Laden. The tragic events of two weeks ago demonstrate how profoundly misplaced such assumptions were. In this respect, we perhaps overestimated the significance of our past successes (e.g., in largely foiling most of bin Laden's terrorist operations from the August 1998 embassy bombings to the November 2000 attack on the *U.S.S. Cole*) and the terrorists' own incompetence and propensity for mistakes (e.g., Ahmad Ressam's bungled attempt to enter the United States from Canada in December 1999). Indeed, both more impressive and disturbing is the fact that there was likely considerable overlap in the planning for these attacks and the one last November against the U.S.S. Cole in Aden: thus suggesting a multi-track operational and organizational capability to coordinate major, multiple attacks at one time.

Attention was also arguably focused too exclusively either on the low-end threat posed by car and truck bombs against buildings or the more exotic high-end threats, involving biological or chemical weapons or cyber-attacks. The implicit assumptions of much of our planning scenarios on mass casualty attacks were that they would involve germ or chemical agents or result from widespread electronic attacks on critical infrastructure and that any conventional or less extensive incident could be addressed simply by planning for the most catastrophic threat. This left a painfully vulnerable gap in our anti-terrorism defenses where a traditional and long-proven tactic—like airline hijacking—was neglected in favor of other, less conventional threats and the consequences of using an aircraft as a suicide weapon seem to have been almost completely discounted. In retrospect, it was not the 1995 sarin nerve gas attack on the Tokyo subway that should have been the dominant influence on our counterterrorist thinking, but the December 1994 hijacking in Algiers of an Air France passenger plane by terrorists belonging to the Armed Islamic Group (GIA). Their plan was to crash the fuel-laden aircraft with its passengers into the heart of Paris. The lesson here is not that we need to be unrealistically omniscient, but rather that we need to consider the entire range of potential attacks and not just those at the extreme end of the technological spectrum.

We also had long consoled ourselves—and had only recently began to question and debate the notion—that terrorists were more interested in publicity than killing and therefore had neither the need nor interest in annihilating large numbers of people. For decades, there was widespread acceptance of the observation made famous by Brian Jenkins in 1975 that, "Terrorists want a lot of people watching and a lot of people listening and not a lot of people dead."[3] Even despite the events of the mid-1980s—when a series of high-profile and particularly lethal suicide car and truck-bombings were directed against American diplomatic and military targets in the Middle East (in one instance resulting in the deaths of 241 Marines)—many analysts saw no need to revise these arguments. In 1985, Jenkins, one of the most perspicacious and acute observers of this phenomenon, again noted that, "simply killing a lot of people has seldom been one terrorist objective . . . Terrorists operate on the principle of the minimum force necessary. They find it unnecessary to kill many, as long as killing a few suffices for their purposes."[4] The events of September 11th prove such notions now to be wishful thinking, if not dangerously anachronistic.

Finally, bin Laden himself has re-written the history of both terrorism and probably of the post-Cold War era—which he arguably single-handedly ended on September 11th. At a time when the forces of globalization, coupled with economic determinism, seemed to have submerged the role the individual charismatic leader of men beneath far more powerful, impersonal forces , bin Laden has cleverly cast himself (admittedly and inadvertently with our assistance) as a David against the American Goliath: one man standing up to the world's sole remaining superpower and able to challenge its might and directly threaten its citizens. To his followers, who may well be growing in the aftermath of the September 11th attacks, bin Laden has proven to be the fabled right man in the right place at the right time: possessing the vision, financial resources, organizational skills and flair for self-promotion to meld together the disparate strands of Islamic fervor, Muslim piety and general enmity towards the West into a formidable global force.

Given these profound changes and development both in the nature of terrorism as we know it and the salient threat now so clearly posed to the United States, how should we begin to organize for "a war on terrorism"? What the U.S. requires is a strategy, a comprehensive understanding of the threat in all its dimensions, and—both to support and help implement these concerted efforts—a reconfigured national security architecture.

A Clear, Comprehensive and Coherent Strategy

It is inaccurate if not delusory to write off the tragic events of September 11th simply as an intelligence failure. The problem is more complex and systemic than a deficiency of any single agency or component of our national security structure. Indeed, it goes beyond the United States and implicates the intelligence and security services of many of our closest allies in Europe and elsewhere as well. But most importantly, it manifestly underscores the conspicuous absence of a national overarching strategy. As the Gilmore Commission noted in its first annual report to the President and the Congress in December 1999, the promulgation of a succession of policy documents and presidential decision directives[5] neither equates to, nor can substitute for, a truly "comprehensive, fully coordinated national strategy."[6] In this respect, the variety of Federal agencies and programs concerned with counterterrorism still remain painfully fragmented and uncoordinated; with overlapping responsibilities, and lacking clear focus.

The articulation and development of such a strategy, as I have argued in other testimony before Congress,[7] is not simply an intellectual exercise, but must be at the foundation of any effective counterterrorism policy. Failure to do so historically has undermined the counterterrorism efforts of other democratic nations: producing frustratingly ephemeral, if not sometimes, nugatory effects and, in some cases, proving counterproductive in actually reducing the threat. Accordingly, as the September 11th attacks demonstrate, the continued absence of a national strategy seriously undermines our ability to effectively counter terrorism. What is now therefore clearly needed is a comprehensive effort that seeks to knit together more tightly, and provide greater organizational guidance and focus, to the formidable array of capabilities and instruments the U.S. can bring to bear in the struggle against terrorism.

Regular Foreign and Domestic Terrorist Threat Assessments

A critical prerequisite in framing such an integrated national strategy is the tasking of a comprehensive net assessment of the terrorist threat, both foreign and domestic, as it exists today and is likely to evolve in the future.[8] The failure to conduct such comprehensive net assessments on a more regular basis is palpable. For example, the last comprehensive national intelligence estimate (NIE) regarding foreign terrorist threats in the United States—a prospective, forward-looking effort to predict and anticipate future terrorist trends directed at this country—was conducted in 1997. In light of last week's events, it is clear that a re-assessment was long overdue. Indeed, the last, formal, comprehensive foreign terrorist assessment astonishingly was undertaken at the time of the 1990/91 Gulf War—nearly a decade ago. Although a new one was tasked this past summer and presumably was in the process of being finalized in recent weeks, given the profound changes in the nature, operations and mindset of terrorists we have seen in recent years, such an estimate was long overdue. Although the National Intelligence Council's wide-ranging Global Trends 2015 effort, published in December 2000, was a positive step in this direction, surprisingly minimal attention was paid to terrorism, in the published open-source version at least.[9]

Intelligence Reform and Reorganization

We also need to be much more confident than we are that the U.S. intelligence community is correctly configured to counter the terrorist threats of today and tomorrow rather than yesterday. Our national security architecture is fundamentally a cold war-era artifice, created more than half a century ago to counter a specific threat from a specific country and a specific ideology. That architecture, which is oriented overwhelmingly towards military threats and hence to gathering military intelligence, was proven anachronistic with last Tuesday's devastating attacks carried out by non-state/non-military adversaries. However, its structure remains fundamentally unchanged since the immediate post-World War II period. An estimated 60% of the intelligence community's efforts, for example, are still focused on military intelligence pertaining to the standing armed forces of established nation-states.[10] Eight of the 13 agencies responsible for intelligence collection report directly to the Secretary of Defense (who also controls their budgets) rather than to the Director of Central Intelligence.[11] It is not surprising therefore that American's HUMINT (human intelligence) assets have proven so anemic given a military orientation that ineluctably feeds on technological intelligence such as MASINT (measurement and signature intelligence), ELINT (electronic intelligence) and SIGNINT (signals intelligence) collected by spy satellites orbiting the planet. Given the emergence of formidable, transnational, non-state adversaries, and the lethally destructive threats that they clearly pose, this balance is no longer appropriate. Moreover, our own HUMINT deficiencies, which forced us to rely on information provided or forthcoming from liaison services, has clearly been shown to be wanting in the wake of the failure of any of our allies to provide warning of the September 11th operations.

Indeed the emergence of a range of new adversaries, with different aims and motivations, that operate on a flat, more linear basis involving networks rather than stove-piped, rigid command and control hierarchies, underscores the need for a re-distribution of our intelligence collection efforts traditional military intelligence threats to the spectrum of enigmatic, non-traditional, non-military and non-state adversaries who now clearly pose a salient threat to our national security. The U.S. intelligence community's roughly $30 billion budget is already greater than the national defense budgets of all but six countries in world.[12] Accordingly, a redistribution of emphasis, personnel, budgets and resources is needed to ensure that the U.S. is fully capable of responding to both current and future terrorist threats. At the very minimum, funding of key elements of our current counterterrorism efforts should be re-oriented towards providing sustained, multi-year budgets that will encourage the development of longer-term, systematic approaches, as opposed to the current year-to-year process.

The country's anachronistic intelligence architecture has also created a dangerous gap in our national defenses. The CIA, of course, is responsible for foreign intelligence collection and assessment and by law is prohibited from operating within the U.S. Domestic counterterrorism, accordingly, falls within the purview of the FBI. The FBI, however, is primarily a law enforcement and investigative agency, not an intelligence agency. Moreover, its investigative activities embrace a broad spectrum—perhaps too broad a spectrum—that includes kidnapping, bank robberies, counter-espionage, serial killings and other even more prosaic crimes, in addition to countering terrorism. The time may be ripe for some new, "out-of-the-box" thinking that would go beyond simple bureaucratic fixes and embrace a radical re-structuring of our domestic counter-terrorism capabilities. For example, just as the narcotics problem is regarded in the U.S. as so serious a problem and so a great a threat to our national security that we have a separate, uniquely oriented, individual agency specifically dedicated to counter-narcotics—the Drug Enforcement Agency (DEA)—we should consider creating a similar organization committed exclusively to counter-terrorism.

Concluding Thoughts

Based on a firm appreciation of terrorism threats, both foreign and domestic, an overarching strategy should now be developed that ensures that the U.S. is capable of responding across the *entire* technological spectrum of potential adversarial attacks. The focus of U.S. counterterrorism policy in recent years has arguably been too weighted towards the "high end" threats from biological and chemical weapons and was based mainly on planning for extreme worst case scenarios.[13] This approach seemed to assume that, by focusing on "worst case" scenarios involving these more exotic weapons, any less serious incident involving a different, even less sophisticated, though still highly lethal weapon, could be addressed simply by planning for the most catastrophic event. Such an assumption ignored the possibility that non-WMD high-casualty incidents, might present unique challenges of their own—such as we have seen in New York and at the Pentagon.

Finally, it should be noted that none of the changes proposed in this testimony are quick fixes or magically conjured solutions to complex and longstanding problems. They all require time, resources and most of all political will and patience. Results will not come quickly. But by taking a comprehensive approach to the terrorist problem and fashioning a cohesive strategy to address it, the U.S. can avoid repeating the mistakes that facilitated last Tuesday's tragic events. The struggle against terrorism is never-ending. Similarly, our search for solutions and new approaches must be continuous and unyielding, proportional to the threat posed by our adversaries in both innovation and determination.

Endnotes

[1]Nor is this a particularly "American-centric" view in reaction to the stunning and tragic events of two weeks ago. For example, an old friend and colleague, who is one of Israel's leading counterterrorist experts, and who has long experience in military, the government and academe was totally shocked by the September 11th attacks—specifically, their coordination, daring and lethality—remarking: "Never could I have imagined that terrorists could or would do that" (telephone conversation, 17 September 2001). I am also reminded of a conversation with a senior, highly decorated Sri Lankan Armed Forces brigade commander and military intelligence operative who once explained in great detail the "difficulties of pulling off even a successful, significant terrorist attack" (discussion, Batticola, Sri Lanka, December 1997)—not least the four orchestrated suicide aircraft hijackings and three crashes that occurred on September 11th.

[2]Celia W. Dugger, "Victims of '93 Bombay Terror Wary of U.S. Motives," *New York Times*, 24 September 2001.

[3]Brian Michael Jenkins, "International Terrorism: A New Mode of Conflict" in David Carlton and Carlo Schaerf (eds.), *International Terrorism and World Security* (London: Croom Helm, 1975), p. 15.

[4]Brian Michael Jenkins, *The Likelihood of Nuclear Terrorism* (Santa Monica, CA: The RAND Corporation, P-7119, July 1985), p. 6.

[5]e.g., the "Five Year Interagency Counter-Terrorism Plan" and PDDs 39, 62 and 63.

[6]The Advisory Panel to Assess Domestic Response Capabilities For Terrorism Involving Weapons of Mass Destruction, *I. Assessing the Threat*, 15 December 1999, p. 56.

[7]Bruce Hoffman, "Combating Terrorism: In Search of A National Strategy," 27 March 2001. This can be accessed at http://www.rand.org/publications/CT/CT175/CT175.pdf.

[8]This same argument has been made repeatedly by Henry L. Hinton, Jr., Assistant Comptroller General, National Security and International Affairs Division, U.S. General Accounting Office, before the Subcommittee on National Security, Veterans Affairs, and International Relations, Committee on Government Reform, U.S. House of Representatives in (1) "Combating Terrorism: Observation on Federal Spending to Combat Terrorism," 11 March 1999; and (2) "Combating Terrorism: Observation on the Threat of Chemical and Biological Terrorism," 20 October 1999; as well as by John Parachini in "Combating Terrorism: Assessing the Threat" before the same House subcommittee on 20 October 1999; and the Hinton testimony "Combating Terrorism: Observation on Biological Terrorism and Public Health Initiatives," before the Senate Committee on Veterans' Affairs and Labor, Health and Human Services, Education, and Related Agencies Subcommittee, Senate Committee on Appropriations, GAO/T-NSIAD-99-12, General Accounting Office Washington, D.C., 16 March 1999.

[9]National Intelligence Council, *Global Trends 2015: A Dialogue About the Future With Non-government Experts*, December 2000.

[10]Richard Stubbing, "Improving The Output of Intelligence Priorities, Managerial Changes and Funding," in Craig Eisendrath (ed.), *National Insecurity: U.S. Intelligence After the Cold War* (Philadelphia: Temple University Press, 2000), pp. 176 & 183.

[11]Reporting to Secretary of Defense: 1. Defense Intelligence Agency, J-2 (through the Joint Chiefs of Staff); 2. Nine Unified/Regional Commands intelligence units; 3. Assistant Secretary for the Air Force for Space; 4. National Reconnaissance Office; 5. National Security Agency; 6. National Imagery and Mapping Agency; 7. Individual services' intelligence divisions (e.g., Deputy Chief of Intelligence, US Army; Chief of Naval Intelligence; US Air **Force** Intelligence); and, 8. Assistant Secretary of Defense's Office for C(3) I (Command, Control, Communications, Coordination and Intelligence).

[12]Stubbing, "Improving The Output of Intelligence Priorities," p. 172.

[13]This argument has similarly been expressed by Henry L. Hinton, Jr., Assistant Comptroller General, National Security and International Affairs Division, U.S. General Accounting Office, Before the Subcommittee on National Security, Veterans Affairs, and International Realtions, Committtee on Government Reform, U.S. House of Representatives in (1) "Combating Terrorism: Observation on Federal Spending to Combat Terrorism," 11 March 1999; and (2) "Combating Terrorism: Observation on the Threat of Chemical and Biological Terrorism," 20 October 1999; as well as by John Parachini in "Combating Terrorism: Assessing the Threat" and Brian Michael Jenkins in their respective testimony before the same House subcommittee on 20 October 1999; and the Hinton testimony "Combating Terrorism: Observation on Biological Terrorism and Public Health Initiatives," before the Senate Committee on Veterans' Affairs and Labor, Health and Human Services, Education, and Related Agencies Subcommittee, Senate Committee on Appropriations, GAO/T-NSIAD-99-12, General Accounting Office Washington, D.C., 16 March 1999.

DOCUMENT NO. 13

STATEMENTS AT A HEARING BEFORE THE SUBCOMMITTEE ON TERRORISM AND HOMELAND SECURITY OF THE HOUSE PERMANENT SELECTED COMMITTEE ON INTELLIGENCE

"PROTECTING THE HOMELAND FROM ASYMETRICAL/UNCONVENTIONAL THREATS"

CHAIRMAN SAXBY CHAMBLISS
THE HONORABLE JANE HARMAN
MR. J. T. CARUSO, FBI

October 3, 2001

COMMENTARY: *Though the submissions in this Document introduce the topic, through the comments of the Chairman and the ranking Minority Member, most of the individuals who appeared did not submit materials which could be distributed to the public. This is unfortunate for the comments which are present indicate, quite clearly, that the Department of Defense has mounted a major initiative to address this topic and it is making progress " the extent of that progress could be gauged if the cited reports in the Hearing material, and the comments made at this Hearing, are made available.*

STATEMENT OF CHAIRMAN SAXBY CHAMBLISS

October 3, 2001

This hearing of the Intelligence Committee's Subcommittee on Terrorism and Homeland Security will come to order.

This is our second public hearing on terrorism matters since the September 11 terrorist attacks on the World Trade Center, the Pentagon, and on U.S. civilian airliners. In the roughly three weeks since this cowardly attack on innocent civilians, the President has made it clear that the country is now at war.

The war we are facing is being fought on a different kind of battlefield. This is a battlefield without clear contours, readily identifiable targets, or defined borders. It crosses national boundaries and stretches right around the globe. This battlefield consists of sometimes nameless and faceless individuals who provide support for cold-blooded murderers and fanatics willing to sacrifice their lives to inflict death and pain on others. It is a battlefield where illicit international financial networks and producers and procurers of false documents run rampant. And it is a battlefield whose complexity and scope greatly complicate both the means by which we will wage war and by which we will defend ourselves against future attacks of the magnitude of those experienced three weeks ago.

More than forty years ago, the Department of Defense created a Defense Science Board to grapple with new developments in warfare and the threats they pose to U.S. national security interests. The Board more recently set up four task forces under the rubric "Protecting the Homeland" to look at new and growing asymmetrical or unconventional threats to the United States from biological, chemical, nuclear, and cyber weapons and techniques. In addition, a fifth task force was established to address intelligence needs for civil support.

Much of the Board's work on these issues remains classified. The Board did, however, begin reporting its findings to the Secretary of Defense earlier this year and began releasing a series of unclassified reports through the summer. The defense against chemical weapons task force is close to completing its work and will issue a formal report in the near future to complete the "Protecting the Homeland" project.

Some of the finest minds in America have been marshaled by the Defense Science Board to address these issues, and much of their substantive work was completed just prior to the September 11 attacks. We thought it would be both timely and helpful to invite the Board to testify before us today, and particularly, to put its key findings and recommendations into the post-September 11 context. In this way, we hope to arrive at some useful conclusions that will aid in legislative action designed to enhance our intelligence, defense, and other capabilities to fight terrorism.

Dr. William Schneider, Chairman of the Defense Science Board, will give us a brief overview of his organization's mandate and will introduce his task force chairmen, who will talk to the specifics of their group's work. Welcome, Dr. Schneider. On behalf of the subcommittee, I commend you and your Board for your work on these critically important issues, and thank you for assembling this fine group of dedicated professionals here before us today.

I would like to extend a warm welcome to all of our other witnesses at this time. Dr. Roger Hagengruber is the Chairman of the Task Force on Unconventional Nuclear Warfare Defense. Mr. Larry Wright is the Chairman of the Task Force on Defensive Information Warfare. Dr. George Whitesides is the Chairman of the Task Force on Defense Against Chemical Weapons. Dr. Tara O'Toole is a senior representative of the Task Force on Defense Against Biological Weapons. And Mr. Peter Marino is Co-Chairman of the Task Force on Intelligence Needs for Civil Support. Welcome, all of you.

I understand that you cleared your calendars for this hearing on short notice, and some of you came from great distances to share your important insights with us. We greatly appreciate your presence here today. We will have many questions for all of you, and I only ask that you keep your opening statements brief, from five to ten minutes maximum, so that all of us have the opportunity to put forward our questions. It would also be useful if you could put your opening remarks and the findings of your respective task forces into the context of the current situation we find ourselves in after the events of September 11.

Following the precedent we established at our hearing last week, we have invited the leaders of the seven key committees with oversight jurisdiction over terrorism and related issues to participate in today's hearing. I welcome all of you who were able to make it today, and encourage you to continue to participate in our public meetings. All of America is looking to us to represent them in the debate on how our government can better protect the citizenry from terrorist attacks. It is incumbent upon us to work hand in hand and in a wholly bi-partisan fashion to help to ensure that the events of September 11 are not repeated in some way, through conventional, biological, chemical, nuclear, or other means.

Before turning the floor over to my friend and distinguished Ranking colleague, Jane Harman, for whatever opening remarks she would care to make, I would like to introduce Mr. Tim Caruso, the FBI's Deputy Director for Counterterrorism and a friend of this subcommittee. Welcome, Tim. It's good to see you again, as we have so often in closed session, and to have you here today to bring us up to date on the present situation.

When the Speaker and Minority Leader directed this subcommittee to spearhead all House efforts to respond to the September 11 attacks, and to coordinate the work of the other committees of jurisdiction, I asked FBI Director Mueller for some special assistance. Specifically, I asked that a senior FBI official appear before our subcommittee at every public hearing to update us to the extent possible in a public forum on inter-agency cooperation and other matters relevant to the current state of play. The FBI Director readily agreed, and on behalf of the subcommittee, I thank him for his support, especially since this is the first time that the FBI has extended this sort of courtesy to anyone.

I think that it is particularly important as we frame our hearings that the FBI continue to participate to help ensure that what we are doing compliments the hard work that the law enforcement and intelligence communities are doing to get to the bottom of the September 11 attacks, and to prevent future incidents. We cannot afford to be working at cross purposes. I also wanted to give the FBI an opportunity to correct some of the erroneous press reports about its investigation that are being reported as fact by many in the media.

Mr. Caruso will be our first witness. He will read a prepared statement and will not answer questions. Dr. Schneider will then have the floor, and when he is finished with his introductory remarks, we'll turn to the Defense Science Board's substantive witnesses for their statements. Questions will follow, and I will defer to subcommittee members first, then to our distinguished visiting colleagues in order of their arrival.

We will use the five-minute rule as we did last week. Members should also be advised that due to time constraints and the number of witnesses, opening statements are limited to myself and the Ranking Member. All participating Members, however, are invited to submit statements to be entered into the record.

With that, I will now turn to Jane Harman for her opening remarks.

REMARKS OF THE HONORABLE JANE HARMAN

October 3, 2001

Thank you, Mr. Chairman. I join with you in welcoming today's witnesses, distinguished members of the Defense Science Board, who will discuss their multi-volume report, "Protecting the Homeland."

Today's hearing is the second in a series of open hearings and is part of the important process of informing the American public and rebuilding their confidence.

More importantly, these hearings are key to the Subcommittee's mission to work with the White House to developing a structure for our intelligence and homeland defense agencies so they can prevent a "second wave" of attacks.

Last week, our hearing focused on the findings of several major commission reports that assessed the likelihood of a terrorist attack. Today, we shift to the subject of homeland defense.

The Defense Science Board is uniquely qualified to discuss this issue. It is the senior advisory body of the Department of Defense and is composed of members appointed from the private sector who advise on a wide range of scientific, technical, manufacturing, and other matters of special importance to the our defense.

The study before us is comprised of the findings of four task forces that assessed a spectrum of threats to the homeland and made a number of specific technological and operational recommendations needed to protect it.

The study that will be discussed paints a grim picture. As it evaluated threats ranging from ballistic missiles, to the use of inexpensive cruise weapons, to the use of weapons of mass destruction, including information warfare, the Board concluded that the technological and operational capabilities to protect the homeland do not exist.

The report examined each of the following five areas

- early capability assessment;
- actions to prevent attack;
- protection of critical assets and infrastructure;
- consequence management;
- and attribution and retaliation;

and concluded that US capabilities were only adequate against unconventional nuclear attacks.

This gloomy assessment is offset by the Board's recognition that the contributions of the Department of Defense and intelligence community have been effective in thwarting past threats posed to the US homeland.

Interestingly, the Board did not make any particular recommendations regarding the coordination of roles and missions between DoD and the intelligence community in countering current threats. It did, however, echo a theme that has emerged in both the full Intelligence Committee and this Subcommittee: there is a disconnect between authority and execution within our defense and intelligence communities.

The Board said:

> "The nation's leaders must become catalysts for (the) change. While there is some formality regarding who is in charge, there seems to be a mismatch between those formally in charge and those that actually have capability."

As we hear about their recommendations, I'd like our witnesses to focus on the importance of aligning the authority and resources of government with the capabilities to execute the strategies required to protect against these new threats. With Governor Ridge assuming at the end of this week his new responsibilities for this nation, I believe this issue will be key to the success of his efforts to organize government to protect our homeland.

Thank you, Mr. Chairman, for convening this hearing.

I look forward to the testimony and assistance of our witnesses as we fulfill the task Speaker Hastert and Leader Gephardt have assigned this Subcommittee.

STATEMENT OF J. T. CARUSO
FBI DEPUTY ASSISTANT DIRECTOR
COUNTERTERRORISM DIVISION

October 3, 2001

Good morning Mr. Chairman, Ms. Harman, and Members of the Subcommittee. On behalf of the men and women of the FBI, I would like to commend you for your leadership in combating terrorism and to pledge the full support and cooperation of the FBI in your efforts.

Like all Americans, I am deeply saddened by the tragic events of September 11th. The terrorist attacks we witnessed are among the most horrific crimes ever committed against the citizens of this country. As you know, the FBI, in conjunction with law enforcement and intelligence agencies throughout the United States and the world, is in the midst of the largest, most complex and perhaps the most critical criminal and terrorism investigation in our history.

Mr. Chairman, I am limited in what l can discuss today in an open forum. I do not want to reveal any strategies planned, actions taken, or information received by the FBI which may jeopardize the pending investigation. Numerous Committees of the United States Congress, including this one, however, receive frequent updates on the investigation from the FBI and other agencies. 'These updates are provided in closed session which allows us to speak candidly about the sensitive and classified aspects of this investigation. The FBI will continue to work with you and your staff in this regard.

Within minutes of the September 11th attacks, the FBI's Command Center, called the Strategic Information and Operations Center, or SIOC, was operational. Our efforts began as a search and rescue mission, with SIOC providing multi-agency analytical, logistical and administrative support for the teams on the ground in New York, Pennsylvania, and at the Pentagon. Sadly, as days passed, the hope of finding survivors amid the debris began to wane. The crash sites became crime scenes and the tedious process of evidence collection began. The focus in SIOC shifted from rescue efforts to a large scale, global terrorism investigation.

Members and staff of this Subcommittee have had the opportunity to visit SIOC . and to observe our operations to action. You were able to witness firsthand the cooperation and coordination of every aspect of this investigation by and between FBI Headquarters, our 56 field offices, and 32 other government agencies present in the Command Center.

The SIOC currently operates with more than 500 personnel representing these 32 different agencies and their components. Criminal Division lawyers front the Department of Justice are also working In SIOC both to facilitate obtaining warrants and to continuously evaluate evidence.

The FBI recognizes that each agency represented in SIOC plays a critical role in this investigation. We are all working side by side in the Command Center setting investigative leads, responding to inquiries, and tracking the hijackers' activities and contacts priorto September 11th, We have enlisted the professional assistance of our state and local law enforcement partners across the nation in two ways: first, through our 35 joint terrorism task forces and regional task forces where federal, state and local law enforcement agencies partner together on terrorism matters; and, second, through the electronic dissemination of threat warnings and law enforcement intelligence to police agencies across the nation. In this way, we reach approximately 18,000 law enforcement agencies instantly.

In addition, the FBI has dedicated significant resources to this investigation, including 4,000 Special Agents and 3,000 support personnel. Over 250 Laboratory personnel and related field personnel are depbyed at the Pentagon and New York crash sites. Thirty of the FBI's Legal Attache offices overseas are pursuing leads and coordinating investigation with their foreign counterparts. This is truly an investigation of global dimension. Attorney General Ashcroft and FBI Director Mueller are present in the 510C on a daily basis, actively overseeing and directing this investigation.

To date, more than 238,000 tips and potential leads have been generated in this investigation. Over 100,000 of those tips were received through the FBI's Internet information form available on our website "www.ifccfbi.gov." Another 20,000 tips were received on the FBI's toil-free hotline at 1-866-483-5137. The remainder have been generated through the dedicated efforts of the FBI field offices.

As you know, the FBI has identified at least 19 hijackers aboard the foar airliners that crashed on September 11th into the North and South Towers of the World Trade Center in New York, the Pentagon, and Stony Creek Township, Pennsylvania. Last week, the FBl released a letter handwritten in Arabic found in three separate locations: the first, in a suitcase of hijacker Mohammed Atta which did not make the connection to American Airlines Flight #11 that crashed into the North Tower of the World Trade Center; the second, in a vehicle parked at Dulles International Airport belonging to hijacker Nawaf Alhazmi; and the third at the crash site in Pennsylvania. Translations of the letter indicate an alarming willingness to die on the part of the hijackers.

We have also located some of the flight recorders and voice data recorders and are in the process of analyzing them for insights into what took place on board those flights. With respect to United Airlines Ftighi #93 that crashed in Pennsylvania, I can confirm that the passengers engaged in a fight for their lives with their four hijackers and most likely saved the lives of unknown individuals on the ground.

In addition to potential evidence collected at the scenes of these attacks, the FBI is working tirelessly to "follow the money" associated with the 19 hijackers. In the investigation of any terrorist organization, identifying and tracing funds used to finance and fund the organizations is a critical step. "Following the money" plays a key role in identifying those involved in criminal activity, establishing links among them, and developing evidence of their involvement in the activity. locating, seizing, andlor freezing assets tied to terrorist organizations plays a key role in cutting off the financial lifeblood of these organizations and in not only dismantling the organization, but in preventing future terrorist acts. Due to the international nature of terrorist organizations, these investigations require considerable coordination with foreign authorities as well as the CIA and the Intelligence Community to ensure that the criminal investigation does not jeopardize or adversely impact sensitive national security matters. This requires careful adherence to restrictions separating criminal investigations from those involving national security and classified intelligence matters.

In the course of this investigation, the level of cooperation by U.S. financial institutwns has been extraordinary. In all respects, the financial institutions have gone to considerable lengths to provide subpoenaed information as expeditiously as possible and have done everything possible within the legal framework to provide any cooperation requested, To date, the federal government has frozen approximately $6 million in assets both at home and abroad.

One of the inherent difficulties the FBI faces in high-profile investigations such as this is the plethora of news article accounts—some accurate, some partially accurate, and some not accurate at all, I would like to comment on some of the more prevalent reports regarding the September 11th attacks.

- Early in the investigation, reports emerged that the FBI had detained two Middle Eastern males found wearing Delta Airlines pilots' uniforms, canying false pilots' licenses as well as box cutters, These reports were untrue.

- According to same media reports, two of the hijackers were on a so-called "FBI Watch List" and were under active FBI surveillance at the time of the attacks. Prior to the events of September 11, the FBI did not maintain a "watch list" and none of the i9 hijackers were under surveillance. In the aftermath of the attacks, the FBI compiled a list of those individuals who the FBI, through investigation, determined may have some information about one or more of the hijackers or about related activities, This list has grown to over 400 names, It is important to note that these are persons the FBI is interested in interviewing; they are not 400 suspected hijackers.

- Just days ago, the FBI was reported to have foiled a terrorist plot to fly a hijacked plane into the Sears Tower in Chicago, The FBI is unaware of any such plot.

- Media reports also contend that the FBI had advance warnings since 1995 of the plot to hijack U.S. airliners. The FBI had no warnings about any hijack plots. There was a widely publicized 1995 conspiracy in the Philippines to remotely blow up 11 U,S. airliners over the Pacific Ocean but that plot was disrupted. As is the practice, the information obtained during that investigation was widely disseminated, even internationally, and thoroughly analyzed by multiple agencies. It does not connect to the current case.

- Most recently, the media has focused on an individual in Minneapolis who has been detained since August 17 on immigration charges. It has been suggested that this individual, Zacarias Moussaoui, was training to be the fifth hijacker on the flight that crashed in Pennsylvania. Media accounts also suggest that the FBI did not actively investigate Moussaoui until after the September 11th attacks. The FBI conducted vigorous investigation of Moussaoui upon teaming of his detention in mid-August, to include seizing his computer, contacting foreign officials for additional information, and seeking a number of authorities under the Foreign Intelligence Surveillance Ad (FISA) to conduct further investigation. In addition, information about Moussaoui was shared throughout the Intelligence Community prior to September 11th, Although there was insufficient . evidence to establish that Moussaoui was an "agent" of a foreign power or terrorist group as required for a FISH warrant, the FBI pursued all reasonable and lawful investigative steps since mid-August.

Mr. Chairman, I want to thank you and the Subcommittee forthis opportunity to address some of these media reports and to describe the extraordinary interagency cooperation in this investigation. The FBI and its sister agencies are literally working around the clock to determine the full scope of these terrorist acts, to identify all those involved in planning, executing, and assisting in the commission of these acts, and to bring those responsible to justice.

Even so, we at the FBI are dear as to our mission. Director Mueller has forcefully and repeatedly articulated our number one priority: to do everything in our power to prevent the occurrence of any additional temarist acts. Mr. Chairman, you and the American people can be assured that the FBI is committed to this fight, To honor the memories of those Who perished on September 11th, we must, and we will; win this war on terrorism.

DOCUMENT NO. 14

STATEMENTS AT A HEARING BEFORE THE
HOUSE COMMITTEE ON INTERNATIONAL RELATIONS

"AL QUEDA AND THE GLOBAL REACH OF TERRORISM"

CHAIRMAN HENRY J. HYDE
MR. CHARLES SANTOS, SBS ASSOCIATES
MR. OLIVER "BUCK" REVELL
MR. VINCENT CANNISTRARO, FORMER CIA EXECUTIVE

October 3, 2001

COMMENTARY: *The comments made before this Hearing provide further insights into the Al Queda, providing policy makers with additional information on which to build new activities. By understanding more of this formidable foe, and by getting further information on the historical underpinnings of Al Queda"s actions, the U.S. public and its policy makers will more likely construct the right vehicles to cope with this organization and its supporters.*

OPENING STATEMENT OF THE HONORABLE HENRY J. HYDE CHAIRMAN, COMMITTEE ON INTERNATIONAL RELATIONS

October 3, 2001

With the September 11 attacks on the United States, the once-distant prospect of terrorism has become an inescapable reality for all Americans. The impact of this assault is greater than the tally of physical destruction, greater even than the tragic loss of life. The images forced into our lives are permanent ones. The realization that human beings are capable of performing such deeds forces us to accept that evil still exists among us, especially in our modern era when many had hoped it might be abolished altogether.

We understand that the challenge before us is a deeply entrenched one, that we face more than a simple emergency. Many have said that we are at the beginning of a new era, one in which our daily lives and routines may be altered significantly.

But what does this mean? Are we now to live in permanent fear in our own country and adopt a defensive crouch as part of our national character? Do we remake our country and our communities into fortresses? Must we sacrifice our entire foreign policy agenda in order to address this suddenly urgent problem?

Clearly, such responses are unacceptable to a free people. Even more, they are unnecessary. Without doubt, we are faced with a malevolent and implacable enemy, but we should not let its sudden emergence or its embrace of horror distort our deliberations. We must remember that we have overcome far more powerful enemies in the past, from Nazi Germany and Imperial Japan to the Soviet Union. Thus, it seems to me that this latest challenge is well within our capacity to overcome, but only if we are fully committed to the struggle that lies before us.

As President Bush has correctly stated, terrorism is not a problem that will be solved easily or quickly. We cannot eliminate this threat overnight because it did not arise overnight. It has taken root in many places, growing steadily as our attention was focused elsewhere, drawing strength from a bottomless reservoir of hatred. Given the nature of the threat, we should not expect quick victories or even a final victory. I have no doubt that we will eliminate Osama bin Laden and the al-Qaeda network, but we should not make the mistake of believing that our battle would then be won.

Let us begin by accepting that there is no single enemy to be defeated, no one network to be eliminated. Al-Qaeda is but our most prominent opponent, but its outlook is shared by many others who are equally committed to our destruction. If we believe that our safety can be secured by destroying any one organization or any single person, we will only ensure that we will remain unsafe and unprepared once again. For we now know that we have permanent, mortal enemies who will seize upon our vulnerabilities to bloody us, to murder our citizens, to commit horror for the purpose of forcing horror upon us.

There can be no dispute that we were unprepared for the assault upon us. In retrospect, the warning signs may seem obvious, but there is no person or organization we can saddle with the blame. We as a nation did not heed them.

We are now moving to correct our failings and to prepare ourselves for the task ahead. Our hopes and prayers are with our men and women in uniform on whose strength and dedication to duty the safety of our country rests, but we cannot place this burden entirely on their shoulders. If we are to be successful, our enemy must be engaged in many areas far from any battlefield, and our efforts must draw upon the energies and resources of our entire country. Our strategy, plans, and actions must be comprehensive, deliberate, and formulated for the long-term. We must be prepared not only to protect ourselves from new assaults, not only to intercept and frustrate them, but to eliminate new threats at their source. This must be a permanent campaign, similar to the ancient one humanity has waged against disease and its neverending assault on our defenses.

The optimism that is so integral a part of the American outlook often leads some to assume an image of the world that is at odds with reality, one that is peaceful and welcoming without effort. I hope that illusion is now gone. In its place should be a new recognition that peace and security exist for us only because we have created them. We have wrested them from an often hostile world, and they will continue only so long as we are prepared to defend them. The world will be safe for us only if we are prepared to make it safe.

America has always triumphed over her enemies. I have no doubt that we will do so again. But to do so, we must cast aside any illusions of an easy victory, we must take up our responsibilities, and commit ourselves to fully and completely prosecuting the conflict ahead.

We did not seek this conflict, and we cannot run from it. We have no choice but to take it up and to prevail. We have more at stake than even our own safety and that of our children and grandchildren. For this is a battle for our future and for the future of our country.

I would now like to recognize Mr. Lantos for an opening statement. [Because of time constraints, I would ask that other members place their opening statements in the record]. And then we will turn to our witnesses and what I expect will be their very enlightening testimony.

CHARLES SANTOS
PARTNER, SBS ASSOCIATES

3 October 2001

Bin Ladin, the Taliban and Terrorism

The Taliban leadership has refused to turn over Bin Ladin, citing their obligations, supposedly under tribal norms, to provide hospitality. But their relationship has nothing to do with hospitality. Mullah Omar and his Taliban provide sanctuary to Bin Ladin because he has helped the Taliban as much—or even more—than they have helped him. Both are part of the same *extremist* reality: dogmatically committed to a wider, Islamic struggle to expel western and secular influences which they view as corrupt, replacing it with their vision of purified Islamic control over the Muslim world. In this sense they are not so much looking to the past but using it to create a future—one particularly intolerant, narrow-minded and alarming. They are also both united by a willingness to pursue these ends by all means necessary.

This was not always the case. When I was the Political Advisor to the United Nations Special Mission to Afghanistan, I was the first member of the Mission to meet the Taliban Council in January 1995, two months after they emerged in Kandahar. The Taliban, as a new movement, was weak and thus inclined to allow certain less extremist, elements within its ruling Council. At that time, Bin Ladin was nowhere to be found in Taliban areas. Instead he had established a base in Eastern Afghanistan not far from Jalalabad. He started living there more permanently in the summer of 1995 under the protection of Islamicist Jihadi commanders who were opposing the Taliban.

During this period, Bin Ladin's low profile and relatively constrained situation were due to civil strife, particularly in Kabul. However, when the Taliban took control of Jalalabad and Kabul in September 1996, instead of expelling Bin Ladin, a logical conclusion given his relationship with their enemies, he was immediately moved south to Kandahar for his safety.

Bin Ladin, his family and some followers lived in Kandahar for several months in a building across from the Taliban foreign ministry offices. He clearly was given the full support and protection of the Taliban, and traveled freely around the city in an easily recognized caravan of approximately eight Toyota Hiluxes and Landcruisers. My residence was located near a complex of houses in central Kandahar, which, he was building for himself. In fact, he next moved to Kandahar Airport where he lived for more than a year. He gave the newly constructed complex in Kandahar to Mullah Omar and his Taliban leadership.

Mullah Omar publicly demonstrated his closeness to Bin Ladin on several occasions. One important occasion occurred in March 1997 during the Eid prayers after the Haj, when Omar pulled Bin Ladin from the large crowd, announcing in front of them that Bin Ladin was a friend, a brother and great holy warrior. The two then led the prayers for the tens of thousands gathered in an open field.

Why did he show such support for Bin Ladin? For Omar, the Saudi exile is first and foremost a powerful symbol of Islamic struggle and defiance, built on their common triumph over Soviet occupation. As the various mujahideen political parties were contesting Kabul, the Taliban rose to power by successfully identifying themselves not in fractious political terms, but in extremist national and religious terms. Their vision fused ethnic Pashtun hegemony with Sunni fundamentalism. The Taliban were able to promote themselves as Afghanistan's true rulers among the Pashtuns with an historic and divine mandate. They effectively consolidated power by masking their political intentions and minimizing talk of power of their political ambitions.

Bin Ladin and extremist links thus not only provided political legitimacy to his Taliban allies, but also important resources in a contest which was otherwise waged with meager means. These resources were not simply monetary: communications, training, technical expertise and crucial recruits were also provided in those campaigns reaching beyond the traditional Pashtun lands, now into areas dominated by the other Afghan ethnic minorities—*This is a crucial point, the extremist international networks fed an ethnic war machine to further their own purposes.*

As the Taliban consolidated their control with these resources, their movement began to expunge the more traditionalist elements, leaving Mullah Omar and his more radical allies in the Taliban unchallenged. At the same time, links to extremist Sunni fundamentalists in Pakistan and the Gulf deepened and expanded, which in turn provided yet more recruits and resources. International Islamicists, including crucial Pakistani support, in turn came to champion the Taliban as the true representative of a pure Islamic State built upon Islam's victory over the Communist infidels. The Taliban thus have become an integral and important part of Sunni fundamentalist mythology and its international networks, connecting them well beyond Afghanistan to Islamicists in Pakistan, the Gulf, Kashmir, Chechnya and Central Asia. Afghanistan became not only a place where extremists from around the world could meet safely, share ideas, develop strategies, and receive training—a physical base of terror— it also became a symbol to extremists of the possibilities of their mission.

Throughout, the Taliban have continued to receive support from the Government of Pakistan, whose policies have led to a growing wave of "extremism" within Pakistan as well. What was Pakistan's interest in Taliban domination of its neighbor? Often it is mentioned that Pakistan sought strategic depth as a counterweight to India as well as reconnecting Pakistan to transit routes and energy resources in Central Asia. I believe that these are valid reasons but not sufficient in explaining Pakistan's actions, which have isolated the country significantly. Most important is the growing Islamic extremism in Pakistan society, resulting from a combination of corruption, growing poverty, a disconnected elite and a government which has actively encouraged Islamicists as a means of holding together a diverse society. That policy is now out of control, producing a stronger more virulent anti-western view and a much less reliable Pakistan.

Pakistani support of the Taliban also allowed them to strengthen their control and expand their influence into the Pashtun areas of Afghanistan, which presented a historic reversal in their favor. It enabled Pakistan to relocate its training camps for Kashmiri separatists to Afghanistan, benefiting from extremist networks in Afghanistan and providing Pakistan with plausible deniability. Pakistani extremist groups have functioned as umbrella organizations for other international terror groups that sought shelter in Afghanistan.

We should be clear: The Taliban see the West through their ethno-nationalist and fundamentalist eyes as being both corrupt and potentially hostile to their campaign to impose their extremist vision, precisely as Bin Ladin and his ideological allies see America as an obstacle to a 'pure' Islamic region, untainted by westernization. Bin Ladin is neither a guest nor a foreigner in Afghanistan: he is one of them, ideologically, politically, and pragmatically.

The Taliban war machine has also benefited significantly from the trade in opium, levying a thirty percent tax and providing security for the illicit shipments.

Nonetheless, Bin Ladin's alliance with the Taliban has significant vulnerabilities: he has taken sides in a civil war in Afghanistan which *is* ethnic more than it is religious. The Taliban are for all intents and purposes Pashtun, a group that represents less than 40 percent of Afghanistan's population.   They are still the largest minority in a country of minorities—including the Shi'a Hazara, Uzbeks, Turkmens and Tajiks, to name the largest of the nine or so ethnic groups that live within the borders of Afghanistan.

The ugly truth is that the Pakistani supported Taliban-Bin Ladin extremist alliance is built on religious, cultural and ethnic domination in Afghanistan. Bin Ladin and his extremist network are vulnerable in the same way the Taliban are vulnerable—their brutal actions have completely antagonized those that live in the North and Central part of the country, and beyond as well.

There are capable leaders currently on the ground such as General Rashid Dostum, an ethnic Uzbek leader with significant forces in Northern Afghanistan; Karim Khalili, leader of the Hazara of Central Afghanitsan; Ismael Khan, an ethnic Tajik leader and former Governor of Western

Afghanistan; and Commander Fahim, an ethnic Tajik, leading forces in the Panshir Valley and Northeast Afghanistan. All are fighting to protect their people and rid their areas of the Taliban and their extremist supporters.

In the end, Osama Bin Ladin must depend on the Taliban's ability to maintain dominance over the other ethnic communities of Afghanistan. If Pashtun chauvinism however buckles, Bin Ladin and his extremist network, and most importantly, the symbol of a true and pure Islamic State that serves as an ideological as well as physical base for extremism and terror, will collapse.

To ensure that Afghanistan will no longer be a base of terror requires not only eliminating the Taliban, but crucially eliminating the idea of ethnic dominance and religious extremism. This can only happen if a system of government emerges that is democratic and provides protection and rights to all the country's ethnic communities, allowing the links of goodwill to be rebuilt among the various peoples. I believe the Alliance between the North and the former king can assist in this regard, but we should make no mistake: this will not come from any one individual. It will require a change in the thinking of many Pashtuns and a decentralized political system of government—a federal system or confederation—that accurately reflects the political aspirations of the diverse communities of Afghanistan.

STATEMENT OF OLIVER "BUCK" REVELL
PRESIDENT OF THE LAW ENFORCEMENT TELEVISION NETWORK (LETN)
FORMER ASSOCIATE DEPUTY DIRECTOR FOR INVESTIGATIONS
FEDERAL BUREAU OF INVESTIGATION

October 3, 2001

Chairman Hyde, I thank you and members of your Committee for the opportunity to testify during these hearings. Yours is an extremely important responsibility and I know that you and your colleagues want to provide the very best support that you can to our President and those in our Government, military, intelligence, diplomatic and law enforcement that must face this challenge. I will try and provide you with my honest and forthright assessment and opinions based upon the forty years that I have now been involved in this arena.

The terrible events of September 11, 2001 shall ever remain in our collective memories. I like so many other Americans lost friends in the attacks. I wish that I could tell you that the attacks could not have been anticipated and that we are unlikely to face such devastation again. I cannot. For it is very clear that we have been the targets of a sustained campaign of terrorism since 1979. The fall of the Shah of Iran and the establishment of a fundamentalist Islamic State in Iran under the Ayatollah Khomeini, and the invasion of Afghanistan by the Soviet Union in 1979 were the predicates of the tragedy that we suffered on September 11th. In Iran the Islamic extremists found that they could take and hold Americans hostage without serious repercussions. Out of that experience the Iranian back Hezbollah bombed our Embassies in Beirut twice and Kuwait once, as well as killing over two hundred Marines in a suicide truck bombing. The Hezbollah took American's hostage and hijacked our airliners and yet we seemed impotent to respond. Before we even knew of Osama bin Laden, Imad Mugniyah of the Hezbollah was the leading terrorist against America. He was directly responsible for the attacks against our personnel and facilities in Lebanon and yet he and his organization have never been punished for their crimes against our nation.

This example was not lost on the founders of al Qaida, primarily members of the Afghan mujahidin from Arab countries. Osama bin Laden and his associates' experienced first hand that guerilla warfare and terrorist tactics could defeat a "Super Power". He learned from Mugniyah that America was not likely to fight back.

Since the attack on the American Special Forces on a humanitarian mission in Somalia in 1992 bin Laden and his associates have carried out a steady and increasingly deadly campaign against America and Americans. The following are but the publicly known events:

1. Somalia 1992

2. World Trade Center, New York, 1993

3. Planned attacks against multiple targets in New York in July 1993

4. Planned assassination of Pope John Paul in the Philippines 1994 (Americans were in the Pope's entourage)

5. Planned assassination of President Clinton in the Philippines 1995

6. Planned bombings of 11-13 American Airliners over Pacific Ocean 1995

7. Car bombing of U.S. military mission in Riyadh, Saudi Arabia 1995

8. Truck bombing of U.S. Air Force housing area Khubar Towers, Dhahran, Saudi Arabia 1996

9. Truck Bombing U.S. Embassy, Kenya 1998

10. Truck Bombing U.S. Embassy, Tanzania 1998

11. Plot to bomb Los Angeles International Airport, Y2K, New Year 2000

12. Plot to bomb East Coast target, Y2K, New Year, 2000

13. Plot to attack U.S. Naval Ship in Yemen, January 2000

14. Suicide boat attack on USS Cole, Yemen October 2000

By September 11th we certainly should have known that we were the principal targets of a terrorist campaign unlike any we had ever faced. And yet we totally failed to recognize the impending disaster that stalked our nation. Some of us in the Counter-terrorist business tried to warn of the danger, but we were generally thought of as alarmists. For the purpose of lessons learned I am citing the concerns I, among others, expressed about our lack of preparedness for the struggle we now face as a war.

In a speech to a conference held by the National Institute of Justice in May of 1999 on "Terrorism & Technology: Threat and Challenge in the 21st Century" I pointed out my concerns for our lack of readiness to deal with the growing threat of terrorism. Some of these remarks are set forth below.

The rather abrupt end to the Cold War was expected to bring about a substantial improvement in international cooperation, and a concordant change in the manner in which governments dealt with transnational issues such as terrorism and organized crime. However, the expected improvements in overall safety and security of U.S. citizens and interests have not materialized except at the strategic level.

Terrorism remains a constant and viable threat to American interests on a global basis even though the sources of the threat may be evolving into heretofore unknown or undetected elements/organizations.

The threat is changing and increasing due to the following factors:

1.) The philosophy, motivation, objectives and modus operandi of terrorists groups both domestic and international has changed.

2.) The new terrorist groups are not concerned with and in many instances are trying to inflict mass causalities.

3.) Terrorist groups now have ready access to massive databases concerning the entire United States infrastructure including key personnel, facilities, and networks.

4.) Aided by state sponsors or international organized crime groups, terrorist can obtain weapons of mass destruction.

5.) The Internet now allows even small or regional terrorist groups to have a worldwide C3I (Command, Control, Communication and Intelligence) system, and propaganda dissemination capability.

6.) Domestic anti-government reactionary extremists have proliferated, and now pose a significant threat to the Federal Government and to law enforcement at all levels. Militia organizations have targeted the Federal Government for hostile actions, and could target any element of our society that is deemed to be their adversary.

7.) Islamic extremism has spread to the point where it now has a global infrastructure, including a substantial network in the United States.

Terrorism has been a tough political, analytical and operational target for years. Nonetheless, twenty years ago, analysts could agree on several "tenets of terrorism." First, terrorists were viewed as falling into one of three categories: those that were politically motivated, and used violence as a means to achieve legitimacy, such as the IRA or PLO, or; those that used violence as a means of uprising, or finally; those that were state-sponsored whose violence was manipulated by foreign powers to achieve political leverage. Second, terrorists were generally thought to calculate thresholds of pain and tolerance, so that their cause was not irrevocably compromised by their actions.

While U.S. officials worried about terrorists "graduating" to the use of weapons of mass destruction, especially nuclear, we believed that most terrorist groups thought mass casualties were counterproductive. This was because mass casualties seemed to de-legitimize the terrorists' cause, would certainly generate strong governmental responses, and erode terrorist group cohesion. In essence, we thought a certain logic and morality line existed beyond which terrorist dared not go.

The different types of terrorist groups had a wide range of motives. The extreme left's motivation for violence has been significantly diminished by the disenchantment with communism on a global scale. These groups find that their message is out-of-fashion, and they can no longer mobilize the public to their causes. This loss of motivation is a major reason for the recent downward trend in international terrorist incidents, as documented in the State Department's report, "Patterns in Global Terrorism." The threat level of all leftist groups globally, once rated high, is now considered moderate. Of the twenty-two known groups, three have denounced violence altogether. Indeed, high collateral casualties are inconsistent with the fundamental message of leftist terrorists who profess their goal to be the betterment of the masses.

State-sponsored terror has seen a notable decline in the last several years for three primary reasons. First, the Middle East peace process has given previously violent groups and states a motive to refrain from terrorism in order to gain leverage and bargaining power at the table. Second, post Cold-War geopolitical realities have brought about many new agreements and growing cooperation among nations in countering terrorism. One of the largest sponsors of terrorism in the past—the former communist East European countries—are now aggressively supporting counter-terrorism initiatives.

However, several state sponsors remain who continue to fund, motivate, support, and train terrorists. Iran is by far the most active of these state sponsors, with the greatest long-term commitment and worldwide reach. Iraq remains of concern, but has a more limited transnational capability. However, attacks within Iraq's own backyard, such as the attempted assassination of former President George Bush in 1993 during his Kuwaiti trip, and the assassinations of dissidents in Jordan, are more likely to threaten the peace and stability of the region. Syria is a more pragmatic sponsor, by providing supplies in transit, but has refrained more recently from terrorism in order to enhance its negotiating position in the peace talks. Its loss of USSR patronage has meant a decline in financial and logistical support, but it nevertheless allows some rejectionists to maintain headquarters in Syria. Hezbollah still receives supplies through the Damascus airport and operates openly in parts of Syria and Syrian controlled territory. The newest sponsor on the list is Sudan, which was added in 1993 because of its provision of safe haven and training for a variety of terrorist groups. Sudan has hosted Osama Bin Laden's facilities. Libya, a notorious state sponsor, has also refrained lately from terrorism in order to obtain some sanctions relief. It continues, however, to target dissidents, fund extremist Palestinians, and provide safe haven for Abu Nidal, all while attempting to avoid accountability for the PanAm 103 bombing. The recent surrender of the PanAm 103 suspects came only after crippling sanctions by the United Nations. For state-sponsored terrorism, the value of deterrence retains credibility, and America should not relinquish this capability.

Radical Islamic groups are now the most active in terms of the rate of incidents. Many of these groups are considered separatists, and desire a seat at the recognition and negotiation table. Others, considered extreme Islamic zealots, operate as loosely affiliated groups, as in the World Trade Center and East African bombings. For these groups deterrence has less effect. And in fact many have stated that they wanted to maximize casualties to punish the United States, which they have demonized as the Great Satan.

Ethnic separatist terrorism, as old as mankind, can be temporarily side-tracked by a few contemporary geopolitical developments, but generally, it is impervious to such developments because its root-cause is invariable long-lived. Most of these groups seek world recognition and endorsement; to date, they have not resorted to the use of weapons of mass destruction.

The "New" Terrorist, the argument has been made that while traditional terrorism—in terms of motivations—is still a large segment of the terrorist population, there is a new breed of terrorist for which the old paradigms either do not apply at all or have limited application. These groups—cults, religious extremists, anarchists, or serial killers—must be regarded as serious threats, and perhaps the most serious of the terrorist groups operating today. These "new" terrorists are driven by a different set of motivations: they seek an immediate reward for their act, and their motivations and objectives may range from rage, revenge, hatred, mass murder, extortion, or embarrassment, or any combination of these. They may desire mass casualties, or at least not care about how many people are killed in their attacks. As such, they do not make traditional calculations of thresholds of pain or tolerance within a society. These groups tend to be loosely affiliated both internationally and domestically, and may have no ties at all to state sponsorship. They change affiliations and identities as needed, and are extremely difficult to detect. Where traditional groups want publicity to further their cause, many "new" terrorists do not desire attribution; this is particularly true of the religious extremists, God knows, and will reward. Religious extremism is growing in numbers, and is not limited to the Islamic faith. While the "new" terrorist may have a variety of motivations, some single issue groups, such as, extremists in the animal rights, environmental, and anti-abortion movements, may also pose a significant threat, and can not be overlooked. Additionally, the new millennium is an important apocalyptic milestone for many religious or extremist cults. Many terrorist groups, both traditional and "new," have privatized their practices through a few standard business techniques (fund-raising, use of technology, etc.)

Also new today is the proliferation of knowledge and technology among many criminal, terrorist, and narcotics groups. Many of these groups are building skills in state-of-the-art communications, and weaponry. They are achieving new global links and support from one another in cooperative ways. While inflicting mass casualties have never been prohibitive, the barriers to their use seem to be falling.

Twenty years ago, intelligence specialists viewed proliferation of Weapons of Mass Destruction primarily through the lens of nation states seeking the ultimate weapon. Chemical and biological weaponry was only a minuscule afterthought of the whole nuclear problem.

One of the outcomes of the globalization of economies and technologies, the phenomenon that President Bush termed the "New World Order" is the relatively new linking and intermingling of disparate crime and narcotics organizations with terrorists. Analysts have been dismayed to find that even the most notorious crime groups with global reach, such as the Italian Mafia, the Russian Mafias, the Nigerian criminal enterprises, the Chinese triads, the Colombian and Mexican cartels, and the Japanese Yakuza, are developing new working relationships. They are developing cooperative arrangements, and networking with one another and with insurgent and terrorist organizations to take advantage of one another's strengths and to make inroads into previously denied regions.

This has allowed terrorists a new means to raise money as well as provide them with a marketplace to purchase sophisticated weaponry and other high tech equipment. This cooperation, for example, has long been seen among Colombian drug lords and Italian crime groups in exploiting the West European drug market, but now is seen in New York City and in Eastern Europe with drug and financial crime networks linking Russian and Italian groups.

As organized crime groups become increasingly international in the scope of their activities, they are also less constrained by national boundaries. The new lowering of political and economic barriers allows them to establish new operational bases in commercial and banking centers around the globe. The willingness and capability of these groups to move into new areas and cooperate with local groups is unprecedented, magnifying the threats to stability and even governability.

All of these transnational groups are becoming more professional criminals, both in their business and financial practices and in the application of technology. Many of them use state-of-the-art communications security that is better than some nation's security forces can crack.

The Challenge of Cyber-terrorism:

While a number of excellent studies—both classified and unclassifie—have been produced on the information warfare threat, popular journalism has also produced a great deal of hyperbole on this subject. That the National Information Infrastructure is vulnerable to an Information Warfare attack is unarguable. A recent National Intelligence Estimate verified this threat. The challenge comes in providing context and a proper appreciation of the nature of the vulnerabilities and the extent of the threat.

Traditionally, the information warfare threat has been associated with the telecommunications infrastructure and the ability to communicate. This remains a primary area of concern. But the government is also growing more and more dependent upon the commercial power, transportation, energy, and finance communities, and these communities are also vulnerable to attack. All of these major national infrastructures share a common dependency on computer driven management and control systems. With the passage of time, technical and economic imperatives have driven these infrastructures to more and more dependence on networked computer driven systems. Indeed, the complexity of the software involved in the "system-of-systems" that drive some of the major infrastructures is a significant concern.

By virtue of this increasing dependence on networked computer driven systems, all of these infrastructures possess some degree of vulnerability to infowar attack. The question is how vulnerable?

Some of the critical infrastructures (e.g., the Public Switched Telephone Network - PSTN) have been the subject of hacker attacks for years. A number of the major companies operating networks that comprise the PSTN have very robust programs to defeat toll fraud and ensure network continuity. Others have placed less emphasis on this problem and, while a structure exists to facilitate cooperation among the various companies, the level and quality of the cooperation is mixed. The continued globalization of the economy, information, and technology will provide significant new opportunities for those seeking to terrorize or intimidate. This is because the interdependencies created by such networking provide a broader base for greater destruction, especially in the areas of infowar. Concurrently, these very trends may also provide new and better means of tracking, capturing, preventing or deterring these same criminal elements. However, our own growing dependency on computer-driven systems in government, within industry, and throughout the Nation's infrastructures of oil and gas, finance, communications, power, and transportation undoubtedly increases our vulnerability. The President's Commission on Infrastructure Protection has vigorously studied the vulnerabilities of our infrastructure, however it remains to be seen if our society can effectively organize itself to protect these key assets of our nation. (The denial of service attacks launched against several major Internet sites in February of 2000 graphically demonstrates this growing threat to our National security and well being).

Whatever tools terrorists select, the fact of increasing cooperation between crime, narcotics and terrorist groups will provide terrorists with new, more creative ways to raise money and a marketplace to shop for weaponry and high tech equipment.

Weapons of mass destruction are not the only highly destructive tools that terrorists may use. As the government becomes more and more dependent upon commercial-off-the-shelf information technologies, products, and networks, it will become more vulnerable to the infowar threat. This vulnerability will not be limited to potential IW attack on the operation of support infrastructures, but also will include potential "time bomb" attack via pre-programmed imbedded software in operating systems, much, of which software is written abroad.

In addition to foreign nations placing more emphasis on developing infowar capabilities, there is growing evidence that drug cartels and other transnational groups—to include some terrorist groups—have recognized the potential for infowar and are developing capabilities. In fact, some groups, like the FARC, ELN, Provisional IRA, and the Sendero Luminoso, already target information infrastructures today for the purposes of collecting intelligence, targeting data, and monitoring of law enforcement and other government activities. In time, with the increasing availability of infowar attack information on the Internet and in other public media, transnational groups will establish some modicum of capability in this arena.

It is the American character to believe we can solve all problems with our ingenuity and hard work. But even if the United States intelligence and law enforcement communities were given the means to correct these gaps, there still would remain a significant portion of terrorist planning, preparation, operations and attacks that will be unpredictable. Just as better defenses have turned some terrorists away from harder targets, the amorphous nature of the "new" terrorism, combined with the uncertainty inherent in predictive analysis of chaotic behaviors, means that some events will remain unforeseen.

We as a nation may not be able to prevent all acts of terrorism given the nature of our democratic society. However, the new vehemence of terrorist groups and their access to both high technology and weapons of mass destruction make it imperative that we do our utmost to prevent terrorist acts and prepare for the dire consequences if we fail.

Not long after I retired from Federal service I was asked to participate in a conference on Terrorism, hosted by the Ethics and Public Policy Center in Washington. On October 11, 1996 I made a presentation to the conference entitled, " Counter-terrorism and Democratic Values: An American Practitioners Experience" This presentation outlined some of the many difficulties that we have in balancing our need for security and our desire to maintain our Constitutional protections. I have edited the remarks for brevity but believe that what I said has relevance to our current situation.

In 1980, I became an Assistant Director of the Federal Bureau of Investigation and was placed in charge of the Criminal Investigative Division of the FBI, which had responsibility for all criminal investigative programs, including Terrorism. At that time, the U.S. was suffering approximately 100–120 terrorist incidents per year. People think the World Trade Center and Oklahoma City, were the first acts of terrorism in the U.S., however, we have a very short collective memory. During this period when we were still attempting to deal with violence associated with Black power, the uproar in the civil rights movement, the anti-war movement, and so forth. We still had a very active level of terrorism by many groups in the U.S. There were a number of Puerto Rican organizations that were carrying out the most acts of terrorism. We also had the remnants of the Weather Underground that was still very active in committing acts of terrorism, including murder, assassination and bombings. We had groups that were committing terrorist acts right here in Washington—placing a bomb in the Capitol building and at the Naval base in the Potomac Basin. We had groups that were targeting the infrastructure of the U.S., carrying out bombings against power stations and communication centers. And we also had groups that were aiming at the military structure, recruit centers, depots, and so forth in the United States. In the FBI we were trying to cope with the aftermath of one of the frequent purges that goes on in our Government.

There had been no consensus in our Nation in the 60s and 70s on how to deal with major national issues, particularly the Vietnam War and anti-war movement, and to some degree the more radical elements of the civil rights movement, and therefore the Executive branch of our Government had taken certain actions, and those actions had not been by consensus. They had been essentially Presidential decisions. Some of these governmental actions included tactics that today would be considered illegal—at the time were not illegal, but were very unwise. The FBI and military intelligence as well as the CIA, engaged in activities, which sought to determine who was behind certain movements, causes and groups that carried out violent acts. Improper activities by these agencies included wiretaps and surreptitious entries into locations seeking intelligence. In most of the world today, including Britain, France, and Germany, these types of activities are still authorized by executive order of their government. In the U.S. they are not. In my view they should not be. But at the time they were.

In the mid-70s, our Nation had gone through Watergate and the turmoil that brought to our political system, and coming out of the Watergate milieu was a series of Congressional hearings called the Church and Pike Committee hearings. In these hearings the intelligence components of the U.S. Government were highly criticized for their activities during this period of time. Particularly, their spying upon elements in our society that were considered radical, but not necessarily a threat to our existence as a Nation. Of course, they never became that. So, there was no consensus in our body-politic as to the degree and extent to which the domestic law enforcement and intelligence services could and should be utilized to determine the root causes, the structure organization, membership and participants in groups, that in fact, descended into the use of systemic violence.

The Church and Pike hearings resulted in a great deal of criticism, it was primarily directed at the CIA, but the FBI got its share, including for a very misconstrued and ill-considered program called COINTELPRO. COINTELPRO was the adoption of counterintelligence methods used against a foreign power for use against domestic groups. In COINTELPRO the FBI used extralegal tactics to determine who was behind certain movements and what they were involved in and so forth. As a result, the Bureau was quite traumatized and not certain of its proper role and the legal use of executive authority in the pursuit of terrorism, although it was not even called that at the time. Terrorism was still considered a domestic security issue. Terrorism was not *en vogue* as a description for a program that the government would use, today "terrorism" or "anti-terrorism."

In the late 1970s, the FBI practically shut down its entire domestic security operation. It was dealing with specific criminal acts after the fact and had virtually no collection, analysis, or utilization of intelligence prior to the commission of any sort of violent action by a politically motivated organization. In 1980, the level of these incidents had climbed to the point where we simply believed that we had to become pro-active again, but to do so very carefully and under a set of guidelines which we had participated in designing called the Attorney General Guidelines. These guidelines were intended not only to tell us the limitations of our authority, but also to sanction those actions that we did take, and to make sure that people understood that this was a legitimate exercise of the legal authority of the President, the Attorney General, and those charged with carrying out their responsibilities. So under the Attorney General Guidelines, we began to build a more pro-active program during the early 80s. In 1982, I recommended and Director Bill Webster, who had been appointed Director of FBI in 1978, agreed to designate Terrorism as a national priority of the FBI, thereby joining counterintelligence, organized crime and white-collar crime as the principal national priorities of the FBI.

In 1982, we incurred 51 terrorist incidents, 7 people being killed and 26 being injured. There were still a number of very active groups. From 1982 until 1988, we were able to reduce terrorism in the U.S. down to the point where we were incurring only 5 to 10 incidents a year, and only three or four groups were actually still functioning. We had been able, through the use of the law, through the use of prosecution, through the use of the legal procedures, to preempt and neutralize organizations both domestic and foreign that were operating and committing acts of terrorism in the U.S.

In the late 1970s and early 1980s, in addition to domestic groups operating in the United States, we had groups that had their cause, and their base overseas. We had Sikh terrorism, Armenian terrorism, Croatian terrorism; we had terrorism from virtually every continent, but with some of their violent acts being perpetrated in the U.S. There were groups carrying out attacks against the Soviet Union, Turkey, and India, all functioning and operating in the U.S. It was a precursor to what we have today.

But because of the renewed vigor of the Counter-Terrorism program and the emphasis we had given it, we were able to prevent 56 terrorist incidents that if they had occurred, would have resulted in massive loss of life in the U.S., including assassination of foreign leaders while they visited the U.S.

Other incidents similar to PanAm 103 were prevented because of our ability to collect and utilize information under the Attorney General Guidelines.

Of course, this was also the time President Reagan's policy in Central America had become very controversial. We had another situation develop that again set back the development of a totally effective counter-terrorism program. That was a case or series of cases called CISPES—the Committee in Solidarity with the People of El Salvador was the organization. In 1982 or 1983, intelligence had been received from the CIA that this entity in the U.S. was actually a front organization for the terrorist apparatus in El Salvador and was largely funded by Cuba and the Sandinista regime in Nicaragua. The FBI developed an informant who was Salvadoran and there was a substantial amount of information coming in that indicated that CISPES was formed to support of the revolutionary element in El Salvador, which directly supported the terrorist organizations in El Salvador, particularly the " Farabundo Marti National Liberation Front" (FMLN). Information was also received that indicated CISPES was using the U.S. for fundraising, arming and even recruiting people to go to El Salvador—all in violation of U.S. law, and was otherwise engaged in activities that were illegal in the U.S. An investigation began within the Terrorism Section, utilizing FBI field offices in several locations—Dallas, New Orleans, and so forth. This case was one of several hundred pending cases in the Terrorism Section at the time. It never reached the level of the Assistant Director in charge of Criminal Investigations, which I was when the case began, or later the Executive Assistant Director for Investigations, which I was at the time that the difficulties developed. The reason it didn't is because no extraordinary investigative techniques were used—there were no wiretaps, there were no undercover operations, the information was gathered from attending public meetings, from physical surveillance, from the use of informants, all of which were authorized under the Attorney General Guidelines. But, because of the heightened political dichotomy and the disagreement between the President and the Congress, we had a Democratic Congress and a Republican President (this became a focal point for a clash of philosophies, and particularly strategies in dealing with Central America), it became very much a *cause celebe.*

While not denying that there had been mistakes made in the investigation and some violations of our own regulations, the charges against the FBI were that: 1) it was involved in a political investigation; 2) that it was using illegal tactics; and 3) it was violating the Constitutional rights of those involved in this movement. In fact the investigations by the FBI, by the Justice Department, and by the Senate Intelligence Committee, found that none of those allegations were true. There was no political involvement whatsoever on the part of the Reagan Administration—they were not even cognizant that we were involved in this investigation when it was opened. The investigation had been reviewed by the Justice Department's Office of Intelligence Policy and Oversight early on and had been sanctioned as a legitimate investigation. There had been no violation of anyone's Constitutional rights. No one had been prohibited from attending meetings, from speaking their piece or from carrying out their activities, from engaging in all of the protected activities. No one had been impeded, obstructed, or in any way intimidated into not engaging in those activities. Nor had any FBI agent committed any violation of law other than the case agent who was involved in a financial fraud in dealing with informant payments. But that had nothing to do with the members of the CISPES organization.

Then *The New York Times* and *The Washington Post* said, "The FBI admits that it was engaged in illegal actives as they did during COINTELPRO," which was nonsense. I testified before the Senate Intelligence Committee although I had not been personally involved in the CISPES investigation; it had never risen to my level for approval. But in looking at case, I felt there was substantial justification for at least part of the investigation and I was extremely worried that we would suffer again what we had gone through in the late 70s and early 80s. In that the Senate inquiry would jeopardize careers of people who were honestly trying to do their very best to prevent acts of terrorism in the U.S., and who had no ulterior motive except to defend their Country. Unfortunately, that's exactly what happened. In 1988 again we almost went down to ground zero in carrying out our counter-terrorism responsibilities. And that's what led us, in my view, to what happened at the 1993 World Trade Center bombing. Before the World Trade Center, there was an assassination in New York of an individual who was known to most of you, Rabbi Meir Kahane. Rabbi Kahane was himself an extremist. He created an organization—the Jew Defense League (JDL)—, which also engaged in acts of terrorism in the U.S. He engendered a group in Israel that ultimately, I think, committed acts of terrorism, or at least facilitated acts of terrorism, including by an American Jewish doctor who had moved to Israel—Dr. Goldstein. And some of his more active followers fled from the U.S. while under investigation for assassinating a Palestinian-American in Los Angeles and were essentially given sanctuary in Israel—which was one of the difficulties that we had at the time. The New York City Police Department carried out the investigation of the assassination of Meir Kahane with the FBI looking over their shoulder to see if there was anything of interest for the Bureau. I was in charge of Bureau operations at the time and I never received any information that the assassin of

Meir Kahane was connected with any sort of organization that might have a terrorist agenda.

As it turns out later, as we see after the World Trade Center, there was substantial information available that if it had been properly translated, processed, authenticated and analyzed, would have led to a direct association between the assassin of Meir Kahane and the group that conspired and eventually did bomb the World Trade Center, and was conspiring to carry out a number of other heinous acts of terrorism. A proper analysis of the Kahane assassination was not conducted. By-and-large the reason it didn't get done was because of the political climate and the fact that FBI agents were loathe to undertake anything that had any appearance of being involved in the political process. That includes religious activity, free speech, etc., that are obviously protected under our Constitution. It had become very difficult to assess how to deal with those issues.

When I left Washington in May 1991, we were feeling pretty good. The Cold War had ended, we believed our side had won, Communism in the U.S. and the affiliated organizations were largely defunct. Communism as a global movement was essentially discredited. Terrorism was held in check in the U.S. and was descending on an international scale, at least the international acts of terrorism, although terrorism still was very evident in certain countries— Algeria, Israel, India, Northern Ireland, etc. But as far as the U.S., we were becoming less and less a victim. We had defeated Saddam Hussein in an unprecedented alliance and in doing so had countered his threat of global terrorism without any serious losses.

All in all we had done a good job in dealing with the threat of terrorism in spite of a lot problems along the way. Of course, the Iran-Contra controversy arose and there were new allegations that we had again been manipulated and used by the Reagan Administration, which were also untrue. But it took a while to sort this out. However by 1991, I felt very good about leaving Washington, finishing my career in Texas and moving on into another life after government.

Then in 1993 the World Trade Center bombing occurred. Although I was in Texas at the time, we started seeing a nexus between certain people in Texas, particularly in the Dallas/Richardson area, and those directly involved in the World Trade Center. This heightened my interest as to what was really involved. Was this the act of a very small group that was independent and now defunct because of the investigation? Or did it really indicate a much larger and perhaps more global conspiracy?

Unfortunately, perhaps the most informative trial, or series of trials, in the history of the United States, as it relates to the issue of international terrorism, was overshadowed. During the entire course of the New York trials for the WTC bombing, some of the most important testimony, some of the most important revelations about an international movement, which had targeted the U.S. for vicious acts of terrorism on a global basis, was almost totally ignored. The Terrorism trial of the Century was totally overshadowed by a tragic soap opera (The O.J. Simpson trial) from Los Angles. It would have been very instructive to academia, to the media, to our Congress, to have paid attention to what was going on in that trial. The trial revealed a global conspiracy not necessarily of a huge magnitude, but with a very sophisticated capability. One of the individuals who escaped the initial arrests, Ramzi Yousef, went on to plan a whole series of additional acts of terrorism, including the simultaneous bombings of between 11 and 13 U.S. airliners flying from Asia to the U.S., which was planned to occur in January 1995. They had already developed the technology, they had tested it, it had in fact worked—it killed a Japanese citizen aboard a Philippine airliner, they had tested it in a theater, it had worked, they had developed the techniques to put explosive devices on board aircraft, and were fully engaged in the plot to carry out these simultaneous bombings of the U.S. air fleet.

Growing out of the investigation into the World Trade Center, the Bureau through the Joint Terrorism Task Force detected a continuing conspiracy, that had not even slowed down because of the arrests, to carry out bombings on July 4, 1993, of the Lincoln and Holland tunnels, the George Washington bridge, the UN building, and the Federal building housing the FBI. This group also planned a number of political assassinations, including the president of Egypt and a senator from New York. If they had been successful these attacks would have cost several thousand lives. The conspirators were already present in the U.S. and were actively utilizing the protections of our Constitution to aid and facilitate their ability to operate and conspire to carry out these terrorist acts. We also saw certain potentially connected activities overseas, the bombing of the Israeli embassy in Buenos Aires, followed up by a terrible bombing of the Jewish Community Center in Buenos Aires, an attempted bombing in Bangkok, and a bombing in London, by an organization that was functioning and operating that neither the U.S. government nor Allied governments had come to grips with as of yet.

We started to get a handle on this group. The investigations were and are being conducted under the Foreign Counterintelligence Guidelines, which gives somewhat more latitude than the domestic guidelines do, and through the help of some people like Yigal Carmon and Steve Emerson, the Bureau started to understand and appreciate that it was dealing with a much wider conspiracy than just those involved in the World Trade Center bombing.

However, the bombing of the Federal Building in Oklahoma City on April 19, 1995, again demonstrated that our government was not properly prepared to address the specter of domestic Terrorism. The FBI was ill prepared to deal with this phenomenon because it was not investigating the growth of the anti-government militias and similar organizations at the time. Oklahoma City occurred on Wednesday. On Sunday morning I was asked to appear on Face the Nation, immediately prior to my appearance was Leon Panetta, the President's Chief of Staff. Mr. Panetta comes on and says, "Not to worry. The FBI knows all about these organizations and it has things in hand." I'm the next person and my comment is, "It isn't so". "The FBI does not have it in hand, the FBI has not been investigating these organizations, the FBI is not even aware of the totality of the militia movement." In fact, if it hadn't been for the Anti-Defamation League and the Southern Poverty Law Center, I don't think many people in the U.S., including the FBI, would have known much about the militia movement at all. The reason is because under the Attorney General Guidelines as interpreted at the time—and still—the FBI did not believe nor did the Justice Department believe that the FBI had the authority to collect information on groups that openly espouse the use of force and violence unless and until there is a criminal predicate. In other words, that there has been an action taken that would be an indication of a criminal offense in progress, or had that already occurred. The espousal of violence, the collections of arms, as long as the arms were not illegal, and organizing to commit violence, these things would not necessarily have predicated an investigation, and in fact with the militias they had not. We were faced with a situation in that not only did we have evidence of a growing militant, extremist element from overseas based on a misinterpretation of Islam, but we also had within our own country a growing network of groups and individuals who misperceived the entire rationale for our Constitutional form of government and blamed the government for all of the ills that they and our society were subject to. So, we had these twin concerns, one totally domestic, one primarily international, both coming to bear upon the safety and the security of the people of the United States.

No government can totally protect all the people, all the locations, all of the activities in their nation, no matter how high the level of security at any given time, if a person or group is prepared to carry out a terrorist act no matter the risks involved and whatever the consequences might be. In the United States today, we're faced with a dilemma, we do not as a people trust our government entirely to protect us from acts of terrorism, particularly if they are motivated by political or religious beliefs, and at the same time, we expect our government to protect us from terrorism and political violence. We have not reached a level of comfort with what authority we should grant to the counter-terrorism agencies and entities of our government with that responsibility. But at the same time we expect them to be effective. And we've had a very strange coalition develop over the last two to three years in our Congress where elements of the left and the elements of the right have coalesced and come together to oppose a President of the Democratic Party and the leadership of the Republican Party in Congress, in putting together anti-terrorism legislation that has been supported through three Administrations. Which would withstand Constitutional scrutiny, most elements of which have already been ruled on by the Supreme Court in other forms, such as the roving wiretap issue, which has already been adjudicated in organized crime and drug cases as being Constitutional.

There is no consensus in our society as to how far we will allow the counter-terrorism forces to proceed. Under the guidelines as they are today, the FBI is in the very unusual position of being perhaps the only people in our society who cannot take official cognizance of what people say, of what people do, of what people pronounce and promulgate that they will do until they do it. A professor, an institute, a newsman, can collect this information, can analyze it, collate it, can make pronouncements on it, can issue statements of concern, can say the government ought to be doing something or ought not to be doing something, but the FBI cannot. It is prohibited under the current guidelines and a provision of the Privacy Act, from collecting public information even from groups who directly espouse the use of violence to accomplish their objectives. We have already seen a terrorist organization, which was in actuality both a political movement and a religious cult, called the Aum Shinrikyo in Japan, turn to the use of a very dangerous gas—Sarin—developed by the Nazi regime before World War II, with the potential loss of life in its use of thousands. A dozen Japanese citizens were killed and thousands were injured, but that was fortunate. They hadn't really perfected their delivery system as yet, but they intended to kill thousands of people of people. The Aum specifically targeted the Japanese National Police in these attacks and tried to assassinate the Commissioner General of the Police. Their ultimate goal was to bring down the Government of Japan.

We've seen chemical weapons used by outlaw regimes; we've seen the capability of use of chemical weapons obtained by terrorist organizations. In the United States we have people that support and are involved in the militia movement, collect biologicals, including anthrax, which is probably one of the most lethal diseases that could ever be released, and yet it is easily obtainable. We have botulism that can be cultured and proliferated by obtaining a small amount of the toxin. We've already seen terrorist organizations and state sponsors of terrorism utilize these types of weapons of mass destruction, and we have a continuing, growing proliferation of nuclear materials coming out of the former Soviet Union that may not lead to the development of a nuclear device but could certainly lead to contamination through spreading nuclear materials by the use of a conventional explosive device.

As the threat escalates, and we've already seen terrorists utilize weapons of mass destruction, we as a society have not yet as even determined how we're going to utilize and authorize our counter-terrorist forces to prevent acts of terrorism. In a discussion with Senator Specter, during the CISPES inquiry, I asked him, "Senator, do you want us to wait until there's blood on the streets to act? Or are you going to authorize us to act on information that any reasonable person would assume to be true?" And he said, "In a democratic society, you may have to wait until there's blood on the street." If that's one person, maybe society can accept it. If 50,000 people are killed in the World Trade Center bombing, which was the intent of the terrorists, will we as a society accept that? 168 people were killed in Oklahoma City and it traumatized our society. What would the death of 50,000 have done? What would the blowing up of 12 or 13 PanAm 103s do to our society? What would be the reaction of our Congress? Do you think they would stop with the FBI being able to collect public information? Or would we see internments, would we see mass expulsions, would we see the *writ of habeas corpus suspended*? Would we see Draconian measures? I'm concerned that our society would overreact.

As a person that has dealt with enforcing the law for thirty years, that concerns me greatly. In the United Kingdom, from which our legal system was developed, they have suspended the right of trial by jury, they've suspended the *writ of habeas corpus*, they've allowed investigative detention without charge, they've engaged in wiretaps and electronic surveillance without court order, and this is in a society that is civil and democratic and certainly is one that we look to as one of the founding nations of democracy. The British, the French, the Germans, all use extralegal means to combat terrorists. We do not, we should not, and we don't have to. But we have to reach a reasonable balance to allow those elements of our society charged with preventing terrorism an opportunity to carry out their duties and do their jobs.

Right now the balance is not there.

I wish that I could tell you it is my belief that we won't have additional World Trade Centers, PanAm 103s, and Oklahoma Citys—I have no such expectation. There have been some improvements, but they are not what they should be to put us in a position to have a reasonable chance to prevent the kind of events and terrible incidents that I've described. As the potential use of even more devastating weapons increases, we have not increased our capabilities.

Do I think that we ought to impose Draconian measures on our society to prevent terrorism? Absolutely not, that would allow the terrorists to win. But we must find a reasonable balance. We can find a reasonable balance under the Constitution. There's no question that we can. We need the political will and we need public attention for more than 24 hours. In our society, that is very difficult to achieve. But this is a battle we must win to protect our nation from the scourge of terrorism.

Chairman Hyde I am certain that you and your Committee will determine that we need better tools to deal with the problems that increase our vulnerabilities. I only ask that we learn from our past mistakes and oversights. I sincerely believe that we must restructure our Intelligence and Federal law enforcement agencies if we are to come to grips with this most elusive and insidious enemy. Our Nation must be able to protect itself from those who come here to attack our citizens and attempt to destroy our Country and our way of life.

Thank you.

TESTIMONY OF VINCENT CANNISTRARO
FORMER CIA CHIEF OF COUNTERTERRORISM OPERATIONS
AND ANALYSIS

October 3, 2001

I am pleased to appear before this committee to provide my views on al-Qaeda, its structure and its objectives. It is important to note that Americans have a difficult time in understanding extremist organizations with a religious orientation like al-Qaeda. It is essential that the agencies of our government involved in law enforcement and intelligence become intimately familiar with the culture of religious zealots whether of foreign or domestic origin. We must understand the nature of the threat before we can successfully confront it. In America, we also have fundamentalists such as Christian Identity, and other religious extremists who kill or maim in the name of God. Comprehending the danger and the mind-set of these groups is a first step to deterring the violence executed by the Osama Bin Laden's of the world. Unless we know what drives these religious extremists, who are willing to kill themselves in the performance of their violent acts, we will see days like September 11, 2001, repeated, perhaps with even greater casualties.

It is worth studying the evolution of the al-Qaeda group. Bin Laden, who opposes the American influence in the Middle East, was outraged by the 1990 Persian Gulf War which saw American and other western troops stationed in Saudi Arabia. Bin Laden considers the country, ruled by the Al-Sau'd family, as the guardian of the Islamic holy places. King Abd'al aziz al-Sau'd, who founded the monarchy, had the support of the Wahabis, the fundamentalist Islamic sect. The al-Sau'd monarchy derives its authority from the Wahabis, who allied with Abd'al aziz, in creating modern Saudi Arabia. In return, the monarchy serves to guarantee the sanctity of Mecca and Medina, the site and magnetic pole for pilgrimages by the world's Muslims. In Bin Laden's view, the Saudi monarchy betrayed that sacred pact by allowing Christian and Jewish soldiers to be stationed on the soil of this Islamic country which had been entrusted with a special protectorate mission for the holy places. Bin Laden's opposition to the monarch resulted in his expulsion from the Kingdom. Shortly after, Bin Laden used his personal fortune and continuing contributions from wealthy Islamic businessmen in Saudi and the Gulf to organize training camps in the Sudan for Islamic activists from every major Islamic country. These contributions, plus revenues from Islamic Charity fronts, such as the International Islamic Relief Organization, headed by Bin Laden's brother-in-law, as well as numerous other charitable fronts, continue to fuel his group today.

The international cadres that comprise many of the networks associated with al-Qaeda, were trained by so-called "Arab-Afghans" with fighting experience from the Soviet-Afghan war, although many of these "mujahedin" did not reach Afghanistan until after the Soviet withdrawal in 1989. The main mission for Bin Laden was to disperse trained fighters to their native lands to fight against the secular Arab regimes and replace them with religious governments based on the Sharia- Islamic rather than civil law. The targets were secular Muslim countries such as Egypt and Algeria, and Muslim dominated provinces such as Chechnya and Dagestan in Russia and in Bosnia and Kosovo. Anti-government movements were also promoted in Libya and Tunisia as well. Indeed, Bin Laden's vision is to re-establish the "Islamic Caliphate" across every Muslim country, a religious restoration of the old Ottoman Empire, this time under the leadership of the Taliban leader, Mullah Omar. Usama sees the United States and its world influence as the principal obstacle to achieving his vision.

Bin Laden relocated his operations to Afghanistan following pressure on the Sudan exerted by Saudi Arabia and the U.S. The Taliban, a group of religious students from Pakistani schools, were successful in establishing control over Afghanistan with the active military support of Pakistan's military intelligence service, the Inter Services Directorate (ISI). Pakistan's concern was to promote ethnic Pashtun control over the country, which was being run by Afghans hostile to Pashtun rule and Pakistani influence. The Pashtuns, or Pathans in common western usage, designates several dozen separate tribes on both sides of the Afghan/Pakistani border. The Taliban, lacking a secular education, is almost medieval in its concept of governance. The Taliban rulers have mismanaged the country, but have been amenable to Pakistani political influence although not totally subservient to it. Pakistan has also used its position and support to the Taliban to establish within Afghanistan a series of training camps for Kashmiri terrorists. ISI personnel are present, in mufti, to conduct the training. This arrangement allowed Pakistan "plausible denial" that it is promoting insurgency in Kashmir. Pakistan also provisioned the Taliban with weapons to fight the "Northern Alliance" which contests Taliban control over the country and had until recently about 7% of Afghan territory, mostly north of Kabul and in the Panshir. The Northern Alliance, while including some Pashtuns, has been commanded by Ahmad Shah Massud, an ethnic Tajik. About three weeks ago, Massud was assassinated by suicide bombers identified as part of Bin Laden's group.

The bonds between Mullah Omar, and Usama Bin Laden, are bonds of blood and Bin Laden has offered "bayat" to Mullah Omar, an offering of submission to his will and his leadership. Bin Laden recently declared Taliban-ruled Afghanistan as the "new Mecca" and Mullah Omar as the new caliph. It is therefore all but impossible for Mullah Omar to turn over Bin Laden to the U.S. for prosecution as the U.S. has demanded. The

Taliban and Bin Laden's estimated 4,000 to 5,000 fighters are intertwined with the Taliban military and Mullah Omar considers Bin Laden as his right hand.

What is Al-Qaeda? The Arabic word means the "Base," or "foundation." Bin Laden does not refer to his international network as al-Qaeda. This word refers to his companion in arms at his headquarters in Southern Afghanistan. In his camps perhaps 10,000 Bangladeshi, Pakistani, Tunisian, Moroccan, Algerian, Egyptian and ethnic Chechens, Dagestanis, Kosovars and dozens of other nationalities have been trained. Some of them are provided specialized intelligence training, some schooled in the arts of making improvised explosive devices, and others given instruction in the production and use of chemical weapons. Those not chosen for specialized tasks are given combat training and either sent back to their native countries to foment insurgency against their secular regimes or enlisted in his combat brigade that fights alongside the Taliban against the Northern opposition. For the past four years, Bin Laden's men have fought with the Taliban against Massud, and have suffered the losses of at least seven hundred to a thousand men in the fighting, including one of Bin Laden's own sons about seven months ago.

It is important to distinguish between the so-called "loose networks" of affiliated groups, and the tightly controlled inner circle of al-Qaeda that conceives and implements their strategic operations. The bombing of the USS Cole, for example, was a tightly controlled al-Qaeda operation that had some local support, drawn from the Islamic Army of Aden, a radical Islamic group in the Yemen set up by Bin Laden's brother-in-law and funded by Usama. The operation was apparently directed by Muhammad Atef, an Egyptian who serves as Bin Laden's Chief of Operations. It was Atef's daughter who married one of Bin Laden's sons last May, a marriage that also symbolized the merger of the Egyptian Islamic Jihad into al-Qaeda, and a new name for the inner circle: "Jidad al-Qaeda."

The Ahmad Ressam case, was an example of the use of affiliated groups by al-Qaeda to promote violence against America. This was the "millennium" plot frustrated when Ressam panicked at the Canadian/US border while transporting materials for five bombs. Ressam, a member of an Algerian terrorist faction funded and supported by Bin Laden, was trained at an al-Qaeda camp in Afghanistan and given $12,000 seed money. He was told to raise the rest of the monies needed through criminal activity in Canada, organize his cell, and choose targets in America to destroy. Ressam planned to plant bombs at Los Angeles International Airport, to kill as many people as possible. At the same time, a more centrally controlled and sensitive al-Qaeda operation was being implemented in the port of Aden, against the USS Sullivans, the sister ship of the Cole. The explosives laden boat sank in the harbor while being piloted by the two would-be suicide bombers. They swam back to shore, and went to ground, certain that their abortive operation would be discovered. It was not. About 8 months later, the same operation, using more sophisticated and lighter explosives, was carried out against the Cole. The devastating results are well known.

How does the al-Qaeda organization fund its worldwide network of cells and affiliated groups? Several businessmen in Saudi Arabia and in the Gulf contribute monies. Many of these contributions are given out of a sense of Islamic solidarity. But much of the money is paid as "protection" to avoid having the enterprises run by these men attacked. There is little doubt that a financial conduit to Bin Laden was handled through the National Commercial Bank, until the Saudi government finally arrested a number of persons and closed down the channel. It was evident that several wealthy Saudis were funneling contributions to Bin Laden through this mechanism. Now, it appears, that these wealthy individuals are siphoning off funds from their worldwide enterprises in creative and imaginative ways. For example, orders may be given to liquidate a stock portfolio in New York, and have those funds deposited in a Gulf, African or Hong Kong bank controlled by a Bin Laden associate. Other channels exist for the flow of monies to Bin Laden, through financial entities in the UAE and Qatar. Cash, carried to intermediaries, is also a source of funding. There are some female members of Bin Laden's own family who have been sending cash from Saudi Arabia to his "front" accounts in the Gulf.

I will stop my remarks here, and I am prepared to address any questions you may have.

DOCUMENT NO.15

STATEMENTS AT A HEARING OF THE SUBCOMMITTEE ON
GOVERNMENT EFFICIENCY, FINANCIAl MANAGEMENT AND
INTERGOVERNMENTAL RELATIONS OF THE HOUSE COMMITTEE
ON GOVERNMENT REFORM

"A SILENT WAR: ARE FEDERAL, STATE AND LOCAL GOVERNMENTS
PREPARED FOR BIOLOGICAL AND CHEMICAL ATTACKS?"

CHAIRMAN STEPHEN HORN
DR. AMY E. SMITHSON
MR. BRUCE P. BAUGHMAN, FEMA
MS. JANET HEINRICH, GAO

October 5, 2001

COMMENTARY: *The short answer to the question posed at this Hearing is probably"no" but the answers given to the problem presented vary. What is still clear, from all perspectives, is that the proliferation of agencies and programs addressing the terrorism problem must stop or the increasing funding for new programs will merely scatter dollars across the States without effecting any improvements in our capability to cope with terrorism.*

OPENING STATEMENT OF
CHAIRMAN STEPHEN HORN

A quorum being present, this hearing of the Subcommittee on Government Efficiency, Financial Management and Intergovernmental Relations will come to order.

On September 11, 2001, the world witnessed the most devastating and horrific attacks ever committed on United States soil. Despite the damage and enormous loss of life those attacks caused, they failed to cripple the nation. To the contrary, this nation has never been more united in its fundamental belief in freedom and its willingness to protect that freedom.

The diabolical nature of those attacks was an unimaginable wake-up call to all Americans: We must be prepared for the unexpected. We must have the mechanisms in place to protect this nation and its people from further attempts to cause such massive destruction.

Today, the subcommittee will examine the nation's ability to respond to the possibility of a biological or chemical attack. Even though most experts believe that the likelihood of such an attack is relatively low, we must ensure that the nation has an emergency management structure that is prepared to handle even the most remote possibility of such an attack.

The aftermath of the September 11th attacks clearly demonstrated the need for adequate communications systems and rapid deployment of well-trained emergency personnel. Yet despite billions of dollars in spending on Federal emergency programs, there are serious questions as to whether the nation's public health system is equipped to handle a massive chemical or biological attack.

A September 2000 report from the General Accounting Office found that the 1999 outbreak of the West Nile Virus severely taxed the New York public health system. This outbreak, which was ultimately contained, affected hundreds of people. A biological attack could affect thousands more.

Today, the subcommittee will examine how effectively Federal, State and local agencies are working together to prepare for such emergencies. We want the people of this nation to know that they can rely on these systems, should the need arise.

I want to note that we had hoped to have Mayor Rudolph Guiliani with us today, but the city's on-going needs, rightly, take a higher priority. At the conclusion of today's hearing, we will recess and reconvene at a later date to allow the Mayor an opportunity to contribute his expertise to this hearing. In addition, the subcommittee will be conducting similar hearings throughout the country.

We are fortunate to have witnesses today whose valuable experience and insight will help the subcommittee better understand the needs of those on the front lines—representatives of the nation's hospitals, and its cities, counties and States. We want to hear about their capabilities and their challenges. And we want to know what the federal government can do to help.

We welcome all of our witnesses and look forward to their testimony.

PREPARED STATEMENT OF AMY E. SMITHSON, PH.D.
DIRECTOR, CHEMICAL AND BIOLOGICAL WEAPONS
NONPROLIFERATION PROJECT
HENRY L. STIMSON CENTER

5 October 2001

Mr. Chairman, members of the committee, allow me to thank you not only for the invitation to appear here today, but for asking several of the key questions that Congress and the Executive Branch must consider if this nation is to achieve heightened preparedness to cope with the aftermath of a terrorist attack. My guidelines from the committee indicated I should address the following questions:

- How are the federal, state, and local levels of government interacting on the terrorism preparedness issue?

- Where are there plans/programs in place? Where do vulnerabilities exist?

- How well are the various levels working together?

- How is the federal government supporting local efforts? Where is the federal government in the way?

- What can Congress do to improve things? What can the Executive Branch do?

- How can the new Office of Homeland Security be most effective?

Should Washington's policy makers not listen closely to the answers to these questions, I am concerned that they will spend taxpayer dollars unwisely in ways that make little preparedness difference.

My answers to these questions amplify the voices of front-line public safety and health officials from 33 cities in 25 states that I interviewed from February 1999 to September 2000. Since the publication of the report that resulted from these interviews, titled *Ataxia: The Chemical and Biological Terrorism Threat and the US Response*, my co-author Leslie-Anne Levy and I continue to interact with front-line officials from these and other cities on an almost daily basis. These individuals draw upon their lengthy experience in responding to all manner of emergencies and disasters for a series of practical recommendations about how federal preparedness programs can be improved. In all candor—and these rescuers rarely mince words—front-line responders are dismayed at the disarray of the federal government's preparedness programs. Any time the subject of federal leadership of terrorism preparedness programs was broached, the local officials gave eerily similar replies, which can be paraphrased as: "They've been at this for five years and they still can't figure out who is in charge." I was told time and time again that "all the federal agencies constantly preach at us about everybody working together at the local level, but it doesn't take a rocket scientist to see they are fighting with each other tooth and nail over the money and missions."

The Case that Started the Hyperbole

Despite what you might have heard over the last couple of weeks, there are meaningful technical hurdles that stand between this nation's citizens and the ability of terrorist groups to engage in mass casualty attacks with chemical and biological agents. The technical obstacles are so high that even terrorists that have had a wealth of time, money, and technical skill, as well as a determination to acquire and use these weapons, have fallen short of their mark. Chapters two and three of *Ataxia* elaborate on this at quite some length, including a re-examination of the lessons that should be learned from the very terrorist group that got the hyperbole started, Aum Shinrikyo. To summarize, although the results of the cult's 20 March 1995 sarin gas attack were unfortunate enough—12 dead, 54 critically and seriously injured, and several thousand more so frightened that they fled to hospitals—Aum's large corps of scientists hit the technical hurdle that is likely to stymie other groups that attempt to follow in its wayward path. They were unable to figure out how to make their $10 million, state-of-the-art sarin production facility work and therefore were unable to churn out the large quantities of sarin that would be needed to kill thousands. As for Aum's germ weapons program, it was a flop from start to finish because the technical obstacles were so significant.

Preparing for More than Terrorism

Now, the sobering news. This country needs to be better prepared to contend with chemical and biological disasters regardless of whether terrorists ever manage to overcome these technical hurdles, for the following reasons. First, according to 1999 statistics from the Environmental Protection Agency, there are about 850,000 facilities in the United States working with hazardous or extremely hazardous substances. Many of these sites are located in urban areas, and transport of hazardous substances is a routine matter. Every year, over 60,500 accidents and incidents occur at these facilities or during the transport of these chemicals. In the past decade, about 95 percent of the counties in this nation have experienced this type of emergency. Accordingly, it stands to reason that US rescue crews and hospitals need to be well prepared to contend with chemical casualties. Also, the truth of the matter is that terrorists intent on causing mass casualties with chemicals could contemplate sabotaging one of these facilities rather than wrestling with the more complex warfare agents.

Readiness for a biological disaster is also essential because even if a future disease calamity never arrives courtesy of terrorists, mankind is still in a race against time to develop new medications before the natural mutation of pathogens renders impotent all of those currently on the shelves. For many a year, the nation's most esteemed scientists and public health watchdog organizations have talked of a looming global public health crisis that would plunge medicine back to the pre-antibiotic era. Human development that encroaches further on previously untouched ecosystems is rousing new diseases. Moreover, physicians increasingly find that their arsenal of medications is powerless against old diseases that keep resurfacing. Penicillin is no longer effective against 30 percent of *Streptococcus pneumoniae* cases, 11 percent of pneumonia cases are also resistant to third generation, cephalosporin antibiotics, and reports have begun to surface of cases that are not susceptible even to the newer fluoroquinolone treatments. Given the crystal clear data on how microbes are ganging up on mankind, the Institute of Medicine, the American Society of Microbiology, the now-defunct Office of Technology Assessment, and the World Health Organization, among other respected bodies, have given virtually identical counsel about the exigency of boosting medical research to counter the twin threats of emerging infectious diseases and antibiotic resistant disease strains. In sum, it is only a matter of time before a strain of influenza as virulent as the one that swept this country in 1918 or some other disease reappears. The nation's public health capabilities and hospitals need to be readied.

Foundations of Preparedness

The bedrocks of chemical and biological disaster preparedness already exist at the local and state levels. Scattered across the country are some 650 city, county, and state hazardous materials (hazmat) response teams composed of specialists who contend on a regular basis with the aforementioned accidents and incidents. Laboratories and personnel at all levels of the nation's public health system would play a critical role in biological disaster response, particularly in the detection and control of an outbreak. Medical personnel, from paramedics to nurses and physicians, are essential for the treatment of both chemical and biological casualties. Law enforcement personnel would be important for security and criminal investigation missions after any such disaster. Finally, emergency management capabilities exist in the country's major cities and at the state level.

Over the last few years, many of those firefighters, police, paramedics, physicians, nurses, emergency managers, and public health officials have become better prepared to handle the specialized demands of a chemical or biological disaster, thanks to the Domestic Preparedness Program initiated in 1996 by Senators Sam Nunn (D-Georgia, ret.), Richard Lugar (R-Indiana), and Pete Domenici (R-New Mexico). This program's initial goal was to enhance unconventional terrorism response capabilities in the country's 120 largest metropolitan areas, through training, equipment, and planning programs.

The backbone of a federal response to a chemical or biological disaster was in place long ago. The Federal Response Plan, which dates to 1992, divvies up key response missions among federal departments and agencies. For example, the branches of government that would be at the forefront of a federal response would be the Federal Emergency Management Agency, the Department of Health and Human Services, and the Federal Bureau of Investigation. The essential role for the federal government to fulfill is mid- and long-term disaster recovery, which is mainly FEMA's bailiwick. In a major disease outbreak, HHS would trigger activation of civilian medical teams and the national pharmaceutical stockpile. In a chemical or biological disaster, some of the Defense Department's chemical decontamination units and medical personnel could be called upon, depending upon the severity of the disaster and the sufficiency of civilian assets at the local, state, and federal level.

Also, recent federal allocations have spurred some critically needed improvements within the nation's public health system, perhaps the most vital player in the case of either a natural or man-made disease outbreak. The object of neglect for decades, the system has benefited from a badly needed infusion of funds that has expanded laboratory capabilities to detect the rarely seen diseases that could be employed if such an outbreak were to occur.

The Need for Federal and Congressional Coordination

Yet, as one might expect, there is always room for improvement. According to the survey that I conducted, local public safety and public health personnel in these cities assessed themselves as being more ready to deal with a chemical disaster than with a biological one. Chapter six of *Ataxia* contains more detail about where the particular problem areas are in each kind of disaster response. Federally, the main challenge is not that more assets need to be built but that federal involvement needs to be coordinated and streamlined. Dozens of federal entities have been fiercely competing for the missions and money associated with unconventional terrorism response, an unfortunate circumstance that has resulted in redundant capabilities, wasteful spending, and, at the local level, confusion as to which agency would spearhead the federal component of a response.

Perhaps it was inevitable that the launch of resource-rich programs with high-profile missions would be accompanied by considerable friction between the federal agencies involved. As the Domestic Preparedness Program training, equipment, and planning efforts unfurled, federal authorities preached the importance of local response agencies working hand-in-hand and claimed that they would do so themselves. Front-line rescuers, however, got the distinct impression that the federal agencies were locked in an intense competition for terrorism preparedness missions and money. Local suspicions of a federal turf battle could be confirmed when the federal partners spoke, as they did at a mid-April 1999 conference. A Pentagon official stated: "We have ramped up tremendously over the last eighteen months. We have new assets, like the [National Guard Civil Support] teams. Some of them make sense and some of them have just been generated through the process." Afterwards, a representative of the Federal Emergency Management Agency added: "We have a fairly small amount of money at stake here. We'd certainly like to have more." Next, an official from HHS chimed in with, "We don't lack for authority. We lack for people and money." Small wonder then, that the locals found the federal "work together" sermon to be hypocritical. The locals continue to have trouble figuring out who is in charge among the many federal agencies and what the overall federal game plan is. Federal programs have varying time lines, slightly different goals, and conflicting views on priorities and how to accomplish certain response tasks. "The more federal agencies that got in the act, the more confusing it got because they each had their own approach," said a state official who watched the whole circus repeatedly come to town. "They weren't bad people or bad agencies, it was just their view of the world." The duplication of effort aside, these circumstances created practical problems locally. For example, the federal agencies did not standardize the terminology and content of their courses, which left the locals puzzling over the discrepancies in what they were taught.

Given that monies to combat terrorism have been buckshot across over 40 federal agencies, the pace and size of the expansion of federal programming led inevitably to efforts that not only waste taxpayer dollars but imperil the overall effectiveness of the federal government's programming to prepare for and respond to terrorism. Duplication of effort certainly exists in the plethora of research and development programs that were launched to find new detectors and other response equipment. Had Washington policy makers consulted experienced first responders before throwing money at the problem, they might have realized that these individuals do not need all of the equipment that is being developed in their name. For example, why is fancy, expensive decontamination equipment needed when front-line firefighters quickly recognized that they could configure their ladders and pumpers to create impromptu mass decontamination capacity? Another case in point was the creation of over 90 terrorism response training courses and several specialized training centers. Not only was training abundant, it was redundant. Befuddled local officials could hardly wade through all of the options. Meanwhile, no one in Washington refereed the explosion of courses or provided guidance about their quality.

In no small part, fractured congressional oversight has contributed to the mess at the federal level. Committee jurisdictions relevant to the unconventional terrorism issue range from armed services to government reform, transportation and infrastructure to the judiciary, commerce to veterans affairs. If the federal bureaucracy is to be streamlined and mean-ingful preparedness is to be achieved, Congress needs to coordinate much more rigorously its oversight activities across committees of jurisdiction and exercise more discipline in the programs it authorizes.

Institutionalization: The Cost-Effective Route to Nationwide Readiness

The time-tested and commonsense alternative to the proliferation of train-ing courses is the one that also underpins the all-hazards, echelons-of-re-sponse system that both states and cities know and advocate: institutionalization. If preparedness is truly to take hold nationwide on the front lines and be sustained in perpetuity, then it belongs in the local and state training academies, as well as in the nursing and medical schools. A few cities surveyed for *Ataxia* have already added a course at some or all of their responder academies, but a great many more indicated they had no plans to do so. Yet, institutionalization is the most cost-effective way to spread training geographically and build a tiered response capability.

The prerequisite for institutionalization is standards, and all of the re-sponse disciplines—fire, police, EMS, hospital care providers—expressed an abundance of frustration over the absence of standards and protocols to guide them. Standards command the attention of rescue and healthcare personnel because they are the backbone of accountability. Other stan-dards are established at the state level, flowing from the responsibility of governors to ensure public safety. In some disciplines, major professional organizations articulate standards, a role played most strongly by the Na-tional Fire Protection Association and to a lesser by the International Asso-ciation of Chiefs of Police. In the healthcare field, treatment protocols and standards of care evolve gradually through the publication of peer-re-viewed journal articles. Eventually, a body such as the Accreditation Council for Graduate Medical Education arbitrates whether a new protocol will be taught in US residency programs. Adding a subject to the curricula of medical and nursing schools takes at least six years. Once standards and protocols are agreed, state academies, universities, and colleges may incor-porate them. The National Governors Association could play a key role in seeing that standards are adopted nationwide.

Another benefit of institutionalization is that it would involve an important feature that has been lacking to date in training programs, namely the reg-ular testing of professional knowledge and skills. Moreover, this approach also involves refresher courses that update materials and skills. After grad-uating from respective professional schools, rescue personnel and healthcare providers are required to take a certain number of continuing education hours each year. First responders also take regular skills tests to remain certified.

Unconventional terrorism preparedness is on the radar screens of several of the above-named organizations. For instance, in 1998, the National Fire Protection Association issued a tentative interim standard on chemical terror attacks for EMS personnel, as well as for hazmat responders. Pre-hospital and hospital treatment protocols are being developed at a sluggish pace. No overarching structure is in place, however, to move any of these organizations or the state governments forward smartly to create and incorporate standards. Given the advantages that institutionalization offers, Washington could best demonstrate its seriousness about nationwide preparedness by bringing together the pertinent organizations in each discipline to lay the groundwork for institutionalization, complete with time lines. The federal government's job is to be the catalyst and convener that prods the tangle of entities involved in institutionalization to articulate and promulgate standards.

Six years after the onset of the domestic preparedness effort, the time has come for Washington to get out of the training business and turn it over to the appropriate organizations that will take preparedness forward more systematically and cost effectively. The hand-off should be concentrated in these organizations and curtailed elsewhere, so that various branches of the federal government, not to mention enterprising universities and contractors, stop churning out training programs at taxpayer expense. Without such reform, ineffective spending will continue at both the federal and local levels and training lacking in standards will be implemented unevenly, in pockets. Specification of standards and institutionalization of training clearly make more sense than that.

Refocusing Domestic Preparedness Efforts

Those who know first-hand the tremendous demands of responding to a disaster have a saying: "All emergencies are local." In a chemical or a conventional terrorist attack, the life-savers are not some federal response team that swoops in from across the country, but the local firefighters, police, paramedics, nurses, and physicians. Terrorist attacks in 1995 and just last month at the Pentagon and in New York City underscore the basic truth of who saves lives when natural or manmade calamity strikes.

In the moments after Aum Shinrikyo's sarin gas attack against the commuters in Tokyo's subway system on 20 March 1995, local transit workers, police, fire, and paramedics came to the aid of people gasping for air, some of whom were in need of quick administration of the nerve agent antidotes that saved their lives. The attack unfolded from 7:46 to 8:01 am. The first patients reached the nearest hospital less than 30 minutes later. The Japanese Self Defense Forces dispatched its special chemical defense units downtown at 10:10am. Although these units were located in the outskirts of Tokyo, the teams, caught in huge traffic jams, did not reach the attack scene until two and a half to roughly five hours later. The victims of the attack had long since been cleared from the scene.

So many survivors from the attacks on the World Trade Center spoke of being knocked to their knees by the force of the blast, of being surrounded by darkness and overcome by a sense of helplessness, and of beginning to succumb to the fumes when all of a sudden they saw a point of light. Then, they heard the voice and they grasped the hand extended to them. That hand belonged to a firefighter, the person who led them out of hell on earth. Even as the fires raged at the top of the twin towers, rescuers from across the Hudson River in New York City's outskirts mobilized and headed to the scene in accordance with pre-agreed plans. The bulk of the federal or state assets were far away in those critical early hours, when sadly far too few were pulled alive from the rubble by New York City's bravest and finest and their mutual aid partners.

These two tales of local heroism in the midst of unthinkable disaster speak loudly to the basic principle that should guide America's domestic preparedness activities. Indeed, that principle was very much in play in the original Domestic Preparedness Program legislation crafted after the events in Tokyo. Somewhere along the way, this effort to train and equip local responders veered way off course. Since the Domestic Preparedness Program began, talk inside the beltway has centered not on improving local response capabilities, but on how to enhance federal roles and capabilities. Accordingly, the federal government and its host of contractors have swallowed most of the domestic preparedness monies. In the year 2000, only $311 million out of the $8.7 billion spent on defense against terrorism went to enhancing the capacities of local emergency personnel to deal with unconventional attacks. If lives are to be saved in the aftermath of disasters, this ratio clearly has to be reversed.

A key part of the problem appears to be the refusal inside the beltway to accept the most appropriate roles for the federal government in a disaster response, mid- and long-term recovery. Instead, the last several years have witnessed a frenzy of enhancing existing chemical and biological response teams or building new ones from scratch. Each of the teams built comes with its own logistical and administrative bureaucracy, an additional drain on resources that could be better invested in front-line readiness where lives can truly be saved.

Understanding all too well that unless federal assistance were pre-deployed for a major event the bulk would not arrive at the disaster site until roughly 48 to 72 hours after an incident, state and local personnel have to assume that they would be on their own during the critical hours immediately after an incident. In the Oklahoma City aftermath, the first wave of federal assistance did not roll in until fifteen hours after the bombing. More recently, New York State's National Guard Civil Support Team was activated, but did not reach the site until twelve hours after the twin towers collapsed. Then, the Civil Support Team proceeded to employ detectors to search for the presence of chemical agents or other hazards. What the Guard does not acknowledge in its press release about this deployment is that this task was being taken care of hours earlier by New York City's own Public Health and Environmental departments as well as by US Environmental Protection Agency personnel.

The refrain heard inside the beltway when the National Guard or federal response teams are criticized as redundant and unable to reach the site to accomplish their asserted missions is that enhancing federal response teams does not really cost much—just a few million dollars here and there. Such a rejoinder truly belies the fact that national policy makers have lost perspective on the purposes of the domestic preparedness program. A million dollars may be pocket change in the Pentagon's budget, but it is serious money on the front lines that can make a real preparedness difference. Moreover, a few million poorly spent in several programs adds up to a tidy lump sum. To illustrate the point, 2,333 hospitals or fire stations could be outfitted with basic decontamination capabilities for the cost of standing up one National Guard Civil Support Team. If the total 1999 budget for these National Guard teams had been used in such a fashion, 49,800 local rescue and health facilities could have been armed for mass casualty decontamination, a critical shortcoming in chemical disaster preparedness across the country.

Challenges for the New Office of Homeland Security

The appointment of Governor Tom Ridge as Director of the new Office of Homeland Security would appear to be a constructive step that could put improved coordination and streamlining of the federal response bureaucracy on a fast track. Conceptually, imposing oversight on the unwieldy terrorism bureaucracy makes tremendous sense, particularly given the readiness of Congress to increase terrorism preparedness spending in the aftermath of September 11th. In practice, that task will be extremely difficult, for the federal agencies will vie even harder for their slice of the pie and congressional oversight remains fractured. Governor Ridge will need three things if he is to succeed in reshaping federal efforts in a more constructive directive. First, he will require strong budgetary authority if he is to bring the federal agencies to heel. Second, he will require congressional cooperation. Third, but certainly not the least important, he will need sage advice if he is to help direct taxpayer dollars where they can do the most to improve preparedness nationwide. Governor Ridge's right hand advisor should be an individual with extensive local disaster response and management experience.

Working in tandem, Governor Ridge's office and Congress can assess the sufficiency of existing federal programs and response teams and begin to eliminate redundant and spurious ones. In the interim until an assessment of the sufficiency of existing assets is made, a government-wide moratorium on any new rescue teams and bureaucracies should be declared, with the exception of the enhanced intelligence, law enforcement, and airport security measures that are being contemplated. Governor Ridge should also move forward with the appropriate steps to see that preparedness training is institutionalized in local police and fire academies, as well as in medical and nursing schools nationwide. In addition, in coordination with the Health and Human Services Department, this office should articulate a plan for jump-starting federal efforts devoted to public health and medical community readiness. Such programming should feature regional hospital planning grants and additional tests of disease syndrome surveillance systems, followed by plans to establish such capabilities nationwide. Last, but certainly not least, Governor Ridge needs to work with Congress to develop a plan to sustain preparedness over the long term.

I will conclude with one more essential task to which each individual member of Congress must attend. Since September 11th, I have received numerous calls from offices on both sides of the Hill and both sides of the aisle, asking me to brief them on these issues and to help fashion legislation that would put Representative "X's" or Senator "Z's" stamp on the legislation that is taking shape. While I have responded as quickly as possible to such requests, they are in some way indicative of the problem that Washington faces if it is to craft meaningful, cost-effective preparedness programs.

With all due respect, I would point out that while the attacks of September 11th occurred in New York City and Northern Virginia, they were attacks on this nation as a whole. Those who risked their lives that day to save the lives of others were not thinking about themselves or their future, they were selflessly acting in the interests of others. Put another way: this is no time for pet projects, whether they be to benefit constituents or a particular branch of government. This is not about job employment, it is about saving American lives. The future well-being of each American, I would contend, is equally important.

On behalf of the local public health and safety officials who have shared their experience and common sense views with me, I urge Congress to waste no time in passing legislation that brings the burgeoning federal terrorism preparedness programs and bureaucracies into line and points them in a more constructive, cost-effective direction. The key to domestic preparedness lies not in bigger terrorism budgets and more federal bureaucracy, but in smarter spending that enhances readiness at the local level. Even if terrorists never strike again in this country, such investments would be well worthwhile because they would improve the ability of hometown rescuers to respond to everyday emergencies.

STATEMENT OF BRUCE P. BAUGHMAN
DIRECTOR, PLANNING AND READINESS DIVISION
READINESS, RESPONSE, AND RECOVERY DIRECTORATE
FEDERAL EMERGENCY MANAGEMENT AGENCY

October 5, 2001

Introduction

Good morning, Mr. Chairman and Members of the Subcommittee. I am Bruce Baughman, Director of the Planning and Readiness Division, Readiness, Response, and Recovery Directorate, of the Federal Emergency Management Agency (FEMA). Director Allbaugh regrets that he is unable to be here with you today. It is a pleasure for me to represent him at this important hearing on biological and chemical terrorism. I will describe how FEMA works with other agencies, our approach to dealing with acts of terrorism, our programs related to terrorism, and new efforts to enhance preparedness and response.

Background

The FEMA mission is to reduce the loss of life and property and protect our nation's critical infrastructure from all types of hazards. As staffing goes, we are a small agency. Our success depends on our ability to organize and lead a community of local, State, and Federal agencies and volunteer organizations. We know who to bring to the table and what questions to ask when it comes to the business of managing emergencies. We provide an operational framework and a funding source.

The Federal Response Plan (FRP) is the heart of that framework. It reflects the labors of interagency groups that meet as required in Washington, D.C. and all 10 FEMA Regions to develop our capabilities to respond as a team. This team is made up of 26 Federal departments and agencies and the American Red Cross, and organized into interagency functions based on the authorities and expertise of the members and the needs of our counterparts at the state and local level.

Since 1992, the Federal Response Plan has been the proven framework time and time again, for managing major disasters and emergencies regardless of cause. It works during all phases of the emergency life cycle, from readiness, to response, recovery, and mitigation. The framework is successful because it builds upon the existing professional disciplines and communities among agencies. Among Federal agencies, FEMA has the strongest ties to the emergency management and the fire service communities. We plan, train, exercise, and operate together. That puts us in position to manage and coordinate programs that address their needs. Similarly, the Department of Health and Human Services (HHS) has the strongest ties to the public health and medical communities, and the Environmental Protection Agency (EPA) has the strongest ties to the hazardous materials community. The Federal Response Plan respects these relationships and areas of expertise to define the decision-making processes and delivery systems to make the best use of available resources.

The Approach to Biological and Chemical Terrorism

We recognize that biological and chemical scenarios would present unique challenges. Of the two I am more concerned about bioterrorism. A chemical attack is in many ways a large-scale hazardous materials incident. EPA and the Coast Guard are well connected to local hazardous materials responders, State and Federal agencies, and the chemical industry. There are systems and plans in place for response to hazardous materials, systems that are routinely used for small and large-scale events. EPA is also the primary agency for the Hazardous Materials function of the Federal Response Plan. We can improvise around that model in a chemical attack.

With a covert release of a biological agent, the 'first responders' will be hospital staff, medical examiners, private physicians, or animal control workers, instead of the traditional first responders such as police, fire, and emergency medical services. While I defer to the Departments of Justice and HHS on how biological scenarios would unfold, it seems unlikely that terrorists would warn us of a pending biological attack. In exercise and planning scenarios, the worst-case scenarios begin undetected and play out as epidemics. Response would begin in the public health and medical community. Initial requests for Federal assistance would probably come through health and medical channels to the Centers for Disease Control and Prevention (CDC). Conceivably, the situation could escalate into a national emergency.

HHS is a critical link between the health and medical community and the larger Federal response. HHS leads the efforts of the health and medical community to plan and prepare for a national response to a public health emergency. FEMA works closely with the Public Health Service, as the primary agency for the Health and Medical Services function of the Federal Response Plan. We rely on the Public Health Service to bring the right experts to the table when the Federal Response Plan community meets to discuss biological scenarios. We work closely with the experts in HHS and other health and medical agencies, to learn about the threats, how they spread, and the resources and techniques that will be needed to control them. By the same token, the medical experts work with us to learn about the Federal Response Plan and how we can use it to work the management issues, such as resource deployment and public information strategies. Alone, the Federal Response Plan is not an adequate solution for the challenge of planning and preparing for a deadly epidemic or act of bioterrorism. It is equally true that, alone, the health and medical community cannot manage an emergency with biological causes. We must work together.

In recent years, Federal, state and local governments and agencies have made progress in bringing the communities closer together. Exercise Top Officials (TOPOFF) 2000 in May 2000 involved two concurrent terrorism scenarios in two metropolitan areas, a chemical attack on the East Coast followed by a biological attack in the Midwest. We are still working on the lessons learned from that exercise. We need time and resources to identify, develop, and incorporate changes to the system between exercises. Exercises are critical in helping us to prepare for these types of scenarios. In January 2001, the FBI and FEMA jointly published the U.S. Government Interagency Domestic Terrorism Concept of Operation Plan (CONPLAN) with HHS, EPA, and the Departments of Defense and Energy, and pledged to continue the planning process to develop specific procedures for different scenarios, including bioterrorism. The Federal Response Plan and the CONPLAN provide the framework for managing the response to an act of bioterrorism.

Synopsis of FEMA Programs

FEMA programs are focused mainly on planning, training, and exercises to build capabilities to *manage* emergencies resulting from terrorism. Many of these program activities apply generally to terrorism, rather than to one form such as biological or chemical terrorism.

Planning

The overall Federal planning effort is being coordinated with the FBI, using existing plans and response structures whenever possible. The FBI is always the Lead Agency for Crisis Management. FEMA is always the Lead Agency for Consequence Management. We have developed plans and procedures to explain how to coordinate the two operations before and after consequences occur. In 1999, we published the second edition of the FRP Terrorism Incident Annex. In 2001, the FBI and FEMA published the United States Government Interagency Domestic Terrorism Concept of Operations Plan (CONPLAN).

We continually validate our planning concepts by developing plans to support the response to special events, such as we are now doing for the 2002 Olympic Winter Games that will take place in Utah.

To support any need for a Federal response, FEMA maintains the Rapid Response Information System (RRIS). The RRIS provides online access to information on key Federal assets that can be made available to assist state and local response efforts, and a database on chemical and biological agents and protective measures.

In FY 2001, FEMA has distributed $16.6 million in terrorism consequence management preparedness assistance grants to the States to support development of terrorism related capabilities, and $100 million in fire grants. FEMA is developing additional guidance to provide greater flexibility for states on how they can use this assistance.

FEMA has also developed a special attachment to its all-hazards Emergency Operations Planning Guide for state and local emergency managers that addresses developing terrorist incident annexes to state and local emergency operations plans. This planning guidance was developed with the assistance of eight Federal departments and agencies in coordination with NEMA and the International Association of Emergency Managers.

FEMA and the National Emergency Management Association (NEMA) jointly developed the Capability Assessment for Readiness (CAR), a self-assessment tool that enables States and Territories to focus on 13 core elements that address major emergency management functions. Terrorism preparedness is assessed relative to planning, procedures, equipment and exercises. FEMA's CAR report presents a composite picture of the nation's readiness based on the individual State and Territory reports.

FEMA's Comprehensive Hazardous Materials Emergency Response Capability Assessment Program (CHER-CAP) helps communities improve their terrorism preparedness by assessing their emergency response capability. Local, State, and Tribal emergency managers, civic leaders, hospital personnel and industry representatives all work together to identify problems, revise their response plans and improve their community's preparedness for a terrorist event. Since February 2000, a total of 55 communities have been selected to participate, initiated, or completed a sequence of planning, training, and exercise activities to improve their terrorism preparedness.

Training

FEMA supports the training of Federal, State, and local emergency personnel through our National Fire Academy (NFA), which trains emergency responders, and the Emergency Management Institute (EMI), which focuses on emergency planners, coordinators and elected and appointed officials. EMI and NFA work in partnership with State and municipal training organizations. Together they form a very strong national network of fire and emergency training. FEMA employs a "train-the-trainer" approach and uses distance-learning technologies such as the Emergency Education Network via satellite TV and web-based instruction to maximize our training impact.

The NFA has developed and fielded several courses in the *Emergency Response to Terrorism (ERT)* curriculum, including a Self-Study course providing general awareness information for responding to terrorist incidents that has been distributed to some 35,000 fire/ rescue departments, 16,000 law enforcement agencies, and over 3,000 local and state emergency managers in the United States and is available on FEMA internet site. Other courses in the curriculum deal with Basic Concepts, Incident Management, and Tactical Considerations for Emergency Medical Services (EMS), Company Officers, and HAZMAT Response. Biological and chemical terrorism are included as integral parts of these courses.

Over one thousand instructors representing every state and major metropolitan area in the nation have been trained under the ERT program. The NFA is utilizing the Training Resources and Data Exchange (TRADE) program to reach all 50 States and all major metropolitan fire and rescue departments with training materials and course offerings. In FY 2001, FEMA is distributing $4 million in grants to state fire-training centers to deliver first responder courses developed by the NFA.

Over 112,000 students have participated in ERT courses and other terrorism-related training. In addition, some 57,000 copies of a Job Aid utilizing a flip-chart format guidebook to quick reference based on the ERT curriculum concepts and principles have been printed and distributed.

NFA is developing a new course in FY 2002 in the Emergency Response to Terrorism series geared toward response to bioterrorism in the pre-hospital recognition and response phase. It will be completed with the review and input of our Federal partners, notably HHS and the Office of Justice Programs.

EMI offers a comprehensive program of emergency management training including a number of courses specifically designed to help communities, states, and tribes deal with the consequences of terrorism and weapons of mass destruction. The EMI curriculum includes an Integrated Emergency Management Course (IEMC)/Consequences of Terrorism. This 4-½ day course combines classroom training, planning sessions, and functional exercises into a management-level course designed to encourage communities to integrate functions, skills, and resources to deal with the consequences of terrorism, including terrorism. To foster this integration, EMI brings together 70 participants for each course that includes elected officials and public health leaders as well as representatives of law enforcement, emergency medical services, emergency management, and public works. The course provides participants with skill-building opportunities in preparedness, response, and recovery. The scenario for the course changes from offering to offering. In a recent offering, the scenario was based on an airborne anthrax release. Bioterrorism scenarios emphasize the special issues inherent in dealing with both infectious and noninfectious biological agents and stresses the partnerships between local, state, and Federal public health organizations.

Exercises

In the area of exercises, FEMA is working closely with the interagency community and the States to ensure the development of a comprehensive exercise program that meets the needs of the emergency management and first responder communities. FEMA is planning to conduct Phase II of a seminar series on terrorism preparedness in each of the ten FEMA Regional Offices. In addition, exercise templates and tools are being developed for delivery to state and local officials.

New Efforts to Enhance Preparedness and Response

In response to guidance from the President on May 8, 2001, the FEMA Director created an Office of National Preparedness (ONP) to coordinate all federal programs dealing with weapons of mass destruction consequence management, with particular focus on preparedness for, and the response to the terrorist use of such weapons. In July, the Director established the ONP at FEMA Headquarters. An ONP element was also established in each of the ten FEMA Regional Offices to support terrorism-related activities involving the States and localities.

On September 21, 2001, in the wake of the horrific terrorist attacks on the World Trade Center and the Pentagon, the President announced the establishment of an Office of Homeland Security (OHS) in the White House to be headed by Governor Tom Ridge of Pennsylvania. In setting up the new office, the President stated that it would lead, oversee and coordinate a national strategy to safeguard the country against terrorism and respond to attacks that occur. It is our understanding that office will coordinate a broad range of policies and activities related to prevention, deterrence, preparedness and response to terrorism.

The new office includes a Homeland Security Council comprised of key department and agency officials, including the FEMA Director. FEMA expects to provide significant support to the office in its role as the lead Federal agency for consequence management.

Conclusion

Mr. Chairman, you convened this hearing to ask about our preparedness to work with State and local agencies in the event of a biological or chemical attack. It is FEMA's responsibility to ensure that the national emergency management system is adequate to respond to the consequences of catastrophic emergencies and disasters, regardless of cause. All catastrophic events require a strong management system built on expert systems for each of the operational disciplines. Terrorism presents tremendous challenges. We rely on our partners in Department of Health and Human Services to coordinate the efforts of the health and medical community to address biological terrorism, as we rely on EPA and the Coast Guard to co-ordinate the efforts of the hazardous materials community to address chemical terrorism. Without question, they need support to further strengthen capabilities and their operating capacity. FEMA must ensure that the national system has the tools to gather information, set priorities, and deploy resources effectively in a biological scenario. In recent years we have made tremendous strides in our efforts to increase cooperation between the various response communities, from fire and emergency management to health and medical to hazardous materials. We need to do more.

The creation of the Office of Homeland Security and other efforts will enable us to better focus our time and effort with those communities, to prepare the nation for response to any incident.

Thank you, Mr. Chairman. I would be happy to answer any questions.

STATEMENT OF JANET HEINRICH
DIRECTOR, HEALTH CARE—PUBLIC HEALTH ISSUES

BIOTERRORISM COORDINATION AND PREPAREDNESS

Mr. Chairman and Members of the Subcommittee:

I appreciate the opportunity to be here today to discuss our work on the activities of federal agencies to prepare the nation to respond to the public health and medical consequences of a bioterrorist attack.[1] Preparing to respond to the public health and medical consequences of a bioterrorist attack poses some challenges that are different from those in other types of terrorist attacks, such as bombings. On September 28, 2001, we released a report[2] that describes (1) the research and preparedness activities being undertaken by federal departments and agencies to manage the consequences of a bioterrorist attack,[3] (2) the coordination of these activities, and (3) the findings of reports on the preparedness of state and local jurisdictions to respond to a bioterrorist attack. My testimony will summarize the detailed findings included in our report, which augments our previous work on combating terrorism.[4]

In summary, we found that federal departments and agencies are participating in a variety of research and preparedness activities, from improving the detection of biological agents to developing a national stockpile of pharmaceuticals to treat victims of disasters. Federal departments and agencies have engaged in a number of efforts to coordinate these activities on a formal and informal basis, such as interagency work groups. Despite these efforts, we found evidence that coordination between departments and agencies is fragmented. We did, however, find recent actions to improve coordination across federal departments and agencies. In addition, we found emerging concerns about the preparedness of state and local jurisdictions, including insufficient state and local planning for response to terrorist events, inadequacies in the public health infrastructure, a lack of hospital participation in training on terrorism and emergency response planning, insufficient capabilities for treating mass casualties, and the timely availability of medical teams and resources in an emergency.

Background

A domestic bioterrorist attack is considered to be a low-probability event, in part because of the various difficulties involved in successfully delivering biological agents to achieve large-scale casualties.[5] However, a number of cases involving biological agents, including at least one completed bioterrorist act and numerous threats and hoaxes,[6] have occurred domestically. In 1984, a group intentionally contaminated salad bars in restaurants in Oregon with salmonella bacteria. Although no one died, 751 people were diagnosed with foodborne illness. Some experts predict that more domestic bioterrorist attacks are likely to occur.

The burden of responding to such an attack would fall initially on personnel in state and local emergency response agencies. These "first responders" include firefighters, emergency medical service personnel, law enforcement officers, public health officials, health care workers (including doctors, nurses, and other medical professionals), and public works personnel. If the emergency required federal disaster assistance, federal departments and agencies would respond according to responsibilities outlined in the Federal Response Plan.[7] Several groups, including the Advisory Panel to Assess Domestic Response Capabilities for Terrorism Involving Weapons of Mass Destruction (known as the Gilmore Panel), have assessed the capabilities at the federal, state, and local levels to respond to a domestic terrorist incident involving a weapon of mass destruction (WMD), that is, a chemical, biological, radiological, or nuclear agent or weapon.[8]

While many aspects of an effective response to a bioterrorism are the same as those for any disaster, there are some unique features. For example, if a biological agent is released covertly, it may not be recognized for a week or more because symptoms may not appear for several days after the initial exposure and may be misdiagnosed at first. In addition, some biological agents, such as smallpox, are communicable and can spread to others who were not initially exposed. These differences require a type of response that is unique to bioterrorism, including infectious disease surveillance,[9] epidemiologic investigation,[10] laboratory identification of biological agents, and distribution of antibiotics to large segments of the population to prevent the spread of an infectious disease. However, some aspects of an effective response to bioterrorism are also important in responding to any type of large-scale disaster, such as providing emergency medical services, continuing health care services delivery, and managing mass fatalities.

Federal Departments and Agencies Reported a Variety of Research and Preparedness Activities

Federal spending on domestic preparedness for terrorist attacks involving WMDs has risen 310 percent since fiscal year 1998, to approximately $1.7 billion in fiscal year 2001, and may increase significantly after the events of September 11, 2001. However, only a portion of these funds were used to conduct a variety of activities related to research on and preparedness for the public health and medical consequences of a bioterrorist attack. We cannot measure the total investment in such activities because departments and agencies provided funding information in various forms—as appropriations, obligations, or expenditures. Because the funding information provided is not equivalent,[11] we summarized funding by department or agency, but not across the federal government (see apps. I and II).[12]

Research Activities Focus on Detection, Treatment, Vaccination, and Equipment

Research is currently being done to enable the rapid identification of biological agents in a variety of settings; develop new or improved vaccines, antibiotics, and antivirals to improve treatment and vaccination for infectious diseases caused by biological agents; and develop and test emergency response equipment such as respiratory and other personal protective equipment. Appendix I provides information on the total reported funding for all the departments and agencies carrying out research, along with examples of this research.

The Department of Agriculture (USDA), Department of Defense (DOD), Department of Energy, Department of Health and Human Services (HHS), Department of Justice (DOJ), Department of the Treasury, and the Environmental Protection Agency (EPA) have all sponsored or conducted projects to improve the detection and characterization of biological agents in a variety of different settings, from water to clinical samples (such as blood). For example, EPA is sponsoring research to improve its ability to detect biological agents in the water supply. Some of these projects, such as those conducted or sponsored by the DOD and DOJ, are not primarily for the public health and medical consequences of a bioterrorist attack against the civilian population, but could eventually benefit research for those purposes.

Departments and agencies are also conducting or sponsoring studies to improve treatment and vaccination for diseases caused by biological agents. For example, HHS' projects include basic research sponsored by the National Institutes of Health to develop drugs and diagnostics and applied research sponsored by the Agency for Healthcare Research and Quality to improve health care delivery systems by studying the use of information systems and decision support systems to enhance preparedness for the delivery of medical care in an emergency.

In addition, several agencies, including the Department of Commerce's National Institute of Standards and Technology and the DOJ's National Institute of Justice are conducting research that focuses on developing performance standards and methods for testing the performance of emergency response equipment, such as respirators and personal protective equipment.

Preparedness Efforts Include Multiple Actions

Federal departments' and agencies' preparedness efforts have included efforts to increase federal, state, and local response capabilities, develop response teams of medical professionals, increase availability of medical treatments, participate in and sponsor terrorism response exercises, plan to aid victims, and provide support during special events such as presidential inaugurations, major political party conventions, and the Superbowl.[13] Appendix II contains information on total reported funding for all the departments and agencies with bioterrorism preparedness activities, along with examples of these activities.

Several federal departments and agencies, such as the Federal Emergency Management Agency (FEMA) and the Centers for Disease Control and Prevention (CDC), have programs to increase the ability of state and local authorities to successfully respond to an emergency, including a bioterrorist attack. These departments and agencies contribute to state and local jurisdictions by helping them pay for equipment and develop emergency response plans, providing technical assistance, increasing communications capabilities, and conducting training courses.

Federal departments and agencies have also been increasing their own capacity to identify and deal with a bioterrorist incident. For example, CDC, USDA, and the Food and Drug Administration (FDA) are improving surveillance methods for detecting disease outbreaks in humans and animals. They have also established laboratory response networks to maintain state-of-the-art capabilities for biological agent identification and characterization of human clinical samples.

Some federal departments and agencies have developed teams to directly respond to terrorist events and other emergencies. For example, HHS' Office of Emergency Preparedness (OEP) created Disaster Medical Assistance Teams to provide medical treatment and assistance in the event of an emergency. Four of these teams, known as National Medical Response Teams, are specially trained and equipped to provide medical care to victims of WMD events, such as bioterrorist attacks.

Several agencies are involved in increasing the availability of medical supplies that could be used in an emergency, including a bioterrorist attack. CDC's National Pharmaceutical Stockpile contains pharmaceuticals, antidotes, and medical supplies that can be delivered anywhere in the United States within 12 hours of the decision to deploy. The stockpile was deployed for the first time on September 11, 2001, in response to the terrorist attacks on New York City.

Federally initiated bioterrorism response exercises have been conducted across the country. For example, in May 2000, many departments and agencies took part in the Top Officials 2000 exercise (TOPOFF 2000) in Denver, Colorado, which featured the simulated release of a biologicalagent.[14] Participants included local fire departments, police, hospitals, the Colorado Department of Public Health and the Environment, the Colorado Office of

Emergency Management, the Colorado National Guard, the American Red Cross, the Salvation Army, HHS, DOD, FEMA, the Federal Bureau of Investigation (FBI), and EPA.

Several agencies also provide assistance to victims of terrorism. FEMA can provide supplemental funds to state and local mental health agencies for crisis counseling to eligible survivors of presidentially declared emergencies. In the aftermath of the recent terrorist attacks, HHS released $1 million in funding to New York State to support mental health services and strategic planning for comprehensive and long-term support to address the mental health needs of the community. DOJ's Office of Justice Programs (OJP) also manages a program that provides funds for victims of terrorist attacks that can be used to provide a variety of services, including mental health treatment and financial assistance to attend related criminal proceedings.

Federal departments and agencies also provide support at special events to improve response in case of an emergency. For example, CDC has deployed a system to provide increased surveillance and epidemiological capacity before, during, and after special events. Besides improving emergency response at the events, participation by departments and agencies gives them valuable experience working together to develop and practice plans to combat terrorism.

Fragmentation Remains Despite Efforts to Coordinate Federal Programs

Federal departments and agencies are using a variety of interagency plans, work groups, and agreements to coordinate their activities to combat terrorism. However, we found evidence that coordination remains fragmented. For example, several different agencies are responsible for various coordination functions, which limits accountability and hinders unity of effort; several key agencies have not been included in bioterrorism-related policy and response planning; and the programs that agencies have developed to provide assistance to state and local governments are similar and potentially duplicative. The President recently took steps to improve oversight and coordination, including the creation of the Office of Homeland Security.

Departments and Agencies Use a Variety of Methods to Coordinate Activities

Over 40 federal departments and agencies have some role in combating terrorism, and coordinating their activities is a significant challenge. We identified over 20 departments and agencies as having a role in preparing for or responding to the public health and medical consequences of a bioterrorist attack. Appendix III, which is based on the framework given in the Terrorism Incident Annex of the Federal Response Plan, shows a sample of the coordination efforts by federal departments and agencies with responsibilities for the public health and medical consequences of a bioterrorist attack, as they existed prior to the recent creation of the Office of Homeland Security. This figure illustrates the complex relationships among the many federal departments and agencies involved.

Departments and agencies use several approaches to coordinate their activities on terrorism, including interagency response plans, work groups, and formal agreements. Interagency plans for responding to a terrorist incident help outline agency responsibilities and identify resources that could be used during a response. For example, the Federal Response Plan provides a broad framework for coordinating the delivery of federal disaster assistance to state and local governments when an emergency overwhelms their ability to respond effectively. The Federal Response Plan also designates primary and supporting federal agencies for a variety of emergency support operations. For example, HHS is the primary agency for coordinating federal assistance in response to public health and medical care needs in an emergency. HHS could receive support from other agencies and organizations, such as DOD, USDA, and FEMA, to assist state and local jurisdictions.

Interagency work groups are being used to minimize duplication of funding and effort in federal activities to combat terrorism. For example, the Technical Support Working Group is chartered to coordinate interagency research and development requirements across the federal government in order to prevent duplication of effort between agencies. The Technical Support Working Group, among other projects, helped to identify research needs and fund a project to detect biological agents in food that can be used by both DOD and USDA.

Formal agreements between departments and agencies are being used to share resources and knowledge. For example, CDC contracts with the Department of Veterans Affairs (VA) to purchase drugs and medical supplies for the National Pharmaceutical Stockpile because of VA's purchasing power and ability to negotiate large discounts.

Coordination Remains Fragmented Within the Federal Government

Overall coordination of federal programs to combat terrorism is fragmented.[15] For example, several agencies have coordination functions, including DOJ, the FBI, FEMA, and the Office of Management and Budget. Officials from a number of the agencies that combat terrorism told us that the coordination roles of these various agencies are not always clear and sometimes overlap, leading to a fragmented approach. We have found that the overall coordination of federal research and development efforts to combat terrorism is still limited by a number of factors, including the compartmentalization or security classification of some research efforts.[16] The Gilmore Panel also concluded that the current coordination structure does not provide for the requisite authority or accountability to impose the discipline necessary among the federal agencies involved.[17]

The multiplicity of federal assistance programs requires focus and attention to minimize redundancy of effort.[18] Table 1 shows some of the federal programs providing assistance to state and local governments for emergency planning that would be relevant to responding to a bioterrorist attack. While the programs vary somewhat in their target audiences, the potential redundancy of these federal efforts highlights the need for scrutiny. In our report on combating terrorism, issued on September 20, 2001, we recommended that the President, working closely with the Congress, consolidate some of the activities of DOJ's OJP under FEMA.[19]

Table 1: Selected Federal Activities Providing Assistance to State and Local Governments for Emergency Planning Relevant to a Bioterrorist Attack

Department or agency	Activities	Target audience
HHS—CDCState and local health agencies	Provides grants, technical support, and performance standards to support bioterrorism preparedness and response planning.	State and local health agencies
HHS—OEP	Enters into contracts to enhance medical response capability. The program includes a focus on response to bioterrorism, including early recognition, mass postexposure treatment, mass casualty care, and mass fatality management.	Local jurisdictions (for fire, police, and emergency medical services; hospitals; public health agencies; and other services)
DOJ—OJP	Assists states in developing strategic plans. Includes funding for training, equipment acquisition, technical assistance, and exercise planning and execution to enhance state and local capabilities to respond to terrorist incidents.	States (for fire, law enforcement, emergency medical, and hazardous materials response services; hospitals; public health departments; and other services)
FEMA	Provides grant assistance to support state and local consequence management planning, training, and exercises for all types of terrorism, including bioterrorism.	State emergency management agencies

Source: Information obtained from departments and agencies.

We have also recommended that the federal government conduct multidisciplinary and analytically sound threat and risk assessments to define and prioritize requirements and properly focus programs and investments in combating terrorism.[20] Such assessments would be useful in addressing the fragmentation that is evident in the different threat lists of biological agents developed by federal departments and agencies.

Understanding which biological agents are considered most likely to be used in an act of domestic terrorism is necessary to focus the investment in new technologies, equipment, training, and planning. Several different agencies have or are in the process of developing biological agent threat lists, which differ based on the agencies' focus. For example, CDC collaborated with law enforcement, intelligence, and defense agencies to develop a critical agent list that focuses on the biological agents that would have the greatest impact on public health. The FBI, the National Institute of Justice, and the Technical Support Working Group are completing a report that lists biological agents that may be more likely to be used by a terrorist group working in the United States that is not sponsored by a foreign government. In addition, an official at USDA's Animal and Plant Health Inspection Service told us that it uses two lists of agents of concern for a potential bioterrorist attack developed through an international process (although only some of these agents are capable of making both animals and humans sick). According to agency officials, separate threat lists are appropriate because of the different focuses of these agencies. In our view, the existence of competing lists makes the assignment of priorities difficult for state and local officials.

Fragmentation has also hindered unity of effort. Officials at the Department of Transportation (DOT) told us that the department has been overlooked in bioterrorism-related planning and policy. DOT officials noted that even though the nation's transportation centers account for a significant percentage of the nation's potential terrorist targets, DOT was not part of the founding group of agencies that worked on bioterrorism issues and has not been included in bioterrorism response plans. DOT officials also told us that the department is supposed to deliver supplies for FEMA under the Federal Response Plan, but it was not brought into the planning early enough to understand the extent of its responsibilities in the transportation process. The department learned what its responsibilities would be during TOPOFF 2000.

Recent Actions Seek to Improve Coordination Across Federal Departments and Agencies

In May 2001, the President asked the Vice President to oversee the development of a coordinated national effort dealing with WMDs.[21] At the same time, the President asked the Director of FEMA to establish an Office of National Preparedness to implement the results of the Vice President's effort that relate to programs within federal agencies that address consequence management resulting from the use of WMDs. The purpose of this effort is to better focus policies and ensure that programs and activities are fully coordinated in support of building the needed preparedness and response capabilities. In addition, on September 20, 2001, the President announced the creation of the Office of Homeland Security to lead, oversee, and coordinate a comprehensive national strategy to protect the country from terrorism and respond to any attacks that may occur. These actions represent potentially significant steps toward improved coordination of federal activities. In a recent report, we listed a number of important characteristics and responsibilities necessary for a single focal point, such as the proposed Office of Homeland Security, to improve coordination and accountability.[22]

Despite Federal Efforts, Concerns Exist Regarding Preparedness at State and Local Levels

Nonprofit research organizations, congressionally chartered advisory panels, government documents, and articles in peer-reviewed literature have identified concerns about the preparedness of states and local areas to respond to a bioterrorist attack. These concerns include insufficient state and local planning for response to terrorist events, inadequacies in the public health infrastructure, a lack of hospital participation in training on terrorism and emergency response planning, insufficient capacity for treating mass casualties from a terrorist act, and questions regarding the timely availability of medical teams and resources in an emergency.

Questions exist regarding how effectively federal programs have prepared state and local governments to respond to terrorism. All 50 states and approximately 255 local jurisdictions have received or are scheduled to receive at least some federal assistance, including training and equipment grants, to help them prepare for a terrorist WMD incident. In 1997, FEMA identified planning and equipment for response to nuclear, biological, and chemical incidents as an area in need of significant improvement at the state level. However, an October 2000 report concluded that even those cities receiving federal aid are still not adequately prepared to respond to a bioterrorist attack.[23]

Components of the nation's infectious disease surveillance system are also not well prepared to detect or respond to a bioterrorist attack. Reductions in public health laboratory staffing and training have affected the ability of state and local authorities to identify biological agents. Even the initial West Nile virus outbreak in 1999, which was relatively small and occurred in an area with one of the nation's largest local public health agencies, taxed the federal, state, and local laboratory resources.[24] Both the New York State and the CDC laboratories were inundated with requests for tests, and the CDC laboratory handled the bulk of the testing because of the limited capacity at the New York laboratories. Officials indicated that the CDC laboratory would have been unable to respond to another outbreak, had one occurred at the same time. In fiscal year 2000, CDC awarded approximately $11 million to 48 states and four major urban health departments to improve and upgrade their surveillance and epidemiological capabilities.

Inadequate training and planning for bioterrorism response by hospitals is a major problem. The Gilmore Panel concluded that the level of expertise in recognizing and dealing with a terrorist attack involving a biological or chemical agent is problematic in many hospitals.[25] A recent research report concluded that hospitals need to improve their preparedness for mass casualty incidents.[26] Local officials told us that it has been difficult to get hospitals and medical personnel to participate in local training, planning, and exercises to improve their preparedness.

Several federal and local officials reported that there is little excess capacity in the health care system for treating mass casualty patients. Studies have reported that emergency rooms in some areas are routinely filled and unable to accept patients in need of urgent care.[27] According to one local official, the health care system might not be able to handle the aftermath of a disaster because of the problems caused by overcrowding and the lack of excess capacity.

Local officials are also concerned about whether the federal government could quickly deliver enough medical teams and resources to help after a biological attack.[28] Agency officials say that federal response teams, such as Disaster Medical Assistance Teams, could be on site within 12 to 24 hours. However, local officials who have deployed with such teams say that the federal assistance probably would not arrive for 24 to 72 hours. Local officials also told us that they were concerned about the time and resources required to prepare and distribute drugs from the National Pharmaceutical Stockpile during an emergency. Partially in response to these concerns, CDC has developed training for state and local officials on using the stockpile and will deploy a small staff with the supplies to assist the local jurisdiction with distribution.

Concluding Observations

We found that federal departments and agencies are participating in a variety of research and preparedness activities that are important steps in improving our readiness. Although federal departments and agencies have engaged in a number of efforts to coordinate these activities on a formal and informal basis, we found that coordination between departments and agencies is fragmented, as illustrated by the many and complex relationships between federal departments and agencies shown in Appendix III. In addition, we found concerns about the preparedness of state and local jurisdictions, including the level of state and local planning for response to terrorist events, inadequacies in the public health infrastructure, a lack of hospital participation in training on terrorism and emergency response planning, capabilities for treating mass casualties, and the timely availability of medical teams and resources in an emergency.

Mr. Chairman, this completes my prepared statement. I would be happy to respond to any questions you or other Members of the Subcommittee may have at this time.

Contact and Acknowledgments

For further information about this testimony, please contact me at (202) 512-7118. Barbara Chapman, Robert Copeland, Marcia Crosse, Greg Ferrante, Deborah Miller, and Roseanne Price also made key contributions to this statement.

Appendix I: Funding for Research

Total Reported Funding for Research on Bioterrorism and Terrorism by Federal Departments and Agencies, Fiscal Year 2000 and Fiscal Year 2001

Dollars in millions

Department or agency	Fiscal year 2000 funding	Fiscal year 2001 funding	Sample activities
U.S. Department of Agriculture (USDA)—Agricultural Research Service	0	$0.5	Improving detection of biological agents
Department of Energy	$35.5	$39.6	Developing technologies for detecting and responding to a bioterrorist attack Developing models of the spread of and exposure to a biological agent after release
Department of Health and Human Services (HHS)—Agency for Healthcare Research and Quality	$5.0	0	Examining clinical training and ability of frontline medical staff to detect and respond to a bioterrorist threat Studying use of information systems and decision support systems to enhance preparedness for medical care in the event of a bioterrorist event
HHS—Centers for Disease Control and Prevention (CDC)	$48.2	$46.6	Developing equipment performance standards Conducting research on smallpox and anthrax viruses and therapeutics
HHS—Food and Drug Administration (FDA)	$8.8	$9.1	Licensing of vaccines for anthrax and smallpox Determining procedures for allowing use of not-yetapproved drugs and specifying data needed for approval and labeling
HHS—National Institutes of Health	$43.0	$49.7	Developing new therapies for smallpox virus Developing smallpox and bacterial antigen detection system
HHS—Office of Emergency Preparedness (OEP)	0	$4.6	Overseeing a study on response systems

Department of Justice (DOJ)—Office of Justice Programs (OJP)	$0.7	$4.6	Developing a biological agent detector
DOJ—Federal Bureau of Investigation	0	$1.1	Conducting work on detection and characterization of biological materials
Department of the Treasury—Secret Service	0	$0.5	Developing a biological agent detector
Environmental Protection Agency (EPA)	0	$0.5	Improving detection of biological agents

Note: Total reported funding refers to budget data we received from agencies. Agencies reported appropriations, actual or estimated obligations, or actual or estimated expenditures. An agency providing appropriations is not necessarily indicating the level of its obligations or expenditures for that year—only the amount of budget authority made available to it by the Congress. Similarly, an agency that provided expenditure information for fiscal year 2000 may have obligated the funds in fiscal year 1999 based on an appropriation for fiscal year 1998.

Source: Information obtained from departments and agencies.Appendix II: Funding for Preparedness

Appendix II: Funding for Preparedness Activities

Total Reported Funding for Preparedness Activities on Bioterrorism and Terrorism by Federal Departments and Agencies, Fiscal Year 2000 and Fiscal Year 2001

Dollars in millions

Department or agency	Fiscal year 2000 funding	Fiscal year 2001 funding	Sample activities
USDA—Animal and Plant Health Inspection Service	0	$0.2	Developing educational materials and training programs specifically dealing with bioterrorism
Department of Defense (DOD)—Joint Task Force for Civil Support	$3.4	$8.7	Planning, and when directed, commanding and controlling DOD's WMD and high-yield explosive consequence management capabilities in support of FEMA
DOD—National Guard	$70.0	$93.3	Managing response teams that would enter a contaminated area to gather samples for on-site evaluation
DOD—U.S. Army	$29.5	$11.7	Maintaining a repository of information about chemical and biological weapons and agents, detectors, and protection and decontamination equipment
HHS—CDC	$124.9	$147.3	Awarding planning grants to state and local health departments to prepare bioterrorism response plans Improving surveillance methods for detecting disease outbreaks Increasing communication capabilities in order to improve the gathering and exchanging of information related to bioterror
HHS—FDA	$0.1	$2.1	Improving capabilities to identify and characterize foodborne pathogens Identifying biological agents using animal studies and microbiological surveillance
HHS—OEP	$35.3	$46.1	Providing contracts to increase local emergency response capabilities Developing and managing response teams that can provide support at the site of a disaster

DOJ—OJP	$7.6	$5.3	Helping prepare state and local emergency responders through training, exercises, technical assistance, and equipment programs Developing a data collection tool to assist states in conducting their threat, risk, and needs assessments, and in developing their preparedness strategy for terrorism, including bioterrorism
EPA	$0.1	$2.0	Providing technical assistance in identifying and decontaminating biological agents Conducting assessments of water supply vulnerability to terrorism, including contamination with biological agents
Federal Emergency Management Agency	$25.1	$30.3	Providing grant assistance and guidance to states for planning and training Maintaining databases of safety precautions for biological, chemical, and nuclear agents

Note: Total reported funding refers to budget data we received from agencies. Agencies reported appropriations, actual or estimated obligations, or actual or estimated expenditures. An agency providing appropriations is not necessarily indicating the level of its obligations or expenditures for that year—only the amount of budget authority made available to it by the Congress. Similarly, an agency that provided expenditure information for fiscal year 2000 may have obligated the funds in fiscal year 1999 based on an appropriation for fiscal year 1998.

Source: Information obtained from departments and agencies.

Appendix III: Examples of Coordination Activities on Bioterrorism Among Federal Departments and Agencies

We identified the following federal departments and agencies as having responsibilities related to the public health and medical consequences of a bioterrorist attack:

- USDA—U.S. Department of Agriculture
    - APHIS—Animal and Plant Health Inspection Service
    - ARS—Agricultural Research Service
    - FSIS—Food Safety Inspection Service
    - OCPM—Office of CrisiPlanning and Management
- DOC—Department of Commerce
    - NIST—National Institute of Standards and Technology
- DOD—Department of Defense
    - DARPA—Defense Advanced Research Projects Agency
    - JTFCS—Joint Task Force for Civil Support
    - National Guard
    - U.S. Army
- DOE—Department of Energy
- HHS—Department of Health and Human Services
    - AHRQ—Agency for Healthcare Research and Quality
    - CDC—Centers for Disease Control and Prevention
    - FDA—Food and Drug Administration
    - NIH—National Institutes of Health
    - OEP—Office of Emergency Preparedness
- DOJ—Department of Justice
    - FBI—Federal Bureau of Investigation
    - OJP—Office of Justice Programs
- DOT—Department of Transportation
    - USCG—U.S. Coast Guard
- Treasury—Department of the Treasury
    - USSS—U.S. Secret Service
- VA—Department of Veterans Affairs
- EPA—Environmental Protection Agency
- FEMA—Federal Emergency Management Agency

Figure 1, which is based on the framework given in the Terrorism Incident Annex of the Federal Response Plan, shows a sample of the coordination activities by these federal departments and agencies, as they existed prior to the recent creation of the Office of Homeland Security. This figure illustrates the complex relationships among the many federal departments and agencies involved. The following coordination activities are represented on the figure:

- OMB Oversight of Terrorism Funding. The Office of Management and Budget established a reporting system on the budgeting and expenditure of funds to combat terrorism, with goals to reduce overlap and improve coordination as part of the annual budget cycle.

- Federal Response Plan—Health and Medical Services Annex. This annex in the Federal Response Plan states that HHS is the primary agency for coordinating federal assistance to supplement state and local resources in response to public health and medical care needs in an emergency, including a bioterrorist attack.

- Informal Working Group—Equipment Request Review. This group meets as necessary to review equipment requests of state and local jurisdictions to ensure that duplicative funding is not being given for the same activities.

- Agreement on Tracking Diseases in Animals That Can Be Transmitted to Humans. This group is negotiating an agreement to share information and expertise on tracking diseases that can be transmitted from animals to people and could be used in a bioterrorist attack.

- National Medical Response Team Caches. These caches form a stockpile of drugs for OEP's National Medical Response Teams.

- Domestic Preparedness Program. This program was formed in response to the National Defense Authorization Act of Fiscal Year 1997 (P.L. 104-201) and required DOD to enhance the capability of federal, state, and local emergency responders regarding terrorist incidents involving WMDs and high-yield explosives. As of October 1, 2000, DOD and DOJ share responsibilities under this program.

- Office of National Preparedness—Consequence Management of WMD Attack. In May 2001, the President asked the Director of FEMA to establish this office to coordinate activities of the listed agencies that address consequence management resulting from the use of WMDs.

- Food Safety Surveillance Systems. These systems are FoodNet and PulseNet, two surveillance systems for identifying and characterizing contaminated food.

- National Disaster Medical System. This system, a partnership between federal agencies, state and local governments, and the private sector, is intended to ensure that resources are available to provide medical services following a disaster that overwhelms the local health care resources.

- Collaborative Funding of Smallpox Research. These agencies conduct research on vaccines for smallpox.

- National Pharmaceutical Stockpile Program. This program maintains repositories of life-saving pharmaceuticals, antidotes, and medical supplies that can be delivered to the site of a biological (or other) attack.

- National Response Teams. The teams constitute a national planning, policy, and coordinating body to provide guidance before and assistance during an incident.

- Interagency Group for Equipment Standards. This group develops and maintains a standardized equipment list of essential items for responding to a terrorist WMD attack. (The complete name of this group is the Interagency Board for Equipment Standardization and Interoperability.)

- Force Packages Response Team. This is a grouping of military units that are designated to respond to an incident.

- Cooperative Work on Rapid Detection of Biological Agents in Animals, Plants, and Food. This cooperative group is developing a system to improve on-site rapid detection of biological agents in animals, plants, and food.

Figure 1: Examples of Coordination Activities on Bioterrorism Among Federal Departments and Agencies

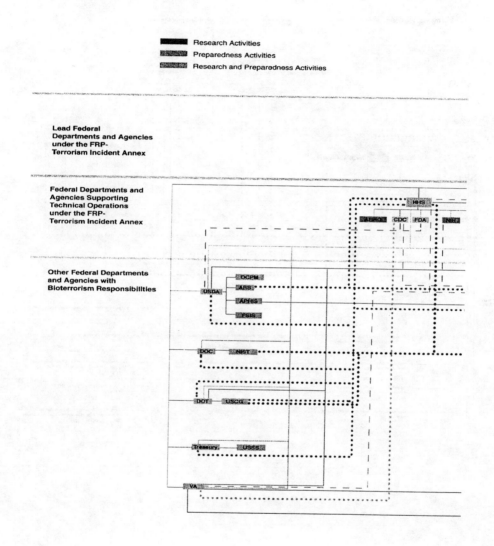

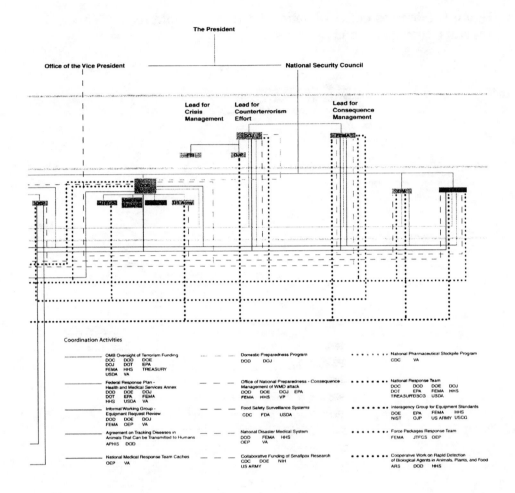

Coordination Activities

OMB Oversight of Terrorism Funding
DOC   DOD   DOE
DOJ   DOT   EPA
FEMA HHS   TREASURY
USDA VA

Federal Response Plan -
Health and Medical Services Annex
DOD   DOE   DOJ
DOT   EPA   FEMA
HHS   USDA VA

Informal Working Group -
Equipment Request Review
DOD   DOE   DOJ
FEMA OEP   VA

Agreement on Tracking Diseases in
Animals That Can be Transmitted to Humans
APHIS   DOD

National Medical Response Team Caches
OEP   VA

Domestic Preparedness Program
DOD   DOJ

Office of National Preparedness - Consequence
Management of WMD attack
DOD   DOE   DOJ   EPA
FEMA HHS   VP

Food Safety Surveillance Systems
CDC   FDA   USDA

National Disaster Medical System
DOD   FEMA   HHS
OEP   VA

Collaborative Funding of Smallpox Research
CDC   DOE   NIH
US ARMY

National Pharmaceutical Stockpile Program
CDC   VA

National Response Team
DOC   DOD   DOE   DOJ
DOT   EPA   FEMA HHS
TREASURY DSCG USDA

Interagency Group for Equipment Standards
DOE   EPA   FEMA   HHS
NIST OJP   US ARMY USCG

Force Packages Response Team
FEMA   JTFCS   OEP

Cooperative Work on Rapid Detection
of Biological Agents in Animals, Plants, and Food
ARS   DOD   HHS

Related GAO Products

Bioterrorism: Federal Research and Preparedness Activities (GAO-01-915, Sept. 28, 2001).

Combating Terrorism: Selected Challenges and Related Recommendations (GAO-01-822, Sept. 20, 2001).

Combating Terrorism: Comments on H.R. 525 to Create a President's Council on Domestic Terrorism Preparedness (GAO-01-555T, May 9, 2001).

Combating Terrorism: Accountability Over Medical Supplies Needs Further Improvement (GAO-01-666T, May 1, 2001).

Combating Terrorism: Observations on Options to Improve the Federal Response (GAO-01-660T, Apr. 24, 2001).

Combating Terrorism: Accountability Over Medical Supplies Needs Further Improvement (GAO-01-463, Mar. 30, 2001).

Combating Terrorism: Comments on Counterterrorism Leadership and National Strategy (GAO-01-556T, Mar. 27, 2001).

Combating Terrorism: FEMA Continues to Make Progress in Coordinating Preparedness and Response (GAO-01-15, Mar. 20, 2001).

Combating Terrorism: Federal Response Teams Provide Varied Capabilities; Opportunities Remain to Improve Coordination (GAO-01-14, Nov. 30, 2000).

West Nile Virus Outbreak: Lessons for Public Health Preparedness (GAO/HEHS-00-180, Sept. 11, 2000).

Combating Terrorism: Linking Threats to Strategies and Resources (GAO/T-NSIAD-00-218, July 26, 2000).

Chemical and Biological Defense: Observations on Nonmedical Chemical and Biological R&D Programs (GAO/T-NSIAD-00-130, Mar. 22, 2000).

Combating Terrorism: Need to Eliminate Duplicate Federal Weapons of Mass Destruction Training (GAO/NSIAD-00-64, Mar. 21, 2000).

Combating Terrorism: Chemical and Biological Medical Supplies Are Poorly Managed (GAO/T-HEHS/AIMD-00-59, Mar. 8, 2000).

Combating Terrorism: Chemical and Biological Medical Supplies Are Poorly Managed (GAO/HEHS/AIMD-00-36, Oct. 29, 1999).

Food Safety: Agencies Should Further Test Plans for Responding to Deliberate Contamination (GAO/RCED-00-3, Oct. 27, 1999).

Endnotes

[1]Bioterrorism is the threat or intentional release of biological agents (viruses, bacteria, or their toxins) for the purposes of influencing the conduct of government or intimidating or coercing a civilian population.

[2]*See Bioterrorism: Federal Research and Preparedness Activities* (GAO-01-915, Sept. 28, 2001). This report was mandated by the Public Health Improvement Act of 2000 (P.L. 106- 505, sec. 102).

[3]We conducted interviews with and obtained information from the Departments of Agriculture, Commerce, Defense, Energy, Health and Human Services, Justice, Transportation, the Treasury, and Veterans Affairs; the Environmental Protection Agency; and the Federal Emergency Management Agency.

[4]See the list of related GAO products at the end of this statement.

[5]*See Combating Terrorism: Need for Comprehensive Threat and Risk Assessments of Chemical and Biological Attacks* (GAO/NSIAD-99-163, Sept. 14, 1999), pp. 10-15, for a discussion of the ease or difficulty for a terrorist to create mass casualties by making or using chemical or biological agents without the assistance of a state-sponsored program.

[6]For example, in January 2000, threatening letters were sent to a variety of recipients, including the Planned Parenthood office in Naples, Florida, warning of the release of anthrax. Federal authorities found no signs of anthrax or any other traces of harmful substances and determined these incidences to be hoaxes.

[7]The Federal Response Plan, originally drafted in 1992 and updated in 1999, is authorized under the Robert T. Stafford Disaster Relief and Emergency Assistance Act (Stafford Act; P.L. 93-288 as amended). The plan outlines the planning assumptions, policies, concept of operations, organizational structures, and specific assignment of responsibilities to lead departments and agencies in providing federal assistance once the President has declared an emergency requiring federal assistance.

[8]Some agencies define WMDs to include large conventional explosives as well.

[9]Disease surveillance systems provide for the ongoing collection, analysis, and dissemination of data to prevent and control disease.

[10]Epidemiological investigation is the study of patterns of health or disease and the factors that influence these patterns.

[11]For example, an agency providing appropriations is not necessarily indicating the level of its commitments (that is, obligations) or expenditures for that year—only the amount of budget authority made available to it by the Congress, some of which may be unspent. Similarly, an agency that provided expenditure information for fiscal year 2000 may have obligated the funds in fiscal year 1999 based on an appropriation for fiscal year 1998. To simplify presentation, we generally refer to all the budget data we received from agencies as "reported funding."

[12]Although there are generally no specific appropriations for activities on bioterrorism, some departments and agencies did provide estimates of the funds they were devoting to activities on bioterrorism. Other departments and agencies provided estimates for overall terrorism activities but were unable to provide funding amounts for activities on bioterrorism specifically. Still others stated that their activities were relevant for bioterrorism, but they were unable to specify the funding amounts. Funding levels for activities on terrorism, including bioterrorism, were reported for activities prior to the 2001 Emergency Supplemental Appropriations Act for Recovery From and Response to Terrorist Attacks on the United States (P.L. 107-38).

[13]Presidential Decision Directive 62, issued May 22, 1998, created a category of special events called National Security Special Events, which are events of such significance that they warrant greater federal planning and protection than other special events.

[14]In addition to simulating a bioterrorism attack in Denver, the exercise also portrayed a chemical weapons incident in Portsmouth, New Hampshire. A concurrent exercise, referred to as National Capital Region 2000, simulated a radiological event in the greater Washington, D.C., area.

[15]See also Combating Terrorism: Comments on Counterterrorism Leadership and National Strategy (GAO-01-556T, Mar. 27, 2001), p. 1.

[16]See Combating Terrorism: Selected Challenges and Related Recommendations (GAO-01-822, Sept. 20, 2001), pp. 79, 84.

[17]Advisory Panel to Assess Domestic Response Capabilities for Terrorism Involving Weapons of Mass Destruction, Toward a National Strategy for Combating Terrorism, Second Annual Report (Arlington, Va.: RAND, Dec. 15, 2000), p. 7.

[18]See also Combating Terrorism: Issues in Managing Counterterrorist Programs (GAO/T-NSIAD-00-145, Apr. 6, 2000), p. 8.

[19]See GAO-01-822, Sept. 20, 2001, pp. 104-106.

[20]See Combating Terrorism: Threat and Risk Assessments Can Help Prioritize and Target Program Investments (GAO/NSIAD-98-74, Apr. 9, 1998) and GAO/NSIAD-99-163, Sept. 14, 1999.

[21]According to the Office of the Vice President, as of June 2001, details on the Vice President's efforts had not yet been determined.

[22]See GAO-01-822, Sept. 20, 2001, pp. 41-42.

[23]A.E. Smithson and L.-A. Levy, Ataxia: The Chemical and Biological Terrorism Threat and the U.S. Response (Washington, D.C.: The Henry L. Stimson Center, Oct. 2000), p. 271.

[24]See West Nile Virus Outbreak: Lessons for Public Health Preparedness (GAO/HEHS-00-180, Sept. 11, 2000), p. 21.

[25]Advisory Panel to Assess Domestic Response Capabilities for Terrorism Involving Weapons of Mass Destruction, p. 32.

[26]D.C. Wetter, W.E. Daniell, and C.D. Treser, "Hospital Preparedness for Victims of Chemical or Biological Terrorism," American Journal of Public Health, Vol. 91, No. 5 (May 2001), pp. 710-16.

[27]J.R. Richards, M.L. Navarro, and R.W. Derlet, "Survey of Directors of Emergency Departments in California on Overcrowding," Western Journal of Medicine, Vol. 172 (June 2000), pp. 385-88.

[28]Smithson and Levy, p. 227.

ROLE OF THE NATIONAL GUARD, RESERVE AND
MILITARY HEALTH SYSTEM IN THE EVENT OF
BIOLOGICAL OR CHEMICAL TERRORIST ATTACKS
BY
MR. CRAIG W. DUEHRING
PRINCIPAL DEPUTY ASSISTANT SECRETARY OF
DEFENSE FOR RESERVE AFFAIRS

Good morning, Mr. Chairman and other distinguished members of this subcommittee. Thank you for the invitation to testify before you today on how the National Guard and Reserves would interface with state and local officials in the aftermath of a chemical or biological attack in the United States. I will also address the preparedness of our Military Health System to assist state and local governments in the event of a biological or chemical terrorist attack. My colleague, Lieutenant General Peake, Surgeon General of the Army, is also here to answer any questions you may have regarding the Military Health System.

The horrific events of Sept. 11th highlighted our nation's vulnerabilities to determined zealots bent on carrying out heinous acts of terrorism. While President Bush, Attorney General Ashcroft, and Secretary Rumsfeld are taking necessary steps to deter and prevent terrorism within the United States, we must consider and prepare ourselves for the very real possibility that these zealots may choose chemical or biological weapons in their next campaign of terror.

The Department of Defense has a wide array of capabilities within our Armed Forces that can be made available to support federal, state and local authorities in dealing with the consequences of a terrorist incident. When disaster strikes, the Reserve Components provide vital capability in the areas of security, search and rescue, water purification, emergency power, communications, temporary shelter, mortuary services, air traffic control and transportation. Every year National Guard, Reserve, and Active Forces respond to domestic emergencies across the nation, from firefighting and riot control to support of citizens victimized by tornadoes, floods and earthquakes.

Located in over 4500 communities across America, our National Guard and Reserves are uniquely suited to help state and local authorities prepare for and respond to chemical or biological incidents in their jurisdictions. They are familiar with emergency response plans and procedures, and they often have close links with the fire, police, and emergency medical personnel who will be first on the scene. As a result, the National Guard and Reserves comprise a highly effective source of trained and ready manpower and expertise. My testimony today focuses on how the National Guard and

Reserves will work with federal, state and local authorities in the event of a domestic chemical or biological event.

Both Guardsmen and Reservists bring critical technical skills and resources to bear during domestic emergencies. Whether fighting forest fires, protecting our communities from the ravages of floods, or assisting federal, state and local authorities in recovering from a terrorist attack, the National Guard and Reserves are ready and trained to preserve life, protect property, and restore essential community services.

Although National Guard and Reserve forces have similar capabilities in responding to emergency situations, there are significant differences in the statutes that apply to their employment. The National Guard operates under different authorities than the Reserves with respect to conditions of employment, command and control structures, and capabilities.

The Reserves operate under the control of the active component or "regular" military forces. These federal military forces typically respond to requests for DoD assistance from a lead federal agency (for example, the FBI or FEMA) during presidentially declared emergencies. Generally, these requests fill special needs or augment state and local level emergency management responders at or near the incident site who may be overwhelmed. If attacks involve the use of chemical or biological agents, casualties may be significant—and Reserve component medical expertise and equipment will likely be needed to both assist state and local health service agencies, and to augment the Department of Health and Human Services' and Department of Veterans Affairs emergency medical support operations. Today, over seventy percent of the Department of Defense's military medical capabilities are assigned to the Army Reserve, Naval Reserve and Air Force Reserve.

The Reserves also possess more than sixty percent of the Department's capability in military chemical-biological detection and decontamination, with the Army Reserve providing the bulk of this capability. These assets will be essential in providing technical expertise and advice to state and local authorities in understanding the nature of a chemical or biological attack and helping to effectively minimize its effect on people, property and public safety.

The Army National Guard and the Air National Guard, on the other hand, may operate under either state control or federal control, depending on the circumstance. The National Guard, while serving in a state active duty status, represents the military force of the state and is controlled by its elected chief executive officer, the governor. It is important for state authorities to be seen as partners with, and not subordinate to, Federal authorities, as recognized in the Terrorism Annex of the Federal Emergency Management Agency's (FEMA) Federal Response Plan. In fact, the plan stipulates that state governments, as opposed to the Federal Government, will have primary responsibility for Weapons of Mass Destruction (WMD) consequence management.

For example, if a domestic biological or chemical incident occurs, the appropriate local medical, firefighter, emergency management or law enforcement official manages the first response. Once the local on-scene incident commander determines that the scope of the incident exceeds the resources and capabilities at that level, state assistance is requested.

The Governor, through the State's Adjutant General, controls National Guard forces in peacetime. The Governor can call the State's Guard members into action to mitigate local or statewide emergencies, such as severe storms, floods, earthquakes, or civil disturbances.

In the event of a terrorist attack, those closest to the problem will be the first to respond. However, the presumption is that if the attack results in catastrophic consequences, state and local capabilities will likely be quickly overwhelmed. If the Governor requests federal support from the President, and the President declares an emergency, a lead federal agency will be designated by the President to direct and coordinate support from other federal agencies (including DoD) to assist state and local responders in responding to the incident.

There is a clearly defined operational structure for the National Guard to respond to emergency situations. As a key component of a Governor's state emergency response force, the National Guard will usually be the first military asset on the scene once deployed for disaster or emergency situations. In 23 states, the State Adjutant General also serves as the State Emergency Management Officer. The State Emergency Management Officer is directly responsible for the planning, operating and executing all state assets for emergency situations. This situation strengthens the effectiveness of emergency response throughout the state and ensures close collaboration and communication between the National Guard and state and local authorities. It also positions the National Guard to facilitate multi-jurisdictional opportunities to jointly train, plan, and exercise with state-based federal, state and local disaster and emergency response agencies.

During the past three years, the Department has established new or strengthened existing capabilities within the National Guard and Reserve to better support federal, state and local authorities in dealing with the consequences of a terrorist event. 27 Weapons of Mass Destruction (WMD) Civil Support Teams have been established to date. We will soon announce the stationing of the 5 additional teams authorized by Congress last year, for a total of 32 Civil Support Teams.

These teams provide specialized expertise and technical assistance to the local incident commander in:

1) Facilitating on-scene communications and command and control among the different responding agencies;

2) Exchanging technical data and information with military laboratory experts on weaponized chemical and biological agents; and

3) Helping to shape/revise the local incident commander's response strategy based on the specific chemical, biological and radiological agents found at the scene.

These WMD Civil Support teams are comprised of 22 highly skilled, full-time, trained and equipped Army and Air National Guard personnel. These teams are unique because of their federal-state relationship. They are federally resourced, federally trained, and operate to support a federal doctrine. But, they will perform their mission primarily under the command and control of the governors of the states in which they are located. Operationally, they fall under the command and control of the Adjutants General of those states for which they have geographic responsibility to respond. As a result, they will be available to respond to an incident as part of a state response, well before federal response assets would be called upon to provide assistance.

If the situation were to evolve into an event that, due to extended operational demands, overwhelmed state and local response assets, the governor could request the President to issue a declaration of national disaster emergency and to provide federal assistance. Other WMD Civil Support teams may be federalized to relieve and further sustain the communications, command and control, and technical support established by the first WMD Civil Support team.

The President of the United States can also activate the National Guard to participate in federal missions. Generally speaking, when federalized for this purpose, Guard units are commanded not by their state Governors, but by the Commander in Chief (CINC) in whose area they operate. These are the CINC, Joint Forces Command (for the continental United States), CINC, Pacific Command (for Hawaii, Alaska, Guam and the Marshall Islands), and CINC, Southern Command (for Puerto Rico and the Virgin Islands.)

Shifting gears a bit, I will now focus on the process by which military medical resources may be used to assist state and local governments in a disaster situation and to identify some of the health and medical assets we can bring to the disaster scene to lend needed assistance. However, before I get into those descriptions, I would like to briefly offer you a summary of what the Military Health System is and why it exists.

The military medical departments' primary mission is to support their combat forces in war and in peacetime to maintain and sustain their well being in the accomplishment of National Military Objectives. The military medical mission is "to provide top quality health services, whenever needed, and to support military operations." Subsequently, military medical readiness is defined as all actions and preparation necessary to respond effectively and rapidly to the entire spectrum of potential military operations—from major regional conflicts, to smaller scale contingency operations, to humanitarian support missions. Military readiness involves both Active and Reserve forces, and is accomplished through a strategy that seamlessly ensures a health and fit force, prevention of casualties from operational threats, and responsive combat casualty care and management. The Military Health System (MHS) must fully integrate its military medical readiness mission with its beneficiary mission to provide quality, cost-effective medical services and support to military families, retirees and their families worldwide. Through the conduct of the MHS beneficiary mission, readiness is promoted in the military medical departments through the maintaining of a fit force; continuous surveillance of health risks pre-, during and post-deployment; the provision of clinical training for medical providers; enhancing recruiting and retention of quality service members; and otherwise fostering quality of life for military families by ensuring access to a world class health care system.

The Military Health System (MHS) consists of 76 hospitals and more than 400 medical clinics worldwide serving an eligible population of 8.3 million. In addition, we maintain medical units capable of deploying with our Armed Forces to provide the preventive and resuscitative care that our troops may require in the conduct of operational contingencies. We emphasize the maintenance of a healthy, hyper-fit force prepared for the rigors of these contingencies, and the prevention of injury and illness. We identify potential hazardous exposures, track immunizations, and record health encounters with information systems designed to provide a continuous life-cycle surveillance that supports the health and fitness of the fighting force.

Concurrently, we provide a comprehensive healthcare delivery system for our service members, retirees, survivors, and family members. This system not only provides a training platform to maintain the technical skills of military clinicians, but also ensures our ability to directly influence the quality of care provided we deliver to our beneficiaries. Our primary responsibility is to provide medical support for our deployed forces, but those capabilities are inextricably linked to our hospital and clinic operations. A robust healthcare delivery system is a strategic lynchpin that ensures a healthy and fit force for National Command Authority-directed contingencies, provides the medical architecture capable of providing combat health support in missions ranging from humanitarian civic assistance to high intensity conflict.

The U.S. military has a history of successfully providing support and assistance to domestic civil authorities during emergencies and other instances of national concern. Examples you may recall include the military's response to natural disasters within the United States, such as hurricanes and earthquakes. The task of supporting civil authorities in a time of crisis is not a new responsibility for either DoD or military medicine.

The process for involving the Federal Government in support of a chemical, biological, radiological, nuclear, or high-yield explosive (CBRNE) event follows closely the process for involvement with domestic natural or man made disasters. Should the local and state assets be overwhelmed, the Governor may request Federal assistance under the Federal Response Plan. Twenty-eight federal agencies, including DoD, support this plan.

Because of our constant vigilance and need to be prepared to support operational forces in any location around the world, military medicine can rapidly mobilize health and medical assets in support of virtually any crisis. Some of these capabilities include field hospitals, specialized medical augmentation teams, field laboratory diagnostic capabilities, medical evacuation, public health, vector control, patient tracking, veterinary support, medical logistics support, and mass casualty care. Additionally, we have our stationary military medical treatment facilities located around the nation that have inpatient capabilities. Specific medical tasks for the Military Health System in a CBRNE incident include triage and stabilization, health and risk assessment, and other life sustaining and supporting measures.

Finally, DoD is a partner with Federal agencies that provide support of validated requirements emerging from FEMA's Federal Response Plan for Emergency Support Function 8, "Health and Medical Services." This includes making available, if requested, a robust bed expansion capability that can be activated by the National Disaster Medical System (NDMS).

The National Disaster Medical System is a Federal system designed to provide a coordinated medical response in time of war, national emergency, or major domestic disaster resulting in mass casualties. Patients are evacuated to designated locations throughout the United States for care that cannot be provided locally. They are placed in a national network of hospitals that have agreed to accept patients in the event of a major disaster. Agencies sharing responsibilities with DoD include the Department of Health and Human Services (DHHS), FEMA, and the Department of Veterans Affairs (VA). The Assistant Secretary of Defense for Health Affairs may activate NDMS in support of military contingencies when casualties exceed the combined capabilities of the VA/DoD Contingency Care System. The Director of FEMA or the Assistant Secretary of Health (Department of Health and Human Services) may activate NDMS in response to a domestic conventional disaster. Under the latter circumstances, DoD components, when authorized, will participate in relief operations to the extent compatible with U.S. national security interests.

We will continue to leverage the wartime capabilities of the men and women in our Armed Forces for domestic consequence management in support of civil authorities. Above all, we will work to ensure that Active, Guard and Reserve forces are readily accessible to support domestic civil emergencies, and that they are trained to seamlessly function as part of the incident command system used by the nation's first responder community.

Our goal is to support America's fire, police, and emergency medical personnel as rapidly as possible with capabilities and tools that complement and enhance their response, not duplicate it. Our ongoing efforts, which leverage the best military technology and expertise available, will help us achieve that goal.

In summary, Mr. Chairman and Distinguished Members of the Subcommittee, the Department of Defense has tremendous capability to support federal, state and local agencies in the event of a biological or chemical terrorist attack. The mechanisms for providing that support are well understood and have been exercised more vigorously in the last few years. The events of September 11, 2001 have invigorated many federal, state and local authorities to review and update their plans in the event of a domestic terrorist attack using chemical or biological weapons. Communications between and among these critical emergency response elements across federal, state and local levels have improved dramatically, and need to be continuously exercised.

It has been my distinct pleasure to be here today, and I thank you again for the opportunity to testify. Lieutenant General Peake and I welcome any questions you may have.

DOCUMENT NO. 16

STATEMENTS AT A HEARING OF THE SUBCOMMITTEE ON NATIONAL SECURITY, VETERANS AFFAIRS AND INTERNATIONAL RELATIONS OF THE HOUSE COMMITTEE ON GOVERNMENT REFORM

"COMBATING TERRORISM: ASSESSING THE THREAT OF A BIOLOGICAL WEAPONS ATTACK"

CHAIRMAN CHRISTOPHER SHAYS
MR. RAYMOND DECKER, GAO
M. JOHN PARACHINI, RAND
DR. JEROLD M. POST,
THE GEORGE WASHINGTON UNIVERSITY

October 12, 2001

COMMENTARY: *Through the comments of Chairman Shays are in the form of a Press Release, the material he provides includes an excellent background paper which sets the stage for the testimony given and the problems to be addressed. Also, the testimony offers distinctly professional commentary from a diverse range of experts.*

CHRISTOPHER SHAYS, CHAIRMAN
SUBCOMMITTEE ON NATIONAL SECURITY, VETERANS AFFAIRS
AND INTERNATIONAL RELATIONS

NEWS RELEASE

For Immediate Release
October 11, 2001
Washington D.C.

National Security Hearing to Examine Bioweapons Threat;
Ex-Soviet Bioweapons Program Official, Dr. Ken Alibek, To Testify

(Washington, DC)—Congressman Christopher Shays (R-CT), Chairman of the Subcommittee on National Security, Veterans Affairs, and International Relations, will convene an oversight hearing October 12 entitled *"Combating Terrorism: Assessing the Threat of a Biological Weapons Attack."* Dr. Ken Alibek, deputy chief of the former Soviet Union's biological weapons program from 1988 to 1992, will testify.

"Many experts believe it is only a matter of time before biological weapons are used by international terrorists," said Chairman Shays. "Although a biological agent can be developed with relative ease, weaponizing the agent and delivering it are more difficult. The purpose of this hearing is to examine U.S. efforts to develop a comprehensive assessment process to address the threat of biological terrorism."

The Friday, October 12 hearing will convene at 10:00 a.m. in Room 2154, the Rayburn Building in Washington, DC. Witnesses will be representatives from the General Accounting Office (GAO), Advanced Bio-Systems Inc., RAND Corporation, and George Washington University (GWU).

Among the witnesses will be Dr. Kenneth Alibek, President of Bio-Systems Inc. and author of the 1999 book "Biohazard." He was first deputy chief of the Biopreparat arm of the former Soviet Union's biological weapons program before defecting to the U.S. in 1992. Formerly known as Kanatjan Alibekov, Dr. Alibek claims that Russia today still conducts research on biological agents under the guise of defensive research activities. He will discuss Russia's biological weapons program, the potential transfer of that technology to states and terrorist groups, and the range of biological agents that might be used as weapons.

According to a TIME Magazine article entitled "The Germ Warrior" (7/19/99), Dr. Alibek's book "Biohazard" is part of "a campaign to warn the world about the danger of biological attacks. Says Alibek, 'Existing defenses against these weapons are dangerously inadequate, and when biological terror strikes, and I'm convinced it will, public ignorance will only heighten the disaster.'"

Other hearing witnesses will be:

Raymond Decker, GAO's Director of Defense Capabilities, who will address the need and requirement for a comprehensive threat and risk assessment;

John Parachini, Policy Analyst at RAND, who will focus on terrorist organizations, including the types of states, groups or individuals most likely to use bioweapons, and what hurdles terrorists face in acquiring and using such weapons;

Jerold Post, Professor of Psychiatry at GWU, who will discuss the mind of the terrorist and the personality traits associated with terrorism.

"We can't defend against every conceivable worst case scenario," Shays said. "Defense against biological warfare depends on a clear-eyed assessment of the real threat and a willingness to confront that threat aggressively."

On October 23, the Subcommittee will examine the role of vaccines in defending against biological weapons attacks.

The Subcommittee on National Security, Veterans Affairs, and International Relations has oversight responsibility over those departments and agencies of government managing programs and activities related to committee jurisdictions, including the DoD, State, VA, FEMA, NASA, CIA, and others involved in national security. This will be the panel's twentieth hearing on U.S. efforts to combat terrorism.

MEDIA ADVISORY

For Immediate Release
October 9, 2001
Washington, D.C.

Congressman Christopher Shays to Hold October 12 Hearing Entitled *"Combating Terrorism: Assessing the Threat of a Biological Weapons Attack."*

(Washington, DC)—Congressman Christopher Shays (R-CT), Chairman of the Subcommittee on National Security, Veterans Affairs, and International Relations, will convene an oversight hearing on October 12 entitled, "Combating Terrorism: Assessing the Threat of a Biological Weapons Attack," as announced by Government Reform Committee, Chairman, Rep. Dan Burton (R-IN). The hearing will identify states, terrorist groups and individuals who allegedly acquired or employed biological weapons, and determine the intent and capabilities of such actors.

The Friday, October 12, 2001 hearing will convene at 10:00 am in room 2154 Rayburn House Office Building.

The Subcommittee on National Security, Veterans Affairs, and International Relations has oversight responsibility over those departments and agencies of government managing programs and activities related to committee jurisdictions, including the DoD, State, FEMA, CIA, and others involved in national security.

Witnesses

Mr. Raymond Decker
Director, Defense Capabilities
Management Team
U.S. General Accounting Office

Accompanied by,
Mr. Stephen Caldwell
Assistant Director

Dr. Ken Alibek
Author, "Biohazard"
President of Advanced Bio-Systems, Inc

John Parachini
Policy Analyst
RAND Corporation

Jerrold Post
Professor of Psychiatry
Political Psychology and
International Affairs
The George Washington University

MEMORANDUM

October 9, 2001

To: Members of the Subcommittee on National Security, Veterans Affairs, and International Relations

From: R. Nicholas Palarino, Senior Policy Analyst

Subject:Briefing memorandum for the hearing *Combating Terrorism: Assessing the Threat of Biological Terrorism*, scheduled for Friday, October 12, 2001, at 10:00 a.m. in room 2154 Rayburn House Office Building.

PURPOSE OF THE HEARING

The purpose of the hearing is to examine the factors that should be considered in assessing the risks of biological terrorism.

HEARING ISSUES

1. To what extent are assessments needed to address the threat of biological terrorism?

2. How are the intentions and capabilities of state and non-state actors measured in assessing the threat of biological terrorism?

BACKGROUND

Many agree a biological weapons attack on the United States could be psychologically devastating and, depending on the microorganism or toxin, kill thousands of people. However, there are opposing views concerning the likelihood and impact of such an event.

Policymakers, scholars, and the news media are becoming increasingly alarmed by the potential for biological weapons terrorism. Driving these concerns are the global spread of scientific knowledge and technology relevant to biological weapons terrorism, the vulnerability of the civilian population, the events of September 11, 2001, which demonstrated the intent of the terrorists to inflict mass casualties, and the recent cases of anthrax discovered in Florida.

Others consider the likelihood of a terrorist attack using biological weapons to be low because of difficulties involved processing biological agents into lethal forms, and problems delivering the weapons in a manner which would achieve large-scale casualties.

Assessing Terrorist Threats

Threat analysis is the continual process of compiling and examining all available information concerning potential terrorist activities by terrorist groups. A threat analysis reviews the factors of a terrorist group's existence, capability, intentions, history, and targeting, as well as the security environment in which they operate. Threat analysis is an essential step in identifying the probability of a terrorist attack and results in a threat assessment.

While agencies continuously assess, and report on various threats, National Intelligence Estimates (NIE) provide analysis on issues of major importance and long-term interest to the United States. They are the intelligence community's most authoritative projection of future developments in a particular subject area. An NIE is intended to help decision-makers think through critical issues by presenting key facts, judgements about the likely course of events, and the implications for the United States.

NIEs are generally focused on foreign-origin threats. The National Intelligence Council (NIC), (an organization composed of 12 National Intelligence Officers, including one from the FBI, and that reports directly to the Director of Central Intelligence) produces NIEs. To prepare an NIE, the NIC brings together analysts from all the intelligence agencies that have expertise on the issue under review. In the end, an NIE is the Director of Central Intelligence's assessment, with which the heads of the U.S. intelligence agencies concur. (**Attachment 1,** p. 5)

Risk management is the deliberate process of understanding risk—the likelihood that a threat will harm an asset or individuals with some severity of consequences—and deciding on and implementing actions to reduce it. A threat analysis, the first step in determining risk, identifies and evaluates each threat on the basis of various factors such as its capability and intent to attack an asset and the likelihood and the severity of the consequences of a successful attack. Valid, current, and documented threat information, including NIEs, in a risk assessment process are crucial to ensuring risk management strategies are not based solely on worst-case scenarios and are not therefore out of balance with the threat.

Risk management principles acknowledge that (1) while risk generally cannot be eliminated, it can be reduced by enhancing protection from validated and credible threats, (2) although many threats are possible, some are more likely to be carried out than others, and (3) all assets are not equally critical. (**Attachment 1,** p. 6)

Risk management establishes priorities for security program requirements. Generally, the process is a deliberate, analytical approach to identify which threats can exploit which vulnerabilities to an organization's specific assets.

These variables are ranked according to predetermined criteria, such as the probability of a threat targeting a specific asset or the impact of vulnerabilities being exploited by a specific threat. The process results in a prioritized list of risks used to select safeguards to reduce vulnerabilities and create a certain level of protection. This process helps prioritize investment in preparedness against a terrorist attack. (**Attachment 1**, p. 19, and **Attachment 2**, p. 4)

Recognizing other countries have more experience dealing with terrorist attacks within their borders, the GAO assessed how other countries allocate their resources to combat terrorism. Canada, France, Germany, Israel, and the United Kingdom were used as case studies. (**Attachment 3**)

The five countries GAO reviewed received terrorist threat information from civilian and military intelligence services and foreign sources. Using various means, each of the countries' intelligence services continuously assess these threats to determine which could result in terrorist activity and require countermeasures, which may be less likely to occur but may emerge later, and which are unlikely to occur.

Officials in all countries told the GAO that because of limited resources, they made funding decisions for programs to combat terrorism based on the likelihood of terrorist activity actually taking place, not vulnerability to terrorist attack. For example, each of the countries may be vulnerable to a chemical, biological, radiological, or nuclear attack by terrorists, but officials believe such attacks are unlikely to occur in the near future for a variety of reasons, including the current difficulty in producing and delivering these types of weapons. (**Attachment 3**, p. 11)

Based on the studies cited above, the GAO recommended the Federal Bureau of Investigation (FBI) conduct a comprehensive threat and risk assessment. The FBI agreed to conduct the assessment. (**Attachment 4**) On September 10, 2001, a member of the Subcommittee staff asked counterterrorism officials within the FBI the status of threat and risk assessment. The FBI officials said they knew nothing about the assessment.

Understanding the Biological Weapons and the Terrorist Threat

A biological weapon is a living microorganism or infective material derived from the organism, intentionally used to cause disease or death in plants and animals. Biological agents are more toxic, more specific, slower acting, and may be more persistent than chemical agents. Biological agents are also less controllable, and may have longer residual effects than chemical agents. The 1975 Biological Weapons Convention (BWC) prohibits the development, production, and stockpiling of biological weapons.

There are a number of biological agents that are cause for concern. Two agents—anthrax and smallpox—are particularly worrisome. Anthrax (bacillus anthracis), within two to four days of exposure, causes coughing, difficult breathing, exhaustion, and eventually terminal shock. If left untreated, the lethality rate is very high—up to 100%. Anthrax can be inhaled, ingested, or absorbed by contact. Anthrax spores are stable and remain viable for many years.

Smallpox is a highly contagious viral disease, declared eradicated in 1980 by the World Health Organization (WHO). Individuals contracting smallpox produce pimplelike pustules on the skin that become pockmarked scars. The mortality rate is high. Even though the virus has been eradicated, the United States and Russia have stocks of the virus. Illicit stocks are thought to exist in rogue nations. (**Attachment 5**)

There are a number of countries that are reported to have biological weapons or biological weapon development programs. (**Attachment 6**)

China, a member of the BWC since 1984, is believed to have maintained an offensive biological weapons program throughout most of the 1980s that included development, production, stockpiling or other acquisition or maintenance of biological warfare agents. Within the US intelligence community there is concern that China may have revived and possibly expanded its offensive biological weapons program in recent years. The concern is based partly on evidence that China is pursuing biological research at two ostensibly civilian-run research centers controlled by the Chinese military. The research centers were known to have been previously involved in the production and storage of biological weapons. Moreover, in 1991 one of the suspected biological centers was expanded.

Egypt, a signatory but not a member of the BWC, has a program of military-applied research in the area of biological weapons dating back to the 1960s. In the 1970s, President Anwar Sadat confirmed that a stockpile of biological agents was stored in refrigerated facilities on Egyptian soil. Egypt has been studying various toxins, and techniques for their production and refinement are presently being developed by a national research center. Egyptian researchers have been cooperating with US military and civilian laboratories in areas related to biological defense research, specifically those based on highly pathogenic micro-organisms and dangerous vectors. The level of bilateral cooperation is such the US military has a military-medical laboratory in Egypt where research is focused on defenses against infectious diseases. This laboratory is recognized as one of the region's leading medical-biological centers, equipped with the latest equipment and staffed with highly qualified American specialists.

Iran has been a member of the BWC since 1973. Iran has the technical infrastructure to support a significant biological warfare program and needs little foreign assistance. Nonetheless, Western countries have noted attempts by Iranian representatives to buy, unofficially, technology and biological materials used specifically for the production of biological weapons.

Iran conducts legitimate biomedical research at various institutes, which are suspected of involvement in this biological weapons program. The Iranian military has used medical, education, and scientific research organizations for many aspects of biological agent procurement, research, and production. The US finding is that Iran probably has produced biological agents and apparently has weaponized a small quantity of those agents.

Israeli officials have been tight-lipped about any national biological weapons program. An Israeli biological weapons program is likely to be patterned, however, after those formerly maintained by the United States and the former Soviet Union. In other words, the agents likely to be involved in an Israeli program are anthrax, botulinum toxin, tularemia, plague, Venezuelan equine encephalitis, and Q-fever. Similarly, Israeli delivery systems are likely to mirror those developed by the United States, namely spray systems or missile warheads. Israel is one of the few states that has not signed the BWC.

Libya has been a member of the BWC since 1972. There is information indicating it is engaged in initial testing of biological weapons. Libyans have expressed interest in information on work overseas involving biological agents. Contacts with representatives of other Arab countries have revealed Libyan specialists are displaying a willingness to fund joint biological programs, including ones of a military-applied nature, provided they are not undertaken on Libyan territory.

North Korea, a member of the BWC since 1987, is one of the most closed and heavily militarized societies on Earth. During the early 1960s, North Korea initiated an offensive biological warfare program. Presently, North Korea is engaged in applied military-biological research at universities, medical institutes, and specialized research centers. Research being conducted at these centers involves pathogens for malignant anthrax, cholera, and bubonic plague. Evidence indicates that North Korea has been testing biological weapons on its island territories.

Syria has signed but not ratified the BWC. Israel has expressed concern that Syria has biological agents for contaminating drinking water. However, no reliable information is available about the existence of biological weapons in Syria or a directed program for the creation of an offensive potential in the biological realm. Syria nonetheless remains among those countries the United States believes to be developing an offensive biological warfare capability.

Taiwan joined the BWC in 1973, and is another country suspected of proliferating both chemical and biological weapons. Taiwan is said not to have biological weapons, but it continues to manifest an active interest in conducting biological research of a military-applied nature. Taiwan has a significant scientific and technical base in microbiology and a large number of skilled biotechnology specialists, mostly trained in America and Western Europe. Taiwan is moving to upgrade its biotechnology sector, which makes wide use of technologies basic to the production of biological weapons. Sufficient evidence to determine if Taiwan is producing or weaponizing biological agents does not exist, but Taiwan's advanced scientific research and industrial base would enable the country to produce biological weapons with relative ease.

Russia is said to have had an extensive biological weapons program. Kenneth Alibek was known as Kanatjan Alibekov as he rose to become first deputy chief of the Biopreparat arm of the Soviet biological weapons program. His tenure inside the weapons complex lasted from 1975 to 1991. Then Alibek, who invented an anthrax strain that is four times more efficient than the standard military variant, defected to the United States in 1992. According to Alibek, the Soviet Union continued a biological weapons program in the 1970s and 1980s out of fear a covert US offensive germ warfare program remained active even after President Richard Nixon terminated the US program in 1969. Alibek claims that today Russia still conducts research on biological agents under the guise of defensive research activities. In addition to their work with the plague, Russian scientists have developed genetically altered strands of tularemia and glanders that are antibiotic resistant. Russian scientists from Obolensk published a research paper in *Vaccine*, a British medical journal, stating they had genetically engineered an anthrax strain so it resists the current vaccine. During the heyday of the Soviet program, Alibek says the Soviet Union stockpiled at least 20 tons of weapons grade smallpox. Other stockpiled agents included the plague and anthrax.

The **United States** maintains a defensive program. On 25 November 1969, during a visit to Fort Detrick, Maryland, President Nixon renounced the development, production, stockpiling, and use of biological warfare agents. He also reaffirmed the US no-first-use policy for chemical weapons. The Department of Defense was required to dispose of existing biological weapons and scale down the program to include research only for defensive measures. In the wake of the announcement, the US Army Medical Unit changed its name to the US Army Medical Research Institute of Infectious Diseases (USAMRIID). The focus of USAMRIID shifted to the development of vaccines, protective measures, and detection systems.

Biological weapons are easier to breed than to disseminate. The lethality of the agent depends on the delivery method, weather conditions, and where victims encounter the germ. With each scenario there are different pluses and minuses. According to experts in the many fields associated with the technical aspects of dealing with biological agents, including those formerly with state-sponsored offensive biological weapon programs, terrorists working outside a state-run laboratory infrastructure would have to overcome extraordinary technical and operational challenges to effectively and successfully weaponize and deliver a biological agent to cause mass casualties. Terrorists would require specialized knowledge from a wide range of scientific disciplines to successfully conduct biological terrorism and cause mass casualties. Moreover, biological agents have varying characteristics.

Information and technical data from these experts, intelligence, and authoritative documented sources indicate that some biological agents such as smallpox are difficult to obtain. In the case of other biological agents such as anthrax and tularemia (both of which are bacteria), it is difficult to obtain a virulent strain (one that causes disease and injury to humans). Other agents such as plague are difficult to produce. Biological toxins such as ricin require large quantities to cause mass casualties, thereby increasing the risk of arousing suspicion or detection prior to dissemination. Furthermore, some agents such as Q fever incapacitate rather than cause death. Finally, many agents are relatively easy to grow, but are difficult to process into a form for a weapon. (**Attachment 1**, p. 13-14)

According to experts from former biological warfare programs, to survive and be effective, a virulent biological agent must be grown, handled, and stored properly. This requires time and effort for research and development. Terrorists would need the means to sterilize the growth medium and dispose of hazardous biological wastes. Processing the biological agent into a weaponized form requires even more specialized knowledge. The most effective way to disseminate a biological agent is by aerosol. This method allows the simultaneous respiratory infection of a large number of people. Microscopic particles that are dispersed must remain airborne for long periods and may be transported by the wind over long distances. The particles must be small enough to reach the tiny air sacs of the lungs (alveoli) and bypass the body's natural filtering and defense mechanisms. If larger particles are dispersed, they may fall to the ground, causing no injury, or become trapped in the upper respiratory tract, possibly causing infections but not necessarily death. From a bio-engineering standpoint, it is easier to produce and disseminate the larger particles than the microscopic particles. Other critical technical hurdles include obtaining the proper size equipment to generate proper size aerosols, calculating the correct output rate (speed at which the equipment operates), and having the correct liquid composition.

Biological agents can also be processed into liquid or dry forms for dissemination. Both forms pose difficult technical challenges for terrorists to effectively cause mass casualties. Liquid agents are easy to produce. However, it is difficult to effectively disseminate aerosolized liquid agents with the right particle size without reducing the strength of the mixture. Further, the liquid agent requires larger quantities and dissemination vehicles that can increase the possibility of raising suspicion and detection. In addition, experts say that in contrast, dry biological agents are more difficult to produce than liquid agents, but dry agents are easier to disseminate. Dry biological agents could be easily destroyed when processed, rendering the agent ineffective for causing mass casualties. The whole process entails risks. For example, powders easily adhere to rubber gloves and pose a handling problem. Effectively disseminating both forms of agent can pose technical challenges in that the proper equipment and energy sources are needed. A less sophisticated product and dissemination method can produce some illness and/or deaths.

Exterior dissemination of biological agents can be disrupted by environmental (e.g., pollution) and meteorological (e.g., sun, rain, mist, and wind) conditions. Once released, an aerosol cloud gradually decays and dies as a result of exposure to oxygen, pollutants, and ultraviolet rays. If wind is too erratic or strong, the agent might be dissipated too rapidly or fail to reach the desired area. Interior dissemination of a biological agent through a heating and air conditioning ventilation system could cause casualties. But this method also has risks. Security countermeasures could intercept the perpetrators or apprehend them after the attack. Successful interior dissemination also requires knowledge of aerodynamics. For example, the air exchange rate in a building could affect the dissemination of a biological agent. Regardless of whether a liquid or dry agent is used in interior or exterior environments, experts believe testing would need to be done to determine if the agent is virulent and disseminates properly. The numerous steps in the process of developing a biological weapon increase the chances of a terrorist being detected by authorities.

Much of the information about terrorist interest and activity in biological weapons is classified. However, some of this activity has been reported. On March 20, 1995, the nerve agent sarin was unleashed in the Tokyo subway system, killing 12 people and injuring 5,500. Thousands did not die from the Tokyo attack because of an impure mixture of the agent. The cult responsible for the sarin attack, Aum Shinrikyo ("Supreme Truth") was developing biological agents as well. (**Attachment 7**)

In October 1992 Shoko Asahara, head of the Aum Shinrikyo cult, and 40 followers traveled to Zaire, ostensibly to help treat Ebola victims. But the group's real intention, according to an October 31, 1995, report by the U.S. Senate's Permanent Subcommittee on Investigations, was probably to obtain virus samples, culture them, and use them in biological attacks.

Interest in acquiring killer organisms for sinister purposes is not limited to groups outside the United States. On May 5, 1995, six weeks after the Tokyo subway incident, Larry Harris, a laboratory technician in Ohio, ordered the bacterium that causes bubonic plague from a Maryland Collection in Rockville, Md., mailed him three vials of Yersinia pestis.

Harris drew suspicion only when he called the firm four days after placing his order to find out why it had not arrived. Company officials wondered about his impatience and his apparent unfamiliarity with laboratory techniques, so they contacted federal authorities. He was later found to be a member of a white supremacist organization. In November 1995 he pled guilty in federal court to mail fraud.

To get the plague bacteria, Harris needed no more than a credit card and a false letterhead. Partially in response to this incident, an antiterrorism law enacted this past April required the Centers for Disease Control and Prevention to monitor more closely shipments of infectious agents.

Fortunately, biological terrorism has thus far been limited to very few cases. One incident occurred in September 1984, when about 750 people became sick after eating in restaurants in Oregon. In 1986 Ma Anand Sheela confessed at a federal trial that she and other members of a nearby cult that had clashed with local Oregonians had spread salmonella bacteria on salad bars in four restaurants; the bacteria had been grown in laboratories on the cult's ranch. (**Attachment 7**)

Osama bin Laden declared in an interview, "We don't consider it a crime if we tried to have nuclear, chemical, biological weapons. Our Holy land is occupied by Israeli and American forces. We have the right to defend ourselves and to liberate our holy land.[1]

Although there have been many studies conducted to understand the mind of a terrorist, the studies did not identify a single personality pattern or trait associated with terrorism. However, two personality types were disproportionately represented among terrorists, especially among leaders. Such individuals had features of narcissistic and sociopathic personality disorders, as well as angry paranoia. These types of individuals seem to be self- absorbed, restless, action-oriented, and have a low level of tolerance. They suffer from an impaired conscience and reduced capacity to empathize with the pain and suffering of others. They tend to externalize their problems, idealizing the group. Such individuals, who often suffer from a lack of personal, educational, and professional success, seek an outside enemy to blame for their problems. The statement "It's not us, it's them; they are responsible" provides a psychologically satisfying explanation for what has gone wrong in their lives. They feel an imperative need to strike out at the external objects they perceive as the source of their misfortune. (**Attachment 8**)

---

1   Jamal Ismail, "I Am Not Afraid of Death" (interview with Osama bin Laden), *Nesweek*, January 11, 1999, p. 37.

The witnesses for the hearing will focus on different aspects of the bioterrorism issue. Mr. Raymond Decker, from GAO, will discuss the need and requirement for a comprehensive threat and risk assessment. Dr. Kenneth Alibek, previously the first deputy chief of the Biopreparat arm of the Soviet biological weapons program, will address the Russian biological weapons program and the transfer of technology to other state and non-state actors. Mr. John Parachini will focus on terrorist organizations, including what type of states, terrorist groups, or individuals are most likely to use biological weapons, and for what purpose, linkage among terrorist groups and individuals, and what hurdles terrorists face in acquiring and using such weapons. Mr. Jerold Post, Professor of Psychiatry, will discuss the mind of the terrorist and personality patterns and traits associated with terrorism.

1. To what extent are assessments needed to address the threat of biological terrorism?

A threat analysis should identify and evaluate each threat on the basis of various factors, such as capability and intent to attack an asset, the likelihood of successful attack, and lethality. The next step is to determinate the likelihood, or risk, a threat will harm an asset or individuals with some severity of consequence, and deciding on and implementing actions to reduce the likelihood. The last step in the process is prioritizing and allocating resources based on the likelihood of an occurrence. This allows funds to be distributed to the most critical areas.

The GAO and Congressional Research Service (CRS) have made numerous recommendations about the need for threat prioritization. In September of 1999, the GAO recommended the Federal Bureau of Investigation (FBI) produce a threat assessment of the more likely chemical and biological agents used by domestic-origin terrorists. Additionally, GAO recommends the FBI sponsor a national-level risk assessment using National Intelligence Estimates (NIE) and other inputs to help guide and prioritize appropriate counter-measures and programs designed to combat chemical and biological terrorism. In May 2000, the GAO stated that there is a lack of linkage between the terrorist threat, national strategy, and agency resources.[2] In July 2000, the GAO stated that the first step in developing sound programs to combat terrorism is to develop a thorough understanding of the terrorist threat. The second step is the development of a threat and risk assessment that can be used to develop a strategy, and guide resource investments.[3] CRS states, "Comprehensive threat and risk

2   Congress, House, Committee on Transportation and Infrastructure. *Combating Terrorism: H. R. 4210*: Hearing before the Subcommittee on Oversight, Investigations and Emergency Management, May 4, 2000.

3   General Accounting Office, *Combating Terrorism: Linking Threat to Strategies and Resources*, GAO/T-SIAD-00-218, July 2000.

assessments concerning the possible use of weapons of mass destruction by terrorists would allow federal authorities to make judgements as to whether funding is at the proper level overall, as well as allocations for specific programs. These same assessments could assist in establishing priorities and reducing or eliminating duplication of effort in combating terrorism programs."[4]

Experts have recommended the Executive Branch develop a national intelligence estimate focusing on the terrorist threat. John Parachini, from the Monterey Institute of International Studies states, "The United States lacks a comprehensive and integrated intelligence assessment to inform policymakers thinking on how to prioritize spending decisions to support the government's programs to counter terrorism." Parachini further points out, "what is missing on how to best combat terrorism is a regular, comprehensive threat assessment that integrates assessments of both domestic and international terrorist threats."[5] Micheal Wermuth, Program Director at the RAND Corporation states, the "United States does not have an integrated threat and risk assessment incorporating terrorist threats to military installations and forces, including international threats and domestic terrorist threats."[6]

Frank J. Cilluffo, from the Center for Strategic and International Studies (CSIS) said, "The common thread is the need for a first rate intelligence capability. More specifically, the breadth, depth, and uncertainty of the terrorist threat demands significant investment, coordination, and re-tooling of the intelligence process across the board for the pre-attack (warning), trans-attack (preemption) and post-attack (whodunit) phases."[7] Cilluffo also said the development of an annual threat assessment of the foreign and domestic threat of chemical, biological, radiological, and nuclear terrorism to provide federal planners with the basis for assessing the emerging risk of such attacks and develop an integrated analysis structure for planning US programs and response.[8]

---

4   Congressional Research Service RL30938. *Terrorism and the Military's Role in Domestic Crisis Management: Background and Issues for Congress.* Report prepared by Jeffrey D. Brake, National Defense Fellow, April 19, 2001, 20.

5   Congress, House, Committee on Government Reform, *Combating Terrorism: Assessing Threats, Risk Management, and Establishing Priorities:* Hearing before the Subcommittee on National Security, Veterans Affairs and International Relations, July 26, 2000.

6   Ibid.

7   Congress, House, Committee on Government Reform, *Combating Terrorism: In Search of a National Strategy:* Hearing before the Subcommittee on National Security, Veterans Affairs and International Relations, March 27, 2001.

8   Frank J. Cilluffo, Sharon L. Cardash, and Gordon N. Lederman, *Combating Chemical, Biological, Radiological and Nuclear Terrorism: A Comprehensive Strategy* (Washington, D.C.: Center for Strategic and International Studies, 2000), 24.

Two government-sponsored commissions agree the United States requires a comprehensive threat assessment. The US Commission on National Security/21st Century recommends development of a national intelligence estimate.[9] The Advisory Panel to Assess Domestic Response Capabilities for Terrorism Involving Weapons of Mass Destruction concludes, initial and continuing, comprehensive and articulate assessments of potential credible terrorist threats within the United States, and ensuring risk and vulnerability assessments are critical for policymakers.[10]

2. How are the intentions and capabilities of state and non-state actors measured in assessing the threat of biological terrorism?

When considering the probability of terrorist attack using biological weapons, several factors should be considered. First there is the history of such events. Although there have been few cases discovered of terrorists using biological weapons, many believe it is only a matter of time before such weapons are used. There are two primary reasons for this conclusion. First, the remnants of state-sponsored biological programs may allow some biological weapons, or even the technology to develop biological weapons, to be transferred to terrorist groups. Second, terrorist groups such as al Queda, have demonstrated they want high profile, mass casualty events like September 11, 2001. Therefore, terrorists could have access to biological weapons, and certainly, have the motivation.

Other factors should be considered in assessing capabilities of terrorists. The technological expertise and means of delivery is problematic for the terrorist. Although, some believe a biological agent can be developed with relative ease, weaponizing the agent and delivering it are more difficult, especially if the desired effect is mass casualties. However, even the threat of a biological weapons attack could have a devastating physchological impact on the citizens of a country. An additional factor to consider is the mind of the terrorist, or his motivation for using biological weapons. Post indicates terrorists are unstable, and will strike out using any means to accomplish their goals.

The United States must make every effort to prevent such an attack, if prevention fails, deal quickly and effectively with the consequences, and last, respond against the perpetrators and sponsors with overwhelming force.

---

9   U.S. Commission on National Strategy/21st Century, *Roadmap for National Security: Imperative for Change*, February 2001, 127.

10   The Advisory Panel to Assess Domestic Response Capabilities for Terrorism Involving Weapons of Mass Destruction, *Second Annual Report to the President and the Congress, Toward a National Strategy*, December 2000.

ATTACHMENTS

1. *Combating Terrorism: Need for Comprehensive Threat and Risk Assessments of Chemical and Biological Attacks*, (GAO/NSIAD-99-163) September 1999. p. 5, 6, 13-14, 19, http://*www.gao.gov/*

2. *Combating Terrorism: Threat and Risk Assessments Can Help Prioritize and Target Program Investments*, (GAO/NSIAD-98-74), April 1998, p. 4,http://*www.gao.gov/*

3. *Combating Terrorism: How Five Countries Are Organized to Combat Terrorism*, (GAO/NSAID-00-85), April 2000, http://*www.gao.gov/*

4. John E. Collingwood, Assistant Director of Public Affairs and Congressional Affairs, Federal Bureau of Investigation letter to Honorable Dan Burton, Chairman, Committee on Government Reform, March 22, 2000.

5. Marilyn Werber Serafini, "Ignorance is No Defense," National Journal, October 6, 2001.

6. The Henry L. Stimson Center, *Chemical and Biological Weapons Nonproliferation Project, www.stimson.org/cwc/bwprolif.*

7. Leonard A. Cole, "The Specter of Biological Weapons," *Scientific American*, December 1996, http://www.sciam.com//1296issue.

8. Jerold M. Post, "Psychological and Motivational Factors in Terrorist Decision-Making: Implications for CBW Terrorism," in *Toxic Terror*, Jonathan B. Tucker, ed. (Cambridge, Mass. MIT Press, 2000), p. 273.

STATEMENT OF RAYMOND J. DECKER
DIRECTOR, DEFENSE CAPABILITIES AND MANAGEMENT

HOMELAND SECURITY:
KEY ELEMENTS OF A RISK MANAGEMENT APPROACH

October 12, 2001

Mr. Chairman and Members of the Committee:

I appreciate the opportunity to be here today to discuss with you an approach to manage the risk from terrorism directed at Americans in our homeland. With the initiation of military operations against terrorist targets in Afghanistan, senior government officials indicated the need to be prepared for the potential of another attack on our homeland. There may be ways to prepare better in the event such an attack does come. We have undertaken a body of work in the area of combating terrorism, which has evaluated various facets of federal efforts to address this challenge. From this work, we identified three essential elements in an effective risk management approach to prepare better against acts of terrorism. My testimony today will focus on the three key elements that the federal government as well as state and local governments and private entities should adopt to enhance their timely preparedness against potential threats.

Summary

Risk management is a systematic and analytical process to consider the likelihood that a threat will endanger an asset, individual, or function and to identify actions to reduce the risk and mitigate the consequences of an attack. Risk management principles acknowledge that while risk generally cannot be eliminated, enhancing protection from known or potential threats can reduce it. A good risk management approach includes three primary elements: a threat assessment, a vulnerability assessment, and a criticality assessment. Threat assessments are important decision support tools that can assist organizations in security-program planning and key efforts. A threat assessment identifies and evaluates threats based on various factors, including capability and intentions as well as the potential lethality of an attack. Over the past several years, we have recommended that a comprehensive, national threat assessment be conducted by the appropriate federal agencies. Nonetheless, we will never know whether we have identified every threat, nor will we have complete information about the threats that we have identified. Consequently, we believe that the two other elements of the approach, vulnerability assessments and criticality assessments, are essential and required to prepare better against terrorist attacks. A vulnerability assessment is a process that identifies weaknesses that may be exploited by terrorists and suggests options to eliminate or mitigate those weaknesses. A criticality assessment is a process designed to systematically identify and evaluate an organization's assets based on the importance of its mission or function, the group of people at risk, or the significance of a structure. Criticality assessments are important because they provide a basis for prioritizing which assets and structures require higher or special protection from an attack. The approach that we have described could help prepare us against the threat we face and permit better direction of our resources to areas of highest priority.

Background

As demonstrated by the terrorist attacks of September 11, 2001, the United States and other nations face increasingly diffuse threats. Potential adversaries are more likely to strike vulnerable civilian or military targets in non-traditional ways to avoid direct confrontation with our military forces on the battlefield, to try to coerce our government to take some action terrorists desire, or simply to make a statement. Moreover, according to the President's December 2000 national security strategy,[1] such threats are more viable today because of porous borders, rapid technological change, greater information flow, and the destructive power of weapons now within the reach of states, groups, and individuals who may aim to endanger our values, way of life, and the personal security of our citizens.

Hostile nations, terrorist groups, and even individuals may target Americans, our institutions, and our infrastructure with weapons of mass destruction—including biological, chemical, radiological, nuclear, or high explosive weapons. Although they would have to overcome significant technical and operational challenges to make and release many chemical or biological agents of a sufficient quality and quantity to kill large numbers of people, the possibility exists that it could be done and it has been attempted. For example, in 1995, the Aum Shinrikyo group succeeded in killing 12 people and injuring thousands by releasing the nerve agent Sarin in the Tokyo subway. Prior to the Aum Shinrikyo attack, in 1984, the Rajneeshee religious cult in Oregon contaminated salad bars in local restaurants with salmonella bacteria to prevent people from voting in a local election. Although no one died, hundreds of people were diagnosed with food-borne illness.

A fundamental role of the government under our Constitution is to protect America from both foreign and domestic threats. The government must be able to prevent and deter attacks on our homeland as well as detect impending danger before attacks or incidents occur. Although it may not be possible to detect, prevent, or deter every attack, steps can be taken to manage the risk posed by the threats to homeland security.

A Risk Management Approach Can Help Prepare Against Terrorism

Risk management is a systematic, analytical process to consider the likelihood that a threat will harm an asset or individuals and to identify actions to reduce the risk and mitigate the consequences on an attack. Risk management principles acknowledge that while risk generally cannot be eliminated, enhancing protection from known or potential threats can reduce it.

A risk management approach exists that may be used to enhance our level of preparedness for terrorist threats. This approach is based on assessments of threat, vulnerabilities, and criticality (importance). A variation of this approach is currently used by DOD, which we discuss in our September 2001 report on combating terrorism.[2] One of the largest U.S. multi-national corporations uses another variation of the approach. In addition, the Interagency Commission on Crime and Security in U.S. Seaports has proposed a similar approach to assess the security of U.S. seaports.

Threat Assessments Are an Important Step in Implementing the Approach

A threat assessment is used to evaluate the likelihood of terrorist activity against a given asset or location. It is a decision support tool that helps to establish and prioritize security-program requirements, planning, and resource allocations. A threat assessment identifies and evaluates each threat on the basis of various factors, including capability, intention, and lethality of an attack. Intelligence and law enforcement agencies assess the foreign and domestic terrorist threats to the United States. The U.S. intelligence community—which includes the Central Intelligence Agency (CIA), the Defense Intelligence Agency, and the State Department's Bureau of Intelligence and Research, among others—monitors the foreign- origin terrorist threat to the United States. The FBI gathers information and assesses the threat posed by domestic sources of terrorism. Threat information gathered by both the intelligence and law enforcement communities can produce threat assessments for use in national security strategy planning. By identifying and assessing threats, organizations do not have to rely on worst-case scenarios to guide planning and resource allocations. Worst-case scenarios tend to focus on vulnerabilities, which are virtually unlimited, and would require extraordinary resources to address. Therefore, in the absence of detailed threat data, it is essential that a careful balance exists using all three elements in preparing and protecting against threats.

Several federal government organizations as well as companies in the private sector apply some formal threat assessment process in their programs, or such assessments have been recommended for implementation. In 1999, and again in our recent report on combating terrorism, we recommended that the FBI prepare a formal intelligence assessment that specifically assesses the chemical and biological agents that could be used by domestic terrorists without the assistance or support of a foreign laboratory.[3] The FBI concurred and expects to complete its assessment in December 2001, although it noted a limitation in its methodology. The FBI stated that its law enforcement role placed limitations on its collection and use of intelligence data, and the Bureau added that it had little intelligence on specific domestic terrorist groups. We also recommended that the FBI sponsor a national-level threat assessment that uses both intelligence estimates[4] and inputs from the intelligence community and others to form the basis for, and to prioritize, programs developed to combat terrorism. The FBI concurred and stated last month that the assessment is being finalized. This latter assessment is expected to be classified. The Department of Defense (DOD) uses threat assessments for its antiterrorism program designed to protect military installations. DOD evaluates threats on the basis of several factors, including a terrorist group's intentions, capabilities, and past activities. The assessments provide installation commanders with a list of credible threats to their installations and can be used in conjunction with other information (such as the state of the installation's preparedness) to prepare against attack, to recover from the effects of an attack, and to adequately target resources.

Similarly, a leading multi-national oil company attempts to identify threats in order to decide how to manage risk in a cost-effective manner. Because the company operates overseas, its facilities and operations are exposed to a multitude of threats, including terrorism, political instability, and religious or tribal conflict. In characterizing the threat, the company examines the historical record of security and safety breaches and obtains location-specific threat information from government organizations and other sources. It then evaluates these threats in terms of company assets that represent likely targets. Additionally, the Interagency Commission on Crime and Security in U.S. Seaports reported that threat assessments would assist seaports in preparing for terrorist threats. [5] The Commission recommended that the federal government establish baseline threat assessments for terrorism at U.S. seaports and, thereafter, conduct these assessments every 3 years.

While threat assessments are a key decision support tool, it should be recognized that, even if updated often, threat assessments might not adequately capture emerging threats posed by some terrorist groups. No matter how much we know about potential threats, we will never know that we have identified every threat or that we have complete information even about the threats of which we are aware. Consequently, we believe that a risk management approach to preparing for terrorism with its two additional assessments can provide better assurance of preparedness for a terrorist attack.

Vulnerability Assessments Are a Way to Identify Weaknesses

A vulnerability assessment is a process that identifies weaknesses in physical structures, personnel protection systems, processes, or other areas that may be exploited by terrorists and may suggest options to eliminate or mitigate those weaknesses. For example, a vulnerability assessment might reveal weaknesses in an organization's security systems or unprotected key infrastructure such as water supplies, bridges, and tunnels. In general, these assessments are conducted by teams of experts skilled in such areas as engineering, intelligence, security, information systems, finance, and other disciplines. For example, at many military bases, experts have identified security concerns including the distance from parking lots to important buildings as being so close that a car bomb detonation would damage or destroy the buildings and the people working in them. To mitigate this threat, experts have advised that the distance between parking lots and some buildings be increased. Another security enhancement might be to reinforce the windows in buildings to prevent glass from flying into the building if an explosion occurs.

For private sector companies, such assessments can identify vulnerabilities in the company's operations, personnel security, and physical and technical security. The Seaport Commission recommended similar vulnerability assessments be conducted. It identified factors to be considered that include the accessibility of vessels or facilities, avenues of ingress and egress, and the ease of access to valuable or sensitive items such as hazardous materials, arms, ammunition, and explosives. With information on both vulnerabilities and threats, planners and decisionmakers are in a better position to manage the risk of a terrorist attack by more effectively targeting resources. However, risk and vulnerability assessments need to be bolstered by a criticality assessment, which is the final major element of the risk management approach.

Criticality Assessments Are Necessary to Prioritize Assets for Protection

A criticality assessment is a process designed to systematically identify and evaluate important assets and infrastructure in terms of various factors, such as the mission and significance of a target. For example, nuclear power plants, key bridges, and major computer networks might be identified as "critical" in terms of their importance to national security, economic activity, and public safety. In addition, facilities might be critical at certain times, but not others. For example, large sports stadiums, shopping malls, or office towers when in use by large numbers of people may represent an important target. Criticality assessments are important because they provide a basis for identifying which assets and structures are relatively more important to protect from an attack. The assessments provide information to prioritize assets and allocate resources to special protective actions. These assessments have considered such factors as the importance of a structure to accomplish a mission, the ability to reconstitute this capability, and the potential cost to repair or replace the asset.

The multi-national company we reviewed uses descriptive values to categorize the loss of a structure as catastrophic, critical, marginal, or negligible. It then assigns values to its key assets. This process results in a matrix that ranks as highest risk, the most important assets with the threat scenarios most likely to occur. The Seaports Commission has also identified potential high-value assets (such as production, supply, and repair facilities; transfer, loading, or storage facilities; transportation modes; and transportation support systems) that need to be included in a criticality analysis, but it reported that no attempt has been made to identify the adverse affect from the loss of such assets. To evaluate the risk to an asset, the Seaports Commission advised that consideration be given to the mission and the military or economic impact of its loss or damage.

Conclusion

After threat, vulnerability, and criticality assessments have been completed and evaluated in this risk-based decision process, key actions vcan be taken to better prepare ourselves against potential terrorist attacks. Threat assessments alone are insufficient to support the key judgements and decisions that must be made. However, in conjunction with vulnerability and criticality assessments, leaders and managers will make better decisions based on this risk management approach. If the federal government were to apply this approach universally and if similar approaches were adopted by other segments of society, we could more effectively and efficiently prepare in-depth defenses against acts of terrorism against our country.

This concludes my prepared statement. I will be pleased to respond to any questions you may have.

Related GAO Products

Homeland Security

Homeland Security: A Framework for Addressing the Nation's Issues (GAO-01-1158T, Sept. 21, 2001).

Combating Terrorism

Bioterrorism: Public health and Medical Preparedness (GAO-02-141T, Oct. 9, 2001).

Bioterrorism: Coordination and Preparedness (GAO-02-129T, Oct. 5, 2001).

Bioterrorism: Federal Research and Preparedness Activities (GAO-01-915, Sept. 28, 2001).

Combating Terrorism: Selected Challenges and Related Recommendations (GAO-01-822, Sept. 20, 2001).

Combating Terrorism: Actions Needed to Improve DOD Antiterrorism Program Implementation and Management (GAO-01-909, Sept. 19, 2001).

Combating Terrorism: Comments on H.R. 525 to Create a President's Council on Domestic Preparedness (GAO-01-555T, May 9, 2001).

Combating Terrorism: Observations on Options to Improve the Federal Response (GAO-01-660T, Apr. 24, 2001).

Combating Terrorism: Accountability Over Medical Supplies Needs Further Improvement (GAO-01-463, Mar. 30, 2001).

Combating Terrorism: Comments on Counterterrorism Leadership and National Strategy (GAO-01-556T, Mar. 27, 2001).

Combating Terrorism: FEMA Continues to Make Progress in Coordinating Preparedness and Response (GAO-01-15, Mar. 20, 2001)

Combating Terrorism: Federal Response Teams Provide Varied Capabilities; Opportunities Remain to Improve Coordination (GAO-01-14, Nov. 30, 2000).

Combating Terrorism: Linking Threats to Strategies and Resources (GAO/T-NSIAD-00-218, July 26, 2000).

Combating Terrorism: Action Taken but Considerable Risks Remain for Forces Overseas (GAO/NSIAD-00-181, July 19, 2000).

Weapons of Mass Destruction: DOD's Actions to Combat Weapons Use Should Be More Integrated and Focused (GAO/NSIAD-00-97, May 26, 2000).

Combating Terrorism: Comments on Bill H.R. 4210 to Manage Selected Counterterrorist Programs (GAO/T-NSIAD-00-172, May 4, 2000).

Combating Terrorism: How Five Foreign Countries Are Organized to Combat Terrorism (GAO/NSIAD-00-85, Apr. 7, 2000).

Combating Terrorism: Issues in Managing Counterterrorist Programs (GAO/T-NSIAD-00-145, Apr. 6, 2000).

Combating Terrorism: Need to Eliminate Duplicate Federal Weapons of Mass Destruction Training (GAO/NSIAD-00-64, Mar. 21, 2000).

Combating Terrorism: Chemical and Biological Medical Supplies Are Poorly Managed (GAO/HEHS/AIMD-00-36, Oct. 29, 1999).

Combating Terrorism: Observations on the Threat of Chemical and Biological Terrorism (GAO/T-NSIAD-00-50, Oct. 20, 1999).

Combating Terrorism: Need for Comprehensive Threat and Risk Assessments of Chemical and Biological Attack (GAO/NSIAD-99-163, Sept. 7, 1999).

Combating Terrorism: Analysis of Federal Counterterrorist Exercises (GAO/NSIAD-99-157BR, June 25, 1999).

Combating Terrorism: Observations on Growth in Federal Programs (GAO/T-NSIAD-99-181, June 9, 1999).

Combating Terrorism: Analysis of Potential Emergency Response Equipment and Sustainment Costs (GAO/NSIAD-99-151, June 9, 1999).

Combating Terrorism: Use of National Guard Response Teams Is Unclear (GAO/NSIAD-99-110, May 21, 1999).

Combating Terrorism: Issues to Be Resolved to Improve Counterterrorist Operations (GAO/NSIAD-99-135, May 13, 1999).

Combating Terrorism: Observations on Biological Terrorism and Public Health Initiatives (GAO/T-NSIAD-99-112, Mar. 16, 1999).

Combating Terrorism: Observations on Federal Spending to Combat Terrorism (GAO/T-NSIAD/GGD-99-107, Mar. 11, 1999).

Combating Terrorism: FBI's Use of Federal Funds for Counterterrorism-Related Activities (FYs 1995-98) (GAO/GGD-99-7, Nov. 20, 1998).

Combating Terrorism: Opportunities to Improve Domestic Preparedness Program Focus and Efficiency (GAO/NSIAD-99-3, Nov. 12, 1998).

Combating Terrorism: Observations on the Nunn-Lugar-Domenici Domestic Preparedness Program (GAO/T-NSIAD-99-16, Oct. 2, 1998).

Combating Terrorism: Observations on Crosscutting Issues (GAO/TNSIAD-98-164, Apr. 23, 1998).

Combating Terrorism: Threat and Risk Assessments Can Help Prioritize and Target Program Investments (GAO/NSIAD-98-74, Apr. 9, 1998).

Combating Terrorism: Spending on Governmentwide Programs Requires Better Management and Coordination (GAO/NSIAD-98-39, Dec. 1, 1997).

Endnotes

[1]*A National Security Strategy for a Global Age*, December 2000.

[2]*Combating Terrorism: Actions Needed to Improve DOD Antiterrorism Program Implementation and Management* (GAO-01-909, Sept. 19, 2001).

[3]*Combating Terrorism: Selected Challenges and Related Recommendations* (GAO-01-822, Sept. 20, 2001).

[4]A national intelligence estimate analyzes issues of major importance and long-term interest to the United States and is the intelligence community's most authoritative projection of future developments in a particular subject area.

[5]*Report of the Interagency Commission on Crime and Security in U.S. Seaports*, Fall, 2000.

STATEMENT OF JOHN PARACHINI
POLICY ANALYST
RAND WASHINGTON OFFICE

Thank you, Mr. Chairman, for the privilege and opportunity to testify before the Committee. Since the tragic events of September 11th, many Americans have become concerned about the prospect of biological terrorism. After all, it seems plausible that hijackers willing to kill themselves, those aboard commercial airliners, and thousands more in the World Trade Center and the Pentagon might be willing to use biological agents to kill indiscriminately. These theoretical concerns have turned into a real fear. Reports that some of the suicide hijackers had shown an interest in crop-duster aircraft played a part in this transformation, as have the recent reports of the apparently deliberate use of anthrax spores in Florida.

The fear over biological terrorism is greater than the fear inspired by more conventional forms of terrorism. Some of this fear is justified and some of it is exaggerated. Some agents are highly contagious and lethal. Indeed, some biological agents if used in certain ways have the potential to deliver a strategic strike with casualty results similar to nuclear weapons. In fact, simply the fear they evoke imbues them with power. And perhaps the most frightening aspect of biological weapons is how they invade the body without notice. We fear threats we cannot see, hear, or feel.

However, in these uncertain times, it is important to maintain some perspective of the relative dangers. The twentieth century history of warfare, terrorism, and crime involving biological agents is much less deadly than that the history with conventional explosives. While history is not a perfect guide to the future, it does provide a context for our thinking about the future. Dramatic advances in the biological sciences could create previously unimaginable opportunities for terrorists bent on using the life sciences for their pernicious purposes. At the same time, biotechnology may provide tools that lessen these dangers. Remedies for enhanced or improvised conventional explosives, such as those used on September 11th, may be equally difficult to handle if not more so. Since the future is impossible to see clearly, we must anticipate a number of possible scenarios. We need to take account of history and hedge against the seeming imponderables of the future.

Given these heightened (and even exaggerated) public fears and given reports that law enforcement and intelligence officials believe that another terrorist attack of some kind is highly likely following the attacks in Afghanistan, there is a real need to conduct a thorough and sober assessment of biological terrorism. Such an assessment entails answering two interrelated questions. First, how feasible is it for terrorists groups to use biological and chemical weapons? And second, given the question of feasibility, how likely is it that terrorist groups would conduct attacks using biological or chemical weapons? The answers to both of these questions vary in terms of the actors involved, that is whether the biological is state-sponsored or whether it is the effort of sub-national groups or individuals acting in concert or independently of a state.

Given the answers to these two questions, I then turn to the question of what the government can and should do to deal with biological and chemical threats. I finish with some overall conclusions.

How Feasible Is It For Terrorist Groups To Use Biological Weapons?

When it comes to the feasibility of using biological or chemical weapons, states are more likely to have the resources, technical capabilities, and organizational capacity to assemble the people, know-how, material, and equipment to produce such weapons and to be able to clandestinely deliver them to valued targets. Nonetheless, mustering the resources and capabilities to inflict a devastating blow with biological agents has proven to be a formidable task even for states. The United States and the former Soviet Union dedicated considerable national defense resources to their biological weapons programs, and both countries encountered significant difficulties along the way. Iraq also dedicated considerable resources to its biological weapons program; although Iraq's effort was more successful than most experts imagined possible, it still encountered a number of significant challenges. Some of these difficulties are unique and inevitable for state programs that aim to achieve a militarily significant capacity with military-grade agents. Lower standards of achievement are certainly possible. On balance, then, a state's ability to command resources and organize them for certain priority scientific and industrial objectives presents the potential for the greatest threat of bioterrorism.

When it comes to the feasibility of biological terrorism perpetrated by sub-national groups and individuals, the range of capability (and level of consequence) depends on whether the groups or individuals are state-sponsored or not. High-consequence biological attacks would require the assistance of a state sponsor or considerable resources. However, even these conditions do not ensure high-consequence attacks by sub-national groups or individuals. There are no widely agreed upon historical examples in the open source literature of states providing sub-national groups with biological weapons for overt or covert use. Money, arms, logistical support, training, and even training on how to operate in a chemically contaminated environment are all forms of assistance states have provided to terrorists. But historically they have not crossed the threshold and provided biological weapons materials to insurgency groups or terrorist organizations. Even if states sought to perpetrate biological attacks for their own purposes, they would probably not trust such an operation to groups or individuals that they do not completely control.

Some argue that Saddam Hussein's Iraq is the type of state that might cross this threshold.[1]However, what is more likely than a conscious decision by a country's command authority is that a unauthorized faction within a state might take it upon itself to use a sub-national group to do its dirty work. The alleged involvement of the Iranian government security services in the attack on American military personnel in Khobar Towers seems to be an example of this type of involvement. Thus, while the probability of states using sub-national groups or individuals to perpetrate a biological warfare attack on its behalf seems low, it is not zero. In these times of dramatic change, American and allied intelligence services should be attentive to this possibility, even though it is without historical precedent and seems unlikely.

Sub-national groups or individuals can develop or acquire their own biological weapon capabilities for clandestine use, but it is not easy. Terrorist groups and individuals have historically not employed biological weapons because of a combination of formidable barriers to acquisition and use and comparatively readily available alternatives and disincentives. Procurement of materials and recruitment of people with skills and know-how are formidable barriers. Even if some of the materials and production equipment are procurable for legitimate scientific or industrial purposes, handling virulent biological materials and fashioning them into weapons capable of producing mass casualties is beyond the reach of most sub-national groups or individuals.

In the last twenty years, there are only two significant cases of sub-national groups using or attempting to use biological weapons and a few cases where groups or individuals made efforts to acquire biological materials. In the first of those cases, the Rajneeshees, a religious cult group located in Oregon, sought to win a local election in 1984 by running its own candidates and sickening local townspeople who they expected would vote against them. Using their medical clinics, cult members ordered a variety of bacterial cultures from the American Type Culture Collection located in Maryland. They intentionally and indiscriminately contaminated ten salad bars with a strain of salmonella, sickening at least 751 people. They used commercially available biological agents to incapacitate people clandestinely, because it was important for them to avoid attracting attention. Indeed, the intentional character of the outbreak was not recognized for over a year, when members of the cult revealed details about the attacks to authorities in exchange for lighter sentences stemming from other charges.

The other case occurred more than ten years later, when another religious cult, a Japanese group called the Aum Shinrikyo, sought to develop and deliver biological agents against a number of targets. The Aum's unsuccessful attempts at biological terrorism came to light after it released liquid sarin on the Tokyo subway. While this attack was heralded as a sign that sub-national groups would begin breaking the taboo on use of unconventional weapons, six years have passed since the attack and no other group has done so.

The clearest explanation for this extremely small historical data set is the difficulty of acquiring and delivering biological weapons, as well as a number of disincentives against doing so.

How Likely Is It That Terrorist Groups Would Use Biological Or Chemical Weapons?

The probability of a major biological attack by either a state or a sophisticated terrorist group seems remote. In contrast, smaller acts of biocriminality, such as the recent anthrax case in Florida, are much more likely biological terrorist attacks. While states can amass the resources and capabilities to wage biological terrorism, considerable disincentives keep them from doing so. A state that undertook a clandestine attack using biological weapons risks the prospect of the attack being traced back to them. The response to an attack with biological weapons could be devastating, which gives states reason for caution. While different U.S. administrations have articulated American policy on responding to known biological attacks in different ways, the basic position is that the United States reserves the right to respond with the full range of capabilities in the arsenal. Strategic ambiguity provides maximum flexibility while leaving no uncertainty about the potential magnitude of the response—devastating. The threat of retaliation is believed to deter states from using biological weapons clandestinely against other states.

However, there are three circumstances when a state might clandestinely wage biological terrorism. First, a state struggling for its existence might be willing to use biological weapons clandestinely as a means to forestall or to prevent a seemingly imminent defeat. There is no historical example of a state responding with a biological weapon in a moment of desperate struggle for its existence, but it is conceivable.

Second, if a state felt it could attack with biological weapons and be undetected, it might do so. In the twentieth century, there are a few examples of states using biological agents clandestinely except during times of war. For example, in the First World War, Germany sought to disrupt allied logistical capabilities by infecting horses with glanders—a contagious and destructive disease caused by a bacterium.[2] There a few other alleged wartime cases, but none in times of peace.

The third situation when a state might engage in biological terrorism would be when it sought to perpetrate an attack against its own citizens. In the 1980s, both the Bulgarian and the South African governments used biological materials to kill domestic political opponents. South Africa had a significant clandestine chemical and biological program that supported a major effort against regime opponents. Little is known about the Bulgarian program. Bulgarian operatives are believed to have assassinated a Bulgarian dissident in London with the toxin ricin, which they received from the Soviet KGB. Aside from state assassinations of perceived regime opponents, historically states have been extremely reluctant to use biological weapons overtly or covertly.[3]

Thus, state biological terrorism is a low probability threat, albeit one with potentially catastrophic consequences. During times of war, this threat increases in probability and is highest when a command authority perceives itself in a desperate situation in which using any means necessary may be its only option for survival.

On a more general level, there are incentives and disincentives for using biological weapons, but the disincentives tend to win out. As for the incentives, the acquisition, transfer, production, and delivery of biological weapons make them comparatively easy to conceal if managed by skilled personnel. (Conversely, of, course, while they are comparatively easy to conceal, some agents can be extremely contagious and some can be extremely deadly, making them difficult to handle.) Because bacteria and viruses are living microorganisms, small amounts can be used to grow much larger quantities. In addition, some biological agents, such as toxins, can be derived from naturally occurring plants or animals. Thus, the physical properties of some biological agents make them effective strategic weapons that can be assembled covertly.

Indeed, biological agents may appeal to terrorist groups because of what they can do or what they represent. As for what they can do, such agents may be desirable because they affect people indiscriminately, have a delayed impact, can be confused with natural disease outbreaks, and, in some cases, incapacitate rather than kill. As noted earlier, the Rajneeshees chose a biological material that would incapacitate people rather then kill, because they did not want their attack to provoke the scrutiny of authorities. Aum, in contrast, was fascinated with poisons. The cult's leader Shoko Asahara wrote songs about sarin. In addition to this pernicious obsession, Aum leaders had delusions of grandeur that far exceeded reality. They imagined a world they sought to create that was not constrained by the world in which they lived. To bring this imaginary world into being, they sought weapons they believed might trigger an apocalypse from which they would emerge as a dominant power. Since Aum leaders viewed their organization as a government and military in waiting, seeking to acquire some of the most potent weapons it believed states possessed. Instead of seeking lower-grade pathogens, Aum sought pathogens that are generally associated with military biological weapons programs. Aum exhibited this unique combination of obsession, delusions of grandeur, and belief in an apocalypse they could launch that would enable them to reign like leaders of a state.

Despite the incentives for seeking and using biological weapons, there are a number of even more compelling disincentives. As noted earlier, terrorists may hesitate in using biological weapons specifically because breaking the taboo on their use may evoke considerable retaliation. In addition, state sponsors of terrorist groups may exert restraint on the weapons the group uses. State sponsors have a great incentive to control the activities of the groups they support, because they fear that retaliation may be directed against them if they are connected to a group that used biological weapons. Moreover, terrorists may be drawn to explosives like arsonists are drawn to fire. The immediate gratification of explosives and the thrill of the blast may meet a psychological need of terrorists that the delayed effects of biological weapons do not.

However, perhaps the greatest disincentive to using biological weapons is that terrorists can inflict (and have inflicted) many more fatalities and casualties with conventional explosives than with unconventional weapons. Putting aside the spectacular quality of the Aum subway attack with liquid sarin, far fewer people died or were injured than in similarly spectacular attacks with conventional explosives. In comparison to the bombings of the Murrah federal building in Oklahoma City, the Khobar Towers military barracks in Saudi Arabia, and the U.S. embassies in Kenya and Tanzania, fewer people died as a result of the sarin release. In comparison with the recent attacks on the World Trade Center and the Pentagon, the Tokyo subway incident, though clearly tragic, was simply an event of much smaller scale.

How Should The Government Deal With The Threat Of Biological And Chemical Terrorism?

Although the prospects of a major biological terrorist attack are remote, they are still possible. Small-scale biocrimes are much more likely. In this light, the challenge before the government is how to put relative dangers in proper perspective and yet still hedge against future eventualities that are unlikely, but possible.

Meeting this challenge is formidable, especially since the prospect of any biological attack, as noted earlier, tends to instill fear that is often disproportionate to the actual threat. In terms of biological terrorism, we have tended to conflate the heightened attention to the prospect of terrorist attacks with unconventional weapons brought on by the Aum subway attack. This has led us to cast the threat in terms of what we fear the most, not necessarily what terrorist can or plan to do. In the last six years, authorities have focused too much on the means by which terrorists might use rather than the outcome of mass destruction and mass casualties.

Put another way, when assessing threats, it is important to search for comparable metrics to gauge scope and magnitude of the threats. A very constructive reassessment of the lessons learned from the Aum experience has begun, which should contribute to our understanding of the scope and magnitude of the biological terrorism threat. [4] The group turned to chemicals after failing with biological agents. A view that is gaining more credence with every new revelation is that "despite the expenditure of substantial time, effort, money and some requisite talent, their efforts totally failed."[5] The Aum's attempt and failure are testament to both the difficulty of procuring or developing a biological weapons capability and the efforts a determined group will undertake in its quest for the capability.

Fears that the Aum attempt to acquire and use biological weapons heralded a new age in such terrorism have been a constant refrain in the years since the attack. Yet so much about the Aum is so unique that it is hard to imagine it ever being repeated. Japanese law enforcement authorities tend to make arrests only when they have an ironclad case against the perpetrator of a crime. There were several incidents prior to the March 1995 sarin attack on the Tokyo subway that in retrospect should have raised suspicion. Additionally, Japanese legal provisions protecting religious organizations from intense government scrutiny inhibited authorities from intervening until long after the group committed a number of heinous acts. The Aum leadership presents another anomaly. Shoko Asahara, Aum's leader, was a controlling leader with an obsession with poisons. He wrote songs in praise of sarin. He also greatly admired another mass poisoner, Adolph Hitler.

While the reassessment of the Aum experience shows that U.S. planning for future biological and chemical attacks should not remain fixated on that experience, the lessons learned from that experience do raise some serious issues about dealing with such threats in general. One of these issues is intelligence. Despite the group's threats to kill the American president and accusations that the U.S. military attacked them with chemical weapons, the U.S. intelligence community overlooked this religious group in an allied country as a potential threat. The former head of the CIAs Nonproliferation Center said in Congressional testimony that the U.S. intelligence community did not view the Aum Shinrikyo as a terrorist entity of concern.[6] At the time, the CIA focused its energies on Islamic terrorism, because many felt that an obscure religious group in an allied country was not a threat. They were wrong. Some of these intelligence "blind spots" have since been addressed, but which ones remain and what new ones have developed?

Two other aspects of the Aum biological weapons experience deserve special note when considering the threat of biological terrorism. Aum's global effort to procure biological materials for its nefarious purposes deserves much greater examination. While there is no open source information indicating that the Aum obtained any radiological, biological, or chemical materials in Russia, it certainly tried. That the group tried and succeeded in getting meetings with Russian scientists, some of whom had weapons expertise, is troubling.

In addition, Aum members traveled to Zaire believing the could obtain samples of the Ebola virus. There is no evidence to indicate that they were successful in their venture. What may have inspired their trip was a newspaper account of a Japanese tourist who developed a hemorrhagic fever after returning from a game safari in Africa. In fact, the time during which Aum members traveled to Zaire there were no reported outbreaks of Ebola. But once again, what is significant is that six years ago a group that may have been interested in acquiring the material for a biological agent traveled to a country seeking to obtain a deadly infectious disease. If the Aum were trying to obtain biological material from infected people or corpses for weapons purposes, this highlights a very different source of material than the weapons laboratories of the former Soviet Union. It is much easier to monitor scientific institutes that were once or are currently affiliated with weapons programs than it is to monitor the sites of deadly disease outbreaks that occur around the globe. Some thought and attention needs to be given to how natural disease outbreaks might be exploited for pernicious purposes.

Conclusions

The terrorists responsible for the tragic attacks on September 11th turned a comparatively ordinary vehicle of modern transportation into a weapon that produced mass destruction and mass casualties. The question the committee is considering today is whether a state, a sub-national group, or individuals would attempt to achieve the same outcome with biological materials used as a weapon. Despite the spectacular and fanatical nature attacks against the World Trade Center and the Pentagon, bioterrorism on a similarly grand scale remains a remote possibility. At the moment, only states are able to perpetrate clandestinely biological attacks on a similar scale, and they are extremely reluctant to do so. While some terrorist groups may attempt large scale biological attacks, perpetrating an attack on the same scale as the September 11th attacks is not likely. Limited attacks using biological agents as common as salmonella and as rare as anthrax are possible. But the scope and scale of such attacks will be modest.

But even if the possibility is remote, the government has a responsibility to do all that it can to prevent, protect against, and respond to events that seem unlikely. The challenge is to determine how much to prepare for a low-probability, albeit potentially catastrophic, attack, while at the same time, guarding against not focusing enough on more probable events with significant, but not necessarily catastrophic, consequences. It is also possible to take a more proactive stance. As noted earlier, one of the reasons that terrorists do not use biological weapons is because they have alternatives that better serve their purposes. Such alternatives and disincentives to terrorist use of biological weapons deserve greater study. If we can augment disincentives for terrorist to choose biological weapons, we can narrow the possibility that they will do so.

Endnotes

[1] Laurie Myroie, *Study of Revenge: Saddam Hussein's Unfinished War against America*, (Washington, DC: The AEI Press), 2000. See also Laurie Myroie, "The Iraqi Connection", *The Wall Street Journal*, September 13, 2001, p. A20. In regard to the 1993 bombing, some of the case for state involvement is based on inferences that are disputed. See John Parachini, "The World Trade Center Bombers (1993)," in Jonathan B. Tucker, ed., *Terror: Assessing Terrorist Use of Chemical and Biological Weapons*, (Cambridge, Massachusetts: MIT Press, 2000).

[2] Mark Wheelis, "Biological sabotage in World War I," in *Biological and Toxin Weapons: Research, Development and Use from the Middle Ages to 1945*, Edited by Erhard Geissler and John Ellis van Courtland Moon, SIPRI Chemical & Biological Warfare Studies No. 18, (Oxford, UK: Oxford University Press), pp. 35-61.

[3] For an insightful discussion historical discussion of weapons of mass destruction and their use by states and terrorist see, David Rapoport, "Terrorism and Weapons of the Apocalypse," *National Security Studies Quarterly*, Vol. V, No. 3, (Summer).

[4] For three recent studies that provide a new assessments of the Aum experience and its implications for biological terrorism see, First Annual Report to the President and the Congress of the Advisory Panel to Assess Domestic Response Capabilities for Terrorism Involving Weapons of Mass Destruction, (hereafter referred to as the Gilmore Commission Report), *I. Assessing the Threat*, December 15, 1999; Milton Leitenberg, "The Experience of the Japanese Aum Shinrikyo Group and Biological Agents," *Terrorism and Political Violence*, Vol. 11, No. 4, Winter, 1999; Amy E. Smithson and Leslie-Anne Levy, *Ataxia: The Chemical and Biological Terrorism Threat and the U.S. Response* (Washington, D.C.: Henry L. Stimson Center, 2000).

[5] Milton Leitenberg, "Biological Weapons in the Twentieth Century: A Review and Analysis," (http://www.fas.org/bwc/papers/review/exp.htm) (Viewed on October 4, 2001)

[6] U.S. Congress, Senate, Committee on Governmental Affairs, Permanent Subcommittee on Investigations, Global Proliferation of Weapons of Mass Destruction, Part I, (Washington, DC: US Government Printing Office, 1996) pp. 27-28.

TESTIMONY OF JERROLD M. POST, M.D.[1]
THE ELLIOTT SCHOOL OF INTERNATIONAL AFFAIRS
THE GEORGE WASHINGTON UNIVERSITY

DIFFERENTIATING THE THREAT OF CHEMICAL/BIOLOGICAL
TERRORISM: MOTIVATIONS AND CONSTRAINTS

October 12, 2001

There is a heightened concern in the United States over the specter of a cat-astrophic domestic chemical or biological terrorist attack. Billions are being invested in training first responders for what is acknowledged to be a high consequence-low probability event. But while substantial investment is being devoted to protecting our vulnerable society from such a devastating act, there is very little attention being devoted to who might do it, and why, and, as important, who might not do it, and why not?

A number of factors have contributed to this heightened concern. The World Trade Center bombing in 1993 dented the wall of denial in the United States that "it can't happen here." However, if the wall of denial was dented by the World Trade Center bombing, the illusion of invulnera-bility was surely shattered by the bombing of the Alfred T. Murah Federal building in Oklahoma City in 1995, which claimed 168 lives in a dramatic act of mass casualty terrorism. And the tragic events of September 11 was an act of mass destruction unprecedented in the history of political terror-ism. This was mass casualty super-terrorism. But this was, it should be em-phasized, conventional terrorism.

The Aum Shinrikyo sarin gas attack on the Tokyo subway in 1995 for the first time focused the international community on the dread prospect of chemical and biological terrorism. As the story emerged, with documenta-tion of the extensive efforts by the leadership of this millennial cult to re-cruit Ph.D. scientists to develop chemical, biological and nuclear weapons, increasing attention was focused on this exotic terrorism as a disaster wait-ing to happen. As Secretary of Defense William Cohen put it, "It isn't a question of if, but when."

On the agenda of a conference sponsored by the Department of Defense in 1998, major attention was devoted to what might happen, i.e. what terror-ists could do, with learned presentations by virologists, microbiologists, in-fectious disease experts, and chemical warfare experts, with no attention being given to the source of and motivations for the threat, i.e. which groups might do it and why. At an American Medical Association confer-ence in April, 2000 on responding to the threat of chemical and biological terrorism, when the author raised the question with the conference plan-ners of the lack of attention on the agenda paid to the magnitude of the threat and to identifying the motivations, incentives and constraints for terrorist groups to commit such attacks, it was dismissed as not relevant to the question at hand.

In fact, there is a major disconnect between the weapons technology community and the community of academic terrorism experts, with the former being focused on vulnerabilities of our society and what might happen in terms of technological possibilities, and the latter , who study terrorist motivation and decision making, being underwhelmed by the probability of such an event *for most—but not all*—terrorist groups. In the Monterey Institute of International Affairs project report, *Toxic Terror* edited by Jonathan Tucker, which consists of a series of detailed case studies following up on reports of chemical or biological terrorism by interviewing primary sources, including alleged perpetrators, most of the alleged cases upon close examination turned out to have reflected media hype and were not in fact *bona fide* cases of chemical or biological terrorism by organized terrorist groups. There were a number of cases of attempts by emotionally disturbed individuals, which, however, really fell more into the sphere of psychopathology or criminal extortion than political terrorism.

This testimony is in the service of differentiating the threat, focusing on which groups are significantly constrained from committing such extreme acts, and which groups might be less inhibited and indeed might find incentives to commit such acts. Moreover, it seeks to differentiate the spectrum of CBW terrorist acts, for a group that assuredly would be constrained from an act of so-called super-terrorism using CBW might well find a focused low-level attack advantageous.[2]

It is useful at this juncture to consider the term "weapons of mass destruction terrorism," usually employed to refer to chemical, biological, radiological or nuclear weapons (CBRN.) It is a semantically confusing term, for conventional weapons, such as the fertilizer bomb used by Timothy McVeigh at the Alfred P. Mural Federal Building in Oklahoma City, the bombs which destroyed the U.S. embassies in Nairobi, Kenya and Dar es Saalan, Tanzania, and the hijacked planes which flew into the World trade Center and the Pentagon can produce mass destruction. Moreover, the so-called weapons of mass destruction, especially biological and chemical weapons, can be employed with exquisite discrimination to produce low-level casualties, to the point of being employed for assassination of lone individuals.

The Spectrum of Terrorism

As reflected in Figure 1, terrorism is not a homogeneous phenomenon. There is a broad spectrum of terrorist groups and organizations, each of which has a different psychology, motivation and decision making structure. Indeed, one should not speak of terrorist psychology in the singular, but rather of terrorist psychologies. In the top tier of the graphic, we differentiate political terrorism from criminal and pathological terrorism. Studies of political terrorist psychology[3] do not reveal severe psychiatric pathology. Indeed, political terrorist groups do not permit emotionally disturbed individuals to join their groups, for they represent a security risk. Seriously disturbed individuals tend to act alone. In fact, many of the cases in *Toxic Terror* fall into this category.

At the middle tier, state terrorism refers to the state turning its resources—police, judiciary, military, secret police, etc— against its own citizenry to suppress dissent, as exemplified by the "dirty wars" in Argentina. When Saddam Hussein used nerve gas against his own Kurdish citizens, this was an example of state CBW terrorism. State-supported terrorism is of major concern to the United States. Currently on the list annually distributed by the Department of State are Iran, Iraq, Syria, Libya, Sudan, North Korea and Cuba. In these situations, when states are acting through terrorist groups, fearing retaliation, the decision making of the state leadership will be a significant constraint upon the group acting under their influence or control.

In the lower tier, a diverse group of sub-state terrorist groups are specified: social-revolutionary terrorism, nationalist-separatist terrorism, right-wing terrorism, religious extremist terrorism, subsuming both religious fundamentalist terrorism and terrorism perpetrated by non-traditional religious groups (such as Aum Shinrikyo), and single issue terrorism

The Spectrum of Terrorist Acts

Now, in considering which groups in the spectrum of terrorist groups might be inclined to carry out acts of biological or chemical terrorism, it is important to differentiate the spectrum of such acts as well. In Figure 2, we discriminate 5 levels—large scale casualties, with conventional weapons, sham CBW attacks, low-level casualties (under 20), large scale casualties (20-hundreds), and catastrophic or super-terrorism, in which thousands of casualties may result. The crucial psychological barrier to cross concerns not the choice of weapon, in my judgment, but rather the willingness to cause mass casualties, and this threshold has been crossed for some groups. Indeed, given the skills and hazards in working with CBW, some groups might well ask, why should we move into this technologically difficult and dangerous area when we can cause mass casualties and mass terror through conventional weapons, as was vividly demonstrated in the attacks of September 11. Sham attacks are included, for the psychological constraints against CBW attacks are missing for sham attacks, which can have devastating effects, especially psychologically. With the attention being given to training first-responders in how to respond to chemical and biological attacks, insufficient attention is being given to the dilemmas of responding to what will likely be much more frequent, sham attacks such as the rash of anthrax hoaxes in 1998, as exemplified by the sham anthrax attack on the B'nai Bri'th Building in Washington, D.C. In this event, even though no actual biological weapon was used, the perpetrators called attention to their cause, dramatically paralyzing the city of Washington, with a televised humiliating public decontamination of individuals at the center of the event. This was assuredly a highly successful terrorist act. Could it be that the indiscreet inquiries concerning crop dusting airplanes by the al Qaeda terrorists before they engaged in their catastrophic mission were designed to be discovered in order to create further panic within the United States?

Writing in *Disorders and Terrorism*, Report of the Task Force on Disorders and Terrorism, more than 20 years ago, Menge[4] distinguishes four different means by which terrorists attempt to achieve their goals. He observes there is a distinct difference between discriminate and random target selection. Whereas discriminate target selection can be used in support of bargaining or to make a political statement, random targeting is associated with the motivation to cause social paralysis, or inflict mass casualties. Groups motivated to cause mass casualties in his estimation are characterized by a group's realization that:

1. They do not have a position of strength from which bargaining can be successful

2. The public will no longer respond to state-(propaganda-)related attacks

3. Popular support ahs been lost because of the social paralysis caused by previous attacks

In evaluating the risk among terrorist groups for using CBW weapons, it is useful to employ this distinction in differentiating among terrorist groups. The asterisk(*) distinguishes discriminate from indiscriminate acts. Some groups might well consider CBW attacks only in a bounded area, limiting casualties, which would significantly militate against negative reactions from their constituents, both local and international. But these groups would be significantly constrained against such acts in a region in which the group's constituents might well be adversely affected as a result of physical proximity to the area of attack, and would accordingly adversely affect constituents. These bounded acts are specified as discriminate. Indiscriminate attacks, in contrast, are attacks in which no consideration is given to the selection of specific victims, or the impact of the act upon internal or external constituents.

The matrix in this graphic evaluates the nature of the act by the terrorist group type, focusing specifically on psychological incentives and constraints. In the remainder of this essay, a description of the motivations and decision making of each group type is described, evaluating the degree of risk for the spectrum of mass casualty/CBW acts. That a check mark appears in the summarizing graphic is intended to convey *not* that the group is at high risk for such acts, but that the balance of incentives and constraints is such that CBW acts could be rationalized as serving the group's goals, with a weakened pattern of disincentives. To say that differently, for the spectrum of terrorist groups, the constraints against use of CBW weapons on a large or catastrophic scale are great, and the likelihood of such acts is quite small. For some groups, those that are designated with a check mark, it is less improbable than for others, as they experience a lesser degree of constraint.

Moreover, this matrix is concerned only with motivations and constraints, and does not consider resource and capability. Weapons experts regularly identify weaponization as a major constraint to mass CBW terrorism. The resources and technological capability to carry out a large scale attack would, in the judgment of many in the weapons community, require resources and technological skill only found at the state level. It should be remembered that Aum Shinrikyo had gathered a remarkable Assemblage of scientific experts, but still were daunted by the dispersal problem. Some of the perpetrators in the matrix, such as individual right-wing extremists, might be highly motivated to cause mass destruction, with no psychological or moral constraint, but would lack the technological capability and resources to mount more than a small local attack.

Social Revolutionaries

Social revolutionary terrorism, also known as terrorism of the left, includes those acts perpetrated by groups seeking to overthrow the capitalist economic and social order. Social revolutionary groups are typified by the European "fighting communist organizations" active throughout the 1970s and 1980s (e.g., the Red Army Faction in Germany and the Red Brigades in Italy). While social-revolutionary terrorist groups have experienced a significant decline over the last two decades, paralleling the collapse of Communism in Europe and the end of the Cold War, social-revolutionary terrorism and insurgency are still underway, as exemplified by the Japanese Red Army (JRA), Sendero Luminosa (the Shining Path), Movement Revolutionaire Tupac Amaru (MRTA) in Peru, several Columbian terrorist groups who are also associated with natrco-terrorism, and Ejército Zapatista de Liberación Nacional (EZLN) of Chiapas, Mexico.

These are complex organizations, however, not groups per se. The decision-making locus is outside of the action cells. In these secret organizations, there is a tension between security and communication. This leads to rather more decision-making latitude for the action cells than might be present in a more open organization. Thus policy guidelines may be laid down, but specific planning concerning the target and the tactics has been delegated to the group. Nevertheless, for a matter so grave as the strategic decision to deploy weapons of mass destruction, the organizational deci-sion-makers would certainly be the prime movers.

Insofar as these groups are seeking to influence their society, they would be significantly constrained from indiscriminate acts that cause significant casualties among their own countrymen, or cause negative reactions in their domestic and international audiences. But discriminate acts against government or symbolic capitalist targets could be rationalized by these groups.

Nationalist-Separatists

Nationalist-separatist terrorism, also known as ethno-nationalist terrorism, includes those groups fighting to establish a new political order or state based on ethnic dominance or homogeneity. The Irish Republican Army, the Liberation Tigers of Tamil Eelam (LTTE) of Sri Lanka, the Basque Fa-therland and Liberty (ETA) in Spain, and radical Palestinian groups such as the Abu Nidal Organization and the Palestinian Front for the Liberation of Palestine-General Command (PFLP-GC) are prominent examples. Nation-alist-separatist terrorists are usually attempting to garner international sympathy for their cause and to coerce the dominant group. Thus ETA is attempting to pressure Spain to yield to its demands for an independent Basque state. These causes of the nationalist-separatist terrorist groups and organizations are particularly intractable, for the bitterness and resent-ment against the dominant ethnic group has been conveyed from genera-tion to generation.[5] Nationalist-separatist groups operating within their nation are particularly sensitive to the responses of their internal constitu-ency, as well as their international audience. This provides a constraint against acts so violent or extra-normal as to offend their constituents, as ex-emplified by the attack by the Real IRA in Omagh in 1998 in which 29, mostly women and children, were killed. The resulting uproar from their Irish constituents was so extreme, that the Real IRA apologized and for-swore future violence.

These groups will be significantly constrained from acts that indiscrimi-nately involve mass casualties and will negatively affect the group's repu-tation with their constituents and their international audience. But discriminate acts against their adversary, in areas where their constituents are not present, can be rationalized. Just as the rash of suicide bombings in Tel Aviv and other predominantly Jewish cities in Israel was implemented by absolutist Palestinian groups (some of which were radical Islamists as well) in order to reverse the peace process, the prospect of tactical CBW weapons in such areas is quite conceivable. Such discriminate attacks could also be implemented in revenge against U.S. targets. But a CBW at-tack in Jerusalem, by secular Palestinian terrorists that might affect their own constituents is considered highly unlikely

Religious Extremists

Religious extremist terrorism is characterized by groups seeking to maintain or create a religious social and political order and includes two types of groups and organizations: those adhering to a radical fundamentalist interpretation of mainstream religious doctrines as well as non-traditional religious groups representing "new religions," such as Aum Shinrikyo, responsible for the 1995 sarin nerve gas attack on the subway system in Tokyo, Japan.

Religious Fundamentalist Terrorism

In the 1970's and 1980s, most of the acts of terrorism were perpetrated by nationalist-separatist terrorists and social-revolutionary terrorists, who wished to call attention to their cause and accordingly would regularly claim responsibility for their acts. They were seeking to influence the West and the establishment. But in the past decades, no responsibility is claimed for upwards of 40% of terrorist acts. We believe this is because of the increasing frequency of terrorist acts by radical religious extremist terrorists. They are not trying to influence the West. Rather the radical Islamist terrorists are trying to expel the secular modernizing West. And they do not need their name identified in a New York Times headline or on a story on CNN. They are "killing in the name of God" and don't need official notice; after all, God knows.

Traditional groups include Islamic, Jewish, Christian and Sikh radical fundamentalist extremists. In contrast to social revolutionary and nationalist-separatist terrorists, for religious fundamentalist extremist groups, the decision-making role of the preeminent leader is of central importance. For these true believers, the radical cleric is seen as the authentic interpreter of God's word, not only eliminating any ambivalence about killing, but endowing the destruction of the defined enemy with sacred significance.

The radical cleric, whether ayatollah, rabbi or priest, has used sacred text to justify killing in the name of God. Ayatollah Khomeini employed a radical interpretation of the Quo'ran to provide the ideological foundation for his Islamic revolution, and selected verses to justify terrorist extremity, such as "And slay them where ye catch them, and turn them out from where they have turned you out...Such is the reward of those who suppress the faith (2:190-193) . In a radio broadcast of June 5, 1983, Khomeini exhorted his followers: "With humility toward God and relying on the power of Islam, they should cut the cruel hands of the oppressors and world-devouring plunderers, especially the United States, from the region." To those who died fighting this holy cause, Khomeini assured a higher place in paradise. In inciting his followers during the Iran-Iraq war, he rhetorically asked: "Why don't you recite the *sura* of killing? Why should you always recite the *sura* of mercy? Don't forget that killing is also a form of mercy." He and his clerical followers regularly found justification for their acts of violence in the Qur'anic *suras* calling for the shedding of blood.[6]

These organizations are hierarchical in structure; the radical cleric provides interpretation of the religious text justifying violence which is uncritically accepted by his "true believer" followers, so there is no ambivalence concerning use of violence which is religiously commanded.   These groups are accordingly particularly dangerous, for they are not constrained by Western reaction, indeed often wish to expel secular modernizing influences. They have shown a willingness to perpetrate acts of mass casualty terrorism, as exemplified by the bombings of Khobar Towers in Saudi Arabia, the World Trade Center in the U.S., the U.S. embassies in Kenya and Tanzania, the U.S.S. Cole, and the mass casualty terrorism on a scale never seen before in the coordinated attacks on the World Trade Center in New York and the Pentagon in Washington, D.C. Usama bin Laden, responsible for these events has actively discussed the use of weapons of mass destruction in public interviews.

While not a religious authority, Osama bin Laden is known for his piety, and has been granted the title emir. Like Khomeini, Osama bin Laden regularly cites verses from the Koran to justify his acts of terror and extreme violence, empoloying many of the same verses earlier cited by Khomeini. Consider this extract from the February 1998 Fatwa, Jihad Against Jews and Crusaders, World Islamic Front Statement:

> **In compliance with God's order, we issue the following fatwa to all Muslims:**
>
>> The ruling to kill the Americans and their allies—civilians and military—is an individual duty for every Muslim who can do it in any country in which it is possible to do it, in order to liberate the al-Aqsa Mosque and the holy mosque [Mecca] from their grip, and in order for their armies to move out of all the lands of Islam, defeated and unable to threaten any Muslim. This is in accordance with the words of Almighty God, "and fight the pagans all together as they fight you all together," and "fight them until there is no more tumult or oppression, and there prevail justice and faith in God."
>
> **We—with God's help—call on every Muslim who believes in God and wishes to be rewarded to comply with God's order to kill the Americans and plunder their money wherever and whenever they find it.**

Note it is not Osama bin laden who is ordering his followers to kill Americans. He is the messenger, relaying the commands of God, which are justified with verses from the Koran.

While from the theoretical perspective of "pure culture" religious fundamentalist terrorism, there would be no constraint upon these groups, in
fact, some of the radical Islamist groups, such as Hamas and Islamic Jihad,
responsible for most of the suicide bombings in Israel, do in fact have domestic constituencies which would provide a measure of constraint against
indiscriminate mass casualty acts, and against "super terrorism."

But as the events of September 11 make clear, for the al Qaeda organization, there is no constraint against mass casualty terrorism. And it is the
willingness, indeed the goal to take as many causalities as possible that is
the dynamic of the "true believers" of the al Qaeda group under the destructive charismatic leadership of Osama bin Laden that places this group
at high risk to move into the area of CBW terrorism, for they have already
crossed the threshold of mass casualties using conventional terrorism,
demonstrating a willingness to perpetrate super-terrorism.

In his prepared statement released after the U.S./British attack on Taliban
military targets on the night of 7 October, bin Laden emphasized the climate of terror in the United States-"America has been filled with fear from
North to South, from East to West, thank God. " And he ended his statement by asserting his intent to keep the Un+ited States in a continuing
state of insecurity-"America and those who live in America won't dream of
having security before we have it in Palestine and all infidel armies depart
from the land of Muhammad." At this point in time, a mass casualty attack
with the requisite technological skills and preparation would not be required to produce mass panic in the United States. As this testimony is being prepared, anthrax has been diagnosed in a second employee of the
supermarket tabloid publisher, America Media Corporation, in West Palm
Beach, Florida, which is only 40 miles from the airstrip where some of the
al Qaeda terrorists made inquiries concerning crop dusting equipment.
While the initial indications are that this is a criminal matter, that this could
represent a small CBW attack is by no means out of the question, and
would fit Osama bin Laden's espoused goals of keeping the United States
in the throes of continuing insecurity.

Non-traditional religious extremist groups

Non-traditional religious extremist groups, such as Aum Shinrikyo, must
also be considered. These generally closed cults are in a struggle for survival against a demonized enemy that must be destroyed. While the majority of millennial apocalyptic cults are waiting for the millennium, some
religious belligerents are seeking to force the end, and, in the case of Aum
Shinrikyo, to precipitate the final struggle. Charismatic leaders of closed
cults, like Shoko Asahara, the leader of Aum Shinrikyo, who see themselves
in a God-like role, a self-perception rewarded by the God-like reverence
with which they are treated by their followers, can become obsessed with
power. Asahara's fascination with high technology led him to recruit

nuclear physicists, nuclear engineers, chemists, and microbiologists, simultaneously exploring nuclear, biological and chemical weapons. Especially for closed religious cults, the dynamic is one of a charismatic leader who holds total sway over his followers. What he declares is moral and required *is* moral and required. The followers yield their individual judgment to the leader and become deskilled, acting as if they have no independent critical faculties of their own. No doubt or doubters are permitted in these powerful hermetically sealed closed organization. The price for defection in Aum Shinrikyo was death. This too had a high-tech aspect to it, for apprehended defectors were incinerated in an industrial microwave oven, ensuring the conforming loyalty of witnessing members.

Asahara, in mounting WMD programs, was attempting to precipitate the final apocalyptic conflict. At the cusp of the millennium, apocalyptic millennial cults can be expected to proliferate and experience a heightened sense of urgency, which may lead other groups to pursue the path of weapons of mass destruction aggression to precipitate the final struggle. As was demonstrated by Aum Shinrikyo, such groups can justify indiscriminate CBW attacks producing mass casualties, and that same rationale could serve as the justification for "super-terrorism." But, Aum Shinrikyo is quite unusual within the spectrum of millennial cults, for most such cults are not religious belligerents seeking to precipitate the apocalypse, as was the case with Aum, but rather tend to withdraw from society, passively awaiting the " final days."

Right-Wing Groups

Right-wing terrorism includes those groups seeking to preserve the dominance of a threatened ethnic majority or to return society to an idealized "golden age" in which ethnic relations more clearly favored the dominant majority. These groups generally espouse fascist ideologies, including racist, anti-Semitic, and anti-government "survivalist" beliefs. These groups in the United States fear the federal government, which they see as contributing to the decline of the majority's dominance. In their view, the government is dominated by Jews—hence ZOG, the Zionist Occupied Government and accordingly is illegitimate.

Because of this dehumanization of their enemies, discriminate attacks on target groups, such as blacks, or, in Europe, on enclaves of foreign workers, are justified by their ideology. Because of their delegitimation and dehumanization of the government, discriminate attacks on government facilities are certainly feasible by such groups, including attacks on the seat of the federal government, Washington, D.C., as represented in *The Turner Diaries*.

Right-Wing Community of Belief

Many of the case studies developed by the Center for Non-Proliferation Studies at the Monterey Institute for International Studies, the first group of which was published as *Toxic Terror,* were committed by individuals hewing to a right-wing ideology, but not belonging to a formal group or organization per se. The case study by Jessica Stern of Larry Wayne Harris, a former neo-Nazi is a case in point. Timothy McVeigh is an exemplar of such individuals seeking to cause mass casualty terrorism, using onventional weapons. McVeigh was enthralled by *The Turner Diaries,* which he sold below cost at gun shows. At the time of his capture, glassined, highlighted pages from this bible of the radical right were found in his car. Individuals in this category are a significant threat for low level CBW attacks, but, because of resource limitations, probably do not represent a threat of mass casualty CBW terrorism.

The role of the internet in propagating the ideology of right wing extremist hatred is of concern, for an isolated individual consumed by hatred can find common cause in the right-wing web sites, feel he is not alone, and be moved along the pathway from thought to action, responding to the extremist ideology of his virtual community.

Implications

Reviewing the spectrum of terrorist groups in terms of motivation, incentives and constraints, for nearly all groups, the feared catastrophic CBW superterrorism, against the prospect of which the United States is preparing, would be highly counter-productive. The constraints are particularly severe for large scale mass casualty terrorism for groups that are concerned with their constituents—social revolutionary and nationalist separatist terrorists—although discriminate low level attacks are possible. Right-wing extremists, including individuals who are members of the right-wing virtual community of hatred, because of their tendency to dehumanize their victims and delegitimize the federal government, represent a distinct danger for low level discriminate attacks against their demonized targets: Jews, blacks, and ethnic minorities, as well as federal buildings. Concerning non-traditional religious extremist groups, should other non-traditional groups resembling Aum Shinrikyo emerge, they would be at great risk, but most millennial cults are not led by religious belligerents, but rather passively await the final days.

Religious fundamentalist terrorist groups, who follow the dictates of destructive charismatic religious leaders, are not constrained by their audience on earth, as their acts of violence are given sacred significance. They are more at risk for mass casualty attacks, although to the degree they have a constituency, as does Hamas, they are also constrained. Having demonstrated an unconstrained goal of committing mass casualty destruction, and of maintaining America in a continuing state of insecurity. The al Qaeda group of Osama bin Laden is not constrained and is particularly dangerous. Because of the series of successes, with ever increasing violence of al Qaeda, and the expanding mission of its grandiose leader, Osama bin laden, this organization is considered at the highest risk to move into CBW terrorism, as Osama bin Laden is innovative and continually seeking to create ever greater terror. Because of the resource and technological constraints, however, small focal attacks are the most likely, rather than CBW super-terrorism. This limitation would be removed were the group supported by a state with the necessary technological resources.

Given the severe constraints against catastrophic CBW terrorism for most groups, this argues for continuing to protect against the greatest danger—conventional terrorism—and to devote significantly increased intelligence resources to monitoring much more closely the groups at greatest risk for CBW terrorism: right-wing extremist groups and religious extremist groups, both non-traditional cults similar to Aum Shinrikyo and especially religious fundamentalist terrorist organizations.

Figure 1. Typology of Terrorism

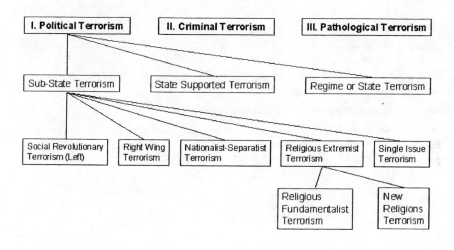

Figure 2. Differentiating Motivations and Constraints for CBW Terrorism by Group Type

	Large-scale Conventional	CBW Hoax	Small-scale CBW Use	Large-scale CBW Use	Catastrophic CBW Use (Superterrorism)

Figure 2. Differentiating Motivations and Constraints for CBW Terrorism by Group Type

Group Type	Large-scale Conventional	CBW Hoax	Small-scale CBW Use	Large-scale CBW Use	Catastrophic CBW Use (Superterrorism)
Social-Revolutionary	✓ *	✓	✓ *	X	X
Nationalist-Separatist	✓ *	✓	✓ *	X	X
Right-Wing	✓	✓	✓	✓	X
Right-Wing Community of Belief	✓	✓	✓	X	X
Religious-Fundamentalist	✓	✓	✓	✓	✓
Non-traditional Religious Extremists (closed cults)	✓	✓	✓	✓	✓

* Discriminate acts: acts which do not alienate supporters or endanger constituents, usually taking place outside regional base/home territory

X Significantly constrained against such acts, extremely unlikely

✓ Less constrained, and while still unlikely, could rationalize such acts. The check does not indicate likelihood of committing such an act, but refers to motivation only. Thus many right-wing extremists might be highly motivated to commit such an act, but would lack the necessary resource and capability to carry it out.

Endnotes

[1]Jerrold Post is Professor of Psychiatry, Political Psychology and International Affairs, and Director of the Political Psychology Program at the George Washington University, Washington, D.C.

[2]This testimony draws on but expands upon analysis presented in *Toxic Terror*. A preliminary version of these remarks was presented at the annual Non-Proliferation Conference of the Carnegie Endowment for International Peace in March, 2000.

[3]Post, J. "Terrorist Psycho-Logic: Terrorist Behavior as a Product of Psychological Forces" in Reich, W.(ed.) *Origins of terrorism: Psychologies, ideologies, theologies, states of mind* Cambridge: Cambridge Univ. Press, 1993

[4]Mengel, R.W. (1977) "Terrorism and new technologies of destruction: An overview of the potential risk" in *Disorders and terrorism*: Report of the Task Force on Disorders and Terrorism. U.S. National Advisory Committee on Criminal Justice Standards and Goals. Washington, D.C. U.S. Government Printing Office, 443-473.

[5]Post, J. "Terrorist Psycho-Logic: Terrorist Behavior as a Product of Psychological Forces," in Reich, W. (ed.) *Origins of Terrorism*. Cambridge: Cambridge University Press, 1990, pp. 25-40.

[6]Robins, R. and Post, J. *Political Paranoia: The Psychopolitics of Hatred*. New Haven, CT: Yale Univ. Press, 1997, pp 153-154.

DOCUMENT NO. 17

STATEMENTS AT A JOINT HEARING OF THE
SENATE COMMITTEE ON GOVERNMENT AFFAIRS AND
THE SUBCOMMITTEE ON INTERNATIONAL SECURITY,
PROLIFERATION AND FEDERAL SERVICES

"FEDERAL EFFORTS TO COORDINATE AND PREPARE THE UNITED
STATES FOR BIOTERRORISM.
ARE THEY READY?"

CHAIRMAN JOE LIEBERMAN
SENATOR FRED THOMPSON
THE HONORABLE TOMMY G. THOMPSON
MR. MICHAEL BROWN, FEMA
DR. ANNA JOHNSON-WINEGAR, OFFICE OF SECDEF
DR. MARGARET A. HAMBURG, NUCLEAR THREAT INITIATIVE
MR. GARY W. MCCONNELL, GEORGE EMERGENCY AGENCY
DR. AMY SMITHSON, HENRY L. STIMSON CENTER
MR. HENRY L. HINTON, JR. GAO

October 17, 2001

COMMENTARY: *The devastating damage associated with the mailed anthrax
packages in the U.S. set the stage for these hearings.*

STATEMENT OF
CHAIRMAN JOE LIEBERMAN

October 17, 2001

This morning, this Committee will try to provide answers to the urgent question of whether our government is organized adequately to respond to biological or chemical attacks on the American homeland. Senator Thompson and I are pleased to hold this hearing in conjunction with the Subcommittee on International Security, Proliferation and Federal Services, and its able chairman and ranking member, Senators Akaka and Cochran.

As we are now painfully and personally aware, the past week has brought one story after another of anthrax attacks—biological attacks—endangering hundreds of innocent people and actually infecting a handful in several states. Here on Capitol Hill, a wing of the Hart Building was quarantined, Senators and staff are undergoing testing, and mail delivery came to a halt when anthrax was identified in a package delivered to the Majority Leader's office. We have received word today that a number of Senator Daschle's staff have been affected. These incidents—and the countless false alarms and hoaxes people are experiencing daily—have put many Americans into an understandable, state of high anxiety over this threat to our public health.

This morning, I hope we can calmly discuss the facts and offer some reassurance to the public that the federal government is on duty and rapidly improving its preparedness to respond to whatever may come. We have entered an era when the previously theoretical has become altogether real. It's clear to me we have a lot of work to do. But the response of our public health system over the last two weeks is almost exactly what it should have been, with quick detection, identification, treatment and containment of the problem—and that has clearly and thankfully minimized casualties.

I want particularly to commend our first witness, Secretary of Health and Human Services Thompson, for his leadership in responding to this crisis, in calming a tense nation and urgently preparing to improve our response systems to what is now a very real threat.

The Governmental Affairs Committee is an oversight committee charged with the specific mandate to assure that the federal government is organized effectively to fulfill its responsibilities. In today's hearing, we will be focusing on the organizational coordination of scores of federal bureaus and departments that are involved in responding to bio-terrorism and chemical terrorism attacks. Ten major agencies and dozens of bureaus—including the Defense Department and the intelligence agencies—are responsible for, among other things, threat assessment, surveillance of disease occurrences, surveillance of food and water supplies, developing and stockpiling vaccines, and assisting state and local governments in planning, training and responding. Secretary Thompson's department, itself, has six different agencies involved in bio-terrorism and chemical terrorism, which, Mr. Secretary, is why it made such good sense for you to appoint a Department coordinator last July.

This morning, we will also look at coordination between the federal government and state and local governments and their public health systems—because those are the people on the front lines of homeland defense, and they will be called upon to respond first.

The possibility of a biological or chemical attack poses a completely different kind of threat, requiring a different kind of response, from a different set of responders, than on the dark day of September 11. That day, events were visibly and immediately seen by millions of people on television, and the catastrophe required conventional fire, rescue and medical capabilities —on a huge scale. A biological or chemical attack would unfold in a very different way. It might not be immediately visible. It could emerge slowly in different locations, in mail rooms, doctors' offices, clinics, emergency rooms, and public health department laboratories, and a completely different set of actors—mostly medical personnel- would be the first to respond. Some biological agents—such as small pox—are contagious and would spread rapidly throughout the population. A government exercise simulating a biological attack conducted earlier this year showed that such diseases could greatly challenge state and local medical capabilities to respond.

The good news is we have systems and equipment in place to respond to an attack of this sort, and, as we will hear today, the federal government has begun to organize the pieces that will be needed to contain biological or chemical attacks on a large scale. The Health and Human Services Department is developing an Internet-based surveillance system to gather data on disease incidence that would allow for real-time analysis. The Pentagon is developing civil support teams within the National Guard in every state. And state and local officials are increasingly well trained to deal with these attacks.

But the systems are in place clearly need to be strengthened. Preparation for these types of attacks didn't even begin at the federal level until the late 1990s, so many agency plans and programs are still incomplete. There is duplication and overlap because of traditional government stove-pipe structures and the inevitable turf battles that accompany this kind of structure. And there appears to be no overarching strategy and no single, focused executive direction. It's hard not to conclude that the government has a series of organizational decisions to make—and quickly.

Federal support for state and local governments and health care systems must grow to meet the challenge before us. These are the agencies that employ the local heroes—the emergency medical technicians, the police, the firemen, the hospital emergency room workers. And yet, while federal funding for response to terrorist attacks involving biological and chemical weapons has increased in the past three or four years, not enough of that money is reaching the state and local levels.

We need to build a more robust public health system capable of aggressive health surveillance programs—early warning systems—to detect the onset of illnesses. We need adequate inventories of pharmaceuticals and we need better coordination and better support for state and local governments and the health care system.

Only the federal government can ensure that the capabilities to protect our citizens in the event of a biological or chemical attack are in place. I hope this hearing and this Committee can help it do that quickly.

OPENING STATEMENT OF
RANKING MEMBER FRED THOMPSON

October 17, 2001

Good morning. I thank Secretary of Health and Human Services Tommy Thompson for being here today. It's a delicate balance he and others have to walk in telling the American people the truth about the dangers we are facing today and I look forward to hearing from him this morning.

Last Friday we held a hearing to discuss the structure of the new Homeland Security Office in the Administration. Today, we look a little closer at some of the more specific challenges which the Director of that new office will face with regard to biological and chemical attacks.

Concerns about these issues are not new. Two months ago the International Security, Proliferation, and Federal Services Subcommittee held a hearing to discuss our level of preparedness for a biological attack. There have been over ten different hearings held in Congress this year on the biological and chemical threat and the federal government's response capabilities. Moreover, in the *Government at the Brink* report I released earlier this year I noted that combating terrorism was an area of potential overlap and fragmentation, issues I believe we will be discussing more today.

While these concerns may not be new, there is a new sense of urgency. There have been anthrax attacks now in three states as well as here in Washington. Our Committee office was shut down yesterday and again today because of its proximity to Sen. Daschle's office and our staff had to undergo testing. Mr. Chairman, your own personal office was shut down. Clearly we no longer have the luxury of time to deal with the bioterrorism threat and our government's response. The challenge we have before us now is to determine how we can, at the federal level, best prepare our country for chemical and biological attacks.

As a nation, we do have certain priorities in this effort. First, ensuring that local officials are prepared for an attack. Especially in dealing with a biological attack, the first responders on the front line will be local medical personnel and community public health officials. How well trained and ready they are will be the biggest factor in our success or failure in dealing with biological and chemical attacks. Second, the federal government must provide proper support to local first responders in the event of an attack. That support could come in the form of response teams, pharmaceutical supplies, law enforcement as well as other efforts. And third, the federal government can continue to provide research to aid in surveillance, detection and treatment for biological and chemical attacks.

The good news is that there are many federal agencies working on all of these issues. The bad news is that there are many federal agencies working on all of these issues. As GAO recently stated in a report, "coordination of federal terrorism research, preparedness, and response programs is fragmented...several different agencies are responsible for various coordination functions, which limits accountability and hinders unity of effort."

This is not just true in this arena. It's endemic of government and we seem to follow a pattern of overlap and duplication throughout government. In my *Government at the Brink* report released this spring, we listed problem upon problem illustrating overlap and duplication. For example, training for local police, firefighters, doctors, emergency room personnel and public health officials is offered by multiple agencies. We seem to have ignored clear and present dangers. We've been holding hearings, following the release of reports, and adding programs upon programs to the mix, later consolidating, and resulting in the same pattern again and again.

Other problems exist. The federal government tends to spend most of its resources at the federal level, rather than on the front lines. As one of our witnesses today, Dr. Amy Smithson, noted in her book on this subject, just 3.7 percent or $315 million of the overall $8.4 billion counterterrorism budget in 2000 went to the front lines in the form of training, equipment grants, and planning assistance. Quote, "Bluntly put, an absurdly small slice of the funding pie has made it beyond the beltway." We are spending a great deal of money on this problem and we will need to make sure it's spent effectively.

Also, the large number of Congressional committees asserting jurisdiction in this area has resulted in several different agencies receiving authorization for activities that overlap.

I look forward to hearing from our witnesses today. I hope that we can discuss not only what problems may exist with regard to coordination and fragmentation in our fight against biological and chemical terrorism, but also ways we can improve the efficiency and effectiveness of the federal response to such attacks.

STATEMENT OF TOMMY G. THOMPSON
SECRETARY, DEPARTMENT OF HEALTH AND HUMAN SERVICES

Wednesday, October 17, 2001

Mr. Chairman and Members of the Committee, thank you for inviting me here today to discuss the Department of Health and Human Services (HHS) role in federal government efforts to coordinate, prepare for and respond to acts of terrorism, particularly those involving biological or chemical agents.

The Federal Emergency Management Agency (FEMA), as overall lead federal agency for consequence management efforts, has designated the Department of Health and Human Services (HHS) as the lead agency to coordinate medical assistance in national emergencies, be they natural disasters or acts of terrorism. When FEMA determines a federal response is warranted, this agency deploys medical personnel, equipment, and drugs to assist victims of a major disaster, emergency, or terrorist attack. Given our critical medical role in any biological, chemical, radiological or nuclear attack, I take HHS preparedness efforts most seriously.

We are working very closely within the Administration to make sure our resource needs are adequately and accurately developed. Areas we have particularly focused on include:

Accelerating development and procurement of vaccines and pharmaceuticals to control and treat critical biological threats, including smallpox and anthrax.

Protecting our food supply by increasing inspections of food imports, and providing the Food and Drug Administration (FDA) more of the modern equipment needed to detect select agents.

Working with cities to ensure that their Metropolitan Medical Response System units have the equipment and training to respond to bioterrorist events and other disasters.

Working with States to ensure they have comprehensive response plans, and increasing their capacity to detect and respond to threats. This includes:

expanding the number of State labs with rapid testing capability;

improving coordination with local response plans, and

expanding the Health Alert Network.

Implementing a new hospital preparedness effort to ensure that our health facilities plan for the equipment and training to respond to mass casualty incidents.

Recent events involving anthrax have highlighted the collaboration between state and local health and law enforcement officials, HHS's Centers for Disease Control and Prevention (CDC) and the Federal Bureau of Investigation (FBI). We are continuing to conduct investigations related to anthrax exposures in Florida, New York, Nevada, and our Nation's Capitol complex. CDC and state and local health officials continue to work closely with medical professionals nationwide to monitor hospitals and out-patient clinics for any possible additional anthrax cases. During this heightened surveillance, cases of illness that may reasonably resemble symptoms of anthrax will be thoroughly reviewed until anthrax can be ruled out.

The public health and medical community continue to be on a heightened level of disease monitoring. This is an example of the disease monitoring system in action, and that system is working.

Coordinated Preparedness Efforts

As you know, much of the initial burden and responsibility for providing an effective response by medical and public health professionals to a terrorist attack rests with local governments. If the disease outbreak reaches any significant magnitude, however, local and state resources will be overwhelmed and the federal government will be required to provide protective and responsive measures for the affected populations.

HHS agencies that play a key role in our Department's overall terrorism preparedness include the CDC, the FDA, the Office of Emergency Preparedness (OEP), and the National Institutes of Health (NIH).

The Department has always valued the cooperation that it has received from its federal, state, and local government partners. We work closely with all of the agency signatories of the Federal Response Plan and have had a particularly close working relationship with FEMA, the Department of Defense (DOD), the Department of Justice (DOJ), the Department of State (DOS), the Department of Veterans Affairs (VA), the U.S. Department of Agriculture (USDA), the Department of Energy (DOE), and the Environmental Protection Agency (EPA).

I will focus the remainder of my testimony on a few examples of HHS's terrorism preparedness efforts conducted in collaboration with our federal, state, and local partners.

National Disaster Medical System

The National Disaster Medical System (NDMS) is the vehicle for providing resources for meeting the medical, mental health, and forensic service requirements in response to major emergencies, federally declared disasters, and terrorist acts. Begun in 1984, NDMS is a partnership among HHS, VA, DoD, FEMA, state and local governments, and the private sector. The

System has three components: direct medical care; patient evacuation; and the non-federal hospital bed system. NDMS was created as a nationwide medical response system to supplement state and local medical resources during disasters and emergencies, to provide back-up medical support to the military and VA health care systems during an overseas conventional conflict, and to promote development of community-based disaster medical systems. The availability of beds in over 2,000 civilian hospitals is coordinated by VA and DoD Federal Coordinating Centers. The NDMS medical response component is comprised of over 7,000 private sector medical and support personnel organized into approximately 70 Disaster Medical Assistance Teams, Disaster Mortuary Operational Response Teams, and speciality teams across the Nation.

When there is a disaster, FEMA, as the Nation's consequence management and response coordinator, tasks HHS to provide critical services, such as health and medical care; preventive health services; mental health care; veterinary services; mortuary activities; and any other public health or medical service that may be needed in the affected area. HHS's Office of Emergency Preparedness directs NDMS, the Public Health Service's Commissioned Corps Readiness Force, and other federal resources, to assist in providing the needed services to ensure the continued health and well being of disaster victims.

Pharmaceutical Stockpiles

The VA is one of the largest purchasers of pharmaceuticals and medical supplies in the world. Capitalizing on this buying power, OEP and VA have entered into an agreement under which the VA manages and stores specialized pharmaceutical caches for OEP's National Medical Response Teams. The VA has purchased many of the items in the pharmaceutical stockpile. The VA is also responsible for maintaining the inventory, ensuring its security, and rotating the stock to ensure that the caches are ready for deployment with the specialized National Medical Response Teams. Additionally, during FY 2001, OEP provided funds to the VA to begin to develop plans and curricula to train NDMS hospital personnel to respond to weapons of mass destruction events.

Research Efforts

With the support of Congress, the President has implemented a government-wide emergency response package to help deal with the tragic events of September 11th. This complements efforts already underway to prepare our nation against such heinous attacks, including threats of bioterrorism. For example, CDC and the National Institutes of Health (NIH) within HHS are collaborating with the Department of Defense (DOD) and other agencies to support and encourage research to address scientific issues related to bioterrorism. The capability to detect and counter bioterrorism depends to a substantial degree on the state of relevant medical science. In some cases, new vaccines, antitoxins, or innovative drug treatments need to be developed or stocked. Moreover, we need to learn more about the pathogenesis and epidemiology of the infectious diseases which do not affect the U.S. population currently. We have only limited knowledge about how artificial methods of dispersion may affect the infection rate, virulence, or impact of these biological agents. Our continuing research agenda in collaboration with CDC, NIH, and DOD is vital to overall preparedness.

Even before the events of September 11, HHS's Food and Drug Administration actively cooperated with DOD in the operation of its vaccine development program and the maintenance of their stockpile program. Any vaccine development, whether by DOD or private industry, must be in accordance with FDA requirements that ensure the safety, effectiveness and manufacturing quality of the finished product. FDA provides assistance to DOD regarding the research required to develop new vaccines, as well as assistance during all phases of development. FDA also works with DOD's office that screens new and unusual ideas for development of products to treat diseases and develop diagnostic tools.

Food Safety

Because food is a possible medium for spreading infectious diseases, FDA and CDC are enhancing their surveillance activities with respect to diseases caused by foodborne pathogens, and are working with our federal, state, and local partners to coordinate these activities. PulseNet, a national network of public health laboratories created, administered and coordinated by CDC in collaboration with FDA and USDA, enables the comparison of bacteria isolated from patients from widespread locations, from foods and from food production facilities. This type of rapid comparison allows public health officials to connect what may appear to be unrelated clusters of illnesses, thus facilitating the identification of the source of an outbreak caused by intentional or unintentional contamination of foods.

FDA also works with the EPA, the Nuclear Regulatory Commission and other agencies to address chemical and nuclear food safety issues of concern.

Training

HHS has used classroom training, distance learning, and hands-on training activities to prepare the health and medical community for contingencies such as bioterrorism and other terrorism events. For example, in Fiscal Year 1999, Congress appropriated funds for OEP to renovate and modernize the Noble Army Hospital at Ft. McClellan, Alabama, so the hospital can be used to train doctors, nurses, paramedics and emergency medical technicians to recognize and treat patients with chemical exposures and other public health emergencies. Working with CDC and the VA, a training program was developed for pharmacists working with distribution of the National Pharmaceutical Stockpile. Expansion of the bioterrorism component of Noble Training Center curriculum is a high priority for HHS.

HHS has been working closely with the Office of Justice Programs (OJP) National Domestic Preparedness Consortium, and we will continue our excellent relationship with them. OJP and HHS have teamed together to develop a health care assessment tool and have also delivered a combined MMRS/first responder training program.

CDC has participated with DOD, most notably to provide distance-based learning for bioterrorism and disease awareness to the clinical community. CDC is now moving to expand such training with organizations, such as the Infectious Disease Society of America (IDSA), and Schools of Public Health, such as the Johns Hopkins Center for Civilian Biodefense.

The recent FEMA-CDC initiative to expand the scope of FEMA's Integrated Emergency Management Course (IEMC) will serve as a vehicle to integrate the emergency management and health community response efforts in a way that has not been possible in the past. It is clear that these communities can best respond together if they are able to train together toward realistic scenarios that leverage the best of both organizations.

Because the initial detection of a biological terrorist attack will most likely occur at the local level, it is essential to educate and train members of the medical community—both public and private—who may be the first to examine and treat the victims. It is also necessary to upgrade the surveillance systems of state and local health departments, as well as within healthcare facilities such as hospitals, which will be relied upon to spot unusual patterns of disease occurrence and to identify any additional cases of illness. HHS and its other partners will continue to provide terrorism-related training to epidemiologists and laboratorians, emergency responders, emergency department personnel and other front-line health-care providers, and health and safety personnel.

State and Local Collaborations

HHS has also had a particularly close working relationship with local and state public health and health care delivery communities. We coordinate closely with the public safety, public health, and health care delivery communities at all of these levels, particularly through the health agencies and emergency management authorities.

As key partners in our response strategy, state and local public health programs comprise the foundation of an effective national strategy for preparedness and emergency response. Preparedness must incorporate not only the immediate responses to threats such as biological terrorism, it also encompasses the broader components of public health infrastructure which provide the foundation for immediate and effective emergency responses.

CDC has used funds provided by the past several Congresses to begin the process of improving the expertise, facilities and procedures of state and local health departments to respond to biological terrorism. For example, over the last three years, the agency has awarded more than $130 million in cooperative agreements to 50 states, one territory and four major metropolitan health departments as part of its overall Bioterrorism Preparedness and Response Program.

CDC has invested $90 million in the Health Alert Network (HAN), a nationwide system that is now in all 50 states, which provides high-speed Internet connections for local health officials; rapid communications with first responder agencies and others; transmission of surveillance, laboratory and other sensitive data; and on-line, Internet- and satellite-based distance learning.

The CDC also has launched an effort to improve public health laboratories. The Laboratory Response Network (LRN), a partnership among the Association of Public Health Laboratories (APHL), CDC, FBI, State Public Health Laboratories, DOD and the Nation's clinical laboratories, will help ensure that the highest level of containment and expertise in the identification of biological agents is available in an emergency event.

Metropolitan Medical Response System

HHS is also working on a number of fronts to assist local hospitals and medical practitioners to deal with the effects of biological, chemical, and other terrorist acts. Since Fiscal Year 1995, for example, HHS through OEP has been developing local Metropolitan Medical Response Systems (MMRS). Through contractual relationships, the MMRS uses existing emergency response systems—emergency management, medical and mental health providers, public health departments, law enforcement, fire departments, EMS and the National Guard—to provide an integrated, unified response to a mass casualty event. As of September 30, 2001, OEP has contracted with 97 municipalities to develop MMRSs. During FY 2002, we intend to award $10 million to 25 additional cities (for a total of 122) through the MMRS to help them improve their medical response capabilities.

MMRS contracts require the development of local capability for mass immunization/prophylaxis for the first 24 hours following an identified disease outbreak; the capability to distribute materiel deployed to the local site from the National Pharmaceutical Stockpile; local capability for mass patient care, including procedures to augment existing care facilities; local medical staff trained to recognize disease symptoms so that they can initiate treatment; and local capability to manage the remains of the deceased.

Conclusion

The Department of Health and Human Services is committed to working with other federal agencies as well as state and local public health partners to ensure the health and medical well-being of our citizens. The mutual and ongoing consultation, assistance, collaborations and support HHS receives from its federal agency partners are useful in identifying not only programmatic overlaps but also gaps in our preparedness efforts. These efforts also allow us to work toward integrating our respective initiatives into a government-wide framework.

Our ongoing relationships with state and local governments have been reinforced in recent years as a result of the investments we have made in bioterrorism preparedness. Without their engagement in this undertaking, we would not be seeing the advances that have been made in recent years.

We have made substantial progress to date in enhancing the nation's capability to respond to biological or chemical acts of terrorism. But there is more we can do to strengthen the response. Priorities include strengthening our local and state public health surveillance capacity, continuing to enhance the National Pharmaceutical Stockpile, improving public health planning and preparedness at the state and local level, and helping our local hospitals and medical professionals better prepare for responding to a biological or chemical terrorist attack.

Mr. Chairman, that concludes my prepared remarks. I would be pleased to answer any questions you or members of the Committee may have.

STATEMENT OF MICHAEL D. BROWN
ACTING DIRECTOR AND GENERAL COUNSEL,
OFFICE OF GENERAL COUNSEL
FEDERAL EMERGENCY MANAGEMENT AGENCY

October 17, 2001

Introduction

Good morning, Mr. Chairman and Members of the Subcommittee. I am Bruce Baughman, Director of the Planning and Readiness Division, Readiness, Response, and Recovery Directorate, of the Federal Emergency Management Agency (FEMA). Director Allbaugh regrets that he is unable to be here with you today. It is a pleasure for me to represent him at this important hearing on biological and chemical terrorism. I will describe how FEMA works with other agencies, our approach to dealing with acts of terrorism, our programs related to terrorism, and new efforts to enhance preparedness and response.

Background

The FEMA mission is to reduce the loss of life and property and protect our nation's critical infrastructure from all types of hazards. As staffing goes, we are a small agency. Our success depends on our ability to organize and lead a community of local, State, and Federal agencies and volunteer organizations. We know who to bring to the table and what questions to ask when it comes to the business of managing emergencies. We provide an operational framework and a funding source.

The Federal Response Plan (FRP) is the heart of that framework. It reflects the labors of interagency groups that meet as required in Washington, D.C. and all 10 FEMA Regions to develop our capabilities to respond as a team. This team is made up of 26 Federal departments and agencies and the American Red Cross, and organized into interagency functions based on the authorities and expertise of the members and the needs of our counterparts at the state and local level.

Since 1992, the Federal Response Plan has been the proven framework time and time again, for managing major disasters and emergencies regardless of cause. It works during all phases of the emergency life cycle, from readiness, to response, recovery, and mitigation. The framework is successful because it builds upon the existing professional disciplines and communities among agencies. Among Federal agencies, FEMA has the strongest ties to the emergency management and the fire service communities. We plan, train, exercise, and operate together. That puts us in position to manage and coordinate programs that address their needs. Similarly, the Department of Health and Human Services (HHS) has the strongest ties to the public health and medical communities, and the Environmental Protection Agency (EPA) has the strongest ties to the hazardous materials community. The Federal Response Plan respects these relationships and areas of expertise to define the decision-making processes and delivery systems to make the best use of available resources.

The Approach to Biological and Chemical Terrorism

We recognize that biological and chemical scenarios would present unique challenges. Of the two I am more concerned about bioterrorism. A chemical attack is in many ways a large-scale hazardous materials incident. EPA and the Coast Guard are well connected to local hazardous materials responders, State and Federal agencies, and the chemical industry. There are systems and plans in place for response to hazardous materials, systems that are routinely used for small and large-scale events. EPA is also the primary agency for the Hazardous Materials function of the Federal Response Plan. We can improvise around that model in a chemical attack.

With a covert release of a biological agent, the 'first responders' will be hospital staff, medical examiners, private physicians, or animal control workers, instead of the traditional first responders such as police, fire, and emergency medical services. While I defer to the Departments of Justice and HHS on how biological scenarios would unfold, it seems unlikely that terrorists would warn us of a pending biological attack. In exercise and planning scenarios, the worst-case scenarios begin undetected and play out as epidemics. Response would begin in the public health and medical community. Initial requests for Federal assistance would probably come through health and medical channels to the Centers for Disease Control and Prevention (CDC). Conceivably, the situation could escalate into a national emergency.

HHS is a critical link between the health and medical community and the larger Federal response. HHS leads the efforts of the health and medical community to plan and prepare for a national response to a public health emergency. FEMA works closely with the Public Health Service, as the primary agency for the Health and Medical Services function of the Federal Response Plan. We rely on the Public Health Service to bring the right experts to the table when the Federal Response Plan community meets to discuss biological scenarios. We work closely with the experts in HHS and other health and medical agencies, to learn about the threats, how they spread, and the resources and techniques that will be needed to control them. By the same token, the medical experts work with us to learn about the Federal Response Plan and how we can use it to work the management issues, such as resource deployment and public information strategies. Alone, the Federal Response Plan is not an adequate solution for the challenge of planning and preparing for a deadly epidemic or act of bioterrorism. It is equally true that, alone, the health and medical community cannot manage an emergency with biological causes. We must work together.

In recent years, Federal, state and local governments and agencies have made progress in bringing the communities closer together. Exercise Top Officials (TOPOFF) 2000 in May 2000 involved two concurrent terrorism scenarios in two metropolitan areas, a chemical attack on the East Coast followed by a biological attack in the Midwest. We are still working on the lessons learned from that exercise. We need time and resources to identify, develop, and incorporate changes to the system between exercises. Exercises are critical in helping us to prepare for these types of scenarios. In January 2001, the FBI and FEMA jointly published the U.S. Government Interagency Domestic Terrorism Concept of Operation Plan (CONPLAN) with HHS, EPA, and the Departments of Defense and Energy, and pledged to continue the planning process to develop specific procedures for different scenarios, including bioterrorism. The Federal Response Plan and the CONPLAN provide the framework for managing the response to an act of bioterrorism.

Synopsis of FEMA Programs

FEMA programs are focused mainly on planning, training, and exercises to build capabilities to *manage* emergencies resulting from terrorism. Many of these program activities apply generally to terrorism, rather than to one form such as biological or chemical terrorism.

Planning

The overall Federal planning effort is being coordinated with the FBI, using existing plans and response structures whenever possible. The FBI is always the Lead Agency for Crisis Management. FEMA is always the Lead Agency for Consequence Management. We have developed plans and procedures to explain how to coordinate the two operations before and after consequences occur. In 1999, we published the second edition of the FRP Terrorism Incident Annex. In 2001, the FBI and FEMA published the United States Government Interagency Domestic Terrorism Concept of Operations Plan (CONPLAN).

We continually validate our planning concepts by developing plans to support the response to special events, such as we are now doing for the 2002 Olympic Winter Games that will take place in Utah.

To support any need for a Federal response, FEMA maintains the Rapid Response Information System (RRIS). The RRIS provides online access to information on key Federal assets that can be made available to assist state and local response efforts, and a database on chemical and biological agents and protective measures.

In FY 2001, FEMA has distributed $16.6 million in terrorism consequence management preparedness assistance grants to the States to support development of terrorism related capabilities, and $100 million in fire grants. FEMA is developing additional guidance to provide greater flexibility for states on how they can use this assistance.

FEMA has also developed a special attachment to its all-hazards Emergency Operations Planning Guide for state and local emergency managers that addresses developing terrorist incident annexes to state and local emergency operations plans. This planning guidance was developed with the assistance of eight Federal departments and agencies in coordination with NEMA and the International Association of Emergency Managers.

FEMA and the National Emergency Management Association (NEMA) jointly developed the Capability Assessment for Readiness (CAR), a self-assessment tool that enables States and Territories to focus on 13 core elements that address major emergency management functions. Terrorism preparedness is assessed relative to planning, procedures, equipment and exercises. FEMA's CAR report presents a composite picture of the nation's readiness based on the individual State and Territory reports.

FEMA's Comprehensive Hazardous Materials Emergency Response Capability Assessment Program (CHER-CAP) helps communities improve their terrorism preparedness by assessing their emergency response capability. Local, State, and Tribal emergency managers, civic leaders, hospital personnel and industry representatives all work together to identify problems, revise their response plans and improve their community's preparedness for a terrorist event. Since February 2000, a total of 55 communities have been selected to participate, initiated, or completed a sequence of planning, training, and exercise activities to improve their terrorism preparedness.

Training

FEMA supports the training of Federal, State, and local emergency personnel through our National Fire Academy (NFA), which t rains emergency responders, and the Emergency Management Institute (EMI), which focuses on emergency planners, coordinators and elected and appointed officials. EMI and NFA work in partnership with State and municipal training organizations. Together they form a very strong national network of fire and emergency training. FEMA employs a "train-the-trainer" approach and uses distance-learning technologies such as the Emergency Education Network via satellite TV and web-based instruction to maximize our training impact.

The NFA has developed and fielded several courses in the *Emergency Response to Terrorism (ERT)* curriculum, including a Self-Study course providing general awareness information for responding to terrorist incidents that has been distributed to some 35,000 fire/ rescue departments, 16,000 law enforcement agencies, and over 3,000 local and state emergency managers in the United States and is available on FEMA internet site. Other courses in the curriculum deal with Basic Concepts, Incident Management, and Tactical Considerations for Emergency Medical Services (EMS), Company Officers, and HAZMAT Response. Biological and chemical terrorism are included as integral parts of these courses.

Over one thousand instructors representing every state and major metropolitan area in the nation have been trained under the ERT program. The NFA is utilizing the Training Resources and Data Exchange (TRADE) program to reach all 50 States and all major metropolitan fire and rescue departments with training materials and course offerings. In FY 2001, FEMA is distributing $4 million in grants to state fire-training centers to deliver first responder courses developed by the NFA.

Over 112,000 students have participated in ERT courses and other terrorism-related training. In addition, some 57,000 copies of a Job Aid utilizing a flip-chart format guidebook to quick reference based on the ERT curriculum concepts and principles have been printed and distributed.

NFA is developing a new course in FY 2002 in the Emergency Response to Terrorism series geared toward response to bioterrorism in the pre-hospital recognition and response phase. It will be completed with the review and input of our Federal partners, notably HHS and the Office of Justice Programs.

EMI offers a comprehensive program of emergency management training including a number of courses specifically designed to help communities, states, and tribes deal with the consequences of terrorism and weapons of mass destruction. The EMI curriculum includes an Integrated Emergency Management Course (IEMC)/Consequences of Terrorism. This 4-½ day course combines classroom training, planning sessions, and functional exercises into a management-level course designed to encourage communities to integrate functions, skills, and resources to deal with the consequences of terrorism, including terrorism. To foster this integration, EMI brings together 70 participants for each course that includes elected officials and public health leaders as well as representatives of law enforcement, emergency medical services, emergency management, and public works. The course provides participants with skill-building opportunities in preparedness, response, and recovery. The scenario for the course changes from offering to offering. In a recent offering, the scenario was based on an airborne anthrax release. Bioterrorism scenarios emphasize the special issues inherent in dealing with both infectious and noninfectious biological agents and stresses the partnerships between local, state, and Federal public health organizations.

Exercises

In the area of exercises, FEMA is working closely with the interagency community and the States to ensure the development of a comprehensive exercise program that meets the needs of the emergency management and first responder communities. FEMA is planning to conduct Phase II of a seminar series on terrorism preparedness in each of the ten FEMA Regional Offices. In addition, exercise templates and tools are being developed for delivery to state and local officials.

New Efforts to Enhance Preparedness and Response

In response to guidance from the President on May 8, 2001, the FEMA Director created an Office of National Preparedness (ONP) to coordinate all federal programs dealing with weapons of mass destruction consequence management, with particular focus on preparedness for, and the response to the terrorist use of such weapons. In July, the Director established the ONP at FEMA Headquarters. An ONP element was also established in each of the ten FEMA Regional Offices to support terrorism-related activities involving the States and localities.

On September 21, 2001, in the wake of the horrific terrorist attacks on the World Trade Center and the Pentagon, the President announced the establishment of an Office of Homeland Security (OHS) in the White House to be headed by Governor Tom Ridge of Pennsylvania. In setting up the new office, the President stated that it would lead, oversee and coordinate a national strategy to safeguard the country against terrorism and respond to attacks that occur. It is our understanding that office will coordinate a broad range of policies and activities related to prevention, deterrence, preparedness and response to terrorism.

The new office includes a Homeland Security Council comprised of key department and agency officials, including the FEMA Director. FEMA expects to provide significant support to the office in its role as the lead Federal agency for consequence management.

Conclusion

Mr. Chairman, you convened this hearing to ask about our preparedness to work with State and local agencies in the event of a biological or chemical attack. It is FEMA's responsibility to ensure that the national emergency management system is adequate to respond to the consequences of catastrophic emergencies and disasters, regardless of cause. All catastrophic events require a strong management system built on expert systems for each of the operational disciplines. Terrorism presents tremendous challenges. We rely on our partners in Department of Health and Human Services to coordinate the efforts of the health and medical community to address biological terrorism, as we rely on EPA and the Coast Guard to co-ordinate the efforts of the hazardous materials community to address chemical terrorism. Without question, they need support to further strengthen capabilities and their operating capacity. FEMA must ensure that the national system has the tools to gather information, set priorities, and deploy resources effectively in a biological scenario. In recent years we have made tremendous strides in our efforts to increase cooperation between the various response communities, from fire and emergency management to health and medical to hazardous materials. We need to do more.

The creation of the Office of Homeland Security and other efforts will enable us to better focus our time and effort with those communities, to prepare the nation for response to any incident.

Thank you, Mr. Chairman. I would be happy to answer any questions.

STATEMENT OF DR. ANNA JOHNSON-WINEGAR
DEPUTY ASSISTANT TO THE SECRETARY OF DEFENSE FOR
CHEMICAL AND BIOLOGICAL DEFENSE

October 17, 2001

Mr. Chairman and distinguished committee members, i am dr. Anna johnson-winegar, deputy assistant to the secretary of defense for chemical and biological defense. My office is the single focal point within the office of the secretary of defense responsible for oversight, coordination, and integration of the joint chemical and biological defense programs.

The tragic events of september 11th and the recently reported anthrax cases in florida and elsewhere have heightened the public's awareness of the threat posed by biological terrorism. For some years, the department of defense has considered the use of biological weapons as a possible means by which states and non-state actors might counter america's overwhelming conventional warfighting strength—often referred to as asymmetric means. In response to this threat congress directed the department of defense to consolidate chemical and biological defense efforts. Since the establishment of a joint chemical and biological defense program in 1994, and with continued congressional support, the department of defense has made significant progress in fielding biological defense equipment for our warfighters and stands ready to meet the most credible threats.

Biological warfare threats. In addition, my office stands ready to assist civilian agencies through technology sharing, technical advice, or as otherwise requested by the appropriate authorities.

In order to meet the challenge of biological warfare across the spectrum, our program must address the need for both materiel improvement and operational concepts to use the new and improved equipment. In order to address the issue of bioterrorism, we have documented gaps and deficiencies in exercises, such as top off, and these will be the focus of reprioritized efforts within the department of defense. One of the lessons of the topoff exercise was that to work effectively during an actual crisis, various governmental agencies must actually exercise beforehand or their "cultural differences" will overcome any plan. We will continue to work with other agencies, including the new office of homeland security, to ensure good working relationships. One specific area we will focus on is to help define what support the department of defense can provide and work with other agencies to define what support they request and need.

While the DOD can provide unique expertise and materiel support, it is not charged with lead federal agent responsibilities as described in the federal response plan. In the area of domestic terrorism medical response, the department of health and human services takes charge and requests support as needed. In my testimony today, i will outline the ways the department of defense provides materiel support to other organizations and how we coordinate efforts.

Materiel support

Congress has provided a number of statutory methods for the department of defense to support other federal, state, and local agencies in preparing for and responding to weapons of mass destruction (wmd) terrorism. Requests may come to the department for operational support or for the purchase of equipment. These requests are approved on a case-by-case basis. My office has dealt with a number of requests from other-federal agencies for individual and collective protective equipment and access to vaccines, while the operational support provided by the department is coordinated through the secretary of the army as the DOD executive agent for such matters. The department will continue to provide this support within statutory and regulatory limits and balance requests against the readiness of military forces to accomplish their warfighting mission.

DOD can offer many of its systems, either in the field or in development, and expertise that may prove useful to civilians. DOD's chemical and biological detection equipment could be applied in civilian situations, as can many of our medical countermeasures. However, the provision of materiel alone does not enhance capability, it needs to be accompanied by valid operational concepts, training, and maintenance.

The mission of the DOD chemical and biological defense program is to provide materiel to allow our armed forces to be trained and equipped to conduct their operational missions in environments contaminated with chemical or biological agents. Our armed forces are trained primarily for traditional warfighting requirements. However, our forces also maintain significant capabilities to support homeland security, through such operational units as the technical escort unit, the wmd-civil support teams, and the marine corps' chemical and biological incident response force (cbirf).

In order to enhance our nation's overall capabilities the department of defense participates in programs to support the transition of military equipment and concepts to other-than-DOD agencies.

Specifically, the technical support working group (tswg), rapidly prototypes emerging technologies for high priority federal interagency requirements (www.tswg.gov);

The interagency board for equipment standardization and interoperability (known as the iab), is a partnership with federal, state, and local agencies focused on the capabilities necessary for fire, medical, and law enforcement responses to wmd terrorism (www.iab.gov);

The domestic preparedness program, mandated under the 1997 nunn-lugar-domenici legislation, trained and equipped municipalities to address wmd terrorism (the program transferred to the department of justice in 2000, reports remain available at www2.sbccom.army.mil/hld/); and

Interagency agreements with departments of justice's office of domestic preparedness to purchase equipment in support of justice's grant program.

Medical training programs from the us army medical research institutes for infectious disease and chemical defense; and

The White House Office of Science and Technology Policy chaired weapons of mass destruction program, research and development subgroup.

These efforts represent a snap shot of the department's procurement and research support to address bioterrorism. As the lead federal agencies assess their needs, DOD anticipates additional requests of or participation in these groups.

Coordination

The department of defense has established a set of requirements for the successful completion of military operations in chemical and biological environments. We submit an annual report to congress documenting our progress in meeting these requirements. My office regularly coordinates its efforts with the department of energy, department of health and human services, and the intelligence community through the counterproliferation program review committee, which reports annually to congress on its progress (provided as a classified document to the congress).

Some of the department's requirements to protect the military force correlate with civilian requirements to protect the population against biological terrorism. For instance, one of the concepts being investigated for the development and production of biological defense vaccines is a vaccine production facility. In order to coordinate the needs of the interested agencies, the DOD, relatively early in the process of considering alternatives for vaccine acquisition, established a federal interagency advisory group. Participants, in addition to those from DOD agencies, have included representatives from:

The White House [Office of Homeland Security, Office of Science and Technology Policy, National Security Council, Office of Management and Budget],

Federal Emergency Management Agency,

Department of Health and Human Services (DHHS) [National Institutes of Health, Public Health Service, Food and Drug Administration, Centers for DIsease Control and Prevention, and the Office of the Assistant Secretary for Health and the Surgeon General].

This group, which I chair, has served as a highly effective and productive forum for discussions concerning U.S. vaccine acquisition—particularly vaccines for defense against biological warfare agents—for force health protection and public health needs for the civilian sector.

Conclusion

DOD works regularly with the lead federal agents to coordinate requirements and development efforts for biological terrorism. In addition to coordination, there are a number of mechanisms for DOD to provide assistance to other-federal, state, and local agencies. In light of recent events, DOD anticipates a greater number of requests for assistance. DOD will address these requests on a case-by-case basis to ensure that public safety is enhanced and DOD can still accomplish its warfighting mission. Thank you for the opportunity to speak here today, I would be happy to respond to any questions. Thank you.

TESTIMONY OF MARGARET A. HAMBURG, M.D.
VICE PRESIDENT OF BIOLOGICAL PROGRAMS,
NUCLEAR THREAT INITIATIVE

October 17, 2001

Mr. Chairman and members of the Committee, thank you for the invitation to discuss the need to enhance our nation 's capacity to respond to the threat of biological terrorism. Your leadership and commitment in addressing this challenge comes at a critical time.

The tragic attacks last month have been a powerful reminder of our nation's vulnerability to terrorism, and have increased fears that we could face even more devastating assaults in the future, including the possible use of biological weapons.

Certainly, the events of recent days have underscored how seriously we must take this emerging threat. Whether an unsophisticated delivery system with a limited number of exposures, as we have seen in several American cities, or the potential of a more high-technology, mass casualty attack, the prospects are frightening. Today, no one is complacent about the possibility that a biological agent might be intentionally used to cause widespread panic, disease and death.

In this time of heightened anxiety and concern, our nation has a real opportunity—and obligation—to make sure that we have in place the programs and policies necessary to better protect ourselves against this threat, and perhaps to prevent such an attack from occurring in the first place. While there are many challenges before us, we do know a great deal about what needs to be done and how to do it. I will address these issues in more detail later in my testimony, but I want to emphasize at the outset that improving the national response to bioterrorism must include several broad elements, such as:

Prevention. Every effort must be made to reduce the likelihood that dangerous pathogens will be acquired or used by those that want to do harm. This must include improving intelligence, limiting inappropriate access to certain biological agents and efforts to establish standards that will help prevent the development and spread of biological agents as weapons;

Strengthening public health. Rapid detection and response will depend on a well-trained cadre of trained public health professionals to enhance disease surveillance and outbreak investigation, educated and alert health care providers, upgraded laboratories to support diagnosis, and improved communications across all levels of government, across agencies and across the public and private sector.

Enhancing medical care capacity. We must improve treatment for victims of an attack by enhancing local and federal emergency medical response teams, training health professionals to diagnose and treat these diseases, developing strategies to improve the ability of hospitals to rapidly increase emergency capacity, and providing necessary drugs or vaccines where they are needed through a national pharmaceutical stockpile.

Research. A comprehensive research agenda will serve as the foundation of future preparedness. Perhaps most urgently, we need improved detectors/diagnostics, along with better vaccines and new medications.

Some of these activities are already underway, but need to be strengthened and extended; other programs and policies still need to be developed and implemented. This hearing represents an important forum to better define the agenda we must pursue to be a nation prepared.

DARK WINTER EXERCISE

I have been asked in my testimony to address "Dark Winter," a recent bioterrorism exercise which involved the intentional release of smallpox and the lessons learned. Although a simulation of a worst-case scenario, it powerfully conveyed the distinctive–and sobering–features of a potential bioterrorist attack and helped to spotlight many of the vulnerabilities that we must urgently and effectively address.

"Dark Winter" simulated a series of National Security Council (NSC) meetings dealing with a terrorist attack involving the covert release of smallpox in three American cities. The exercise was conducted by the Center for Strategic and International Studies, the Johns Hopkins Center for Civilian Biodefense Studies, and the ANSER Institute for Homeland Defense, under the leadership of John Hamre, Tara O'Toole and Randy Larsen, respectively. Many of the participants in "Dark Winter" had served previous Presidents in cabinet or sub-cabinet positions. Most knew how the NSC worked, and they were all individuals with considerable expertise and perspective in the security, law enforcement and health fields. I served as the Secretary of Health and Human Services.

In the opening minutes of "Dark Winter" we learned that cases of smallpox had just been diagnosed by the Centers for Disease Control. Given the propensity of this disease to spread person-to-person, the 30% fatality rate of the disease, and the limited supply of smallpox vaccine, it was not surprising that we were soon dealing with an epidemic of devastating, if not catastrophic, potential.

In the 20th century, more than 300 million people died from smallpox— more than those killed in all wars of the century combined. Thanks to a massive and highly collaborative international campaign, smallpox as a naturally occurring disease was eradicated, and vaccination against the disease stopped. Consequently, each passing year has seen the birth of new generations of unvaccinated citizens, and a decrease in the potency of previous vaccinations among adults. So although the eradication of smallpox has saved thousands of lives, the end of vaccination against it has paradoxically left the world more vulnerable to the disease.

This fact would be of little consequence if we did not know that smallpox was made into a weapon by the Soviet Union, and that other nations or groups may have successfully acquired stocks of the virus.

Today, a single case of smallpox anywhere in the world would constitute a global medical concern. An example of the seriousness of this disease is the wave of smallpox that was touched off in Yugoslavia in 1972 by a single infected individual. The epidemic was stopped in its fourth wave by quarantines, aggressive police and military measures, and 18 million emergency vaccinations, this to protect a population of 21 million that was already highly vaccinated.

By comparison, in America today we have less than 15 million effective doses of vaccine to protect a population of 275 million that is highly vulnerable to the disease. The Yugoslavia crisis mushroomed from one case; the "Dark Winter" exercise began with 20 confirmed cases in Oklahoma City, 30 suspected cases spread out in Oklahoma, Georgia, and Pennsylvania, and many more individuals who were infected but not yet ill. Initially, we did not know the time, place or size of the release, so we had no way to judge the true magnitude of the crisis. We could easily predict, however, that it would get worse before it would get better.

Over a 24-hour period at Andrews Air Force Base, our NSC "war gamers" dealt with three weeks of simulated shock, stress and horror. We learned that on December 9, 2002, some dozen patients reported to the Oklahoma City Hospital with a strange illness confirmed quickly by the CDC to be smallpox. While we knew only about the Oklahoma cases the first day, we later learned the scope of the initial infections and the sites of three simultaneous attacks in shopping centers in Oklahoma, Georgia and Pennsylvania. The initial infection quickly spread to five states and 3,000 victims, although at this point, most infected individuals had not displayed symptoms or gone to the hospital, so it was impossible to tell who or where they were.

The two primary tools for containing a smallpox epidemic are isolation of cases and vaccination of contacts. In accordance with this, a strategy was devised to include strict isolation of those with disease and a firewall of vaccine protection around those cases, but from the beginning, that strategy was limited by the large numbers of people initially infected, the rapid spread of the disease, and our limited supply of vaccine. Unfortunately, we had only enough vaccine for one out of every 23 Americans. (This remains the case in America today, although a contract is in place and is being accelerated to produce at least 40 million new doses by the end of 2002).

The Secretary of Defense demanded that all 2.3 million of U.S. military personnel be immediately vaccinated wherever they were in the world. In his wisdom, the President decided against this policy. Instead, we administered vaccine to U.S. military, including the National Guard, and security and medical service personnel who were on the front lines locally, and also those who were in areas of the world where a smallpox attack was more likely to occur.

So, on the first night of decision-making, we designed the vaccination strategy, and we ordered accelerated production of new stock. We even asked the Secretary of State to try to find surplus stock from other countries, but we were doubtful that they would comply with our request in the face of a smallpox epidemic that would in all likelihood become global.

On Day Six of the crisis, very little vaccine was left. The situation required that we consider measures considered draconian by modern standards, including enforced isolation, restrictions on travel, and providing food and other essential supplies to affected areas in the face of these restrictions. These problems were exacerbated by the fact that, by this point, we could no longer provide vaccine to essential providers.

On Day Twelve, when the war game ended, we were beginning the next stage of the epidemic—those who caught smallpox from the original 3,000 people who were infected in the initial terrorist attack. Epidemiologic models predicted that without effective intervention, every two to three weeks the number of cases would increase ten-fold.

At the conclusion of the exercise, the epidemic had spread to 25 states and 10 foreign countries. Civil disorder was erupting sporadically around the nation. Interstate commerce had ceased in large areas of the country. Financial markets had suspended trading. We were out of vaccine and were using isolation as the primary means of disease control.

For each of us around the table, the lessons learned were somewhat different, depending on our various backgrounds, experience and expectations. It was fascinating to see the differing perspectives that were brought to bear on the same fundamental sets of data and decision-points. At times, the old adage "what you see depends on where you sit" came to mind. Yet I think we all agreed that the exercise was indeed plausible—even conservative—in the framing of the scenario and the assumptions made about disease exposure, transmission and treatment. Certainly, we all left the room humbled by what we did not know and could not do, and convinced of the urgent need to better prepare our nation against this gruesome threat.

In my role as the Secretary of Health and Human Services, the perspective I brought to the table was that of someone who served first as a local health officer (New York City Health Commissioner) and then as a federal public health official (Assistant Secretary for Planning and Evaluation,

Department of Health and Human Services). I felt first hand the devastation of terrorism as New York City's Health Commissioner when the World Trade Center was first bombed in 1993. Today, the horror of that event is dwarfed by the attacks of September 11th. Yet despite the incredible scale of these attacks, it is clear that an attack with a biological weapon has the potential to inflict even greater damage upon our country, both in terms of the extended timescale of the unfolding disaster and the numbers of people affected.

I should state that my bias is to approach the bioweapons issue in the broader context of infectious disease threats, both naturally occurring and intentionally caused. There is a continuum. A bioterrorist attack such as that depicted in "Dark Winter" would certainly represent the extreme end of that continuum, both in terms of its potentially catastrophic consequences for health and because of the disruption and panic that it would cause.

ISSUES RAISED BY DARK WINTER EXERCISE

"Dark Winter" raised many important issues and provided an opportunity to enhance awareness about the complexities of a bioterrorist attack. It served as a compelling illustration of just how much an attack caused by biological weapons would differ from conventional terrorism, military strikes or even attacks caused by other weapons of mass destruction.

It demonstrated how such an attack would unfold slowly—over days, weeks, months—as an infectious disease epidemic, with the potential to cause enormous suffering and death, as well as panic, destabilization and quite possibly civil disorder. There was little doubt that this would be a true public health emergency, for which our nation is ill-prepared to respond. Moreover, it showed how a bioterrorist attack would represent a national security crisis of enormous proportions, yet many of the traditional strategies to manage such an event would not apply. For example, identification of the perpetrator, as well as avenues for possible retaliation, might not be feasible. "Dark Winter" also underscored the interwined legal, ethical, political and logistical difficulties that attend contagious disease containment and control.

"Dark Winter" further demonstrated how poorly current organizational structures and capabilities fit with the management needs and operational requirements of an effective bioterrorism response. Responding to a bioterrorist attack will require new levels of partnership between public health and medicine, law enforcement and intelligence. However, these communities have little past experience working together and vast differences in their professional cultures, missions and needs. The "Dark Winter" scenario also underscored the pivotal role of the media, and how a productive partnership with media will be paramount in communicating important information to the public and reducing the potential for panic.

Another clear lesson that emerged from "Dark Winter" was that effective response will also require stronger working relationships across levels of government. While national leadership, guidance and support will be essential, it must be recognized that much of the initial crisis response and subsequent consequence management will unfold on the local level. " On-the-ground" local providers—public health and medical professionals, emergency response personnel, law enforcement officials and government and community leaders—will provide the foundation of the response and will deal with the problem from the moment the first cases emerge until the crisis is over.

The "Dark Winter" scenario also brought into bold relief the fact that management of such a crisis would almost certainly occur in the context of an already strained health care system and severe limitations on certain critical resources, including shortages of vaccine, hospital beds and isolation capacity.

CHALLENGES FOR THE FUTURE

As an exercise, "Dark Winter" was not designed to provide answers, but rather to raise critical questions and issues about our current preparedness to address the bioterrorist threat—Certainly it achieved that goal, but how do we begin to address these critical concerns? Building on lessons learned from "Dark Winter" from the perspective of public health and medicine, let me emphasize several key challenges as we move forward.

(1) *Focus on the real threat/strengthen public health.* In previous testimony before Congress, I have emphasized the need to convince policymakers and the public that the threat of bioterrorism is real. However, the recent cases of anthrax in Florida and New York City have made this point more forcefully than I ever could. However, even in the context of current events, I believe that a major challenge remains the need to get policymakers, legislators, and program planners to really comprehend that the threat of bioterrorism is fundamentally different than the other threats we face, such as "conventional" terrorism, or attack with a chemical or nuclear weapon.

Meaningful progress against this threat depends on understanding it in the context of an infectious and epidemic disease. It requires different investments and different partners. Until bioterrorism's true nature as an epidemic disease event is fully recognized, our nation's preparedness programs will continue to be inadequately designed: the wrong first responders will be trained and equipped; we will fail to fully build the critical infrastructure we need to detect and respond; the wrong research agendas will be developed; and we will never effectively grapple with the long-term consequence management needs that such an event would entail.

Unfortunately, if we look at our current preparedness efforts to date, necessary public health and medical care activities have been underdeveloped and underfunded. Of the roughly $10 billion budget for counterterrorism efforts in FY 2001, only a very small percentage has supported activities that truly can be considered as core elements of a coherent program to address the bioterrorist threat. In the current environment, it is clear that very substantial new monies will be available, and we must ensure that a significant component of those resources are targeted to address these critical concerns.

(2) *Build on existing strategies.*   Effective strategies must build on existing systems where possible, but build in flexibility. We do not want to develop an entire ancillary system for responding to the bioterrorist threat. Rather, we should strive to integrate our thinking and planning into the continuum of infectious disease threats and potential disasters that public health agencies are already charged to respond to. The last thing we want is to find ourselves trying out a plan for the very first time in the midst of a crisis. Instead, we want to find the systems that work in routine activities and then identify what we need to do to amplify or modify them to be appropriately responsive for these more acute and catastrophic situations.

(3) *Support the health care system's capacity for mass casualty care .* Controlling disease and caring for the sick will require a deep engagement of the public health and medical community. There are currently many pressures on health care providers and the hospital community that limit their ability to prepare in some of the critical ways necessary for effective planning in the face of the bioterrorist threat. The enormous downsizing that has occurred, the competitive pressures to cut costs, the just-in-time pharmaceutical supplies and staffing approaches, and the limited capacity for certain specialty services such as respiratory isolation beds and burn units that may become critical in a biological or chemical terrorist attack, all need to be recognized and addressed.

We must be realistic about the potential costs that would be incurred by these institutions and individuals, as well as the enormous up-front investments needed if they are truly to prepare. And in many ways, if you are a health care institution today, making those preparatory investments is a high-risk undertaking. By preparing, you are also almost setting yourself up to incur a series of costs that may not be reimbursed after the crisis is over.

We know that we must find better ways to strategically support our health care institutions, both because of the implications of a bioterrorist attack but also because of the existing demands on the system, as evidenced this past year when a routine flu season overwhelmed hospital capacity in several cities.

There is an urgent need to develop programs that target dollars for health care disaster planning and relief, including training, templates for preparedness, and efforts to develop strategies in collaboration with other critical partners for providing ancillary hospital support in the event of a crisis. This could be done either through the army field hospital model or what was done in the 1918 pandemic flu, when armories, school gymnasiums and the like were taken over to provide medical care. In doing this, we need to support local and state planning efforts to assess community assets and capabilities, and we need to look at what federal supports can be brought to bear locally in a crisis.

(4) *Invest in research.* Today's investment in research and development will be the foundation of tomorrow's preparedness. A comprehensive research agenda should be developed and pursued that extends across many important research domains. For example, our capability to detect and respond to a bioterrorist attack depends largely on the state of the relevant medical science and technology. Without rapid techniques for accurate identification of pathogens and assessment of their antibiotic sensitivities, planning for the medical and public health response will be significantly compromised. Without efficacious prophylactic and treatment agents, even the best planned responses are likely to fail. Biomedical research is needed to develop new tools for rapid diagnostics, as well as improved drugs and vaccines. At an even more basic level, we must invest in research to enhance the fundamental study of genomics, disease pathogenesis and the human immune response.

In addition to biomedical research, further research into such diverse concerns as defining appropriate personal protective gear or decontamination procedures under different circumstances will be important to our overall preparedness for a bioterrorist attack.

Research to support deeper understanding of the behavioral issues and psychosocial consequences of a catastrophic event of this kind is currently very limited but should be made a high priority. I believe that the importance of all of these areas has been underscored by our recent experience in responding to the mounting set of anthrax cases and exposures. These events have demonstrated critical gaps in our knowledge as well as deficiencies in our tools for detection, response and consequence management that we can and should swiftly address.

5) *Understanding the public response.* Sadly, the many fears, anxieties and uncertainties that have surrounded the current anthrax scare reinforce another major gap identified in current preparedness and planning efforts. This involves how to engage the public, and importantly, how to most effectively work with the public in the event of a crisis. The recent small-scale anthrax attacks, although they have sickened only a handful people, have given new insights into how complex these issues may be. Certainly, the specter of a silent, invisible killer such as an infectious agent evokes a different level of fear and panic than other disaster scenarios. Indeed, response to previous major disease epidemics—such as the outbreak of pneumonic plague in Seurat, India in 1994—suggests a level of panic and civil disruption on a far greater scale.

Anyone who has ever dealt with disaster response knows that how the needs of the public are handled from the very beginning is critical to the overall response. In the context of a biological event, this will no doubt be even more crucial. Managing the worried well may interfere with the ability to manage those truly sick or exposed. In fact, implementation of disease control measures may well depend on the constructive recruitment of · the public to behave in certain ways, such as avoiding congregate settings or following isolation orders. In the final analysis, clear communication and appropriate engagement of the public will be the key to preventing mass chaos and enabling disease control as well as critical infrastructure operations to move forward. Correspondingly, the needs and concerns of response personnel, including health care workers, must also be addressed. Again, prior experience with serious infectious disease outbreaks tells us that when this does not occur, essential frontline responders and key workers are just as likely as the public to panic, if not flee. The mass exodus of health care workers following onset of the Ebola epidemic in Kikwit, Zaire in the mid 1990s serves witness to this point.

(7) *Engage the media.* The media is key to efforts in a crisis to communicate important information to protect health and control disease, as well as to reduce the potential for panic. Over the past days, we have seen both the press and the public receive a crash course on anthrax. They have been fast learners, and for the most part, the media has done a credible and responsible job in communicating this important information. But there must be a clear plan for providing the news media with timely and accurate information. Furthermore, the credible and consistent voice of well-informed health officials is critical to this effort.

Stepping back, it is clear that the ability of the media to mobilize effectively in a crisis is greatly enhanced by a process of ongoing and continuing mutual communication and education in calmer times. We must strive for the development of a set of working relationships grounded in trust—trust that they will be provided with information in a timely and appropriate manner, and in turn, that they will use that information in a responsible, professional way.

No doubt there will always be tensions between the desire to get out a good story and an appreciation of the complexities, sensitivities and uncertainties inherent in such a crisis. But stonewalling the press or viewing them as the enemy is virtually guaranteed to make the situation worse.

(8) *Clarify legal authorities.* In planning for an effective response, an array of legal concerns need to be addressed. Issues include such basic ones as the declaration of emergency—what are the existing authorities? Are they public health, or do they rest in other domains that will be relevant? What are the criteria for such a declaration? What are the authorities that still need to be established?

Other outstanding legal questions concern the ability to isolate, quarantine, or detain groups or individuals; the ability to mandate treatment or mandate work; restrictions on travel and trade; the authority to seize community or private property such as hospitals, utilities, medicines, or vehicles; or the ability to compel production of certain goods. Also, questions concerning emergency use of pharmaceuticals or diagnostics that are not yet approved or labeled for certain uses need to be answered.

These questions involve many different levels of government, many different laws and authorities, and raise many complex and intertwined ethical, political and economic issues. In a systematic and coherent way, we must address this array of pressing issues and concerns. And not just what laws are in place or could be put in place, but then also what policies and procedures would be necessary to actually implement them.

(9) *Plan, prepare and practice.* Perhaps most fundamentally, "Dark Winter" signaled the need for more planning and preparation—across all the domains mentioned above and more. Planning can make a difference, but we cannot begin to prepare in the midst of a crisis. As "Dark Winter" unfolded, it was evident that a sense of desperation about what needed to be done arose, at least in part because the country had not produced sufficient vaccine; had not prepared top officials to cope with this new type of security crisis; had not invested adequately in the planning and exercises needed to implement a coordinated response; and had not educated the American people or developed strategies to constructively engage the media to educate people about what was happening and how to protect themselves.

Prior planning and preparation can greatly mitigate the death and suffering that would result from a serious bioweapons attack. As a nation, we need comprehensive, integrated planning for how we will address the threat of bioterrorism, focusing both on prevention and response. We need to define the relative roles and responsibilities of the different agencies involved, and identify the mechanisms by which the varying levels of government will interact and work together. We need true national leadership to address the bioweapons threat to our homeland. Planning efforts must be backed by the necessary resources and authority to translate planning into action. Moreover, we must practice what we plan. Preparations must be exercised, evaluated and understood by decision-makers if they are to prove useful in a time of crisis.

(10) *The importance of prevention.* The many intrinsic challenges involved in mounting an effective response to a bioterrorism attack—and the many casualties that will inevitably occur—should compel us to make a greater commitment to what can be accomplished to reduce the fundamental threat of their use. Clearly, measures that will deter or prevent bioterrorism will be the most cost effective means to counter such threats to public health and social order—both in human and economic terms.

Are there strategies to limit or prevent these often frightening microbes from getting into the hands of those who might misuse them, and how do we reduce the likelihood that they would be misused?

On a policy level, such prevention efforts require a global approach, including the need to find ways to meaningfully strengthen and enforce the Biological Weapons Convention, as well as international scientific cooperation to create opportunities for scientists formerly engaged in bioweapons research to redirect their often considerable talents and energy into more constructive and open research arenas. For example, a number of scientific collaborations have begun in Russia in an attempt to address this goal.

We must also strengthen and expand efforts to control access to and handling of certain dangerous pathogens, including proactive measures by the scientific community to monitor more closely the facilities and procedures involved in the use of such biological agents.

THE NUCLEAR THREAT INITIATIVE—A New Foundation

Encouraging and supporting our government to deter, prevent, and defend against biological terrorism is a central part of our mission at the Nuclear Threat Initiative (NTI)—an organization founded by Ted Turner and guided by a distinguished board co-chaired by him and former Senator Sam Nunn. We are dedicated to reducing the global threat from biological, nuclear, and chemical weapons by increasing public awareness, encouraging dialogue, catalyzing action, and promoting new thinking about these dangers in this country and abroad.

We fully recognize that only our government can provide the leadership and resources to achieve our security and health priorities. But within that context, NTI is:

Seeking ways to reduce the threat from biological weapons and their consequences.

Exploring ways to increase education, awareness and communication among public health experts, medical professionals, and scientists, as well as among policy makers and elected officials—to make sure more and more people understand the nature and scope of the biological weapons threat.

Considering ways to improve infectious disease surveillance around the globe—including rapid and effective detection, investigation, and response. This is a fundamental defense against any infectious disease threat, whether it occurs naturally or is released deliberately.

Stimulating and supporting the scientific community in its efforts to limit inappropriate access to dangerous pathogens and to establish standards that will help prevent the development and spread of biological agents as weapons.

And finally, NTI is searching for ways to help our government and the Russian government to facilitate the conversion of Russian bioweapons facilities and know-how to peaceful purposes, to secure biomaterials for legitimate use or destruction, and to improve security of dangerous pathogens worldwide.

CONCLUSION

In conclusion, let me re-emphasize that a sound strategy for addressing bioterrorism will need to be quite different from those that target other types of terrorist acts. While a large-scale event most likely remains a relatively low probability event, the high consequence implications of bioterrorism place it in a special category that requires immediate and comprehensive action. Yet as we move forward to address this disturbing new threat, it is heartening to recognize that the investments we make to strengthen the public health infrastructure, to improve medical consequence management and to support fundamental and applied research, will also benefit our efforts to protect the health and safety of the public from naturally occurring disease.

To be effective, we will need to define new priorities, forge new partnerships, make new investments to build capacity and expertise, and support planning. We may never be truly prepared for some of the most catastrophic scenarios, but there is a great deal that can and should be done.

I look forward to working with you on these important issues and would be happy to answer any questions you may have.

STATEMENT Of GARY W. McCONNELL
DIRECTOR, GEORGIA EMERGENCY MANAGEMENT AGENCY
ON BEHALF OF
NATIONAL EMERGENCY MANAGEMENT ASSOCIATION

October 17, 2001

Mr. Chairman and Members of the Subcommittee:

Thank you for the opportunity to appear before you today to offer comments on preparedness for chemical and biological attacks. My name is Gary W. McConnell and I am the Director of the Georgia Emergency Management Agency (GEMA). In Georgia, my agency, as part of the Governor's Office, is responsible for directing terrorism consequence management activities, and serves as the central coordination point for the State's response and coordination with local governments and federal agencies. I have been the director of GEMA for over ten years, serving as the governor's representative for 16 Presidential Disaster Declarations. During this same period, I had the privilege of serving as the Chief of Staff of the State Olympic Law Enforcement Command for the 1996 Olympic Games and was responsible for the security and safety operations of 29 state agencies and 5,000 law enforcement officers. Previously, I was sheriff of Chattooga County, Georgia for 22 years. My comments today are a product of these experiences.

I am here today representing the National Emergency Management Association (NEMA) whose members are the directors of emergency management for the states and territories. We are responsible to our governors for disaster mitigation, preparedness, response and recovery. This includes responsibility for terrorism consequence management and preparedness at the state level by serving as the central coordination point for all state response activities and interface with federal agencies when federal assistance is requested.

I would like to begin this afternoon by thanking Chairman Lieberman and Ranking Member Thompson and the members of the Committee for recognizing the importance of preparing for acts of terrorism.

Since the September 11, 2001 attacks and the recent exposures to Anthrax, our nation has been reevaluating our preparedness for acts of terrorism. Particularly at the state level, we have been assessing the preparedness levels our federal, state, and local governments and our private sector partners must attain to deal with incidents of terrorism, including chemical and biological attacks.

States have been in the forefront of preparing for and responding to all types of disasters, both natural and man-made. We take an all-hazards approach to disaster preparedness and have integrated into our domestic preparedness efforts those proven systems we already use for dealing with natural and technological disasters. We also recognize clearly the value of prevention and mitigation in minimizing the consequences of disaster and we incorporate those considerations in all our efforts. Our nation needs to build on the existing "all hazards" approach since we cannot afford to "recreate the wheel" when addressing biological and chemical terrorism threats.

NEMA's members developed a list of recommended enhancements to be incorporated into a nation-wide strategy for attaining better preparedness for catastrophic events. The full text of these recommendations is included in the attached 'NEMA White Paper' for your reference. I would like to highlight the highest priority items in my testimony today.

The lessons learned from the September attacks are not brand new ideas. Many are concepts we have been working on for years and just have not been able to fully implement. The immediate lessons learned also include the suggestions of the state emergency management directors from New York, Pennsylvania, and Virginia.

Now is the time for federal, state, and local governments to take action. It is not the time to prepare reports or criticize past actions. We should all follow New York City Mayor Rudolph Guiliani's comments to the United Nations. He said, "Now is the time . . . to unite our strength . . . this is not a time for further study or vague directives."

MEDICAL SURGE (MASS CASUALTY) CAPABILITY

The most immediate need that we found necessary to effectively address chemical and biological events, as well as weapons of mass destruction (WMD) is our nation's medical surge capacity. We need to guarantee that the surge capability is strengthened. The emergency management, medical and public health professions must work with lawmakers on all levels to ensure that each region has a certain minimum surge capacity to deal with mass casualty events.

Hospitals should agree to provide defined and standardized levels of resources, capabilities and assistance to handle mass casualties, especially those contaminated by chemical and biological agents. Funding for equipment and supplies to accomplish this mission should be provided to develop this additional capability, in exchange for agreeing to participate as a local receiving hospital and as part of the U.S. Public Health Service's National Disaster Medical System (NDMS).

The incremental costs to the health care system of developing and maintaining mass casualty emergency response capacity are significant. Funding to cover those costs not available from any other sources must be provided by the federal government.

This means that for-profit hospitals and clinics must have an incentive to participate since business plans and the managed care approach make it difficult to justify paying for capabilities like decontamination units if they would be used only sporadically. Also, poison control centers have a role in assisting in response and their funding streams need to be addressed since budget crunches have forced many regional operations to consolidate or down-grade their activities.

States also need assistance to fully implement the National Pharmaceutical Stockpile Plan. While the final TOPOFF Exercise report is not yet available, one of the lessons we learned was that the federal government could only get the pharmaceutical push package to the Mobilization Centers. There were insufficient plans in place to then get the pharmaceutical "push pack" broken down into useable packages and distributed from the airport to the population in immediate need. This is being addressed, but demands emphasis and funding and must be addressed as soon as possible.

We must ensure that the medical treatment reaches the patients in the hardest hit areas quickly. I would further suggest that we look to keeping multiple stockpiles in regionally centralized locations near transportation assets needed to rapidly move those push packages. There should also be back-up stockpiles in several locations around the country to bolster the national surge capacity and to enable a flexible response to multiple events.

Providing this regionally based medical surge capacity in the health care community will take some time. In the interim, the best truly rapid response surge capacity we do have is a combination of the Veteran's Administration (VA) health care system, the Disaster Medical Assistance Teams and the military Reserve Component medical units. We particularly need to ensure that those military Reserve assets are trained, equipped and empowered to provide rapid medical capacity under "imminent and serious" conditions. They are, in many cases, the closest deployable assets.

We need to change our focus and begin thinking of health professionals as first responders. State and Local Disaster Medical Assistance Teams should be developed across the country with standardized equipment, personnel and training. These teams would serve as the first line of response to support impacted communities within impacted states, and could be required to respond outside the state as a mutual aid resource upon request. Self contained capability to respond outside the team's jurisdiction would be best provided by military Reserve Component assets available in each state.

Additionally, the less than 60 U.S. Public Heath Service NDMS Disaster Medical Assistance Teams (DMAT) should be uniformly enhanced for Weapons of Mass Destruction (WMD) response, including focus on personnel protection and training for WMD. Currently, only four of the teams have been upgraded and equipped to serve as National Medical Response Teams (NMRTS).

INTELLIGENCE SHARING

The key to an effective terrorism response lies in intelligence sharing. The right people need to know information key to responding and preparing at all times. This means reciprocity for security clearances, no matter what department or level of government the personnel are representing. In addition, an expedited process is needed for state and local officials to obtain clearances.

INTERSTATE MUTUAL AID AND REGIONAL PLANNING

An existing system we need to take advantage of for all domestic preparedness planning is the Emergency Management Assistance Compact (EMAC). EMAC is an interstate mutual aid agreement that allows states to assist one another in responding to all kinds of natural and man-made disasters. EMAC offers a quick and easy way for states to send personnel and equipment to help disaster relief efforts in other states. There are times when state and local resources are overwhelmed and federal assistance is inadequate, inappropriate, too far away or unavailable. Out-of-state aid through EMAC helps fill such shortfalls. There are 42 states and two territories that are members of EMAC and other states and territories are considering joining. Currently, emergency managers from several states are providing technical assistance to New York through EMAC. EMAC support is in place at the state emergency operations center and in New York City and has been used in conjunction with the federal emergency support team. A system like this enables experts to be used across jurisdictions and regions based on the nature of a particular event.

State and local governments have established regional approaches to building capacity to deal with catastrophic events. The regional approach gives us a flexible response capability, both regionally and nationally, which can adapt to catastrophic events as they occur and most effectively use the limited resources we share. Regional planning is invaluable since we can develop common, flexible preparedness strategies which capitalize on sharing limited resources within regions. Because necessary capabilities cannot be afforded by all jurisdictions, we can use mutual aid to respond to multiple simultaneous events in different parts of the state, the region or the nation.

STATE COORDINATION

Coordination with the states is a critical issue that I would like to reiterate that requires attention. Too often, each of the federal agencies deals directly with their state counterpart thereby creating a stovepipe effect for funding that limits states' abilities to leverage federal funding to its maximum benefit and to ensure at least a minimum statewide prepared-ness and response capability. We look forward to working with Governor Ridge and his new Office of Homeland Security. In order for the office to be successful, it is essential that the Office of Homeland Security integrates input from state emergency management agencies. We hope that state emergency managers and first responders from the state and local level will be invited to participate in developing the national preparedness strategy.

The majority of the nation's governors designated their state emergency management agencies as the single point of contact to coordinate the De-partment of Justice terrorism grants program created in 1999 for equip-ment and planning. At the state level, the program requires a single point of contact for the nation's governors and the mayor of the District of Co-lumbia to administer the grant. Forty-two governors and the District of Co-lumbia designated the state emergency management agency. These same state emergency management agencies, in many cases, also administer FEMA terrorism grant funding. We are strongly encouraging that all federal programs and funding should be coordinated through the governor's desig-nated single point of contact for the state terrorism preparedness program.

Currently, The Department of Justice needs assessment process requires the development of statewide strategic plans to assure the federal govern-ment that state planning and assessment of state capacity is an ongoing, coordinated and inclusive process in the states. Many states are currently in the process of conducting these needs assessments. NEMA recom-mends that any new federal planning requirements not be a duplication of the current DOJ requirement, but rather build off plans and programs al-ready in place in the states. We would also recommend that the DOJ should immediately release the FY00 and FY01 equipment funds in order to begin implementation of preparedness plans and to enhance our capa-bilities, and then require a basic statewide strategy in order to receive the FY02 funds.

NEMA believes it would be extremely helpful to allow states to administer the equipment programs and to provide greater flexibility with the ap-proved equipment list. We specifically would like the ability to use the funds for the purchase of necessary equipment for hospitals and the health care industry, regardless of private sector ownership of these critical "first receiver" response system components. Congress could help by increas-ing the funding for these grants to provide for detection, personnel protec-tion and decontamination equipment for the nation's emergency response agencies. We need to assure that federal training and maintenance money must be included in any national terrorism response plan. This funding must include money for federal, state, and local governments to exercise together. Finally, with all of the new proposals and funding mechanisms to address domestic preparedness needs, now more than ever is the time to continue using states as the single point of contact and to allow the funding to be flexible to maintain a current focus.

CONCLUSION

In summary, NEMA supports efforts to improve federal coordination on domestic preparedness, especially with chemical and biological preparedness. We also believe that medical surge capacity needs to be addressed immediately. The greater safety of the nation is at stake and all responders and policymakers at the federal, state, and local level need to work together to ensure that we are prepared for an incident of domestic terrorism. We pledge our cooperation to continue to work with you and this committee to ensure that our nation is at the highest level of preparedness to deal with a terrorist event. Thank you again for inviting NEMA to present testimony on this important issue. I would like to thank the Committee for their dedication on this issue. We look forward to working with you, the Administration, and local responders to make this country a safer place for all.

PREPARED STATEMENT OF
AMY E. SMITHSON, PH.D.
DIRECTOR, CHEMICAL AND BIOLOGICAL WEAPONS
NONPROLIFERATION PROJECT
HENRY L. STIMSON CENTER

With the interplay of politics, institutional interests, and differences of opinion, complex public policy decisions can be difficult enough to make in times of peace and prosperity. In times of turmoil and war, such decisions can be even more challenging. In recent weeks, US citizens have been on edge about the prospects of chemical and biological terrorist attacks. The occurrence of isolated anthrax incidents in Florida, New York City, and now the nation's capital has made it difficult for the country to regain a sense of normalcy in the aftermath of the September 11th tragedies. Americans are looking to their leaders to make sage decisions that will enhance the ability of local, state, and federal assets to promptly and effectively respond to a chemical calamity and to detect a disease outbreak in time to take life-saving intervention. Mr. Chairman, I know that this responsibility weighs heavily on the minds of this committee's members, as well as the broader Senate membership, so I appreciate the invitation to testify on matters that in light of recent events carry a sense of greater urgency and importance.

No matter where one comes out in the debate about whether terrorists can pull off a biological attack that causes massive casualties, the debate itself is moot. One need only consult public health journals to understand that it is only a matter of time before a strain of influenza as virulent as the one that swept this country in 1918 naturally resurfaces. Further confirmation of a looming public health crisis can be secured through reports from the World Health Organization and the Institutes of Medicine, which describe how a growing list of common diseases (e.g., pneumonia, tuberculosis) are becoming resistant to antibiotics. These public health watchdogs are also justifiably worried about the array of new diseases emerging as mankind ventures into previously uninhabited areas. Even with everything in the modern medical arsenal, public health authorities will find it difficult to handle with disease outbreaks in the future. Global travel will facilitate the spread of communicable diseases through huge population concentrations and will in turn hinder use of the traditional means of containing a contagious disease outbreak, namely quarantine.

As for the prospects of a large-scale chemical disaster, one needs to keep in mind what America's first responders and health care workers have to deal with on a routine basis. According to the US Chemical Health and Safety Investigation Board, between 1987 and 1996, a hazardous chemical incident of some severity took place in 95 percent of US counties. An average of 60,500 chemical incidents occurred per year at fixed facilities and in transit, injuring or killing roughly 2,550 annually. This country is peppered with roughly 850,000 facilities that work with hazardous or extremely hazardous chemical substances. While the chemical industry takes site security seriously and emergency responders in many US cities began long ago take extra security precautions with these sites, my main chemical terrorism concern relates to the possible sabotage of these industrial facilities.

Thus, there is a need for this nation's front line responders—from firefighters, police, and paramedics to doctors, nurses, laboratory workers, and public health officials—to be prepared to cope with chemical and biological disasters. This need will remain constant for the indefinite future, regardless of whether or not terrorists turn to chemical and biological weapons to inflict mass casualties.

A Roadmap to Better Coordinated, More Cost-Effective Programs

The appointment of Governor Tom Ridge as Director of the new Office of Homeland Security would seem to be a constructive step that could put improved coordination and streamlining of the federal response bureaucracy on a fast track. That may not be the case, however, if he lacks sufficiently strong budgetary authority. An initial review of section 3(k) of the Executive Order establishing the Office of Homeland Security and the Homeland Security Council does not appear to vest such power in this new office. To aid Governor Ridge in his efforts, Congress should grant him czar-like budgetary authority. Alone, Governor Ridge will have difficulty taming the federal bureaucracy.

The other essential element of streamlining and coordinating government programs lies here, in Congress. Anyone that attempts to tally the number of congressional committees with terrorism prevention and preparedness oversight very quickly runs out of fingers and toes. So long as that is the case, individual federal agencies may continue to exploit the situation to the advantage of their own institutional interests and the detriment of co-ordinated, cost-effective programming. A consolidation of congressional oversight committees is sorely needed.

Also in order is a reassessment of the true value of politically popular placebo programs like the National Guard's Civil Support Teams. I urge you to consider the evaluation of these teams offered by the public safety and health officials, including members of the National Guard, that I interviewed in 33 cities in 25 states. Their views are presented fully in *Ataxia: The Chemical and Biological Terrorism Threat and the US Response*, a report co-authored with Leslie-Anne Levy and released last October and available at: www.stimson.org/cwc.

Briefly, the message from the front line about these National Guard teams is unified and clear: They have minuscule, if not negative, utility. In the mid-May 2000 TOPOFF exercise, the Civil Support Team in Denver insisted that it had identified the mystery biological agent with SMART tickets, which have such high false positive and false negative rates that numerous cities have refused to buy them. The team in Portsmouth lacked the technical expertise to understand the minimal hazard posed by mustard on a chilly, 49-degree day. To veterans of epidemiological investigations and hazardous material operations, the absurdity of these two anecdotes is readily apparent. The deputy director of one city's Office of Emergency Management said, "The good thing about those teams is that it takes them as long as it does to get here."

To further illustrate the problem, called to duty after the planes struck the World Trade Towers, the New York Civil Support Team arrived at the scene roughly 12 hours later and proceeded to conduct environmental monitoring that was redundant of efforts undertaken hours earlier by New York City agencies as well as the US Environmental Protection Agency. The dynamics of a chemical disaster response are such that these teams cannot arrive in time to make a life-saving difference. As for their applicability to a biological disaster, their four-person medical component is a drop in the bucket of what would be needed in a major disease outbreak.

To those accustomed to overseeing billion dollar budgets, this National Guard program might not seem so ill-advised. Please consider how this program's budget could be put to uses that would make a real preparedness difference on the front lines, for example, to begin fixing the glaring lack of decontamination capacity in US hospitals that results in recurrent hospital closures even after small hazmat incidents. In most of the cities that I surveyed for *Ataxia*, the central game plan for hospitals in the event of a major chemical catastrophe was to "lockdown," meaning to shut their doors to incoming patients. For the cost of standing up one National Guard Civil Support Team, 2,333 hospitals or fire stations could be outfitted with decontamination capabilities. With the total 1999 budget for this program, 49,800 local rescue and health facilities could have been armed for decontamination. Civil Support Team funds, in other words, could be used to make a genuine preparedness difference were they applied to overcoming the decontamination bottleneck at US hospitals. Proposals are now circulating for each state to have its own Civil Support Team. Common sense calls for the existing teams to be disbanded, their equipment to be disbursed within the respective states to front-line rescue units and laboratories, where any leftover training monies would also be placed.

The National Guard's Civil Support Teams aside, both Congress and Governor Ridge have their work cut out for them. A series of expert studies and panels, as well as Congress' own General Accounting Office, have labeled the federal preparedness programs a fractured mess and urged a national strategy to guide programs better. For the past several years, over 40 federal agencies have been competing for the money and missions associated with combating terrorism. The section of chapter 7 in *Ataxia* entitled "Preparedness Versus Pork" discusses in more detail how lack of coordination and redundant programs handicap the federal effort. This competition has been confusing for local and state officials, who have difficulty figuring which agency is in charge, not to mention how to decipher the varying sets of priorities and guidelines that accompany the different federal grant programs.

In addition, this sparring among federal agencies has contributed to a drift in the Domestic Preparedness Program away from the initial objectives of its trio of Senate designers, Senators Richard Lugar (R-Indiana), Sam Nunn (D-Georgia, ret.), and Pete Domenici (R-New Mexico). The initial objective was to enhance the readiness of local public safety and public health officials to grapple with an unconventional terrorism attack. Instead, according to Office of Management and Budget figures, this year federal government is spending $8.7 billion to combat terrorism but only $311 million of that amount is making it to the local level in the form of training, planning, and equipment grants for unconventional attacks. More specifically in the area of biodisaster readiness, in 2000, an estimated $206 million from the weapons of mass destruction budget line items were put toward hospital preparations, the public health infrastructure, and biomedical research *combined*. Those interested in a detailed breakdown of that spending can consult table 7.2 in *Ataxia*.

If you take no other message away from my testimony today, let it be an understanding that the key to domestic preparedness lies not in bigger federal bureaucracy, but in getting taxpayers' dollars channeled to readiness at the local level, where training and enhanced response capacities will better arm public safety and medical personnel to contend with disease outbreaks and chemical incidents, whether natural, accidental, or intentional. Federal spending priorities sorely need to be redressed, and unless reforms are made and mindsets change on both ends of Pennsylvania Avenue, a few years from now a great deal of money will have been spent with marginal impact on front-line preparedness.

The Route to Enhanced Readiness Nationwide

While the signs of a chemical disaster would materialize very quickly, perhaps the first challenge facing the health care community in a biological disaster would be figuring out that something is amiss. Many diseases present with flu-like symptoms, and the physicians and nurses who could readily recognize the finer distinctions between influenza and more exotic diseases are few in number indeed. As medical science eradicated a series of diseases, medical and nursing schools concentrated training on the ailments that health care givers are more likely to see.

Exotic disease recognition problems are not limited to the medical community. In the nation's laboratories, microbiologists and other technicians who analyze the samples (e.g., blood, throat cultures) that physicians order to help them figure out what ails their patients are much more likely to have encountered exotic diseases in textbook photographs rather than under their microscopes. Thanks to the laboratory enhancement program initiated by the Centers for Disease Control and Prevention (CDC), the ability to identify out-of-the-ordinary diseases more rapidly is on the rise in several dozen laboratories across the country. However, such is not the case in the 158,000 laboratories that serve hospitals, private physicians, and health maintenance organizations and form the backbone of disease detection in this nation. Enhanced training certainly contributed to the early diagnosis of the first anthrax case in Florida. A CDC official has noted that the Florida Department of Health laboratory in Jacksonville where the blood sample taken from Bob Stevens was identified as anthrax had recently completed a special course in the identification of biowarfare diseases.

Still, an illustration of the need for better education of health care professionals about bioterrorism matters can be found in the far too many recent reports of physicians prescribing antibiotics for patients worried about a possible bioterrorist attack. Of all people, physicians should understand how such prescriptions could backfire, not just in adverse reactions to the antibiotics if citizens begin self-medicating their children and themselves when they come down with the sniffles, but in the lessened ability of those very drugs to help their patients in a time of true medical need. Moreover, over-prescription of antibiotics contributes to the rise in the number of antibiotic-resistant diseases.

To date, Domestic Preparedness Program training, now administered by the Justice Department, has managed to draw some health care personnel, mostly emergency department physicians and nurses, into the classroom in the cities where training is being provided. To enhance the disease detection and treatment skills of the medical community nationwide over the long term, however, a different strategy is required. If a long-term difference is to be made, then more comprehensive instruction in medical, nursing, microbiology, and other pertinent schools is required. Knowledge of exotic diseases should be necessary to obtain diplomas, and the topic should become a mainstay of the refresher courses offered to maintain professional credentials. Those involved in setting the curricula for these schools should waste no time in adjusting their course offerings, requirements, and other professional activities accordingly. In the near term, compressed training should be made available to all practicing US physicians via presentations during grand rounds or via satellite hookup. Both forms of training, by the way, already exist, so it is just a matter of making it more widely available. Moreover, in conjunction with the CDC and the Association of Public Health Laboratories, the American Society of Microbiology is developing protocols to assist clinical microbiology laboratories in identifying bioterrorist agents. Although the protocols have yet to be published, volume number 33 in the *Cumulative Techniques and Procedures in Clinical Microbiology* series addresses bioterrorism issues and is available from the American Society of Microbiology.

Similarly, for chemical and biological disaster readiness, preparedness standards need to be established for the various response disciplines and training needs to be institutionalized in fire and police academies, as well as in paramedic schools across the country. Roughly six years into the domestic preparedness effort, the time has passed for Washington to turn training over to the appropriate professional and local entities that will take preparedness forward more systematically and cost effectively. The hand-off should be concentrated in these organizations (e.g., the National Fire Protection Association, the Accreditation Council for Graduate Medical Education) and curtailed elsewhere, so that various branches of the federal government, not to mention enterprising contractors and universities, stop churning out redundant training programs at taxpayers' expense. Already, over 90 such training courses exist. Without such reform, ineffective spending will continue at both the federal and local levels and training lacking in standards will be implemented unevenly, in pockets. Specification of standards and institutionalization of training clearly make more sense than that.

Establishing an Early Warning Capability for Disease Outbreak Detection

With modern data collection and analysis capabilities, one need not rely solely on the ability of laboratories and medical personnel to pick up the telltale early signs of a disease outbreak. In a few areas of the United States, public health and emergency management officials are teaming to test ways to get a head start on detection. The concept focuses on early signs of syndromes (e.g., flu-like illness, fever and skin rash) that might indicate the presence of diseases of concern. They are compiling historical databases to supply a baseline of normal health patterns at various times of the year, against which contemporary developments can be measured. Since people feeling ill tend to take over-the-counter medications, consult their physicians, or request emergency medical care, some areas are beginning to track the status of health in their communities via select Emergency Medical Services call types (e.g., respiratory distress, adult asthma); sales of certain medications (e.g., over-the-counter flu remedies); reports from physicians, sentinel hospitals, and coroners about select disease symptoms or unexplained deaths; or some combination of these markers. This tracking allows abnormal activity levels can be detected. For instance, should EMS calls rise above the expected rate in the fall season, public health officials and emergency managers would get the earliest possible indication that something was amiss, which would enable them to cue medical personnel and laboratories to search more diligently for what might be causing a possible disease outbreak. This concept of syndrome surveillance will be key to allowing public health officials to get the jump on prophylaxis and other control measures. For more on this approach, see the groundbreaking work of New York City's Department of Public Health and Office of Emergency Management, which is summarized in box 6.7 of *Ataxia*.

What is now called for is a more systematic approach to institutionalizing syndrome surveillance across the nation. A model should be refined and then made available nationally, along with funds to allow metropolitan areas to conduct the necessary historical analysis and establish the computer database, communications, and other components needed to put syndrome surveillance in place. Again, the data and the computing capabilities are available; it is just a matter of harnessing them for the purposes of early disease outbreak recognition. In their own ways, the Kennedy-Frist and the Edwards-Hagel bills address these matters. Coordination of congressional action is necessary so that the most readiness can be gained for taxpayers' dollars.

The Need for Regional Hospital Planning

The next challenge facing a metropolitan area in the midst of a chemical disaster or a major disease outbreak would be contending with the flood of humanity that would seek health care services. If one examines what transpired in Tokyo after Aum Shinrikyo's 20 March 1995 morning release of sarin in the subway, demand for patient care would peaked rapidly and then began subsiding by mid-afternoon on the day of the attack. The best medical care in the world can be found in this country, but in general US hospitals are at present poorly prepared to handle either a chemical disaster or an epidemic. With regard to a pandemic, those familiar with what is happening on the front lines of health care in America know that US hospitals already have difficulty handling the patient loads that accompany a regular influenza season. Ambulances wait for hours in emergency department bays, unable to unload patients until bed space is available. The press of genuinely ill and worried citizens clamoring for medical attention in the midst of a plague or smallpox epidemic would so far outstrip a normal flu season that local health care systems could collapse.

To prevent hospitals from being quickly overwhelmed, it will be critical for regional health care facilities to have a pre-agreed plan that divides responsibilities and locks in arrangements to bring emergency supplies in the interim until federal assistance can arrive. In the era of managed care, hospitals compete with each other for business and rely on just-in-time supply of inventory, keeping an average of two or three days supplies on hand. Since community-wide hospital planning has fallen by the wayside, precious time could be wasted if hospitals lack prior agreement as to which facilities would convert to care of infectious disease cases—particularly important if a communicable disease is involved—and which ones would attend to the other medical emergencies that would persist throughout an epidemic. Business competitors, in other words, must convert within hours to work as a team.

Regionally, hospitals must plan to handle an overflow of patients and provide prophylaxis to thousands upon thousands of people. Whether the approach involves auxiliary facilities near major hospitals, the conversion of civic or sporting arenas to impromptu hospitals, or the use of fire stations or other neighborhood facilities to conduct patient screening and prophylaxis, such a plan needs to be put in place. Other factors that regional hospital planning must address are how to tap into local reserves of medical personnel (e.g., nursing students, retired physicians), how to break down and distribute securely the national pharmaceutical stockpile, and how to enable timely delivery of emergency supplies of everything from intravenous fluids to sheets, tongue depressors, and food. Obviously, regional hospital plans that address how to overcome problems of decontamination, training, security, critical medical supplies (e.g., respirators, antidotes), and burden-sharing would also be of great utility should a chemical disaster bring a surge of patients to health care facilities.

The Role of the Federal Government

Washington's willingness to fund preparedness efforts at the local level across the country will be critical to chemical or biological disaster readiness. With a few exceptions, the federal government's role in responding to a chemical or biological terrorism attack would fall under the general heading of mid- to long-term disaster recovery assistance. FEMA's capabilities have risen steadily over the last decade and little, if anything, would need to be added to its existing capabilities and regular Stafford Act assistance activities. Local officials noted that they would probably call upon federal assets to help decontaminate a site after a chemical disaster, but that does not mean that additional federal capacity needs to be built. Prior to the 1995 Aum Shinrikyo attack, as chapter 4 of *Ataxia* describes, numerous Pentagon and Environmental Protection Agency teams that could be brought in to assist a stricken community already existed. While little, if any, additional federal capacity needs to be constructed to aid local and state authorities in a chemical disaster, appreciable work remains the area of biological disaster readiness at the federal level. Aside from continuing to infuse funds into the improvement of the public health system at the local and state levels, the federal government needs to sort out once and for all who is in charge and attend to its important roles in the development and production of essential medicines and in the provision of medical manpower during an emergency.

Calling the Shots in a Public Health Crisis

How many FBI special agents or Federal Emergency Management Agency (FEMA) officials know off the top of their heads the appropriate adult dosages of ciprofloxacin for prophylaxis in the event of a terrorist release of anthrax? Darned few, if any. No, the FBI excels at catching criminals and FEMA at providing mid- and long-term recovery support to communities stricken with all manner of disasters. An outbreak of disease is first and foremost a public health problem, so let's not be confused about who should be calling the shots in an epidemic—public health officials. Yet, this simple fact is certainly not reflected in what is taking place with regard to bioterrorism preparedness, inside or outside the beltway.

Inside of Washington's beltway, concepts of crisis and consequence management not only linger, they predominate. With an apparent lack of budgetary authority and proposals circulating anew to have the Justice Department retain a leadership and coordination role despite the Bush administration's earlier appointment of FEMA in this capacity, it is fair to say that Governor Ridge's office will have difficulty presiding over the tug of war about which federal agency should lead the federal component of unconventional terrorism response. In America's cities, counties, and states there is also a fair amount of jostling as to who exactly would have the authority to make certain decisions during an epidemic. Only a handful of states, unfortunately, have untangled the cross-cutting jurisdictions left over from more than a century of contradictory laws passed as authorities scrambled to deal with the different diseases that were sweeping the country. Prompt, decisive action could make a lifesaving difference in the midst of an outbreak, but the experience of various terrorism exercises and drills gives ample reason to believe that precious time would be squandered as local, state, and federal officials squabbled over who has the authority to do what.

These circumstances beg for a clear vision and a firm hand to untangle this mess and put the people who know the most about disease control and eradication—public health officials—unquestionably in charge of any biological disaster, whether natural or manmade. FEMA, the FBI, the Pentagon, and other federal and local agencies should be playing support roles, not reshaping and second-guessing the directions of public health professionals as they manage the crisis *and* consequences of a major eruption of disease.

Research, Development, and Production of Medications

Long before the current concerns about bioterrorism, I was at a loss to explain how the federal government could have known about the extent of the Soviet Union's biowarfare program—including the production of tons of agents such as smallpox and antibiotic resistant plague and anthrax—as early as 1992 and not kicked this nation's vaccine research, development, and production programs into a higher gear until 1997.

The extent of the problem is illustrated by the fact that only one company is under contract to produce the anthrax vaccine, no company currently produces the plague vaccine, and it was not until recently that steps were taken to meaningfully jumpstart smallpox vaccine production. Such matters should have been promptly addressed if only to enable protection of US combat troops, not to mention producing enough vaccine to cover the responders on the domestic front lines, namely the medical personnel, firefighters, police, paramedics, public health officials, and emergency managers who would be called upon to aid US citizens in the event of a biological disaster.

As for the effort that was mounted, many nongovernmental experts have been taken aback at the structuring and relatively meager funding of the Joint Vaccine Acquisition Program. With a $322 million budget over ten years, this program aims to bring seven candidate biowarfare vaccines through the clinical trials process. Giving credit where it is due, one must acknowledge that this program—as well as Defense Advanced Research Projects Agency-sponsored research into innovative medical treatments—is making headway. However, the federal government must find ways to shrink the nine to 15 year timeline that it takes to bring a new drug through clinical trials to the marketplace. Food and Drug Administration officials are already wrestling with how to adjust the clinical trials process for testing of new vaccines and additional bumps are to be expected on the road ahead.

Next, the National Institutes of Health and the pharmaceutical industry, not the Defense Department, are this country's experts at clinical testing and production of medications. My point is not that the Defense Department should not have a role—perhaps even a lead role since the candidate vaccines originated with the US Army Medical Research Institute for Infectious Diseases—but these other important players need to be at the table if an accelerated program is to be achieved. As I noted, Governor Ridge will have his hands full, no matter which direction he turns. Moreover, close congressional oversight of this particular aspect of the nation's biological disaster readiness is warranted.

On the chemical side of the house, by the way, the picture is similarly discouraging. The Pentagon now turns to one company for supply of the nerve agent antidote kits, known as Mark 1 kits, that the Health and Human Services Office of Emergency Preparedness has encouraged cities participating in the Metropolitan Medical Response System program to purchase. Many a city is still waiting to receive the Mark 1 kits ordered long ago, and when they do, these kits will have a considerably shorter shelf life than the kits made available to the military.

Emergency Medical Manpower Needs During a Major Disease Outbreak

Secretary of Health and Human Services Tommy Thompson stated on September 30th in an interview with "60 Minutes" that his department has "7,000 medical personnel that are ready to go" in the event of a bioterrorist attack. While that statement may be true in theory, in practice it may not hold. Somewhat lost in the late 1990s rush to soup up federal teams for hot zone rescues was the one major non-FEMA federal support capability that would clearly be needed after an infectious disease outbreak and perhaps after a chemical incident as well—medical assistance. The National Disaster Medical System was one of several improvements made to federal disaster recovery capabilities over the last decade, a time during which the federal government demonstrated that it could bring appreciable humanitarian and logistical assets to bear after natural catastrophes and conventional terrorist bombings. While these events flexed the muscles of the FEMA-led recovery system, including the deployment of Disaster Medical Assistance Teams, they did not even approach the type of monumental challenge that a full-fledged infectious disease outbreak would present. Prior to Secretary Thompson's recent statement, officials from the Health and Human Services Department and the Pentagon have also stated that they could mobilize significant medical assets quickly.

Yet considerable skepticism exists that these two departments combined could have met the medical aid requests made from Denver after the release of plague was simulated during the mid-May 2000 TOPOFF drill, much less a call for even more help. During that hypothetical event, health care officials quickly found their medical facilities sinking under the patient load and concluded that 2,000 more medical personnel were needed on the ground within a day to prevent the flight of citizens that would have further spread the disease. Getting that number of physicians and nurses to a city and into hospitals and field treatment posts would be a tremendous logistical achievement. No one that interviewed for *Ataxia*, including members of the Disaster Medical Assistance Teams and other medical and public health professionals, felt that the federal government could deliver 2,000 civilian medical professionals within the required timeframe. For its part, the Pentagon has yet to articulate clearly or commit to civilians at the federal or local level just how much medical manpower it could deliver and in what timeframe.

Quite frankly, the time has come for the Pentagon to stop being coy about what medical assets it could bring bear in a domestic emergency. Articulation of this capability, even if it needs to be done in classified forums, is necessary for sound planning on the civilian side.

Furthermore, there have been no large-scale dress rehearsals to confirm whether civilian or military medical assets could muster that many medical professionals that quickly, or even over a few days. Even so, the 2,000 figure from the Denver segment of TOPOFF seems almost quaint when compared to one US city's rough estimate that 45,000 health care providers—many of whom would have to be imported—would be required to screen and treat its denizens.

The only way to find out whether the federal government is truly up to the most important role it may have to perform after a bioterrorist attack or a natural disease outbreak is to hold a large-scale medical mobilization exercise. Despite the expense, Congress should mandate a realistic test of how much civilian and military medical assistance can be delivered, how fast. Unlike TOPOFF, where federal assets were pre-picked and pre-staged, the terms of the exercise should specify that teams deploy as notified. While the general nature and identity of the exercise location(s) would certainly be known beforehand and the timeframe of the drill agreed within a window of several months, local officials should trigger the onset of the exercise. In short, dispense with the tabletop games that allow everyone the comfort of claims of what they could do and see what a real exercise brings. A genuine and probably sobering measure of federal capabilities could be taken, and the lessons of the exercise could inform the structure of federal and local plans and programs.

Conclusions

In the 33-city survey done for *Ataxia*, cities felt far better prepared to contend with a chemical disaster than they did a biological one. The higher state of chemical disaster preparedness is not surprising given that over 650 hazmat teams, which would form the core of an on-scene response, already existed nationwide prior to the onset of federal domestic preparedness programs. Local officials consistently identified the need for enhancement of hospital readiness, the institutionalization of training, the replenishment of personal protection gear, the maintenance of key equipment items, and the regular conduct of major field drills as critical to improving overall chemical disaster preparedness.

When it comes to biological disaster readiness, one need not resort to hyperbole when it comes to how difficult it would be for major US cities to handle a pandemic; the truth is sobering enough. Even though the basic components of the ability to handle a disease outbreak—hospitals, public health capabilities at the federal, state, and local levels, and a wealth of medical professionals—are already in place, there is ample room for improvement. The pragmatic steps that the federal government should take are clear.

Mr. Chairman, Members of the Committee, Washington can take the smart route to enhance chemical and biological disaster preparedness nationwide or it can continue to go about this in an expensive and inefficient way. The keys to national chemical and biological disaster readiness lie not in bigger budgets and more federal bureaucracy but in common-sense policies and programs such as the following:

The sufficiency of existing federal programs, response teams, and bureaucracies needs to be assessed and redundant and spurious ones need to be eliminated. In the interim until an assessment of the sufficiency of existing assets is made, a government-wide moratorium on any new rescue teams and bureaucracies should be declared, with the exception of the enhanced intelligence, law enforcement, and airport security measures that are being contemplated.

The bulk of federal funds need to be devoted to enhancing readiness at the local level, where an increase in skills, training, and equipment would make a genuine life-saving difference. Even if terrorists never strike again in this country, such investments would be well worthwhile because they would improve the ability of hometown rescuers to respond to everyday emergencies.

Defense Department programs related to the development and production of new vaccines, antibiotics, and chemical antidotes need to be put on a faster track, incorporating as appropriate industrial expertise in such matters.

The federal government should continue to revive the nation's public health system, an endeavor that involves sending funds to the local and state levels, not keeping them inside the beltway. In addition, the federal government should fund regional hospital planning grants and additional tests of disease syndrome surveillance system, followed by plans and funds to establish such capabilities nationwide.

Appropriate steps should be taken to see that firefighters, police, paramedics, physicians, nurses, laboratory workers, and public officials benefit from training that is institutionalized in the nation's training academies, universities, and schools.

Last, but certainly not least, Washington needs to develop a plan to sustain preparedness over the long term. Drills at the local and federal levels are necessary because plans that sit on the shelf for extended periods of time are often plans that do not work well when emergencies occur.

On behalf of the local public health and safety officials who have shared their experience and common sense views with me, I urge Congress to waste no time in passing legislation that brings the burgeoning federal terrorism preparedness programs and bureaucracies into line and points them in a more constructive, cost-effective direction.

STATEMENT OF HENRY L. HINTON, JR.
MANAGING DIRECTOR, DEFENSE CAPABILITIES AND MANAGEMENT

COMBATING TERRORISM:
CONSIDERATIONS FOR INVESTING RESOURCES IN
CHEMICAL AND BIOLOGICAL PREPAREDNESS

Mr. Chairman and Members of the Committee

I appreciate the opportunity to be here today to discuss GAO's work on efforts to prepare for and respond to chemical and biological terrorist attacks. With the coordinated terrorist attacks against the World Trade Center and the Pentagon on September 11, 2001, the threat of terrorism rose to the top of the country's national security and law enforcement agendas. With the current investigations into anthrax incidents, the threat remains at the top of those agendas. My comments are based upon four of our recent reports.[1] The first report was on the West Nile Virus outbreak in New York City and its implications for public health preparedness. The second was on federal teams that could respond to chemical, biological, radiological, or nuclear terrorist attacks. The third was on federal research and preparedness programs specific to biological terrorism. And finally, the fourth report summarized our overall work on combating terrorism over the last 5 years. In these reports, and the earlier work that preceded them, we have taken a detailed look at programs to prepare for and respond to terrorism, including chemical and biological terrorism.[2]

My statement, after providing some background, will first discuss the growing uncertainties regarding the terrorist threat and the need for a risk management approach. Next, I will discuss some of the specific federal programs to prepare for and respond to chemical and biological agents or weapons. Third, I will discuss some of the problems identified in evaluations of chemical and biological preparedness. Finally, I will make some suggestions for the Congress to consider for investing resources in chemical and biological preparedness.

In summary, the nature of the terrorist threat appears to be more uncertain since the September 11 attacks. Preparing for all possible contingencies is not practical, so a risk management approach should be used. This would include a threat assessment to determine which chemical or biological agents are of most concern. The federal government has a variety of programs to prepare for and respond to chemical and biological terrorism, including response teams, support laboratories, training and equipment programs, and research efforts. Evaluations of chemical and biological preparedness have identified a number of problems and their solutions. Some of these solutions to improve the response to chemical and biological terrorism have broad applicability across a variety of contingencies while other response requirements are applicable to only a specific type of attack. For example, efforts to improve public health surveillance would be useful in any disease outbreak, whereas efforts to provide vaccines for smallpox would be useful only if terrorists used smallpox in a biological attack. The Congress faces competing demands for spending as it seeks to invest resources to better prepare our nation for chemical and biological terrorism. Funding to combat terrorism, which was originally budgeted to be less than $13 billion, may exceed $50 billion for fiscal year 2002, including supplemental emergency contingency funding. Given the uncertainty of the chemical and biological threat, the Congress may want to initially invest resources in efforts with broad applicability over those that are only applicable under a specific type of chemical or biological attack. As threat information becomes more certain, it may be more appropriate to invest in efforts only applicable to specific chemical or biological agents.

Background on Federal Policies, Plans, and Coordination Problems

Federal programs to prepare for and respond to chemical and biological terrorist attacks operate under an umbrella of various policies and contingency plans. Federal policies on combating terrorism are laid out in a series of presidential directives and implementing guidance.[3] These documents divide the federal response to terrorist attacks into two categories—crisis management and consequence management. Crisis management includes efforts to stop a terrorist attack, arrest terrorists, and gather evidence for criminal prosecution. Crisis management is led by the Department of Justice, through the Federal Bureau of Investigation. All federal agencies and departments, as needed, would support the Department of Justice and the Federal Bureau of Investigation on-scene commander. Consequence management includes efforts to provide medical treatment and emergency services, evacuate people from dangerous areas, and restore government services. Consequence management activities of the federal government are led by the Federal Emergency Management Agency in support of state and local authorities. Unlike crisis management, the federal government does not have primary responsibility for consequence management; state and local authorities do. Crisis and consequence management activities may overlap and run concurrently during the emergency response and are dependent upon the nature of the incident.

In a chemical or biological terrorist incident, the federal government would operate under one or more contingency plans. The U.S. Government Interagency Domestic Terrorism Concept of Operations Plan establishes conceptual guidelines for assessing and monitoring a developing threat, notifying appropriate agencies concerning the nature of the threat, and deploying necessary advisory and technical resources to assist the lead federal agency in facilitating interdepartmental coordination of crisis and consequence management activities. In the event that the President declares a national emergency, the Federal Emergency Management Agency also would coordinate the federal response using a generic disaster contingency plan called the Federal Response Plan. This plan—which has an annex specific for terrorism—outlines the roles of federal agencies in consequence management during terrorist attacks. More specifically, the plan outlines the planning assumptions, policies, concept of operation, organizational structures, and specific assignment of responsibilities to lead departments and agencies in providing federal assistance. The plan categorizes the types of assistance into specific "emergency support functions." Examples of emergency support functions include mass care and health and medical services. In addition, several individual agencies have their own contingency plans or guidance specific to their activities.[4]

Our September 20, 2001, report found significant coordination and fragmentation problems across the various federal agencies that combat terrorism.[5] In May 1998, the President established a National Coordinator within the National Security Council to better lead and coordinate these federal programs; however, the position's functions were never detailed in either an executive order or legislation. Many of the overall leadership and coordination functions that we had identified as critical were not given to the National Coordinator. In fact, several agencies performed interagency functions that we believed would have been performed more appropriately above the level of individual agencies. The interagency roles of these various agencies were not always clear and sometimes overlapped, which led to a fragmented approach. For example, the Department of Justice, the National Security Council, the Federal Bureau of Investigation, and the Federal Emergency Management Agency all had been developing or planning to develop potentially duplicative national strategies to combat terrorism. In a more recent report and testimony, we provide additional examples of coordination difficulties specific to biological terrorism.[6]

To improve overall leadership and coordination of federal efforts to combat terrorism, the President announced the creation of an Office of Homeland Security on September 20, 2001, and specified its functions in Executive Order 13228 on October 8, 2001. These actions represent potentially significant steps toward improved coordination of federal activities and are generally consistent with our recent recommendations.[7] Some questions that remain to be addressed include how this new office will be structured, what authority the Director will have, and how this effort can be institutionalized and sustained over time.

New Uncertainties Regarding the Terrorist Threat

There appears to be additional uncertainties about the terrorist threat in general since the September 11 attacks. Before those attacks, the Federal Bureau of Investigation had identified the largest domestic threat to be the "lone wolf" terrorist—an individual who operated alone. U.S. intelligence agencies had reported an increased possibility that terrorists would use chemical or biological weapons in the next decade. However, terrorists would have to overcome significant technical and operational challenges to successfully produce and release chemical or biological agents of sufficient quality and quantity to kill or injure large numbers of people without substantial assistance from a foreign government sponsor. In most cases, specialized knowledge is required in the manufacturing process and in improving an effective delivery device for most chemical and nearly all biological agents that could be used in terrorist attacks. Moreover, some of the required components of chemical agents and highly infective strains of biological agents are difficult to obtain. Finally, terrorists may have to overcome other obstacles to successfully launch an attack that would result in mass casualties, such as unfavorable meteorological conditions and personal safety risks.

On September 11, terrorists redefined the term "weapon of mass destruction." Up to that point, that term generally referred to chemical, biological, radiological, or nuclear agents or weapons. As clearly shown on September 11, a terrorist attack would not have to fit that definition to result in mass casualties, destruction of critical infrastructures, economic losses, and disruption of daily life nationwide. The attack increased the uncertainties regarding the threat, although terrorists would still face the technical challenges described above in conducting chemical or biological attacks. The uncertainty has increased because the attacks on the World Trade Center and the Pentagon were conducted by a large group of conspirators rather than one individual. In addition, the terrorists were executing a long-planned coordinated attack, showing a level of sophistication that may not have been anticipated by the Federal Bureau of Investigation—the agency responsible for monitoring national security threats within the United States. Also, the terrorists were willing to commit suicide in the attacks, showing no concern for their own personal safety, which was considered one of the barriers to using chemical or biological agents. And most recently, the threat of anthrax has gone from a series of hoaxes to actual cases under investigation by the Federal Bureau of Investigation.

Given the uncertainty about the threat, we continue to believe that a risk management approach is necessary to enhance domestic preparedness against terrorist threats. Risk management is a systematic and analytical process to consider the likelihood that a threat will endanger an asset, individual, or function and to identify actions to reduce the risk and mitigate the consequences of an attack. While the risk cannot be eliminated entirely, enhancing protection from known or potential threats can reduce the risk. This approach includes three key elements: a threat assessment, a vulnerability assessment, and a criticality assessment (assessing the importance or significance of a target). This approach would include a threat assessment to determine which chemical or biological agents are of most concern. Without the benefits that a risk management approach provides, many agencies have been relying on worst case chemical, biological, radiological, or nuclear scenarios to generate countermeasures or establish their programs. By using worst case scenarios, the federal government is focusing on vulnerabilities (which are unlimited) rather than credible threats (which are limited). As stated in our recent testimony, a risk management approach could help the United States prepare for the threats it faces and allow us to focus finite resources on areas of greatest need.[8]

Federal Programs to Respond to Chemical and Biological Terrorism

A terrorist attack using chemical or biological weapons presents an array of complex issues to state and local first responders. These responders would include police, firefighters, emergency medical services, and hazardous material technicians. They must identify the agent used so as to rapidly decontaminate victims and apply appropriate medical treatments. If the incident overwhelms state and local response capabilities, they may call on federal agencies to provide assistance. To provide such assistance, the federal government has a variety of programs to prepare for and respond to chemical and biological terrorism, including response teams, support laboratories, training and equipment programs, and research efforts, as follows.

- Federal agencies have special teams that can respond to terrorist incidents involving chemical or biological agents or weapons. These teams perform a wide variety of functions, such as hands-on response; providing technical advice to state, local, or federal authorities; or coordinating the response efforts of other federal teams. Figure 1 shows selected federal teams that could respond to a chemical or biological terrorist incident.[9]

- Federal agencies also have laboratories that may support response teams by performing tests to analyze and test samples of chemical and biological agents. In some incidents, these laboratories may perform functions that enable federal response teams to perform their role. For example, when a diagnosis is confirmed at a laboratory, response teams can begin to treat victims appropriately.

- Federal agencies also have programs to train and equip state and local authorities to respond to chemical and biological terrorism. The programs

- Federal Programs to Respond to Chemical and Biological Terrorism have improved domestic preparedness by training and equipping over 273,000 first responders. The programs also have included exercises to allow first responders to interact with themselves and federal responders.

- Finally, federal agencies have a number of research and development projects underway to combat terrorism. Examples of recently developed and fielded technologies include products to detect and identify chemical and biological weapons. Additional research and/or development projects include chemical monitoring devices and new or improved vaccines, antibiotics, and antivirals.

Figure 1: Federal Response Teams for Chemical and Biological Terrorism

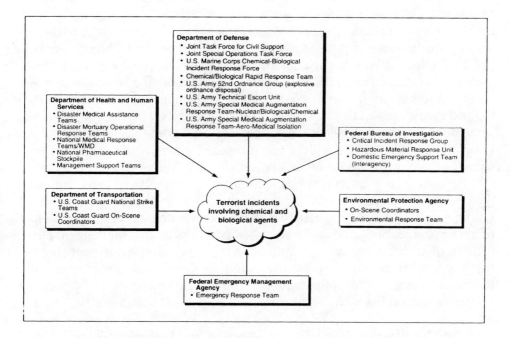

Note: This figure includes federal teams for both crisis and consequence management in a terrorist incident involving chemical or biological agents. Federal agencies have additional teams not shown that might be used in conventional, radiological, or nuclear incidents.

Source: GAO analysis.

Characteristics of Chemical Terrorism

There are a variety of chemical agents potentially used by terrorists. These chemical agents could be dispersed as a gas, vapor, liquid, or aerosol. A chemical agent could be disseminated by explosive or mechanical delivery. Some chemicals disperse rapidly and others remain toxic for days or weeks and require decontamination and clean up. Rapid exposure to a highly concentrated agent would increase the number of casualties. Federal, state, and local officials generally agree that a chemical terrorist incident would look like a major hazardous material emergency. According to the

International Association of Fire Chiefs, over 600 local and state hazardous material teams will be the first to respond to a chemical incident. If local responders are unable to manage the situation or are overwhelmed, the incident commander has access to state and federal assets. A variety of federal teams could be deployed to provide assistance.[10]

Characteristics of Biological Terrorism

Terrorists also can potentially use a variety of biological agents. Biological agents must be disseminated by some means that infects enough individuals to initiate a disease epidemic. According to a wide range of experts in science, health, intelligence, and biological warfare and a technical report, the most effective way to disseminate a biological agent is by aerosol. This method allows the simultaneous respiratory infection of a large number of people. A few biological agents (e.g., plague and smallpox) are communicable and can be spread beyond those directly affected by the weapon or dissemination device. The release of a biological agent or weapon may not be known for several days until victims present themselves to medical personnel in doctors' offices, clinics, and emergency rooms where the symptoms might easily be confused with influenza or other less virulent illnesses. Accordingly, the critical detection of the biological agent begins with the public health infrastructure that detects outbreaks of illness, identifies the sources and modes of transmission, and performs rapid agent laboratory identification. Once diagnosis of a biological agent is confirmed, treating victims may require the use of federal consequence management teams and the items from the National Pharmaceutical Stockpile. Again, a variety of federal teams could be deployed to provide assistance.[11]

Problems Identified in Preparing for Chemical and Biological Terrorism

We have identified a number of problems that require solutions in order to improve preparedness for chemical and biological terrorism. Some of these are included in our recent reports and testimony. For example, our report on the West Nile Virus outbreak identified specific weaknesses in the public health system that need to be addressed to improve preparedness for biological terrorism.[12] Our recent report on biological terrorism examined evaluations of the effectiveness of federal programs to prepare state and local authorities.[13] For this statement, we also conducted an analysis of federal exercise evaluations to identify problems associated with chemical and biological terrorism that needed to be solved. In doing this, we examined 50 evaluations representing 40 separate exercises with chemical or biological scenarios.

Based upon our review, the problems and their solutions fell into two categories. These categories were (1) generic problems and solutions that are generally applicable to any type of terrorist incident, major accident, or natural disaster, and (2) problems and solutions that are applicable to both chemical and biological terrorist events. Specific examples of each category follow.

The first category of problems and their solutions are generally applicable to any type of terrorist incident. These would apply not only to chemical and biological terrorism but also to all hazards including emergencies unrelated to terrorism, such as major accidents or natural disasters.

- Command and control. The roles, responsibilities, and the legal authority to plan and carry out a response to a weapon of mass destruction terrorist incident are not always clear, which could result in a delayed and inadequate response.

- Planning and operations. State and local emergency operations plans do not always conform to federal plans. The operational procedures for requesting federal assistance are not always compatible with state and local procedures.

- Resource management and logistics. State and local governments can be overwhelmed with the resource management and logistical requirements of managing a large incident, particularly after the arrival of additional state and federal assets. For example, state and local officials could have difficulty providing support to numerous military units that might be needed.

- Communication. Interoperability difficulties exist at the interagency and intergovernmental levels. Also, the public health community lacks robust communication systems, protocols, equipment, and facilities.

- Exercises. Many exercises focus primarily on crisis management, which often ends in a successful tactical resolution of the incident and do not include more likely scenarios where terrorist attacks are successful, requiring a consequence management exercise component.

- Mass casualties. Overall planning and integration among agencies are needed for mass casualty management, including conventional terrorist incidents. Also, medical surge capacity for any type of weapon of mass destruction event may be limited. Disposition of bodies would also be an issue.

The second category of problems and their solutions are applicable to chemical or biological incidents. They would not be relevant in a conventional, radiological, or nuclear terrorist incident; however, they would be relevant in other chemical or biological events not related to terrorism, such as an accidental release of chemicals or a natural outbreak of a disease. They vary in their level of applicability, with some only being applicable to specific chemical or biological agents.

- Public health surveillance. Basic capacity for public health surveillance is lacking. Improved public health-coordinated surveillance for biological terrorism and emerging infectious diseases is an urgent preparedness requirement at the local level.

- Detection and risk assessment. The capability of first responders and specialized response teams to rapidly and accurately detect, recognize, and identify chemical or biological agents and assess the associated health risks can be slow. Also, following the release of a chemical or biological agent, emergency hazardous material teams do not always conduct a downwind analysis of the toxic cloud, which could delay a decision to evacuate potentially affected populations.

- Protective equipment and training. First responders often lack special personal protective equipment (level-A protective clothing and masks) to safeguard them from chemical or biological agents and could become contaminated themselves. Training curricula deal with the technical level of response, such as treatment protocols, but do not describe operational guidelines and strategies for responding to large-scale public health emergencies. Physicians sometimes lack adequate training to recognize chemical and biological agents.

- Chemical and biological-specific planning. Emergency operations plans and "all-hazard" plans do not adequately address the response to a large- scale chemical or biological terrorism event. Plans often do not address chemical or biological incidents.

- Hospital notification and decontamination. Delays could occur in the notification of local hospitals that a biological incident has occurred. By the time the hospitals are notified, they could become contaminated by self-referred patients, have to close, and not treat other victims. First responders could become victims themselves and contaminate emergency rooms.

- Distribution of pharmaceuticals. State and local health officials have found it difficult to break down and distribute tons of medical supplies contained in push-packages from the National Pharmaceutical Stockpile.

- Vaccines and pharmaceuticals. Some pharmaceuticals, such as antibiotics, are generic and can be used to treat several different biological agents, whereas others, such as vaccines, are agent-specific. An example would be the smallpox vaccine, which would only be useful if terrorists used smallpox in an attack.

- Laboratories. Even a small outbreak of an emerging disease would strain resources. There is a need for broadening laboratory capabilities, ensuring adequate staffing and expertise, and improving the ability to deal with surges in testing needs.

- Medical and veterinary coordination. Problems exist in communication between public health officials and veterinary officials. The local and state veterinary disaster response plan may not adequately address the impact of a biological incident on the animal population, which could have dramatic health, economic, and public relations implications.

- Quarantine. Quarantine would be resource-intensive and would require a well-planned strategy to implement and sustain. Questions that have to be addressed include implementation authority, enforcement, logistics, financial support, and the psychological ramifications of quarantine.

Suggestions to Consider for Investing Resources

The Congress may want to consider several factors before investing resources in the rapidly growing budget for combating terrorism. Even before September 11, funding to combat terrorism had increased 78 percent from the fiscal year 1998 level of about $7.2 billion to the proposed fiscal year 2002 budget of about $12.8 billion. After September 11, the Congress approved the President's request for $20 billion in emergency assistance and provided an additional $20 billion to supplement existing contingency funds. Thus, terrorism-related funding in fiscal year 2002 may exceed $50 billion. Further, a number of additional funding proposals have been introduced in the Congress that could further raise that amount.

The challenge facing the Congress and the nation is to invest new resources where they will make the most difference in protecting people and responding to terrorist attacks, including those involving chemical and biological agents or weapons. The terrorist attacks of September 11 have profoundly changed the management agendas of the Congress, the White House, federal agencies, and state and local governments. However, as we respond to the urgent priorities and the enduring requirements of combating terrorism, our nation still must address the short-term and long- term fiscal challenges that were present before September 11 and that remain today. It is important to remember that the long-term pressures on the budget from competing programs have not lessened. In fact, long-term pressures have increased due to the slowing economy and the spending levels expected for fiscal year 2002. As a result, the ultimate task of addressing today's urgent needs without unduly exacerbating our long- range fiscal challenges has become more difficult.

As discussed above, the nature of the threat appears to have become more uncertain since the September 11 attacks. Despite this uncertainty, preparing for all possible contingencies is not practical because vulnerabilities are unlimited, so a risk management approach is needed to help focus resource investments. Efforts to better prepare for chemical and biological attacks include solutions that have broad applicability across a variety of contingencies and solutions that are applicable to only a specific type of attack. For example, efforts to improve public health surveillance would be useful in any disease outbreak, whereas efforts to provide vaccines for smallpox would be useful only if terrorists used smallpox in a biological attack. Given the uncertainty of the chemical and biological terrorist threat and continued fiscal concerns, the Congress may want to initially invest resources in efforts with broad applicability rather than those that are only applicable under a specific type of chemical or biological attack. As threat information becomes more certain, it may be more appropriate to invest in efforts only applicable to specific chemical or biological agents. This approach would focus finite resources on areas of greatest need using a risk management approach.

Scope and Methodology

As stated initially, this testimony is based largely upon recent GAO reports. In addition, we sought to determine what types of problems might arise in responding to chemical and biological terrorist attacks. To do so, we analyzed after-action reports and other evaluations from federal exercises that simulated chemical and biological terrorist attacks. The scope of this analysis was governmentwide. Our methodology initially identified and catalogued after-action reports and evaluations from federal exercises over the last 6 fiscal years (fiscal years 1996 to 2001). The analysis was limited to those 50 after-action reports (representing 40 different exercises) that had a chemical and/or biological terrorism component. The analysis did not include exercises involving radiological and/or nuclear agents, and it does not represent all federal after-action reports for combating terrorism exercises during that period. We then identified specific problems and issues associated with chemical and biological terrorism exercises. We compared those specific problems and solutions to determine which ones were specific to chemical and to biological incidents.

Mr. Chairman, this concludes my prepared statement. I would be happy to respond to any questions you or other members of the Committee may have.

Contact and Acknowledgments

For further information about this testimony, please contact me at (202) 512-4300. For information specifically on biological terrorism please contact Janet Heinrich at (202) 512-7250. Stephen L. Caldwell, Mark A. Pross, James C. Lawson, Harry L. Purdy, Jason G. Venner, and M. Jane Hunt made key contributions to this statement.

Related GAO Products

Homeland Security: Key Elements of a Risk Management Approach (GAO-02-150T, Oct. 12, 2001).

Bioterrorism: Review of Public Health Preparedness Programs (GAO-02-149T, Oct. 10, 2001).

Bioterrorism: Public Health and Medical Preparedness (GAO-02-141T, Oct. 9, 2001).

Bioterrorism: Coordination and Preparedness (GAO-02-129T, Oct. 5, 2001).

Bioterrorism: Federal Research and Preparedness Activities (GAO-01-915, Sept. 28, 2001).

Combating Terrorism: Selected Challenges and Related Recommendations (GAO-01-822, Sept. 20, 2001).

Combating Terrorism: Comments on H.R. 525 to Create a President's Council on Domestic Terrorism Preparedness (GAO-01-555T, May 9, 2001).

Combating Terrorism: Accountability Over Medical Supplies Needs Further Improvement (GAO-01-666T, May 1, 2001).

Combating Terrorism: Observations on Options to Improve the Federal Response (GAO-01-660T, Apr. 24, 2001).

Combating Terrorism: Accountability Over Medical Supplies Needs Further Improvement (GAO-01-463, Mar. 30, 2001).

Combating Terrorism: Comments on Counterterrorism Leadership and National Strategy (GAO-01-556T, Mar. 27, 2001).

Combating Terrorism: FEMA Continues to Make Progress in Coordinating Preparedness and Response (GAO-01-15, Mar. 20, 2001).

Combating Terrorism: Federal Response Teams Provide Varied Capabilities; Opportunities Remain to Improve Coordination (GAO-01-14, Nov. 30, 2000).

West Nile Virus Outbreak: Lessons for Public Health Preparedness (GAO/HEHS-00-180, Sept. 11, 2000).

Combating Terrorism: Linking Threats to Strategies and Resources (GAO/T-NSIAD-00-218, July 26, 2000).

Chemical and Biological Defense: Observations on Nonmedical Chemical and Biological R&D Programs (GAO/T-NSIAD-00-130, Mar. 22, 2000).

Combating Terrorism: Need to Eliminate Duplicate Federal Weapons of Mass Destruction Training (GAO/NSIAD-00-64, Mar. 21, 2000).

Combating Terrorism: Chemical and Biological Medical Supplies Are Poorly Managed (GAO/T-HEHS/AIMD-00-59, Mar. 8, 2000).

Combating Terrorism: Chemical and Biological Medical Supplies Are Poorly Managed (GAO/HEHS/AIMD-00-36, Oct. 29, 1999).

Food Safety: Agencies Should Further Test Plans for Responding to Deliberate Contamination (GAO/RCED-00-3, Oct. 27, 1999).

Endnotes

[1]The four reports discussed are *West Nile Virus Outbreak: Lessons for Public Health Preparedness* (GAO/HEHS-00-180, Sept. 11, 2000); *Combating Terrorism: Federal Response Teams Provide Varied Capabilities; Opportunities Remain to Improve Coordination* (GAO-01-14, Nov. 30, 2000); *Bioterrorism: Federal Research and Preparedness Activities* (GAO-01-915, Sept. 28, 2001); *and Combating Terrorism: Selected Challenges and Related Recommendations* (GAO-01-822, Sept. 20, 2001).

[2]A more complete list of GAO products related to terrorism appears at the end of this statement.

[3]For a compendium of relevant federal policy and planning documents for combating terrorism, see app. I of GAO-01-822. In addition to documents mentioned in that report, the President signed Executive Order 13228 on Oct. 8, 2001, which established a new Office of Homeland Security.

[4]An example of agency-specific guidance would be the U.S. Coast Guard's Interim Guidance Regarding Coast Guard Response to Weapons of Mass Destruction Incidents of June 2000. For a list of additional plans and guidance by individual agencies, see app. II of GAO-01-822.

[5]GAO-01-822, pp. 31-43.

[6]For example, fragmentation is evident in the different threat lists of biological agents developed by federal departments and agencies (see GAO-01-915, p.18). Our recent testimony, *Bioterrorism: Public Health and Medical Preparedness* (GAO-02-141T, Oct. 9, 2001) also included a graphic representation of the complicated coordination networks involved (see its app. III, fig. 1).

[7]Our recent summary report highlighted a number of important characteristics and responsibilities necessary for a single focal point, such as the Office of Homeland Security, to improve coordination and accountability (see GAO-01-822, pp. 41-42).

[8]*Homeland Security: Key Elements of a Risk Management Approach* (GAO-02-150T, Oct. 12, 2001).

[9]For a more detailed description of these federal teams, including their mission, authority, personnel, and response times, see GAO-01-14, app. I.

[10]For a detailed discussion of what teams would perform what functions in a chemical terrorist incident, see GAO-01-14, app. III.

[11]For a detailed discussion of what teams would perform what functions in a biological terrorist incident, see GAO-01-14, app. IV.

[12]See GAO/HEHS-00-180.

[13]See GAO-01-915.

INTERNATIONAL DOCUMENTS

United Nations

DOCUMENT NO. 18

RESOLUTION 1368

Adopted by the United Nations Security Council at Its 4370th Meeting

September 12, 2001

COMMENTARY: This brief Declaration emphasizes the United Nations opposition to all forms of terrorism and asks the international community to extend increased cooperation as called for in the previous Resolution 1269 of October 19, 1999.

The Security Council

Reaffirming the principles and purposes of the Charter of the United Nations,

Determined to combat by all means threats to international peace and security caused by terrorist acts,

Recognizing the inherent right of individual or collective self-defence in accordance with the Charter,

1. *Unequivocally condemns* in the strongest terms the horrifying terrorist attacks which took place on 11 September 2001 in New York, Washington, D.C. And Pennsylvania and *regards* such acts, like any act of international terrorism, as threat to international peace and security;

2. *Expresses* its deepest sympathy and condolences to the victims and their families and to the people and Government of the United States of America;

3. *Calls* on all States to work together urgently to bring to justice the perpetrators, organizers and sponsors of these terrorist attacks and stresses that those responsible for aiding, supporting or harbouring the perpetrators, organizers and sponsors of these acts will be held accountable;

4. *Calls also* on the international community to redouble their efforts to prevent and suppress terrorist acts including by increased cooperation and full implementation of the relevant international anti-terrorist conventions and Security Council resolutions, in particular resolution 1269 (1999) of 19 October 1999;

5. *Expresses* its readiness to take all necessary steps to respond to the terrorist attacks of 11 September 2001, and to combat all forms of terrorism, in accordance with its responsibilities under the Charter of the United Nations;

6. *Decides* to remain seized of the matter.

DOCUMENT NO. 19

UNITED NATIONS RESOLUTION 1373 (2001) ON ANTI-TERRORISM

September 28, 2001

COMMENTARY: In addition to stating its opposition to all forms of terrorism, this Declaration established a Committee of the Council to monitor the implementation of the Resolution, giving all States 90 days to report on what actions they are taking.

Security Council SC/7158 4385th Meeting (Night)28 September 2001

SECURITY COUNCIL UNANIMOUSLY ADOPTS WIDE-RANGING ANTI-TERRORISM RESOLUTION;

CALLS FOR SUPPRESSING FINANCING, IMPROVING INTERNATIONAL COOPERATION

Resolution 1373 (2001) Also Creates Committee to Monitor Implementation

Reaffirming its unequivocal condemnation of the terrorist acts that took place in New York, Washington, D.C., and Pennsylvania on 11 September, the Security Council this evening unanimously adopted a wide-ranging, comprehensive resolution with steps and strategies to combat international terrorism.

By resolution 1373 (2001) the Council also established a Committee of the Council to monitor the resolution's implementation and called on all States to report on actions they had taken to that end no later than 90 days from today.

Under terms of the text, the Council decided that all States should prevent and suppress the financing of terrorism, as well as criminalize the wilful provision or collection of funds for such acts. The funds, financial assets and economic resources of those who commit or attempt to commit terrorist acts or participate in or facilitate the commission of terrorist acts and of persons and entities acting on behalf of terrorists should also be frozen without delay.

The Council also decided that States should prohibit their nationals or persons or entities in their territories from making funds, financial assets, economic resources, financial or other related services available to persons who commit or attempt to commit, facilitate or participate in the commission of terrorist acts. States should also refrain from providing any form of support to entities or persons involved in terrorist acts; take the necessary steps to prevent the commission of terrorist acts; deny safe haven to those who finance, plan, support, commit terrorist acts and provide safe havens as well.

By other terms, the Council decided that all States should prevent those who finance, plan, facilitate or commit terrorist acts from using their respective territories for those purposes against other countries and their citizens. States should also ensure that anyone who has participated in the financing, planning, preparation or perpetration of terrorist acts or in supporting terrorist acts is brought to justice. They should also ensure that terrorist acts are established as serious criminal offences in domestic laws and regulations and that the seriousness of such acts is duly reflected in sentences served.

By further terms, the Council decided that States should afford one another the greatest measure of assistance for criminal investigations or criminal proceedings relating to the financing or support of terrorist acts. States should also prevent the movement of terrorists or their groups by effective border controls as well.

Also by the text, the Council called on all States to intensify and accelerate the exchange of information regarding terrorist actions or movements; forged or falsified documents; traffic in arms and sensitive material; use of communications and technologies by terrorist groups; and the threat posed by the possession of weapons of mass destruction.

States were also called on to exchange information and cooperate to prevent and suppress terrorist acts and to take action against the perpetrators of such acts. States should become parties to, and fully implement as soon as possible, the relevant international conventions and protocols to combat terrorism.

By the text, before granting refugee status, all States should take appropriate measures to ensure that the asylum seekers had not planned, facilitated or participated in terrorist acts. Further, States should ensure that refugee status was not abused by the perpetrators, organizers or facilitators of terrorist acts, and that claims of political motivation were not recognized as grounds for refusing requests for the extradition of alleged terrorists.

The Council noted with concern the close connection between international terrorism and transnational organized crime, illicit drugs, money laundering and illegal movement of nuclear, chemical, biological and other deadly materials. In that regard, it emphasized the need to enhance the coordination of national, subregional, regional and international efforts to strengthen a global response to that threat to international security.

Reaffirming the need to combat by all means, in accordance with the Charter, threats to international peace and security caused by terrorist acts, the Council expressed its determination to take all necessary steps to fully implement the current resolution.

The meeting, which began at 10:50 p.m., adjourned at 10:53 p.m.

Resolution

The full text of resolution 1373 (2001) reads as follows:

"The Security Council,

"Reaffirming its resolutions 1269 (1999) of 19 October 1999 and 1368 (2001) of 12 September 2001,

"Reaffirming also its unequivocal condemnation of the terrorist attacks which took place in New York, Washington, D.C., and Pennsylvania on 11 September 2001, and expressing its determination to prevent all such acts,

"Reaffirming further that such acts, like any act of international terrorism, constitute a threat to international peace and security,

"Reaffirming the inherent right of individual or collective self-defence as recognized by the Charter of the United Nations as reiterated in resolution 1368 (2001),

"Reaffirming the need to combat by all means, in accordance with the Charter of the United Nations, threats to international peace and security caused by terrorist acts,

"Deeply concerned by the increase, in various regions of the world, of acts of terrorism motivated by intolerance or extremism,

"Calling on States to work together urgently to prevent and suppress terrorist acts, including through increased cooperation and full implementation of the relevant international conventions relating to terrorism,

"Recognizing the need for States to complement international cooperation by taking additional measures to prevent and suppress, in their territories through all lawful means, the financing and preparation of any acts of terrorism,

"Reaffirming the principle established by the General Assembly in its declaration of October 1970 (resolution 2625 (XXV)) and reiterated by the Security Council in its resolution 1189 (1998) of 13 August 1998, namely that every State has the duty to refrain from organizing, instigating, assisting or participating in terrorist acts in another State or acquiescing in organized activities within its territory directed towards the commission of such acts,

"Acting under Chapter VII of the Charter of the United Nations,

"1. Decides that all States shall:

"(a) Prevent and suppress the financing of terrorist acts;

"(b) Criminalize the wilful provision or collection, by any means, directly or indirectly, of funds by their nationals or in their territories with the intention that the funds should be used, or in the knowledge that they are to be used, in order to carry out terrorist acts;

"(c) Freeze without delay funds and other financial assets or economic resources of persons who commit, or attempt to commit, terrorist acts or participate in or facilitate the commission of terrorist acts; of entities owned or controlled directly or indirectly by such persons; and of persons and entities acting on behalf of, or at the direction of such persons and entities, including funds derived or generated from property owned or controlled directly or indirectly by such persons and associated persons and entities;

"(d) Prohibit their nationals or any persons and entities within their territories from making any funds, financial assets or economic resources or financial or other related services available, directly or indirectly, for the benefit of persons who commit or attempt to commit or facilitate or participate in the commission of terrorist acts, of entities owned or controlled, directly or indirectly, by such persons and of persons and entities acting on behalf of or at the direction of such persons;

"2. Decides also that all States shall:

"(a) Refrain from providing any form of support, active or passive, to entities or persons involved in terrorist acts, including by suppressing recruitment of members of terrorist groups and eliminating the supply of weapons to terrorists;

"(b) Take the necessary steps to prevent the commission of terrorist acts, including by provision of early warning to other States by exchange of information;

"(c) Deny safe haven to those who finance, plan, support, or commit terrorist acts, or provide safe havens;

"(d) Prevent those who finance, plan, facilitate or commit terrorist acts from using their respective territories for those purposes against other States or their citizens;

"(e) Ensure that any person who participates in the financing, planning, preparation or perpetration of terrorist acts or in supporting terrorist acts is brought to justice and ensure that, in addition to any other measures against them, such terrorist acts are established as serious criminal offences in domestic laws and regulations and that the punishment duly reflects the seriousness of such terrorist acts;

"(f) Afford one another the greatest measure of assistance in connection with criminal investigations or criminal proceedings relating to the financing or support of terrorist acts, including assistance in obtaining evidence in their possession necessary for the proceedings;

"(g) Prevent the movement of terrorists or terrorist groups by effective border controls and controls on issuance of identity papers and travel documents, and through measures for preventing counterfeiting, forgery or fraudulent use of identity papers and travel documents;

"3. Calls upon all States to:

"(a) Find ways of intensifying and accelerating the exchange of operational information, especially regarding actions or movements of terrorist persons or networks; forged or falsified travel documents; traffic in arms, explosives or sensitive materials; use of communications technologies by terrorist groups; and the threat posed by the possession of weapons of mass destruction by terrorist groups;

"(b) Exchange information in accordance with international and domestic law and cooperate on administrative and judicial matters to prevent the commission of terrorist acts;

"(c) Cooperate, particularly through bilateral and multilateral arrangements and agreements, to prevent and suppress terrorist attacks and take action against perpetrators of such acts;

"(d) Become parties as soon as possible to the relevant international conventions and protocols relating to terrorism, including the International Convention for the Suppression of the Financing of Terrorism of 9 December 1999;

"(e) Increase cooperation and fully implement the relevant international conventions and protocols relating to terrorism and Security Council resolutions 1269 (1999) and 1368 (2001);

"(f) Take appropriate measures in conformity with the relevant provisions of national and international law, including international standards of human rights, before granting refugee status, for the purpose of ensuring that the asylum seeker has not planned, facilitated or participated in the commission of terrorist acts;

"(g) Ensure, in conformity with international law, that refugee status is not abused by the perpetrators, organizers or facilitators of terrorist acts, and that claims of political motivation are not recognized as grounds for refusing requests for the extradition of alleged terrorists;

"4. Notes with concern the close connection between international terrorism and transnational organized crime, illicit drugs, money-laundering, illegal arms-trafficking, and illegal movement of nuclear, chemical, biological and other potentially deadly materials, and in this regard emphasizes the need to enhance coordination of efforts on national, subregional, regional and international levels in order to strengthen a global response to this serious challenge and threat to international security;

"5. Declares that acts, methods, and practices of terrorism are contrary to the purposes and principles of the United Nations and that knowingly financing, planning and inciting terrorist acts are also contrary to the purposes and principles of the United Nations;

"6. Decides to establish, in accordance with rule 28 of its provisional rules of procedure, a Committee of the Security Council, consisting of all the members of the Council, to monitor implementation of this resolution, with the assistance of appropriate expertise, and calls upon all States to report to the Committee, no later than 90 days from the date of adoption of this resolution and thereafter according to a timetable to be proposed by the Committee, on the steps they have taken to implement this resolution;

"7. Directs the Committee to delineate its tasks, submit a work programme within 30 days of the adoption of this resolution, and to consider the support it requires, in consultation with the Secretary-General;

"8. Expresses its determination to take all necessary steps in order to ensure the full implementation of this resolution, in accordance with its responsibilities under the Charter;

"9.Decides to remain seized of this matter."

(Distributed by the Office of International Information Programs, U.S. Department of State. Web site: http://usinfo.state.gov)

INTERNATIONAL DOCUMENTS

Canada

DOCUMENT NO. 20

JOINT U.S.-CANADA DECLARATION FOR THE CREATION OF A SMART BORDER FOR THE 21ST CENTURY

December 12, 2001

COMMENTARY: This Declaration is a blue print for addressing many questions concerning the flow of persons and goods across the borders. It is clearly one more weapon to cope with terrorists and it was prompted, in part, by the ease with which terrorists have been moving in and out of the respective countries.

CANADA AND THE UNITED STATES SIGN SMART BORDER DECLARATION

John Manley, Minister of Foreign Affairs and Chairman of the Ad Hoc Cabinet Committee on Public Security and Anti-Terrorism, and Governor Tom Ridge, Director of the Office of Homeland Security in the United States, today signed a declaration for the creation of a Smart Border for the 21st century between the United States and Canada.

The Smart Border Declaration outlines the 30-point Action Plan, based on four pillars, to collaborate in identifying and addressing security risks while efficiently and effectively expediting the legitimate flow of people and goods back and forth across the Canada-U.S. border. The Declaration includes 21 new objectives and builds on nine other recent Canada-U.S. initiatives set out in the eight-point, December 3 Joint Statement of Cooperation on Border Security and Regional Migration Issues and in the RCMP-FBI agreement to improve the exchange of fingerprint data of the same date.

"We have agreed to an aggressive action plan that will allow the safest, most efficient passage of people and goods between our two countries, as part of our ongoing commitment to the creation of a Smart Border," said Minister Manley. "This action plan will enhance the technology, coordination and information sharing that are essential to safeguard our mutual security and strengthen cross-border commerce for the world's largest binational trading relationship."

"On behalf of President Bush, I was pleased to visit Canada to meet with Minister Manley and senior Canadian officials to discuss how to build a smart and secure border that allows the free flow of people and goods between our two countries. We look forward to working together to achieve real-time real solutions as quickly as possible," said Governor Ridge.

The new objectives contained in the Secure and Smart Border Action Plan are as follows:

Secure Flow of People:

- develop and deploy a secure card for permanent residents;
- resume, evaluate and expand the NEXUS pilot project at the Sarnia-Port Huron border point and discuss its expansion to air travel;
- review practices and procedures for the screening of refugee/asylum claimants;
- implement the Canada-U.S. Pre-clearance Agreement, resume in-transit pre-clearance at Vancouver and expand it to other airports;
- share Advance Passenger Information and agreed-to Passenger Name Records for flights in transit and between Canada and the U.S.;
- review customs and immigration presence and practices at international ferry terminals;
- develop jointly an automated immigration database; and
- provide international technical assistance.

Secure Flow of Goods:

- establish complementary systems for commercial processing, including audit-based programs;
- develop an integrated approach for processing truck, rail and marine cargo away from the border;
- establish criteria for the creation of small, remote joint border facilities;
- share customs data; and
- exchange information and analysts to target marine in-transit containers.

Secure Infrastructure:

- work to secure resources for joint and coordinated physical and technological improvements to border and trade corridor infrastructure;
- deploy interoperable technologies for the secure movement of goods and people;

- assess threats and protect transborder transportation and other critical infrastructure; and
- finalize agreement on comparable/equivalent aviation security and training standards.

Coordination and Information Sharing:

- address legal and operational challenges to joint removals of deportees;
- bring into force legislation on terrorism;
- exchange advance information on individuals and organizations designated as engaging in terrorist fundraising; and
- increase dialogue and commitment to joint counterterrorism training and exercises.

Minister Manley and Governor Ridge agreed to meet again early in the new year. They will review the critical paths that they have asked officials to develop for realizing each of the objectives set out in the Action Plan. The two governments are committed to building on this Action Plan by identifying and implementing measures that can be taken to secure a Smart Border. Minister Manley and Governor Ridge will consult regularly on this plan in order to achieve the goals outlined as quickly as possible. These measures are regarded by both governments as matters of the highest priority.

BUILDING A SMART BORDER FOR THE 21st CENTURY ON THE FOUNDATION OF A NORTH AMERICAN ZONE OF CONFIDENCE

The terrorist actions of September 11 were an attack on our common commitment to democracy, the rule of law and a free and open economy. They highlighted a threat to our public and economic security. They require our governments to develop new approaches to meet these challenges. This declaration commits our governments to work together to address these threats to our people, our institutions and our prosperity.

Public security and economic security are mutually reinforcing. By working together to develop a zone of confidence against terrorist activity, we create a unique opportunity to build a smart border for the 21st century; a border that securely facilitates the free flow of people and commerce; a border that reflects the largest trading relationship in the world.

Our countries have a long history of cooperative border management. This tradition facilitated both countries' immediate responses to the attacks of September 11. It is the foundation on which we continue to base our cooperation, recognizing that our current and future prosperity and security depend on a border that operates efficiently and effectively under all circumstances.

Action Plan

The attached *Action Plan for Creating a Secure and Smart Border* includes the measures already identified by our colleagues as well as new initiatives. Four pillars support the action plan:

(1) *The Secure Flow of People*

- We will implement systems to collaborate in identifying security risks while expediting the flow of low risk travellers.
- We will identify security threats before they arrive in North America through collaborative approaches to reviewing crew and passenger manifests, managing refugees, and visa policy coordination.
- We will establish a secure system to allow low risk frequent travellers between our countries to move efficiently across the border.

(2) *The Secure Flow of Goods*

- We will implement a system to collaborate in identifying high risk goods while expediting the flow of low risk goods.
- We will identify security threats arriving from abroad by developing common standards for screening cargo before it arrives in North America, while working to clear goods at the first port of entry.

- We will adopt compatible security standards at production and distribution facilities to minimize security threats. We will expedite the flow of low risk traffic between our countries by establishing compatible commercial processes at the border.

- We will expedite the flow of low risk goods between our countries by establishing secure procedures to clear goods away from the border, including at rail yards and at marine ports.

(3) *Secure Infrastructure*

- We will relieve congestion at key crossing points by investing reciprocally in border infrastructure and identifying technological solutions that will help to speed movement across the border.

- We will identify and minimize threats to our critical infrastructure including the airports, ports, bridges, tunnels, pipelines and powerlines that link our countries.

(4) *Coordination and Information Sharing in the Enforcement of these Objectives*

- We will put the necessary tools and legislative framework in place to ensure that information and intelligence is shared in a timely and coherent way within our respective countries as well as between them.

- We will strengthen coordination between our enforcement agencies for addressing common threats.

Next Steps

- We will meet again early in the new year to review the critical paths that we have asked our officials to develop for realizing each of the objectives set out in the action plan. We will consult regularly to ensure continued progress on this plan to achieve the goals outlined as quickly as possible.

- This joint action plan is an important step. Our governments are committed to building on this plan to continually identify and implement measures that can be taken to secure a smart border.

- These measures are regarded by both governments as matters of the highest priority.

Ottawa, Canada
December 12, 2001

ACTION PLAN FOR CREATING A SECURE AND SMART BORDER

The Secure Flow of People

1) Biometric Identifiers

Jointly develop on an urgent basis common biometric identifiers in documentation such as permanent resident cards, NEXUS, and other travel documents to ensure greater security.

2) Permanent Resident Cards

Develop and deploy a secure card for permanent residents which includes a biometric identifier.

3) Single Alternative Inspection System

Resume NEXUS pilot project, with appropriate security measures, for two-way movement of pre-approved travelers at Sarnia-Port Huron, complete pilot project evaluation and expand a single program to other areas along the land border. Discuss expansion to air travel.

4) Refugee/Asylum Processing

Review refugee/asylum practices and procedures to ensure that applicants are thoroughly screened for security risks and take necessary steps to share information on refugee and asylum claimants.

5) Managing of Refugee/Asylum Claims

Negotiate a safe third-country agreement to enhance the managing of refugee claims.

6) Visa Policy Coordination

Initiate joint review of respective visa waiver lists and share look-out lists at visa issuing offices.

7) Air Preclearance

Finalize plans/authority necessary to implement the Preclearance Agreement signed in January 2001. Resume intransit preclearance at Vancouver and expand to other airports per Annex I of the Agreement.

8) Advance Passenger Information / Passenger Name Record

Share Advance Passenger Information and agreed-to Passenger Name Records on flights between Canada and the United States, including in-transit flights. Explore means to identify risks posed by passengers on international flights arriving in each other's territory.

9) Joint Passenger Analysis Units

Establish joint units at key international airports in Canada and the United States.

10) Ferry Terminals

Review customs and immigration presence and practices at international ferry terminals.

11) Compatible Immigration Databases

Develop jointly an automated database, such as Canada's Support System for Intelligence, as a platform for information exchange, and enhance sharing of intelligence and trend analysis.

12) Immigration Officers Overseas

Increase number of Canadian and US immigration officers at airports overseas and enhance joint training of airline personnel.

13) International Cooperation

Undertake technical assistance to source and transit countries.

The Secure Flow of Goods

14) Harmonized Commercial Processing

Establish complementary systems for commercial processing, including audit-based programs and partnerships with industry to increase security. Explore the merits of a common program.

15) Clearance Away from the Border

Develop an integrated approach to improve security and facilitate trade through away-from-the-border processing for truck/rail cargo (and crews), including inland preclearance/post-clearance, international zones and pre-processing centers at the border, and maritime port intransit preclearance.

16) Joint Facilities

Establish criteria, under current legislation and regulations, for the creation of small, remote joint border facilities. Examine the legal and operational issues associated with the establishment of international zones and joint facilities, including armed protection or the arming of law enforcement officers in such zones and facilities.

17) Customs Data

Sign the Agreement on Sharing Data Related to Customs Fraud, exchange agreed upon customs data pursuant to NAFTA, and discuss what additional commercial and trade data should be shared for national security purposes.

18) Intransit Container Targeting at Seaports

Jointly target marine intransit containers arriving in Canada and the United States by exchanging information and analysts. Work in partnership with the industry to develop advance electronic commercial manifest data for marine containers arriving from overseas.

Secure Infrastructure

19) Infrastructure Improvements

Work to secure resources for joint and coordinated physical and technological improvements to key border points and trade corridors aimed at overcoming traffic management and growth challenges, including dedicated lanes and border modeling exercises.

20) Intelligent Transportation Systems

Deploy interoperable technologies in support of other initiatives to facilitate the secure movement of goods and people, such as transponder applications and electronic container seals.

21) Critical Infrastructure Protection

Conduct binational threat assessments on trans-border infrastructure and identify necessary additional protection measures, and initiate assessments for transportation networks and other critical infrastructure.

22) Aviation Security

Finalize Federal Aviation Administration-Transport Canada agreement on comparability/equivalence of security and training standards.

Coordination and Information Sharing in the Enforcement of These Objectives

23) Integrated Border and Marine Enforcement Teams

Expand IBET/IMET to other areas of the border and enhance communication and coordination.

24) Joint Enforcement Coordination

Works toward ensuring comprehensive and permanent coordination of law enforcement, anti-terrorism efforts and information sharing, such as by strengthening the Cross-Border Crime Forum and reinvigorating Project Northstar.

25) Integrated Intelligence

Establish joint teams to analyze and disseminate information and intelligence, and produce threat and intelligence assessments. Initiate discussions regarding a Canadian presence on the U.S. Foreign Terrorist Tracking Task Force.

26) Fingerprints

Implement the Memorandum of Understanding to supply equipment and training that will enable the RCMP to access FBI fingerprint data directly via real-time electronic link.

27) Removal of Deportees

Address legal and operational challenges to joint removals, and coordinate initiatives to encourage uncooperative countries to accept their nationals.

28) Counter-Terrorism Legislation

Bring into force legislation on terrorism, including measures for the designation of terrorist organizations.

29) Freezing of Terrorist Assets

Exchange advance information on designated individuals and organizations in a timely manner.

30) Joint Training and Exercises

Increase dialogue and commitment for the training and exercise programs needed to implement the joint response to terrorism guidelines. Joint counter-terrorism training and exercises are essential to building and sustaining effective efforts to combat terrorism and to build public confidence.

DOCUMENT NO. 21

THE CANADIAN ANTI TERRORIST ACT
BILL C-36

Assented to on December 18, 2001

COMMENTARY: *Through there are differences in specifics, this legislative initiative mirrors, in depth and timeliness, the actions taken in the United States and in the United Kingdom (see Document No. 22 following). Great care has been taken to assure the Canadian people that individual freedoms will not be jeopardized, with the same assurances being given both in the United States and in the United Kingdom where other new legislation is being passed.*

Anti-Terrorism Act Receives Royal Assent

OTTAWA December 18, 2001—The Government of Canada announced today that tough new legislation targeting terrorists has received Royal Assent. The new measures are a part of the Government's Anti-Terrorism Plan which takes aim at terrorist organizations and strengthens investigation, prosecution and prevention of terrorist activities at home and abroad.

"This legislation strikes at the new face of modern terrorism that we saw in the horrific events of September 11," said the Honourable Anne McLellan, Minister of Justice and Attorney General of Canada. "It reassures Canadians and our allies that Canada is serious about dealing with this long term threat to our peace and human security through effective laws that safeguard our rights and freedoms, including our most fundamental right to live in a secure and peaceful society."

The provisions under Bill C-36 will come into force soon after measures for implementation have been arranged with the provinces, territories, police and others responsible for enforcement.

Since the introduction of Bill C-36, the Government of Canada has listened carefully to the concerns of Canadians to ensure that the anti-terrorism legislation meets their needs. Canadians want measures that will protect their security and they support strong laws that deal effectively with terrorism. Canadians also want assurances that safeguards are in place to protect their rights and freedoms. The provisions in the *Anti-Terrorism Act* meet the need for protection of both human security and human rights.

The *Anti-Terrorism Act* includes measures to **deter, disable, identify, prosecute, convict and punish terrorists**, such as:

- defining and designating terrorist groups and activities to make it easier to prosecute terrorists and those who support them;
- making it an offence to knowingly participate in, contribute to or facilitate the activities of a terrorist group or to instruct anyone to carry out a terrorist activity or an activity on behalf of a terrorist group or to knowingly harbour a terrorist; and
- cutting off financial support for terrorists by making it a crime to knowingly collect or give funds, either directly or indirectly, in order to carry out terrorism, denying or removing charitable status from those who support terrorist groups, and by making it easier to freeze and seize their assets.

The Act will give law enforcement and national security agencies **new investigative tools** to gather knowledge about and prosecute terrorists and terrorist groups, as well as protect Canadians from terrorist acts, including:

- enhancing the ability to use electronic surveillance against terrorist groups with measures similar to those already in place for organized crime investigations;
- within carefully defined limits, allowing the arrest and imposition of supervisory conditions of release on suspected terrorists to prevent terrorist acts and save lives; and
- requiring individuals who have information related to a terrorist group or offence to appear before a judge to provide that information.

Measures have been included in the Act to address the root causes of hatred and to ensure Canadian values of equality, tolerance and fairness are affirmed in the wake of the September 11 attacks. These include:

- amending the *Criminal Code* to eliminate online hate propaganda and create a new offence of mischief against places of religious worship or religious property; and
- amending the *Canadian Human Rights Act* to clarify that the prohibition against spreading repeated hate messages by telephonic communications includes all telecommunications technologies.

The *Anti-Terrorism Act* contains rigorous **safeguards** to uphold the rights and freedoms of Canadians, which were further strengthened as a result of recommendations made by the House of Commons and Senate committees that studied the bill. These safeguards include:

- the Attorney General and Solicitor General of Canada, provincial Attorneys General and Ministers responsible for policing will be required to report annually to Parliament on the use of the preventive arrest and investigative hearing provisions in Bill C-36. In addition, the whole Act will be subject to a Parliamentary review in three years;

- provisions in the Act dealing with preventive arrest and investigative hearing powers will sunset after five years unless a resolution is passed by both the House of Commons and Senate to extend either or both of these powers for up to five more years. A provision will also be added to grandfather proceedings that have already started prior to the sunset date so that they can be completed, if the powers are not extended;

- the scope of *Criminal Code* provisions is clearly defined to ensure that they only apply to terrorists and terrorist groups; and

- the *Anti-Terrorism Act* is consistent with Canada's legal framework, including the *Canadian Charter of Rights and Freedoms*, the requirement for due process, and the consent of the Attorney General and judicial review where appropriate.

The *Anti-Terrorism Act* is a key component of the Government of Canada Anti-Terrorism Plan, and it parallels the actions taken by our international partners to combat terrorism.

Together with our international partners, Canada signed the Council of Europe's *Convention on Cybercrime* on November 23, 2001. The Convention is the first international agreement to facilitate the detection and prosecution of computer and computer-related crime, including cyberterrorism, money laundering and terrorist financing activities. Canada, led by the Department of Justice, played an important role in the drafting and negotiation of the convention.

Ref.:

Farah Mohamed
Minister's Office
Department of Justice
(613) 992-4621

Backgrounder

Royal Assent of Bill C-36
The Anti-Terrorism Act

The Government of Canada has taken steps to combat terrorism and terrorist activities at home and abroad through tough new anti-terrorism measures. The new package of legislation: creates measures to **deter, disable, identify, prosecute, convict and punish** terrorist groups; provides **new investigative tools** to law enforcement and national security agencies; and ensures that Canadian values of respect and fairness are preserved and the root causes of hatred are addressed through **stronger laws against hate crimes and propaganda**. The package also includes rigorous safeguards to ensure that the fundamental rights and freedoms of Canadians are upheld.

IDENTIFY, PROSECUTE, CONVICT AND PUNISH TERRORIST ACTIVITY

Under the *Criminal Code*, terrorists can already be prosecuted for hijacking, murder and other acts of violence. The Government of Canada has signed all 12 United Nations Conventions and under the new anti-terrorism measures, Canada will ratify the remaining two counter-terrorism conventions:

- *The Suppression of Terrorist Financing Convention* relates to the freezing of terrorist property by prohibiting dealing in any property of a person engaged in terrorist activities and prohibiting making available funds and financial or other related services to terrorists. Bill C-36 fulfils Canada's obligations under this convention and allows a Federal Court judge to order the seizure and forfeiture of property used in or related to terrorist activity. Fifteen other states have ratified this convention.

- *The Suppression of Terrorist Bombings Convention* contains provisions relating to the targeting of public places, government or infrastructure facilities or transportation systems with explosives or other lethal devices, including chemical or biological agents. Forty-five states have ratified this convention.

Through the *Anti-Terrorism Act*, Canada will also ratify the *Safety of United Nations and Associated Personnel Convention*, which relates to ensuring the safety of UN personnel, including peacekeepers, from attacks against their person, official premises, private accommodation and modes of transport.

Under Bill C-36, the *Criminal Code* will also be amended to establish provisions aimed at disabling and dismantling the activities of terrorist groups and those who support them. These include:

- defining "terrorist activity" in the *Criminal Code* as an action that takes place either within or outside of Canada that:
  - is an offence under one of the UN anti-terrorism conventions and protocols; or

- is taken for political, religious or ideological purposes and intimidates the public concerning its security, or compels a government to do something, by intentionally killing, seriously harming or endangering a person, causing substantial property damage that is likely to seriously harm people or by seriously interfering with or disrupting an essential service, facility or system.

Under this definition, there is an interpretive clause that states for greater clarity that an expression of political, religious or ideological beliefs alone is not a "terrorist activity," unless it is part of a larger conduct that meets all of the requirements of the definition of "terrorist activity." (i.e., conduct that is committed for a political, religious or ideological purpose, is intended to intimidate the public or compel a government, and intentionally causes death or serious physical harm to people.)

The definition makes it clear that disrupting an essential service is not a terrorist activity if it occurs during a protest or a work strike and is not intended to cause death or serious harm to persons.

- permitting the designation of groups whose activities meet the definition of terrorist activity as "terrorist groups."

This definition and designation framework forms the basis for new offences in the *Criminal Code* that will make it a crime to:

- knowingly collect or provide funds, either directly or indirectly, in order to carry out terrorist crimes. Using this definition, the Crown must prove that the accused collected, provided or made available funds that he or she knew would be used to help a terrorist group. Canadian courts will be given the jurisdiction to try this offence even if it has been committed outside Canada, when the accused is found in Canada. The maximum sentence will be 10 years.

- knowingly participate in, contribute to or facilitate the activities of a terrorist group. The participation or contribution itself does not have to be a criminal offence and will include knowingly recruiting new individuals for the purpose of enhancing the ability of the terrorist group to facilitate or commit terrorist activities. The maximum sentence for participating or contributing offences will be 10 years. The maximum sentence for facilitating will be 14 years.

- instruct anyone to carry out a terrorist activity on behalf of a terrorist group (a "leadership" offence). This offence carries a maximum life sentence.

- knowingly harbour or conceal a terrorist. The maximum sentence under this offence will be 10 years.

In addition, any indictable offence under any Act of Parliament that is committed for the benefit of, at the direction of, or in association with a terrorist group carries a maximum sentence of life imprisonment. An offender convicted of any indictable offence that is also a terrorist activity will be liable to life imprisonment.

The *Criminal Code* will also stipulate that the sentences imposed for each of these offences are to be served consecutively to any other sentence imposed relating to the same activity or event. The offender will also be ineligible for parole for half of the sentence imposed unless the accused can demonstrate that it is not in the public interest.

In addition to these *Criminal Code* reforms, the new definition and designation schemes will make it easier to remove or deny charitable status to those who support terrorist groups under the *Income Tax Act*.

To ensure that the courts can deal with an expected increase in enforcement, appeals and reviews connected to the Government's new Anti-Terrorism Plan, the Act will increase the number of Federal Court judge positions by up to 15. Of these new positions, 13 can be added to the Trial Division, while two can be added to the Court of Appeal.

STRONGER INVESTIGATIVE TOOLS

The new anti-terrorist measures will give new investigative tools to security, intelligence and law enforcement agencies and will ensure that the prosecution of terrorist offences can be undertaken efficiently and effectively. Measures will include:

- The investigatory powers currently in the *Criminal Code* and in Bill C-24 that make it easier to use electronic surveillance against criminal organizations will be applied to terrorist groups. This includes eliminating the need to demonstrate that electronic surveillance is a last resort in the investigation of terrorists. The proposed legislation will extend the period of validity of a wiretap authorization from the current 60 days to up to one year when police are investigating a terrorist group offence. A Superior Court judge will still have to approve the use of electronic surveillance to ensure that these powers are used appropriately. Further, the requirement to notify a target after surveillance has taken place can be delayed for up to three years.

- The *Criminal Code* will be amended to require individuals with information relevant to an ongoing investigation of a terrorist crime to appear before a judge to provide that information. This will require the consent of the Attorney General. This measure will increase the ability of law enforcement to effectively investigate and obtain evidence about terrorist organizations, subject to legal safeguards to protect the witness. For example, information given by a witness cannot be used against the witness in any current or future criminal proceedings.

- The *Criminal Code* will be amended to create a "preventive arrest" power to impose conditions of release where appropriate on suspected terrorists. This will prevent terrorist activity and protect the lives of Canadians. This will allow a peace officer to arrest and bring a person before a judge to impose reasonable supervisory conditions if there are reasonable grounds to suspect that the person is about to commit a terrorism activity. A warrant will be required except where exigent circumstances exist, and the person will have to be brought before a judge within 24 hours of an arrest. This will require the consent of the Attorney General.

- The *Official Secrets Act* will be amended to address national security concerns, including threats of espionage by foreign powers and terrorist groups, and the intimidation or coercion of ethnocultural communities in Canada. The Act will also have a new title, the *Security of Information Act*.

  New offences will be created to improve and modernize the "spying" provisions of the Act, taking into account new realities, including new players and new threats. These offences will focus upon those situations in which it is appropriate for Canada to protect its institutions and citizenry from information-related conduct that is harmful or likely to be harmful to Canada.

  New players other than the governments of traditional states include governments-in-waiting, governments in exile and other foreign powers, as well as terrorist groups.

  New threats that are being recognized include threats against ethnocultural communities in Canada, threats to trade secrets and threats to essential infrastructures, both public and private.

  The bill also includes specific new offences dealing with unauthorized communication, or purported communication, of special operational information (for example, the identity of confidential sources, covert agents or targets of CSIS) by persons permanently bound to secrecy.

- The *Canada Evidence Act* will be amended to address the judicial balancing of interests when the disclosure of information in judicial or other proceedings would encroach upon a specified public interest or be injurious to international relations or national defence or national security. Information that could be protected from disclosure might, for example, be information that, if disclosed, would threaten another country's vital interests or jeopardize intelligence networks.

- The *National Defence Act* will be amended to clarify the mandate of the Communications Security Establishment (CSE), under strict controls, to:
  - intercept the communications of foreign targets abroad; and
  - undertake security checks of government computer networks to protect them from terrorist activity.

The permission of the Minister of National Defence will be required to authorize any interception of private communications of foreign targets abroad in order to ensure that the privacy of individual Canadians is protected.

- The *Proceeds of Crime (Money Laundering) Act* will be amended to authorize the Financial Transactions and Reports and Analysis Centre (FINTRAC) to detect financial transactions that may constitute threats to the security of Canada and to disclose this information to the Canadian Security Intelligence Service (CSIS) and other law enforcement agencies.

- The DNA warrant scheme and data bank will be extended to include terrorist offences in the list of "primary designated offences" for which DNA samples can be taken and stored.

- On November 23, Canada signed the *Council of Europe Convention on Cyber-Crime*, which requires states to criminalize certain forms of abuse of computer systems and certain crimes, like hacking, when they are committed through the use of computer systems. The convention also supports international cooperation to detect, investigate and prosecute these criminal offences, as well as to collect electronic evidence of any criminal offence, including terrorist crimes, terrorist financing and money laundering offences. Some of the other prohibited activities covered by the Convention include interference of computer systems, computer fraud and forgery.

STRONGER LAWS AGAINST HATE CRIMES AND PROPAGANDA

Following the attack on September 11, Canadians have called for a renewed commitment to values of respect, equality, diversity and fairness and a strong condemnation of hate-motivated violence. Bill C-36 contains legislation that addresses the root causes of hatred, reaffirms Canadian values and ensures that Canada's respect for justice and diversity is reinforced. These measures include:

- amendments to the *Criminal Code* that allow the courts to order the deletion of publicly available hate propaganda from computer systems such as an Internet site. Individuals who post the material will be given the opportunity to convince the court that the material is not hate propaganda. The provision applies to hate propaganda that is located on Canadian computer systems, regardless of where the owner of the material is located or whether he or she can be identified.

- *Criminal Code* amendments that create a new offence of mischief motivated by bias, prejudice or hate based on religion, race, colour or national or ethnic origin, committed against a place of religious worship or associated religious property, including cemeteries. This offence carries a maximum penalty of 10 years when prosecuted on indictment, or to a maximum penalty of eighteen months on summary conviction.

- amending the *Canadian Human Rights Act* to clarify that the prohibition against spreading repeated hate messages by telephonic communications includes all telecommunications technologies.

COMPREHENSIVE SAFEGUARDS

Canadians have expressed concerns about their security and support strong laws that deal effectively with terrorism. Canadians also want assurances that safeguards are in place to protect their rights and freedoms. Bill C-36 contains measures to protect both human security and human rights under the *Canadian Charter of Rights and Freedoms*. These safeguards include:

- the Attorney General and Solicitor General of Canada, provincial Attorneys General and Ministers responsible for policing will be required to report annually to Parliament on the use of preventive arrest and investigative hearing provisions in Bill C-36.

- a Parliamentary review of the anti-terrorism legislation as a whole in three years.

- provisions in the Act dealing with preventive arrest and investigative hearing powers will sunset after five years unless a resolution is passed by both the House of Commons and Senate to extend either or both of these powers for up to five more years. Proceedings that have already started prior to the sunset date will be grandfathered so that they could be completed, if the powers are not extended

- the scope of the *Criminal Code* provisions is clearly defined so that they are targeted at terrorists and terrorist groups. This is a campaign against terrorists and not against any one community, group or faith. Legitimate political activism and protests are also protected through the precise definition of terrorist activities.

- Attorney General certificates prohibiting the release of information will be subject to review by a judge of the Federal Court of Appeal. In addition, the existing provisions and process for the collection, use and protection of information will be preserved under the *Privacy Act* and the *Personal Information Protection and Electronic Documents Act*.

- the burden of proof is on the state to establish that there was knowledge or intent on the part of the accused "for the purpose of facilitating or carrying out terrorist activity."

- the process of adding a group to the list of terrorists incorporates a number of protections including provisions for removal from the list, judicial review and safeguards to address cases of mistaken identity. As well, the list must be reviewed every two years by the Solicitor General.

- the Attorney General's consent is required to prosecute all of the new terrorism offences.

- the Minister of Defence's authorization is required for the Communications and Security Establishment to intercept foreign communications targeted against a non-Canadian abroad that may have a Canadian connection.

Department of Justice
December 18, 2001

RECOMMENDATION

Her Excellency the Governor General recommends to the House of Commons the appropriation of public revenue under the circumstances, in the manner and for the purposes set out in a measure entitled "*An Act to amend the Criminal Code, the Official Secrets Act, the Canada Evidence Act, the Proceeds of Crime (Money Laundering) Act and other Acts, and to enact measures respecting the registration of charities, in order to combat terrorism*".

SUMMARY

This enactment amends the *Criminal Code*, the *Official Secrets Act*, the *Canada Evidence Act*, the *Proceeds of Crime (Money Laundering) Act* and a number of other Acts, and enacts the *Charities Registration (Security Information) Act*, in order to combat terrorism.

Part 1 amends the *Criminal Code* to implement international conventions related to terrorism, to create offences related to terrorism, including the financing of terrorism and the participation, facilitation and carrying out of terrorist activities, and to provide a means by which property belonging to terrorist groups, or property linked to terrorist activities, can be seized, restrained and forfeited. It also provides for the deletion of hate propaganda from public web sites and creates an offence relating to damage to property associated with religious worship.

Part 2 amends the *Official Secrets Act*, which becomes the *Security of Information Act*. It addresses national security concerns, including threats of espionage by foreign powers and terrorist groups, economic espionage and coercive activities against émigré communities in Canada. It creates new offences to counter intelligence-gathering activities by foreign powers and terrorist groups, as well as other offences, including the unauthorized communication of special operational information.

Part 3 amends the *Canada Evidence Act* to address the judicial balancing of interests when the disclosure of information in legal proceedings would encroach on a specified public interest or be injurious to international relations or national defence or security. The amendments impose obligations on parties to notify the Attorney General of Canada if they anticipate the disclosure of sensitive information or information the disclosure of which could be injurious to international relations or national defence or security, and they give the Attorney General the powers to assume carriage of a prosecution and to prohibit the disclosure of information in connection with a proceeding for the purpose of protecting international relations or national defence or security.

Part 4 amends the *Proceeds of Crime (Money Laundering) Act*, which becomes the *Proceeds of Crime (Money Laundering) and Terrorist Financing Act*. The amendments will assist law enforcement and investigative agencies in the detection and deterrence of the financing of terrorist activities, facilitate the investigation and prosecution of terrorist activity financing offences, and improve Canada's ability to cooperate internationally in the fight against terrorism.

Part 5 amends the *Access to Information Act, Canadian Human Rights Act, Canadian Security Intelligence Service Act, Corrections and Conditional Release Act, Federal Court Act, Firearms Act, National Defence Act, Personal Information Protection and Electronic Documents Act, Privacy Act, Seized Property Management Act* and *United Nations Act*. The amendments to the *National Defence Act* clarify the powers of the Communications Security Establishment to combat terrorism.

Part 6 enacts the *Charities Registration (Security Information) Act*, and amends the *Income Tax Act*, in order to prevent those who support terrorist or related activities from enjoying the tax privileges granted to registered charities.

BILL C-36

TABLE OF PROVISIONS

AN ACT TO AMEND THE CRIMINAL CODE, THE OFFICIAL SECRETS ACT, THE CANADA EVIDENCE ACT, THE PROCEEDS OF CRIME (MONEY LAUNDERING) ACT AND OTHER ACTS, AND TO ENACT MEASURES RESPECTING THE REGISTRATION OF CHARITIES, IN ORDER TO COMBAT TERRORISM

SHORT TITLE

An Act respecting the registration of charities having regard to security and criminal intelligence information

SHORT TITLE

PURPOSE AND PRINCIPLES

INTERPRETATION

CERTIFICATE BASED ON INTELLIGENCE

JUDICIAL CONSIDERATION OF CERTIFICATE

EVIDENCE

REVIEW OF CERTIFICATE

PART 7
COORDINATING, REVIEW AND COMMENCEMENT PROVISIONS

Coordinating Amendments

SCHEDULES 1 AND 2

(The text of Bill C-36 is not reproduced.)

INTERNATIONAL DOCUMENTS

United Kingdom

DOCUMENT 22

ANTI-TERRORISM, CRIME AND SECURITY BILL

Introduced on November 13, 2001

EXPLANATORY NOTES

Explanatory notes to the Bill, prepared by the Home Office, Her Majesty's Treasury, the Department of Trade and Industry, the Department for Transport, Local Government and the Regions, and the Foreign and Commonwealth Office, will be published as Bill 49—EN.

EUROPEAN CONVENTION ON HUMAN RIGHTS

Mr Secretary Blunkett has made the following statement under section 19(1)(a) of the Human Rights Act 1998:

In my view the provisions of the Anti-terrorism, Crime and Security Bill are compatible with the Convention rights.

A BILL TO

Amend the Terrorism Act 2000; to make further provision about terrorism and security; to provide for the freezing of assets; to make provision about immigration and asylum; to amend or extend the criminal law and powers for preventing crime and enforcing that law; to make provision about the control of pathogens and toxins; to provide for the retention of communications data; to provide for implementation of Title VI of the Treaty on European Union; and for connected purposes.

Be it enacted by the Queen's most Excellent Majesty, by and with the advice and consent of the Lords Spiritual and Temporal, and Commons, in this present Parliament assembled, and by the authority of the same, as follows:—

PART 1

TERRORIST PROPERTY

1 Forfeiture of terrorist cash

(1) Schedule 1 (which makes provision for enabling cash which—

(a) is intended to be used for the purposes of terrorism,

(b) consists of resources of an organisation which is a proscribed organisation, or

(c) is, or represents, property obtained through terrorism, to be forfeited in civil proceedings before a magistrates' court or (in Scotland) the sheriff) is to have effect.

(2) The powers conferred by Schedule 1 are exercisable in relation to any cash whether or not any proceedings have been brought for an offence in connection with the cash.

(3) Expressions used in this section have the same meaning as in Schedule 1.

(4) Sections 24 to 31 of the Terrorism Act 2000 (c. 11) (seizure of terrorist cash) are to cease to have effect.

(5) An order under section 123 bringing Schedule 1 into force may make any modifications of any code of practice then in operation under Schedule 14 to the Terrorism Act 2000 (exercise of officers' powers) which the Secretary of State thinks necessary or expedient.

2 Amendments relating to section 1

(1) In Schedule 2 to the Access to Justice Act 1999 (c. 22) (services excluded from the Community Legal Service), paragraph 2 (exclusion of advocacy: exceptions) is amended as follows.

(2) In paragraph 2(2) (Crown Court), after paragraph (c) insert—

"or

(d) which relate to an order under paragraph 6 of Schedule 1 to the Anti-terrorism, Crime and Security Act 2001",

and omit the "or" at the end of paragraph (b).

(3) In paragraph 2(3) (magistrates' courts), in paragraph (j), after "1998" insert—

"or

(k) for an order or direction under paragraph 3, 5, 6 or 9 of Schedule 1 to the Anti-terrorism, Crime and Security Act 2001",

and omit the "or" at the end of paragraph (i).

(4) Schedule 14 to the Terrorism Act 2000 (c. 11) (exercise of officers' powers) is amended as follows.

(5) In paragraph 1—

(a) in paragraph (a), for "section 24" substitute "the terrorist cash provisions", and

(b) after paragraph (b) insert—

"and "the terrorist cash provisions" means Schedule 1 to the Anti-terrorism, Crime and Security Act 2001".

(6) In paragraphs 2, 3 and 6(1), at the end insert "or the terrorist cash provisions".

(7) In paragraph 5, after "Act" insert "or the terrorist cash provisions".

(8) In Part I of Schedule 1 to the Legal Aid, Advice and Assistance (Northern Ireland) Order 1981 (S.I.1981/228 (N.I.8)) (proceedings for which legal aid may be given under Part II of the Order), in paragraph 3 (courts of summary jurisdiction) after sub-paragraph (h) insert—

"(i) proceedings under paragraphs 3, 5, 6 and 9 of Schedule 1 to the Anti-terrorism, Crime and Security Act 2001".

3 Terrorist property: amendments

Schedule 2 contains amendments to the Terrorism Act 2000.

PART2

FREEZING ORDERS

Orders

4 Power to make order

(1) The Treasury may make a freezing order if the following two conditions are satisfied.

(2) The first condition is that the Treasury reasonably believe that—

(a) action to the detriment of the United Kingdom's economy (or part of it) has been or is likely to be taken by a person or persons, or

(b) action constituting a threat to the life or property of one or more nationals of the United Kingdom or residents of the United Kingdom has been or is likely to be taken by a person or persons.

(3) If one person is believed to have taken or to be likely to take the action the second condition is that the person is—

(a) the government of a country or territory outside the United Kingdom, or

(b) a resident of a country or territory outside the United Kingdom.

(4) If two or more persons are believed to have taken or to be likely to take the action the second condition is that each of them falls within paragraph (a) or(b) of subsection (3); and different persons may fall within different paragraphs.

5 Contents of order

(1) A freezing order is an order which prohibits persons from making funds available to or for the benefit of a person or persons specified in the order.

(2) The order must provide that these are the persons who are prohibited—

(a) all persons in the United Kingdom, and

(b) all persons elsewhere who are nationals of the United Kingdom or are bodies incorporated under the law of any part of the United Kingdom or are Scottish partnerships.

(3) The order may specify the following (and only the following) as the person or persons to whom or for whose benefit funds are not to be made available—

(a) the person or persons reasonably believed by the Treasury to have taken or to be likely to take the action referred to in section 4;

(b) any person the Treasury reasonably believe has provided or is likely to provide assistance (directly or indirectly) to that person or any of those persons.

(4) A person may be specified under subsection (3) by—

(a) being named in the order, or

(b) falling within a description of persons set out in the order.

(5) The description must be such that a reasonable person would know whether he fell within it.

(6) Funds are financial assets and economic benefits of any kind.

6 Contents: further provisions

Schedule 3 contains further provisions about the contents of freezing orders.

7 Review of order

The Treasury must keep a freezing order under review.

8 Duration of order

A freezing order ceases to have effect at the end of the period of 2 years starting with the day on which it is made.

Interpretation

9 Nationals and residents

(1) A national of the United Kingdom is an individual who is—

(a) a British citizen, a British Dependent Territories citizen, a British National (Overseas) or a British Overseas citizen,

(b) a person who under the British Nationality Act 1981 (c. 61) is a British subject, or

(c) a British protected person within the meaning of that Act.

(2) A resident of the United Kingdom is—

(a) an individual who is ordinarily resident in the United Kingdom,

(b) a body incorporated under the law of any part of the United Kingdom, or

(c) a Scottish partnership.

(3) A resident of a country or territory outside the United Kingdom is—

(a) an individual who is ordinarily resident in such a country or territory, or

(b) a body incorporated under the law of such a country or territory.

(4) For the purposes of subsection (3)(b) a branch situated in a country or territory outside the United Kingdom of—

(a) a body incorporated under the law of any part of the United Kingdom, or

(b) a Scottish partnership,

is to be treated as a body incorporated under the law of the country or territory where the branch is situated.

(5) This section applies for the purposes of this Part.

Orders: procedure etc.

10 Procedure for making freezing orders

(1) A power to make a freezing order is exercisable by statutory instrument.

(2) A freezing order—

(a) must be laid before Parliament after being made;

(b) ceases to have effect at the end of the relevant period unless before the end of that period the order is approved by a resolution of each House of Parliament (but without that affecting anything done under the order or the power to make a new order).

(3) The relevant period is a period of 28 days starting with the day on which the order is made.

(4) In calculating the relevant period no account is to be taken of any time during which Parliament is dissolved or prorogued or during which both Houses are adjourned for more than 4 days.

(5) If the Treasury propose to make a freezing order in the belief that the condition in section 4(2)(b) is satisfied, they must not make the order unless they consult the Secretary of State.

11 Procedure for making certain amending orders

(1) This section applies if—

(a) a freezing order is made specifying by description (rather than by name) the person or persons to whom or for whose benefit funds are not to be made available,

(b) it is proposed to make a further order which amends the freezing order only so as to make it specify by name the person or persons (or any of the persons) to whom or for whose benefit funds are not to be made available, and

(c) the further order states that the Treasury believe that the person or persons named fall within the description contained in the freezing order.

(2) This section also applies if—

(a) a freezing order is made specifying by name the person or persons to whom or for whose benefit funds are not to be made available,

(b) it is proposed to make a further order which amends the freezing order only so as to make it specify by name a further person or further persons to whom or for whose benefit funds are not to be made available, and

(c) the further order states that the Treasury believe that the further person or persons fall within the same description as the person or persons specified in the freezing order.

(3) This section also applies if—

(a) a freezing order is made, and

(b) it is proposed to make a further order which amends the freezing order only so as to make it specify (whether by name or description) fewer persons to whom or for whose benefit funds are not to be made available.

(4) If this section applies, a statutory instrument containing the further order is subject to annulment in pursuance of a resolution of either House of Parliament.

12 Procedure for revoking orders

A statutory instrument containing an order revoking a freezing order (without re-enacting it) is subject to annulment in pursuance of a resolution of either House of Parliament.

13 De-hybridisation

If apart from this section an order under this Part would be treated for the purposes of the standing orders of either House of Parliament as a hybrid instrument, it is to proceed in that House as if it were not such an instrument.

14 Orders: supplementary

(1) Where this Part confers a power to make provision, different provision may be made for different purposes.

(2) An order under this Part may include supplementary, incidental, saving or transitional provisions.

(3) Nothing in this Part affects the generality of subsection (2).

Miscellaneous

15 The Crown

(1) A freezing order binds the Crown, subject to the following provisions of this section.

(2) No contravention by the Crown of a provision of a freezing order makes the Crown criminally liable; but the High Court or in Scotland the Court of Session may, on the application of a person appearing to the Court to have an interest, declare unlawful any act or omission of the Crown which constitutes such a contravention.

(3) Nothing in this section affects Her Majesty in her private capacity; and this is to be construed as if section 38(3) of the Crown Proceedings Act 1947 (c. 44) (meaning of Her Majesty in her private capacity) were contained in this Act.

16 Repeals

(1) These provisions shall cease to have effect—

   (a) section 2 of the Emergency Laws (Re-enactments and Repeals) Act 1964 (c. 60) (Treasury's power to prohibit action on certain orders as to gold etc);

   (b) section 55 of the Finance Act 1968 (c. 44) (meaning of security in section 2 of 1964 Act).

(2) Subsection (1) does not affect a reference which—

   (a) is to a provision referred to in that subsection, and

   (b) is contained in a provision made under an Act.

PART 3

DISCLOSURE OF INFORMATION

17 Extension of existing disclosure powers

(1) This section applies to the provisions listed in Schedule 4, so far as they authorise the disclosure of information.

(2) Each of the provisions to which this section applies shall have effect, in relation to the disclosure of information by or on behalf of a public authority, as if the purposes for which the disclosure of information is authorised by that provision included each of the following—

   (a) the purposes of any criminal investigation whatever which is being or may be carried out, whether in the United Kingdom or elsewhere;

(b) the purposes of any criminal proceedings whatever which have been or may be initiated, whether in the United Kingdom or elsewhere;

(c) the purposes of the initiation or bringing to an end of any such investigation or proceedings;

(d) the purpose of facilitating a determination of whether any such investigation or proceedings should be initiated or brought to an end.

(3) The Treasury may by order made by statutory instrument add any provision contained in any subordinate legislation to the provisions to which this section applies.

(4) A statutory instrument containing an order under subsection (3) shall be subject to annulment in pursuance of a resolution of either House of Parliament.

(5) Nothing in this section shall be taken to prejudice any power to disclose information which exists apart from this section.

(6) The information that may be disclosed by virtue of this section includes information obtained before the commencement of this section.

18 Restriction on disclosure of information for overseas purposes

(1) Subject to subsections (2) and (3), the Secretary of State may give a direction which—

(a) specifies any overseas proceedings or any description of overseas proceedings; and

(b) prohibits the making of any relevant disclosure for the purposes of those proceedings or, as the case may be, of proceedings of that description.

(2) In subsection (1) the reference, in relation to a direction, to a relevant disclosure is a reference to a disclosure authorised by any of the provisions to which section 17 applies which—

(a) is made for a purpose mentioned in subsection (2)(a) to (d) of that section; and

(b) is a disclosure of any such information as is described in the direction.

(3) The Secretary of State shall not give a direction under this section unless it appears to him that the overseas proceedings in question, or that overseas proceedings of the description in question, relate or would relate—

(a) to a matter in respect of which it would be more appropriate for any jurisdiction or investigation to be exercised or carried out by a court or other authority of the United Kingdom, or of a particular part of the United Kingdom;

(b) to a matter in respect of which it would be more appropriate for any jurisdiction or investigation to be exercised or carried out by a court or other authority of a third country; or

(c) to a matter that would fall within paragraph (a) or (b)—

(i) if it were appropriate for there to be any exercise of jurisdiction or investigation at all; and

(ii) if (where one does not exist) a court or other authority with the necessary jurisdiction or functions existed in the United Kingdom, in the part of the United Kingdom in question or, as the case may be, in the third country in question.

(4) A direction under this section shall not have the effect of prohibiting—

(a) the making of any disclosure by a Minister of the Crown or by the Treasury; or

(b) the making of any disclosure in pursuance of a Community obligation.

(5) A direction under this section—

(a) may prohibit the making of disclosures absolutely or in such cases, or subject to such conditions as to consent or otherwise, as may be specified in it; and

(b) must be published or otherwise issued by the Secretary of State in such manner as he considers appropriate for bringing it to the attention of persons likely to be affected by it.

(6) A person who, knowing of any direction under this section, discloses any information in contravention of that direction shall be guilty of an offence and liable—

(a) on conviction on indictment, to imprisonment for a term not exceeding two years or to a fine or to both;

(b) on summary conviction, to imprisonment for a term not exceeding three months or to a fine not exceeding the statutory maximum or to both.

(7) The following are overseas proceedings for the purposes of this section—

(a) criminal proceedings which are taking place, or will or may take place, in a country or territory outside the United Kingdom;

(b) a criminal investigation which is being, or will or may be, conducted by an authority of any such country or territory.

(8) References in this section, in relation to any proceedings or investigation, to a third country are references to any country or territory outside

the United Kingdom which is not the country or territory where the proceedings are taking place, or will or may take place or, as the case may be, is
not the country or territory of the authority which is conducting the investigation, or which will or may conduct it.

(9) In this section "court" includes a tribunal of any description.

19 Disclosure of information held by revenue departments

(1) This section applies to information which is held by or on behalf of the
Commissioners of Inland Revenue or by or on behalf of the Commissioners
of Customs and Excise, including information obtained before the coming
into force of this section.

(2) No obligation of secrecy imposed by statute or otherwise prevents the
disclosure, in accordance with the following provisions of this section, of
information to which this section applies if the disclosure is made—

   (a) for the purpose of facilitating the carrying out by any of the intelligence services of any of that service's functions;

   (b) for the purposes of any criminal investigation whatever which is being or may be carried out, whether in the United Kingdom or elsewhere;

   (c) for the purposes of any criminal proceedings whatever which have
   been or may be initiated, whether in the United Kingdom or elsewhere;

   (d) for the purposes of the initiation or bringing to an end of any such
   investigation or proceedings; or

   (e) for the purpose of facilitating a determination of whether any such
   investigation or proceedings should be initiated or brought to an end.

(3) Information to which this section applies shall not be disclosed by virtue of this section except by the Commissioners by or on whose behalf it is
held or with their authority.

(4) Information obtained by means of a disclosure authorised by subsection
(2) shall not be further disclosed except—

   (a) for a purpose mentioned in that subsection; and

   (b) with the consent of the Commissioners by whom or with whose authority it was initially disclosed;

and information so obtained otherwise than by or on behalf of any of the
intelligence services shall not be further disclosed (with or without such
consent) to any of those services, or to any person acting on behalf of any
of those services, except for a purpose mentioned in paragraphs (b) to (e) of
that subsection.

(5) A consent for the purposes of subsection (4) may be given either in relation to a particular disclosure or in relation to disclosures made in such circumstances as may be specified or described in the consent.

(6) Nothing in this section authorises the making of any disclosure which is prohibited by any provision of the Data Protection Act 1998 (c. 29).

(7) References in this section to information which is held on behalf of the Commissioners of Inland Revenue or of the Commissioners of Customs and Excise include references to information which—

(a) is held by a person who provides services to the Commissioners of Inland Revenue or, as the case may be, to the Commissioners of Customs and Excise; and

(b) is held by that person in connection with the provision of those services.

(8) In this section "intelligence service" has the same meaning as in the Regulation of Investigatory Powers Act 2000 (c. 23).

(9) Nothing in this section shall be taken to prejudice any power to disclose information which exists apart from this section.

20 Interpretation of Part 3

(1) In this Part—

"criminal investigation" means an investigation of any criminal conduct, including an investigation of alleged or suspected criminal conduct and an investigation of whether criminal conduct has taken place; "information" includes—

(a) documents; and

(b) in relation to a disclosure authorised by a provision to which section 17 applies, anything that falls to be treated as information for the purposes of that provision;

"public authority" has the same meaning as in section 6 of the HumanRights Act 1998 (c. 42); and

"subordinate legislation" has the same meaning as in the Interpretation

Act 1978 (c. 30).

(2) Proceedings outside the United Kingdom shall not be taken to be criminal proceedings for the purposes of this Part unless the conduct with which the defendant in those proceedings is charged is criminal conduct or conduct which, to a substantial extent, consists of criminal conduct.

(3) In this section—

"conduct" includes acts, omissions and statements; and

"criminal conduct" means any conduct which—

(a) constitutes one or more criminal offences under the law of a part of the United Kingdom; or

(b) is, or corresponds to, conduct which, if it all took place in a particular part of the United Kingdom, would constitute one or more offences under the law of that part of the United Kingdom.

PART 4

IMMIGRATION AND ASYLUM

Suspected international terrorists

21 Suspected international terrorist: certification

(1) The Secretary of State may issue a certificate under this section in respect of a person if the Secretary of State—

(a) believes that the person's presence in the United Kingdom is a risk to national security, and

(b) suspects that the person is an international terrorist.

(2) In subsection (1)(b) "international terrorist" means a person who—

(a) is or has been concerned in the commission, preparation or instigation of acts of international terrorism,

(b) is a member of or belongs to an international terrorist group, or

(c) has links with a person who is a member of or belongs to an international terrorist group.

(3) A group is an international terrorist group for the purposes of subsection (2)(b) and (c) if—

(a) it is subject to the control or influence of persons outside the United Kingdom, and

(b) the Secretary of State suspects that it is concerned in the commission, preparation or instigation of acts of international terrorism.

(4) In this Part—

"terrorism" has the meaning given by section 1 of the Terrorism Act 2000 (c. 11), "international terrorism" does not include terrorism concerned only with the affairs of a part of the United Kingdom, and

"suspected international terrorist" means a person certified under subsection (1).

(5) Where the Secretary of State issues a certificate under subsection (1) he shall as soon as is reasonably practicable—

(a) take reasonable steps to notify the person certified, and

(b) send a copy of the certificate to the Special Immigration Appeals Commission.

(6) The Secretary of Sate may revoke a certificate issued under subsection (1).

22 Deportation, removal, &c.

(1) An action of a kind specified in subsection (2) may be taken in respect of a suspected international terrorist despite the fact that (whether temporarily or indefinitely) the action cannot result in his removal from the United Kingdom because of—

(a) a point of law which wholly or partly relates to an international agreement, or

(b) a practical consideration.

(2) The actions mentioned in subsection (1) are—

(a) refusing leave to enter or remain in the United Kingdom in accordance with provision made by or by virtue of any of sections 3 to 3B of the Immigration Act 1971 (c. 77) (control of entry to United Kingdom),

(b) varying a limited leave to enter or remain in the United Kingdom in accordance with provision made by or by virtue of any of those sections,

(c) recommending deportation in accordance with section 3(6) of that Act (recommendation by court),

(d) taking a decision to make a deportation order under section 5(1) of that Act (deportation by Secretary of State),

(e) making a deportation order under section 5(1) of that Act,

(f) refusing to revoke a deportation order,

(g) cancelling leave to enter the United Kingdom in accordance with paragraph 2A of Schedule 2 to that Act (person arriving with continuous leave),

(h) giving directions for a person's removal from the United Kingdom under any of paragraphs 8 to 10 or 12 to 14 of Schedule 2 to that Act (control of entry to United Kingdom),

(i) giving directions for a person's removal from the United Kingdom under section 10 of the Immigration and Asylum Act 1999 (c. 33) (person unlawfully in United Kingdom), and

(j) giving notice to a person in accordance with regulations under paragraph 1 of Schedule 4 to that Act of a decision to make a deportation order against him.

(3) Action of a kind specified in subsection (2) which has effect in respect of a suspected international terrorist at the time of his certification under section 21 shall be treated as taken again (in reliance on subsection (1) above) immediately after certification.

23 Detention

(1) A suspected international terrorist may be detained under a provision specified in subsection (2) despite the fact that his removal or departure from the United Kingdom is prevented (whether temporarily or indefinitely) by—

(a) a point of law which wholly or partly relates to an international agreement, or

(b) a practical consideration.

(2) The provisions mentioned in subsection (1) are—

(a) paragraph 16 of Schedule 2 to the Immigration Act 1971 (c. 77) (detention of persons liable to examination or removal), and

(b) paragraph 2 of Schedule 3 to that Act (detention pending deportation).

24 Bail

(1) A suspected international terrorist who is detained under a provision of the Immigration Act 1971 may be released on bail.

(2) For the purpose of subsection (1) the following provisions of Schedule 2 to the Immigration Act 1971 (control on entry) shall apply with the modifications specified in Schedule 3 to the Special Immigration Appeals Commission Act 1997 (c. 68) (bail to be determined by Special Immigration Appeals Commission) and with any other necessary modifications—

(a) paragraph 22(1A), (2) and (3) (release),

(b) paragraph 23 (forfeiture),

(c) paragraph 24 (arrest), and

(d) paragraph 30(1) (requirement of Secretary of State's consent).

(3) Rules of procedure under the Special Immigration Appeals Commission Act 1997—

   (a) may make provision in relation to release on bail by virtue of this section, and

   (b) subject to provision made by virtue of paragraph (a), shall apply in relation to release on bail by virtue of this section as they apply in relation to release on bail by virtue of that Act subject to any modification which the Commission considers necessary.

25 Certification: appeal

(1) A suspected international terrorist may appeal to the Special Immigration Appeals Commission against his certification under section 21.

(2) On an appeal the Commission must cancel the certificate if—

   (a) it does not agree with the belief or suspicion referred to in section 21(1)(a) or (b), or

   (b) it considers that for some other reason the certificate should not have been issued.

(3) If the Commission determines not to cancel a certificate it must dismiss the appeal.

(4) Where a certificate is cancelled under subsection (2) it shall be treated as never having been issued.

(5) An appeal against certification may not be commenced after the period of three months beginning with the date on which the certificate is issued.

26 Certification: review

(1) The Special Immigration Appeals Commission must review each certificate issued under section 21—

   (a) in a case where an appeal is brought under section 25, as soon as is reasonably practicable after the expiry of the period of six months beginning with the date on which the appeal is finally determined, and

   (b) in a case where no appeal is brought, as soon as is reasonably practicable after the expiry of the period of six months beginning with the date on which the certificate is issued.

(2) The Commission must review each certificate issued under section 21 as soon as is reasonably practicable after the expiry of the period of six months beginning with the date on which a review under subsection (1) or this subsection is finally determined.

(3) The Commission may review a certificate during a period mentioned in subsection (1) or (2) if—

(a) the person certified applies for a review, and

(b) the Commission considers that a review should be held because of a change in circumstance.

(4) On a review the Commission—

(a) must cancel the certificate if it does not agree with the belief or suspicion referred to in section 21(1)(a) or (b), and

(b) otherwise, may not make any order (save as to leave to appeal).

(5) A certificate cancelled by order of the Commission under subsection (4) ceases to have effect at the end of the day on which the order is made.

(6) Where the Commission reviews a certificate under subsection (3), the period for determining the next review of the certificate under subsection (2) shall begin with the date of the final determination of the review under subsection (3).

27 Appeal and review: supplementary

(1) The following provisions of the Special Immigration Appeals Commission Act 1997 (c. 68) shall apply in relation to an appeal or review under section 25 or 26 as they apply in relation to an appeal under section 2 of that Act—

(a) section 6 (person to represent appellant's interests),

(b) section 7 (further appeal on point of law), and

(c) section 7A (pending appeal).

(2) The reference in subsection (1) to an appeal or review does not include a reference to a decision made or action taken on or in connection with—

(a) an application under section 26(3)(a) of this Act, or

(b) subsection (8) below.

(3) Subsection (4) applies where—

(a) a further appeal is brought by virtue of subsection (1)(b) in connection with an appeal or review, and

(b) the Secretary of State notifies the Commission that in his opinion the further appeal is confined to calling into question one or more derogation matters within the meaning of section 30 of this Act.

(4) For the purpose of the application of section 26(1) and (2) of this Act the determination by the Commission of the appeal or review in connection

with which the further appeal is brought shall be treated as a final determination.

(5) Rules under section 5 or 8 of the Special Immigration Appeals Commission Act 1997 (general procedure; and leave to appeal) may make provision about an appeal, review or application under section 25 or 26 of this Act.

(6) Subject to any provision made by virtue of subsection (5), rules under section 5 or 8 of that Act shall apply in relation to an appeal, review or application under section 25 or 26 of this Act with any modification which the Commission considers necessary.

(7) Subsection (8) applies where the Commission considers that an appeal or review under section 25 or 26 which relates to a person's certification under section 21 is likely to raise an issue which is also likely to be raised in other proceedings before the Commission which relate to the same person.

(8) The Commission shall so far as is reasonably practicable—

(a) deal with the two sets of proceedings together, and

(b) avoid or minimise delay to either set of proceedings as a result of compliance with paragraph (a).

(9) Cancellation by the Commission of a certificate issued under section 21 shall not prevent the Secretary of State from issuing another certificate, whether on the grounds of a change of circumstance or otherwise.

(10) The reference in section 81 of the Immigration and Asylum Act 1999 (c. 33) (grants to voluntary organisations) to persons who have rights of appeal under that Act shall be treated as including a reference to suspected international terrorists.

28 Duration of sections 21 to 23

(1) Sections 21 to 23 shall, subject to the following provisions of this section, expire at the end of the period of 15 months beginning with the day on which this Act is passed.

(2) The Secretary of State may by order—

(a) repeal sections 21 to 23;

(b) revive those sections for a period not exceeding one year;

(c) provide that those sections shall not expire in accordance with subsection (1) or an order under paragraph (b) or this paragraph, but shall continue in force for a period not exceeding one year.

(3) An order under subsection (2)—

(a) must be made by statutory instrument, and

(b) may not be made unless a draft has been laid before and approved by resolution of each House of Parliament.

(4) An order may be made without compliance with subsection (3)(b) if it contains a declaration by the Secretary of State that by reason of urgency it is necessary to make the order without laying a draft before Parliament; in which case the order—

(a) must be laid before Parliament, and

(b) shall cease to have effect at the end of the period specified in subsection (5) unless the order is approved during that period by resolution of each House of Parliament.

(5) The period referred to in subsection (4)(b) is the period of 40 days—

(a) beginning with the day on which the order is made, and

(b) ignoring any period during which Parliament is dissolved or prorogued or during which both Houses are adjourned for more than four days.

(6) The fact that an order ceases to have effect by virtue of subsection (4)—

(a) shall not affect the lawfulness of anything done before the order ceases to have effect, and

(b) shall not prevent the making of a new order.

29 Exclusion of legal proceedings

(1) No court or tribunal may, except as provided by a provision of this Part, entertain proceedings for questioning—

(a) a decision or action of the Secretary of State in connection with certification under section 21 or a provision of sections 21 to 31, or

(b) a decision or action of the Special Immigration Appeals Commission taken by virtue of or in connection with a provision of sections 21 to 27.

(2) No court or tribunal other than the Special Immigration Appeals Commission may entertain proceedings for questioning an action of the Secretary of State taken in reliance on section 22 or 23.

(3) A certificate of the Secretary of State that specified action is taken in reliance on section 22 or 23 shall be conclusive of the matter certified.

30 Legal proceedings: derogation

(1) In this section "derogation matter" means—

(a) a derogation by the United Kingdom from Article 5(1) of the Convention on Human Rights which relates to the detention of a person where there is an intention to remove or deport him from the United Kingdom, or

(b) the designation under section 14(1) of the Human Rights Act 1998 (c. 42) of a derogation within paragraph (a) above.

(2) Except as provided by this section, no court or tribunal may entertain proceedings if or in so far as they call a derogation matter into question.

(3) The Special Immigration Appeals Commission may entertain proceedings which call a derogation matter into question; and the Commission—

(a) is the appropriate tribunal for the purpose of section 7 of the Human Rights Act 1998 in relation to proceedings all or part of which call a derogation matter into question; and

(b) may hear proceedings which could, but for subsection (2), be brought in the High Court or the Court of Session.

(4) In relation to proceedings brought by virtue of subsection (3)—

(a) section 6 of the Special Immigration Appeals Commission Act 1997 (c. 68) (person to represent appellant's interests) shall apply with the reference to the appellant being treated as a reference to any party to the proceedings,

(b) rules under section 5 or 8 of that Act (general procedure; and leave to appeal) shall apply with any modification which the Commission considers necessary, and

(c) in the case of proceedings brought by virtue of subsection (3)(b), the Commission may do anything which the High Court may do (in the case of proceedings which could have been brought in that court) or which the Court of Session may do (in the case of proceedings which could have been brought in that court).

(5) The Commission's power to award costs (or, in Scotland, expenses) by virtue of subsection (4)(c) may be exercised only in relation to such part of proceedings before it as calls a derogation matter into question.

(6) In relation to proceedings brought by virtue of subsection (3)(a) or (b)—

(a) an appeal may be brought to the appropriate appeal court (within the meaning of section 7 of the Special Immigration Appeals Commission Act 1997) with the leave of the Commission or, if that leave is refused, with the leave of the appropriate appeal court, and

(b) the appropriate appeal court may consider and do only those things which it could consider and do in an appeal brought from the High Court or the Court of Session in proceedings for judicial review.

(7) In relation to proceedings which are entertained by the Commission under subsection (3) but are not brought by virtue of subsection (3)(a) or (b), subsection (5) shall apply in so far as the proceedings call a derogation matter into question.

(8) In this section "the Convention on Human Rights" has the meaning given to "the Convention" by section 21(1) of the Human Rights Act 1998.

31 Interpretation

A reference in section 22, 23 or 24 to a provision of the Immigration Act 1971 (c. 77) includes a reference to that provision as applied by—

(a) another provision of that Act, or

(b) another Act.

32 Channel Islands and Isle of Man

Her Majesty may by Order in Council direct that sections 21 to 31 shall extend, with such modifications as appear to Her Majesty to be appropriate, to any of the Channel Islands or the Isle of Man.

Refugee Convention

33 Certificate that Convention does not apply

(1) This section applies to an asylum appeal before the Special Immigration Appeals Commission where the Secretary of State issues a certificate that—

(a) the appellant is not entitled to the protection of Article 33(1) of the Refugee Convention because Article 1(F) or 33(2) applies to him (whether or not he would be entitled to protection if that Article did not apply), and

(b) the removal of the appellant from the United Kingdom would be conducive to the public good.

(2) In this section—

"asylum appeal" means an appeal under section 2 of the Special Immigration Appeals Commission Act 1997 (c. 68) in which the appellant makes a claim for asylum (within the meaning given by section 167(1) of the Immigration and Asylum Act 1999 (c. 33)), and

"the Refugee Convention" has the meaning given by that section.

(3) Where this section applies the Commission must begin its substantive deliberations on the asylum appeal by considering the statements in the Secretary of State's certificate.

(4) If the Commission agrees with those statements it must dismiss such part of the asylum appeal as amounts to a claim for asylum (before considering any other aspect of the case).

(5) If the Commission does not agree with those statements it must quash the decision or action against which the asylum appeal is brought.

(6) Where a decision or action is quashed under subsection (5)—

(a) the quashing shall not prejudice any later decision or action, whether taken on the grounds of a change of circumstance or otherwise, and

(b) the claim for asylum made in the course of the asylum appeal shall be treated for the purposes of section 15 of the Immigration and Asylum Act 1999 (interim protection from removal) as undecided until it has been determined whether to take a new decision or action of the kind quashed.

(7) The Secretary of State may revoke a certificate issued under subsection (1).

(8) No court may entertain proceedings for questioning—

(a) a decision or action of the Secretary of State in connection with certification under subsection (1),

(b) a decision of the Secretary of State in connection with a claim for asylum (within the meaning given by section 167(1) of the Immigration and Asylum Act 1999 (c. 33)) in a case in respect of which he issues a certificate under subsection (1) above,

(c) a decision or action of the Secretary of State taken as a consequence of the dismissal of all or part of an asylum appeal in pursuance of subsection (4), or

(d) a decision of the Special Immigration Appeals Commission on or in connection with an asylum appeal to which this section applies.

(9) Subsection (8) shall not prevent an appeal under section 7 of the Special Immigration Appeals Commission Act 1997 (c. 68) (appeal on point of law).

(10) Her Majesty may by Order in Council direct that this section shall extend, with such modifications as appear to Her Majesty to be appropriate, to any of the Channel Islands or the Isle of Man.

34 Construction

(1) Articles 1(F) and 33(2) of the Refugee Convention (exclusions: war criminals, national security, &c.) shall not be taken to require consideration of the gravity of—

(a) events or fear by virtue of which Article 1(A) would or might apply to a person if Article 1(F) did not apply, or

(b) a threat by reason of which Article 33(1) would or might apply to a person if Article 33(2) did not apply.

(2) In this section "the Refugee Convention" means the Convention relating to the Status of Refugees done at Geneva on 28th July 1951 and the Protocol to the Convention.

Fingerprints

35 Destruction of fingerprints

(1) In section 143 of the Immigration and Asylum Act 1999 (destruction of fingerprints)—

(a) subsections (3) to (8) (requirement to destroy fingerprints on resolution of asylum and immigration cases) shall cease to have effect,

(b) in subsection (9) (dependants) after "F" insert "(within the meaning of section 141(7))", and

(c) subsection (14) (interpretation) shall cease to have effect.

(2) Subsection (1)—

(a) shall have effect in relation to fingerprints whether taken before or after the coming into force of this section, and

(b) in relation to fingerprints which before the coming into force of this section were required by section 143 to be destroyed, shall be treated as having had effect before the requirement arose.

PART 5

RACE AND RELIGION

36 Meaning of racial hatred

In section 17 of the Public Order Act 1986 (c. 64) (racial hatred defined by reference to a group of persons in Great Britain) omit the words "in Great Britain".

37 Meaning of fear and hatred

In Article 8 of the Public Order (Northern Ireland) Order 1987 (S.I. 1987/463 (N.I. 7)) in the definition of fear and the definition of hatred (fear and hatred defined by reference to a group of persons in Northern Ireland) omit the words "in Northern Ireland".

38 Religious hatred offences

(1) Part 3 of the Public Order Act 1986 (racial hatred offences) is amended as set out in subsections (2) to (6).

(2) For the heading substitute "RACIAL OR RELIGIOUS HATRED".

(3) After section 17 insert—

"Meaning of "religious hatred"

17A Meaning of "religious hatred"

In this Part "religious hatred" means hatred against a group of persons defined by reference to religious belief or lack of religious belief."

(4) In the following provisions for "racial hatred" substitute "racial or religious hatred"—

(a) the cross-heading preceding section 18;

(b) section 18(1) and (5) (use of words or behaviour or display of written material);

(c) section 19(1) and (2) (publishing or distributing written material);

(d) section 20(1) and (2) (public performance of play);

(e) section 21(1) and (3) (distributing, showing or playing a recording);

(f) section 22(1), (3), (4), (5) and (6) (broadcasting or including programme in cable programme service);

(g) section 23(1) and (3) (possession of racially inflammatory material).

(5) In the sidenote to section 23 and the preceding cross-heading for "racially inflammatory" substitute "inflammatory".

(6) In section 29 (interpretation) after the definition of "recording" insert—

""religious hatred" has the meaning given by section 17A;".

(7) In section 24(2) of the Police and Criminal Evidence Act 1984 (c. 60) (arrestable offences) in paragraph (i) (offences under section 19 of the Public Order Act 1986) for "racial hatred" substitute "racial or religious hatred".

39 Religiously aggravated offences

(1) Part 2 of the Crime and Disorder Act 1998 (c. 37) is amended as set out in subsections (2) to (6).

(2) In the cross-heading preceding section 28 for "Racially-aggravated" substitute "Racially or religiously aggravated".

(3) In section 28 (meaning of racially aggravated)—

(a) in the sidenote and subsection (1) for "racially aggravated" substitute "racially or religiously aggravated";

(b) in subsections (1) and (2) for "racial group" substitute "racial or religious group";

(c) in subsection (3) for the words from "on" to the end of the subsection substitute "on any other factor not mentioned in that paragraph."

(4) In section 28 after subsection (4) insert—

"(5) In this section "religious group" means a group of persons defined by reference to religious belief or lack of religious belief."

(5) In each of the provisions listed in subsection (6)—

(a) in the sidenote for "Racially-aggravated" substitute "Racially or religiously aggravated";

(b) in subsection (1) for "racially aggravated" substitute "racially or religiously aggravated".

(6) The provisions are—

(a) section 29 (assaults);

(b) section 30 (criminal damage);

(c) section 31 (public order offences);

(d) section 32 (harassment etc.).

(7) In section 153 of the Powers of Criminal Courts (Sentencing) Act 2000 (c. 6) (increase in sentences for racial aggravation)—

(a) in the sidenote for "racial aggravation" substitute "racial or religious aggravation";

(b) in subsection (1) for the words from "racially-aggravated assaults" to the end of the subsection substitute "racially or religiously aggravated assaults, criminal damage, public order offences and harassment etc).";

(c) in subsections (2) and (3) for "racially aggravated" substitute "racially or religiously aggravated".

(8) In section 24(2) of the Police and Criminal Evidence Act 1984 (c. 60) (arrestable offences) in paragraph (p) (offences falling within section 32(1)(a) of the Crime and Disorder Act 1998) for "racially-aggravated" substitute "racially or religiously aggravated".

40 Racial or religious hatred offences: penalties

In section 27(3) of the Public Order Act 1986 (c. 64) (penalties for racial or religious hatred offences) for "two years" substitute "seven years".

41 Hatred and fear offences: penalties

In Article 16(1) of the Public Order (Northern Ireland) Order 1987 (S.I. 1987/ 463 (N.I. 7)) (penalties for offences involving stirring up hatred or arousing fear) for "2 years" substitute "7 years".

42 Saving

This Part does not apply to anything done before it comes into force.

PART 6

WEAPONS OF MASS DESTRUCTION

Amendment of the Biological Weapons Act 1974 and the Chemical Weapons Act 1996

43 Transfers of biological agents and toxins

In section 1 of the Biological Weapons Act 1974 (c. 6) (restriction on development etc. of certain biological agents and toxins and of biological weapons), after subsection (1) insert—

"(1A) A person shall not—

(a) transfer any biological agent or toxin to another person or enter into an agreement to do so, or

(b) make arrangements under which another person transfers any biological agent or toxin or enters into an agreement with a third person to do so, if the biological agent or toxin is likely to be kept or used (whether by the transferee or any other person) otherwise than for prophylactic, protective or other peaceful purposes and he knows or has reason to believe that that is the case."

44 Extraterritorial application of biological weapons offences

After section 1 of the Biological Weapons Act 1974 insert—

"**1A Extraterritorial application of section 1**

(1) Section 1 applies to acts done outside the United Kingdom, but only if they are done by a United Kingdom person.

(2) Proceedings for an offence committed under section 1 outside the United Kingdom may be taken, and the offence may

for incidental purposes be treated as having been committed, in any place in the United Kingdom.

(3) Her Majesty may by Order in Council extend the application of section 1, so far as it applies to acts done outside the United Kingdom, to bodies incorporated under the law of any of the Channel Islands, the Isle of Man or any colony.

(4) In this section "United Kingdom person" means a United Kingdom national, a Scottish partnership or a body incorporated under the law of a part of the United Kingdom .

(5) For this purpose a United Kingdom national is an individual who is—

(a) a British citizen, a British Dependent Territories citizen, a British National (Overseas) or a British Overseas citizen;

(b) a person who under the British Nationality Act 1981 (c. 61) is a British subject; or

(c) a British protected person within the meaning of that Act.

(6) Nothing in this section affects any criminal liability arising otherwise than under this section."

45 Customs and Excise prosecutions for biological weapons offences

Before section 2 of the Biological Weapons Act 1974 (c. 6) insert—

"1B Customs and Excise prosecutions

(1) Proceedings for a biological weapons offence may be instituted by order of the Commissioners of Customs and Excise if it appears to them that the offence has involved either—

(a) the movement of any thing mentioned in section 1(1)(a) or (b) above into or out of any country or territory; or

(b) any proposal or attempt to move any such thing into or out of any country or territory.

(2) In this section "biological weapons offence" means an offence under section 1 of this Act or section 50 of the Anti-Terrorism, Crime and Security Act 2001 (including an offence of aiding, abetting, counselling, procuring or inciting the commission of, or attempting or conspiring to commit, such an offence).

(3) Any proceedings for an offence which are instituted under subsection (1) above shall be commenced in the name of an officer, but may be continued by another officer.

(4) Where the Commissioners of Customs and Excise investigate, or propose to investigate, any matter with a view to determining—

(a) whether there are grounds for believing that a biological weapons offence has been committed, or

(b) whether a person should be prosecuted for such an offence, that matter shall be treated as an assigned matter within the meaning of the Customs and Excise Management Act 1979.

(5) Nothing in this section affects any power of any person (including any officer) apart from this section.

(6) In this section "officer" means a person commissioned by the Commissioners of Customs and Excise.

(7) This section does not apply to proceedings in Scotland."

46 Customs and Excise prosecutions for chemical weapons offences

Before section 31 of the Chemical Weapons Act 1996 (c. 6) insert—

"30A Customs and Excise prosecutions

(1) Proceedings for a chemical weapons offence may be instituted by order of the Commissioners of Customs and Excise if it appears to them that the offence has involved either—

(a) the movement of any chemical weapon into or out of any country or territory; or

(b) any proposal or attempt to move any chemical weapon into or out of any country or territory.

(2) In this section "chemical weapons offence" means an offence under section 2 above or section 50 of the Anti-Terrorism Act 2001 (including an offence of aiding, abetting, counselling, procuring or inciting the commission of, or attempting or conspiring to commit, such an offence).

(3) Any proceedings for an offence which are instituted under subsection (1) shall be commenced in the name of an officer, but may be continued by another officer.

(4) Where the Commissioners of Customs and Excise investigate, or propose to investigate, any matter with a view to determining—

(a) whether there are grounds for believing that a chemical weapons offence has been committed, or

(b) whether a person should be prosecuted for such an offence, that matter shall be treated as an assigned matter within the meaning of the Customs and Excise Management Act 1979.

(5) Nothing in this section affects any power of any person (including any officer) apart from this section.

(6) In this section "officer" means a person commissioned by the Commissioners of Customs and Excise.

(7) This section does not apply to proceedings in Scotland."

Nuclear weapons

47 Use etc. of nuclear weapons

(1) A person who—

(a) knowingly causes a nuclear weapon explosion;

(b) develops or produces, or participates in the development or production of, a nuclear weapon;

(c) has a nuclear weapon in his possession;

(d) participates in the transfer of a nuclear weapon; or

(e) engages in military preparations, or in preparations of a military nature, intending to use, or threaten to use, a nuclear weapon,

is guilty of an offence.

(2) Subsection (1) has effect subject to the exceptions and defences in sections 48 and 49.

(3) For the purposes of subsection (1)(b) a person participates in the development or production of a nuclear weapon if he does any act which—

(a) facilitates the development by another of the capability to produce or use a nuclear weapon, or

(b) facilitates the making by another of a nuclear weapon, knowing or having reason to believe that his act has (or will have) that effect.

(4) For the purposes of subsection (1)(d) a person participates in the transfer of a nuclear weapon if—

(a) he buys or otherwise acquires it or agrees with another to do so;

(b) he sells or otherwise disposes of it or agrees with another to do so; or

(c) he makes arrangements under which another person either acquires or disposes of it or agrees with a third person to do so.

(5) A person guilty of an offence under this section is liable on conviction on indictment to imprisonment for life.

(6) In this section "nuclear weapon" includes a nuclear explosive device that is not intended for use as a weapon.

(7) This section applies to acts done outside the United Kingdom, but only if they are done by a United Kingdom person.

(8) Paragraph (a) of subsection (1) shall cease to have effect on the coming into force of the Nuclear Explosions (Prohibition and Inspections) Act 1998 (c. 7).

48 Exceptions

(1) Nothing in section 47 applies—

    (a) to an act which is authorised under subsection (2); or

    (b) to an act done in the course of an armed conflict.

(2) The Secretary of State may—

    (a) authorise any act which would otherwise contravene section 47 in such manner and on such terms as he thinks fit; and

    (b) withdraw or vary any authorisation given under this subsection.

(3) Any question arising in proceedings for an offence under section 47 as to whether anything was done in the course of an armed conflict shall be determined by the Secretary of State.

(4) A certificate purporting to set out any such determination and to be signed by the Secretary of State shall be received in evidence in any such proceedings and shall be presumed to be so signed unless the contrary is shown.

49 Defences

(1) In proceedings for an offence under 47(1)(c) or (d) relating to an object it is a defence for the accused to show that he did not know and had no reason to believe that the object was a nuclear weapon.

(2) But he shall be taken to have shown that fact if—

    (a) sufficient evidence is adduced to raise an issue with respect to it; and

    (b) the contrary is not proved by the prosecution beyond reasonable doubt.

(3) In proceedings for such an offence it is also a defence for the accused to show that he knew or believed that the object was a nuclear weapon but, as soon as reasonably practicable after he first knew or believed that fact, he took all reasonable steps to inform the Secretary of State or a constable of his knowledge or belief.

Assisting or inducing weapons-related acts overseas

50 Assisting or inducing certain weapons-related acts overseas

(1) A person who aids, abets, counsels or procures, or incites, a person who is not a United Kingdom person to do a relevant act outside the United Kingdom is guilty of an offence.

(2) For this purpose a relevant act is an act that, if done by a United Kingdom person, would contravene any of the following provisions—

(a) section 1 of the Biological Weapons Act 1974 (offences relating to biological agents and toxins);

(b) section 2 of the Chemical Weapons Act 1996 (offences relating to chemical weapons); or

(c) section 47 above (offences relating to nuclear weapons).

(3) Nothing in this section applies to an act mentioned in subsection (1) which—

(a) relates to a relevant act which would contravene section 47; and

(b) is authorised by the Secretary of State; and section 48(2) applies for the purpose of authorising acts that would otherwise constitute an offence under this section.

(4) A person accused of an offence under this section in relation to a relevant act which would contravene a provision mentioned in subsection (2) may raise any defence which would be open to a person accused of the corresponding offence ancillary to an offence under that provision.

(5) A person convicted of an offence under this section is liable on conviction on indictment to imprisonment for life.

(6) This section applies to acts done outside the United Kingdom, but only if they are done by a United Kingdom person.

(7) Nothing in this section prejudices any criminal liability existing apart from this section.

Supplemental provisions relating to sections 47 and 50

51 Extraterritorial application

(1) Proceedings for an offence committed under section 47 or 50 outside the United Kingdom may be taken, and the offence may for incidental purposes be treated as having been committed, in any part of the United Kingdom.

(2) Her Majesty may by Order in Council extend the application of section 47 or 50, so far as it applies to acts done outside the United Kingdom, to

bodies incorporated under the law of any of the Channel Islands, the Isle of Man or any colony.

52 Powers of entry

(1) If—

(a) a justice of the peace is satisfied on information on oath that there are reasonable grounds for suspecting that evidence of the commission of an offence under section 47 or 50 is to be found on any premises; or

(b) in Scotland a justice (within the meaning of section 307 of the Criminal Procedure (Scotland) Act 1995 (c. 46)) is satisfied by evidence on oath as mentioned in paragraph (a) above,

he may issue a warrant authorising a constable or an authorised officer to enter the premises, if necessary by force, at any time within one month from the time of the issue of the warrant and to search them.

(2) The powers of a person who enters the premises under the authority of the warrant include power—

(a) to take with him such other persons and such equipment as appear to him to be necessary;

(b) to inspect, seize and retain any substance, equipment or document found on the premises;

(c) to require any document or other information which is held in electronic form and is accessible from the premises to be produced in a form—

(i) in which he can read and copy it; or

(ii) from which it can readily be produced in a form in which he can read and copy it;

(d) to copy any document which he has reasonable cause to believe may be required as evidence for the purposes of proceedings in respect of an offence under section 47 or 50.

(3) A constable who enters premises under the authority of a warrant or by virtue of subsection (2)(a) may—

(a) give such assistance as an authorised officer may request for the purpose of facilitating the exercise of any power under this section; and

(b) search or cause to be searched any person on the premises who the constable has reasonable cause to believe may have in his possession any document or other thing which may be required as evidence for the purposes of proceedings in respect of an offence under section 47 or 50.

(4) No constable shall search a person of the opposite sex.

(5) The powers conferred by a warrant under this section shall only be exercisable, if the warrant so provides, in the presence of a constable.

(6) A person who—

(a) wilfully obstructs an authorised officer in the exercise of a power conferred by a warrant under this section; or

(b) fails without reasonable excuse to comply with a reasonable request made by an authorised officer or a constable for the purpose of facilitating the exercise of such a power,

is guilty of an offence.

(7) A person guilty of an offence under subsection (6) is liable—

(a) on summary conviction, to a fine not exceeding the statutory maximum; and

(b) on conviction on indictment to imprisonment for a term not exceeding two years or a fine (or both).

(8) In this section "authorised officer" means an authorised officer of the Secretary of State.

53 Customs and Excise prosecutions

(1) Proceedings for a nuclear weapons offence may be instituted by order of the Commissioners of Customs and Excise if it appears to them that the offence has involved either—

(a) the movement of a nuclear weapon into or out of any country or territory; or

(b) any proposal or attempt to move a nuclear weapon into or out of any country or territory.

(2) In this section "nuclear weapons offence" means an offence under section 47 or 50 (including an offence of aiding, abetting, counselling, procuring or inciting the commission of, or attempting or conspiring to commit, such an offence).

(3) Any proceedings for an offence which are instituted under subsection (1) shall be commenced in the name of an officer, but may be continued by another officer.

(4) Where the Commissioners of Customs and Excise investigate, or propose to investigate, any matter with a view to determining—

(a) whether there are grounds for believing that a nuclear weapons offence has been committed, or

(b) whether a person should be prosecuted for such an offence, that matter shall be treated as an assigned matter within the meaning of the Customs and Excise Management Act 1979 (c. 2).

(5) Nothing in this section affects any powers of any person (including any officer) apart from this section.

(6) In this section "officer" means a person commissioned by the Commissioners of Customs and Excise.

(7) This section does not apply to proceedings in Scotland.

54 Offences

(1) A person who knowingly or recklessly makes a false or misleading statement for the purpose of obtaining (or opposing the variation or withdrawal) of authorisation for the purposes of section 47 or 50 is guilty of an offence.

(2) A person guilty of an offence under subsection (1) is liable—

(a) on summary conviction, to a fine of an amount not exceeding the statutory maximum;

(b) on conviction on indictment, to imprisonment for a term not exceeding two years or a fine (or to both).

(3) Where an offence under section 47, 50 or subsection (1) above committed by a body corporate is proved to have been committed with the consent or connivance of, or to be attributable to any neglect on the part of—

(a) a director, manager, secretary or other similar officer of the body corporate; or

(b) any person who was purporting to act in any such capacity,

he as well as the body corporate shall be guilty of that offence and shall be liable to be proceeded against and punished accordingly.

(4) In subsection (3) "director", in relation to a body corporate whose affairs are managed by its members, means a member of the body corporate.

55 Consent to prosecutions

Proceedings for an offence under section 47 or 50 shall not be instituted—

(a) in England and Wales, except by or with the consent of the Attorney General;

(b) in Northern Ireland, except by or with the consent of the Attorney General for Northern Ireland.

56 Interpretation of Part 6

(1) In this Part "United Kingdom person" means a United Kingdom national, a Scottish partnership or a body incorporated under the law of a part of the United Kingdom.

(2) For this purpose a United Kingdom national is an individual who is—

(a) a British citizen, a British Dependent Territories citizen, a British National (Overseas) or a British Overseas citizen;

(b) a person who under the British Nationality Act 1981 (c. 61) is a British subject; or

(c) a British protected person within the meaning of that Act.

Extension of Part 6 to dependencies

57 Power to extend Part 6 to dependencies

Her Majesty may by Order in Council direct that any of the provisions of this Part shall extend, with such exceptions and modifications as appear to Her Majesty to be appropriate, to any of the Channel Islands, the Isle of Man or to any British overseas territory.

PART 7

SECURITY OF PATHOGENS AND TOXINS

58 Pathogens and toxins in relation to which requirements under Part 7 apply

(1) Schedule 5 (which lists the pathogens and toxins in relation to which the requirements of this Part apply) has effect.

(2) The Secretary of State may by order modify any provision of Schedule 5 (including the notes).

(3) The Secretary of State may not add any pathogen or toxin to that Schedule unless he is satisfied that the pathogen or toxin is capable of endangering life or causing serious harm to human health.

(4) In this Part "dangerous substance" means—

(a) anything which consists of or includes a substance for the time being mentioned in Schedule 5; or

(b) anything which is infected with or otherwise carries any such substance.

59 Duty to notify Secretary of State before keeping or using any dangerous substance

(1) The occupier of any premises must give a notice to the Secretary of State before any dangerous substance is kept or used there.

(2) Subsection (1) does not apply to premises in respect of which a notice has previously been given under that subsection (unless it has been withdrawn).

(3) The occupier of any premises in respect of which a notice has been given may withdraw the notice if no dangerous substance is kept or used there.

(4) A notice under this section must—

   (a) identify the premises in which the substance is kept or used;

   (b) identify any building or site of which the premises form part; and

   (c) contain such other particulars (if any) as may be prescribed.

(5) The occupier of any premises in which any dangerous substance is kept or used on the day on which this section comes into force must give a notice under this section before the end of the period of one month beginning with that day.

(6) Where—

   (a) a substance which is kept or used in any premises becomes a dangerous substance by virtue of a modification of Schedule 5, but

   (b) no other dangerous substance is kept or used there, the occupier of the premises must give a notice under this section before the end of the period of one month beginning with the day on which that modification comes into force.

60 Power to require information about security of dangerous substances

(1) A constable may give to the occupier of any relevant premises a notice requiring him to give the chief officer of police such information as is specified or described in the notice by a time so specified and in a form and manner so specified.

(2) The required information must relate to the measures taken (whether by the occupier or any other person) to ensure the security of any dangerous substance kept or used in the premises.

(3) In this Part references to measures taken to ensure the security of any dangerous substance kept or used in any relevant premises include—

   (a) measures taken to ensure the security of any building or site of which the premises form part; and

(b) measures taken for the purpose of ensuring access to the substance is given only to those whose activities require access and only in circumstances that ensure the security of the substance.

(4) In this Part "relevant premises" means any premises in which any dangerous substance is kept or used.

61 Power to require information about persons with access to dangerous substances

(1) A police officer of at least the rank of inspector may give to the occupier of any relevant premises a notice requiring him to give the chief officer of police a list of—

(a) each person who has access to any dangerous substance kept or used there;

(b) each person who, in such circumstances as are specified or described in the notice, has access to such part of the premises (if any) as may be so specified or described;

(c) each person who, in such circumstances as are specified or described in the notice, has access to the premises; and

(d) each person who, in such circumstances as are specified or described in the notice, has access to any building or site of which the premises form part.

(2) A list under subsection (1) must be given before the end of the period of one month beginning with the day on which the notice is given.

(3) Where a list under subsection (1) is given, the occupier of the premises for the time being—

(a) must secure that only the persons mentioned in the list are given the access identified in the list relating to them; but

(b) may give a supplementary list to the chief officer of police of other persons to whom it is proposed to give access.

(4) Where a supplementary list is given under subsection (3)(b), the occupier of the premises for the time being must secure that persons mentioned in that list do not have the proposed access relating to them until the end of the period of 30 days beginning with the day on which that list is given.

(5) The chief officer of police may direct that a person may have such access before the end of that period.

(6) The Secretary of State may by order modify the period mentioned in subsection (4).

(7) Any list under this section must—

(a) identify the access which the person has, or is proposed to have;

(b) state the full name of that person, his date of birth, his address and his nationality; and

(c) contain such other matters (if any) as may be prescribed.

62 Duty to comply with security directions

(1) A constable may give directions to the occupier of any relevant premises requiring him to take such measures to ensure the security of any dangerous substance kept or used there as are specified or described in the directions by a time so specified.

(2) The directions may—

(a) specify or describe the substances in relation to the security of which the measures relate; and

(b) require the occupier to give a notice to the chief officer of police before any other dangerous substance specified or described in the directions is kept or used in the premises.

63 Duty to dispose of dangerous substances

(1) Where the Secretary of State has reasonable grounds for believing that adequate measures to ensure the security of any dangerous substance kept or used in any relevant premises are not being taken and are unlikely to be taken, he may give a direction to the occupier of the premises requiring him to dispose of the substance.

(2) The direction must—

(a) specify the manner in which, and time by which, the dangerous substance must be disposed of; or

(b) require the occupier to produce the dangerous substance to a person specified or described in the notice in a manner and by a time so specified for him to dispose of.

64 Denial of access to dangerous substances

(1) The Secretary of State may give directions to the occupier of any relevant premises requiring him to secure that the person identified in the directions—

(a) is not to have access to any dangerous substance kept or used there;

(b) is not to have, in such circumstances (if any) as may be specified or described in the directions, access to such part (if any) of the premises as may be so specified or described;

(c) is not to have, in such circumstances (if any) as may be specified or described in the directions, access to the premises; and

(d) is not to have, in such circumstances (if any) as may be specified or described in the directions, access to any building or site of which the premises form part.

(2) The directions must be given under the hand of the Secretary of State.

(3) The Secretary of State may not give the directions unless he believes that they are necessary in the interests of national security.

65 Powers of entry

(1) A constable may, on giving notice under this section, enter any relevant premises, or any building or site of which the premises form part, at a reasonable time for the purpose of assessing the measures taken to ensure the security of any dangerous substance kept or used in the premises.

(2) The notice must be given to the occupier of the premises, or (as the case may be) the occupier of the building or site of which the premises form part, at least 2 working days before the proposed entry.

(3) The notice must set out the purpose mentioned in subsection (1).

(4) A constable who has entered any premises, building or site by virtue of subsection (1) may for the purpose mentioned in that subsection—

(a) search the premises, building or site;

(b) require any person who appears to the constable to be in charge of the premises, building or site to facilitate any such inspection; and

(c) require any such person to answer any question.

(5) The powers of a constable under this section include power to take with him such other persons as appear to him to be necessary.

66 Search warrants

(1) If on an application made by a constable a justice of the peace is satisfied that there are reasonable grounds for believing—

(a) that a dangerous substance is kept or used in any premises but that no notice under section 59 is in force in respect of the premises, or

(b) that the occupier of any relevant premises is failing to comply with any direction given to him under section 62 or 63,

and that any of the conditions mentioned in subsection (3) apply, he may issue a warrant authorising a constable to enter the premises, if necessary by force, and to search them.

(2) A constable may seize and retain anything which he believes is or contains a dangerous substance.

(3) The conditions mentioned in subsection (1) are—

(a) that it is not practicable to communicate with any person entitled to grant entry to the premises;

(b) that it is practicable to communicate with a person entitled to grant entry to the premises but it is not practicable to communicate with any person entitled to grant access to any substance which may be a dangerous substance;

(c) that entry to the premises will not be granted unless a warrant is produced;

(d) that the purpose of a search may be frustrated or seriously prejudiced unless a constable arriving at the premises can secure immediate entry to them.

(4) In the application of subsection (1) to Scotland the reference to a justice of the peace is to a justice within the meaning of section 307 of the Criminal Procedure (Scotland) Act 1995 (c. 46).

67 Offences

(1) An occupier who fails without reasonable excuse to comply with any duty or direction imposed on him by or under this Part is guilty of an offence.

(2) A person who, in giving any information to a person exercising functions under this Part, knowingly or recklessly makes a statement which is false or misleading in a material particular is guilty of an offence.

(3) A person guilty of an offence under this section is liable—

(a) on conviction on indictment, to imprisonment for a term not exceeding five years or a fine (or both); and

(b) on summary conviction, to imprisonment for a term not exceeding six months or a fine not exceeding the statutory maximum (or both).

68 Offences: bodies corporate

(1) If an offence under this Part committed by a body corporate is shown to have been committed with the consent or connivance of, or to be attributable to any neglect on the part of—

(a) any officer, or

(b) any other employee of the body corporate who is in charge of any relevant premises or the access to any dangerous substance kept or used there,

he, as well as the body corporate, is guilty of the offence and liable to be proceeded against and punished accordingly.

(2) In this section "officer", in relation to a body corporate, means—

(a) any director, manager, secretary or other similar officer of the body corporate; or

(b) any person purporting to act in any such capacity.

(3) Where the affairs of a body corporate are managed by its members, this section applies in relation to the acts and defaults of a member in connection with his functions of management as if he were a director of the body corporate.

69 Offences: partnerships and unincorporated associations

(1) Proceedings for an offence alleged to have been committed by a partnership or an unincorporated association must be brought in the name of the partnership or association (and not in that of any of its members).

(2) A fine imposed on the partnership or association on its conviction of an offence is to be paid out of the funds of the partnership or association.

(3) Rules of court relating to the service of documents are to have effect as if the partnership or association were a body corporate.

(4) In proceedings for an offence brought against the partnership or association—

(a) section 33 of the Criminal Justice Act 1925 (c. 86) and Schedule 3 to the Magistrates' Courts Act 1980 (c. 43) (procedure) apply as they do in relation to a body corporate;

(b) sections 70 and 143 of the Criminal Procedure (Scotland) Act 1995 (c. 46) (procedure) apply as they do in relation to a body corporate;

(c) section 18 of the Criminal Justice (Northern Ireland) Act 1945 (c. 15 (N.I.)) and Schedule 4 to the Magistrates' Courts (Northern Ireland) Order 1981 (S.I. 1981/1675 (N.I. 26)) (procedure) apply as they do in relation to a body corporate.

(5) If an offence under this Part committed by a partnership is shown to have been committed with the consent or connivance of, or to be attributable to any neglect on the part of—

(a) a partner or a person purporting to act as a partner, or

(b) any employee of the partnership who is in charge of any relevant premises or the access to any dangerous substance kept or used there,

he, as well as the partnership, is guilty of the offence and liable to be proceeded against and punished accordingly.

(6) If an offence under this Part committed by an unincorporated association is shown to have been committed with the consent or connivance of, or to be attributable to any neglect on the part of—

(a) any officer, or

(b) any employee of the association who is in charge of any relevant premises or the access to any dangerous substance kept or used there,

he, as well as the association, is guilty of the offence and liable to be proceeded against and punished accordingly.

(7) In subsection (6) "officer", in relation to any association, means—

(a) any officer of the association or any member of its governing body; or

(b) any person purporting to act in such a capacity.

70 Denial of access to dangerous substances: appeals

(1) There shall be a commission, to be known as the Pathogens Access Appeal Commission.

(2) Any person aggrieved by directions given under section 64 may appeal to the Commission.

(3) The Commission must allow an appeal if it considers that the decision to give the directions was flawed when considered in the light of the principles applicable on an application for judicial review.

(4) A party to any appeal under this section which the Commission has determined may bring a further appeal on a question of law to—

(a) the Court of Appeal, if the first appeal was heard in England and Wales;

(b) the Court of Session, if the first appeal was heard in Scotland; or

(c) the Court of Appeal in Northern Ireland, if the first appeal was heard in Northern Ireland.

(5) An appeal under subsection (4) may be brought only with the permission of—

(a) the Commission; or

(b) where the Commission refuses permission, the court to which the appeal would be brought.

(6) Schedule 6 (constitution of the Commission and procedure) has effect.

71 Other appeals

(1) Any person who is required to do any act in response to—

(a) any notice under section 60, or

(b) any directions under section 62 or 63,

may appeal to a magistrates' court against the requirement on the ground that, having regard to all the circumstances of the case, it is unreasonable to be required to do that act.

(2) An appeal may not be brought after the end of the period of one month beginning with the day on which the notice or directions were given.

(3) If the magistrates' court allows the appeal, it may—

(a) direct that the required act need not be done; or

(b) make such modification of the requirement as it considers appropriate.

(4) An appeal shall lie to the Crown Court against any decision of the magistrates' court.

(5) In the application of this section to Scotland—

(a) references to a magistrates' court are to the sheriff; and

(b) the reference to the Crown Court is to the High Court of Justiciary.

(6) In the application of this section to Northern Ireland references to a magistrates' court are to a court of summary jurisdiction.

72 Giving of directions or notices

Any direction or notice under this Part may be given by post.

73 Orders and regulations

(1) The power to make an order or regulations under this Part is exercisable by statutory instrument.

(2) A statutory instrument containing an order under section 58 shall not be made unless a draft of it has been laid before and approved by a resolution of each House of Parliament.

(3) A statutory instrument containing—

(a) an order under section 61, or

(b) regulations under section 59 or 61 or Schedule 5, shall be subject to annulment in pursuance of a resolution of either House of Parliament.

74 Interpretation

(1) In this Part—

"chief officer of police" means—

(a) in relation to any premises in Great Britain, the chief officer of police for the area in which the premises are situated; and

(b) in relation to any premises in Northern Ireland, the Chief Constable of the Police Service of Northern Ireland;

"dangerous substance" has the meaning given in section 58; "direction" means a direction in writing;

"notice" means a notice in writing;

"occupier" includes a partnership or unincorporated association and, in relation to premises that are unoccupied, means any person entitled to occupy the premises;

"prescribed" means prescribed in regulations made by the Secretary of State; and

"relevant premises" has the meaning given in section 60.

(2) In this Part references to measures taken to ensure the security of any dangerous substance are to be construed in accordance with section 60.

75 Power to extend Part 7 to animal or plant pathogens, pests or toxic chemicals

(1) The Secretary of State may, in relation to anything to which this section applies, make an order applying, or making provision corresponding to, any provision of this Part, with or without modifications.

(2) This section applies to—

(a) toxic chemicals (within the meaning of the Chemical Weapons Act 1996 (c. 6));

(b) animal pathogens;

(c) plant pathogens; and

(d) pests.

(3) The power under this section may be exercised in relation to any chemical only if the Secretary of State is satisfied that the chemical is capable of endangering life or causing serious harm to human health.

(4) The power under this section may be exercised in relation to any pathogen or pest only if the Secretary of State is satisfied that there is a risk that the pathogen or pest is of a description that could be used to cause—

(a) widespread damage to property;

(b) significant disruption to the public; or

(c) significant alarm to the public.

(5) An order under this section may—

(a) provide for any reference in the order to an instrument or other document to take effect as a reference to that instrument or document as revised or re-issued from time to time;

(b) make different provision for different purposes; and

(c) make such incidental, supplementary and transitional provision as the Secretary of State thinks fit.

(6) A statutory instrument containing an order under this section shall not be made unless a draft of it has been laid before and approved by a resolution of each House of Parliament.

PART 8

SECURITY OF NUCLEAR INDUSTRY

76 Atomic Energy Authority special constables

(1) Section 3 of the Special Constables Act 1923 (c. 11) shall have effect as if all nuclear sites that are not for the time being designated under subsection (2) were premises under the control of the United Kingdom Atomic Energy Authority.

(2) The Secretary of State may by order made by statutory instrument designate any nuclear sites which appear to him to be used wholly or mainly for defence purposes as premises to which subsection (1) does not apply.

(3) An AEA constable shall have the powers and privileges (and be liable to the duties and responsibilities) of a constable anywhere within 5 kilometres of the limits of the nuclear sites to which subsection (1) applies.

(4) An AEA constable shall have the powers and privileges (and be liable to the duties and responsibilities) of a constable anywhere it appears to him expedient to go—

(a) in order to safeguard any nuclear material which is being carried (or being trans-shipped or stored incidentally to its carriage) before its delivery at its final destination; or

(b) in order to pursue, arrest, place in the custody of the police, or take to any premises within which the constable was appointed to act, a person who the constable reasonably believes has (or has attempted to) unlawfully remove or interfere with any nuclear material being safeguarded by the constable.

(5) An AEA constable shall have the powers and privileges (and be liable to the duties and responsibilities) of a constable at any place at which he reasonably believes a particular consignment of nuclear material will be trans-shipped or stored incidentally to its carriage, in order to ensure the security of the nuclear material on its arrival at that place.

(6) This section has effect in United Kingdom waters adjacent to Great Britain as it applies in Great Britain.

(7) In this section—

"AEA constable" means a person appointed on the nomination of the United Kingdom Atomic Energy Authority to be a special constable under section 3 of the Special Constables Act 1923 (c. 11);

"nuclear material" means—

(a) any fissile material in the form of uranium metal, alloy or chemical compound, or of plutonium metal, alloy or chemical compound; or

(b) any other fissile material which may be prescribed by regulations made by the Secretary of State;

"nuclear site" means premises in respect of which a nuclear site licence (within the meaning of the Nuclear Installations Act 1965 (c. 57)) is for the time being in force; and

"United Kingdom waters" means waters within the seaward limits of the territorial sea.

(8) An order under subsection (2) shall be laid before Parliament after being made.

(9) The power to make regulations under subsection (7) is exercisable by statutory instrument subject to annulment in pursuance of a resolution of either House of Parliament.

77 Regulation of security of civil nuclear industry

(1) The Secretary of State may make regulations for the purpose of ensuring the security of—

(a) nuclear sites and other nuclear premises;

(b) nuclear material used or stored on nuclear sites or other nuclear premises and equipment or software used or stored on such sites or premises in connection with activities involving nuclear material;

(c) other radioactive material used or stored on nuclear sites and equipment or software used or stored on nuclear sites in connection with activities involving other radioactive material;

(d) sensitive nuclear information which is in the possession or control of anyone who is (or is expected to be) involved in activities on, or in relation to, any nuclear site or other nuclear premises;

(e) nuclear material which is being (or is expected to be)—

(i) transported within the United Kingdom or its territorial sea;

(ii) transported (outside the United Kingdom and its territorial sea) to or from any nuclear site or other nuclear premises in the United Kingdom; or

(iii) carried on board a United Kingdom ship;

(f) information relating to the security of anything mentioned in paragraphs (a) to (e).

(2) The regulations may, in particular—

(a) require a person to produce for the approval of the Secretary of State a plan for ensuring the security of anything mentioned in subsection (1) and to comply with the plan as approved by the Secretary of State;

(b) require compliance with any directions given by the Secretary of State;

(c) impose requirements in relation to any activities by reference to the approval of the Secretary of State;

(d) create summary offences or offences triable either way;

(e) make provision for the purposes mentioned in subsection (1) corresponding to any provision which may be made for the general purposes of Part 1 of the Health and Safety at Work etc. Act 1974 (c. 37) by virtue of section 15(2), (3)(c) and (4) to (8) of that Act (health and safety regulations);

(f) make provision corresponding to any provision which may be made by virtue of section 43(2) to (5), (8) and (9) of that Act (fees), in connection with the performance by or on behalf of the Secretary of State or any other specified body or person of functions under the regulations; and

(g) apply (with or without modifications), or make provision corresponding to, any provision contained in sections 19 to 42 and 44 to 47 of that Act.

(3) An offence under the regulations may be made punishable—

(a) in the case of an offence triable either way, with imprisonment for a term not exceeding two years or a fine not exceeding the statutory maximum (or both); or

(b) in the case of a summary offence, with imprisonment for a term not exceeding six months or a fine not exceeding level 5 on the standard scale (or both).

(4) The regulations may make—

(a) provision applying to acts done outside the United Kingdom by United Kingdom persons;

(b) different provision for different purposes; and

(c) such incidental, supplementary and transitional provision as the Secretary of State considers appropriate.

(5) Before making the regulations the Secretary of State shall consult—

(a) the Health and Safety Commission; and

(b) such other persons as he considers appropriate.

(6) The power to make the regulations is exercisable by statutory instrument subject to annulment in pursuance of a resolution of either House of Parliament.

(7) In this section—

"nuclear material" and "nuclear site" have the same meaning as in section 76;

"other nuclear premises" means premises other than a nuclear site on which nuclear material is used or stored;

"sensitive nuclear information" means—

(a) information relating to, or capable of use in connection with, any treatment of uranium that increases the proportion of the isotope 235 contained in the uranium; or

(b) information relating to activities carried out on or in relation to nuclear sites or other nuclear premises which appears to the Secretary of State to be information which needs to be protected in the interests of national security;

"United Kingdom ship" means a ship registered in the United Kingdom under Part 2 of the Merchant Shipping Act 1995 (c. 21)

(8) Any sums received by virtue of provision made under subsection (2)(f) shall be paid into the Consolidated Fund.

78 Repeals relating to security of civil nuclear installations

(1) In Schedule 1 to the Nuclear Installations Act 1965 (c. 57) (security provisions applicable by order under section 2 of that Act), paragraphs 5 and 6 shall cease to have effect.

(2) In section 19(1) of the Atomic Energy Authority Act 1971 (c. 11) (application of certain security provisions to designated companies), for "Paragraphs 4 to 6 " and "they apply" substitute respectively "Paragraph 4" and "it applies"

79 Prohibition of disclosures in relation to nuclear security

(1) A person is guilty of an offence if he discloses any information or thing the disclosure of which might prejudice the security of any nuclear site or of any nuclear material—

(a) with the intention of prejudicing that security; or

(b) being reckless as to whether the disclosure might prejudice that security.

(2) The reference in subsection (1) to nuclear material is a reference to—

(a) nuclear material which is being held on any nuclear site, or

(b) nuclear material anywhere in the world which is being transported to or from a nuclear site or carried on board a British ship,

(including nuclear material which is expected to be so held, transported or carried).

(3) A person guilty of an offence under subsection (1) is liable—

(a) on conviction on indictment, to imprisonment for a term not exceeding seven years or a fine (or both); and

(b) on summary conviction, to imprisonment for a term not exceeding six months or a fine not exceeding the statutory maximum (or both).

(4) In this section—

"British ship" means a ship (including a ship belonging to Her Majesty) which is registered in the United Kingdom;

"disclose" and "disclosure", in relation to a thing, include parting with possession of it;

"nuclear material" has the same meaning as in section 76; and

"nuclear site" means a site in the United Kingdom (including a site occupied by or on behalf of the Crown) which is (or is expected to be) used for any purpose mentioned in section 1(1) of the Nuclear Installations Act 1965 (c. 57).

(5) This section applies to acts done outside the United Kingdom by a United Kingdom person.

(6) Proceedings for an offence committed outside the United Kingdom may be taken, and the offence may for incidental purposes be treated as having been committed, in any place in the United Kingdom.

(7) Nothing in this section affects any criminal liability arising otherwise than under this section.

80 Prohibition of disclosures of uranium enrichment technology

(1) This section applies to—

(a) any information about the enrichment of uranium; or

(b) any information or thing which is, or is likely to be, used in connection with the enrichment of uranium;

and for this purpose "the enrichment of uranium" means any treatment of uranium that increases the proportion of the isotope 235 contained in the uranium.

(2) The Secretary of State may make regulations prohibiting the disclosure of information or things to which this section applies.

(3) A person who contravenes a prohibition is guilty of an offence and liable—

(a) on conviction on indictment, to imprisonment for a term not exceeding seven years or a fine (or both); and

(b) on summary conviction, to imprisonment for a term not exceeding six months or a fine not exceeding the statutory maximum (or both).

(4) The regulations may, in particular, provide for—

(a) a prohibition to apply, or not to apply—

(i) to such information or things; and

(ii) in such cases or circumstances,

as may be prescribed;

(b) the authorisation by the Secretary of State of disclosures that would otherwise be prohibited; and

(c) defences to an offence under subsection (3) relating to any prohibition.

(5) The regulations may—

(a) provide for any prohibition to apply to acts done outside the United Kingdom by United Kingdom persons;

(b) make different provision for different purposes; and

(c) make such incidental, supplementary and transitional provision as the Secretary of State thinks fit.

(6) The power to make the regulations is exercisable by statutory instrument.

(7) The regulations shall not be made unless a draft of the regulations has been laid before and approved by each House of Parliament.

(8) In this section—

"disclosure", in relation to a thing, includes parting with possession of it;

"information" includes software; and

"prescribed" means specified or described in the regulations.

81 Part 8: supplementary

(1) Proceedings for an offence under section 79 or 80 shall not be instituted—

(a) in England and Wales, except by or with the consent of the Attorney General; or

(b) in Northern Ireland, except by or with the consent of the Attorney General for Northern Ireland.

(2) In this Part "United Kingdom person" means a United Kingdom national, a Scottish partnership or a body incorporated under the law of any part of the United Kingdom.

(3) For this purpose a United Kingdom national is an individual who is—

(a) a British citizen, a British Dependent Territories citizen, a British National (Overseas) or a British Overseas citizen;

(b) a person who under the British Nationality Act 1981 (c. 61) is a British subject; or

(c) a British protected person within the meaning of that Act.

PART 9

AVIATION SECURITY

82 Arrest without warrant

(1) At the end of section 24(2) of the Police and Criminal Evidence Act 1984 (c. 60) (arrest without warrant: particular offences) insert—

"(u) an offence under section 21C(1) or 21D(1) of the Aviation Security Act 1982 (c. 36) (unauthorised presence in restricted zone or on aircraft);

(v) an offence under section 39(1) of the Civil Aviation Act 1982 (c. 16) (trespass on aerodrome)."

(2) At the end of Article 26(2) of the Police and Criminal Evidence (Northern Ireland) Order 1989 (S.I. 1989/1341 (N.I. 12) (arrest without warrant: particular offences)) insert—

"(j) an offence under section 21C(1) or 21D(1) of the Aviation Security Act 1982 (unauthorised presence in restricted zone or on aircraft);

(k) an offence under section 39(1) of the Civil Aviation Act 1982 (trespass on aerodrome)."

(3) Where, in Scotland, a constable has reasonable grounds for suspecting that a person has committed—

(a) an offence under section 21C(1) or 21D(1) of the Aviation Security Act 1982 (unauthorised presence in restricted zone or on aircraft);

(b) an offence under section 39(1) of the Civil Aviation Act 1982 (trespass on aerodrome),

he may arrest that person without warrant.

(4) This section shall have effect in relation to an offence committed or alleged to have been committed after the end of the period of two months beginning with the day on which this Act is passed.

83 Trespass on aerodrome: penalty

(1) In section 39(1) of the Civil Aviation Act 1982 (c. 16) (trespass on aerodrome) for "level 1 on the standard scale" substitute "level 3 on the standard scale".

(2) This section shall have effect in relation to an offence committed after the end of the period of two months beginning with the day on which this Act is passed.

84 Removal of intruder

(1) At the end of section 21C of the Aviation Security Act 1982 (c. 36) (unauthorised presence in aerodrome) add—

"(4) A constable, the manager of an aerodrome or a person acting on his behalf may use reasonable force to remove a person who fails to comply with a request under subsection (1)(b) above."

(2) At the end of section 21D of that Act (unauthorised presence on aircraft) add—

"(3) A constable, the operator of an aircraft or a person acting on his behalf may use reasonable force to remove a person who fails to comply with a request under subsection (1)(b) above."

85 Aviation security services

After section 20 of the Aviation Security Act 1982 (security directions: inspection) insert—

"20A Aviation security services: approved providers

(1) In this section "aviation security service" means a process or activity carried out for the purpose of—

(a) complying with a requirement of a direction under any of sections 12 to 14, or

(b) facilitating a person's compliance with a requirement of a direction under any of those sections.

(2) Regulations may provide for the Secretary of State to maintain a list of persons who are approved by him for the provision of a particular aviation security service.

(3) The regulations may—

(a) prohibit the provision of an aviation security service by a person who is not listed in respect of that service;

(b) prohibit the use or engagement for the provision of an aviation security service of a person who is not listed in respect of that service;

(c) create a criminal offence;

(d) make provision about application for inclusion in the list (including provision about fees);

(e) make provision about the duration and renewal of entries on the list (including provision about fees);

(f) make provision about training or qualifications which persons who apply to be listed or who are listed are required to undergo or possess;

(g) make provision about removal from the list (which may include provision for appeal);

(h) make provision about the inspection of activities carried out by listed persons;

(i) confer functions on the Secretary of State or on a specified person;

(j) confer jurisdiction on a court.

(4) Regulations under subsection (3)(c)—

(a) may not provide for a penalty on summary conviction greater than a fine not exceeding the statutory maximum,

(b) may not provide for a penalty of imprisonment on conviction on indictment greater than imprisonment for a term not exceeding two years (whether or not accompanied by a fine), and

(c) may create a criminal offence of purporting, with intent to deceive, to do something as a listed person or of doing something, with intent to deceive, which purports to be done by a listed person.

(5) A direction under any of sections 12 to 14 may—

(a) include a requirement to use a listed person for the provision of an aviation security service;

(b) provide for all or part of the direction not to apply or to apply with modified effect where a listed person provides an aviation security service.

(6) Regulations under this section—

(a) may make different provision for different cases,

(b) may include incidental, supplemental or transitional provision,

(c) shall be made by the Secretary of State by statutory instrument,

(d) shall not be made unless the Secretary of State has consulted organisations appearing to him to represent persons affected by the regulations, and

(e) shall be subject to annulment in pursuance of a resolution of either House of Parliament."

86 Detention of aircraft

(1) After section 20A of the Aviation Security Act 1982 (c. 36) (aviation security services) (inserted by section 85)) insert—

"Detention of aircraft

20B Detention direction

(1) An authorised person may give a detention direction in respect of an aircraft if he is of the opinion that—

(a) a person has failed to comply or is likely to fail to comply with a requirement of a direction under section 12 or 14 of this Act in respect of the aircraft,

(b) a person has failed to comply with a requirement of an enforcement notice in respect of the aircraft,

(c) a threat has been made to commit an act of violence against the aircraft or against any person or property on board the aircraft, or

(d) an act of violence is likely to be committed against the aircraft or against any person or property on board the aircraft.

(2) A detention direction in respect of an aircraft—

(a) shall be given in writing to the operator of the aircraft, and

(b) shall require him to take steps to ensure that the aircraft does not fly while the direction is in force.

(3) An authorised person who has given a detention direction in respect of an aircraft may do anything which he considers necessary or expedient for the purpose of ensuring that the aircraft does not fly while the direction is in force; in particular, the authorised person may—

(a) enter the aircraft;

(b) arrange for another person to enter the aircraft;

(c) arrange for a person or thing to be removed from the aircraft;

(d) use reasonable force;

(e) authorise the use of reasonable force by another person.

(4) The operator of an aircraft in respect of which a detention direction is given may object to the direction in writing to the Secretary of State.

(5) On receipt of an objection to a detention direction under subsection (4) the Secretary of State shall—

(a) consider the objection,

(b) allow the person making the objection and the authorised person who gave the direction an opportunity to make written or oral representations to the Secretary of State or to a person appointed by him,

(c) confirm, vary or cancel the direction, and

(d) give notice of his decision in writing to the person who made the objection and to the authorised person who gave the direction.

(6) A detention direction in respect of an aircraft shall continue in force until—

(a) an authorised person cancels it by notice in writing to the operator of the aircraft, or

(b) the Secretary of State cancels it under subsection (5)(c).

(7) A person commits an offence if—

(a) without reasonable excuse he fails to comply with a requirement of a detention direction, or

(b) he intentionally obstructs a person acting in accordance with subsection (3).

(8) A person who is guilty of an offence under subsection (7) shall be liable—

(a) on summary conviction, to a fine not exceeding the statutory maximum, or

(b) on conviction on indictment, to a fine, to imprisonment for a term not exceeding two years or to both.

(9) A detention direction may be given in respect of—

(a) any aircraft in the United Kingdom, and

(b) any aircraft registered or operating in the United Kingdom.

(10) A detention direction may be given in respect of a class of aircraft; and for that purpose—

(a) a reference to "the aircraft" in subsection (1) shall be treated as a reference to all or any of the aircraft within the class, and

(b) subsections (2) to (9) shall apply as if the direction were given in respect of each aircraft within the class."

(2) In section 23 of the Aviation Security Act 1982 (c. 36) (annual report)—

(a) in subsection (1) after "enforcement notices" insert "and detention directions", and

(b) in subsection (2) for "and enforcement notices" substitute ", enforcement notices and detention directions".

(3) At the end of section 24 of that Act add—

"(9) Subsections (6) to (8) above shall apply to a detention direction as they apply to an enforcement notice."

87 Air cargo agent: documents

After section 21F of the Aviation Security Act 1982 (air cargo agents) insert—

"**21FA Air cargo agents: documents**

(1) A person commits an offence if with intent to deceive he issues a document which purports to be issued by a person on a list of approved air cargo agents maintained under section 21F(2)(a) of this Act.

(2) A person guilty of an offence under subsection (1) shall be liable on summary conviction to imprisonment for a term not exceeding six months or to a fine not exceeding level 5 on the standard scale or to both."

PART 10

POLICE POWERS

Identification

88 Fingerprinting of terrorist suspects

(1) Schedule 8 to the Terrorism Act 2000 (c. 11) (persons detained under terrorism provisions) is amended as follows.

(2) In paragraph 10, at the beginning of sub-paragraph (6) (grounds on which officer may authorise fingerprinting or taking of sample), insert "Subject to sub-paragraph (6A)"; and after that sub-paragraph insert—

"(6A) An officer may also give an authorisation under sub-paragraph (4)(a) for the taking of fingerprints if—

(a) he is satisfied that the fingerprints of the detained person will facilitate the ascertainment of that person's identity; and

(b) that person has refused to identify himself or the officer has reasonable grounds for suspecting that that person is not who he claims to be.

(6B) In this paragraph references to ascertaining a person's identity include references to showing that he is not a particular person."

(3) In paragraph 20(2), for the subsection (2) substituted by way of modification of section 18 of the Criminal Procedure (Scotland) Act 1995 (c. 46) substitute—

"'(2) Subject to subsection (2A), a constable may take from a detained person or require a detained person to provide relevant physical data only if—

(a) in the case of a person detained under section 41 of the Terrorism Act 2000, he reasonably suspects that the person has been involved in an offence under any of the provisions mentioned in section 40(1)(a) of that Act and he reasonably believes that the relevant physical data will tend to confirm or disprove his involvement; or

(b) in any case, he is satisfied that it is necessary to do so in order to assist in determining whether the person falls within section 40(1)(b).

(2A) A constable may also take fingerprints from a detained person or require him to provide them if—

(a) he is satisfied that the fingerprints of that person will facilitate the ascertainment of that person's identity; and

(b) that person has refused to identify himself or the constable has reasonable grounds for suspecting that that person is not who he claims to be.

(2B) In this section references to ascertaining a person's identity include references to showing that he is not a particular person.'"

(4) For paragraph 20(3) substitute—

"(3) Subsections (3) to (5) shall not apply, but any relevant physical data or sample taken in pursuance of section 18 as applied by this paragraph may be retained but shall not be used by any person except for the purposes of a terrorist investigation or for purposes related to the prevention or detection of crime, the investigation of an offence or the conduct of a prosecution.

(4) In this paragraph—

(a) a reference to crime includes a reference to any conduct which—

(i) constitutes one or more criminal offences (whether under the law of a part of the United Kingdom or of a country or territory outside the United Kingdom); or

(ii) is, or corresponds to, any conduct which, if it all took place in any one part of the United Kingdom, would constitute one or more criminal offences; and

(b) the references to an investigation and to a prosecution include references, respectively, to any investigation outside the United Kingdom of any crime or suspected crime and to a prosecution brought in respect of any crime in a country or territory outside the United Kingdom."

89 Searches, examinations and fingerprinting: England and Wales

(1) After section 54 of the Police and Criminal Evidence Act 1984 (c. 60) (searches of detained persons) insert—

"54A Searches and examination to ascertain identity

(1) If an officer of at least the rank of inspector authorises it, a person who is detained in a police station may be searched or examined, or both—

(a) for the purpose of ascertaining whether he has any mark that would tend to identify him as a person involved in the commission of an offence; or

(b) for the purpose of facilitating the ascertainment of his identity.

(2) An officer may only give an authorisation under subsection (1) for the purpose mentioned in paragraph (a) of that subsection if—

(a) the appropriate consent to a search or examination that would reveal whether the mark in question exists has been withheld; or

(b) it is not practicable to obtain such consent.

(3) An officer may only give an authorisation under subsection (1) in a case in which subsection (2) does not apply if—

(a) the person in question has refused to identify himself; or

(b) the officer has reasonable grounds for suspecting that that person is not who he claims to be.

(4) An officer may give an authorisation under subsection (1) orally or in writing but, if he gives it orally, he shall confirm it in writing as soon as is practicable.

(5) Any identifying mark found on a search or examination under this section may be photographed—

(a) with the appropriate consent; or

(b) if the appropriate consent is withheld or it is not practicable to obtain it, without it.

(6) Where a search or examination may be carried out under this section, or a photograph may be taken under this section, the only persons entitled to carry out the search or examination, or to take the photograph, are—

(a) constables; and

(b) persons who (without being constables) are designated for the purposes of this section by the chief officer of police for the police area in which the police station in question is situated;

and section 117 (use of force) applies to the exercise by a person falling within paragraph (b) of the powers conferred by the preceding provisions of this section as it applies to the exercise of those powers by a constable.

(7) A person may not under this section carry out a search or examination of a person of the opposite sex or take a photograph of any part of the body of a person of the opposite sex.

(8) An intimate search may not be carried out under this section.

(9) A photograph taken under this section—

(a) may be used by, or disclosed to, any person for any purpose related to the prevention or detection of crime, the investigation of an offence or the conduct of a prosecution; and

(b) after being so used or disclosed, may be retained but may not be used or disclosed except for a purpose so related.

(10) In subsection (9)—

(a) the reference to crime includes a reference to any conduct which—

(i) constitutes one or more criminal offences (whether under the law of a part of the United Kingdom or of a country or territory outside the United Kingdom); or

(ii) is, or corresponds to, any conduct which, if it all took place in any one part of the United Kingdom, would constitute one or more criminal offences;

and

(b) the references to an investigation and to a prosecution include references, respectively, to any investigation outside the United Kingdom of any crime or suspected crime and to a prosecution brought in respect of any crime in a country or territory outside the United Kingdom.

(11) In this section—

(a) references to ascertaining a person's identity include references to showing that he is not a particular person; and

(b) references to taking a photograph include references to using any process by means of which a visual image may be produced, and references to photographing a person shall be construed accordingly.

(12) In this section 'mark' includes features and injuries; and a mark is an identifying mark for the purposes of this section if its existence in any person's case facilitates the ascertainment of his identity or his identification as a person involved in the commission of an offence."

(2) In section 61(4) of that Act (grounds on which fingerprinting of person detained at a police station may be authorised)—

(a) in paragraph (b), after "his involvement" insert "or will facilitate the ascertainment of his identity (within the meaning of section 54A), or both";

(b) after that paragraph insert—

"but an authorisation shall not be given for the purpose only of facilitating the ascertainment of that person's identity except where he has refused to identify himself or the officer has reasonable grounds for suspecting that he is not who he claims to be."

90 Searches, examinations and fingerprinting: Northern Ireland

(1) After Article 55 of the Police and Criminal Evidence (Northern Ireland) Order 1989 (S.I. 1989/1341 (N.I. 12)) (searches of detained persons) insert—

"55A Searches and examination to ascertain identity

(1) If an officer of at least the rank of inspector authorises it, a person who is detained in a police station may be searched or examined, or both—

(a) for the purpose of ascertaining whether he has any mark that would tend to identify him as a person involved in the commission of an offence; or

(b) for the purpose of facilitating the ascertainment of his identity.

(2) An officer may only give an authorisation under paragraph (1) for the purpose mentioned in sub-paragraph (a) of that paragraph if—

(a) the appropriate consent to a search or examination that would reveal whether the mark in question exists has been withheld; or

(b) it is not practicable to obtain such consent.

(3) An officer may only give an authorisation under paragraph (1) in a case in which paragraph (2) does not apply if—

(a) the person in question has refused to identify himself; or

(b) the officer has reasonable grounds for suspecting that that person is not who he claims to be.

(4) An officer may give an authorisation under paragraph (1) orally or in writing but, if he gives it orally, he shall confirm it in writing as soon as is practicable.

(5) Any identifying mark found on a search or examination under this Article may be photographed—

(a) with the appropriate consent; or

(b) if the appropriate consent is withheld or it is not practicable to obtain it, without it.

(6) Where a search or examination may be carried out under this Article, or a photograph may be taken under this Article, the only persons entitled to carry out the search or examination, or to take the photograph, are—

(a) constables; and

(b) persons who (without being constables) are designated for the purposes of this Article by the Chief Constable;

and Article 88 (use of force) applies to the exercise by a person falling within sub-paragraph (b) of the powers conferred by the preceding provisions of this Article as it applies to the exercise of those powers by a constable.

(7) A person may not under this Article carry out a search or examination of a person of the opposite sex or take a photograph of any part of the body of a person of the opposite sex.

(8) An intimate search may not be carried out under this Article.

(9) A photograph taken under this Article—

(a) may be used by, or disclosed to, any person for any purpose related to the prevention or detection of crime, the investigation of an offence or the conduct of a prosecution; and

(b) after being so used or disclosed, may be retained but may not be used or disclosed except for a purpose so related.

(10) In paragraph (9)—

(a) the reference to crime includes a reference to any conduct which—

(i) constitutes one or more criminal offences (whether under the law of a part of the United Kingdom or of a country or territory outside the United Kingdom); or

(ii) is, or corresponds to, any conduct which, if it all took place in any one part of the United Kingdom, would constitute one or more criminal offences;

and

(b) the references to an investigation and to a prosecution include references, respectively, to any investigation outside the United Kingdom of any crime or suspected crime and to a prosecution brought in respect of any crime in a country or territory outside the United Kingdom.

(11) In this Article—

(a) references to ascertaining a person's identity include references to showing that he is not a particular person; and

(b) references to taking a photograph include references to using any process by means of which a visual image may be produced, and references to photographing a person shall be construed accordingly.

(12) In this Article 'mark' includes features and injuries; and a mark is an identifying mark for the purposes of this Article if its existence in any person's case facilitates the ascertainment of his identity or his identification as a person involved in the commission of an offence."

(2) In Article 61(4) of that Order (grounds on which fingerprinting of person detained at a police station may be authorised)—

(a) in sub-paragraph (b), after "his involvement" insert "or will facilitate the ascertainment of his identity (within the meaning of Article 55A), or both"; and

(b) after that sub-paragraph insert—

"but an authorisation shall not be given for the purpose only of facilitating the ascertainment of that person's identity except where he has refused to identify himself or the officer has reasonable grounds for suspecting that he is not who he claims to be."

91 Photographing of suspects etc.: England and Wales

After section 64 of the Police and Criminal Evidence Act 1984 (c. 60) insert—

"64A Photographing of suspects etc.

(1) A person who is detained at a police station may be photographed—

(a) with the appropriate consent; or

(b) if the appropriate consent is withheld or it is not practicable to obtain it, without it.

(2) A person proposing to take a photograph of any person under this section—

(a) may, for the purpose of doing so, require the removal of any item or substance worn on or over the whole or any part of the head or face of the person to be photographed; and

(b) if the requirement is not complied with, may remove the item or substance himself.

(3) Where a photograph may be taken under this section, the only persons entitled to take the photograph are—

(a) constables; and

(b) persons who (without being constables) are designated for the purposes of this section by the chief officer of police for the police area in which the police station in question is situated; and section 117 (use of force) applies to the exercise by a person falling within paragraph (b) of the powers conferred by the preceding provisions of this section as it applies to the exercise of those powers by a constable.

(4) A photograph taken under this section—

(a) may be used by, or disclosed to, any person for any purpose related to the prevention or detection of crime, the investigation of an offence or the conduct of a prosecution; and

(b) after being so used or disclosed, may be retained but may not be used or disclosed except for a purpose so related.

(5) In subsection (4)—

(a) the reference to crime includes a reference to any conduct which—

(i) constitutes one or more criminal offences (whether under the law of a part of the United Kingdom or of a country or territory outside the United Kingdom); or

(ii) is, or corresponds to, any conduct which, if it all took place in any one part of the United Kingdom, would constitute one or more criminal offences;

and

(b) the references to an investigation and to a prosecution include references, respectively, to any investigation outside the United Kingdom of any crime or suspected crime and to a prosecution brought in respect of any crime in a country or territory outside the United Kingdom.

(6) References in this section to taking a photograph include references to using any process by means of which a visual image may be produced; and references to photographing a person shall be construed accordingly."

92 Photographing of suspects etc.: Northern Ireland

After Article 64 of the Police and Criminal Evidence (Northern Ireland) Order 1989 (S.I. 1989/1341 (N.I. 12)) insert—

"64A Photographing of suspects etc.

(1) A person who is detained at a police station may be photographed—

(a) with the appropriate consent; or

(b) if the appropriate consent is withheld or it is not practicable to obtain it, without it.

(2) A person proposing to take a photograph of any person under this Article—

(a) may, for the purpose of doing so, require the removal of any item or substance worn on or over the whole or any part of the head or face of the person to be photographed; and

(b) if the requirement is not complied with, may remove the item or substance himself.

(3) Where a photograph may be taken under this Article, the only persons entitled to take the photograph are—

(a) constables; and

(b) persons who (without being constables) are designated for the purposes of this Article by the Chief Constable; and Article 88 (use of force) applies to the exercise by a person falling within sub-paragraph (b) of the powers conferred by the preceding provisions of this Article as it applies to the exercise of those powers by a constable.

(4) A photograph taken under this Article—

(a) may be used by, or disclosed to, any person for any purpose related to the prevention or detection of crime, the investigation of an offence or the conduct of a prosecution; and

(b) after being so used or disclosed, may be retained but may not be used or disclosed except for a purpose so related.

(5) In paragraph (4)—

(a) the reference to crime includes a reference to any conduct which—

(i) constitutes one or more criminal offences (whether under the law of a part of the United Kingdom or of a country or territory outside the United Kingdom); or

(ii) is, or corresponds to, any conduct which, if it all took place in any one part of the United Kingdom, would constitute one or more criminal offences;

and

(b) the references to an investigation and to a prosecution include references, respectively, to any investigation outside the United Kingdom of any crime or suspected crime and to a prosecution brought in respect of any crime in a country or territory outside the United Kingdom.

(6) References in this Article to taking a photograph include references to using any process by means of which a visual image may be produced; and references to photographing a person shall be construed accordingly."

93 Powers to require removal of disguises: Great Britain

(1) After section 60 of the Criminal Justice and Public Order Act 1994 (c. 33) insert—

"60AA Powers to require removal of disguises

(1) Where—

(a) an authorisation under section 60 is for the time being in force in relation to any locality for any period, or

(b) an authorisation under subsection (3) that the powers conferred by subsection (2) shall be exercisable at any place in a locality is in force for any period, those powers shall be exercisable at any place in that locality at any time in that period.

(2) This subsection confers power on any constable in uniform—

(a) to require any person to remove any item which the constable reasonably believes that person is wearing wholly or mainly for the purpose of concealing his identity;

(b) to seize any item which the constable reasonably believes any person intends to wear wholly or mainly for that purpose.

(3) If a police officer of or above the rank of inspector reasonably believes—

(a) that activities may take place in any locality in his police area that are likely (if they take place) to involve the commission of offences, and

(b) that it is expedient, in order to prevent or control the activities, to give an authorisation under this subsection, he may give an authorisation that the powers conferred by this section shall be exercisable at any place within that locality for a specified period not exceeding twenty-four hours.

(4) If it appears to an officer of or above the rank of superintendent that it is expedient to do so, having regard to offences which—

(a) have been committed in connection with the activities in respect of which the authorisation was given, or

(b) are reasonably suspected to have been so committed, he may direct that the authorisation shall continue in force for a further twenty-four hours.

(5) If an inspector gives an authorisation under subsection (3), he must, as soon as it is practicable to do so, cause an officer of or above the rank of superintendent to be informed.

(6) Any authorisation under this section—

(a) shall be in writing and signed by the officer giving it; and

(b) shall specify—

(i) the grounds on which it is given;

(ii) the locality in which the powers conferred by this section are exercisable;

(iii) the period during which those powers are exercisable; and a direction under subsection (4) shall also be given in writing or, where that is not practicable, recorded in writing as soon as it is practicable to do so.

(7) A person who fails to remove an item worn by him when required to do so by a constable in the exercise of his power under this section shall be liable, on summary conviction, to imprisonment for a term not exceeding one month or to a fine not exceeding level 3 on the standard scale or both.

(8) The preceding provisions of this section, so far as they relate to an authorisation by a member of the British Transport Police Force (including one who for the time being has the same powers and privileges as a member of a police force for a police area), shall have effect as if references to a locality or to a locality in his police area were references to any locality in or in the vicinity of any policed premises, or to the whole or any part of any such premises.

(9) In this section 'British Transport Police Force' and 'policed premises' each has the same meaning as in section 60.

(10) The powers conferred by this section are in addition to, and not in derogation of, any power otherwise conferred."

(2) In section 60A(1) of that Act (retention of things seized under section 60), after "section 60" insert "or 60AA".

(3) In section 60B of that Act (offence under section 60(8) to be an arrestable offence in Scotland), after "60(8)" insert "or 60AA(7)".

(4) In section 24(2) of the Police and Criminal Evidence Act 1984 (c. 60) (arrestable offences), in paragraph (o), for "section 60(8)(b)" substitute "section 60AA(7)".

94 Powers to require removal of disguises: Northern Ireland

(1) In Part 5 of the Public Order (Northern Ireland) Order 1987 (S.I. 1987/463 (N.I. 7)), before Article 24 insert—

"Temporary powers to deal with activities in a locality

23A Powers to require removal of disguises

(1) Where—

(a) an authorisation under paragraph (3) that the powers conferred by paragraph (2) shall be exercisable at any place in a locality is in force for any period, or

(b) an authorisation under Article 23B is for the time being in force in relation to any locality for any period, those powers shall be exercisable at any place in that locality at any time in that period.

(2) This paragraph confers power on any constable in uniform—

(a) to require any person to remove any item which the constable reasonably believes that person is wearing wholly or mainly for the purpose of concealing his identity;

(b) to seize any item which the constable reasonably believes any person intends to wear wholly or mainly for that purpose.

(3) If a police officer of or above the rank of inspector reasonably believes—

(a) that activities may take place in any locality that are likely (if they take place) to involve the commission of offences, and

(b) that it is expedient, in order to prevent or control the activities, to give an authorisation under this paragraph, he may give an authorisation that the powers conferred by this Article shall be exercisable at any place within that locality for a specified period not exceeding twenty-four hours.

(4) If it appears to an officer of or above the rank of superintendent that it is expedient to do so, having regard to offences which—

(a) have been committed in connection with the activities in respect of which the authorisation was given, or

(b) are reasonably suspected to have been so committed, he may direct that the authorisation shall continue in force for a further twenty-four hours.

(5) If an officer below the rank of superintendent gives an authorisation under paragraph (3), he must, as soon as it is practicable to do so, cause an officer of or above that rank to be informed.

(6) Any authorisation under this Article—

(a) shall be in writing and signed by the officer giving it; and

(b) shall specify—

(i) the grounds on which it is given;

(ii) the locality in which the powers conferred by this Article are exercisable;

(iii) the period during which those powers are exercisable; and a direction under paragraph (4) shall also be given in writing or, where that is not practicable, recorded in writing as soon as it is practicable to do so.

(7) A person who fails to remove an item worn by him when required to do so by a constable in the exercise of his power under this Article shall be liable, on summary conviction, to imprisonment for a term not exceeding one month or to a fine not exceeding level 3 on the standard scale or both.

(8) The powers conferred by this Article are in addition to, and not in derogation of, any power otherwise conferred."

(2) In Article 26(2) of the Police and Criminal Evidence (Northern Ireland) Order 1989 (S.I. 1989/1341 (N.I. 12)) (arrestable offences), after sub-paragraph (i) insert—

"(j) Article 23A(7) of the Public Order (Northern Ireland) Order 1987 (S.I. 1987/463 (N.I. 7)) (failing to comply to requirement to remove disguise)."

Powers of stop, search and seizure in Northern Ireland

95 Power to stop and search in anticipation of violence

In the Public Order (Northern Ireland) Order 1987, after Article 23A (which is inserted by section 94) insert—

"23B Powers to stop and search in anticipation of violence

(1) If a police officer of or above the rank of inspector reasonably believes—

> (a) that incidents involving serious violence may take place in any locality, and that it is expedient to give an authorisation under this Article to prevent or control their occurrence, or

> (b) that persons are carrying dangerous instruments or offensive weapons in any locality without good reason,

he may give an authorisation that the powers conferred by this Article are to be exercisable at any place within that locality for a specified period not exceeding twenty-four hours.

(2) This Article confers power on any constable in uniform—

> (a) to stop any pedestrian and search him or anything carried by him for offensive weapons or dangerous instruments;

> (b) to stop any vehicle and search the vehicle, its driver and any passenger for offensive weapons or dangerous instruments;

and a constable may in the exercise of those powers stop any person or vehicle and make any search he thinks fit whether or not he has any grounds for suspecting that the person or vehicle is carrying weapons or dangerous instruments.

(3) If it appears to an officer of or above the rank of superintendent that it is expedient to do so, having regard to offences which—

> (a) have been committed in connection with the activities in respect of which the authorisation was given, or

> (b) are reasonably suspected to have been so committed, he may direct that the authorisation shall continue in force for a further twenty-four hours.

(4) If an officer below the rank of superintendent gives an authorisation under paragraph (1) he must, as soon as it is practicable to do so, cause an officer of or above that rank to be informed.

(5) If in the course of a search under this Article a constable discovers a dangerous instrument or an article which he has reasonable grounds for suspecting to be an offensive weapon, he may seize it.

(6) This Article applies (with the necessary modifications) to ships, aircraft and hovercraft as it applies to vehicles.

(7) A person who fails to stop or (as the case may be) fails to stop a vehicle when required to do so by a constable in the exercise of his powers under this Article shall be liable on summary conviction to imprisonment for a term not exceeding one month or to a fine not exceeding level 3 on the standard scale or both.

(8) Any authorisation under this Article—

(a) shall be in writing and signed by the officer giving it; and

(b) shall specify—

(i) the grounds on which it is given;

(ii) the locality in which the powers conferred by this Article are exercisable;

(iii) the period during which those powers are exercisable;

and a direction under paragraph (3) shall also be given in writing or, where that is not practicable, recorded in writing as soon as it is practicable to do so.

(9) Where a vehicle is stopped by a constable under this Article the driver shall be entitled to obtain a written statement that the vehicle was stopped under the powers conferred by this Article if he applies for such a statement not later than the end of the period of 12 months from the day on which the vehicle was stopped.

(10) A person who is searched by a constable under this Article shall be entitled to obtain a written statement that he was searched under the powers conferred by this Article if he applies for such a statement not later than the end of the period of 12 months from the day on which he was searched.

(11) The powers conferred by this Article are in addition to, and not in derogation of, any power otherwise conferred.

(12) For the purposes of this Article, a person carries a dangerous instrument or an offensive weapon if he has it in his possession.

(13) In this Article—

'caravan' has the meaning given by section 25(1) of the Caravans Act (Northern Ireland) 1963 (N.I. c. 17);

'dangerous instrument' means an instrument which has a blade or is sharply pointed;

'offensive weapon' has the meaning given by Article 22(1); 'vehicle' includes a caravan."

96 Seized articles

In the Public Order (Northern Ireland) Order 1987 (S.I. 1987/463 (N.I. 7)), after Article 23B insert—

"**23C Retention and disposal of things seized under Article 23A and 23B**

(1) Anything seized by a constable under Article 23A or 23B may be retained in accordance with regulations made by the Secretary of State under this Article.

(2) The Secretary of State may make regulations regulating the retention and safe keeping, and the disposal and destruction in prescribed circumstances, of such things.

(3) Regulations made under this Article shall be subject to annulment in pursuance of a resolution of either House of Parliament in like manner as a statutory instrument and section 5 of the Statutory Instruments Act 1946 (c. 36) shall apply accordingly."

MoD and transport police

97 Jurisdiction of MoD police

(1) Section 2 of the Ministry of Defence Police Act 1987 (c. 4) (jurisdiction of members of the Ministry of Defence Police) is amended as follows.

(2) In subsection (2) (places where members of Ministry of Defence Police have powers and privileges of constables), omit paragraph (d) (which is superseded by the amendment made by subsection (4) of this section).

(3) In subsection (3) (circumstances in which members of Ministry of Defence Police have powers and privileges of constables in places in United Kingdom not mentioned in subsection (2)), after paragraph (b) insert—

"(ba) in connection with offences against persons within paragraph (b) above, with the incitement of such persons to commit offences and with offences under the Prevention of Corruption Acts 1889 to 1916 in relation to such persons;".

(4) After that subsection insert—

"(3A) Where a member of the Ministry of Defence Police has been requested by a constable of—

(a) the police force for any police area;

(b) the Police Service of Northern Ireland;

(c) the British Transport Police Force; or

(d) the United Kingdom Atomic Energy Authority Constabulary, to assist him in the execution of his duties in relation to a particular incident, investigation or operation, members of the Ministry of Defence Police shall have the powers and privileges of constables for the purposes of that incident, investigation or operation but subject to subsection (3B) below.

(3B) Members of the Ministry of Defence Police have the powers and privileges of constables for the purposes of an incident, investigation or operation by virtue of subsection (3A) above—

(a) if the request was made under paragraph (a) of that subsection by a constable of the police force for a police area, only in that police area;

(b) if it was made under paragraph (b) of that subsection, only in Northern Ireland;

(c) if it was made under paragraph (c) of that subsection, only to the extent that those powers and privileges would in the circumstances be exercisable for those purposes by a constable of the British Transport Police Force by virtue of subsection (1A) or, in Scotland, subsection (4) of section 53 of the British Transport Commission Act 1949 (c. xxix); or

(d) if it was made under paragraph (d) of that subsection, only to the extent that those powers and privileges would in the circumstances be exercisable for those purposes by a constable of the United Kingdom Atomic Energy Authority Constabulary.

(3C) Members of the Ministry of Defence Police shall have in any police area the same powers and privileges as constables of the police force for that police area, and in Northern Ireland the same powers and privileges as constables of the Police Service of Northern Ireland,—

(a) in relation to persons whom they suspect on reasonable grounds of having committed, being in the course of committing or being about to commit an offence; or

(b) if they believe on reasonable grounds that they need those powers and privileges in order to save life or to prevent or minimise personal injury.

(3D) But members of the Ministry of Defence Police have powers and privileges by virtue of subsection (3C) above only if—

(a) they are in uniform or have with them documentary evidence that they are members of the Ministry of Defence Police; and

(b) they believe on reasonable grounds that a power of a constable which they would not have apart from that subsection ought to be exercised and that, if it cannot be exercised until they secure the attendance of or a request under subsection (3A) above by a constable who has it, the purpose for which they believe it ought to be exercised will be frustrated or seriously prejudiced."

(5) In subsection (4) (territorial waters)—

(a) for "to (3)" substitute "to (3D)", and

(b) for "subsections (1) and (3)" substitute "those subsections".

(6) In subsection (5)—

(a) after the definition of "appropriate Gazette" insert—

""British Transport Police Force" means the constables appointed under section 53 of the British Transport Commission Act 1949;", and

(b) after the definition of "service authorities" insert—

""United Kingdom Atomic Energy Authority Constabulary" means the special constables appointed under section 3 of the Special Constables Act 1923 (c. 11) on the nomination of the United Kingdom Atomic Energy Authority;".

98 Provision of assistance by MoD police

After section 2 of the Ministry of Defence Police Act 1987 (c. 4) insert—

"2A Provision of assistance to other forces

(1) The Chief Constable of the Ministry of Defence Police may, on the application of the chief officer of any relevant force, provide constables or other assistance for the purpose of enabling that force to meet any special demand on its resources.

(2) Where a member of the Ministry of Defence Police is provided for the assistance of a relevant force under this section—

(a) he shall be under the direction and control of the chief officer of that force; and

(b) he shall have the same powers and privileges as a member of that force.

(3) Constables are not to be regarded as provided for the assistance of a relevant force under this section in a case where assistance is provided under section 2 above.

(4) In this section—

"British Transport Police Force" has the same meaning as in section 2 above;

"chief officer" means—

(a) the chief officer of the police force for any police area;

(b) the Chief Constable of the Police Service of Northern Ireland;

(c) the Chief Constable of the British Transport Police Force; or

(d) the Chief Constable of the United Kingdom Atomic Energy Authority Constabulary;

"relevant force" means—

(a) the police force for any police area;

(b) the Police Service of Northern Ireland;

(c) the British Transport Police Force; or

(d) the United Kingdom Atomic Energy Authority Constabulary; and "United Kingdom Atomic Energy Authority Constabulary" has the same meaning as in section 2 above."

99 Jurisdiction of transport police

(1) Where a member of the British Transport Police Force has been requested by a constable of—

(a) the police force for any police area,

(b) the Ministry of Defence Police, or

(c) the United Kingdom Atomic Energy Authority Constabulary,

("the requesting force") to assist him in the execution of his duties in relation to a particular incident, investigation or operation, members of the British Transport Police Force have for the purposes of that incident, investigation or operation the same powers and privileges as constables of the requesting force.

(2) Members of the British Transport Police Force have in any police area the same powers and privileges as constables of the police force for that police area—

(a) in relation to persons whom they suspect on reasonable grounds of having committed, being in the course of committing or being about to commit an offence, or

(b) if they believe on reasonable grounds that they need those powers and privileges in order to save life or to prevent or minimise personal injury.

(3) But members of the British Transport Police Force have powers and privileges by virtue of subsection (2) only if—

(a) they are in uniform or have with them documentary evidence that they are members of that Force, and

(b) they believe on reasonable grounds that a power of a constable which they would not have apart from that subsection ought to be exercised and that, if it cannot be exercised until they secure the attendance of or a request under subsection (1) by a constable who has it, the purpose for which they believe it ought to be exercised will be frustrated or seriously prejudiced.

(4) In this section—

"British Transport Police Force" means the constables appointed under section 53 of the British Transport Commission Act 1949 (c. xxix), and

"United Kingdom Atomic Energy Authority Constabulary" means the special constables appointed under section 3 of the Special Constables Act 1923 (c. 11) on the nomination of the United Kingdom Atomic Energy Authority.

100 Further provisions about transport police and MoD police

Schedule 7 contains amendments relating to the British Transport Police Force and the Ministry of Defence Police.

PART 11

RETENTION OF COMMUNICATIONS DATA

101 Codes and agreements about the retention of communications data

(1) The Secretary of State shall issue, and may from time to time revise, a code of practice relating to the retention by communications providers of communications data obtained by or held by them.

(2) The Secretary of State may enter into such agreements as he considers appropriate with any communications provider about the practice to be followed by that provider in relation to the retention of communications data obtained by or held by that provider.

(3) Before issuing or revising a code of practice under this section the Secretary of State shall consult with the communications providers to whom the code will apply or, as the case may be, who will be affected by the revisions, or with the persons appearing to him to represent those providers.

(4) Where the Secretary of State issues or revises a code of practice under this section, he shall publish the code or, as the case may be, the revised

code in such manner as he considers appropriate for bringing it to the attention of the communications providers to whom it applies.

(5) A code of practice or agreement under this section may contain any such provision as appears to the Secretary of State to be necessary—

(a) for the purpose of safeguarding national security; or

(b) for the purposes of the prevention or detection of crime or the prosecution of offenders.

(6) A failure by any person to comply with a code of practice or agreement under this section shall not of itself render him liable to any criminal or civil proceedings.

(7) A code of practice or agreement under this section shall be admissible in evidence in any legal proceedings in which the question arises whether or not the retention of any communications data is justified on the grounds that a failure to retain the data would be likely to prejudice national security, the prevention or detection of crime or the prosecution of offenders.

102 Directions about retention of communications data

(1) If, after reviewing the operation of any requirements contained in the code of practice and any agreements under section 101, it appears to the Secretary of State that it is necessary to do so, he may by order made by statutory instrument authorise the giving of directions under this section.

(2) Where any order under this section is in force, the Secretary of State may give such directions as he considers appropriate about the retention of communications data—

(a) to communications providers generally;

(b) to communications providers of a description specified in the direction; or

(c) to any particular communications providers or provider.

(3) An order under this section must specify the maximum period for which a communications provider may be required to retain communications data by any direction given under this section while the order is in force.

(4) Before giving a direction under this section the Secretary of State shall consult—

(a) with the communications provider or providers to whom it will apply; or

(b) except in the case of a direction confined to a particular provider, with the persons appearing to the Secretary of State to represent the providers to whom it will apply.

(5) A direction under this section must be given or published in such manner as the Secretary of State considers appropriate for bringing it to the attention of the communications providers or provider to whom it applies.

(6) It shall be the duty of a communications provider to comply with any direction under this section that applies to him.

(7) The duty imposed by subsection (6) shall be enforceable by civil proceedings by the Secretary of State for an injunction, or for specific performance of a statutory duty under section 45 of the Court of Session Act 1988 (c. 36), or for any other appropriate relief.

(8) The Secretary of State shall not make an order under this section unless a draft of it has been laid before Parliament and approved by a resolution of each House.

103 Lapsing of powers in section 102

(1) Section 102 shall cease to have effect at the end of the initial period unless an order authorising the giving of directions is made under that section before the end of that period.

(2) Subject to subsection (3), the initial period is the period of two years beginning with the day on which this Act is passed.

(3) The Secretary of State may by order made by statutory instrument extend, or (on one or more occasions) further extend the initial period.

(4) An order under subsection (3)—

(a) must be made before the time when the initial period would end but for the making of the order; and

(b) shall have the effect of extending, or further extending, that period for the period of two years beginning with that time.

(5) The Secretary of State shall not make an order under subsection (3) unless a draft of it has been laid before Parliament and approved by a resolution of each House.

104 Arrangements for payments

(1) It shall be the duty of the Secretary of State to ensure that such arrangements are in force as he thinks appropriate for authorising or requiring, in such cases as he thinks fit, the making to communications providers of appropriate contributions towards the costs incurred by them—

(a) in complying with the provisions of any code of practice, agreement or direction under this Part, or

(b) as a consequence of the retention of any communications data in accordance with any such provisions.

(2) For the purpose of complying with his duty under this section, the Secretary of State may make arrangements for the payments to be made out of money provided by Parliament.

105 Interpretation of Part 11

(1) In this Part—

"communications data" has the same meaning as in Chapter 2 of Part 1 of the Regulation of Investigatory Powers Act 2000 (c. 23);

"communications provider" means a person who provides a postal service or a telecommunications service;

"legal proceedings", "postal service" and "telecommunications service" each has the same meaning as in that Act;

and any reference in this Part to the prevention or detection of crime shall be construed as if contained in Chapter 2 of Part 1 of that Act.

(2) References in this Part, in relation to any code of practice, agreement or direction, to the retention by a communications provider of any communications data include references to the retention of any data obtained by that provider before the time when the code was issued, the agreement made or the direction given, and to data already held by that provider at that time.

PART 12

BRIBERY AND CORRUPTION

106 Bribery and corruption: foreign officers etc.

(1) For the purposes of any common law offence of bribery it is immaterial if the functions of the person who receives or is offered a reward have no connection with the United Kingdom and are carried out in a country or territory outside the United Kingdom.

(2) In section 1 of the Prevention of Corruption Act 1906 (c. 34) (corrupt transactions with agents) insert this subsection after subsection (3)—

"(4) For the purposes of this Act it is immaterial if—

(a) the principal's affairs or business have no connection with the United Kingdom and are conducted in a country or territory outside the United Kingdom;

(b) the agent's functions have no connection with the United Kingdom and are carried out in a country or territory outside the United Kingdom."

(3) In section 7 of the Public Bodies Corrupt Practices Act 1889 (c. 69) (interpretation relating to corruption in office) in the definition of "public body" for "but does not include any public body as above defined existing elsewhere than in the United Kingdom" substitute "and includes any body which exists in a country or territory outside the United Kingdom and is equivalent to any body described above".

(4) In section 4(2) of the Prevention of Corruption Act 1916 (c. 64) (in the 1889 and 1916 Acts public body includes local and public authorities of all descriptions) after "descriptions" insert "(including authorities existing in a country or territory outside the United Kingdom)".

107 Bribery and corruption committed outside the UK

(1) This section applies if—

(a) a national of the United Kingdom or a body incorporated under the law of any part of the United Kingdom does anything in a country or territory outside the United Kingdom, and

(b) the act would, if done in the United Kingdom, constitute a corruption offence (as defined below).

(2) In such a case—

(a) the act constitutes the offence concerned, and

(b) proceedings for the offence may be taken in the United Kingdom.

(3) These are corruption offences—

(a) any common law offence of bribery;

(b) the offences under section 1 of the Public Bodies Corrupt Practices Act 1889 (c. 69) (corruption in office);

(c) the first two offences under section 1 of the Prevention of Corruption Act 1906 (c. 34) (bribes obtained by or given to agents).

(4) A national of the United Kingdom is an individual who is—

(a) a British citizen, a British Dependent Territories citizen, a British National (Overseas) or a British Overseas citizen,

(b) a person who under the British Nationality Act 1981 (c. 61) is a British subject, or

(c) a British protected person within the meaning of that Act.

108 Presumption of corruption not to apply

Section 2 of the Prevention of Corruption Act 1916 (c. 64) (presumption of corruption in certain cases) is not to apply in relation to anything which would not be an offence apart from section 106 or section 107.

PART 13

MISCELLANEOUS

Third pillar of the European Union

109 Implementation of the third pillar

(1) An authorised Minister may by regulations make provision—

(a) for the purpose of implementing any obligation of the United Kingdom created or arising by or under the third pillar (whether before or after the passing of this Act), or enabling any such obligation to be implemented,

(b) for the purpose of enabling any rights enjoyed or to be enjoyed by the United Kingdom under or by virtue of the third pillar to be exercised, or

(c) for the purpose of dealing with matters arising out of or related to any such obligation or rights.

(2) "The third pillar" means—

(a) Title VI of the Treaty on European Union signed at Maastricht on 7th February 1992, together with the other provisions of the Treaty so far as they relate to that Title,

(b) the Protocol integrating the Schengen acquis into the framework of the European Union, so far as it relates to that Title, and

(c) agreements referred to in Article 24 of the Treaty, so far as they cover matters falling under that Title.

(3) In subsection (2) a reference to a provision of the Treaty on European Union includes a reference to that provision as amended by any provision of—

(a) the Treaty signed at Amsterdam on 2nd October 1997, or

(b) the Treaty signed at Nice on 26th February 2001.

(4) The provision that may be made under subsection (1) includes, subject to subsection (5), any such provision (of any such extent) as might be made by Act of Parliament.

(5) The powers conferred by subsection (1) do not include power—

(a) to make any provision imposing or increasing taxation,

(b) to make any provision taking effect from a date earlier than that of the making of the instrument containing the provision,

(c) to confer any power to legislate by means of orders, rules, regulations or other subordinate instrument, other than rules of procedure for a court or tribunal, or

(d) to create, except in accordance with subsection (7), a criminal offence which is punishable—

(i) on conviction on indictment, with imprisonment for more than two years,

(ii) on summary conviction, with imprisonment for more than three months,

(iii) on summary conviction, with a fine (not calculated on a daily basis) of more than level 5 on the standard scale or (for an offence triable either way) more than the statutory maximum, or

(iv) on summary conviction, with a fine of more than £100 a day.

(6) Subsection (5)(c) does not preclude the modification of a power to legislate conferred otherwise than under subsection (1), or the extension of any such power to purposes of the like nature as those for which it was conferred, and a power to give directions as to matters of administration is not to be regarded as a power to legislate within the meaning of subsection (5)(c).

(7) Subsection (5)(d) does not preclude the creation of an offence punishable on conviction on indictment with imprisonment for a term of any length if—

(a) the offence is one for which a term of that length, a term of at least that length, or a term within a range of lengths including that length, is required for the offence by an obligation created or arising by or under the third pillar,

(b) the offence, if committed in particular circumstances, would be an offence falling within paragraph (a), or

(c) the offence is not committed in the United Kingdom but would, if committed in the United Kingdom, or a part of the United Kingdom, be punishable on conviction on indictment with imprisonment for a term of that length.

110 Third pillar: supplemental

(1) "Authorised Minister" in section 109(1) has the meaning given by sub-sections (2) and (3).

(2) The Scottish Ministers are authorised Ministers for any purpose for which powers under section 109(1) are exercisable within devolved competence (within the meaning of the Scotland Act 1998 (c. 46)).

(3) For any other purpose, the following are authorised Ministers—

(a) the Secretary of State,

(b) the Lord Chancellor,

(c) the Treasury,

(d) the National Assembly for Wales, if designated under subsection (4),

(e) the First Minister and deputy First Minister acting jointly, a Northern Ireland Minister or a Northern Ireland department, if the Ministers are, or the Minister or the department is, designated under subsection (4).

(4) A designation under this subsection may be made by Order in Council in relation to any matter or for any purpose, and is subject to any restriction or condition specified in the Order.

(5) An Order in Council under subsection (4) is subject to annulment in pursuance of a resolution of either House of Parliament.

(6) The power to make regulations under section 109(1)—

(a) in the case of the First Minister and deputy First Minister acting jointly, a Northern Ireland Minister or a Northern Ireland Department, is exercisable by statutory rule for the purposes of the Statutory Rules (Northern Ireland) Order 1979 (S.I.1979/1573 (N.I. 12)),

(b) in any other case, is exercisable by statutory instrument.

(7) No regulations may be made under section 109(1) unless a draft of the regulations has been laid before and approved by a resolution of each House of Parliament.

(8) Subsection (7) has effect, so far as it relates to the exercise of powers under section 109(1) by the Scottish Ministers, as if the reference to each House of Parliament were a reference to the Scottish Parliament.

(9) Subsection (7) does not apply to a statutory instrument containing regulations made by the National Assembly for Wales unless the statutory instrument contains regulations—

(a) made by the Secretary of State, the Lord Chancellor or the Treasury (whether or not jointly with the Assembly),

(b) relating to an English border area, or

(c) relating to a cross-border body (and not relating only to the exercise of functions, or the carrying on of activities, by the body in or with respect to Wales or a part of Wales);

and in this subsection expressions used in the Government of Wales Act 1998 (c. 38) have the same meaning as in that Act.

(10) Subsection (7) has effect, so far as it relates to the exercise of powers under section 109(1) by the First Minister and deputy First Minister acting jointly, a Northern Ireland Minister or a Northern Ireland department, as if the reference to each House of Parliament were a reference to the Northern Ireland Assembly.

Dangerous substances

111 Use of noxious substances to cause harm and intimidate

(1) A person who takes any action which—

(a) involves the use of a noxious substance or other noxious thing;

(b) has an effect falling within subsection (2); and

(c) is designed to influence the government or to intimidate the public or a section of the public,

is guilty of an offence.

(2) Action falls within this subsection if it—

(a) involves serious violence against a person;

(b) involves serious damage to property;

(c) endangers human life or creates a serious risk to the health or safety of the public or a section of the public; or

(d) is likely to induce in members of the public the fear that the action is likely to endanger their lives or create a serious risk to their health or safety; but any effect on the person taking the action is to be disregarded.

(3) A person who—

(a) makes a threat that he or another will take any action falling within subsection (1); and

(b) intends thereby to induce in any person the fear that the threat will be carried out,

is guilty of an offence.

(4) A person guilty of an offence under this section is liable—

(a) on summary conviction, to imprisonment for a term not exceeding six months or a fine not exceeding the statutory maximum (or both); and

(b) on conviction on indictment, to imprisonment for a term not exceeding fourteen years or a fine (or both).

(5) In this section—

"person" includes a person outside the United Kingdom;

"property" means tangible property (whether real or personal) anywhere in the world;

"the public" includes the public of a country other than the United Kingdom; and

"the government" means the government of the United Kingdom, a part of the United Kingdom or of a country other than the United Kingdom.

112 Hoaxes and threats involving noxious substances or things

(1) A person is guilty of an offence if he—

(a) places any substance or other thing in any place whatever; or

(b) sends any substance or other thing from one place to another (by post, rail or any other means whatever);

with the intention of inducing in any person a belief that it is likely to be (or contain) a noxious substance or other noxious thing and thereby endanger human life or create a serious risk to human health.

(2) A person is guilty of an offence if he communicates any information which he knows or believes to be false with the intention of inducing in any person a belief that a noxious substance or other noxious thing is or will be present in any place whatever and thereby likely to endanger human life or create a serious risk to human health.

(3) A person guilty of an offence under this section is liable—

(a) on summary conviction, to imprisonment for a term not exceeding six months or a fine not exceeding the statutory maximum (or both); and

(b) on conviction on indictment, to imprisonment for a term not exceeding seven years or a fine (or both).

113 Sections 111 and 112: supplementary

(1) For the purposes of sections 111 and 112 "substance" includes any biological agent and any other natural or artificial substance (whatever its form, origin or method of production).

(2) For a person to be guilty of an offence under section 111(3) or 112 it is not necessary for him to have any particular person in mind as the person in whom he intends to induce the belief in question.

Intelligence Services Act 1994

114 Amendments of Intelligence Services Act 1994

(1) In section 7 of the Intelligence Services Act 1994 (c. 13) (authorisation of acts outside the British Islands), in subsection (3) —

(a) in paragraphs (a) and (b)(i), after "the Intelligence Service" insert, in each case, "or GCHQ"; and

(b) in paragraph (c), after "2(2)(a)" insert "or 4(2)(a)".

(2) After subsection (8) of that section insert—

"(9) For the purposes of this section the reference in subsection (1) to an act done outside the British Islands includes a reference to any act which—

(a) is done in the British Islands; but

(b) is or is intended to be done in relation to apparatus that is believed to be outside the British Islands, or in relation to anything appearing to originate from such apparatus; and in this subsection 'apparatus' has the same meaning as in the Regulation of Investigatory Powers Act 2000 (c. 23)."

(3) In section 11(1A) of that Act (prevention and detection of crime to have the same meaning as in Chapter 1 of Part 1 of the Regulation of Investigatory Powers Act 2000), for the words from "for the purposes of this Act" to the end of the subsection substitute—

"(a) for the purposes of section 3 above, as it applies for the purposes of Chapter 1 of Part 1 of that Act; and

(b) for the other purposes of this Act, as it applies for the purposes of the provisions of that Act not contained in that Chapter."

Terrorism Act 2000

115 Information about acts of terrorism

(1) The Terrorism Act 2000 (c. 11) is amended as follows.

(2) After section 38 insert—

"38A Information about acts of terrorism

(1) This section applies where a person has information which he knows or believes might be of material assistance—

(a) in preventing the commission by another person of an act of terrorism, or

(b) in securing the apprehension, prosecution or conviction of another person, in the United Kingdom, for an offence involving the commission, preparation or instigation of an act of terrorism.

(2) The person commits an offence if he does not disclose the information as soon as reasonably practicable in accordance with subsection (3).

(3) Disclosure is in accordance with this subsection if it is made—

(a) in England and Wales, to a constable,

(b) in Scotland, to a constable or a procurator fiscal, or

(c) in Northern Ireland, to a constable or a member of Her Majesty's forces.

(4) It is a defence for a person charged with an offence under subsection (2) to prove that he had a reasonable excuse for not making the disclosure.

(5) A person guilty of an offence under this section shall be liable—

(a) on conviction on indictment, to imprisonment for a term not exceeding five years, or to a fine or to both, or

(b) on summary conviction, to imprisonment for a term not exceeding six months, or to a fine not exceeding the statutory maximum or to both.

(6) Proceedings for an offence under this section may be taken, and the offence may for the purposes of those proceedings be treated as having been committed, in any place where the person to be charged is or has at any time been since he first knew or believed that the information might be of material assistance as mentioned in subsection (1)."

(3) In section 39(3) (disclosure of information etc.), after "21" insert "or 38A".

116 Port and airport controls for domestic travel

(1) Schedule 7 to the Terrorism Act 2000 (c. 11) (port and border controls) is amended as follows.

(2) In paragraph 2(2)(b), at the end insert "or his travelling by air within Great Britain or within Northern Ireland."

(3) In paragraph 2(3), for "in Great Britain or Northern Ireland." substitute "at any place in Great Britain or Northern Ireland (whether from within or outside Great Britain or Northern Ireland)."

(4) For paragraph 9(2) substitute—

"(2) This paragraph applies to—

(a) goods which have arrived in or are about to leave Great Britain or Northern Ireland on a ship or vehicle, and

(b) goods which have arrived at or are about to leave any place in Great Britain or Northern Ireland on an aircraft (whether the place they have come from or are going to is within or outside Great Britain or Northern Ireland)."

117 Passenger information

(1) Paragraph 17 of Schedule 7 to the Terrorism Act 2000 (c. 11) (port and border controls: passenger information) is amended as follows.

(2) For sub-paragraph (1) substitute—

"(1) This paragraph applies to a ship or aircraft which—

(a) arrives or is expected to arrive in any place in the United Kingdom (whether from another place in the United Kingdom or from outside the United Kingdom), or

(b) leaves or is expected to leave the United Kingdom."

(3) In sub-paragraph (4)—

(a) omit the "or" at the end of paragraph (b), and

(b) after paragraph (c) add—

", or

(d) to goods."

118 Weapons training for terrorists

(1) In section 54(1) and (2) of the Terrorism Act 2000 (weapons training for terrorists), after paragraph (a) insert—

"(aa) radioactive material or weapons designed or adapted for the discharge of any radioactive material,".

(2) In section 55 of that Act (definitions)—

(a) for the definition of "biological weapon" substitute—

""biological weapon" means a biological agent or toxin (within the meaning of the Biological Weapons Act 1974) in a form capable of use for hostile purposes or anything to which section 1(1)(b) of that Act applies,";

(b) after the definition of "chemical weapon" insert—

""radioactive material" means radioactive material capable of endangering life or causing harm to human health,"; and

(c) the definition of "nuclear weapon" shall cease to have effect.

119 Crown Court judges: Northern Ireland

(1) The Terrorism Act 2000 is amended as follows.

(2) In paragraph 18 of Schedule 5 (terrorist investigations: application to Northern Ireland)—

(a) omit paragraph (e);

(b) in paragraph (g) for "county court judge" substitute "Crown Court judge".

(3) In paragraph 3(c) of Schedule 6 (persons by whom financial information orders may be made) for "county court judge" substitute "Crown Court judge".

(4) In paragraph 20 of that Schedule (powers of Secretary of State), in sub-paragraphs (2) and (3)(a) for "county court judge" substitute "Crown Court judge".

PART 14

SUPPLEMENTAL

120 Consequential and supplementary provision

(1) A Minister of the Crown may by order make such incidental, consequential, transitional or supplemental provision as he thinks necessary or

expedient for the general purposes, or any particular purpose, of this Act or in consequence of any provision made by or under this Act or for giving full effect to this Act or any such provision.

(2) An order under this section may, in particular, make provision—

(a) for applying (with or without modifications) or amending, repealing or revoking any provision of or made under an Act passed before this Act or in the same Session,

(b) for making savings, or additional savings, from the effect of any repeal or revocation made by or under this Act.

(3) Amendments made under this section are in addition, and without prejudice, to those made by or under any other provision of this Act.

(4) No other provision of this Act restricts the powers conferred by this section.

(5) An order under this section may make different provision for different purposes.

(6) An order under this section shall be made by statutory instrument which shall be subject to annulment in pursuance of a resolution of either House of Parliament.

(7) In this Part, "Minister of the Crown" has the same meaning as in the Ministers of the Crown Act 1975 (c. 26).

121 Repeals and revocation

The enactments mentioned in Schedule 8 are repealed or revoked to the extent specified in the second column of that Schedule.

122 Expenses

There shall be paid out of money provided by Parliament—

(a) any expenditure incurred by a Minister of the Crown by virtue of this Act, and

(b) any increase attributable to this Act in the sums payable out of money so provided under any other enactment.

123 Commencement

(1) Except as provided in subsections (2) and (3), this Act comes into force on such day as the Secretary of State may appoint by order.

(2) The following provisions come into force on the day on which this Act is passed—

(a) Parts 2 to 5,

(b) Part 7,

(c) Part 8, except section 78,

(d) Part 9, except sections 84 and 87,

(e) sections 88 to 92,

(f) sections 94 to 96,

(g) Part 11,

(h) Part 13, except section 119,

(i) this Part, except section 121 and Schedule 8 so far as they relate to the entries—

  (i) in Part 1 of Schedule 8,

  (ii) in Part 5 of Schedule 8, in respect of the Nuclear Installations Act 1965,

  (iii) in Part 7 of Schedule 8, in respect of Schedule 5 to the Terrorism Act 2000.

(3) The following provisions come into force at the end of the period of two months beginning with the day on which this Act is passed—

  (a) section 84,

  (b) section 87.

(4) Different days may be appointed for different provisions and for different purposes.

(5) An order under this section—

  (a) must be made by statutory instrument, and

  (b) may contain incidental, supplemental, consequential or transitional provision.

124 Extent

(1) The following provisions do not extend to Scotland—

  (a) Part 5,

  (b) Part 12.

(2) The following provisions do not extend to Northern Ireland—

  (a) section 76,

  (b) section 99.

(3) Except as provided in subsections (1) and (2), an amendment, repeal or revocation in this Act has the same extent as the enactment amended, repealed or revoked.

125 Short title

This Act may be cited as the Anti-terrorism, Crime and Security Act 2001.

SCHEDULES

SCHEDULE 1

FORFEITURE OF TERRORIST CASH

PART 1

INTRODUCTORY

Terrorist cash

1 (1) This Schedule applies to cash ("terrorist cash") which—

   (a) is within subsection (1)(a) or (b) of section 1, or

   (b) is property earmarked as terrorist property.

(2) "Cash" means—

   (a) coins and notes in any currency,

   (b) postal orders,

   (c) cheques of any kind, including travellers' cheques,

   (d) bankers' drafts,

   (e) bearer bonds and bearer shares, found at any place in the United Kingdom.

(3) Cash also includes any kind of monetary instrument which is found at any place in the United Kingdom, if the instrument is specified by the Secretary of State by order.

(4) The power to make an order under sub-paragraph (3) is exercisable by statutory instrument, which is subject to annulment in pursuance of a resolution of either House of Parliament.

PART 2

SEIZURE AND DETENTION

Seizure of cash

2 (1) An authorised officer may seize any cash if he has reasonable grounds for suspecting that it is terrorist cash.

(2) An authorised officer may also seize cash part of which he has reasonable grounds for suspecting to be terrorist cash if it is not reasonably practicable to seize only that part.

Detention of seized cash

3 (1) While the authorised officer continues to have reasonable grounds for his suspicion, cash seized under this Schedule may be detained initially for a period of 48 hours.

(2) The period for which the cash or any part of it may be detained may be extended by an order made by a magistrates' court or (in Scotland) the sheriff; but the order may not authorise the detention of any of the cash—

(a) beyond the end of the period of three months beginning with the date of the order, and

(b) in the case of any further order under this paragraph, beyond the end of the period of two years beginning with the date of the first order.

(3) A justice of the peace may also exercise the power of a magistrates' court to make the first order under sub-paragraph (2) extending the period.

(4) An order under sub-paragraph (2) must provide for notice to be given to persons affected by it.

(5) An application for an order under sub-paragraph (2)—

(a) in relation to England and Wales and Northern Ireland, may be made by the Commissioners of Customs and Excise or an authorised officer,

(b) in relation to Scotland, may be made by a procurator fiscal, and the court, sheriff or justice may make the order if satisfied, in relation to any cash to be further detained, that one of the following conditions is met.

(6) The first condition is that there are reasonable grounds for suspecting that the cash is intended to be used for the purposes of terrorism and that either—

(a) its continued detention is justified while its intended use is further investigated or consideration is given to bringing (in the United Kingdom or elsewhere) proceedings against any person for an offence with which the cash is connected, or

(b) proceedings against any person for an offence with which the cash is connected have been started and have not been concluded.

(7) The second condition is that there are reasonable grounds for suspecting that the cash consists of resources of an organisation which is a proscribed organisation and that either—

(a) its continued detention is justified while investigation is made into whether or not it consists of such resources or consideration is given to bringing (in the United Kingdom or elsewhere) proceedings against any person for an offence with which the cash is connected, or

(b) proceedings against any person for an offence with which the cash is connected have been started and have not been concluded.

(8) The third condition is that there are reasonable grounds for suspecting that the cash is property earmarked as terrorist property and that either—

(a) its continued detention is justified while its derivation is further investigated or consideration is given to bringing (in the United Kingdom or elsewhere) proceedings against any person for an offence with which the cash is connected, or

(b) proceedings against any person for an offence with which the cash is connected have been started and have not been concluded.

Payment of detained cash into an account

4 (1) If cash is detained under this Schedule for more than 48 hours, it is to be held in an interest-bearing account and the interest accruing on it is to be added to it on its forfeiture or release.

(2) In the case of cash seized under paragraph 2(2), the authorised officer must, on paying it into the account, release so much of the cash then held in the account as is not attributable to terrorist cash.

(3) Sub-paragraph (1) does not apply if the cash is required as evidence of an offence or evidence in proceedings under this Schedule.

Release of detained cash

5 (1) This paragraph applies while any cash is detained under this Schedule.

(2) A magistrates' court or (in Scotland) the sheriff may direct the release of the whole or any part of the cash if satisfied, on an application by the person from whom it was seized, that the conditions in paragraph 3 for the detention of cash are no longer met in relation to the cash to be released.

(3) A authorised officer or (in Scotland) a procurator fiscal may, after notifying the magistrates' court, sheriff or justice under whose order cash is being detained, release the whole or any part of it if satisfied that the detention of the cash to be released is no longer justified.

(4) But cash is not to be released—

(a) if an application for its forfeiture under paragraph 6, or for its release under paragraph 9, is made, until any proceedings in pursuance of the application (including any proceedings on appeal) are concluded,

(b) if (in the United Kingdom or elsewhere) proceedings are started against any person for an offence with which the cash is connected, until the proceedings are concluded.

PART 3

FORFEITURE

Forfeiture

6 (1) While cash is detained under this Schedule, an application for the forfeiture of the whole or any part of it may be made—

(a) to a magistrates' court by the Commissioners of Customs and Excise or an authorised officer,

(b) (in Scotland) to the sheriff by the Scottish Ministers.

(2) The court or sheriff may order the forfeiture of the cash or any part of it if satisfied that the cash or part is terrorist cash.

(3) In the case of property earmarked as terrorist property which belongs to joint tenants one of whom is an excepted joint owner, the order may not apply to so much of it as the court or sheriff thinks is attributable to the excepted joint owner's share.

(4) An excepted joint owner is a joint tenant who obtained the property in circumstances in which it would not (as against him) be earmarked; and references to his share of the earmarked property are to so much of the property as would have been his if the joint tenancy had been severed.

Appeal against forfeiture

7 (1) Any party to proceedings in which an order is made under paragraph 6 ("a forfeiture order") who is aggrieved by the order may appeal—

(a) in relation to England and Wales, to the Crown Court,

(b) in relation to Scotland, to the Court of Session,

(c) in relation to Northern Ireland, to a county court.

(2) An appeal under sub-paragraph (1) must be made—

(a) within the period of 30 days beginning with the date on which the order is made, or

(b) if sub-paragraph (6) applies, before the end of the period of 30 days beginning with the date on which the order under section 3(3)(b) of the Terrorism Act 2000 (c. 11) referred to in that sub-paragraph comes into force.

(3) The appeal is to be by way of a rehearing.

(4) The court hearing the appeal may make any order it thinks appropriate.

(5) If the court upholds the appeal, it may order the release of the cash.

(6) Where a successful application for a forfeiture order relies (wholly or partly) on the fact that an organisation is proscribed, this sub-paragraph applies if—

(a) a deproscription appeal under section 5 of the Terrorism Act 2000 is allowed in respect of the organisation,

(b) an order is made under section 3(3)(b) of that Act in respect of the organisation in accordance with an order of the Proscribed Organisations Appeal Commission under section 5(4) of that Act (and, if the order is made in reliance on section 123(5) of that Act, a resolution is passed by each House of Parliament under section 123(5)(b)), and

(c) the forfeited cash was seized under this Schedule on or after the date of the refusal to deproscribe against which the appeal under section 5 of that Act was brought.

Application of forfeited cash

8 (1) *Cash forfeited under this Schedule, and any accrued interest on it—*

(a) *if forfeited by a magistrates' court in England and Wales or Northern Ireland, is to be paid into the Consolidated Fund,*

(b) *if forfeited by the sheriff, is to be paid into the Scottish Consolidated Fund.*

(2) But it is not to be paid in—

(a) before the end of the period within which an appeal under paragraph 7 may be made, or

(b) if a person appeals under that paragraph, before the appeal is determined or otherwise disposed of.

PART 4

MISCELLANEOUS

Victims

9 (1) A person who claims that any cash detained under this Schedule, or any part of it, belongs to him may apply to a magistrates' court or (in Scotland) the sheriff for the cash or part to be released to him under this section.

(2) The application may be made in the course of proceedings under paragraph 3 or 6 or at any other time.

(3) If it appears to the court or sheriff concerned that—

(a) the applicant was deprived of the cash claimed, or of property which it represents, by criminal conduct,

(b) the property he was deprived of was not, immediately before he was deprived of it, property obtained by or in return for criminal conduct and nor did it then represent such property, and

(c) the cash claimed belongs to him, the court or sheriff may order the cash to be released to the applicant.

Compensation

10 (1) If no forfeiture order is made in respect of any cash detained under this Schedule, the person to whom the cash belongs or from whom it was seized may make an application to the magistrates' court or (in Scotland) the sheriff for compensation.

(2) If, for any period after the initial detention of the cash for 48 hours, the cash was not held in an interest-bearing account while detained, the court or sheriff may order an amount of compensation to be paid to the applicant.

(3) The amount of compensation to be paid under sub-paragraph (2) is the amount the court or sheriff thinks would have been earned in interest in the period in question if the cash had been held in an interest-bearing account.

(4) If the court or sheriff is satisfied that, taking account of any interest to be paid under this Schedule or any amount to be paid under sub-paragraph (2), the applicant has suffered loss as a result of the detention of the cash and that the circumstances are exceptional, the court or sheriff may order compensation (or additional compensation) to be paid to him .

(5) The amount of compensation to be paid under sub-paragraph (4) is the amount the court or sheriff thinks reasonable, having regard to the loss suffered and any other relevant circumstances.

(6) *If the cash was seized by a customs officer, the compensation is to be paid by the Commissioners of Customs and Excise.*

(7) *If the cash was seized by a constable, the compensation is to be paid as follows—*

(a) *in the case of a constable of a police force in England and Wales, it is to be paid out of the police fund from which the expenses of the police force are met,*

(b) in the case of a constable of a police force in Scotland, it is to be paid by the police authority or joint police board for the police area for which that force is maintained,

(c) *in the case of a police officer within the meaning of the Police (Northern Ireland) Act 2000 (c. 32), it is to be paid out of money provided by the Chief Constable.*

(8) *If the cash was seized by an immigration officer, the compensation is to be paid by the Secretary of State.*

(9) If a forfeiture order is made in respect only of a part of any cash detained under this Schedule, this paragraph has effect in relation to the other part.

(10) This paragraph does not apply if the court or sheriff makes an order under paragraph 9.

PART 5

PROPERTY EARMARKED AS TERRORIST PROPERTY

Property obtained through terrorism

11 (1) A person obtains property through terrorism if he obtains property by or in return for acts of terrorism, or acts carried out for the purposes of terrorism.

(2) In deciding whether any property was obtained through terrorism—

(a) it is immaterial whether or not any money, goods or services were provided in order to put the person in question in a position to carry out the acts,

(b) it is not necessary to show that the act was of a particular kind if it is shown that the property was obtained through acts of one of a number of kinds, each of which would have been an act of terrorism, or an act carried out for the purposes of terrorism.

Property earmarked as terrorist property

12 (1) Property obtained through terrorism is earmarked as terrorist property.

(2) But if property obtained through terrorism has been disposed of (since it was so obtained), it is earmarked as terrorist property only if it is held by a person into whose hands it may be followed.

(3) Property may be followed into the hands of a person obtaining it on a disposal by—

(a) the person who obtained the property through terrorism, or

(b) a person into whose hands it may (by virtue of this sub-paragraph) be followed.

Tracing property

13 (1) Where property obtained through terrorism ("the original property") is or has been earmarked as terrorist property, property which represents the original property is also earmarked.

(2) If a person enters into a transaction by which—

(a) he disposes of the original property or of property which (by virtue of this Part) represents the original property, and

(b) he obtains other property in place of it, the other property represents the original property.

(3) If a person disposes of property which represents the original property, the property may be followed into the hands of the person who obtains it (and it continues to represent the original property).

Mixing property

14 (1) Sub-paragraph (2) applies if a person's property which is earmarked as terrorist property is mixed with other property (whether his property or another's).

(2) The portion of the mixed property which is attributable to the property earmarked as terrorist property represents the property obtained through terrorism.

(3) Property earmarked as terrorist property is mixed with other property if (for example) it is used—

(a) to increase funds held in a bank account,

(b) in part payment for the acquisition of an asset,

(c) for the restoration or improvement of land,

(d) by a person holding a leasehold interest in the property to acquire the freehold.

Accruing profits

15 (1) This paragraph applies where a person who has property earmarked as terrorist property obtains further property consisting of profits accruing in respect of the earmarked property.

(2) The further property is to be treated as representing the property obtained through terrorism.

General exceptions

16 (1) If—

(a) a person disposes of property earmarked as terrorist property, and

(b) the person who obtains it on the disposal does so in good faith, for value and without notice that it was earmarked, the property may not be followed into that person's hands and, accordingly, it ceases to be earmarked.

(2) If—

(a) in pursuance of a judgment in civil proceedings (whether in the United Kingdom or elsewhere), the defendant makes a payment to the claimant or the claimant otherwise obtains property from the defendant,

(b) the claimant's claim is based on the defendant's criminal conduct, and

(c) apart from this sub-paragraph, the sum received, or the property obtained, by the claimant would be earmarked as terrorist property,

the property ceases to be earmarked.

In relation to Scotland, "claimant" and "defendant" are to be read as "pursuer" and "defender"; and, in relation to Northern Ireland, "claimant" is to be read as "plaintiff".

(3) If—

(a) a payment is made to a person in pursuance of a compensation order under Article 14 of the Criminal Justice (Northern Ireland) Order 1994 (S.I. 1994/2795 (N.I. 15)), section 249 of the Criminal Procedure (Scotland) Act 1995 (c. 46) or section 130 of the Powers of Criminal Courts (Sentencing) Act 2000 (c. 6), and

(b) apart from this sub-paragraph, the sum received would be earmarked as terrorist property,

the property ceases to be earmarked.

(4) If—

(a) a payment is made to a person in pursuance of a restitution order under section 27 of the Theft Act (Northern Ireland) 1969 (c.16 (NI)) or section 148(2) of the Powers of Criminal Courts (Sentencing) Act 2000 or a person otherwise obtains any property in pursuance of such an order, and

(b) apart from this sub-paragraph, the sum received, or the property obtained, would be earmarked as terrorist property,

the property ceases to be earmarked.

(5) If—

(a) in pursuance of an order made by the court under section 382(3) or 383(5) of the Financial Services and Markets Act 2000 (c. 8) (restitution orders), an amount is paid to or distributed among any persons in accordance with the court's directions, and

(b) apart from this sub-paragraph, the sum received by them would be earmarked as terrorist property, the property ceases to be earmarked.

(6) If—

(a) in pursuance of a requirement of the Financial Services Authority under section 384(5) of the Financial Services and Markets Act 2000 (c. 8) (power of authority to require restitution), an amount is paid to or distributed among any persons, and

(b) apart from this sub-paragraph, the sum received by them would be earmarked as terrorist property,

the property ceases to be earmarked.

(7) Where—

(a) a person enters into a transaction to which paragraph 13(2) applies, and

(b) the disposal is one to which sub-paragraph (1) applies, this paragraph does not affect the question whether (by virtue of paragraph 13(2)) any property obtained on the transaction in place of the property disposed of is earmarked.

PART 6

INTERPRETATION

Property

17 (1) Property is all property wherever situated and includes—

(a) money,

(b) all forms of property, real or personal, heritable or moveable,

(c) things in action and other intangible or incorporeal property.

(2) Any reference to a person's property (whether expressed as a reference to the property he holds or otherwise) is to be read as follows.

(3) In relation to land, it is a reference to any interest which he holds in the land.

(4) In relation to property other than land, it is a reference—

(a) to the property (if it belongs to him), or

(b) to any other interest which he holds in the property.

Obtaining and disposing of property

18 (1) References to a person disposing of his property include a reference—

(a) to his disposing of a part of it, or

(b) to his granting an interest in it, (or to both); and references to the property disposed of are to any property obtained on the disposal.

(2) If a person grants an interest in property of his which is earmarked as terrorist property, the question whether the interest is also earmarked is to be determined in the same manner as it is on any other disposal of earmarked property.

(3) A person who makes a payment to another is to be treated as making a disposal of his property to the other, whatever form the payment takes.

(4) Where a person's property passes to another under a will or intestacy or by operation of law, it is to be treated as disposed of by him to the other.

(5) A person is only to be treated as having obtained his property for value in a case where he gave unexecuted consideration if the consideration has become executed consideration.

General interpretation

19 (1) In this Schedule—

"authorised officer" means a constable, a customs officer or an immigration officer,

"cash" has the meaning given by paragraph 1,

"constable", in relation to Northern Ireland, means a police officer within the meaning of the Police (Northern Ireland) Act 2000 (c. 32),

"criminal conduct" means conduct which constitutes an offence in any part of the United Kingdom, or would constitute an offence in any part of the United Kingdom if it occurred there,

"customs officer" means an officer commissioned by the Commissioners of Customs and Excise under section 6(3) of the Customs and Excise Management Act 1979 (c. 2),

"forfeiture order" has the meaning given by paragraph 7,

"immigration officer" means a person appointed as an immigration officer under paragraph 1 of Schedule 2 to the Immigration Act 1971 (c. 77), "interest", in relation to land—

(a) in the case of land in England and Wales or Northern Ireland, means any legal estate and any equitable interest or power,

(b) in the case of land in Scotland, means any estate, interest, servitude or other heritable right in or over land, including a heritable security,

"interest", in relation to property other than land, includes any right (including a right to possession of the property),

"part", in relation to property, includes a portion,

"property obtained through terrorism" has the meaning given by paragraph 11, "property earmarked as terrorist property" is to be read in accordance with Part 5,

"proscribed organisation" has the same meaning as in the Terrorism Act 2000 (c. 11),

"terrorism" has the same meaning as in the Terrorism Act 2000,

"terrorist cash" has the meaning given by paragraph 1,

"value" means market value.

(2) Paragraphs 17 and 18 and the following provisions apply for the purposes of this Schedule.

(3) For the purpose of deciding whether or not property was earmarked as terrorist property at any time (including times before commencement), it is to be assumed that this Schedule was in force at that and any other relevant time.

(4) References to anything done or intended to be done for the purposes of terrorism include anything done or intended to be done for the benefit of a proscribed organisation.

(5) An organisation's resources include any cash which is applied or made available, or is to be applied or made available, for use by the organisation.

(6) Proceedings against any person for an offence are concluded when—

(a) the person is convicted or acquitted,

(b) the prosecution is discontinued or, in Scotland, the trial diet is deserted simpliciter, or

(c) the jury is discharged without a finding.

SCHEDULE 2

TERRORIST PROPERTY: AMENDMENTS

PART 1

ACCOUNT MONITORING ORDERS

1 (1) The Terrorism Act 2000 is amended as follows.

(2) The following section is inserted after section 38—

"38A Account monitoring orders

Schedule 6A (account monitoring orders) shall have effect."

(3) The following Schedule is inserted after Schedule 6—

"SCHEDULE 6A

ACCOUNT MONITORING ORDERS

Introduction

1 (1) This paragraph applies for the purposes of this Schedule.

(2) A judge is—

(a) a Circuit judge, in England and Wales;

(b) the sheriff, in Scotland;

(c) a Crown Court judge, in Northern Ireland.

(3) The court is—

(a) the Crown Court, in England and Wales or Northern Ireland;

(b) the sheriff, in Scotland.

(4) An appropriate officer is—

(a) a police officer, in England and Wales or Northern Ireland;

(b) the procurator fiscal, in Scotland.

(5) "Financial institution" has the same meaning as in Schedule 6.

Account monitoring orders

2 (1) A judge may, on an application made to him by an appropriate officer, make an account monitoring order if he is satisfied that—

(a) the order is sought for the purposes of a terrorist investigation,

(b) the tracing of terrorist property is desirable for the purposes of the investigation, and

(c) the order will enhance the effectiveness of the investigation.

(2) The application for an account monitoring order must state that the order is sought against the financial institution specified in the application in relation to information which—

(a) relates to an account or accounts held at the institution by the person specified in the application (whether solely or jointly with another), and

(b) is of the description so specified.

(3) The application for an account monitoring order may specify information relating to—

(a) all accounts held by the person specified in the application for the order at the financial institution so specified,

(b) a particular description, or particular descriptions, of accounts so held, or

(c) a particular account, or particular accounts, so held.

(4) An account monitoring order is an order that the financial institution specified in the application for the order must—

(a) for the period specified in the order,

(b) in the manner so specified,

(c) at or by the time or times so specified, and

(d) at the place or places so specified, provide information of the description specified in the application to an appropriate officer.

(5) The period stated in an account monitoring order must not exceed the period of 90 days beginning with the day on which the order is made.

Applications

3 (1) An application for an account monitoring order may be made ex parte to a judge in chambers.

(2) The description of information specified in an application for an account monitoring order may be varied by the person who made the application.

(3) If the application was made by a police officer, the description of information specified in it may be varied by a different police officer.

Discharge or variation

4 (1) An application to discharge or vary an account monitoring order may be made to the court by—

(a) the person who applied for the order;

(b) any person affected by the order.

(2) If the application for the account monitoring order was made by a police officer, an application to discharge or vary the order may be made by a different police officer.

(3) The court—

(a) may discharge the order;

(b) may vary the order.

Rules of court

5 (1) Rules of court may make provision as to the practice and procedure to be followed in connection with proceedings relating to account monitoring orders.

(2) In Scotland, rules of court shall, without prejudice to section 305 of the Criminal Procedure (Scotland) Act 1995 (c. 46), be made by Act of Adjournal.

Effect of orders

6 (1) In England and Wales and Northern Ireland, an account monitoring order has effect as if it were an order of the court.

(2) An account monitoring order has effect in spite of any restriction on the disclosure of information (however imposed).

Statements

7 (1) A statement made by a financial institution in response to an account monitoring order may not be used in evidence against it in criminal proceedings.

(2) But sub-paragraph (1) does not apply—

(a) in the case of proceedings for contempt of court;

(b) in the case of proceedings under section 23 where the financial institution has been convicted of an offence under any of sections 15 to 18;

(c) on a prosecution for an offence where, in giving evidence, the financial institution makes a statement inconsistent with the statement mentioned in sub-paragraph (1).

(3) A statement may not be used by virtue of sub-paragraph (2)(c) against a financial institution unless—

(a) evidence relating to it is adduced, or

(b) a question relating to it is asked, by or on behalf of the financial institution in the proceedings arising out of the prosecution."

PART 2

RESTRAINT ORDERS

2 (1) Part 1 of Schedule 4 to the Terrorism Act 2000 (c. 11) (forfeiture orders under section 23 of that Act: England and Wales) is amended as follows.

(2) In paragraph 5 (restraint orders) for sub-paragraph (2) substitute—

"(2) The High Court may also make a restraint order under this paragraph where—

(a) a criminal investigation has been started in England and Wales with regard to an offence under any of sections 15 to 18,

(b) an application for a restraint order is made to the High Court by the person who the High Court is satisfied will have the conduct of any proceedings for the offence, and

(c) it appears to the High Court that a forfeiture order may be made in any proceedings for the offence."

(3) In paragraph 5(3) for "the proceedings" substitute "any proceedings".

(4) In paragraph 5 after sub-paragraph (5) insert—

"(6) In this paragraph "criminal investigation" means an investigation which police officers or other persons have a duty to conduct with a view to it being ascertained whether a person should be charged with an offence."

(5) For paragraph 6(3) substitute—

"(3) A restraint order made under paragraph 5(1) shall in particular be discharged on an application under sub-paragraph (2) if the proceedings for the offence have been concluded.

(4) A restraint order made under paragraph 5(2) shall in particular be discharged on an application under sub-paragraph (2)—

(a) if no proceedings in respect of offences under any of sections 15 to 18 are instituted within such time as the High Court considers reasonable, and

(b) if all proceedings in respect of offences under any of sections 15 to 18 have been concluded."

(6) In paragraph 8(3) for "the proposed proceedings" substitute "any proceedings for an offence under any of sections 15 to 18".

(7) In paragraph 9(1) (compensation where restraint order discharged) for "paragraph 6(3)(a)" substitute "paragraph 6(4)(a)".

3 (1) Part 2 of Schedule 4 to the Terrorism Act 2000 (c. 11) (forfeiture orders under section 23 of that Act: Scotland) is amended as follows.

(2) In paragraph 18 (restraint orders) for sub-paragraph (2) substitute—

"(2) The Court of Session may also make a restraint order on such an application where—

(a) a criminal investigation has been instituted in Scotland with regard to an offence under any of sections 15 to 18, and

(b) it appears to the Court of Session that a forfeiture order may be made in any proceedings for the offence."

(3) In paragraph 18(3) for "the proceedings" substitute "any proceedings".

(4) In paragraph 18 after sub-paragraph (5) insert—

"(6) In this paragraph "criminal investigation" means an investigation which police officers or other persons have a duty to conduct with a view to it being ascertained whether a person should be charged with an offence."

(5) In paragraph 19(3) for "the proceedings" substitute "proceedings".

4 (1) Part 3 of Schedule 4 to the Terrorism Act 2000 (forfeiture orders under section 23 of that Act: Northern Ireland) is amended as follows.

(2) In paragraph 33 (restraint orders) for sub-paragraph (2) substitute—

"(2) The High Court may also make a restraint order under this paragraph where—

(a) a criminal investigation has been started in Northern Ireland with regard to an offence under any of sections 15 to 18,

(b) an application for a restraint order is made to the High Court by the person who the High Court is satisfied will have the conduct of any proceedings for the offence, and

(c) it appears to the High Court that a forfeiture order may be made in any proceedings for the offence."

(3) In paragraph 33(3) for "the proceedings" substitute "any proceedings".

(4) In paragraph 33 after sub-paragraph (5) insert—

"(6) In this paragraph "criminal investigation" means an investigation which police officers or other persons have a duty to conduct with a view to it being ascertained whether a person should be charged with an offence."

(5) For paragraph 34(3) substitute—

"(3) A restraint order made under paragraph 33(1) shall in particular be discharged on an application under sub-paragraph (2) if the proceedings for the offence have been concluded.

(4) A restraint order made under paragraph 33(2) shall in particular be discharged on an application under sub-paragraph (2)—

(a) if no proceedings in respect of offences under any of sections 15 to 18 are instituted within such time as the High Court considers reasonable, and

(b) if all proceedings in respect of offences under any of sections 15 to 18 have been concluded."

(6) In paragraph 38(4), in the definition of "prosecutor", for "the proposed proceedings" substitute "any proceedings for an offence under any of sections 15 to 18".

(7) In paragraph 39(1) (compensation where restraint order discharged) for "paragraph 34(3)(a)" substitute "paragraph 34(4)(a)".

PART 3

DISCLOSURE OF INFORMATION

5 (1) The Terrorism Act 2000 (c. 11) is amended as follows.

(2) The following sections are inserted after section 21—

"21A Failure to disclose: regulated sector

(1) A person commits an offence if each of the following three conditions is satisfied.

(2) The first condition is that he—

(a) knows or suspects, or

(b) has reasonable grounds for knowing or suspecting, that another person has committed an offence under any of sections 15 to 18.

(3) The second condition is that the information or other matter—

(a) on which his knowledge or suspicion is based, or

(b) which gives reasonable grounds for such knowledge or suspicion, came to him in the course of a business in the regulated sector.

(4) The third condition is that he does not disclose the information or other matter to a constable or a nominated officer as soon as is practicable after it comes to him.

(5) But a person does not commit an offence under this section if—

(a) he has a reasonable excuse for not disclosing the information or other matter;

(b) he is a professional legal adviser and the information or other matter came to him in privileged circumstances.

(6) In deciding whether a person committed an offence under this section the court must consider whether he followed any relevant guidance which was at the time concerned—

(a) issued by a supervisory authority or any other appropriate body,

(b) approved by the Treasury, and

(c) published in a manner it approved as appropriate in its opinion to bring the guidance to the attention of persons likely to be affected by it.

(7) A disclosure to a nominated officer is a disclosure which—

(a) is made to a person nominated by the alleged offender's employer to receive disclosures under this section, and

(b) is made in the course of the alleged offender's employment and in accordance with the procedure established by the employer for the purpose.

(8) Information or other matter comes to a professional legal adviser in privileged circumstances if it is communicated or given to him—

(a) by (or by a representative of) a client of his in connection with the giving by the adviser of legal advice to the client,

(b) by (or by a representative of) a person seeking legal advice from the adviser, or

(c) by a person in connection with legal proceedings or contemplated legal proceedings.

(9) But subsection (8) does not apply to information or other matter which is communicated or given with a view to furthering a criminal purpose.

(10) Schedule 3A has effect for the purpose of determining what is—

(a) a business in the regulated sector;

(b) a supervisory authority.

(11) For the purposes of subsection (2) a person is to be taken to have committed an offence there mentioned if—

(a) he has taken an action or been in possession of a thing, and

(b) he would have committed the offence if he had been in the United Kingdom at the time when he took the action or was in possession of the thing.

(12) A person guilty of an offence under this section is liable—

(a) on conviction on indictment, to imprisonment for a term not exceeding five years or to a fine or to both;

(b) on summary conviction, to imprisonment for a term not exceeding six months or to a fine not exceeding the statutory maximum or to both.

(13) An appropriate body is any body which regulates or is representative of any trade, profession, business or employment carried on by the alleged offender.

(14) The reference to a constable includes a reference to a person authorised for the purposes of this section by the Director General of the National Criminal Intelligence Service.

21B Protected disclosures

(1) A disclosure which satisfies the following three conditions is not to be taken to breach any restriction on the disclosure of information (however imposed).

(2) The first condition is that the information or other matter disclosed came to the person making the disclosure (the discloser) in the course of a business in the regulated sector.

(3) The second condition is that the information or other matter—

(a) causes the discloser to know or suspect, or

(b) gives him reasonable grounds for knowing or suspecting, that another person has committed an offence under any of sections 15 to 18.

(4) The third condition is that the disclosure is made to a constable or a nominated officer as soon as is practicable after the information or other matter comes to the discloser.

(5) A disclosure to a nominated officer is a disclosure which—

(a) is made to a person nominated by the discloser's employer to receive disclosures under this section, and

(b) is made in the course of the discloser's employment and in accordance with the procedure established by the employer for the purpose.

(6) The reference to a business in the regulated sector must be construed in accordance with Schedule 3A.

(7) The reference to a constable includes a reference to a person authorised for the purposes of this section by the Director General of the National Criminal Intelligence Service."

(3) In section 19 after subsection (1) insert—

"(1A) But this section does not apply if the information came to the person in the course of a business in the regulated sector."

(4) In section 19 after subsection (7) insert—

"(7A) The reference to a business in the regulated sector must be construed in accordance with Schedule 3A.

(7B) The reference to a constable includes a reference to a person authorised for the purposes of this section by the Director General of the National Criminal Intelligence Service."

(5) In section 20 after subsection (4) insert—

"(5) References to a constable include references to a person authorised for the purposes of this section by the Director General of the National Criminal Intelligence Service."

(6) The following Schedule is inserted after Schedule 3—

"SCHEDULE 3A

REGULATED SECTOR AND SUPERVISORY AUTHORITIES

PART 1

REGULATED SECTOR

Business in the regulated sector

1 (1) A business is in the regulated sector to the extent that it engages in any of the following activities—

(a) accepting deposits by a person with permission under Part 4 of the Financial Services and Markets Act 2000 (c. 8) to accept deposits (including, in the case of a building society, the raising of money from members of the society by the issue of shares);

(b) the business of the National Savings Bank;

(c) business carried on by a credit union;

(d) any home-regulated activity carried on by a European institution in respect of which the establishment conditions in paragraph 13 of Schedule 3 to the Financial Services and Markets Act 2000, or the service conditions in paragraph 14 of that Schedule, are satisfied;

(e) any activity carried on for the purpose of raising money authorised to be raised under the National Loans Act 1968 (c. 13) under the auspices of the Director of Savings;

(f) the activity of operating a bureau de change, transmitting money (or any representation of monetary value) by any means or cashing cheques which are made payable to customers;

(g) any activity falling within sub-paragraph (2);

(h) any of the activities in points 1 to 12 or 14 of Annex 1 to the Banking Consolidation Directive, ignoring an activity described in any of paragraphs (a) to (g) above;

(i) business which consists of effecting or carrying out contracts of long term insurance by a person who has received official authorisation pursuant to Article 6 or 27 of the First Life Directive.

(2) An activity falls within this sub-paragraph if it constitutes any of the following kinds of regulated activity in the United Kingdom—

(a) dealing in investments as principal or as agent;

(b) arranging deals in investments;

(c) managing investments;

(d) safeguarding and administering investments;

(e) sending dematerialised instructions;

(f) establishing (and taking other steps in relation to) collective investment schemes;

(g) advising on investments.

(3) Paragraphs (a) and (i) of sub-paragraph (1) and sub-paragraph (2) must be read with section 22 of the Financial Services and Markets Act 2000, any relevant order under that section and Schedule 2 to that Act.

2 (1) This paragraph has effect for the purposes of paragraph 1.

(2) "Building society" has the meaning given by the Building Societies Act 1986.

(3) "Credit union" has the meaning given by the Credit Unions Act 1979 (c. 34) or the Credit Unions (Northern Ireland) Order 1985 (S.I. 1985/1205 (N.I. 12)).

(4) "European institution" means an EEA firm of the kind mentioned in paragraph 5(b) or (c) of Schedule 3 to the Financial Services and Markets Act 2000 (c. 8) which qualifies for authorisation for the purposes of that Act under paragraph 12 of that Schedule.

(5) "Home-regulated activity" in relation to a European institution, means an activity—

(a) which is specified in Annex 1 to the Banking Consolidation Directive and in respect of which a supervisory authority in the home State of the institution has regulatory functions, and

(b) if the institution is an EEA firm of the kind mentioned in paragraph 5(c) of Schedule 3 to the Financial Services and Markets Act 2000, which the institution carries on in its home State.

(6) "Home State", in relation to a person incorporated in or formed under the law of another member State, means that State.

(7) The Banking Consolidation Directive is the Directive of the European Parliament and Council relating to the taking

up and pursuit of the business of credit institutions (No. 2000/12 EC).

(8) The First Life Directive is the First Council Directive on the coordination of laws, regulations and administrative provisions relating to the taking up and pursuit of the business of direct life assurance (No. 79/267/EEC).

Excluded activities

3 A business is not in the regulated sector to the extent that it engages in any of the following activities—

(a) the issue of withdrawable share capital within the limit set by section 6 of the Industrial and Provident Societies Act 1965 (c. 12) by a society registered under that Act;

(b) the acceptance of deposits from the public within the limit set by section 7(3) of that Act by such a society;

(c) the issue of withdrawable share capital within the limit set by section 6 of the Industrial and Provident Societies Act (Northern Ireland) 1969 (N.I. c. 24) by a society registered under that Act;

(d) activities carried on by the Bank of England;

(e) any activity in respect of which an exemption order under section 38 of the Financial Services and Markets Act 2000 has effect if it is carried on by a person who is for the time being specified in the order or falls within a class of persons so specified .

PART 2

SUPERVISORY AUTHORITIES

4 (1) Each of the following is a supervisory authority—

(a) the Bank of England;

(b) the Financial Services Authority;

(c) the Council of Lloyd's;

(d) the Director General of Fair Trading;

(e) a body which is a designated professional body for the purposes of Part 20 of the Financial Services and Markets Act 2000 (c. 8).

(2) The Secretary of State is also a supervisory authority in the exercise, in relation to a person carrying on a business in the regulated sector, of his functions under the enactments relating to companies or insolvency or under the Financial Services and Markets Act 2000.

(3) The Treasury are also a supervisory authority in the exercise, in relation to a person carrying on a business in the regulated sector, of their functions under the enactments relating to companies or insolvency or under the Financial Services and Markets Act 2000.

PART 3

POWER TO AMEND

5 (1) The Treasury may by order amend Part 1 or 2 of this Schedule.

(2) An order under sub-paragraph (1) must be made by statutory instrument subject to annulment in pursuance of a resolution of either House of Parliament."

PART 4

FINANCIAL INFORMATION ORDERS

6 (1) Paragraph 1 of Schedule 6 to the Terrorism Act 2000 (c. 11) (financial information orders) is amended as follows.

(2) In sub-paragraph (1) after "financial institution" insert "to which the order applies".

(3) After sub-paragraph (1) insert—

"(1A) The order may provide that it applies to—

(a) all financial institutions,

(b) a particular description, or particular descriptions, of financial institutions, or

(c) a particular financial institution or particular financial institutions."

SCHEDULE 3

FREEZING ORDERS

Interpretation

1 References in this Schedule to a person specified in a freezing order as a person to whom or for whose benefit funds are not to be made available are to be read in accordance with section 5(4).

Funds

2 A freezing order may include provision that funds include gold, cash, deposits, securities (such as stocks, shares and debentures) and such other matters as the order may specify.

Making funds available

3 (1) A freezing order must include provision as to the meaning (in relation to funds) of making available to or for the benefit of a person.

(2) In particular, an order may provide that the expression includes—

(a) allowing a person to withdraw from an account;

(b) honouring a cheque payable to a person;

(c) crediting a person's account with interest;

(d) releasing documents of title (such as share certificates) held on a person's behalf;

(e) making available the proceeds of realisation of a person's property;

(f) making a payment to or for a person's benefit (for instance, under a contract or as a gift or under any enactment such as the enactments relating to social security);

(g) such other acts as the order may specify.

Licences

4 (1) A freezing order must include—

(a) provision for the granting of licences authorising funds to be made available;

(b) provision that a prohibition under the order is not to apply if funds are made available in accordance with a licence.

(2) In particular, an order may provide—

(a) that a licence may be granted generally or to a specified person or persons or description of persons;

(b) that a licence may authorise funds to be made available to or for the benefit of persons generally or a specified person or persons or description of persons;

(c) that a licence may authorise funds to be made available generally or for specified purposes;

(d) that a licence may be granted in relation to funds generally or to funds of a specified description;

(e) for a licence to be granted in pursuance of an application or without an application being made;

(f) for the form and manner in which applications for licences are to be made;

(g) for licences to be granted by the Treasury or a person authorised by the Treasury;

(h) for the form in which licences are to be granted;

(i) for licences to be granted subject to conditions;

(j) for licences to be of a defined or indefinite duration;

(k) for the charging of a fee to cover the administrative costs of granting a licence;

(l) for the variation and revocation of licences.

Information and documents

5 (1) A freezing order may include provision that a person—

(a) must provide information if required to do so and it is reasonably needed for the purpose of ascertaining whether an offence under the order has been committed;

(b) must produce a document if required to do so and it is reasonably needed for that purpose.

(2) In particular, an order may include—

(a) provision that a requirement to provide information or to produce a document may be made by the Treasury or a person authorised by the Treasury;

(b) provision that information must be provided, and a document must be produced, within a reasonable period specified in the order and at a place specified by the person requiring it;

(c) provision that the provision of information is not to be taken to breach any restriction on the disclosure of information (however imposed);

(d) provision restricting the use to which information or a document may be put and the circumstances in which it may be disclosed;

(e) provision that a requirement to provide information or produce a document does not apply to privileged information or a privileged document;

(f) provision that information is privileged if the person would be entitled to refuse to provide it on grounds of legal professional privilege in proceedings in the High Court or (in Scotland) on grounds of confidentiality of communications in proceedings in the Court of Session;

(g) provision that a document is privileged if the person would be entitled to refuse to produce it on grounds of legal professional privilege in proceedings in the High Court or (in Scotland) on grounds of confidentiality of communications in proceedings in the Court of Session;

(h) provision that information or a document held with the intention of furthering a criminal purpose is not privileged.

Disclosure of information

6 (1) A freezing order may include provision requiring a person to disclose information as mentioned below if the following three conditions are satisfied.

(2) The first condition is that the person required to disclose is specified or falls within a description specified in the order.

(3) The second condition is that the person required to disclose knows or suspects, or has grounds for knowing or suspecting, that a person specified in the freezing order as a person to whom or for whose benefit funds are not to be made available—

(a) is a customer of his or has been a customer of his at any time since the freezing order came into force, or

(b) is a person with whom he has dealings in the course of his business or has had such dealings at any time since the freezing order came into force.

(4) The third condition is that the information—

(a) on which the knowledge or suspicion of the person required to disclose is based, or

(b) which gives grounds for his knowledge or suspicion, came to him in the course of a business in the regulated sector.

(5) The freezing order may require the person required to disclose to make a disclosure to the Treasury of that information as soon as is practicable after it comes to him.

(6) The freezing order may include—

(a) provision that Schedule 3A to the Terrorism Act 2000 (c. 11) is to have effect for the purpose of determining what is a business in the regulated sector;

(b) provision that the disclosure of information is not to be taken to breach any restriction on the disclosure of information (however imposed);

(c) provision restricting the use to which information may be put and the circumstances in which it may be disclosed by the Treasury;

(d) provision that the requirement to disclose information does not apply to privileged information;

(e) provision that information is privileged if the person would be entitled to refuse to disclose it on grounds of legal professional privilege in proceedings in the High Court or (in Scotland) on grounds of confidentiality of communications in proceedings in the Court of Session;

(f) provision that information held with the intention of furthering a criminal purpose is not privileged.

Offences

7 (1) A freezing order may include any of the provisions set out in this paragraph.

(2) A person commits an offence if he fails to comply with a prohibition imposed by the order.

(3) A person commits an offence if he engages in an activity knowing or intending that it will enable or facilitate the commission by another person of an offence under a provision included under sub-paragraph (2).

(4) A person commits an offence if—

(a) he fails without reasonable excuse to provide information, or to produce a document, in response to a requirement made under the order;

(b) he provides information, or produces a document, which he knows is false in a material particular in response to such a requirement or with a view to obtaining a licence under the order;

(c) he recklessly provides information, or produces a document, which is false in a material particular in response to such a requirement or with a view to obtaining a licence under the order;

(d) he fails without reasonable excuse to disclose information as required by a provision included under paragraph 6.

(5) A person does not commit an offence under a provision included under sub- paragraph (2) or (3) if he proves that he did not know and had no reason to suppose that the person to whom or for whose benefit funds were made available, or were to be made available, was the person (or one of the persons) specified in the freezing order as a person to whom or for whose benefit funds are not to be made available.

(6) A person guilty of an offence under a provision included under sub-paragraph (2) or (3) is liable—

(a) on summary conviction, to imprisonment for a term not exceeding 6 months or to a fine not exceeding the statutory maximum or to both;

(b) on conviction on indictment, to imprisonment for a term not exceeding 2 years or to a fine or to both.

(7) A person guilty of an offence under a provision included under sub-paragraph (4) is liable on summary conviction to imprisonment for a term not exceeding 6 months or to a fine not exceeding level 5 on the standard scale or to both.

Offences: procedure

8 (1) A freezing order may include any of the provisions set out in this paragraph.

(2) Proceedings for an offence under the order are not to be instituted in England and Wales except by or with the consent of the Treasury or the Director of Public Prosecutions.

(3) Proceedings for an offence under the order are not to be instituted in Northern Ireland except by or with the consent of the Treasury or the Director of Public Prosecutions for Northern Ireland.

(4) Despite anything in section 127(1) of the Magistrates' Courts Act 1980 (c. 43) (information to be laid within 6 months of offence) an information relating to an offence under the order which is triable by a magistrates' court in England and Wales may be so tried if it is laid at any time in the period of one year starting with the date of the commission of the offence.

(5) In Scotland summary proceedings for an offence under the order may be commenced at any time in the period of one year starting with the date of the commission of the offence.

(6) In its application to an offence under the order Article 19(1)(a) of the Magistrates' Courts (Northern Ireland) Order 1981 (S.I. 1981/1675 (N.I. 26)) (time limit within which complaint charging offence must be made) is to have effect as if the reference to six months were a reference to twelve months.

Offences by bodies corporate etc.

9 (1) A freezing order may include any of the provisions set out in this paragraph.

(2) If an offence under the order—

(a) is committed by a body corporate, and

(b) is proved to have been committed with the consent or connivance of an officer, or to be attributable to any neglect on his part,

he as well as the body corporate is guilty of the offence and liable to be proceeded against and punished accordingly.

(3) These are officers of a body corporate—

(a) a director, manager, secretary or other similar officer of the body;

(b) any person purporting to act in any such capacity.

(4) If the affairs of a body corporate are managed by its members sub-paragraph

(2) applies in relation to the acts and defaults of a member in connection with his functions of management as if he were an officer of the body.

(5) If an offence under the order—

(a) is committed by a Scottish partnership, and

(b) is proved to have been committed with the consent or connivance of a partner, or to be attributable to any neglect on his part, he as well as the partnership is guilty of the offence and liable to be proceeded against and punished accordingly.

Compensation

10 (1) A freezing order may include provision for the award of compensation to or on behalf of a person on the grounds that he has suffered loss as a result of—

(a) the order;

(b) the fact that a licence has not been granted under the order;

(c) the fact that a licence under the order has been granted on particular terms rather than others;

(d) the fact that a licence under the order has been varied or revoked.

(2) In particular, the order may include—

(a) provision about the person who may make a claim for an award;

(b) provision about the person to whom a claim for an award is to be made (which may be provision that it is to be made to the High Court or, in Scotland, the Court of Session);

(c) provision about the procedure for making and deciding a claim;

(d) provision that no compensation is to be awarded unless the claimant has behaved reasonably (which may include provision requiring him to mitigate his loss, for instance by applying for a licence);

(e) provision that compensation must be awarded in specified circumstances or may be awarded in specified circumstances (which may include provision that the circumstances involve negligence or other fault);

(f) provision about the amount that may be awarded;

(g) *provision about who is to pay any compensation awarded (which may include provision that it is to be paid or reimbursed by the Treasury);*

(h) provision about how compensation is to be paid (which may include provision for payment to a person other than the claimant).

Treasury's duty to give reasons

11 A freezing order must include provision that if—

(a) a person is specified in the order as a person to whom or for whose benefit funds are not to be made available, and

(b) he makes a written request to the Treasury to give him the reason why he is so specified,

as soon as is practicable the Treasury must give the person the reason in writing.

SCHEDULE 4

EXTENSION OF EXISTING DISCLOSURE POWERS

PART 1

ENACTMENTS TO WHICH SECTION 17 APPLIES

Agricultural Marketing Act 1958 (c. 47)

1 Section 47(2) of the Agricultural Marketing Act 1958.

Harbours Act 1964 (c. 40)

2 Section 46(1) of the Harbours Act 1964.

Cereals Marketing Act 1965 (c. 14)

3 Section 17(2) of the Cereals Marketing Act 1965.

Agriculture Act 1967 (c. 22)

4 Section 24(1) of the Agriculture Act 1967.

Trade Descriptions Act 1968 (c. 29)

5 Section 28(5A) of the Trade Descriptions Act 1968.

Sea Fish Industry Act 1970 (c. 11)

6 Section 14(2) of the Sea Fish Industry Act 1970.

National Savings Bank Act 1971 (c. 29)

7 Section 12(2) of the National Savings Bank Act 1971.

Employment Agencies Act 1973 (c. 35)

8 Section 9(4) of the Employment Agencies Act 1973.

Fair Trading Act 1973 (c. 41)

9 Section 133(3) of the Fair Trading Act 1973 so far only as it relates to information obtained under or by virtue of any provision of Part 3 of that Act (protection of consumers).

Prices Act 1974 (c. 24)

10 Paragraph 12(2) of the Schedule to the Prices Act 1974.

Consumer Credit Act 1974 (c. 39)

11 Section 174(3) of the Consumer Credit Act 1974.

Health and Safety at Work etc. Act 1974 (c. 37)

12 Section 28(7) of the Health and Safety at Work etc. Act 1974.

Sex Discrimination Act 1975 (c. 65)

13 Section 61(1) of the Sex Discrimination Act 1975.

Race Relations Act 1976 (c. 74)

14 Section 52(1) of the Race Relations Act 1976.

Energy Act 1976 (c. 76)

15 Paragraph 7 of Schedule 2 to the Energy Act 1976.

National Health Service Act 1977 (c. 49)

16 Paragraph 5 of Schedule 11 to the National Health Service Act 1977.

Estate Agents Act 1979 (c. 38)

17 Section 10(3) of the Estate Agents Act 1979.

Public Passenger Vehicles Act 1981 (c. 14)

18 Section 54(8) of the Public Passenger Vehicles Act 1981.

Fisheries Act 1981 (c. 29)

19 Section 12(2) of the Fisheries Act 1981.

Merchant Shipping (Liner Conferences) Act 1982 (c. 37)

20 Section 10(2) of the Merchant Shipping (Liner Conferences) Act 1982.

Civil Aviation Act 1982 (c. 16)

21 Section 23(4) of the Civil Aviation Act 1982.

Diseases of Fish Act 1983 (c. 30)

22 Section 9(1) of the Diseases of Fish Act 1983.

Telecommunications Act 1984 (c. 12)

23 Section 101(2) of the Telecommunications Act 1984.

Companies Act 1985 (c. 6)

24 Section 449(1) of the Companies Act 1985.

Airports Act 1986 (c. 31)

25 Section 74(2) of the Airports Act 1986.

Legal Aid (Scotland) Act 1986 (c. 47)

26 Section 34(2) of the Legal Aid (Scotland) Act 1986.

Consumer Protection Act 1987 (c. 43)

27 Section 38(2) of the Consumer Protection Act 1987.

Companies Act 1989 (c. 40)

28 Section 87(1) of the Companies Act 1989.

Broadcasting Act 1990 (c. 42)

29 Section 197(2) of the Broadcasting Act 1990.

Property Misdescriptions Act 1991 (c. 29)

30 Paragraph 7(1) of the Schedule to the Property Misdescriptions Act 1991.

Water Industry Act 1991 (c. 56)

31 Section 206(3) of the Water Industry Act 1991.

Water Resources Act 1991 (c. 57)

32 Section 204(2) of the Water Resources Act 1991.

Timeshare Act 1992 (c. 35)

33 Paragraph 5(1) of Schedule 2 to the Timeshare Act 1992.

Railways Act 1993 (c. 43)

34 Section 145(2) of the Railways Act 1993.

Coal Industry Act 1994 (c. 21)

35 Section 59(2) of the Coal Industry Act 1994.

Shipping and Trading Interests (Protection) Act 1995 (c. 22)

36 Section 3(4) of the Shipping and Trading Interests (Protection) Act 1995.

Pensions Act 1995 (c. 26)

37 (1) Section 105(2) of the Pensions Act 1995.

(2) Section 108(2) of that Act.

Goods Vehicles (Licensing of Operators) Act 1995 (c. 23)

38 Section 35(4) of the Goods Vehicles (Licensing of Operators) Act 1995.

Chemical Weapons Act 1996 (c. 6)

39 Section 32(2) of the Chemical Weapons Act 1996.

Bank of England Act 1998 (c. 11)

40 (1) Paragraph 5 of Schedule 7 to the Bank of England Act 1998.

(2) Paragraph 2 of Schedule 8 to that Act.

Audit Commission Act 1998 (c. 18)

41 Section 49(1) of the Audit Commission Act 1998.

Data Protection Act 1998 (c. 29)

42 Section 59(1) of the Data Protection Act 1998.

Police (Northern Ireland) Act 1998 (c. 32)

43 Section 63(1) of the Police (Northern Ireland) Act 1998.

Landmines Act 1998 (c. 33)

44 Section 19(2) of the Landmines Act 1998.

Health Act 1999 (c. 8)

45 Section 24 of the Health Act 1999.

Disability Rights Commission Act 1999 (c. 17)

46 Paragraph 22(2)(f) of Schedule 3 to the Disability Rights Commission Act 1999.

Access to Justice Act 1999 (c. 22)

47 Section 20(2) of the Access to Justice Act 1999.

Nuclear Safeguards Act 2000 (c. 5)

48 Section 6(2) of the Nuclear Safeguards Act 2000.

Finance Act 2000 (c. 21)

49 Paragraph 34(3) of Schedule 22 to the Finance Act 2000.

Local Government Act 2000 (c. 22)

50 Section 63(1) of the Local Government Act 2000.

Postal Services Act 2000 (c. 26)

51 Paragraph 3(1) of Schedule 7 to the Postal Services Act 2000.

Utilities Act 2000 (c. 27)

52 Section 105(4) of the Utilities Act 2000.

Transport Act 2000 (c. 38)

53 (1) Section 143(5)(b) of the Transport Act 2000.

(2) Paragraph 13(3) of Schedule 10 to that Act.

PART 2

NORTHERN IRELAND LEGISLATION TO WHICH SECTION 17 APPLIES

Transport Act (Northern Ireland) 1967 (c. 37 (N.I.))

54 Section 36(1) of the Transport Act (Northern Ireland) 1967.

Sex Discrimination (Northern Ireland) Order 1976 (S.I. 1976/1042 (N.I. 15))

55 Article 61(1) of the Sex Discrimination (Northern Ireland) Order 1976.

Health and Safety at Work (Northern Ireland) Order 1978 (S.I. 1978/1039 (N.I. 9))

56 Article 30(6) of the Health and Safety at Work (Northern Ireland) Order 1978.

Legal Aid, Advice and Assistance (Northern Ireland) Order 1981 (S.I. 1981/228 (N.I. 8))

57 Article 24(1) of the Legal Aid, Advice and Assistance (Northern Ireland) Order 1981.

Agricultural Marketing (Northern Ireland) Order 1982 (S.I. 1982/1080 (N.I. 12))

58 Article 29(3) of the Agricultural Marketing (Northern Ireland) Order 1982.

Companies (Northern Ireland) Order 1986 (S.I. 1986/1032 (N.I. 6))

59 Article 442(1) of the Companies (Northern Ireland) Order 1986.

Consumer Protection (Northern Ireland) Order 1987 (S.I. 1987 (N.I. 20))

60 Article 29(2) of the Consumer Protection (Northern Ireland) Order 1987.

Electricity (Northern Ireland) Order 1992 (S.I. 1992/231 (N.I. 1))

61 Article 61(2) of the Electricity (Northern Ireland) Order 1992.

Airports (Northern Ireland) Order 1994 (S.I. 1994/426 (N.I. 1))

62 Article 49(2) of the Airports (Northern Ireland) Order 1994.

Pensions (Northern Ireland) Order 1995 (S.I. 1995/3213 (N.I. 22))

63 (1) Article 103(2) of the Pensions (Northern Ireland) Order 1995.

(2) Article 106(2) of that Order.

Gas (Northern Ireland) Order 1996 (S.I. 1996/275 (N.I. 2))

64 Article 44(3) of the Gas (Northern Ireland) Order 1996.

Race Relations (Northern Ireland) Order 1997 (S.I. 1997/869 (N.I. 6))

65 Article 50(1) of the Race Relations (Northern Ireland) Order 1997.

Fair Employment and Treatment (Northern Ireland) Order 1998 (S.I. 1998/3162 (N.I. 21))

66 Article 18(1) of the Fair Employment and Treatment (Northern Ireland) Order 1998.

SCHEDULE 5

PATHOGENS AND TOXINS

VIRUSES

Chikungunya virus

Congo-crimean haemorrhagic fever virus

Dengue fever virus

Eastern equine encephalitis virus

Ebola virus

Hantaan virus

Japanese encephalitis virus

Junin virus

Lassa fever virus

Lymphocytic choriomeningitis virus

Machupo virus

Marburg virus

Monkey pox virus

Rift Valley fever virus

Tick-borne encephalitis virus (Russian Spring-Summer encephalitis virus)

Variola virus

Venezuelan equine encephalitis virus

Western equine encephalitis virus

White pox

Yellow fever virus

RICKETTSIAE

Coxiella burnetii

Bartonella quintana

(Rochalimea quintana, Rickettsia quintana)

Rickettsia prowazeki

Rickettsia rickettsii

BACTERIA

Bacillus anthracis

Brucella abortus

Brucella melitensis

Brucella suis

Chlamydia psittaci

Clostridium botulinum

Francisella tularensis

Burkholderia mallei (Pseudomonas mallei)

Burkholderia pseudomallei (Pseudomonas pseudomallei)

Salmonella typhi

Shigella dysenteriae

Vibrio cholerae

Yersinia pestis

TOXINS

Botulinum toxins

Clostridium perfringens toxins

Conotoxin

Ricin

Saxitoxin

Shiga toxin

Staphylococcus aureus toxins

Tetrodotoxin

Verotoxin

Microcystin (Cyanginosin)

Aflatoxins

Notes

1 Any reference in this Schedule to a micro-organism includes—

(a) any genetic material containing any nucleic acid sequence associated with the pathogenicity of the micro-organism; and

(b) any gentically modified organism containing any such sequence.

2 Any reference in this Schedule to—

(a) a biological agent does not include an agent in the form of a vaccine;

(b) a toxin does not include any immunotoxin (but does include subunits of a toxin); and

(c) a botulinum toxin does not include a botulinum toxin which satisfies prescribed conditions.

SCHEDULE 6

THE PATHOGENS ACCESS APPEAL COMMISSION

Constitution and administration

1 (1) The Commission shall consist of members appointed by the Lord Chancellor.

(2) The Lord Chancellor shall appoint one of the members as chairman.

(3) A member shall hold and vacate office in accordance with the terms of his appointment.

(4) A member may resign at any time by notice in writing to the Lord Chancellor.

2 The Lord Chancellor may appoint officers and servants for the Commission.

3 *The Lord Chancellor—*

(a) *may pay sums by way of remuneration, allowances, pensions and gratuities to or in respect of members, officers and servants;*

(b) *may pay compensation to a person who ceases to be a member of the Commission if the Lord Chancellor thinks it appropriate because of special circumstances; and*

(c) *may pay sums in respect of expenses of the Commission.*

Procedure

4 (1) The Commission shall sit at such times and in such places as the Lord Chancellor may direct.

(2) The Commission may sit in two or more divisions.

(3) At each sitting of the Commission—

(a) three members shall attend;

(b) one of the members shall be a person who holds or has held high judicial office (within the meaning of the Appellate Jurisdiction Act 1876 (c. 59)); and

(c) the chairman or another member nominated by him shall preside and report the Commission's decision.

5 (1) The Lord Chancellor may make rules—

(a) regulating the exercise of the right of appeal to the Commission;

(b) prescribing practice and procedure to be followed in relation to proceedings before the Commission;

(c) providing for proceedings before the Commission to be determined without an oral hearing in specified circumstances;

(d) making provision about evidence in proceedings before the Commission (including provision about the burden of proof and admissibility of evidence);

(e) making provision about proof of the Commission's decisions.

(2) In making the rules the Lord Chancellor shall, in particular, have regard to the need to secure—

(a) that decisions which are the subject of appeals are properly reviewed; and

(b) that information is not disclosed contrary to the public interest.

(3) The rules may, in particular—

(a) provide for full particulars of the reasons for denial of access to be withheld from the applicant and from any person representing him;

(b) enable the Commission to exclude persons (including representatives) from all or part of proceedings;

(c) enable the Commission to provide a summary of evidence taken in the absence of a person excluded by virtue of paragraph (b);

(d) permit preliminary or incidental functions to be discharged by a single member;

(e) permit proceedings for permission to appeal under section 70(5) to be determined by a single member;

(f) make provision about the functions of persons appointed under paragraph 6;

(g) make different provision for different parties or descriptions of party.

(4) Rules under this paragraph—

(a) shall be made by statutory instrument; and

(b) shall not be made unless a draft of them has been laid before and approved by resolution of each House of Parliament.

(5) In this paragraph a reference to proceedings before the Commission includes a reference to proceedings arising out of proceedings before the Commission.

6 (1) The relevant law officer may appoint a person to represent the interests of an organisation or other applicant in proceedings in relation to which an order has been made by virtue of paragraph 5(3)(b).

(2) The relevant law officer is—

(a) in relation to proceedings in England and Wales, the Attorney General;

(b) in relation to proceedings in Scotland, the Advocate General for Scotland; and

(c) in relation to proceedings in Northern Ireland; the Attorney General for Northern Ireland.

(3) A person appointed under this paragraph must—

(a) have a general qualification for the purposes of section 71 of the Courts and Legal Services Act 1990 (c. 41) (qualification for legal appointments);

(b) be an advocate or a solicitor who has rights of audience in the Court of Session or the High Court of Justiciary by virtue of section 25A of the Solicitors (Scotland) Act 1980 (c. 46); or

(c) be a member of the Bar of Northern Ireland.

(4) A person appointed under this paragraph shall not be responsible to the applicant whose interests he is appointed to represent.

(5) In paragraph 5 of this Schedule a reference to a representative does not include a reference to a person appointed under this paragraph.

SCHEDULE 7

TRANSPORT POLICE AND MOD POLICE: FURTHER PROVISIONS

Firearms Act 1968 (c. 27)

1 The Firearms Act 1968 has effect subject to the following amendments.

2 In section 54 (Crown servants etc.), after subsection (3) insert—

"(3A) An appropriately authorised person who is either a member of the British Transport Police Force or an associated civilian employee does not commit any offence under this Act by reason of having in his possession, or purchasing or acquiring, for use by that Force anything which is—

(a) a prohibited weapon by virtue of paragraph (b) of section 5(1) of this Act; or

(b) ammunition containing or designed or adapted to contain any such noxious thing as is mentioned in that paragraph.

(3B) In subsection (3A) of this section—

(a) "appropriately authorised" means authorised in writing by the Chief Constable of the British Transport Police Force or, if he is not available, by a member of that Force who is of at least the rank of assistant chief constable; and

(b) "associated civilian employee" means a person employed by the Strategic Rail Authority who is under the direction and control of the Chief Constable of the British Transport Police Force."

3 In section 57(4), after the definition of "Article 7 authority" insert—

""British Transport Police Force" means the constables appointed under section 53 of the British Transport Commission Act 1949 (c. xxix);".

Police and Criminal Evidence Act 1984 (c. 60)

4 The Police and Criminal Evidence Act 1984 has effect subject to the following amendments.

5 In section 35 (designated police stations), after subsection (2) insert—

"(2A) The Chief Constable of the British Transport Police Force may designate police stations which (in addition to those designated under subsection (1) above) may be used for the purpose of detaining arrested persons."

6 (1) Section 36 (custody officers at designated police stations) is amended as follows.

(2) In subsection (2), for "a designated police station" substitute "a police station designated under section 35(1) above".

(3) After that subsection insert—

"(2A) A custody officer for a police station designated under section 35(2A) above shall be appointed—

(a) by the Chief Constable of the British Transport Police Force; or

(b) by such other member of that Force as that Chief Constable may direct."

7 In section 118(1), after the definition of "arrestable offence" insert—

""British Transport Police Force" means the constables appointed under section 53 of the British Transport Commission Act 1949;".

Criminal Justice and Public Order Act 1994 (c. 33)

8 The Criminal Justice and Public Order Act 1994 has effect subject to the following amendments.

9 (1) Section 60 (powers to stop and search) is amended as follows.

(2) After subsection (9) insert—

"(9A) The preceding provisions of this section, so far as they relate to an authorisation by a member of the British Transport Police Force (including one who for the time being has the same powers and privileges as a member of a police force for a police area), shall have effect as if the references to a locality in his police area were references to any locality in or in the vicinity of any policed premises, or to the whole or any part of any such premises."

(3) In subsection (11), before the definition of "dangerous instruments" insert—

""British Transport Police Force" means the constables appointed under section 53 of the British Transport Commission Act 1949 and "policed premises" has the meaning given by section 53(3) of that Act;".

10 In section 136(1) and (2) (cross-border enforcement: execution of warrants), after "country of execution" insert ", or by a constable appointed under section 53 of the British Transport Commission Act 1949 (c. Xxix),".

11 In section 137 (cross-border powers of arrest), after subsection (2) insert—

"(2A) The powers conferred by subsections (1) and (2) may be exercised in England and Wales and Scotland by a constable appointed under section 53 of the British Transport Commission Act 1949."

12 In section 140 (reciprocal powers of arrest), after subsection (6) insert—

"(6A) The references in subsections (1) and (2) to a constable of a police force in Scotland, and the references in subsections (3) and (4) to a constable of a police force in England and Wales, include a constable appointed under section 53 of the British Transport Commission Act 1949."

Police Act 1996 (c. 16)

13 The Police Act 1996 has effect subject to the following amendments.

14 In section 23 (collaboration agreements between police forces), after subsection (7) insert—

"(7A) For the purposes of this section—

(a) the British Transport Police Force shall be treated as if it were a police force,

(b) the Chief Constable of that Force shall be treated as if he were the chief officer of police of that Force,

(c) "police functions" shall include the functions of the British Transport Police Force, and

(d) the British Transport Police Committee shall be treated as if it were the police authority maintaining that Force for the purposes of subsections (1), (2) and (7) and the Strategic Rail Authority shall be so treated for the purposes of subsection (3)."

15 In section 24 (aid of one police force by another), after subsection (4) insert—

"(4A) This section shall apply in relation to the Strategic Rail Authority, the British Transport Police Force and the Chief Constable of that Force as it applies to a police authority, a police force and a chief officer of police respectively, and accordingly the reference in subsection (3) to section 10(1) shall be construed, in a case where constables are provided by that Chief Constable, as including a reference to the scheme made under section 132 of the Railways Act 1993 (c. 43)."

16 In section 25 (provision of special services), after subsection (1) insert—

"(1A) The Chief Constable of the British Transport Police Force may provide special police services at the request of any person, subject to the payment to the Strategic Rail Authority of charges on such scales as may be determined by that Authority."

17 In section 30 (jurisdiction of constables), after subsection (3) insert—

"(3A) A member of the British Transport Police Force who is for the time being required by virtue of section 23 or 24 to serve with a police force maintained by a police authority shall have all the powers and privileges of a member of that police force."

18 In section 90(4) (impersonation etc.), before the word "and" at the end of paragraph (a) insert—

"(aa) "member of a police force" includes a member of the British Transport Police Force,";

19 In section 91(2) (causing disaffection), after "applies to" insert "members of the British Transport Police Force and".

20 In section 101(1), before the definition of "chief officer of police" insert—

""British Transport Police Force" means the constables appointed under section 53 of the British Transport Commission Act 1949 (c. xxix);".

Terrorism Act 2000 (c. 11)

21 The Terrorism Act 2000 has effect subject to the following amendments.

22 (1) Section 34 (power of superintendent for police area to designate cordoned area in the police area) is amended as follows.

(2) In subsection (1), for "subsection (2)" substitute "subsections (1A), (1B) and (2)".

(3) After that subsection insert—

"(1A) A designation under section 33 may be made in relation to an area (outside Northern Ireland) which is in, on or in the vicinity of any policed premises (within the meaning of section 53(3) of the British Transport Commission Act 1949) by a member of the British Transport Police Force who is of at least the rank of superintendent.

(1B) A designation under section 33 may be made by a member of the Ministry of Defence Police who is of at least the rank of superintendent in relation to an area outside or in Northern Ireland—

(a) if it is a place to which subsection (2) of section 2 of the Ministry of Defence Police Act 1987 (c. 4) applies,

(b) if a request has been made under paragraph (a), (b) or (d) of subsection (3A) of that section in relation to a terrorist investigation and it is a place where he has the powers and privileges of a constable by virtue of that subsection as a result of the request, or

(c) if a request has been made under paragraph (c) of that subsection in relation to a terrorist investigation and it is a place in, on or in the vicinity of policed premises (within the meaning of section 53(3) of the British Transport Commission Act 1949).

(1C) But a designation under section 33 may not be made by—

(a) a member of the British Transport Police Force, or

(b) a member of the Ministry of Defence Police, in any other case."

23 In section 44 (power to authorise stopping and searching), after subsection (4) insert—

"(4A) In a case (within subsection (4)(a), (b) or (c)) in which the specified area or place is in, on or in the vicinity of policed premises (within the meaning of section 53(3) of the British Transport Commission Act 1949 (c. xxix)), an authorisation may also be given by a member of the British Transport Police Force who is of at least the rank of assistant chief constable.

(4B) In a case in which the specified area or place is a place to which section 2(2) of the Ministry of Defence Police Act 1987 (c. 4) applies, an authorisation may also be given by a member of the Ministry of Defence Police who is of at least the rank of assistant chief constable.

(4C) But an authorisation may not be given by—

(a) a member of the British Transport Police Force, or

(b) a member of the Ministry of Defence Police, in any other case."

24 In section 121, after the definition of "article" insert—

""British Transport Police Force" means the constables appointed under section 53 of the British Transport Commission Act 1949,".

25 In section 122, after the entry relating to the expression "Authorised officer" insert—

"British Transport Police Force Section 121"

SCHEDULE 8
REPEALS AND REVOCATION

PART 1
TERRORIST PROPERTY

Short Title and Chapter	Extent of Repeal
Access to Justice Act 1999 (c. 22)	In Schedule 2, in paragraph 2(2), the "or" at the end of paragraph (b), and in paragraph 2(3) the "or" at the end of paragraph (i).
Terrorism Act 2000 (c. 11)	Sections 24 to 31. In section 122, the entries for "Authorised officer" and "Cash".

PART 2
FREEZING ORDERS

Short title and chapter	Extent of repeal
Emergency Laws (Reenactments and Repeals) Act 1964 (c. 60)	Section 2. In section 7(1) the words ", and any general direction given under section 2 of this Act,". In section 14(1) and (2) the words "or direction" and ", section 2".
Finance Act 1968 (c. 44)	Section 55.

These repeals have effect subject to section 16(2).

PART 3
IMMIGRATION AND ASYLUM

Short title and chapter	Extent of repeal
Immigration and Asylum Act 1999 (c. 33)	In section 143, subsections (3) to (8) and (14).

PART 4
RACE AND RELIGION

Short title and chapter	Extent of repeal or revocation
Public Order Act 1986 (c. 64)	In section 17 the words "in Great Britain".
Public Order (Northern Ireland) Order 1987 (S.I. 1987/463 (N.I. 7))	In Article 8 in the definition of fear and the definition of hatred the words "in Northern Ireland".

This repeal and this revocation have effect subject to section 42.

PART 5
CIVIL NUCLEAR SECURITY

Nuclear Installations Act 1965 (c. 57)	In Schedule 1, paragraphs 5 and 6.
Atomic Energy Authority (Special Constables) Act 1976 (c. 23).	Section 3. In section 4(2), the definitions of "specified body corporate" and "designated company".

PART 6
POLICE POWERS

Short title and chapter	Extent of repeal
British Transport Commission Act 1962 (c. xlii)	Section 43(3).
Ministry of Defence Police Act 1987 (c. 4)	In section 2, subsection (2)(d), in subsection (3), the words ", but only" and, in subsection (4), the words "as they have effect in the United Kingdom".
Criminal Justice and Public Order Act 1994 (c. 33)	In section 60, subsection (4A) and, in subsection (8), paragraph (b) and the word "or" immediately preceding it.
Crime and Disorder Act 1998 (c. 37)	Section 25(1).

PART 7
MISCELLANEOUS

Short title and chapter	Extent of repeal
Terrorism Act 2000 (c. 11)	In section 55, the definition of "nuclear weapon". In Schedule 5, paragraph 18(e). In Schedule 7, in paragraph 17(4) the "or" at the end of paragraph (b).